Robert Creeley

Robert Creeley

A Biography

EKBERT FAAS
with Maria Trombacco

Including excerpts from the memoirs and 1944 diary of
the poet's first wife, Ann MacKinnon

University Press of New England
Hanover and London

University Press of New England, Hanover, NH 03755

© 2001 by McGill Queen's University Press

All rights reserved

Published simultaneously in Canada by McGill-Queen's University Press, Montreal, Quebec

Printed in Canada   5 4 3 2 1

This book has been published with the help of a grant from the Humanities and Social Sciences Federation of Canada, using funds provided by the Social Sciences and Humanities Research Council of Canada.

McGill-Queen's University Press acknowledges the financial support of the Government of Canada through the Book Publishing Industry Development Program (BPIDP) for its activities. It also acknowledges the support of the Canada Council for the Arts for its publishing program.

Library of Congress Control Number: 2001091501

ISBN: 1-58465-170-9

This book was typeset by Dynagram Inc. in 10.5/13 Janson.

Contents.

Preface.

What is attempted here is a life-writing, or rather, a life writing itself, the biographer letting the documents speak, speaking through them, impersonating voices, senses of humour, ironies, sarcasms, hypocrisies. Rather than by the urge to ascertain certain facts, it is carried by the awareness of how our lives' "events" inevitably come filtered through memory, of how imagination's decaying sense constantly reinvents what we forget, even seconds after the fact. Hence the often discordant accounts of a particular incident reported by different witnesses or by the same witness from different removes in time. Discrepancies such as these, normally streamlined into a single, "objective" tale, variously form part of the following one – as does the archaeological process of digging through layers of conflicting records, of laying bare earlier, "original" writings in the ultimately indecipherable palimpsests of personal self-reification, and sometimes distortion. Especially in Creeley's case, such auto-fictionalization, as we shall see, reaches from his 1989 essay, "Autobiography," back through his critical writings to his novel, *The Island*, and even to some of the early stories. A main endeavour, then, has been to unearth the poet's younger self from underneath the older one's reinventions.

Here the biographer, though otherwise hiding behind his sources, shows his undisguised bias: that is, his predilection for the younger poet's not so "decent" character and "crotchety purview" on life, as denounced by his older double; his fascination with the Rimbaud-type "monstrosity" and unself-pitying candour manifest in much of Creeley's early work; and finally, his disaffection with what followed – preferences more fully accounted for in the afterword. Hence also this biography's primary focus on the period from 1926–66, the first forty years of a poet still alive and productive today.

This biography's archival approach also guided my including, in an appendix, excerpts of Ann MacKinnon's memoirs and early diaries about her life as Creeley's first love and wife. These came to my notice only after completing the respective chapters, which I let stand even where they conflict with Ms MacKinnon's parallel accounts. This should provide the reader with a useful counterpoint to what, in my own narrative, derives to an overwhelming degree from source materials coming from Robert Creeley himself.

Acknowledgments.

For someone like myself, working in relative isolation, indebtedness to the help and advice of a few stands out all the more clearly. First and foremost, I'd like to thank Maria Trombacco, who joined me on various research trips in Europe and North America, organized the source materials for individual chapters, helped me get these into shape, prepared the end notes, as well as checked paraphrases and citations. Second, I would like to acknowledge my debt to Adam Chalmers for his (privately funded) work on the index and proofs. Without his dedication and reliability, this book could not have appeared before 2002. Thanks for help with the same process is also due to Sarah Amaral for some final checking as well as to Maureen Garvie for her painstaking, judicious, and unimposing editorial labours. Earlier research assistance paid for out of two SSHRC research grants, for which I'd like to express my gratitude, was carried out by Sabrina Reed, Michael Holmes, Terri Doughty, Mary Lou McKenna, Keith Findlay, Stephen Hayward, and Michael Hale.

I also acknowledge my indebtedness for the assistance provided by the numerous archives and institutions listed in the bibliography, while – mentioning a peculiarity I had not encountered in researching my prior *Young Robert Duncan* (Black Sparrow Press, 1983). Thus, the initial welcome given to my requests changed, sometimes within minutes, to grudging reluctance or downright refusal on several occasions in recent years. I can only guess at why this should have been so, while the ultimate, factual cause for it has remained a mystery to me throughout. If this sounds vague, it is primarily said by way of apologizing for the absence of some photographs described in the text as well as for my paraphrases of what, on occasion, I would have preferred to quote instead. To say more could only confound what this book may well bring into the open.

Something like the reverse of my relations with this biography's main subject has marked those with the poet's first wife, Ann MacKinnon: an initial misunderstanding, then, years later, a renewed acquaintance and, I hope, friendship, as well as my growing esteem for her candour, high spirits, and multiple talents as autobiographer, essayist, novelist, and poet (most recently *The High Intemperance*, 2000). Many thanks for allowing me to include excerpts from her memoirs and from a 1944 diary in this volume.

In any case, it's been a long haul, dating back to 6 August 1981 when Robert Creeley gave me his authorization to write this biography.

Robert Creeley

I

Childhood.

His birth was a much-anticipated event. His father, Dr Oscar Slade Creeley, had been married twice before. The first marriage had ended in a bitter divorce. Two sons, Thomas and Philip, allied themselves with their mother, Philip even taking the name of her new husband. Oscar's second wife died in the flu epidemic of 1918. He married once again, a nurse, Genevieve Jules, though hardly because of some wild romance. Oscar was an established medical man, well advanced in years when he met his future wife in a tent at the Marchfield Fair, teaching proper nutrition and child care for the Massachusetts Department of Health. It was a marriage between two adults united by shared professional interests. Soon Genevieve was doing her husband's paper work, helping to collect bills, and accompanying him on house calls when he didn't feel well. Their first child was a girl, Helen. Perhaps the second, born four years later when Genevieve was thirty-nine, might be a boy.

Robert White Creeley came into the world on 21 May 1926 at Arlington-Symmes Hospital in Arlington, Massachusetts.

> I was born at seven in
> the morning and my
> father had a monument
> of stone, a pillar, put
> at the entrance of the
> hospital, of which he was head.

Fate struck when Bob was two. He was in a car driven by his father, sitting in his nurse's lap and peering out onto the road, when somewhere around Boston they passed a truck from which a man was shovelling coal into a chute. A lump bounced off, hitting the windscreen and smashing it, sending splinters into little Bob's face. One splinter penetrated his eye, right through the cornea.

Oscar Creeley had the splinter removed immediately, but the damage was done. For a while the injured eye could still make out things faintly, but soon it deteriorated. Having barely learned to walk, Bob now had to be kept from bumping into corners. He was told not to cry, for that could irritate the eye. The doctors feared the infection might travel from the left eye to the right, eventually making him completely blind.

Oscar took it terribly to heart. After the debacle of his first marriage and the estrangement from his first sons, Bob's birth had promised a new start. No wonder the child became the focal point of his father's obsessive worries.

>   my sister
>
> older speaks of
> him, "He felt
>
> that with Bob
> he was starting
>
> over, perhaps, and
> resolved not
>
> to lose this son
> as he had Tom and Phil … "

The summer after the accident Dr Creeley whisked his family off to Lincoln, Massachusetts. His intention was to get Bob away from the heat and dust of Watertown which might aggravate his eye. For further protection the boy was made to wear a straw cap with a bill, the sort worn for tennis. Then his father decided to move the family out to the country altogether. After some searching, he decided on a forty-two acre property in West Acton, about thirty miles west of downtown Boston. Though it was no longer worked as a farm, it still had some of the accoutrements of one: a big barn, a rambling, rustic house, a charming old horse named Major and another reputed to be half mustang, lots of birch, fir, and black maple trees, and a number of great old elms dating back to the American Revolution. There were chickens and a turkey that chased anyone who came out of the house. In summer the kids could swim in nearby lakes, in winter go sleigh riding in the forest that stretched from the edge of their field to the horizon, and from there,

Bob was told, right up to Canada. After some renovating and remodel-
ling, Dr Creeley had the name Four Winds Farm spelt on the barn in
big letters. He put up a flagpole so tall it could be seen from far away.

Bob and his sister, Helen, saw little of their father. Dr Creeley was a
busy man running a practice in Watertown, head of staff at Arlington-
Symmes Hospital, and doctor for various other organizations like the
Perkins Institute for the Blind. He had also begun setting up his own
clinic like the one started by the famous Mayo and Lahey brothers he
had known at Harvard. Thus the personal traces Oscar Creeley left in
the adult poet's memory are scarce and faint: the smell of the cigarettes
he smoked, a whiff from the occasional whiskey and soda.

>   a
> smell I remember
>
> of cigarette box, a
> highball glass,
>
> man in bed with
> mother, the voice
>
> lost now.

Or less clearly, perhaps partly fictionally, Bob in bed, with Father reading
something like Thornton Burgess to him and Helen from the *Boston Herald*.

By contrast, the memories stand out with stark distinctness of the ambulance that, to Bob's and Helen's surprise, drove right across the lawn to the
front door; of Father, wrapped in blankets, being carried out on a stretcher;
of the grooves left by the wheels that stayed in the lawn for a long time.

>   I sit, intent, fat,
>
> the youngest of the suddenly
> disjunct family, whose father is
>
> being then driven in an ambulance
> across the lawn, in the snow, to die.

So as not to upset them, Genevieve did not tell her children that Oscar had
died. Life with Father ended with those "tracks fading in the spring thaws."

Oscar Creeley had died from pneumonia. His skinny body and highly
strung mind, strained by overwork and worry, lacked the stamina to fight

it off. The start of the Great Depression had caused problems for the clinic; expensive technical equipment was never put to use. But Oscar's greatest grief was over the continuing deterioration of Bob's eye. He had begun to consult with a psychiatrist, but to little avail.

His father's death left a vacuum Bob would try to fill over the ensuing months and years. All he had were tantalizing scraps of information that made him yearn for more. For instance, his father had adopted their mentally handicapped servant, Theresa, into the family. He had been a brilliant conversationalist. He had worked hard and saved his money to get a degree from the Harvard Medical School and gone on to become an accomplished surgeon and diagnostician. His widow kept his prescription pads, surgical instruments, and medical bag in the house for a long time. Knowing that the children would play doctor with them, she replaced the pills in the bag with candy. Meanwhile, Bob had learned next to nothing about his father's prior marriages and the two sons born into the first. "I didn't know where the hell anything was," he recalls. "My father had died … other echoes of the family were out there but never located."

His father's ancestry was shrouded in similar mystery. The one person who stood out was Oscar's father, Thomas Laurie Creeley. Helen remembered Oscar talking about how he accompanied his father driving a wagon full of asparagus and strawberries to Faneuil Hall Market, starting at three in the morning so they'd be there at five. They rattled across all the bridges between Belmont and Boston, Oscar trying to sleep in the wagon. T.L., as they called Thomas Laurie, had been as successful in life as he'd been powerful physically, with a long, handsome, steady face. An enterprising market gardener, he came to own a big house as well as eight acres of Belmont land. The Creeley Road still recalls him. T.L. was eventually elected into the Massachusetts state legislature, sold his farm, and died a rich old man.

"His house was numbered 375
Common st.

and his farm lands,
through the heart of which the present Creeley
rd. runs, adjoined

the Chenery holdings and extended
toward Waverly from upper
Common st."

......

But I saw a picture of him once, T.L.
in a chair in Belmont, or it was his invalid
and patient wife they told me sat there, he
was standing, long and steady faced,
a burden to him she was, and the son. The
other child had died.

But what about the rest of T.L.'s family? It seemed as if Bob's informants tried to obscure the facts. Most of the Creeleys had apparently finished their lives under an unlucky star. Two children, Thomas and
Charlotte, died of dysentery; their mother, Helen, née Severns, passed
away soon after. T.L.'s life too took a sharp decline towards the end. As an
old man he roamed Harvard Square in his bathrobe and slippers, buying
gewgaws with his housekeeper, to whom he left all his money. This provided grounds for a colossal lawsuit that continued into Bob's childhood,
coming to an end only when the lawyers' fees exhausted most of the con-
tested inheritance. Great-Aunt Lou, one of Oscar's opponents in the
quarrel, lost out even in death. Her ashes sat in a crypt in Mount Auburn
Cemetery for some twenty-five years. No one among the former combatants would have her buried. It took an outsider to the family, Bob's
mother, Genevieve, to finally lay her to rest. By that time the lawsuit had
long since ripped apart the family. Oscar, a slight figure compared with
his giant but half-demented father, proved to be the family's lone survivor
– and he too died prematurely.

Was the Creeley family doomed? It certainly seemed so at the time of
Oscar's death, because he had left his widow mainly unresolved problems.
But Genevieve, whose maternal ancestors included celebrities like Governor Edward Everett of Massachusetts, was made of sterner stuff than
her husband. One of her first decisions after his death was to prevent Bob
and Helen from attending his funeral. Again, she felt that might prove
too upsetting for them. Genevieve next liquidated the technical equipment for Oscar's clinic and returned to her original profession. She became a public health nurse for Stowe and later the Actons, averaging
some $2,700 to $3,000 a year. The family wasn't badly off, especially by
Depression standards, yet for the children it seemed like going from
riches to rags. Oscar had made $30,000 annually and, apart from Four
Winds Farm, there had been the fancy cars, a chauffeur, maids, all the
paraphernalia of affluence and status.

After settling financial matters, Genevieve next tackled the problem that
had broken Oscar's heart: Bob's injured eye. The doctors were still insisting that the recurring infections might spread to the healthy one and result in total blindness. The safest course would be to remove it. Genevieve

once again decided that it was in her son's best interest not to explain things but to act, and quickly. One day when Bob accompanied her to the hospital, she asked him to come in with her. That was odd: usually he was asked to wait in the car. Then, just minutes before the operation, he was told that a doctor would remove his eye. When he awoke from the anaesthetic, a big bandage covered his head. The eye was gone. He felt a sense of betrayal at "being tricked in this curious way" – understandably. "I so wish she had told me, although I rationally understand why she did not." But what could he do against his stern, well-meaning mother, except secretly hold it against her, which he did, as he remembers, "for some time."

From now on he had to wear a glass eye. It was expensive and couldn't be replaced too often. As the empty socket expanded with time, the glass eye would wobble around in it and sometimes fall out. That might happen at school, as he was bending over a book: the eye dropped onto the floor and rolled along under the desks, where another kid would pick it up. At recess, boys he wasn't friendly with would tease him about it. When he was finally allowed a new glass eye, sitting in the doctor's antechamber waiting to have the socket measured, he noticed those around him exchanging compassionate murmurs or casting sideways pitying glances.

At least he could cry now. However, he soon found out how little good that did him. His mother was a firm believer in proper nutrition and preventive medicine, while his grandmother enforced regular sleeping hours, summer or winter. This meant afternoon naps and the children having to be in bed at 7:30 every night, whether it was still daylight outside or not. Now you can cry, she would tell Bob: "You can do anything, but you stay there."

What could he do? He was gradually starting to resent all the control and to hate those who enforced it. He had flat feet, so a friend of his mother's who was a podiatrist provided him with arch supports. He developed bad posture, so he must wear special canvas straps to pull back his shoulders. He was made to play the violin, a shamefully unmanly instrument, he thought.

The only male support came from his grandfather, Ira Jules. A 1930 photograph shows Ira and Bob with hunting caps and rifles, Ira holding a dog by its collar. A "one-time-cabin-boy-to-second-mate of the last Yankee clipper out of Maine to the Far East," Bob's grandfather was a tough, impatient man, prone to outbursts of fury. Unlike Genevieve who, when reprimands didn't suffice, spanked Bob with a hairbrush, Ira Jules never had to lay a finger on him. Bob knew when Grandpa was down on him. Yet at the same time Ira seemed a broken man amongst all the women. That was obviously what killed him. Watching the women mismanage the lawn mower, he took over, and suffered a heart attack. Bob heard him swear behind the closed bedroom door. When the corpse was laid out in the parlour, Bob put something he valued in his grandfather's hand, perhaps a coin, and was shocked by the unhuman coldness of the skin. The death left a void never again to be filled by anyone in the family.

Sure, there was Genevieve's brother, Uncle Hap, an intensely ambitious man with narrow bourgeois aspirations who would have willingly played surrogate father to Bob. But though well intentioned and humorous, Hap became emotionally confused when his authority was challenged, and substituted violence for discipline. At times he angrily beat his own son, Laurie, with a big black belt.

Uncle Hap was not much of a role model professionally either. For all his apparent successes – working in real estate, for Harvard University Press, or even for Howard Hughes – he was a lifelong dilettante running from job to job. Out of work once during the Depression, he felt so ashamed he carefully concealed his old car from his son's classmates at Phillips Andover, a prestigious boys' academy he had persuaded to admit Laurie. And what a married life he led! Hap was at the beck and call of his hypochondriac wife who, because of this or that health problem, made him move from one part of the country to another, eventually realizing the climate was wrong everywhere they went. Clearly Uncle Hap had neither real authority nor genuine dignity.

In any case, he was hardly part of Bob's immediate domestic surroundings. Those, with his father and grandfather dead, consisted entirely of women, five in all: Bob's sister, mother, grandmother, Genevieve's sister Aunt Bernice, and the servant, Theresa. "I was the youngest in the household," Creeley recalls, "and increasingly the experience of being the growing male became almost awkward. There was the company of women, but there was no company of men. It was a very simple division; I mean, we used to laugh about it. I remember this camping trip we all go on up to Mount Desert Island, off the coast of Maine. We have a wall tent, and a pup tent. And ... the women all sleep in the wall tent – my aunt, my mother, my sister – and I slept in the pup tent." Women everywhere and at all times, controlling him with their puritanical restrictions and petty schemes, talking in "soft, sly voices."

Aunt Bernice was typical, though there was also a lot about her that Bob liked. He was obviously a favourite of hers. They did puzzles together and she told him and Helen stories, condensed and simplified versions of novels she'd read. She particularly liked Dickens, so Bob got a taste of works like *Oliver Twist, Bleak House, The Mystery of Edwin Drood*, and *Nicholas Nickleby* at an age when he was hardly able to read. But when Aunt Bernice retold them, she made sure he understood, sometimes devoting weeks to the same book.

Bernice also wrote poems, parodies of classics of the time such as Housman, or the occasional funny couplet composed when Social Security came into existence in the 1930s: "Cheer up grandma, keep alive, / Life begins at 65." Many of these appeared in print. Her last poem on George Washington's birthday, "along with a very dignified report of her," was published in the Sarasota paper. A substantial scrapbook containing some fifty of her pieces remains in Creeley's possession.

Aunt Bernice was "endlessly, really wittily quotable." She had a sharp tongue which, to Bob's delight, she exercised on Uncle Hap and even on his mother, who was hopeless at repartee. No wonder Bernice had already gone through two husbands, one estranged, the other dead. An intellectually gifted girl at school, she had been advised to go to college by a minister, but Grandfather Ira Jules wouldn't hear of it. Instead she ended up marrying a cabinetmaker, who, when she was pregnant with his child, asked her to pretend the baby was illegitimate to save the costs for its delivery. Unsurprisingly, she had rejoined her parents in Vermont. Genevieve interrupted her studies to take care of her, but the baby was stillborn. Bernice later went to meet her estranged husband at North Station in Boston to see if she had any feelings left for him. She decided she didn't, and divorced him.

Via a lonely hearts newspaper column, she next started corresponding with someone who signed his letters "Hermit of the Woods." She eventually met and married him, Herbert Elkins, a postmaster in Laconia, New Hampshire, who died a few months before Bob's father. Bernice then went to work for a Boston law office, spending the weekends at Four Winds Farm, and when that job folded in the mid 1930s, she moved in with the Creeleys altogether.

Later on she married a third time, a hippie before there were hippies. Her third husband, who came to be known as Uncle Ward, was a schoolteacher who had a daughter from a previous marriage, christened Thoreau. Aunt Bernice used a ruse to ensnare Ward. Although three years older than Genevieve, she persuaded her sister to make Ward believe she was six years younger.

Women talking in "soft, sly voices!"

The third woman presiding over Bob's childhood was his grandmother Caroline Everett, Ira Jules's widow. Grandmother was a great one at telling stories, some about herself. When she sat down and smoothed her impeccable white apron over her knees, Bob and Helen knew it was time to gather around and listen. Old enough to have lived through the American Civil War, as a young woman she had accompanied abolitionist Wendell Phillips on one of his missionary tours out west and met Mark Twain. The trip had had a secret purpose: young Caroline, a poor relative of the famous Boston Everetts, had fallen in love with the wrong man. Surely gifted Caroline could do better than share the life of a sailor, oldest of six sons from a poor Maine family of French-Canadian origin, who had gone to sea at twelve and often wouldn't come home for months or even years at a time. By spiriting her away, the family hoped Caroline might forget the sailor and find someone else. But she remained faithful to her true love, a man who was the very antipode to all her rich, powerful relatives in Boston.

The Everetts' worst predictions came true once Caroline married Ira Jules and settled at Head of the Tide, Maine. Though she bore him nine children, nothing stopped him from taking ship. But Grandmother coped with it all. She might consult the Ouija board about how he was doing, and go about her daily chores, and then, later in the day, sing songs and recite poems for her children. Did she never get lonely with her husband roaming some faraway ocean? Not as long as she could see the smoke from the house in the next valley. Every so often her neighbours would stop by and ask her if everything was all right.

At more than eighty years, Grandmother decided one day to again go out west, this time by Greyhound Bus. She made it to Riverside, California, her purpose to bring back her long lost son Archie who had left home at eighteen. Uncle Hap had the *Globe* photograph the old woman with her family on her return. Had she met Archie? Yes. Had she been successful? No. Archie, foolish as ever, had tried to convert her to his fundamentalist religion:

The Teachings

of my grandmother
who at over eighty
went west from West Acton,
to see a long lost son named
Archie – by Greyhound, my
other uncle, Hap, got the *Globe*
to photograph her, and us –
came back from Riverside, California,
where Archie was – he'd left
at eighteen – and he'd tried,
she told us, to teach her
religion, "at her age" – "as
much a fool as ever" – and
she never spoke of him again.

Stern in some ways, Grandmother was extremely whimsical in others, intriguing Bob and Helen with her weird responses and strange conundrums. In every marriage there are two bears, she told them: bear and forebear – which wasn't easy to figure out. She also had a way of saying things in reverse, like "What are you laughing at?" when Bob looked glum. That never failed to bring a smile to his face, however forced. His mother's name, Genevieve Rivers Jules, had been made up in similarly capricious fashion: Grandmother had put it together after reading a story about a Genevieve St Aubin in the *Bangor Daily Commercial*, and Mary Jane Holmes's popular novel *Lena Rivers*.

Importantly for Bob's later life, Grandmother recited poems and sang songs to him and Helen, just as she had half a century earlier with her own children. She knew reams of poetry and had decided favourites, Browning among them. Some of his poems, like "Evelyn Hope," she repeated so often that Bob and Helen learned them by heart.

She also told them stories about her own father. Once, coming home, Great-Grandfather found an Indian trying to steal from the hogshead of molasses in the back of his wagon. A powerful man, he angrily threw the thief off into the snow. Later that winter, passing the same man on his wagon, he asked him to get on, to make up for having been so rough with him and to show he had no hard feelings. When the Indian asked if he could feel his biceps, Great-Grandfather let him, flexing his muscles. But suspecting a trick, he in turn asked to feel the Indian's biceps. The Indian refused, pleading that he would be ashamed because his were so much smaller. Great-Grandfather insisted, discovered a big knife up the man's sleeve, and threw him off into the snow once again. Obviously, the Indian had been trying to find out whether his opponent carried a knife as well.

Grandmother Caroline stood out from the other women at Four Winds Farm in staying committed, at least in memory, to this patriarchal world of her pioneer ancestors, so much more adventurous and glamorous than the embattled and petty one surrounding most of Bob's childhood. But then she died, depriving him of the last witness of that valiant and sometimes heroic past.

She had fallen ill with the flu, and Bob was told to keep quiet around the house to let her rest. One day he went to a pond with an icehouse next to it, and when he returned at night, a storm was brewing, with big clouds being tossed around in the sky and "lots of moon popping in and out." As soon as he entered the house, his mother told him it was time to see his grandmother. Everyone was already gathered around her bed, from which she was delegating the diverse authorities she had exercised in the family to its survivors, saying: Now, Genevieve, you see to it that Hap does this or that! And: Bernice, you help Genevieve with such and such. Then she suddenly announced that she was tired, and Bob was sent to bed. Next morning she was dead.

If Caroline lived on in her daughter Genevieve, it was mainly in her hardheaded, no-nonsense puritanism. Typical here was the proverbial advice both lavished on the children: The devil has work for idle hands. Early to bed, early to rise, makes a man healthy, wealthy and wise. It never stopped. Everything had to be regimented, compartmentalized, carried out according to an order, or subjected to some authority. It felt like being whipped, first by the women, then by one's guilty conscience. "It's a weird tension," Creeley remembered in 1967, "and the torque that's created by that systematization of experience is just awful. Just incredible. It can *whip* ... I called a book *The Whip*. And that's why."

Meanwhile there was further betrayal, similar to what had happened before the doctor cut out his eye. In 1935, when Bob was away at camp, Nero, the Great Dane he had grown up with, attacked a junk dealer's son. The boy had come with his father to collect some odds and ends in the barn at Genevieve's request. Nero only raked the kid with his paws and scared him, but for Genevieve it was enough to have the dog put down. In her opinion, Nero was far too old. When Bob found out, he shed bitter tears, less of sadness than of anger.

Most unsettling to him, however, was the move from Four Winds Farm to a smaller suburban house on Willow Street in 1936. Genevieve had cogent reasons for selling the farm. With her husband and both parents gone, the farm struck her more than ever as the absurdity it had been all along. Oscar, who had tried to recreate in it his happy childhood, had died shortly after buying it. But unlike Grandfather Thomas Laurie's farm, Four Winds had been a sham. With the little that Genevieve could spend on it, the place had increasingly fallen into disrepair. What happened to it two years after it was sold seemed ordained by fate: a hurricane hit it so badly that some of the elms dating back to the American Revolution were devastated and had to be taken out.

It was a fitting image of what happened to Bob when his family transferred to Willow Street. To him the move entailed the collapse of a deeply cherished world. At the farm he had inhabited a charmed realm of magical creatures like his woodland fairies, and full of the games, objects, sights and sounds that had become very dear to him. Now little more than memories remained – of the solitary old lady whom he and his friends searched out on rambles through the woods and who gave him milk and molasses or gingerbread cookies; of playing knights and joust, charging full tilt with spears, using grain barrel lids as shields.

In Bob's dreams Four Winds Farm kept reappearing for a long time. Every time he woke he had to confront the bitter fact that his rural paradise and everything that lay buried there – his pets, Nero, certain small treasures – had passed into someone else's possession. He resented it. Deprived of his habitual escapes, he more than ever felt subject to the oppressive restrictions of home: "There was an unending restlessness now, because nothing was in its place and all the continuity was just another fight."

And fight he suddenly did, pent-up anger erupting on every front except at home. For a long time he had put up with hostile kids teasing him about his glass eye. Was it round? Did he scoop it out with a spoon? One day, before realizing what he was doing, he jumped on one of his tormentors, pounding the boy's head against the metal supports of the swings until friends pulled him off. It was like an attack of madness, as when during an argument with his cousin Laurie he suddenly battered him with a rake handle, really hitting him. It became a kind of addiction: clubbing a boy with a shovel in the middle of a snowball fight, pushing another's head into the dirt with all his strength, "fighting, trying with all his mind to win, win. He had to."

2

School.

West Acton Grammar School, Creeley remembers, "was two grades to a room, and my mother was the school nurse by the time I got there. Miss Dickenson was a sharp, specific teacher of the third and fourth grades, was it? Miss Allard, bosomy and young, taught the primary ones. Then Miss Suhusky prepared us for the shift to junior high and the further world."

Bob had a rough start. Everyone noticed his missing eye. His teachers soon found out that he also suffered from frequent colds and minor illnesses. There were fifty-one absences during Grade One alone.

Yet otherwise things didn't turn out too badly. From the start, he behaved impeccably, making every possible effort to succeed, which during 1931–32 earned him an A for both effort and conduct. Further results: a B+ for penmanship, and A's for both drawing and arithmetic. Only his grade in reading and literature suffered, mainly because of his many absences. He received a B.

He liked school. The photograph attached to his final school record shows a neatly dressed boy in jacket, shirt, and tie with a shy but radiant smile. Going to school meant an escape from the worst aspects of family life, yet still being able to enjoy the best of it. Coming home, he'd take off to attend to his diverse animals or to play with friends. "Best were the woods well back of the barn that we'd go off into ... without being bothered by adamant, boxed-in people. There we kids played endless patterns of Robin Hood (my friend Harry Scribner would be Robin – I was Will Scarlet), and occasionally Tarzan."

Bob continued to live this essentially rural life up to age fourteen. West Acton was still a small farm town, surrounded by low hills, orchards, pastures, and huge forests; there was the predictable U.S. post office, a drugstore, the town square with a watering trough, and a railway line running through the centre.

Even after the Creeleys moved to the new house on Willow Street when he was ten, Bob held on to as much as he could of the life he'd led earlier. Whatever new creatures he collected had to be corralled into the narrow confines of a garage. His greatest passion became breeding pigeons, a hobby to which he was introduced by Ernest Knippel, a German from Westphalia. He would go to an ice house on a nearby pond where they nested, steal a few two to three week old squeakers, as they were called, and raise them. Soon he had a whole collection of fantails, homers, and rollers, each of which he carefully registered in a special journal.

Occasionally he also visited his cousin Laurie, now a neighbour, who had a barn and a pony. It wasn't a big barn like the Creeleys' had been, just large enough for a good-sized box stall, a place for the saddle and harness, and the pony's winter ration of hay. Characteristically, Uncle Hap had been in a rush moving and rebuilding the barn, and finally left it unfinished. Some of the planks, where the pony couldn't reach, were attached with only one nail. Under one of these boards the two boys had a cache for illicit objects like cigarettes or even a semi-pornographic book.

Meanwhile, the games Bob played with his other friends had been getting rougher by the year. There was an abandoned slaughterhouse where they liked to swing from the meat hooks. As boy scouts, they were so rowdy that nobody wanted to act as their leader. Once on an outing to the edge of someone's orchard, they started an apple fight and within minutes stripped the trees of all their fruit. Naturally, neither the owner nor the scout leader was amused. Their water games would turn so wild that the leader was in constant fear that someone might drown. Roaming around as a gang, once they'd lost their leader, they bragged about how little it would take them to get rid of the next one.

Bob's grade for "conduct" suffered accordingly. It dropped to a c during 1936, the year the Creeleys moved from Four Winds Farm to Willow Street. Right through junior high school, his grades for behaviour were in the b or satisfactory range, though in ninth grade there was another decline to fair.

His marks for effort, after a much slighter drop, remained in the straight a or excellent range. Such effort bore fruit. During 1937–39 he was still hovering around a b+ average, his least outstanding results in English; then during the final year of 1939–40, he pulled himself up to a straight a average.

In principle, he loved school. "I played hookey occasionally," Creeley recalls, "but the action was at school. I mean our social life was there." On the whole, he also liked his teachers. Only one, a math instructor in her forties, treated him so badly he could never forget it. She called him a sneak, which was the one thing he thought he wasn't. If someone confronted him, he would tell the truth, a habit learnt from his mother.

More to his liking was Richard B. Greenman, a teacher with whom he felt a certain affinity. Greenman was an outsider like himself, though for different reasons. A Harvard trained historian, he had come out to Acton from teaching in Concord and Boston, hoping to escape the anti-Semitism that had plagued him in both places. He eventually advanced to becoming a superintendent, but again ran into trouble for disagreeing with the townspeople over some school policy. But the deeper cause "was a tacit dislike of him because he was Jewish. He wasn't one of them ... They were hard people."

Greenman became Bob's teacher during that crisis year, 1935–6, when his grades seemed about to take a nose-dive. Creeley remembers that his "world changed remarkably" when Greenman stepped into it. Obviously, the sympathy was mutual. In 1942 Greenman would sponsor his former pupil and neighbour as the first Acton candidate in at least ten years for the prestigious Harvard Club of Concord Fellowship, calling him ambitious and deserving. Once again in 1944, he supported Bob's application of admission to the American Field Service, extolling him as a cooperative person of excellent character and high standards.

What most spurred Bob to success in high school, however, was a rivalry with his sister. There were rumours that Bob just wasn't as smart as Helen. Bob's senior by four years, she wrote poems which had earned her praise from poet P. Tristram Coffin. She was going to be a writer. Meanwhile, she was doing everything in her power to bring him up to her level, making him read books by Conrad and Dostoyevsky. She later recalled how proud and proprietory she'd felt about her younger brother. She wanted him to have every possible opportunity and advantage. Her girlfriend's brother attended Holderness school near Plymouth, New Hampshire; perhaps Bob might gain admittance to the same prestigious institution. Helen got the application and prodded her mother to arrange for scholarhip tests. Genevieve did, prompting Holderness's headmaster, the Reverend Edric A. Weld, to ask her for more information about Bob. By mid-June the reverend received a detailed, hand-written letter from Mrs Creeley. It praised her son's high honour freshman work, his active involvement in student affairs, his reading interests, his knowledge of current affairs, his playing a fairly good game of tennis, and his skills as a swimmer. He seemed to have many friends and was very popular among his school fellows.

Other bits of information about Bob were rather puzzling.

After four years of practice, the letter said, Bob had learned to play the violin credibly, yet without displaying any unusual musical ability. As a devotee of symphonic music, he had attempted minor compositions of his own, yet his motivation for doing so was an interest in the mechanics of orchestration and the mere working out of themes. Genevieve had noticed that the analysis of the contribution of separate instruments to the whole appealed to him more than the general effect of the music. He also dabbled in photography and had built himself a makeshift darkroom where he printed films for friends. He also had definite political opinions.

A rather slight boy, he had an engaging smile, but the artificial eye he was forced to wear due to an accident in early childhood of course detracted from his appearance. It was greatly to his credit that he had managed as well as he had in overcoming this handicap, Genevieve concluded.

But overcome at what price, the reverend was left to wonder. The boy's fondness for animals, his mother admitted, bordered on the obsessive. His sister had remarked that he preferred his zoo to human society. Apparently, Bob had converted the family's garage into a veritable menagerie of guinea pigs and several rabbits, an alligator, hens, pigeons, a little scotch terrier called Annie Laurie, and a small red pig. An ardent member of the American Society of Pigeon Fanciers, he devoted a lot of time to the breeding of such fowl. The least bit of encouragement made him launch himself into detailed discussions of pigeons from fantails to helmets, Mrs Creeley explained.

But God only knew – perhaps this weird boy might become the Linné or Darwin of his age. After all, there was a serious directedness to his main obsession. The boy, so his mother said, wished to become a veterinarian and had already made plans towards attending a six year program at the University of Pennsylvania.

Mrs Creeley proposed bringing her son to Holderness for inspection. In any case, to be awarded a Holderness scholarship, Bob would have to jump the hurdle of several high speed multiple-choice tests, a cherished part of the Holderness screening system. There one would see how his obviously high but eccentric intelligence stood up to the pressure.

Bob passed his tests with flying colours, the Reverend Weld had to admit. His score on the English reading was at the 97th percentile for his grade, and in English usage was equally outstanding. His work in Latin was so excellent as to render him well prepared for their second-year course. In view of such feats, and of his high-school grade of 90 in algebra, Bob was awarded his scholarship.

He worked hard to fulfil what was expected of him. In his first report card, for the period ending 12 October 1940, he earned himself "High Honors." Weld remarked that he was off to a splendid start. The school was much pleased with his uniformly high level of work. Bob seemed to be making many friends as well as building a good scholastic record.

In turn, the reverend had reason to congratulate himself on an unconventional decision he had taken before these results came in. Bob had been allowed to transfer part of his miniature zoo from West Acton to an old garage on the Holderness campus. Soon there were problems with that, but the headmaster let it pass. From time to time one of Bob's pigeons fell down the chimney of the gym, so that they ended up in the – thank God – unlit furnace whence they could be retrieved by the kindly janitor and returned to their owner.

Creeley remembers Holderness as a very benign school run by the Reverend Weld who, though perhaps not a first-class teacher, was a great headmaster with an uncanny way of assessing the integrity of those in his charge. Others who had watched Weld's career from the time he had taken over at Holderness knew him to be a somewhat more enigmatic person.

The reverend displayed multiple, often intriguingly contradictory character traits. Though interested in anything from batting averages to Buber, he would pertinaciously zero in on important issues, always getting to the heart of things. Particularly misleading to people was his seemingly typical professorial absentmindedness. "After a series of 'yaht, yahts,' convincing the listener that the Rector's mind was etherealizing elsewhere, he would give a benign, slightly vacant smile and then deftly drop the perfect response." Hidden behind Weld's vacant benignity was a steel-trap mind, which before long was to close in on disputatious Bob by way of setting the decisive mark towards his later calamitous career at Harvard.

Yet how promising things looked at first! Bob knew he was one of the youngest and brightest boys at Holderness. He was there on a scholarship while most others were on the payroll of their wealthy parents. Also, he was finally free of the world of females that had oppressed him throughout childhood. At Holderness his instructors were men.

And the campus! Built on a small plateau above Plymouth, on the one hand falling off towards the Pemigewasset River, on the other surrounded by wooded hills, it has preserved its magical isolation to date. Time seems to have stood still here: now as then, there is the handmade iron entrance sign, HOLDERNESS 1879 SCHOOL, with the Earl of Holderness's escutcheon over the entrance; past it, a road curving round towards Livermore Hall and the old wooden school house, the austere New England chapel to the left, picturesque Grey Cottage, Niles and Webster House to the right, with here and there groups of formally dressed pupils filing along the pathways across the lawns. To Bob, when he arrived in

1940, the campus must have appeared as somehow reaching back to that grander world he had come to associate with his ancestors.

Though shy at first, he quickly found himself in his element. Classes were small, so he dared speak up and felt understood. Learning, once past those multiple-choice entrance tests, was conducted in a spirit of experiment and free enquiry. There was no corporal punishment. Increasingly during the years Bob was there, discipline was handled by the pupils themselves.

Rector Weld had managed to attract high-calibre academics to Holderness of both conservative and modernist orientation. Latin teacher William Judge insisted on grammar and gave Bob, who loved Latin poetry (especially Virgil and Catullus), a firm grounding in classical prosody.

Though Bob's physical handicap did not allow him to participate in football or baseball, he played tennis. He also took part in the school's skiing program which involved competitions with other schools like Tilton or Brewster and, before wartime rationing began to limit transportation, ranged from local slopes like Wendy's and Huckins' Hill as far as Proctor and Northwood, Lake Placid.

Anyone who still felt the need for an escape from the restrictions of school was allowed to roam Plymouth after five, perhaps for a soda at the Pemigewasset Hotel or, in summer, an ice cream at the York's Corner Drugstore. Though the boys had to be back in time to put on jacket, shirt, and tie for the formal evening dinner, they were given fair scope to pursue their extracurricular interests or play pranks – except those who, because of low grades, had to do study hall from 7:30 to 9 p.m. But that wasn't Bob's problem.

Blanket-tossing parties defused aggressive energy, and so-called bull-sessions, according to the 1942 yearbook, provided "relief from the tedium of classes or a sour reiteration of common griefs." Participants debated each others' views on people, politics, religion, life in general, or traded stories about their recent exploits with the female sex. There was plenty to talk about: during 1941–42 alone, the dance in the hills of Holderness with the girls of St Mary's-in-the-Mountains; followed by the biggest social event, the weekend mid-winter house-party with skiing and skating as well as a barn dance; then, finally, the Commencement dance, the last one of the year. Fifth and sixth formers were allowed to have dates with the Normal School girls for the first time in Holderness's history.

Bob, alias "Creaky," alias "Hook," took an active part in these events as well as in the subsequent bull-session braggadocio about them. He became known to be familiar with "more young women than a marriage broker." These various affairs of the heart, we read in the 1943 yearbook, "were followed with great interest and jocosity by the rest of the school ... his faux pas when he got a pair of letters to two fair admirers in the wrong envelopes is still savoured with much glee by his many admirers."

Readers took similar pleasure in figuring out the "personal experiences" hidden in Bob's literary contributions to the *Holderness Dial*. One, entitled "How Should I Then Reply," describes the narrator's friendship with a man who, unlike himself, has no interest in money or success. Instead, he searches for "the reason of life," suspecting that there "must be a soul in every man." The narrator is amused by the "obvious absurdity" of these speculations, yet at the same time feels how the man's words "bit into [his] conventional thoughts," causing him distinct uneasiness. With its surrealistic flashes of horror, its sudden change in perspective, and its final turn towards Creeleyan annihilation, the narrative looks forward to the short stories of a later date:

"I stood in my bathroom, a man, shaving, a man who was known in his community as not exactly the most perfect among them, but the point is that I was in essence the conventional conception of man. But as I looked into the mirror I became aware of the fact that I saw before me not my face but the back of a head, and behind that head I saw the mirror. There was no reflection of my face in it. My range of vision increased, and I saw a man, standing looking into a mirror. I did not know that man. He was as unfamiliar to me as any complete stranger might have been. Then my face, without warning, leaped before me. I think my soul had returned to my body. Now what do you think of that, eh?"

He looked at his companion who sat before him. There was no answer to his inquiry. He chuckled to himself and yawned. The fire had nearly given up its fight against the shadows on the wall, and the entire room was clouded with smoke and night.

I looked down at the men sitting in their chairs. Their slumped positions indicated their slumber. Who were they, I wondered. I did not know them.

A door in an adjoining room banged shut. Then all yielded to night.

Another story, "The Passionate Percival Pappit," like "How Should I Then Reply" published in the *Holderness Dial* with Creeley as editor-in-chief, strikes an even more directly autobiographical note. Percival is a compulsive talker who "soared into oratory like a lark. He was not even shaken by the rather dubious compliments, which he received from passing hecklers. The subject matter bounced from war to women, until at last Pappit found common ground, namely love." Otherwise, Percival displays a strange mixture of extreme shyness and wilful resolution in pursuit of the opposite sex, as well as an unusual preference for another man's sexual partner. A self-proclaimed monster, he forces himself upon a woman who's just seen off her football-captain fiancé on a railway platform, and, in spite of the ridicule he suffers as a result, comes out of the event with a perverse sense of elation: "He had attempted to kiss an engaged woman. Why that put him in the class of a Casanova, a wolf, a man! A pure sigh of contentment rattled through Percival's chest. Pappit was at peace."

From early on, Creeley's creative efforts translated into an acute sense of other writers' deficiencies. To the irritation of his English teacher, he would criticize or even rephrase certain lines of poetry they were reading in class. Thus Emily Dickinson's "Inebriate of Air – am I –," which sounded silly to him, he changed into the more straightforward "I am an inebriate of air." Or he ridiculed a line such as Robert Frost's "Two roads diverged in a yellow wood." Irritated by its patness, he wondered how the speaker, in travelling along one of these two roads, could know where the other one led to. Why was Frost so *smug* about it? The questions got the other boys laughing and Bob thrown out of class, the only time that ever happened to him.

Asked to see his teacher later that day, Bob expected to be severely reprimanded, even punished. But the teacher's response was more effective. He acknowledged how Bob felt about Frost's line, yet at the same time put him to shame for trying to impose his dislike on the others who might in fact like it.

A more serious incident elicited an equally effective response from the Reverend Weld in person. Irritated by the frequency with which the boys were served prune whip with their meals, Bob interviewed the school nurse, Mrs Ella Judge, and, catching her off guard, made her say something about the possibly harmful effect of such excess on the pupils' health. A front page editorial quoting that statement which somehow escaped the faculty advisor's censorship appeared in the next issue of *The Bull*, an unofficial student paper Bob had started. The editorial had devastating repercussions.

After the usual prayers and announcements at assembly, the Reverend Weld announced that the school cook, after reading the editorial, had quit, and that unless he could be made to reverse his decision, the school would have to close. Would the author of the editorial please come to see him immediately afterwards in his study. Expecting an outburst of anger, Bob was once again taken by surprise. Weld merely explained that this was wartime, so it would be next to impossible to find someone willing and able to cook for a school. A cook could make more money in Boston, for instance. So Bob and his headmaster worked out a solution: each and every student in the school would have to apologize to the cook. It was a memorable sight: the boys, Bob leading the vanguard, moving single file through the kitchen towards the chef and his wife to offer their apologies. Previously, Bob and his co-contributors to *The Bull* had been ardent muck-rakers filled with high hopes for reforms. After the prune-whip incident the paper became more reserved in all particulars.

Meanwhile, Bob had suffered a slight lapse in his grades as a result of his increasing extracurricular activities. The December 1940 report card still gave him real credit for keeping his level of effort as well as accomplishment consistently high. In spite of a slackening off in the exams *vis-à-vis* his daily work, he also received high honours for the entire first term as well as for the year as a whole. But an interim report card of 8 March sounded a warning: Bob, it said, had a tendency to work too fast on his tests and to make careless errors. Altogether, his grades had been suffering due to the time he invested in his debating.

Creeley's later comment that between the ages of seven and fourteen he couldn't have said more than half a dozen words "to anyone more than three years older" also testifies to the urgency of this endeavour. Though shy with his elders, he soon became compulsively voluble and outspoken amongst peers. At least according to himself, his debating club and bull-session talents improved so rapidly as to make him a self-proclaimed "authority" on the subject of "oratory," to which he devoted a short essay in the official student paper *The Dial* of Spring 1942. Characteristically, true oratory to Bob was not necessarily a public act or a result of rhetorical skill. Instead, it often was brought on by the speaker's need to "break the silence that is strangling him."

Soon mere debate proved an insufficient challenge in exercising his talents. One of his teachers remembers him as a forceful spokesman "on behalf of the students." "His shyness didn't come out that way at all ... And as he grew in his self-assertiveness, he would sound off on almost any subject." He acquired yet another nickname: "Senator." He was always talking, Creeley recalls: "I never shut up."

Bob's final two years at Holderness coincided with a period of increasing student initiative and reform, in all of which he took a leading part. And as usual, the Reverend Weld showed himself as open to these endeavours as one could expect from so benign and liberal a rector. The year book staff for 1941 had in a small supplement complained that the Student Council was "too much of a figurehead" and not enough of "an active, representative body constantly working to improve School life." So Weld invited the Sixth Form of 1942 to return a day early in the fall to discuss plans for the coming year. As one of the editors of the 1942 year book, Bob had a hand in describing the changes to the Student Council initiated during these talks: "Its membership was to be increased to nine boys elected twice a year, meetings were to be held at regular intervals, the minutes were to be read at morning Assembly and then posted, giving the Student Body a better idea of what their elected representatives were doing."

But this was not all. Before meeting the students, Weld, in consultation with his faculty, had drawn up a proposal that he now handed to the young reformers. It provided for a "complete change in the School's disciplinary system." Masters would only *report* on an infraction, leaving the "absolute control of punishment and supervision" to the Student Council. A master in the role of "Faculty Advisor," rather than meting out punishment, would plead on behalf of the culprit before the offence was voted on. If guilty, the offender was given the appropriate demerit on a scale of 1 to 50 ½, at which point he had "earned for himself a permanent vacation from the stress and strain of life at Holderness." The Student Council also controlled part of the smoking-off-bounds problem, administered the Wednesday movie permissions, worked out plans for a club system, and obtained permission for the two upper forms to visit and date girls from the Normal School in Plymouth.

By the end of the year the *Dial Year Book* editors felt ready to assess the relative success of these innovations, some of which the Student Council pursued in disagreement "with measures passed by the Faculty." Proudly they recounted their achievements: the introduction of "many new improvements into the life of the School"; diminished friction "between boys and masters," allowing the latter to treat the boys as friends rather than as suspected culprits; and improved relations between the school and town.

One wonders how Weld felt about these reforms some nine months after he had helped introduce them; or about Bob, who more than anyone else, was pushing them from every angle. By 1943 he was editor of *The Dial, The Bull,* and the year book. Out of the nine editors of the 1942 *Dial Year Book,* he and Robert Edward Vickerman were the only two who were simultaneously members on the Student Council and *The Dial* board as well. Weld, while himself sitting in on the Student Council, also kept himself informed about Bob's activities in his two other functions through his son, Edric A. Weld, Jr, who was both a year book editor and a member of *The Dial* board.

Photographs from 1942 and '43 bring out the personality changes these various activities must have wrought on Bob. Photographed on his own, he glares out at us with an air of grim determination. In the class photograph he is the only one who has firmly interlaced his fingers. Both on the Student Council picture, in which he stands at the centre of the top row, diagonally above the Reverend Weld, and on *The Dial* board photograph, in which he is positioned diagonally above Weld's son, he is the only one sporting a bow tie.

By 1943, even the residue of childlike innocence still softening his stare in the 1942 year book pictures has gone. His face, when photographed on his own, has assumed a stern, adult handsomeness; in groups, a sullen wilfulness is accentuated by his suddenly sharply angular features and large, upward pointed ears. Of the twenty-one pupils of his senior class, as well as of diverse members of the student disciplinary committees, he is the only one who, in a seeming posture of defiance, has firmly crossed his arms. In *The Dial* board photograph, he is holding centre stage, his right fist resolutely planted on the table in front of him; all the other members display both hands in poses of nonchalant relaxation.

New, too, is a tone of jocular aggressiveness with which *The Dial* board extolls its activities: "After a year of activity the DIAL Board can now sink to rest. Although this particular group has been violently criticized for its laziness, inertia, and general state of lethargy, it still can shove the BULL, the DIALS, and this YEAR BOOK before its attackers and say with condescending tone, 'Well?'"

The Bull, that "less dignified member of the DIAL Publications," was full of "those bits of humor upon which its more stately brothers are forced to frown," yet gave "the school a long needed voice." Started as a spontaneous student paper, it put into print some of the concerns previously vented in the popular bull-sessions. Typed up on stencils, the bi-weekly was distributed to paying subscribers before breakfast. Its main objective, explained "Editor-in-Chief" Robert Creeley of the 1943 winter issue of *The Dial*, was "to give the boys a humorous tabulation of the events of the two weeks."

Considering his many extracurricular activities, Bob's scholastic record suffered a relatively minor decline from a grades average of 85.8 per cent at the end of 1940–41, to one of 84 after 1941-42, and 80.4 by the time he left for Harvard. A major portion of that drop is accounted for by a final 72 in chemistry, which he disliked, along with German, in which he finished with a 75. The decline in Latin was from an initial 87 to a final 80, that in English from 87 to 86, his grade in history remaining steady at 89.

This slight scholastic decline had physical reasons as well. Throughout his stay at Holderness Bob continued to suffer from severe head colds, chills, coughing fits, the odd inflammation of the eye socket, or the results of minor accidents. He was hardly careful about his health. Around January 1943, he seemed to be living on almost nothing. The school nurse, Mrs Judge, advised him to eat well-rounded meals if he wished to stay healthy.

Particularly harmful to his scholastic career was an accident on 24 November 1942, in which he received a wound about two inches long and two and a half inches deep in his left thigh. It happened on a Saturday morning under otherwise unexplained circumstances. According to the rector's somewhat implausible report to Mrs Creeley, Bob grabbed another boy's hand not realizing that it held an open knife and forced him to drop it so that the point struck the inner side of his leg. The accident made him miss the monthly tests. Otherwise, he would have probably made the Honour Roll, though "with not much of a margin to spare," as his report card says.

Such seemingly gratuitous afterthoughts, nagging reprimands, or doublespeak eulogies abound in his report cards from then on. Though his work in English was excellent, that in the other subjects was not quite up to his ability. While impressed by his editorials, the Reverend Weld felt that Bob was putting in too much work for *The Dial*: Bob could have done a lot better if he'd been more careful about not wasting time at odd moments and really concentrating during study periods. By 13 March 1943 he had improved in three subjects, sufficiently so to be credited, again somewhat duplicitly, with having made a special endeavour to avoid demerits and increase his cooperation.

All this sounds harmless enough, and none of it could have caused Bob to guess at the devastating blow dealt him by a confidential report Weld sent to Harvard in the spring of 1943.

3

Harvard, 1943–44.

Perhaps Bob didn't need psychiatric attention, Harvard's dean of freshmen, Delmar Leighton, informed Dr Fleming of the Department of Hygiene on 7 February 1944, but he was so unkempt (cigarette-stained fingers, dirty shirt, no tie, etc.) that Leighton felt like sending him to Fleming for "a going over." After some initial diffidence during their interview, Bob had talked quite freely about himself, stating among other things that he wanted to be a writer. But in general he struck the dean as not working effectively and as being low in spirits.

What had happened?

It had started so hopefully when he had arrived in the summer of 1943. He had been offered a scholarship towards becoming a veterinarian from both the University of Massachusetts in Amherst and the University of Pennsylvania, but the lure of being accepted by Harvard proved more tempting. It literally turned his head. Perhaps he might get a scholarship there as well. Also, his professional plans had changed. He now wanted to become a journalist, and hoped that Harvard, as he explained in his application, could provide him with a broad enough education to allow him to do varied types of writing for various types of publications.

Asked to provide a report on her son, his mother had stressed that Bob was going to Harvard with high hopes and was very proud to be a Harvard freshman. With characteristic frankness, she pointed out that Bob was not athletic, possibly because of his missing eye. She also remarked upon his smoking too much and his unhealthy appetite, probably due to a chronic sinus infection, causing him to get easily run down. Some of his Holderness grades could have been higher if he hadn't devoted so much time to writing.

As for Bob himself, he had very much looked forward to his career at Harvard. His final grades at Holderness, though not as high as his earlier ones, had remained in the honours range. And how much time he had invested in developing his journalistic skills editing and writing for various school publications! Moreover, the college board exam results obviously held excellent promise. Bob felt confident, even a bit cocky. In applying, he exchanged his middle name "White" for the more interesting "Whitney" and stated that he would prefer as a roommate a New England private school graduate with interests similar to his. In regard to religion, the roommate might be anything but Catholic.

He had nothing to be apprehensive about, and he wasn't. Hence, the sudden decline of his grades took him by surprise. By August 1943, he had dropped to the c range in most subjects including English, German, and Latin. By October, his mathematics too had dropped to a c, while his grade in Latin had declined to a d.

Granted this was a time thrown into turmoil by World War II. "I can remember the constant shift and change of the educational form," Creeley explained later. "They were using an accelerated program trying to rush people through before they became involved with the army. A very chaotic time indeed." But that alone hardly explains his suddenly deteriorating scholastic record.

Needless to say, his failure was depressing to him, as it was acutely alarming to his mother. Since her son had been refused the anticipated Harvard scholarship, she had to finance his studies herself, partly drawing on a $3,500 award granted him for his eye injury. As she had written to Harvard on 27 June 1943, the family was putting everything into this year, hoping that he might at some point be considered for the scholarship he had been denied earlier.

Genevieve had more to worry about than that. At Christmas Bob had come up to Northeast Harbor, Maine, where she had taken the job of Red Cross nurse to be closer to her daughter, Helen. She was perturbed by Bob's new outlook and attitude. Harvard, she concluded, was quite a letdown for him. She duly wrote another letter to Dean Leighton, appealing for his help. Bob was obviously finding he wasn't the big fellow he'd thought he was, hoping to work for the *Lampoon* and excelling in other ways. He seemed to have lost faith in himself. Worse, he didn't seem to care. What a steady and well-poised boy he had been, beyond his years, and now, unfortunately, so very immature. Either he had been built up too much, or he'd simply become indifferent to his studies. Genevieve later claimed she had mailed the letter by mistake, but at that point Dean Leighton had already summoned Bob for an interview and sent him to Dr Fleming for "a going over."

What must have helped the Dean make that decision was a confidential report in Bob's file drawn up earlier in response to his application for a Harvard scholarship. It confirmed Mrs Creeley's sense that her son had no faith in himself. Bob, the anonymous assessor stated, had a certain amount of intellectual curiosity and was a likable chap when he wanted to be. On the other hand, he was disputatious, moody, a follower not always working for the best of his group, and not too stable emotionally. It all added up to a denial, the assessor concluded. For better computability, he summed up Bob's scholastic abilities and general character traits on a ten point scale. The chart gave Bob an average of five, his optimum achievement being his sociability (seven), his lowest in the area of "initiative" (three), "dependability," and "strength of character" (both four).

What motivated the Harvard assessor to peg Bob so much lower than what was suggested by his Holderness grades? The answer is simple: an equally confidential report by Bob's headmaster, the Reverend Edric Amory Weld. Here are some of its highlights: after extolling Bob's ability to write and his outstanding work in Latin, which even won him a prize, Weld rates Bob's general record not unsatisfactory; he answers the question as to whether the applicant would be willing to do college work with a "probably." How about Bob's intellectual curiosity and ambition? He seemed to have a reasonable amount of both. Was his scholastic record due to conscientious industry or rather brilliance of mind? He worked pretty nearly up to his ability. Was Bob a loner? Not at all. He was gregarious by disposition and rather depended on other people. Any leadership qualities? He had held class offices but, in the reverend's mind, lacked independence of judgment. His opinions tended to be coloured by the particular group he was with.

Two further questions regarding the candidate's possible emotional instability and principal weaknesses gave Weld a chance to make sure the Harvard reader would get the main point – which he did, concluding that Bob was disputatious, moody, a follower who did not always work for the best in a group and not very stable emotionally.

Bob didn't have a rugged physique and at times his reactions showed physical fatigue – though the reverend, open-minded as ever, did not want to call this a fundamental emotional instability. But Bob was sometimes unduly swayed by the cleverness of others, especially if they were more mature or sophisticated. He was only sixteen, and felt his social insecurity. For all his very good possibilities, his success would depend on the crowd in which he travelled.

Looking at Bob's stained fingers, and dirty, tie-less shirt, Dean Leighton could only marvel at the reverend's prophetic warning. Obviously the boy had fallen in with the wrong crowd.

And so he had. As he remembered in 1950, all those close to him then "were in trouble of some sort." Right after moving into Adams House,

Bob came to be close friends with Herbie Cole, a "sad, bright kid" from New York "whose face was like a map of endless acne and dilemmas." Bob liked his new friend's funny, hip manner and his broad, sardonic humour which got other people's backs up. They thought Herbie was a raving homosexual or weirdo. The way he would come down into the common room before dinner and start playing slow tunes on the piano, accompanying himself with grand dramatic gestures! An aficionado of jazz and cabaret singing, Herbie owned a huge record collection that was to absorb much of the time Bob might otherwise have spent studying.

He could go to Herbie's room and play his records any time he wanted: "They started way back with the classic New Orleans, and went all the way up through Kansas City, St Louis, Chicago … He had me located on everything up to the Forties, really, up through Coleman Hawkins … He would love, for example, 'I wish I could shimmy like my sister Kate … ' He liked the humor in it, the funkiness. And Bessie Smith, for example, things like that. And then Kid Ory. Jack Teagarden I remember getting very hooked on; I liked that really wild sound he had. Muggsy Spanier I liked a lot also." At Holderness a friend had introduced Bob to traditional music from the baroque, through classical and Romantic right up to Mahler's *Das Lied von der Erde* or Stravinsky's *Mouvements de Petrouchka*. Now his musical education increasingly immersed him in the *demi-monde* of cabarets, music halls, and jazz clubs.

But the interview with Dr Fleming didn't go badly, the psychiatrist concluding that at least for the time being there was no occasion for alarm. Dean Leighton, though continuing to be concerned by Bob's pallor and untidy appearance, told Bob's mother that her son was entirely polite and took in good humour his suggestion that he wasn't living up to his promise. Moreover, Bob was meeting his requirements and working fairly steadily, if not with enthusiasm. The process of maturing was not always an easy thing to manage, he added. In any case, they had no real grounds for complaint.

Bob's report cards tell a different story. After his initial drop to a c average by August 1943, he further declined to a low c by October. The prize-winning Latin scholar at Holderness finally got a D in the subject and concluded his first term with a c- and c+ in his two English courses, a c- in German, and a c+ in Mathematics. Then in June 1944, after receiving his grades for the third term (D, D+, c, c-, B-), he petitioned for a leave of absence for the summer, arguing that having turned eighteen and hence being of draft age, he felt it would be wise to arrange his affairs before he was called.

The request was granted, then rescinded a few weeks later, the administrative board suggesting that he withdraw in the understanding that readmission would be conditional. In a letter, Dean Hanford pointed out that in case of further complaint, more drastic action would be taken and that Bob was well advised to move away from the Harvard community and from Harvard Square. If he should think of re-applying, he would have to convince the administrative board of his worthiness by a good long service record and by demonstrating that he'd learnt to be more careful and responsible.

What had happened?

Bob had been arrested. The occasion earned him the distinction of being called a "man" rather than a "boy" for the first time at Harvard. He and two others, David Harris and Robert Kelly, had been going around to different dormitory rooms looking for liquor and then had carried a door, which had been taken off the hinges to be painted, out of Lowell House. That was on the night of August 13. Shortly afterwards, the calamitous news, communicated by Dean Hanford, reached Mrs Creeley in her house on Summit Road in Northeast Harbor up in Maine where Bob came to visit her several months later.

4

Sex.

That Christmas in 1943 when he went to Maine to discuss his problems, Bob also talked a lot about a certain Ann MacKinnon. Doing so, he sounded compassionate, high spirited, and witty, like a young man in love rather than the depressed, defeated person his mother and sister expected. So there was a woman in his life now. Helen found this amusing, but to Genevieve it was a cause for additional worry.

Apparently Bob's girl was a troubled, insecure loner, yet full of spunk. She had clearly taken to Bob, telling him what a brilliant conversationalist he was and what a lovely smile he had: it changed his whole face, she had told him.

One of her teachers at Radcliffe who had asked her what she wanted to do with her life was told: have babies. She said it provocatively, perhaps, but there was a serious angle to it. Ann had made a vow: she would never allow herself to forget what it had been like to be a child. Certainly, she would never do to *her* children what people had done to her.

Her childhood had been awful. An orphan, she had grown up without ever knowing her natural parents. At the orphanage she had been adopted once but then brought back. She'd increasingly been forced to act cute under the scrutinizing of visiting would-be parents. Meanwhile, there'd been less and less chance of her being chosen over the other younger and cuter kids. Finally she'd been adopted by a well-to-do Wellesley professor, and then, only two years after, her new "mother" had died, to be replaced by an unsympathetic guardian, Constance Rathburn. Her mother had left Ann lots of money and a house, but Constance vigorously cut back on Ann's food. Constance also undermined her ward's self-esteem, calling her fat, gauche, ugly, and stupid.

Yet there was more to Ann than the downtrodden, innocent waif that all these stories made her out to be. Helen, thoroughly amused, got Bob to tell it all.

What did Ann look like?

A pretty but plain face with wide apart eyes, the nose with a slight snub.

Once at a friend's birthday party, Ann, normally allowed no more than one or two cookies per dinner, glutted herself on cake and ice cream. The house resounded with the screaming and laughter of neighbourhood kids. Ann let three boys feel her small breasts while they hid with her behind a couch.

Or listen to this: Later Ann had been sent to spend the summer at a farm run by a clergyman who took on female boarders of good social background: that is, wealthy, nice girls. The trouble was that one of the parson's sons, unbeknownst to his father, would sneak into Ann's room at night, lie down beside her, and ask to hold her. Feeling lonely, she let him.

Was Ann a brazen hussy out to ruin Bob? Had they made love? No, according to Bob, they had only just met. The way he described that sounded so innocent and romantic – except that he and his friends, performing some charade at a college house celebration, had been drunk. Ann had sat cross-legged in a green velvet dress, looking "so quietly careful, hopeful, watching with such childlike intentness." Later on, Bob had asked her to dance, which they did, "his own shyness lost in her shy trust of him."

Overflowing with happiness, he arranged for them both to ride back to her dormitory in someone's big car, which, after filling up with all their friends, took off without him. Bob ran after it through the snow, calling her name.

It was another few months before Ann and Bob made love. How inexperienced he was! And the strange stories he told her about that. He was just as open with her as she was with him. Growing up to be a man in a household dominated by fiercely puritanical women must have been extremely awkward. "I didn't have a clue as to what men did, except literally I was a man." To his mother, sexual matters had been taboo.

The dark games he had played with his older sister had only compounded his confusion. At first Helen had been extremely jealous of her baby brother and treated him rather nastily, but she eventually turned Bob into an ally against their controlling mother. They staged veritable pageants involving numerous dolls to expand their two-person cast. A very large doll, christened Clara Bow after the movie star of the 1920s and early '30s, was subjected to a ritual murder one Saturday morning. Bob did the stabbing to the accompaniment of a solemn chant. That was so exciting they decided to bring her back to life. After going through yet another life of Hollywood glamour, Clara could be massacred again.

Also, there were the sadistic pranks Bob and his friends perpetrated on a gullible, younger boy named Bateman, playing settlers and Indians on the clearing back of the Creeleys' house. The kid believed everything he was told: that the Indians were massing for an attack on their defences; that an offence was the best defence against them; and that he had to keep watch at the camp while the rest went to fight the Indians in the woods. What followed was a long drawn-out ritual of psychological terror. Once out of young Bateman's sight, the settlers turned Indians, howling about the white dogs who'd robbed them of their land and about how they'd chop off hands, feet, testicles, and heads of all they could get hold of. Meanwhile, someone retransformed into a settler would come dashing out of the forest past the camp site screaming, "They're right behind me!," then again disappear in the woods. And there was young Bateman, bawling with terror. "Only literal fatigue ever ended that one, and it always worked." Poor sobbing Bateman, being assured it was all a game, stopped crying. Then it could start all over again, like slaying Clara Bow. "We just couldn't believe it was so simple."

Bob also told Ann about his bizarre relationship with their family servant, Theresa. Though of an extremely open, affectionate, and uncomplicated cast of mind, she had only deepened his insecurity about his sexual identity. Over the years she had virtually become his body servant. She could barely read or write; instead she drew pictures for him, always the same, round moon faces in profile with full faces on the side. Or she read to him, haltingly, Bob barely listening to her words but attentive to her soothing, affectionate bodily presence.

Theresa came from a Catholic family, the Turners, originally from Ireland. She had friends in town, like the Curleys whom she visited, Bob in tow, on her days off or after church: all "old-time Irish families, most of them very poor" and "intensely and terrifically emotional. I mean the father would cry a lot, there'd be lots of hugging – lots of physical touching and emotion which our family didn't avoid, but we just didn't have it as a habit."

> From the outset charmed
> by the soft, quick speech
> of those men and women,
> Theresa's friends – and the church
>
> she went to, the "other,"
> not the white plain Baptist
> I tried to learn God in.

Wasn't it rather strange for a teenager to be involved in this physically intimate relationship with a grown up, yet still young woman? Theresa was about thirty when Bob turned thirteen. What had that relationship done to semi-retarded, affectionate Theresa, so obviously scared of sex? Had Bob, as he'd grown older, become Theresa's substitute for a lover? Ann liked to figure out such matters.

Perhaps in a psychological sense, but his relations with Theresa had never trespassed beyond what was socially acceptable, Bob explained. Her "emotions were certainly real. But I realized at about eleven or twelve that I could confuse her by tricks, by making up rhetorical patterns."

One thing was certain: sexually Bob had remained an innocent, at least when measured by the standards of that new breed of "hipsters," some of whom Ann had met in her new friend's company. Though known for being familiar with more young women than a marriage broker as early as 1943, Bob had no sexual experience with women at all. All he'd done was talk a lot about sex or avidly listen to others talk about it: like "Rat" working at MacGregor's garage in Acton, "a bullet-headed, muscled young man with slicked back blond hair and scary insistent eyes" who would hint darkly at "women seduced, fucked, buggered, raped, torn, eaten." Bob had also heard the older boys brag about their exploits at the swimming hole, all of them naked. But for him there had been little action, except for a bit of masturbating, alone or in the company of his older cousin Laurie. That had lasted for about two to three months until Laurie had gone away to a caddy camp, leaving Bob behind to indulge in his solitary vices.

For these he drew inspiration from a book which, along with some cigarettes, he kept hidden in Laurie's barn. It had a picture of a woman, her beautiful breasts just big enough to fill the hands of a fourteen year old, a slip undulating down her otherwise naked body, across from her a man reaching to tear off the slip. Bob could still describe every detail many years later, just as he could still remember the accompanying text describing how "she did not at first understand what he expected of her. But he came closer and then she knew that he was about to …" Otherwise, he knew next to nothing about real women: not even where exactly they had their vagina, he told Ann, smiling his lovely smile.

That secret was finally revealed to him one night in the early spring of 1944 in Cambridge. To get out of the cold, they'd gone into a shed, lying on the earth floor among the tools, Ann's head against a lawnmower. According to the later fictionalized account in *The Island*, it was she who took the initiative: "She said to him, please, fuck me. The words were strange. He tried to, fumbling, because he didn't know clearly where even he might, or how to, till the excitement brought him hard against her but not in, and he spurted in a trembling incompetence all over her legs. Then, with his own hand, he rubbed her gently, slowly, insistently, until she gripped tight to him, shaking, and relaxed."

With summer approaching, they went for picnics, the further away from people the better. Their favourite spot was a large open meadow skirted by trees on the top of a hill, with no houses visible anywhere – "lying in the grass with her there, unbuttoning her dress, then pulling down his own clothes, and making inept love to her." Yet even here they weren't safe from occasional intruders like the man in a "neat blue suit" whose brazen persistence jolted Bob out of his precarious new male identity: "[He] wanted to shout at him, *now*, fuck off you old fart, you vicious prying lascivious old monster … Shaking with shame and embarrassment, he got up, pulled up his pants, feeling the man watching him but unable to look, knelt to cover [Ann] as she straightened her own clothes, and then, incredibly, collected the picnic things, picked up the basket, and with [Ann] walked in utter shaken fear away from the man, who stood still watching, and down the hill."

Meanwhile, Bob had other things to worry about. In an attempt to make good for his recent misdemeanour at Harvard, he applied for admittance to the American Field Service. But who would write references for him? There was little point in asking his teachers at Harvard; instead Bob wrote to his previous headmasters at West Acton and Holderness.

In response, Greenman described Bob as a cooperative person of excellent character and high standards whom he recommended without hesitation. The Reverend Weld expressed himself more guardedly. Though unsure as to the applicant's technical competence as an ambulance driver and motor mechanic, he felt that Bob was anxious to have a part in the war effort which had so far been rendered impossible under his classification for limited service only. Mindful of Bob's one-time gregariousness at Holderness, Weld speculated that Bob should get on well with his fellow ambulance drivers. What's more, he had a love of adventure and an excellent mind intent upon practical details. However, the final paragraph, while half-heartedly supporting Bob's application, added a major reservation: though Bob would probably live up to the expectations and responsibilities of the American Field Service as such, it was much harder to judge the steadiness of his character under conditions of great strain.

Nonetheless Bob was admitted, and instantly sent a note to Dean Hanford pleading his future readmission to Harvard. In reply, Hanford reiterated his former discouraging warnings, but also held out a glimpse of hope. Should Bob come back with an outstanding record and the approval of the Medical Department, he would be willing to talk with him about readmission and to lay his request before the board.

Meanwhile, Ann had gone to study art and music at Black Mountain College in North Carolina where Bob went to join her for a few days. This place, which would play such a crucial role in his later life, filled him with little else than disgust now. Walking up the long, sandy road, he was struck by the bleakness, the horror of the edifices, especially the Orwellian-type Studies Building. If it hadn't been for Ann, he wouldn't have lasted even the three days he stayed, sleeping in a room just below Alfred Kazin's, blabbing with a housekeeper, watching some bleak young man wander around aimlessly, or overflowing with contempt at the music several young people were improvising with flutes, drums, and other instruments: "there was no quiet, or no root, in any of it. And I hated it, frankly, loathed them all. And wanted: exact out."

Back at his mother's in Northeast Harbor, Bob received a phone call from Ann reporting that she was pregnant. The news sent him into a tailspin of panic and dithering. "Leaving her, but by a vicious twist not leaving, saying, I can't leave you like this, I must do something. What can we do. The fact was in her, not him."

Ann also told Bob that she no longer loved him and that she was going to marry someone else: a soldier, severely shocked in the war and recovering in a nearby rehabilitation centre.

5

American Field Service, 1944–45.

According to Richard E. Paulson, his commanding officer in the Burma campaign, Bob had a "terrific inferiority complex" when in the company of men of his own age or a few years older. He had obviously had some bad breaks previously, his mother having kept too close a rein on him, the major speculated.

Genevieve's hold over her son had indeed become tighter than ever. Rejected by both Harvard and Ann, all Bob's freshman bravado had collapsed. He could think of little else but his failures and follies. During the long hours on the boat from Baltimore via Gibraltar and the Suez Canal to Bombay, he pondered his dire past. It was like waking from a nightmare that had been nothing else but himself, he wrote home. All he had done was to ruin himself and hurt those who loved and trusted him. How childish and headstrong he had been!

Meanwhile, his mother assured him there would always be a home to return to for her lost and repentant son. Bob was eager to jump at the offer. He and his mother, he wrote back, had become so unified by circumstance that only death could part them. And even then the influence they had on each other would survive. All bonds except those tying him to his mother and sister had become illusory. He was rather glad that Ann had broken off the engagement; there wouldn't have been any room for her.

Meanwhile, he did everything to render himself worthy of so wonderful a family. He began to build a new life that would allow him to grow up at last. Before leaving for India he'd bought himself books so he could continue his studies of literature. He read *Murder in the Cathedral*, wondering why he had avoided it for so long; it so clearly bore out his previous appreciation of T.S. Eliot. A friend lent him books in French and German so he could start learning the one and deepening his knowledge of the other. He would work his way through Proust, which alone would require a good year. His library grew. Some books he bought, others he was given; a lot he picked out of piles left behind by people who were going home.

He couldn't imagine a more congenial group than the one he was with, he kept reassuring the women back home. He would be grateful all his life for the experience it gave him. For once he had made no mistake. Writing to Helen, Bob occasionally retained the self-deprecatory, tongue-in-cheek humour – as when sending her some rhymed doggerel appealing to "ye little childers" to pity "poor Bob Creeley." But on the whole he sounded glum and solemn. He was concerned that his verbose style might have made Helen and Genevieve suspect him of insincerity. He certainly wasn't insincere, he protested, though he might have been so earlier. Over-serious perhaps. But that was only too natural since he was readying himself for whatever he would have to face in the war.

During the long tedious voyage across the Atlantic, there was little to distract him from reading, other than his remorseful meditations in the company of an older man. John Forbes Amery turned out to be the more mysterious the more Bob found out about him. He had insisted on serving in World War II even though combat service in the previous one had already deprived him of most of one lung and severely damaged his head. Nonetheless, he was hardly a warmonger or martyr. From an old Boston family with connections to Lord Louis Mountbatten, he talked in what struck Bob as a near parody of the Harvard accent. Meanwhile Amery had obviously taken to poor Bob with his troubled university career and short-lived hipster existence. He listened attentively, gave thoughtful advice, and helped Bob find his way without being condescending.

After voyaging through the Mediterranean, the Suez Canal, and the Red Sea, there was Aden, sitting on a hill as if looking down on the boats crowding the harbour, and finally, in January 1945 after about a month at sea, Bombay. At Bombay's Green's Hotel, where they lodged before continuing to Calcutta by rail, something happened that would drastically change Bob's appearance.

Going to bed, he wrapped his artificial eye in a handkerchief and placed it on the bedside table. The next morning before he woke, a servant, in straightening out the table, dropped the eye on the floor where it smashed. Bob tried to get a replacement from the American Army Resources, but none fit. The English proposed to send him back to Britain to be fitted properly, but, given flight priorities, that might take two to three months. Bob decided to wear a patch instead. In Calcutta he obtained another glass eye from the American Army Hospital to make sure that the socket would remain unharmed until he would get back to the States. But a look in the mirror quickly made him put back the patch.

The artificial eye seemed to be staring straight up to heaven, which, he concluded, people might find disconcerting. By mid-May, the new artificial eye had cracked as well. He sent it to his mother; if a replacement were posted right away, he suggested, it might reach him within four months. By that time he was already on his way home.

Meanwhile, his eagerness to join the war effort remained unfulfilled for several weeks. From Calcutta he was sent to Number One Company Headquarters in Sudanggi, Burma, then to Advance Headquarters at Monywa, and finally to a Jeep Section in Shwebo, northwest of Mandalay. He was assigned to a Dodge 1500 water truck used for general transport and for towing a water trailer. There was little to do for several weeks, so he had ample time for further study and reflection, or he simply tried to cope with the heat while yearning for a New England spring.

Nonetheless, he was happy, he kept insisting to his family, as well as resigned to his lot. Naturally, one had to wait for an opening, but when he recalled last year's work or the lack thereof, he was glad to be allowed to just sit it out like this. And there was always something to break the boredom – such as the time when they couldn't find a water point with a pump, so he and two IORS (Indian Other Ranks) had to improvise an extremely ineffectual bucket brigade in the sweltering heat. Yet he was thoroughly enjoying the situation watching the pants of the IOR in the middle fall down every time he passed the bucket up to him on the truck. Thank God for British-issue belts!

Bob's idleness had a cause he wasn't aware of. Once his commanding officer had noticed Bob's "terrific inferiority complex," he had stationed him near headquarters to keep an eye on him. But after one and a half months of such scrutiny, Major Paulson felt it was time to send him "into a tough spot."

At that point the Burma campaign was already nearing its end. Earlier in 1945 General Slim had managed a military feat without equal in the war by putting two entire army corps across the Irrawaddy, one of the world's widest rivers. By 9 March his 19th Division recaptured Mandalay after fierce fighting. Next fell Meiktila, some one hundred miles further south. By 28 March the Japanese under the command of Lieutenant-General Heitara Kimura broke off efforts to retake that city and began to withdraw. Only six weeks remained until the monsoon would inundate everything. Before that Slim wanted to complete operation "Sea or Burst" – the reconquering of Rangoon by land. After some debate with Mountbatten, he was ready to launch himself south on 11 April. An eyewitness saw the leading division crash pass the start point, with Slim, 4 Corps Commander Frank Messervy, and three divisional commanders in attendance: "The dust thickened under the trees lining the road until the column was motoring into a thunderous yellow tunnel, first the tanks, infantry all over them, then trucks filled with men, then more tanks going fast, nose to tail, guns, more trucks, more guns – British, Sikhs, Gurkhas, Madrassis, Pathans ... this was the old Indian Army, going down to the attack."

That's an event Bob didn't see, of course. Nor did he witness the various battles as these troops moved the three hundred miles south in a *blitzkrieg* advance. All he had contact with were the casualties incurred in this heroic but ultimately futile campaign: like the soldier with his entire side shot off lying only six feet away from Bob's bed. There was nothing they could do for him. As Bob was about to doze off, he could hear the man's death rattle, but he was too tired to think about it, he admitted to his family. It was just impossible to figure out what was happening. The atmosphere was always changing, from grotesque to absurdly funny, poignantly sad and pointlessly ugly.

Nothing made sense.

Repeatedly, Bob witnessed how some Ghurkas, while being operated on, simply wouldn't pass out even though they had been given the required anaesthetic. "I saw a man thus in his sixties walking out after having been hit three times by .45 caliber bullets two of them right through the solar plexus." Later, he tried to account for these incredible events in terms of a fundamental difference between Caucasians and Indians. Whereas whites, when given an anaesthetic, usually passed out once they get to eight or nine, some Indians were known to have counted till one hundred. Obviously they had "a central nervous system that just won't quit."

Bob's first assignment in this disconcertingly confusing war was to drive a Chevrolet three-ton ambulance with the 53rd Field Ambulance, 19th Division, attached to both 4th and 33rd Corps, 14th British Army. Then, three weeks after the fall of Mandalay, he joined 76th Field Ambulance in the vicinity of Chank-Padaung on the eastern banks of the Irrawaddy, some thirty miles west of Meiktila. From here, following the advancing troops, he moved further south, first to Yenangyaung, next to Allanmyo, and finally to a position just above Prome where he remained with the 75th Field Ambulance until his platoon moved its headquarters to Rangoon after the recapture of that city on 3 May.

The routine remained more or less the same throughout: waking up around six to the chatter of the Indian Other Ranks; a quick wash; breakfast – on good days tea, eggs and bacon or sausages, on bad ones something indescribable; then a bit of occupational therapy such as sweeping out the ambulance or straightening out the kit. Once the casualties arrived around 9:30 a.m., they were treated as quickly as possible, loaded onto the ambulance, and driven some four miles along a bumpy dirt road to the main one, a journey of usually about an hour. Occasionally the groans and screams of the wounded, especially those hit in the stomach, made him slow down. The rest of the journey to the Casualty Clearing Station along a tarmac road proceeded at a faster pace. There were further delays once they arrived. Often Bob's shouts for the stretcher bearers remained unanswered, so he'd have to ferret them out from wherever they were sleeping to help him move his patients. Then he would drive back to the Advanced Dressing Station where the rest of the day was his own.

Once in a while he and his buddies would take their jeep careening along bullock tracks past trees "so huge, so steamy, they looked like par-boiled fingers coming out of the earth" to fetch some girls from a neigh-bouring village. Remembering his time with Ann, sex with someone you couldn't even understand proved surprisingly easy and uncomplicated: the lively, vigorous girl's giggles, as she stood with the others, an instinc-tual choice between her and Bob, her hands busy around his body as they drove back to the station, the two of them climbing into the back of the ambulance, letting the back flap fall, then making love, just love:

You don't share a language, like they say. Few cultural pursuits in common. Just one of each. Amazing how factually and persistently it works out. Thuds, shudders, grunts of body's delight. She is *pleased*, she is *happy*, she is *laughing*! No joke. Later, leaving, you give her carton of cigarettes *in memoriam*. She breaks up!

Bob saw little of the actual fighting but formed idiosyncratic opinions from what he heard about it. He had little good to say about his own countrymen, the victorious British, and their Indian allies. He hated, even loathed the Americans. He held in contempt the British who knew nothing but bad food and poor clothing. He poured scorn on the Sikh soldiers, who, as soon as they got a scratch, prepared themselves to meet their maker by a "long involuted wail / shaping itself over a range of abt 6 octaves."

By contrast, the badly mauled Japanese appeared to him as "great / great / great: men." He reflected admiringly upon stragglers picked up by the British, who still shot at their captors as they were being taken. An-other Japanese, riddled by slugs, jerked erect on the operating table and knifed the surgeon. "They used to look like men from Mars: most of them / small as monkeys, come out from trees, ground, the works." These mythical creatures led by some unidentified heroic general, rather than Slim's troops, are credited with the feat of crossing a river two miles wide "on vines, stretched the distance ... Three fucking divisions waiting.

Woosters, Gurkhas / Sikhs, Queens own, & 7th, 5th, 11th. Waiting, for them. On a road / high sides, bullock carts passing all day, long. Real tension. Then he comes / the whole works, 1000 with him, he right at the back, they open a strip of the road, half a mile long, and they're over and gone, back, back, back, into the hills, sat in back of us, I cd look at each morning." These stylistically erratic accounts from letters written to a friend, Charles Olson, five years later, also record an aspect of Bob's wartime experience carefully concealed from his family. Apparently, his other self as the hipster rebel had survived alongside the repentant sinner. In his words to Olson, he was "out of [his] head those days: with or without stimulus."

A letter to Aunt Bernice written in June 1945 gives the reformed sinner's urbane description of Rangoon where, after doing service in another tough spot around Pegu, he spent a month in a hospital recovering from accumulated ailments such as foot rot and jungle sores. He enjoyed the wonderful feeling of being dry, sleeping without noisy interruptions, and eating other things than bully beef and biscuits. He reflected upon the very modern architecture of Rangoon's business section, the luxuriant and shady seclusion boasted by its residential area, and the fact that it had obviously been a very pleasant city before the war.

An altogether different way of looking at things is evident from the later reminiscences recorded for Olson during the 1950s. To this other Creeley, everything is paradoxical and unreal – "hundreds of people ... yelling & squatting, & kids, dozens, running around, playing ... and at the center, these Buddhas, going way the hell up, some 150 ft., static, with all this fucking movement around them, at their feet." Everywhere around him looms the "sudden grotesqueness" of death: "two men dead on the ground, blankets over them, and a crazy flower or bird very close to them;" or there are the ubiquitous emissaries of an other-worldly order, seemingly unperturbed by the slaughter around them: meditating Buddhist priests "dressed in deep fine orange cloth," oblivious of nearby machine gun fire.

Increasingly, Bob learned to enhance these surrealist experiences by taking diverse stimulants. One was drinking tea Oriental fashion, tasting herbs from a little dish, savouring the taste on the tongue, and then spitting it out. Other stimulants were more potent. While repentant of his past Bohemian follies, he had obviously never stopped drinking, though the booze went down far less smoothly in Burma and India than at home. The rye imbibed in the back of the ambulance truck, for instance, made your mouth feel like fur or caused you to sweat even more than usual. But here a Sikh provided a remedy.

Bob found that these men, of whose soldierly prowess he thought so little, could be intriguingly charming, or signal more in one phrase or gesture than a European in a whole evening's conversation. He played bridge with one Sikh, an older man, delightedly watching him dominate the entire table. A fellow ambulance driver, also a Sikh, one day observed Bob drinking rye, laughed, then asked Bob how it tasted. When told: like hell, he went away, came back with an onion, cut off a slice, and told Bob to rub a little on his tongue. The effect, at least according to Creeley's later memories, was miraculous: "too much! i.e., the onion cuts all the shit taste out, & it tastes very damn good."

Towards the end of his stay in the East, Bob's drinking became so bad again that even the onion trick wasn't enough to cut out the unpleasant side effects. The Burma campaign was virtually over. Bob's platoon, along with a majority of field service personnel, had already returned to India during Bob's convalescence in the Rangoon hospital. Upon his release, he joined them in Calcutta, and from there moved on to Secunderabad. It was a time of waiting, at first for the 14th Army's next operation, then, after Hiroshima and Nagasaki, and Japan's surrender on 14 August 1945, for the journey back home.

As Creeley recalled in 1967, he was in a barrack with about forty men, most of whom were "turned on almost all day long." There was nothing to do except drink – until you got sick and started vomiting. At this juncture "a friend from Southern California" suggested an alternative to alcohol – marijuana: "After literally bile for the last two hours coming out of your guts, he said, 'Try this.' There was nothing mystical. It was ... like, 'Here, have an aspirin.' So we switched and everything became very delightful."

More and more frequently experience became a whirl of hallucinogenic visions. One night in Hyderabad in the pitch black dark, he was stopped dead in his tracks by strange drum beats and a distant glow, then immersed in a synaesthetic orgy of sounds, colours, smells, and motions: a funeral procession, like a mirage, appeared as mysteriously as it vanished. A glow of light coming towards him, the wonderfully looping drum beats, the full deep smell of flowers, hundreds and hundreds of them, being swept along about two blocks, then, suddenly, nothing again: "Not a trace."

Increasingly, even his memories of these events seemed to disintegrate. On the flight back to England a fire broke out, so his plane with "all these flames shooting back" came in low over the Persian Gulf and set down two hundred miles from Babylon, "the land, flat low, damn endless, under all these fantastic stars." Tel Aviv, where he spent a fortnight before proceeding via North Africa, Marseilles, Cambridge, and London to

Barry, just above Cardiff, appeared as a babel of voices: "yiddish, german, french, spanish, italian, arabic, polish, russian ... SPEECH ... was rolling in it, for 2 damn weeks."

After carrying a paper bag full of marijuana through British customs at Cardiff, Bob was well equipped for the two-month wait in Barry as well as for the voyage home. On the *Queen Elizabeth* going from Southhampton to Halifax, Nova Scotia, he and a friend took to smoking in a toilet serving some fifteen to twenty other people. These, lined up in front and banging on the door, came to suspect that the toilet was being used for homosexual activities. Suspicion deepened when Bob missed his bunk bed one night and climbed into someone else's. From then on the two friends smoked their marijuana up on the deck, even though it was restricted. "So it was absolutely silent and isolate, seeing that whole sea in a beautiful full moon. Just beautiful." They docked in Halifax on 19 November 1945.

6

Harvard, 1946–47.

Anyone who had watched Bob fall apart during his odyssey home was in for a surprise to see the same man back in Cambridge. Burma had taught him self-reliance, though hardly of a conventional kind. Instead of relying on just one self, Bob had taught himself to depend on at least two.

What would have broken a more sensitive man had made him more tenacious and complex. In petitioning for readmission to Harvard, he explained: Often he had found himself completely ignorant of everything but his immediate situation. Everywhere he had been confronted with seemingly unjustifiable death and suffering. He'd had to reduce his own beliefs to basics, almost to the point where these beliefs became concrete like the food one ate. He was forced to discover himself and to believe in himself. It was the only way to maintain his identity. The time wasted in the army, in spite of his efforts to keep busy reading books, had made him realize how immature and foolish he'd been earlier in ignoring the opportunities to study and learn at Harvard.

Everyone was impressed to hear him speak in such a forthright manner. He talked without the slightest suggestion that he was putting on an act, testified Douglas Bush. Bob's account of his experiences at Harvard and in the field service struck the professor, who was asking him pointed questions, as admirable in both candour and intelligence. Bob left such an impression of thoughtful maturity that Bush was surprised to find he was only nineteen; Bush had thought he was at least twenty-one.

Others came to share the professor's unequivocally good opinion. Bob made a favourable impression on Dr Fleming and also impressed Dean Hanford who clearly remembered the unsettled young man who had made something of a mess of things at Harvard earlier. He found Bob to have matured and settled down.

Who could have further doubts about the genuineness of Bob's transformation after reading the testimonies of those who had seen him in action in Burma? One, John A. Lester from Rutgers University, drawing on many months of such observation, wrote that Bob was certainly mature enough to handle work at the sophomore level: definitely college material. Even in Burma he had displayed a real interest in and talent for literary criticism. Under the circumstances, that was such a remarkable feat that Lester had written to Professor Harry Levin to keep an eye out for Creeley. Creeley had the calibre worthy of Levin's attention. Major Paulson, his commanding officer in Burma, wrote that Bob, rather unexpectedly for a man with a terrific inferiority complex, had "made good." He had been an asset throughout the remainder of the campaign, had matured and developed a definite purpose in life. Paulson spoke warmly in favour of Bob's readmittance, hoping that the administration would drop him a note about how Bob was getting along in case they did. Obviously, the major had become fond of his protégé. Bob had been popular with the other men. With so many "blow-hards" around, his modesty had been refreshing.

Only one person, psychiatrist Dr Wells, sounded a more cautious note. Bob, he suggested, was at least able *to simulate* the favourable impression he made on others. Thus he had developed a seemingly very mature and insightful attitude towards his previous difficulties at Harvard. However, even Dr Wells had only good things to say about the applicant. There was no question about Bob's intellectual competence. He displayed a very active and original mind which, once brought under proper social control, would render intellectual contributions of considerable value. Hence, Wells concluded that Creeley should be given another chance, though only one more.

The administrative board decided that he would be allowed to register at the opening of the spring term 1946, in sophomore standing. Bob's mother was delighted. Obviously her son was keeping the promises he'd made in his letters. And so did she, offering Bob to share her home on 61 Sparks Street, Cambridge, where she had come to work as a nurse shortly before his departure for Burma. Her regenerate son had come back from the war a hero, decorated with both the 1939–45 Star and the Burma Star. And the determination Bob had shown in getting back into Harvard!

At first Bob seemed to fulfil his mother's expectations. By the summer of 1946, his grades had risen from an initial c to a b average which he maintained and even slightly improved upon by the fall. His extracurricular activities as associate editor of a special e.e. cummings issue of the Harvard *Wake*, along with friends Race Newton and Buddy Berlin, did not detract from his scholastic accomplishments. The *Wake*, which was set up in protest against Harvard's establishment literary magazine, the *Advocate*, also published Bob's first poem.

But gradually, during Bob's senior year at Harvard, his marks dropped back to a c average, the only exception being a b+ in English 60b. By 23 May 1947, he presented himself to the administration to apologize for missing the Philosophy 6 exam. He didn't fail to make his by-now habitual good impression. According to the official report, he was wearing a black patch over one eye, soft spoken and sorry to hear he had caused some inconvenience. Two months later he petitioned to withdraw from Harvard for the remainder of the term. The administration advised him to do so, noting his unsatisfactory mid-term record giving him an e in English and Mathematics as well an Absent in Fine Arts. Once things became more stable for him, he could always return. But that was never to be.

What turned Bob, within less than a year, from a repentant, eager sophomore into a jaded last-semester senior? By this time he was a married man and father-to-be, commuting to classes from Cape Cod. He was disillusioned with Harvard. After his first troubled year, he'd still hoped the university could provide him with a rounded education. Why had he undergone the gruesome ordeal of driving an ambulance in Burma except that it had promised to get him readmitted to Harvard? But the war had only widened the gap between what was taught at Harvard and his evolving personal values. These had first been shaken by the turmoil of the Depression, then reduced to factual basics during his year in Burma. He had come to feel that the coherence that had held things together at one time was no longer possible. "There seemed no logic, so to speak, that could bring together all the violent disparities of that experience. The arts especially were shaken and the *picture of the world* that might previously have served them had to be reformed."

The war appeared to have had the opposite effect on his teachers at Harvard, who tried to hold on with almost paranoid resolve to what had so irrevocably fallen apart. Their militant need for rational structures, reflected in book titles such as *The Rage for Order* or *The Armed Vision*, made them impose on students what they'd decided were right ways of thinking or proper taste. The lone exception who showed some interest in what Bob was after did so almost grudgingly. Fred McCreary, a writer turned professor, taught an English A course "for students unable to bypass it by scoring well on the qualifying test," Bob being one of them. McCreary once asked Bob to see him after class. "When all the others had left," Creeley recalls, "he spoke to me quite sternly, asking if I had thought of what I might like to do after college. It seemed an ironic emphasis upon my uselessness in all respects, but I answered that I hoped to be a writer. He answered that if I kept at it long enough, I just might make it – or words to that effect. It was the only literal encouragement of that kind I ever got at Harvard."

Though Bob studied under renowned scholars like Douglas Bush, Delmore Schwartz, Harry Levin, Werner Jaeger, and F.O. Matthiessen, he found little inspiration in their teaching. In one course he was taught that in writing a poem you ought to escape from yourself, or in reading it ignore all possible biographical innuendos; in another class he was told that autobiographical material was the only thing useful in interpretation for it was all one really knew. Where the method misfired, it had a curious way of stubbornly following through on its dynamics. Once Delmore Schwartz, long-time editor of the *Partisan Review*, began a writing class with the assumption that there must be *one* writer that all the students respected in common. Even though it turned out that there wasn't, he kept insisting, so the class had to work its way through this dilemma for the full length of the semester.

Creeley remembers his classes at Harvard with bitterness and frustration: "My eager thirst for knowledge, almost Jude-the-Obscurian in its innocence, was all but shut down by the sardonic stance of my elders. It was Andrew Wanning, for example, who began a second lecture on Wallace Stevens's poetry with a remark I *think* I will never forget: 'The only thing I can find to say about the later poetry of Wallace Stevens is that it is very obscure.' He then played us a record of Stevens reading."

Woe betide the student who dared venture beyond the academically sanctioned canon. Even an otherwise sensitive, open-minded teacher like F.O. Matthiessen, whom Bob kept querying about his personal heroes, hardly escaped the trend of his time. Why hadn't he put the *Cantos* on his course on contemporary poetry? Bob asked. Because he understood Pound's work too poorly, Matthiessen answered, hedging the issue of Pound's political views, which he, as a devout Christian and committed socialist, found most suspect.

But what was wrong with Walt Whitman who, in the hands of the self-same literary custodians, seemed to fare little better? Prolix and generalizing, went on and on. He lacked structure. Sorry, but he was really a bit of a dumbbell. The typical self-taught man. Just pathetic, not to mention his abnormal sexuality. As a historical figure, yes, but to take an active interest in him as a poet would be simply in bad taste. The students were "herded past him as quickly as possible."

Once again Bob insisted. Worse, he decided to make known his heretical interest in Whitman via another *persona non grata*, the author of *The Bridge*. Hart Crane? Potentially a major poet, though *The Bridge* was ultimately a failure. Of course! Everybody said so – though people were less sure as to how and why. Matthiessen relented. Bob was allowed to give a paper on Crane, even though Crane, like Pound, had been excluded from the course. But even more difficult to overcome than the resistance of the professors was that of fellow students intent upon their own sophistication. Bob read them a sample:

> Yes, Walt,
> Afoot again, and onward without halt, –
> Not soon, nor suddenly, – no, never to let go
> My hand
> in yours,
> Walt Whitman –
> so

Even while reading the lines, he noticed their blasé smiles, the odd titter. But couldn't they hear, he insisted: the intently human tone, the pacing of the rhythm? Or couldn't they see the syntax, or simply the punctuation? Couldn't they read? To their precociously cynical outlook, there was little more than the awkward rhymes, the pathetic articulations of sentimental camaraderie, and, most embarrassingly, Crane's openly stated wish to hold hands with a fellow homosexual.

It was simply asphyxiating. For one couldn't dispute Matthiessen's scholarly accomplishment or his being a "man of deep commitment and care for his students." Just as one couldn't deny fellow students like Kenneth Koch or Donald Hall their intelligence and brilliance. What's more, guys like them were writing and publishing while Bob was mostly *aspiring* to be a writer. Nonetheless, he couldn't look up to them. Kenneth, one day, invited him to his living quarters decorated with tasteful reproductions and carefully chosen furniture. They had a drink, listened to some classical records, then to a few of Kenneth's poems. Kenneth was courteous enough, but Bob felt totally out of place in this well-financed ambience of choice taste and obsolete genteelism.

Donald Hall was a more decisive *non sequitur*: an *Advocate* man, pink cheeks, about twenty-two years old, a tub, an idiot, Creeley wrote later. Somehow these guys continued in the social situation of writers, while the pre-war sense of the professional had all but disintegrated for Bob. Another one was Bunny (alias V.R.) Lang, successfully active in the Cambridge Actors Workshop group. Lang only confirmed Bob in his sense that if there still was a social possibility for artists, he certainly didn't fit into it himself. He seemed to be from the other side of the tracks. Even outsiders like Craig Gilbert, feeling alienated from academia and looking for a way out, aroused mixed feelings at best. Craig had embraced the classic Hemingway pose complete with hat, trench coat, and bottle of bourbon – an impressive attempt but hardly one Bob felt tempted to emulate.

A foray into left-wing politics did little to change his sense of general dis-orientation. After receiving his ideological training from the Young Com-munists League, he ended up working for the Progressive Citizens of America. The PCA sought the election of Henry Agard Wallace, whose Pro-gressive Party was equally backed by the Communist Political Association.

From its inception in 1919, American communism had had a che-quered turncoat career, for the most part dancing to the fiddle of the So-viet-dominated Comintern and, back of it, the most recent development in Soviet power politics. Initially it attacked socialists as worse than fas-cists, then called for a "popular front" uniting all anti-fascist groups. After the signing of the Hitler-Stalin non-aggression pact, it denounced France and Britain for unleashing an "imperialist" war, then after Ger-many's attack on Russia threw its full support behind the U.S. govern-ment in assisting Britain and Russia to wage the "democratic" war against the axis. The Cold War, which, needless to say, communists blamed on U.S. actions, again had brought a major change in directive. When Henry Agard Wallace, former vice-president (1941–45) under F.D. Roosevelt, accused the Truman administration of war-mongering, the Communist Political Association, under the new chairmanship of William Foster, gave its full backing to Wallace's presidential candidacy.

Predictably, the constraints of party discipline in the Cape Cod Pro-gressive Citizens of America chapter, which Bob joined, soon proved as irksome as or worse than those he had experienced at Harvard. He found the assumption of good fellowship amongst the members both annoying and bewildering. On the one hand, he wished to establish himself in a social context; on the other, in being defined by political goals not strictly his own, he had to constantly play the hypocrite. It was unbearable. Years later, he recalled the incident that put an abrupt end to this political career. He was giving his treasurer's report "with recommendations," but the whole situation simply struck him as fright-eningly unreal. "I felt I was floating abt 5 ft. off the floor, couldn't for a minute HEAR what I was saying, & became conscious, slowly, of a kind of amazement on the part of those who were listening. Abt a week later, I was relieved of the job."

Meanwhile, he had long resumed the bohemian life begun before Burma, going back to alcohol and taking up dope; he was back to fre-quenting the bar scene like Jim's Place near Harvard Square; back to the endless talk sessions which occasionally made him feel that he had never talked to anyone but himself; and, above all, back to the jazz clubs listen-ing to Charlie Parker, Thelonias Monk, Max Roach, Al Haig, Jaki Byard, Dick Twardzik, and others. In this growing realm of interest, Bob's sister, Helen, played the role of a major catalyst. Her friends Hugh Whitehouse and Don Mishara had their own band. Her second husband, Dick Axt, was a "classic university jazz clarinetist."

Most of Bob's new friends were part of the jazz world as well: like Race Newton, pianist, Joe Leach, trumpet player and hipster in a pork pie hat, and Buddy Berlin, a short man with black curly hair, and, unlike Bob, neatly dressed to the latest hipster fashion. Buddy was friends with the big jazz stars, a world compelling to Bob for both the music and its glamour. One morning in New York City, Buddy had taken off with Dizzy Gillespie, and then, while Race and Bob were sitting on a sidewalk up on Morningside Drive, reappeared in a black Lincoln Continental – Coleman Hawkins driving, Dizzy on the far side, and Buddy in the middle.

An older musician, Joe Laconi, a student at the New England Conservatory of Music, even thought he might turn one-time violinist Robert White Creeley into a jazz musician. Joe wanted Bob to teach himself bass and join a band. Bob and Joe temporarily shared an apartment on Tremont Street just down from the Hi Hat, where Jaki Byard was the house pianist, and around the corner from the Club Savoy, starring Charlie Parker and other celebrities.

Increasingly Bob felt drawn to search out those who were "in trouble of some sort" like himself: bums, thieves, hitmen, street kids, everyone speaking in a different lingo, – "making it" or finding this or that "the most." At one point he started to hang out with a petty thief. Initially, he was spellbound by the man's compulsive storytelling, then appalled reading in the newspaper about his more sordid exploits. A musician friend from Cleveland who had started taking drugs found a way of supporting his habit by selling books "taken out" of the *Advocate* library, which housed precious items like signed T.S. Eliot editions. One night in a bar in East Cambridge, then notorious for its gangs, a friend came over to warn Bob that someone was out to kill him. Better get out of there, he was told. Bob did, moving "from bar to bar." Four hours later, the friend caught up with him again to tell him that "the mistake had been corrected." What mistake? The hitman had confused him with someone named Curley.

Before long Bob's outward appearance started to blend in with the underground of outcasts and down-and-outs. Driving down a one-way street in the wrong direction, he and four others were stopped by a policeman who looked at them, grinned, and said: You boys are from Columbus Avenue. When did you get out?

Columbus Avenue? Get out? The policeman explained: No one who lives there is without a record. Race Newton remembers first meeting Bob at a Schönberg concert in Cambridge: "His hands were really shaking, and he was smoking a cigarette, and his fingers were all yellow. He was a total wreck."

Via friends like Race, Seymour Lawrence, and Walter Adams, drug expert and literary anarchist, there were indirect links between Creeley's Cambridge circle and the corresponding one in New York around Allen Ginsberg, later to become the Beat Generation's most famous exponent. Typical of both groups was Bill Canastra, an ex-Harvard lawyer known to have caused traffic jams by lying down on an avenue crossing or to have danced drunk along the parapet of his building.

Creeley later analysed such pranks as stemming from a suicidal impulse that at the time amounted to an almost "societal condition" – "a sort of terrifying need to demonstrate the valuelessness of one's own life." Canastra's suicidal urge soon found its sad fulfilment. One night on the subway just as the train was pulling out of Bleeker Street station, Canastra, as a joke performed for the benefit of his friends, threw himself towards the open window, as if he had changed his mind and was going to the Bleeker Tavern. But this time he had overdone it. His body, hanging far out of the subway carriage, hit a pillar inside the tunnel and was yanked out. He was dragged along the tracks for fifty-five feet before the train stopped. Bill Canastra died on his way to Columbus Hospital.

7

Marriage.

A Beat before the Beats, Bob Creeley bears more resemblance to Bill Burroughs than to Bill Canastra. If he didn't spare himself, he spared others even less. He was "charged," as Mitch Goodman remembers, yet he knew how to externalize his inner turmoil, hit back when attacked, and, especially when drunk, keep himself at a high pitch of potential aggressiveness. Nagging friends and enemies alike, he was sort of pulling the wings off flies, tormenting people, Race Newton recalls. Word got around about the wild man. Creeley was fast becoming legendary.

Some people felt provoked even by his appearance: the very image of Satan, usually dressed in black. Hair unkempt, as if it hadn't been washed for weeks, the left eye fixed or covered by a black patch, the other glancing at you surreptitiously, you never quite knew whether out of curiosity or hostility, the mouth muttering. Hauling you up short with a piercing stare, then overwhelming you with his fierce opinions.

Self-absorption made him largely unaware of the effect he had on others. A friend remembers once accompanying him in his rattle-trap truck. They stopped at a red light, where someone in another car kept staring. "What the hell is he looking at me for?" Bob burst out, oblivious to how his appearance, like the devil incarnate, struck others.

Many people, even friends, were afraid of him. His smouldering aggressiveness, fuelled by his provocations, could erupt into actual violence at any moment. More than once he had taught those deceived by his slender body what his strong hands could accomplish when propelled by red-hot fury.

Such physical belligerence went hand in hand with his tough-guy attitude towards friendship. With few exceptions, Bob explained to Jacob Leed, he would need reminding to tell enemies and friends apart. What's more, some of the latter would only get a good spit in the face for their friendship.

His plans for marriage were devised in similarly contentious fashion.

His self-proclaimed strategy of reifying his existence was to marry a woman who would be ultimately responsible for him. There were at least three candidates: one was Ann Hershon, whom he liked very much but ultimately didn't feel attracted to. By contrast, Jacob Leed's girlfriend, Alison, presented a genuine temptation, as well as a moral dilemma that Bob resolved in characteristically unorthodox fashion. He had wanted Alison one very drunken night. He said to her that he was no longer Jacob's friend. This, as he explained to the very same Jacob in a subsequent letter, was not an unreasonable thing to say as he was about to make love to Alison. How could he, drunk or not, feel he was Jacob's friend while being on the verge of betraying the trust Jacob had placed in him? Once the affair was over, Bob decided it had been occasioned largely by Alison's unfortunate attraction to him. Hence, the lady should not, after all, be allowed to come between himself and their friend Jacob. Besides, he had renewed relations with someone who offered a more promising target. He loved Ann MacKinnon, and was going to marry her.

Ann had been one of the first persons Bob had searched out upon his return to Cambridge around Thanksgiving Day of 1945. Trying to locate her in a Radcliffe dorm, he was still wearing his wartime uniform as well as a black patch, looking "kind of dramatic" and enjoying the odd "charming flash response" from diverse young ladies. "I did literally locate this girl who was as dislocated as I was," Creeley remembers. *Mabel: A Story* recalls their reunion, as arranged via a mutual friend:

He sees her sitting at a booth toward the back of the restaurant, talking to the friend, the other girl, who has arranged the meeting at his request. The first girl does not know that he is to be there. He gets up, walks toward the table, already practising gestures of greeting. Hi! He constructs love for her in his head, over and over. He is serious.

... When she sees him, she seems to scream, looks at the other girl, moves back against the booth. He sits down beside her. He wants her now.

He quickly learned that Ann had neither married the soldier nor given birth to their child, but had aborted spontaneously. Bob's decision to marry Ann was made almost as quickly. "Really I all but – no, I don't think I forced her to marry me," Creeley mused in 1975. "I think we had the mutual need for somebody to locate, so we grabbed on to each other. I think I really did insist upon marriage just to be real, to take up a real role as I assumed it to be."

Before the wedding could take place, Bob still had to suffer through some more of the calamities incurred by the "grossness of his own incapabilities, the treachery of his self-assurance." Before long, Ann was pregnant again. This time the decision to abort the child was made jointly. "How can there be a world so finally bleak that all impulse ends as that child," Creeley wondered later. As suggested by *The Island*, the pregnancy terminated in his mother's bathroom, after everyone else but he and Ann had gone to sleep.

The pills again. The cramps started, he ... felt the contractions through her arms, her body, and then it was born, the half developed foetus, into the toilet ... a tiny blunted child, a boy. He had retrieved it from the water, because it was too large to go down, and wrapping it in some old newspaper, put it out in the ashcan in the alley. But they were safe, and they had to be. It was nothing they wanted, and it seemed at last that nothing they wanted would even be.

For all his determination to marry Ann, Bob kept wondering what she might do to him, or, worse, he to her. No intelligent man can marry without fear, he mused to Leed. The German poet Rilke, for instance who had failed so miserably in marriage, thought that husband and wife could remain separate individuals. It was all very well to allege that trust in one another was all that was necessary: what if those "one anothers" should turn into different persons in a year or so? Bob was convinced that was precisely what would happen.

Nonetheless, he felt confident that he and Ann could achieve the *sine qua non* of any real bond between man and woman, i.e., the final blending provided by the most complete fulfillments of sexual intercourse. Also, Ann had money; a small monthly payment of $185 from a trust fund left her by her adoptive mother that would allow him to devote himself to his writing. Friends like Mitch Goodman came to suspect that he married Ann primarily for the money. But given the bridegroom's unpredictable temper, they were afraid to say so.

Cid Corman, a writer and editor who had no idea about Ann's private means, found out in a situation several years later that strikingly revealed to him Bob's own attitude towards the issue. They were driving along in Bob's rattle-trap truck when Bob burst out, saying he hoped Corman didn't think he'd married Ann for her money. That was the first time he realized that Bob had, Corman recalls: he wouldn't have quit school otherwise.

The wedding, as Creeley reported to Leed, was completely successful. Present were a justice of the peace, Buddy Berlin, Bob's mother (who beamed throughout the ceremony), unfortunate Connie (who dripped tears), and Bob, who was very happy. The only person Creeley's account overlooks was the bride. Best man Buddy Berlin later remembered how the justice of the peace, a normally casual man, suddenly became very formal, harumphing, hemming and hawing. Buddy and Bob had a laughing fit.

Less hilarious was the beginning of marriage. Bob had been drinking heavily and showed no signs of slowing down. "Not all the way gone, but shot: 3/4 of any day." At first the young couple lived at the Hotel Bruns-wick, on 520 Boylston Street in Boston, a Harvard project for married vet-erans. Bob found the place quiet and comfortable, and duly proceeded to change that by playing his stereo so loud the general fuse blew.

Next, the Creeleys moved to Provincetown, a Bohemian artists' colony which Bob liked even better than the Hotel Brunswick. After Cambridge, he found people out there surprisingly friendly and helpful. But in the relative isolation of Cape Cod, his drinking only worsened. Trying to set-tle down and write, he couldn't sit still, feeling drawn back to the scene he was trying to escape. He would take off, leaving behind his once-again pregnant young wife, then come back two or three days later.

Officially he was still studying at Harvard, but the will to continue, let alone graduate, was long gone. Commuting between Provincetown and Boston on old boats like the S.S. *Steel Pier* or the S.S. *Chauncey Depew*, which served liquor during the three-hour crossing, he was usually stoned by the time they reached their destination. Finally, he managed to lose his books on the way to Cambridge. On 31 July 1947 he petitioned to withdraw from Harvard.

Slater Brown, who had convinced Bob to move to Provincetown, was an unlikely person to make him shake his drinking. When Bob met him at McBride's, a Cambridge tavern, Brown was a de facto alcoholic. "I'd gone in to get away from the usual company, and also to drink," Creeley recalls, "and found myself at the far end of the crowded bar with just one older man at the wall beyond me. It was Slater. As we talked, he asked me my interests as a student, and then, as I made clear my reading and hopes to write, he told me … that he was the character 'B' in Cummings's *The Enormous Room*." To Bob's growing amazement, Slater also turned out to have been friends with Hart Crane.

Otherwise, Bob's new acquaintance seemed down on his luck. The one-time prolific writer and translator was working as a gardener in Bel-mont. During the autumn of 1947, he had been drinking so hard that his wife had him shipped off to dry out at the Washingtonian on Dover Street in downtown Boston. Yet with the El running right by the clinic, Brown's shattered nerves couldn't take the noise and stress. He took ref-uge with artist John Berks on Charles Street close to a neighbourhood bar. Here he one day told the regulars that he was a writer, causing them to laugh so hard he had to leave. Race Newton remembers Slater Brown as a man of medium height, with a moustache, wearing a fedora hat and a velvet collar on his overcoat, "all in urgent need of repair."

A contemporary portrait of him made by Berks, otherwise known for his busts of Frank Sinatra, showed Brown seated in a chair with a book in his hands, looking like he would die if someone didn't give him a beer, and quick. Meanwhile Berks missed everything about the man that had impressed Bob – such as his willingness, in spite of his own troubles, to take Bob seriously in his desire to become a writer at a point when he had as yet written next to nothing.

Brown, the first writer Bob ever knew personally, became not just a very good friend but a "tacit father surrogate." He would comment, give advice, tell fascinating anecdotes about Hart Crane, or psychoanalyse e.e. cummings's megalomania in terms of his allegedly miniscule prick. Or he told Bob that he'd turn out to be another Yvor Winters. Obligingly, Bob more and more played the Oedipal son who loved and respected but also infuriated the older man for refusing to take his advice. To make matters worse, Brown felt strongly drawn to Bob's wife. One night the couple was looking for Brown, who once again had been drinking hard. And suddenly, there he was stepping in from out of the rain, saying he'd heard Ann calling him. Obviously, there was a deep bond between them, Bob concluded.

Remembering the incident two years later, it still struck Bob that Brown was "I expect, just that, my father." But at that point Charles Olson had already begun to replace Brown in that paternal role. There were aspects to Brown's personality which Bob found pathetic. Who would put up with being called a drunken degenerate, or an utter waste who ought to be shot for the protection of society? That's what the president of Bobbs-Merrill, publisher of Brown's novel *The Burning Wheel*, had told him after he'd asked for the money the publisher owed him. Not only that: after swallowing these insults, Brown had pleaded with the president that he allocate a little money with his grocery store so that he'd at least be able to get some food. "He gets so deep in the bitterness," Bob complained to Olson, "he just goes sour."

A father surrogate in one sense, Slater Brown was a solemn warning in another. Never would Bob want to turn into a pathetic and bitter man like him. Meanwhile, life on the Cape provided ample opportunity for becoming just that. The Provincetown artist colony swarmed with phonies and hangers-on, many of them spending large amounts of money on looking bohemian and poor. The Creeleys' gloomy, "jerry-built" summer cottage in nearby Truro with its drawn shades and a big black dog called Lina slinking around the furniture reminded one of an Edward Hopper painting. As a friend recalls, "there was food and dirty dishes. I remember this horrible meat on the table. Why the dog didn't eat it, I don't know. Maybe she couldn't stand it either." Present, besides the Creeleys, were Race Newton, Buddy Berlin, and Ann Hershon. Suddenly a man, perhaps a real-estate agent, all buffed up in a hat, suit and tie, turned up on the doorstep. He had obviously never seen anything like it. When Lina got up, he tipped his hat to the dog and left.

More and more often, Bob just wanted to escape either for one more drinking spree in Boston or for another of his increasingly crazy drives. Once he went to New York, and then realized he had forgotten his friends' addresses, so he drove straight back to Truro.

Bob's companion on these escapades was not Ann but Lina. One night he smashed the car on his way to Boston near Buzzard's Bay. Dog and master first got a ride to a house in which some thirty people were celebrating an old lady's seventieth birthday. Lina was served a big bowl of hot soup, while Bob was given whiskey and cake as well as permission to dance with a pretty girl to a record from an old Wurlitzer juke-box.

Next, some cops stopped for them but drove off before Lina could get in as well, assuring Bob that the dog would follow on its own. They dropped Bob off at a diner some five miles down the road. Bob waited, and sure enough, suddenly there was Lina, running towards him through the snow. From the diner, where Lina ate doughnuts, they got a ride in a truck to Hyannis, from where they tried to continue by bus. But the driver wouldn't take Lina. The only alternative was a taxi, but Bob didn't have the money. For four hours he answered calls at the taxi stand and finally got a reduced rate back home, though not quite all the way. The stretch from the main road to the house was too drifted to get through. There was nothing else to do but to walk – in sneakers. "Real cold it was. Both of us, dog & me, just abt done when we got in."

Later on, Bob found out what had caused the accident. A man at whose house Bob and Ann had spent the previous evening had tried to stop Bob from driving in his drunkenness and deflated the rear tire of his car. Had he done it out of real concern or out of a subliminal wish to kill him? All Bob knew was that the man hated him while feeling drawn to Ann.

Was he behaving like a proper husband? Things were becoming more and more impossible, especially with Ann heavily pregnant and expecting to give birth any day. That happened at the hospital in Hyannis, Massachusetts. Bob, who kept pestering the nurse at reception for news of his wife's progress, was told "Wife? You're too young to have a wife, much less a baby!" Creeley was twenty-one, like Ann. Their first child, a boy they named David, was born on 5 October 1947. It was time for them to find a proper home away from it all where Bob could settle down, stop drinking, and get on with his writing.

Wake, revived by Seymour Lawrence and Jack Hawkes, had recently accepted Bob's "Poem for D.H. Lawrence" and "Greendoon's Song" for publication in their Spring 1948 issue. He had also started a novel, drafted some short stories, and was planning more. Now he needed time and, above all, inner peace to carry out these projects. He decided that a return to the rural life of his childhood might provide that. The money from the sale of the house Ann had inherited would furnish the means. Bill Gordon, a Harvard acquaintance, suggested that they buy the option to purchase Rock Pool Farm near Littleton, New Hampshire, and Bob went to inspect it. Race Newton, who accompanied him, remembers how, after an endless drive through the snow, they arrived there late at night. "There was no electricity, so we went around striking matches, and he was asking me: What do you think? Think it's sound? Do you think it will be all right? So I said: just don't burn it down, and it'll probably be okay."

Though not as stately as Four Winds Farm, the new abode exceeded Bob's childhood dwelling in natural beauty and wildness. Now as then, Rock Pool Farm is reached by driving for about half a dozen miles along the road from Littleton towards Lisbon up to Barrett Crossing, where a bridge on the left takes you across the Ammonoosuc River. Past some railway tracks, a dirt road winds up into a forest, skirting a gabled hut, appropriately called the Witch's House. Then it suddenly opens onto a small hillside plateau surrounded by trees. Here, two deep roofed, wood-planked structures, each with a towering chimney stack, face each other across the clearing. Certainly, the Creeleys and visiting friends would find ample space to live here. The building on the left, the so-called barn, though without water or toilet, had separate living quarters with three rooms and a good-sized fireplace. The main house, in addition to a spacious kitchen and living room with another massive fireplace on the ground floor, had four upper floor bedrooms reached by a steep staircase. But why "Rock Pool" Farm? The secret of the name was revealed after a climb through the forest towards another opening where the Gale River, originating from Mt Washington, traverses two gigantic stone ledges on either side, then tumbles through massive boulders towards the Ammonoosuc.

The place was in fairly decent shape, requiring paint but little plastering. Nonetheless, Bob, Ann, the baby, Lina, some chickens, and a small army of mice spent two months in the barn while fixing up the main house. Once that was done, Bob set about to populate Rock Pool Farm with further inhabitants until the whole place was teeming with life, just as Four Winds Farm had once done. Mainly there were geese, chickens, and pigeons – a fowl menagerie to which he added some rabbits or a goat at various points. For the first time in years, he felt settled. Moving back to the country had been the right choice. He was not a freak after all, he announced to his friends: "wife snoozin on the sofa / dog under the table: little boy upstairs – pretty cool, I'd say." Most importantly, he had stopped drinking.

Also, there were older men, like backwoods lumberjack neighbour Kenneth Ainsworth and Hanover house painter Ira Grant, over seventy years old, to give advice. Ainsworth taught Bob how to sharpen axes or file saws, Ira Grant how to breed pigeons, and exhibit them. Grant also knew how to go about dowsing – for water as well as for lost objects like money; or he'd paint little pictures which, though crude, somehow captured the subject's inner life or imminent fate. Ira Grant's "extraordinarily practical" way of doing things, Creeley later claimed, taught him more about poetry than he had ever learned from any professor.

Less promising aspects of country life emerged with the arrival of winter. Bob found himself furiously cutting and splitting wood while still just managing to keep a few days ahead of the family's needs. One night, with the truck broken down, he had to walk up the road into the forest in the dark to a pile of logs, load one onto his shoulder, and then stagger back. Meanwhile, the odd invitation from city folks in Boston aroused his unmitigated contempt. On one such occasion, he insisted on wearing his cap all through dinner – "hated them. Couldn't eat – even choked." The bohemian hipster, as he portrayed himself to friends, had turned mean, poker-face hick. He gloated over the embarrassment caused amongst other party guests by Ann's telling an indecorous joke. Or he thoroughly enjoyed playing pranks on persons he disliked. One, a fellow called Jesseman, allegedly a "real shit" ("has garage, & plays politics, vicious man"), got close to breaking his neck while helping Bob lift a stove out of the truck. Jesseman "gets abt two inches from the end of the tailgate, him ABT to step back off, into space, & nice concrete floor, NOT A WORD! I keep my mouth SHUT, & old J/hovers on edge, says, MY I almost fell. NOT A LAUGH. Too much."

Another such story involved a lady wearing tweed which Bob found ridiculous in the country setting. She had recently been given a purebred cow by her gawky son. To Bob's delight, the animal fell off the truck, on its way to being displayed at a show, so mother and son "stopped, to find the cow ... was being dragged along by the neck." Too bad the animal survived, instead of affording Bob the spectacle of mother and son making "their grand entrance to the fair, dragging the carcass, of a once: nize cow."

Intent on cultivating his new image, Bob also reported to friends how he fed chickens, hoed potatoes, or, in breach of his virtuous resolutions, planned on growing a few acres of pot. For all that, neighbours Kenneth and Alice Ainsworth remembered Bob as "strange" – essentially a city person. He was so "different" from them. Alice recalled that it was Ann who for the most part took care of animals, farm, and household, and that it was she who drove the truck except for the rare occasions when Bob took off on trips to Boston and New York. This coincides with Ann's memories of her former husband. To her, Bob "lived in complete idleness except for 20 or so ornamental chickens and for 6 months, a goat. I had a tiny income from my mother's estate and we and the kids lived in poverty indeed. He had a horror of farming or any other work. His ambition was to be a writer and live something like Hemingway although he wrote very little and finally settled on poems as being the least taxing."

8

The Emerging Writer
and Publicist.

The urge to be a poet came to Creeley late in life; and for a long time the wish preceded the act. "I wanted to write desperately; I wanted that to be it. But at the same time I couldn't demonstrate any competence in it."

Slowly that competence emerged amid self-doubt and reflection; yet even after it did, comments upon his writing continued to fill many more pages than did his published literary output. Creeley's *Collected Essays*, most of them criticism, even now constitute his most substantial publication. In turn, his creative writings, including a novel, numerous short stories, and, of course, the poems, remain slim when compared with the thousands of letters he wrote from the late 1940s onwards. Coming into his own as a poet, to Creeley, also meant finding himself within a widening, though for the most part epistolary, circle of literary and artistic associates. From the beginning he was more than just a writer: for years most of his time would be spent on his correspondence and, through it, on an ever-broadening range of activities as literary theorist, editor, publisher, and promoter of his and others' works.

His earliest professional plans had been far removed from literature. He originally wanted to be a doctor like his father; and then, since he'd always loved animals, a veterinarian. But by the time he entered Harvard, these plans had drastically changed. After contributing to various Holderness publications, he wanted to become a journalist. During the summer of 1944, he worked as a copy-boy for the *Boston Globe*. "I thought that if one wanted to be a writer then that was the obvious way: you work on a paper."

His finally deciding to be a poet coincided with getting to know Ann. Falling in love with her proved liberating all around. She helped him shed his puritanically deprived habits, not only of sensuality but also of speech. He turned into a compulsive talker. He talked in bars or at parties, for hours on end, pouring out a stream of words, no one else getting a word in edgewise. He would zero in on someone, screening out everybody else. Once he talked right through the night to the host of a party he hadn't even been invited to; finally leaving to have breakfast somewhere, he realized he had forgotten to tell the man three more things, and went right back to do so.

Though shy and taciturn as a child, Bob had always listened carefully and absorbed it all like a sponge: every speech rhythm and tone of voice – Theresa's inarticulate mumblings, Aunt Bernice's or his sister Helen's speedy loquacity, the New England country folk's tight-lipped, laconic, and compressed way of speaking, as well as, more recently, the fast-talking black and hipster lingos of his friends around Boston. What he had absorbed in the past, he now began to mimic, often not realizing what he was doing until people reacted in panic – like a woman at a Provincetown booze-up whom he harangued in Slater Brown's voice, with Slater, who had just passed out, still there at the party.

Bob's letters project a similarly protean disposition. When addressed to Charles Olson, they are full of the latter's headlong, syntactical cascades and terminological razzle-dazzle; when to an established journal, they speak in a tone of casual civility and tight-lipped matter-of-factness. After reading D.H. Lawrence, he might adopt that writer's self-righteously impassioned tone, or after perusing a text by André Gide, assume a stance of studiously urbane remoteness. And welling up from the deepest layers of his linguistic consciousness were the words, shouts, and screams he had heard as a child roaming the Acton countryside and, along with it, a contempt for the pat formulas of a formally literary language.

Still, from the time the unkempt, chain-smoking freshman told Dean Leighton that he wanted to write until the end of his stay in Burma, the plan to become a poet largely remained wishful thinking. In the meantime, he had read what might help him along the way. During the 1943 Christmas break, he had surprised Helen with his amusing anecdotes about poor Ann but also impressed her with his enthusiasm and intelligence in talking about Donne. Meanwhile, Helen's husband had bought Bob a copy of Pound's *Make It New* for his birthday. The text proved a revelation to Bob.

Unlike his Harvard professors, Pound spoke of writing as a practical activity rather than a finished structure embodying a certain content. He taught Bob how one first had to "*learn* to learn what one had to." For an impecunious student, that entailed other than strictly theoretical problems – like persuading a girlfriend to steal a copy of William Carlos Williams's *The Wedge*, which turned out to be another eye-opener. How Williams described the process of writing a poem was exactly the way he wished to write himself: "When a man makes a poem, makes it, mind you, he takes words as he finds them interrelated about him and composes them ... into an intense expression of his perceptions and ardors that they may constitute a revelation in the speech that he uses. It isn't what he *says* that counts as a work of art, it's what he makes, with such intensity of perception that it lives with an intrinsic movement of its own to verify its authenticity."

Still, his own attempts to write bore little fruit. On the boat from Baltimore to Bombay he had had plenty of time to try, but very little of it struck him as successful. Failure merely confirmed him in his determination to be a poet, however. He simply couldn't alter his wish to write, he confessed to his family back home. So he just kept on reading, all the way from Bombay to Calcutta, then under the watchful eye of Major Paulson while waiting to be put into a "tough spot," and thereafter, in his spare time between ambulance driving, while following the combat troops down from Mandalay towards Rangoon. It was an odd assortment of books to be read in the Burmese jungle: Yeats, cummings, Proust, Pound's first thirty cantos, and Grierson's *Metaphysical Lyrics and Poems of the Seventeenth Century.* They laid the cornerstone for his emerging poetics.

Yet still there were no poems. Obviously, Pound's and Williams's sober-minded instructions about how to write lacked an important catalyst to produce poetry in Bob's mind. Perhaps the universe they inhabited was still too rationalist for someone of his generation. In a world whose traditional order had so obviously disintegrated, the poet would have to derange his senses à la Rimbaud, even perhaps annihilate them, before he could come to grips with what mattered.

Here marijuana opened up never-before-entered doors of surreal perception. While leaving its traces in his reminiscences of that period, it also helped him compose his first poem, "Return," on his "coming back from India to Cambridge in the winter of 1945":

Quiet as is proper for such places;
The street, subdued, half-snow, half-rain,
Endless, but ending in the darkened doors.
Inside, they who will be there always,
Quiet as is proper for such people –
Enough for now to be here, and
To know my door is one of these.

The poem was published in the special e.e. cummings issue of the Harvard *Wake*.

Writing further poems over the following months and years remained an arduous, largely unrewarding struggle; but struggle he did, making every effort to stimulate his costive creativity – like starting to translate Rilke's "Sonnets to Orpheus," rereading Williams and Pound, or steeping himself in D.H. Lawrence to the point where the novelist's creeds struck him as what he'd believed in all along. He emulated in verse the kind of whimsy Miles Davis achieved in bebop, attempted formal experiments like breaking down the rather intellectual opening lines of "My Inarticulate Grandmother" in the lyric hysteria of the concluding ones, or invoked Lawrence or Pound in poems dedicated to them.

Above all he theorized and pontificated. Criticism of his work – such as Slater Brown's comments regarding his clipped lines, general constraint, and overuse of one-syllable words – were of no use to him, Bob felt. Writing from a Dostoyevskian underground, he had become a stranger to his own poems, he explained to Jacob Leed. He had things to say, but still lacked a proper form. To be loose and free in that pursuit struck him as all too easy.

More clearly defined were his ideas about poetic content. What he was after, he told Leed, was a Lawrentian *Ding an sich*, which, though related to human life, had to have its proper distinctness and force. A tree, rather than being charged with our pathetic fallacies, for instance, should be poetically re-enacted, as driven by a powerful will of its own, a will thrusting green hands and huge limbs at the light above and sending huge legs and gripping toes down. Imagination, in combining intellect with emotion, must get to the life, force, and animation of things. To achieve ultimate reality, things must be allowed to realize themselves to their fullest possible degree.

Such Lawrentian spirituality is strangely at odds with both his poetry and critical prose of the period. Especially this latter remained hamstrung by the academic fetters put on him at school and university. The new voice emerging in his solipsistic loquacity had not yet found its way into his poetry and criticism. As he remembered later, he was "probably more articulate in prose than in poetry at first." But even that is only a half-truth. From early on, he tried to write novels, but usually ended up either burning the manuscripts or literally using them as toilet paper.

His first novel, begun on the Cape, was about a young man named Paul like Bob himself. Creeley might claim to a friend that his protagonist got to be less like himself with every page, yet the surviving fragments barely rise above their autobiographical moorings. Couched in the jargon of a Proustian reminiscence, Paul's ruminations on losing his glass eye fuse with others on war casualties in Burma or on his favourite pornographic reading in Uncle Hap's barn: stories of women's slips falling down, of men's pants coming undone, stories even of the fearful losses of arms and legs and eyes. Yet to remember the eye lying on the floor where he could see, even at that distance, the carefully traced veins, was something else again. It was so forgotten that even in remembering it he could not say for certain that it had been his eye.

In a similarly autobiographical vein, Paul describes himself as a man who felt no urge to marry his mother or kill his father who had died before such Oedipal fantasies could mature. Instead, Paul goes to visit the cemetery where his father lies buried alongside his wife. He reflects on the few things he knows about the deceased man – his father's graduation picture; the photograph showing him standing on the concrete steps of their house, holding Paul by the hand; never-collected bills in his father's handwriting; a watch and a pen-knife; what his mother had told him about dad. Who was it down there, six feet under, with a woman he didn't even know, Paul wondered, feeling sure that if he were to dig, he would find nothing at all.

After burning his first novel, Bob began another. Again his materials would be autobiographical. But rather than have the setting forced upon him by memory, he would make it up. These problems solved, there remained the vexing problem of form. Buddy Berlin (the novel's Mr Leo) called what he had read of it at Rock Pool Farm disjointed. But how else than through the large expanse of a novel would Bob be able to convince his readers that his loose, colourless, undistinguished, and roundabout style had some meaning? Rereading Mann's *The Magic Mountain* while planning to write his own novel, he felt as if he were slowly turning into tubercular Hans Castorp – tiring quickly and breathing with difficulty. In more critical moods, he came close to suspecting he might not be a writer at all. One day, sitting on the toilet reading the manuscript, he decided to literally wipe his behind with it.

The genre he had most success with during those years was the short story. In writing stories, he experienced the same intense seizures as in composing poems, usually remaining unaware of how much time it took him to do one until after he had finished it. Beginning "The Unsuccessful Husband," for instance, he wondered if his wife, who'd gone out to the store, would be annoyed by it. But by the time she'd come back, he was so much into it he simply couldn't stop.

With short stories he felt neither the constraints experienced in composing poems nor the need for structural cohesion required by the novel. He knew he was on to something. Damn the editors of the *Kenyon Review*, who felt that "The Unsuccessful Husband" was lacking in incident, plot, and proper character presentation. Irritated by such criticisms, he explained the story's roundabout methods to Leed: its opaqueness was precisely what he had intended. The husband misconceives the relationship with his wife in a way neither fully understood by him nor completely explained in the story, leaving the reader to assume that the wife, who seems to loathe her spouse, may very well love him. The same was true of "Three Fate Tales," in which each tale marks a different step towards an acceptance of reality or fate by three different characters. Hence, readers are invited to view the central issue from as many perspectives as they wish.

While "The Unsuccessful Husband" reflects Creeley's marital problems, "The Other Women" harks back to his troubled relationship with his mother. It was based on what Genevieve, while visiting at Rock Pool Farm, told her son about a colleague at the Board of Health. In the story, Mrs Williams (alias Mrs Creeley) talks about a certain Miss Brittin without realizing that the latter is a lesbian. That Miss Brittin is bestowing special favours on a girl called Harriet (alias Helen) strikes her as an act of benevolence even though Harriet let her know that the two climb into bed together whenever she visits her benefactress. Though seemingly unaware of these discrepancies, Mrs Williams expresses doubt as to why she is telling Miss Brittin's story or what its point is. Meanwhile, the reader becomes increasingly aware of the incongruities Mrs Williams either fails to grasp or refuses to admit. Apparently, Miss Brittin had adopted a blind, older woman, which Mrs Williams once again interprets as a humanitarian gesture, while at the same time conceding that Miss Brittin didn't strike her as humanitarian in character. "The Other Women" helped Creeley ostracize the antagonism he felt for his mother. Hatred was turned into abhorrence, pity, and sorrow. He had never felt more of a brute, he conceded. After all, in writing the story it was his mother he had destroyed so blithely. Being, as Leed had said, a cruel poet, he would never deign to make concessions to an audience. Never! The story remained unpublished.

So, for some time, did the others. In fact, for a period of nearly two years, he met with little else but rejection. Seymour Lawrence of *Wake*, while accepting two of his poems, harshly criticized and rejected his stories. One piece struck him as awkwardly written and kittenish, another, "Pages de Journal," as baffling and lacking in continuity. Theodor Weiss of the *Quarterly Review of Literature* couldn't see how "Pages de Journal" united into one single climax of impression; the pieces insisted on their independence. The whole seemed rather nebulous and static. Bob's style struck Weiss as rather undistinguished, loose, colourless, long and roundabout; the stories read too much like essays or tracts. Weiss also turned down several of Bob's poems, feeling nonplussed by them. Didn't this verbal interplay become too much of a tongue-twisting, and exert a force destructive to the meaning and feeling of the poems, he wondered.

Everyone feigned interest, Bob felt. Phillip Blair Rice of the *Kenyon Review* was impressed by the muffled irony and muted philosophy of his stories as well as fascinated by his oblique way of telling them. He proposed to retain "Leonardo's Nephew" (one of four Bob had sent him along with "The Cemetery," "Pages de Journal," and "Three Fate Tales") for another two to three weeks to see how it would stand up to subsequent readings – only to find that it didn't. Similarly, the *Kenyon Review* accepted and paid for "The Unsuccessful Husband" but then reversed its decision, suggesting that Bob revise the story. They felt it lacked plot, or at least a frame. John Crowe Ransom consulted with his advisory editor, Robert Penn Warren, who argued that "The Unsuccessful Husband" missed out on the necessary progression through the various stages every successful story must pass through.

It was infuriating. The acceptance of "Gangster" and "The Late Comer" by *Accent* made Bob shriek with happiness but brought little relief from these frustrations in the long run. Increasingly, he was sick to death of the piddling responses of the little magazines. What he got from them was at best a kind of schoolgirl fairness. *Partisan Review*, while printing a horrible poem by "money bags" Laughlin, had taken on a shut-mouth policy toward him. *Kenyon Review* reeked with smugness, *Poetry* (Chicago) printed its coterie of a half dozen "poets" that should be led out and shot. As for the rest, they were just awful.

Reflecting on his impotent rages, he slumped into angry self-loathing. Self-pity in quiet, he found, turned to rage, which, inwardly articulate, made him both read and write out of hatred. He was filled so with spleen that he felt his writing had become a mockery of himself. One story he had written sounded pontifical, another oh so clever. His poetry, or the little he could write, was turning into almost pure hate.

Meanwhile, Bob had been thinking for a long time about alternatives to the established journals. On his return from Burma he had helped edit the special e.e. cummings issue of *Wake*, set up as an alternative to the conservative *Advocate*. At some point he had also written to Malcolm Cowley about ideas towards starting a magazine on his own; or he'd discussed the possibilities of private printing with John Hawkes. During the summer of 1949, he and Buddy Berlin had discussed plans toward a magazine propagating I.A. Richards's and C.K. Ogden's ideas about a simplified language called Basic English. Behind all these impulses was his own need for exposure – which, before long, was offered to him by a stranger.

At the time the two men got to know each other, Cid Corman, two years Bob's senior, could already look back on a colourful career as a writer and literary publicist. Decisive in this had been a kidney ailment exempting him from military service and, more importantly, taking him out of university for a year while he was a sophomore at Tufts. During his absence from academia he discovered Baudelaire and Rimbaud, both of whom changed his sense of language and poetry once and for all. Back at Tufts and later at the University of Michigan, everything now was new, because self-directed. Also there were older men who helped him find himself: John Holmes, "a minor poet, but genuinely driven to poetry," and John Ciardi who became "a friend and valued advisor."

At Michigan, as in Medford and Ann Arbor, Corman became involved in editorial work. It made him realize that a magazine, if ever he'd edit one, had to be directed by a single intelligence to avoid the compromises several editors inevitably have to make among themselves.

In 1947 Corman took a "long jaunt around America," from which he finally returned to Boston eager to foment a poetic community there. The first result was a series of poetry discussion groups held in public libraries all over Boston, from its affluent sections to an immigrant slum area like the West End. Realizing how much potential for poetry there was, he propositioned a friend at the local radio station WMEX, Nat Hentoff, about a modern poetry program. A regular announcer, Hentoff also ran a lively folk music program, in which he offered Corman a half-hour spot for two consecutive weeks. The idea was to elicit letters from listeners asking for the poetry insert to be carried as a regular feature. As hoped for, the letters arrived in great numbers, allowing Hentoff to dump some fifty or sixty of them on the station manager's desk with the request that he allow Corman a regular fifteen-minute spot each week. To Corman's surprise, the station manager did.

The first two programs were dedicated to D.H. Lawrence and William Carlos Williams. It was a daring opening which almost killed the fledgling project. One listener sent a rabid letter complaining about the poetry host's "use of profanity." Luckily, another letter from a local minister applauded the program as well as the poem that had irked the offended listener. "This Is Poetry" was allowed to go on.

It did so uninterruptedly for three years, featuring live readings by poets like Ransom, Wilbur, Roethke, and Spender as well as recordings by Eliot, Joyce, and Olson. Towards the end of the first year, when Corman had started to look for younger poets, someone suggested Robert Creeley. Corman had seen his poems in *Accent* and *Wake*. Though hardly earth-shaking, they struck him as sufficiently alive to make him write to Bob.

Creeley's own version of how he ended up reading on Corman's program is different. It has him tuning into the program featuring Wilbur, deciding he would damn well read on it himself, and "set abt to that end. And did, damnit, did."

The Creeley-Corman correspondence, as far as it survives, tells yet another story. Bob's first extant letter to Corman (in response to a note outlining Corman's plans as well as his progress to date) makes no mention of the Wilbur program. Instead, it states that Bob had heard the past week's program with a certain Miss Hoskins. It praises "This Is Poetry" for teaching people to unlearn what they had learned about poetry at school, then concludes with a number of recommendations. Had Corman considered playing existing recordings of other poets reading their works, like Yeats's disturbing recital of "I will arise and go now ..." in that powerful voice of his? Was he making recordings of his current programs? As yet, there was no mention of a projected Creeley reading on "This Is Poetry," which finally occurs in his third surviving letter to Corman.

Bob felt the prospect was a great honour. He was not at all sure he merited it. At the same time, he volunteered a possible date between 18 and 22 January, the 21st being the Saturday of "This Is Poetry," when he would be in Boston for a poultry show, and "free." He also included some yet unpublished verse like "Note on Poetry," "The Primitives," "Go to Sleep, Old Cat," "Still Life Or," and "A Local Celebration." In case Corman might be interested in his stories, Creeley advised him to contact Jack Hawkes who had a bunch of them, "The Cemetery" being the best. Jack worked for Harvard University Press and ran their Grolier's bookstore on Harvard Square. Corman should go see him. Bob had already written Hawkes about "This Is Poetry," so he would know who Corman was.

The planned visit to Boston was an all-round success. At the poultry show Bob exhibited several chickens and pygmy pouters, one young cock of his winning Best Red and also third Best Young Pygmy, all colours competing. On Saturday night he read his poems and talked about them to show host Cid Corman on WMEX. Probably none of his listeners, some of whom sent him fan letters about how dedicated, impressive, and lucid he'd been, guessed at his stage fright. Trembling and groaning at first, he finally recovered his voice, only to start roaring so loud the engineer in the little studio had to yank the microphone away from his mouth.

Buoyed by success, he next decided to settle some old scores. Alison Lurie, whom he had courted at Harvard, and her present boyfriend, Jonathan, had long been grating on his nerves. Jonathan was turning into a critic (God help him!), Alison into a formally accomplished but shallow writer. And how condescending they were towards Corman! Not that Cid had impressed Bob by his brilliance or accomplishments; rather Bob had found him to be just about the person he had expected – serious, honest, and well-intentioned, in short, someone one couldn't possibly dislike. When he noticed how Alison and Jonathan cut down this defenceless man with their snide remarks, he decided it was payback time.

He caught Alison alone, Jonathan sitting in the bathtub. Asking her to show him her poems, he found them technically impressive but without guts. He went on to bait her pretending to suffer from *Weltschmerz*, like someone who had lost all values. She produced a long story. Bob started to read it. After five pages he just looked at her with a pained expression on his face: he couldn't possibly continue any further, it was so awful. According to Bob, his carefully choreographed revenge had a devastating effect. Alison suddenly looked as if she had broken apart, her attractive features becoming wry and ugly – like a beautiful princess turning into a witch in one's arms, someone to spit at, stamp on. Or was he still the little boy feeling rejected for not being paid attention to, Bob wondered in retrospect.

Inspired by Cid's radio program, Bob set about to launch his own at a local station in St Johnsbury. When the hoped-for response to his letter did not come as promptly as expected, he decided to tackle things in person. He'd get a haircut, have his pants creased, then, weather and money permitting, drive over to St Johnsbury in person. Or might he scare people off with his eagerness and enthusiasm? But things went unexpectedly well: the radio station not only accepted his proposal but gave him free rein to do whatever he wanted. He'd start that coming Wednesday at 2 p.m., he proudly wrote to Cid on 12 March 1950. The program, talking about and reading poetry and prose, would be broadcast once a week.

Actually running it became an experience in nervousness and isolation. Bob listened to his own gaps of silence, or as if spellbound, stared out at the logging site on the hill facing the studio. Was he getting through to his listeners? Were they interested in the stuff he was reading from his scripts? For a while audience response was practically nil. Instead of the numerous letters he had received after the reading in Boston, there was one lone phone call. People up here just weren't given to writing letters, he told himself. And gradually he *was* getting through to people. Someone who had come up to Rock Pool Farm to buy a pup was surprised to hear that it was Bob Creeley who was running the program. The visitor assured him that many of his neighbours *were* listening.

However, after about a month the radio station cancelled the program. Until the fall, all afternoons would have to be devoted to baseball games from Boston. After that they would put him back on at night. Bob was sceptical and concluded they had simply grown tired of him.

As it turned out, he had already gotten involved in more portentous matters. His old friend Jacob Leed, now living in Lititz, Pennsylvania, had access to a venerable George Washington hand press on which he proposed to print a volume of Bob's writings. Bob instantly set about making plans. He decided it should be a volume of either poems or stories, not both together. He made suggestions regarding size (possibly smaller than Simpson's book), type (like that used for Paul Goodman's novels), the printing (black, clear, and well spaced), and possible marketing strategies: perhaps the volume should be introduced by I.A. Richards, or even by *several* celebrities. How else could one sell a meagre volume of some twenty or so poems by a nonentity?

At first excited and happy, Creeley lapsed into a more sombre mood after taking a hard look at his slender lyrical output since 1946. All he wished to see in print for the moment, he assured Leed, were some sixteen poems, leaving out eleven others from his grand total of twenty-seven. Yet his determination to see the volume published remained as strong as ever. Also, he had come up with further plans. Would Jacob care to bring out their own magazine? One might run one along the lines of I.A. Richards's Basic English and call it either the *Lititz* or *Littleton Review*. Bob had recently discussed Richards's method with their mutual friend Buddy Berlin. More generally speaking, he wanted to steer the projected magazine away from the flabby and incidental "point of view" evident in *Partisan Review* or *Poetry* and give it real purpose.

Tongue in cheek, he proposed that Jake should edit the journal. If he were to do it himself, he might prove all too obstinate, sullen, uncooperative, and petulant. Taking the hint, Jacob reversed the proposal. In response, Bob decided that it be "Leed & Creeley, edts," adding that this offer, of course, was merely nominal. For he, he, he would be the power. And he was, as Leed remembered in 1993: "It was Bob, not I, who had the ideas, the drive, and a sense for people."

He instantly got down to work, writing letters with requests for contributions to I.A. Richards, Wallace Stevens, Richard Wilbur, Marianne Moore, John Berryman, and William Carlos Williams. His general plan for the first issue was to gather contributions from writers he knew and respected which, he speculated, would attract other, yet unknown writers of like persuasion to send in their work.

Initial responses were not encouraging. The letter to Williams was returned unclaimed so Bob had to send it on to Williams's publisher, New Directions. I.A. Richards, the "pivot" on which the magazine was to swing, was away in the Far East. In his absence, a certain Miss Gibson offered possible future contributions on condition that Bob showed her what he had done so far. Only thereafter might he be allowed to make use of her contacts. Marianne Moore replied that she would be willing to offer part of her translations of La Fontaine's fables, but that might not be for almost another year. If she should unexpectedly produce something suitable in the meantime, she would remember Bob's review. She liked his concept of severity and simplicity, hoping that all the care he was taking would bring him the expected rewards. Wallace Stevens's response was similarly evasive. Though greatly interested in the proposed journal, he was so behind with promises to other people that it would be some little time before he'd get around to sending something. There were further setbacks. Buddy, who had initially volunteered to do the magazine's "Basic" section, was backing out. Meanwhile, reservations about Basic English, at least as handled by Ogden, were arising in Bob's own mind.

Most disappointing was Pound's reaction. E.P. much too exhausted to advise on the project, Dorothy Pound wrote back. Creeley insisted, and Dorothy adopted a more conciliatory stance. Might Creeley with his press be interested in printing Dallam Simpson's *Four Pages*? Sadly, the English collaborators had made a hash of it. Or was he aware of the forty-odd volumes by E.P. out of print? Or of the mass of unpublished stuff he had written since 1930? As far as her husband was concerned, she remained adamant. He was "emphaticly" not writing. Who could expect a man to carry on an argument from a madhouse?

Intrigued by this Creeley who kept barraging them with letters, E.P., of course, did write, eventually sending "the Creel" one "strickly ANONYMOUS" letter after another. He gave practical advice regarding the projected magazine, let Bob in on his network of Poundian associates, gave him reading lists, loaned him magazines and books, or just cursed – against the educational system, the falsification of history, the evils of the monetary system, etc., etc.

His cohorts too got in on the act. T.D. Horton, who'd recently seen "the old man" and Bob's letter to him, announced that neither Ezra Pound nor himself could make out whether Bob had a very definite program. Subsequent letters revealed Horton's own. In attacking the great disease of Western "Syphilisation," Bob's journal should avoid all mention of Freud or that kind of stale, dead, and subjective twaddle. Instead, it had better follow the lead of Alexander Del Mar, author of a history of monetary crimes and, according to Horton, the founder of modern historiography. Why not call the projected journal the *Del Mar Quarterly*?

Though he obediently set about studying Del Mar, Bob quickly came to suffer the strains of his proselytizing devotions. Writing to Mrs Pound, he explained the extreme difficulty of finding material to concur with the limited program she proposed. He also used the opportunity to lash out against Horton. He had asked him to contribute something on his programmatic notions about education, but nothing was forthcoming. Others who were holding down jobs as professors and instructors were prepared to stick out their necks, and so did William Carlos Williams or

E.P. himself. So why not "Horton & Co?" Bob used a different strategy for distancing himself from Dallam Simpson, another Poundian, who had suggested that he and Bob meet in New York City or Washington to form an alliance. Fair enough, Bob commented to Dorothy, except he would have to walk there, having no money for transportation.

The biggest problem was Ezra Pound himself. Bob bent over backwards not to offend him. He conceded that Del Mar might indeed be the pivot on which the magazine would swing; or that its explicitly stated program could be something like: We resent the falsifying of history. We resent the misrepresentation of thought. We resent the misuse of ideas. He even made concessions regarding the "anti-semite biz," which he otherwise branded as a bitter mistake. Anti-Semitism, he wrote to Dorothy Pound, was the fog used to obfuscate the real issue, which was money. Nonetheless, they should do everything to avoid any tie-in with such labels.

Williams's letters, when they arrived at last, offered a welcome relief from such embarrassing tangles. Rather than trying to turn the *Lititz Review* into a journal propagating his ideas, he simply offered enthusiastic support. Though he had nothing to contribute for the moment, he completely agreed with Creeley's plans. Follow-up letters reinforced the same commitment. On 13 April he assured Bob that he would go with him to the limit, giving him permission to reprint "With Rude Fingers Forced," his attack on T.S. Eliot's about-face espousal of Milton and Eliot's condemnation of any "revolution in literature."

Williams's support also provided the proper perspective on further letters from Pound and his followers. Bob was supposed to devote his *Del Mar Quarterly* to furthering the liberation of American culture from false history; Dorothy urged him to adopt a partisan line while remaining noncommittal herself. All they did, Bob felt, was to "fubdub around." So in the end he gladly decided to make Williams the patron saint of the *Lititz Review*.

The question of the journal's spiritual guardianship taken care of, he set out on the final sprint of gathering materials for the first issue. He worked day and night. Sometimes he felt exhausted and fed up with having done nothing else for the last few months, at other times exhilarated by a new sense of power. Turning people down right and left was as gratifying as making enemies over taste and method.

The first issue was taking final shape. It was to feature Williams's attack on Eliot, Williams's brief "moral" program about how distortions of language produce crime, and poetry by Charles Olson, Donald Paquette, Vincent Ferrini, Samuel French Morse, Jacques Prévert, Byron Vazakas, William Bronk, and W.J. Smith. Also, much after Bob's own heart, there was to be an open forum for criticism of the American universities along the lines of Pound's sense of how these institutions had increasingly betrayed the students. Already, Bob was planning a second issue. This was to be organized around a letter from Kenneth Rexroth stating that the absorption of u.s. poets by the academic world had all but destroyed poetry in their generation, resulting in the production of feeble, overcooked stuff, designed solely to win the author enough prestige to hold down a teaching job. Meanwhile, Bob remained in desperate straits for prose for his first issue, pressing hard to get a piece from Paul Goodman which, he felt, would be like a touch of fine spring weather. Failing that, he suggested printing a story of his own, though he'd hate to start off by showing his face in the first issue.

As it turned out, he didn't have to. By the end of June the entire project – both *Lititz Review* and the volume of his poems – collapsed. Leed, who was supposed to print both by hand, broke his wrist in a car accident. At first Bob wouldn't give up and travelled to Lititz to see if he could handle the press himself. He tried for days, but found he just couldn't. He came up with another scheme: for $350 Leed could have someone else print a thousand copies. On the way back to Littleton, Bob tried to wheedle the amount out of a millionaire on Central Park West in Manhattan. "Talked from abt 11 in the morning to five in aft (without food: they ate)," he later reported. Nothing worked.

Back at Rock Pool Farm, an unannounced visit from Slater Brown brought Bob temporary distraction from his growing rages. Slater had become quainter than ever. He quietly dealt himself a hand of cards while Bob was hammering away at the typewriter; he inspected flowers through a small jeweller's magnifying glass and a little microscope he had brought with him. He built a milking stand for the goat, cleaned the shop, and put a treadle on the grindstone.

There were other distractions. Bob acquired three new rabbits, white, with dark brown noses and ears; he trained a few young rollers by flagging them up with a square of cloth, then taught them to come back to the loft. Or he experienced a moment of fairyland mysticism watching Ann in a chair by the window reading, the light coming down yellow on her, with outside the deep green leaves of a lilac tree illumined by the moon – "making TWO lights, two kinds. Two, two: worlds."

But none of his efforts to sidestep his frustrations over the collapse of the magazine brought proper relief. He felt raving mad twenty out of twenty-four hours a day, looking for blood, someone's, somewhere. Such imaginary violence, other than turning into self-loathing, vented itself on the unwitting guests at a party who had to watch Bob wear his cap throughout dinner, give them hateful stares, and choke on his food; or it made him curse political matters he otherwise paid little attention to: the Korean war was a fucking bunch of shit. He hoped that everyone there would have their throats cut. But for the most part, he just felt impotence and rage.

9

Charles Olson.

He was a giant of a man, six foot eight, with a bear-like hairy chest and long, gorilla-like arms. Nonetheless, he felt vulnerable in body and spirit, he confided to his diary in early 1945, staying on Key West, hosted by Hemingway's ex-wife Pauline. His wife, Connie, Olson wrote, "makes firm my genitals, the South could strengthen my muscles, and life will toughen my spirit." But they all became fragile when his faith was low. "How to have faith? How to assume the illusion of one's self!"

His first major poem, "The κ," was written around this time. In Shakespearean terms and with Yeatsian, vatic grandiloquence, it announces his imminent mythic destiny.

Take, then, my answer:
there is a tide in a man
moves him to his moon and,
though it drop him back
he works through ebb to mount
the run again and swell
to be tumescent I.

More so even than to Creeley, the decision to turn poet had come late to Olson. Prior to 1945, he had devoted several years to politics. He held a job with the Foreign Language Division of the Office of War Information from which he resigned when censorship of his press releases proved intolerable, then another as an advisor and strategist for the Democratic Party's National Committee. Now, after Inauguration Day on 20 January 1945, it would have been time to reap the fruits of these endeavours by landing a job with the new administration. But Olson decided otherwise. He wanted to be an artist, even if a poor and struggling one. He had just turned thirty-four.

His first major endeavour was to pay tribute to the man whom, second only to D.H. Lawrence, he ranked highest among the leaders in this pursuit. Ezra Pound, fascist, anti-Semite, and traitor, had recently been removed from an open cage in the u.s. military detention camp at Pisa and flown to Washington. He was awaiting trial, the outcome of which might be death.

Olson jumped to Pound's defence. Donning the mask of W.B. Yeats, he proclaimed that Pound should be judged not by the courts but by his fellow writers. Pound's destiny, like the one awaiting Olson himself, had to be assessed in mythical, not political terms. It had to be measured according to Yeats's cyclical view of history, not along teleological lines. It could only be seen as a tragic one. An "ender out of phase," Pound was paying the price for opposing historical trends in the closing phase of his historical cycle, one that the new generation would have to surpass. But who else in this endeavour, except for D.H. Lawrence, was of greater relevance? Certainly Pound's ideas about poetry remained imperative. As for the rest, Olson, alias Yeats, would "undo no single word" of whatever Pound had published. "This Is Yeats Speaking" appeared in the Winter 1946 issue of *Partisan Review*.

Meanwhile Olson had had a first glimpse of his mythic hero during Pound's arraignment on 27 November 1945. He looked older and weaker than Olson had imagined him. He sat in abject silence, his eyes "full of pain," yet hostile, listening to the nineteen counts of treason, one for each of his Italian radio broadcasts. Several weeks later Olson visited him in Howard Hall, the neo-Gothic wing of St Elizabeth's Federal Hospital for the Insane. The defence had entered an insanity plea on his behalf. Closed off from the rest of the world by a high surrounding wall, the place looked daunting: a labyrinth of gloomy, airless wards and corridors roamed by inmates in various guises of insanity. Olson was led through a black iron door into a holding room dimly illuminated by a barred window and watched over by an armed guard.

And here was Pound, coming to greet the giant stranger. The frail man in the courtroom seemed transmogrified. Grizzled, lion-maned, and red bearded, he seemed like a wounded animal struggling for life. He was lashing out against his opponents. He bitterly complained about how he was treated. Olson barely got a word in edgewise. For Olson to have just listened to him, Pound felt, was enough of a favour. Shortly after the fifteen-minute interview, he told his lawyer that the stranger "had saved his life." According to his own sense of the visit, Olson had at last entered the domain of literary history which he would preside over in subsequent years.

In 1947 Olson published *Call Me Ishmael*, a drastically condensed rewrite of an originally 400-page study of Melville he had drafted in 1939, working under a Guggenheim grant after abandoning his PhD studies at Harvard. In 1948 his first collection of poetry, *y & x*, appeared. A slim volume of five poems, it sold a handful of copies, remained unreviewed except for a single, perfunctory notice in *The Nation*, and lost its publisher Caresse Crosby $1,200. Private comments from mentor Edward Dahlberg as well as from future Black Mountain cohort Robert Duncan were equally unpromising. Dahlberg thought the poems lacked the "darkling speaking heart," were "too abstruse," "too cerebral," and "too sententiously dried out." "Oh, what does the professor know about writing poems?" sneered Duncan.

There was one exception. To this female admirer, "The κ" was the greatest American poem written in the century. "Trinacria," she wrote, evoked "an aristocrat [who had] entered the door and left his armor there." The five poems collected in *y & x* were to her "the purest, hardest, most perfect diamonds since Villon." They placed their author among the ranks of "the bravest and the best" such as Joyce, Rimbaud, Blake, Beethoven, and Michelangelo.

Olson's admirer had first written him regarding the publication of *Call Me Ishmael*. He had saved her, she had told him. Another of his poems, "In Praise of the Fool," which she'd read in *Harper's Bazaar*, had revealed to her his spirit in all its uncovered nakedness. Eager for comparable revelations in the flesh, she invited the poet to meet her in Woodward, the hill-country hamlet in Pennsylvania where she lived. Though intrigued, Olson declined.

Frances Motz Boldereff was no starry-eyed, adolescent admirer. Nearly five years Olson's senior, she had been married to a White Russian nobleman, had held various posts in the fields of publishing, visual arts and education, and was currently working as a book designer at Pennsylvania State College. Equally surprising to Olson when they finally did meet in the 42nd Street New York Public Library was her physical appearance. Instead of the dark and exotic Russian he had expected, there was a petite, fair, almost girlish lady reminding him of early pictures of his mother. Yet Frances's irreverent, "terrific laugh and down, down, derry down throat speech," suggested "sex-all-over-the-place."

Shortly thereafter it was Olson's turn to be "saved." That happened at an exclusive local inn in Tarrytown on the Hudson. His "wizardess," he found, had powers to transform him. He was particularly impressed by her unabashed sexual inventiveness which, as he wrote her on his way back home to rejoin his wife, Connie, had given him a second life. Tarrytown, the site of his resurrection, was renamed the "Woodhenge," the druidlike ground of their union. Olson had finally managed to launch himself on his mythic path. "I am / of use," he proclaimed in "Epigon," written for Frances after his return to Washington.

The riot in Olson's soul was on. Tied to the typewriter like "some manacled mad thing," he drafted world-shattering schemes, wrote poems and essays, or reported on the latest stage in his Herculean labours to his Lawrentian muse. Even more frequently than he to her, Frances wrote to him – up to three separate letters in a single post. She was a passionate woman who had given herself once and for all into his hands, she kept reminding him.

She was also extremely erudite, providing her disciple with choice bits from the treasure-trove of her archaic wisdom. Almost instantly these would be recast in Olson's poetry. The fixed gaze of the Babylonian priest celebrant officiating in a Zeus-Baal temple, which she asked him to look up in Franz Cumont's colour plate reproductions of Mesopotamian frescos at Dura-Europos in Iran, became the strange "look in the sacrificer's eyes / the archaic sought, the harshness / unsought" in Olson's "Dura." Some Sumerian religio-poetic fragments translated by Samuel Noah Kramer inspired the hieratic tone of Olson's poetic descent into the underworld in "La Chute."

"God teaches me and I teach Charles and he teaches the world," Frances announced. During secret meetings, the giant poet and his petite "She Bear" rekindled the psychosexual living flame of their Lawrentian amours, creating "acts for men and women to come."

The sexual fulfilment Olson found with Frances gave an unprecedented boost to his creativity. By February 1950 he sent her a first draft of his essay on Projective Verse, which William Carlos Williams was to hail as the most admirable piece of thinking about the poem that he had recently, perhaps ever, encountered. After another meeting in Knoxville he wrote an early draft of "I, Maximus" that was to become the opening piece of the future long poem. As Tom Clark writes, it is "boldly sexual, thrust forward on images of phallic masts, beaks and lances directed with propulsive energy toward receptive female nests." His once fragile potency had become a source of powerful creativity: "potency man's measure, all, ALL, he liveth for."

Yet writing profusely was one thing, getting published another. The established literary journals were as unreceptive to Olson's volcanic outbursts as they were to Creeley's minimalist pronouncements. But early in 1950 Vincent Ferrini, a General Electric assembly-line worker and fellow poet living in Gloucester, set about to amend this situation. In 1949 Olson had favoured him with a spontaneous, unannounced visit, then in March 1950 sent him a batch of poems to show what he was doing. Ferrini liked them and, without telling Olson, forwarded two, "Lost Aboard U.S.S. 'Growler'" and "The Laughing Ones," to Robert Creeley, who had contacted Ferrini regarding contributions for the *Lititz Review*. The remainder of the story has often been told. Creeley, writing back to Ferrini, turned down the poems, scoffing that Olson was "looking around for a language." By coincidence Ferrini's letter, relaying Creeley's remark and negative verdict, reached Olson along with another by Williams suggesting he write to Creeley who had some ideas and wanted to use them. Together, they prompted the famous opening piece, dated 21 April 1950, to a correspondence that was to last until Olson's death and comprises some one thousand items not counting the many that were lost.

To Creeley the letter was a revelation. There was humour, bravado, and provocation, yet at the same time the decisiveness of a man who had obviously thought about many issues vital to Creeley himself. What's more, Olson had done so more thoroughly. He clearly knew what he was talking about. And how he did had an instant, irresistible appeal for someone with Creeley's contempt for pat formulas.

Perhaps this stranger might help free him from the New Critical jargon that still encumbered him whenever he hit the typewriter to compose an essay or letter. Olson's ways of spacing his prose suggested the pulsations of some vital rhythm propelling his utterances. The headlong rush of his original, folksy, and informal way of speaking reminded Creeley of the laconic compressions of the West Acton dialect he had absorbed as a kid. And there was Olson himself, introducing himself as an "ex-letter carrier, ex-fisherman, ex-character," as if to make sure what he was saying would be taken from the proper, personal perspective.

In reply Creeley proposed to print Olson's "Morning News" in the first, and his "Move Over" in a subsequent issue of his prospective review. He also apologized for having turned down the poems sent earlier. Yet he did so with a new buoyancy that instantly picked up on Olson's. "Not to back down on that matter – NEVER." Also, there is the first of many subsequent attempts to rope Olson into a union of exclusive intimacy. "Nota: I am still laughing, like they say. I hope people can pick up on this thing (MORNING NEWS). I think, with horror, of those who are not amused, etc." You should have told me that gun was loaded, he told Ferrini.

Olson never once in his future, voluminous correspondence with Creeley referred to his epistolary muse and lover, Frances. In turn he was hesitant to talk to her about his new male associate with whom, before long, he came to exchange letters at a rate exceeding those traded with her. Writing to Frances, Olson granted that Creeley was "the best young writer" he knew. At the same time he described him as "this nut (a former peddler of narcotics, a former drinker, a former musician, now a hen farmer)." The Creeley whom Olson by mid-1951 introduced to Robert Duncan as his "running mate" and "tandem" is conspicuous for his near-complete absence from the remaining letters Olson wrote to Frances.

Almost immediately Creeley also began to supplant Frances in the role as advisory muse to Olson's creative efforts. The essay on Projective Verse, a first draft of which had been sent to her, was completed under his tutelage. Creeley suggested several changes and contributed the crucial phrase: "form is never more than an *extension* of content." Another essay, "The Gate and the Center," about the need for a return to the "primordial & phallic energies" – ideas Olson had first worked out with Frances – was started as a letter to Creeley rather than to her. There was the first draft, then a second one, Creeley's critical responses becoming more and more vehement. The second draft slowed down to explain, he complained. Its increase of detail overreached its usefulness. At the same time Olson had allowed too much of his vatic (Frances-inspired) ego to intrude into the argument: "damn you, that IS impertinence ... into yr CENTER, to intrude so, : explanation. Fuck yez, Chas Olson."

Instead of resenting such criticism, Olson congratulated the younger poet on the "wild & true things" he'd said about symbol and mask, then on the "immense *clarities*" of his prose. Responding to a moment of depression in Creeley's life, Olson, as early as 9 May 1950, assured his friend of how much he valued his companionship in their joint foray into postmodern literary history. "Above all things resist, to be sick at heart," he advised: "we are forward, and it is such gratification, that you are ready to go with me."

Creeley paid similar tribute to Olson. Olson had been the first reader to give him a clear sense of the effect of his writing. At the same time he enabled Creeley to finally retrieve the childhood speech patterns acquired in West Acton and to infuse them into his poetry. Here Olson's sense of how he might make the line intimate to his speaking habits proved liberating. Altogether, Olson was the person with the energy he so badly needed. Lacking that, he'd go dead on his feet, he explained to Pound. How marvellous to have found someone shaking things up.

Creeley's apprenticeship took time. Though we find him echo Olson's maxim "the HEART, by way of the BREATH, to the LINE" as early as 7 July 1950, revisions of earlier poems such as "Still Life Or," while carried out under Olson's influence, still amount to no more than post factum formal rearrangements. As yet he had not "begun to rhythmically *think* with his poems." That breakthrough was first achieved in "Hart Crane" and "Le Fou," written in June and July of 1950, in which Creeley, while deep in correspondence with his mentor, first entrusted "himself to the newly emerging projectivism and the rhythms of indigenous speech."

Meanwhile he kept lavishing praise on Olson and his writings. *y & x*, sent to him on 21 April, contained "wonderful things." In his comments on Pound and Williams, Olson showed "fantastic precision." Olson's

"Introduction to Robert Creeley," to be published in *New Directions* 13 (1951), was "very damn wonderful." "Right there in front of your eyes," a poem dedicated to Creeley, "was a fucking fine thing." Altogether, Olson was granted the status of a "fucking genius." As such he was the only man Creeley had "complete & utter respect for, the only man that SHOW[ED him] a thing."

Increasingly the two men's admiration for each other excluded others from their solipsistic partnership. Rather than just running mates, they had come to consider themselves as literary champions running outside competition: "PLEASE, C., tell me abt somebody besides thee & me, quick, or I shall quit this profession as I have quit all previous ones," Olson joked on 8 June 1950. "Let's you and I, by God, write for each other! IT's the only deal. I swear," he suggested in a less humorous vein on 3 July 1950, cursing others. Creeley began to pay similar tribute to the exclusiveness of their partnership. "You have the only *possible* influence, for me," he assured Olson on 19 September 1951, "you are the only one who can give me that sense of my own work, which allows me to make it *my own work*. Damn them all."

More to the point was the strategy of intimidation and realignment Olson had proposed earlier: "I swear – what we have to do is, quick, intimidate 'EM. And then go right ahead sans regard, sans anything but, make use of 'em." A first requirement here was to sort out the older modernist writers. Most of these, such as T.S. Eliot and his followers amongst the New Critical academic poets, received short shrift by being either dismissed or ignored. Others like Stevens, Pound, and Williams had to be assigned their proper places in the new, postmodernist pecking order.

Pondering *r&x*, Creeley as early as 28 April 1950 felt that Olson was pushing for a "movement beyond what the Dr., Stevens, etc., have made for us." As for himself, Creeley kept insisting, they couldn't develop a proper program by simply adopting the present concerns of Williams and Pound, even though the former might serve as a focus. Olson couldn't agree more: "right, right," he replied, "love the Dr, love the Master, still, even they, are in the way. There is new work to be done, new." At least for now, Olson too favoured Williams over Pound.

The one-time champion of Pound had long since come to suspect the master's continuing fascist persuasions. The final break had occurred early in 1948. Back from a trip to California, Olson had gone to visit Pound at St Elizabeth's and volunteered a provocative bit of new information: Poundian George Leite, the Berkeley editor of *Circle*, was of Portuguese rather than the Aryan descent favoured by the master. The remark unleashed a slew of racist comments causing Olson to leave in protest. Next time, he would deliberately bait Pound's anti-Semitic feelings, pretending that his own father's mother had been called Lybeck, suggesting that his blood line was tainted by an either Jewish or gypsy admixture. Pound, as expected, rose to the occasion, but in his own cunningly idiosyncratic fashion. Williams, he remarked, was "confused" because of his "mixed blood." Following this, their last encounter, Olson had sent the St Elizabeth's inmate a sharp note discussing the issues of "mixed blood" and democracy which Pound dismissed as a "lot of 2nd hand mass produced brickabrak."

In "GrandPa, GoodBye," his valedictory epitaph to their friendship, Olson repudiated his former allegiance to Pound by aligning himself with Williams. Unlike E.P., "Bill never faked," Olson wrote, "and that's why he has been of such use to all of us young men who grew up after him. There he was in Rutherford to be gone to, and seen, a clean animal, the only one we had on the ground." While turned down by several editors including James Laughlin, the piece met with the predictably positive response from Williams, a man as disgusted with Pound's anti-Semitism as Olson. Olson was "one of the few men [he took] pleasure in reading," Williams wrote to him.

Though cooped up in an asylum, Pound knew how to stick the knife to defectors where it hurt. A note Creeley received from him in June of 1950 not surprisingly made him wonder what was happening between Olson and the old man. "Believe Olson FUNDAMENTALLY (not superficially) wrong," it said, "tendency which will sterilize anything it touches. i.e., AGAINST nature's increase. But Cr/ must judge for himself." Olson's response confused Creeley even further. Olson hinted that in Pound's eyes he was "BUT a fellows jew." A letter Olson proposed to send to Pound, but first submitted to Creeley, sounded an even more irate note. "Look you old bastard," it said, "if you want open war come on and get it. Only fercrissake stop this goddame sly dirty old sneak trick stuff you're spreading around."

Unaware of the reasons for the break between the two men, Creeley advised caution, while at the same time assuring Olson of his unfailing support. Why get hung up on Ezra's or Dorothy's bigotry? Hadn't Olson himself suggested that their actual task lay in going beyond Pound? In response Olson explained that the big struggle, after his leaving politics, had been to leave Ez, and revealed how he had achieved that by encouraging him and Dorothy to think he was a Jew. Also, there had been another one of Pound's jibes, reported by a third party: "Wot Olson don't know iz, / I hate Swedes as much as I do Jewz."

Creeley increasingly sympathized with Olson's attitude to Pound. In addition to E.P.'s unacceptable anti-Semitism, he noted his total ignorance about prose. This was evident from what Pound had said about Henry James or about prose in general in *Make It New*. Was there anything more

idiotic than to suggest that most good prose arose from an instinct of negation, or that neither prose nor drama could attain poetic intensity except
by construction?

While re-evaluating their modernist forebears, the Olson-Creeley
team also set about to determine the varying roles their postmodernist
contemporaries would be allowed to play in their new literary set-up.
The planning of the *Lititz Review* and, after its collapse, of its successor,
Cid Corman's *Origin*, provided the arena for these decisions. A few, like
Paul Blackburn and William Bronk, would form a circle centred around
Olson-Creeley, others gyrate around this inner core at varying distances,
the rest be subjected to oblivion, ridicule, and damnation. A rare excep-
tion to resist such rigorous classification was Robert Duncan.

Heavenly City, Earthly City, the only Duncan book he had seen, struck
Creeley as rather poor except "for certain technics." Nonetheless, he repeatedly conceded to Olson that the West Coast poet "might be one to
figure in," while at the same time reassuring Olson of his key position in
the general configuration, this time for the American issue of Gerhardt's
Fragmente: "you for the center; substantial Blackburn & Bronk; divers
single items from a few others. All this headed by yr: PRO/VERSE." Olson
agreed. He had just received Duncan's "Africa Revisited," liked it, hoped
that its author would come in, and that *Origin* editor Corman would take
to the poem as well. Creeley too by now felt good about the West Coast
poet – Duncan's star was clearly on the rise. It even threatened to eclipse
others with whom the duovirate had had recent difficulties: "By all means
add Duncan," Olson urged, "... and subtract? Emerson? Bronk? ... I hate
the lot of em, & figure only Duncan acts like a man." For a fleeting moment, Duncan even seemed close to enlarging the two-man core to a tri-
umvirate: the three of them together, so Olson announced on 18
November 1951, deserved a swiftness of publishing and distribution
which the commercial idiots couldn't manage. Even Creeley's former reservations had almost vanished. Figuring in Duncan might accomplish the
purges Olson had suggested earlier. "*Do* send DUNCAN; that cuts down
the others; Emerson was already out."

But as swiftly as fortune wheels her favourites to the pinnacle of power
and fame, as rapidly she plunges them into infamy. The reasons for Duncan's sudden fall were old ones. Even while defending Duncan against
Creeley's animadversions, Olson continued to have doubts about the San
Francisco poet. How could he forget meeting him during a trip West in
the late 1940s – "Robert sitting on a kind of velvet throne, looking like
Hermes himself?"

Still, all that was pardonable given Duncan's poetic talents. Not so was
a suddenly revealed aspect to the man that had so far escaped both Olson

and Creeley. Duncan was not only a homosexual but also had the gall to write like one. That "Third Sex deal" was just too "goddamned EASY" for "a diehard, axehead, Puritan" like himself, Olson unequivocally announced towards the end of November 1951. Rereading "Africa Revisited," he found it to be full of major flaws. Much of it came "out tricky – & ending bad, miserable." Creeley, too, suddenly found fault with the ending. Come to think of it, he disliked the entire poem. Duncan "crowds the whole deal," Olson decided on 15 January 1952: "now sending me a Selected Duncan, as tho i were a publisher!" More generally speaking, Creeley retained his respect for Duncan's craft but concluded that in terms of content his damn head seemed "awfully fuzzed most times." At least for the time being, Duncan had become *persona non grata*.

10

Origin.

When he had first met Cid Corman in early 1950, Creeley found him a serious, earnest sort of person. Other more negative aspects were revealed in due time. Some of his poetry, Creeley felt, was pathetically organized, laboured into a rigid form; his epistolary prose pompous, inflated drivel full of flatulent generalities; his English damn well obscene. He and Olson agreed. Tenacious, honest, devoted as a dog, boy Cid surely was. Otherwise neither Olson nor Creeley found much good in him except that he was printing their works. Kid Korman, the Kid, Cad Cid, or old elephant cid was twisty, fatuous, thick-skinned, fucking coy, and goddamned inarticulate. He was full of pomposity, thickness, dullness, and fucking impertinence. Altogether, he was an idiot, a fuckup, miserly little prick, fucking little fixer, a complete and utter fool.

Shortly after Creeley and Olson enlightened each other in attributing the failures of Duncan's poetry to his unabashed homosexuality, the two "diehard, axehead, Puritan" macho-men analysed Corman in similarly sexuo-pathological terms. Creeley couldn't stand Corman's "sexlessness," his "kind of dirty whiteness like peeling skin," he protested. "We can't live, or I can't, allowing such eunuchism."

To reinforce their consensus, Olson described a visit with Cid's family. "Christ, you shld meet the father: a tailor, here, and formerly in Russia, a man with all the Jewish respect for the intellect, & for true knowledge, but a guy whom the American economic machine & social values has run over, flattened out like one of his pairs of pressed pants. Yet, he has schnapps with his meal, sits at his table like a wan patriarch." Or meet "his bitch of a kind & able wife" who just "because it is America, got the jump" on her husband. Typically, she "dresses her daughter like the daughter of a Saltonstall (she thinks) to go out to the theatre with a courting Merchant-Marine student officer." "And right in the middle of this sad heap of immigrant Jones ... in the midst of the calendar-right furnished apartment, is Cid's room! His study! And what is it? a correct NY apartment! Modern. Comfortable. And his mother bringing us in a card-table for coffee and cakes in the midst of this 'important' conference of the son's! Not like a secretary, but like a shrewd modern mother. Shit!"

Granted, this cocoon of domesticity had allowed Cid to run his radio program as well as to launch *Origin*. But it had also left him "inert, stunned, passive, unbegun," a man with a "hidden hate for woman," a "capon," "ballless like a priest." By comparison, even sodomistic practices à la Duncan suddenly struck Olson as admirable, relatively speaking. "Christ, for one thing, I don't think he ever fucked a girl – or, for that matter, was even buggered": "god, you shld have seen both him and his father rise to it when i dusted off ... and the three of us sat over the kitchen table with schnapps and cigars talking – christ, to repossess both of these two men of their balls!" Hence, the only way to coerce Corman into doing what one wanted from him was to push, slap, shake, and whack him, if need be stick one's "words right up his arse," write him "a real pisser" of a letter, "which will set him on his heels." If only he "could hold him," Olson proposed, while Creeley "punched sense into him!"

Creeley gleefully pondered the anticipated results of this shock-therapy diplomacy. He congratulated himself on his perfect play-off in pitting Corman against competitor Richard Emerson, who, like Cid, was offering to feature Olson and Creeley in print and on the air. Or he'd gloat about playing it like a master right from behind the old curtain after Corman asked him and Olson to serve as contributing editors for *Origin*. In response, he had set an ultimatum: either Olson and Creeley would be the magazine's only contributing editors and have equal voting rights with Corman, or nothing. What wonderful fun it is, Creeley bragged to Leed, to hug this prick like a fucking bear, get his guts, and turn his fucking belly inside out.

Considered in hindsight, it all worked well enough. *Origin*, more than any other magazine of the period, Creeley remembered in 1968, "undertook to make place for the particular poets who later come to be called the 'Black Mountain School.'" Meanwhile Creeley's input into *Origin* at the time was mostly along the lines of negative reinforcement. After turning over to Corman some of the materials collected for the *Lititz Review*, he almost instantly balked at Corman's editorial suggestions. As an editor, Corman simply had no policy. Instead, he cast about for help – as from "Creeley's ideas." How the hell would readers ever know what Corman was up to unless he dropped that "Creeley's ideas" shit, Bob cursed. There were just too many points of dissent between them. Creeley, still dreaming of one day bringing out one of the finest magazines in the country, wanted *Origin* to have a definite program, and to be on the attack. He wanted a short sharp magazine, Corman a long one. He wanted to tackle broader issues like education, Corman to deal with strictly literary matters.

Even more pronounced were their differences over possible contributors. Creeley was aghast to find that the same man who was to feature Olson in the first issue was also contemplating printing the likes of Coffield, Hanson, Burgess, or Hoskins. What else than a mere hodgepodge, a huge, gooey mess could result from lumping together such names with Olson's! Creeley made up his mind: there would be no overt tie-in of himself with the journal. He might pass others on to Cid, if he thought them worthwhile, but he wouldn't have a damn thing to do with the editing.

Imperturbable in his devotions, Corman returned generosity for insult. After all, he had met Creeley and knew he would follow up on a letter full of bitterest *ad hominem* invective with another admitting that, as so often before, he'd gone off the deep end. Perhaps he should feature Creeley in the second issue of *Origin*, Corman suggested. Temporarily, the proposal made Creeley retreat into shamefaced disavowal of his achievements as stilted as when the host of "This Is Poetry" had invited him to read on the program.

Yet in the long run Creeley was an unlikely person to become more conciliatory simply because Corman offered to publish him. On the contrary, it only made him more aggressive. Publish Dr Berkowitz in *Origin*? All right, but not in the company of Robert Creeley! If that mealy-mouthed, belching fathead was in on the gig, he didn't want to hear another word about it. Or the flatulent criticism of Ludwig Lewissohn? Or Lerner? He damn well couldn't see how Corman proposed to print decent new work while at the same time tying himself in with such men. Corman's tireless insistence on the creative had come to sound like a synonym for the altogether ball-less.

The barrage never stopped. If Corman couldn't make up his mind, he should damn well shut up, instead of being blown about like a weathervane. An editor shouldn't drown in a morass of laxity, sloppiness, tired and slack words. Someone supposed to bring down the literary establishment should be guided by a complete and utter fixity of purpose.

Corman finally got the message. On 12 November 1950 he admitted to Creeley that the way he had approached the editing of the magazine had been wrong. But that was a thing of the past. Henceforth, his own judgment was to be the last court of appeals on editorial decisions. All he required was some assistance for which he would like to have Creeley and/or Olson work along with him. What's more, he had decided to push projective writing as propagated by Olson and to enlarge the journal's boundaries beyond the strictly literary into whatever area would be of human pertinence.

For once Creeley was satisfied. He was even prepared to key Corman in on his widening network of international relations, he told him. Rainer Gerhardt, the editor of a little German magazine, *Die Gruppe der Fragmente*, had recently asked him to become his American representative. It was Pound who had suggested that Gerhardt write him. Like *Origin*, Gerhardt's magazine would feature Olson in its first issue; thereafter Creeley would put together an American section for every subsequent one. As a casual afterthought he mentioned to Corman that he'd given Gerhardt Corman's name as one interested in new German work. The manoeuvre was followed by extensive discussions of the terrific letters Gerhardt was sending him and of the poets he promoted.

Creeley also kept reminding Corman of his multiple other options. Despite the long drawn-out wrangling over "The Unsuccessful Husband," the *Kenyon Review* had accepted the story for publication. A Japanese Poundian, Katue Kitasono, was to publish "Mr. Blue" and "In the Summer" in his magazine *Vou*. Unless the *Kenyon Review* printed "The Unsuccessful Husband" in its winter issue, it looked very much like Creeley's first prose would appear in Japanese translation, he proudly announced on 29 December 1950. Also, there was Corman's competitor Richard Emerson with his *Golden Goose Press*, based in Columbus, Ohio.

Creeley's attitude towards Corman had visibly mellowed. To have gone so far with the *Lititz Review* and gone bust at the last minute had been one of the real disappointments of the past few years, he confessed. He credited Corman with the feat of picking up where he had left off, integrating some of his materials into the new magazine, and, like himself, adopting Olson as centre. Hence his jumping in and out like a frog, saying he wanted no part of it, next sticking his hand in up to the elbow. For the time being, Corman, above anyone else including Emerson, would have first whack at everything including "Mr. Blue," which Emerson still hoped to bring out in *Golden Goose*.

But such rueful friendliness towards the man offering him the first major outlet for his writing didn't last for long. A letter by Corman suggesting that Creeley let him arrange the possible tie-in directly with Rainer Gerhardt unleashed an especially colourful avalanche of abuse. His biz with Gerhardt was his, Creeley protested. If Corman kept on like this, he could take his fucking magazine and shove it up his fucking ass. What followed were the habitual PS and PPS of vituperative escalation and shamefaced apology, Creeley pleading the deplorable state of his nerves. Further exchanges as well as two straight days spent in Corman's company brought Creeley the necessary reassurances. For once, he went as far as to grant the long-suffering Corman damn well admirable tenacity and openness. He even admitted that his constant baiting had to do with envy. He'd had a hell of a time forgetting the past summer in which he had failed to launch his own journal, he confessed to Olson.

Yet with one row settled, the next several ones were only around the corner – over Corman's proposal to use varitype and photo offset instead of regular print, over Paul Blackburn, and once again over the printing process. To simply admit he had no loot for the printing was one thing, Bob told Corman. But to argue that print was pretentious was damn idiotic, even pernicious. He might just as well get his friends to make carbons of said material and bind them with what string they could salvage from the weekly groceries – which would probably bring his costs down to a minimum.

The usual apologies came along soon. Creeley granted that he was ashamed of his last outburst and certainly didn't expect Cid to put up with these rages. He even conceded that the samples of varitype Corman had sent him (though somewhat deficient in the spacings) were fair enough, and that he had been blustering. But this time Corman felt deeply hurt by the disaffection of the person who had become so central to what he was doing. On the eve of the appearance of the first issue, he "ran off to New York for a few days and wandered around the Village disconsolately, having no one with whom to share [his] dismay."

That first issue, when it finally appeared in April 1951, was "no marvel of printing" in the editor's opinion. Thus all the more rewarding were the responses of some of the contributors. Vincent Ferrini, whom Cid had gone to join in Gloucester to celebrate the occasion, was thrilled. Olson, whose contributions claimed the bulk of the issue, was ecstatic. To read the magazine had given him the fullest satisfaction he'd ever had from print. However, the most exuberant praise, first by telegram of 20 April, then by letter, came from the man who had but a single poem in the issue. It was a very fine job, Creeley admitted, clean, wonderfully flexible, and altogether without pretension. The printing of Olson's poems was as clear and neat as any he had ever seen; the letters of a very precise beauty; the prose without any of the spacing problems he had anticipated. As far as his own poem, "Hart Crane," was concerned, it was the finest printing of anything of his to date. Thank you, thank you, thank you.

From then on it was clear sailing until the publication of *Origin* #2. Creeley might suggest the odd revision in what was to be published, or simply express his impatience or misgivings towards its appearance. Holding his damn breath waiting for the issue had him very shaky. He only hoped *Origin* #2 wouldn't come out a flat tire. Meanwhile, he simply continued to thank Corman for his faith in him.

Whatever aggression Creeley continued to experience vented itself on Corman's competitors. Gardiner's *Poetry Quarterly* had him groaning. It was so very damn horrible. Emerson, whose financial troubles had still struck a sympathetic chord in him half a year before, came in for similar derision. Even when, to Creeley's surprise, the first issue of *Golden Goose* did appear, his contempt for its editor hardly diminished. By comparison to *Origin*, it was a horrible-looking job, smeared, a mess. Olson's contributions were smudged nearly beyond recognition.

Most conducive towards relaxing his relationship with Corman was a letter from New Directions. Laughlin's response to the short stories Creeley had sent him was not flattering: frankly, he found them "awfully dry and dull reading." At the same time, he felt the struggle in them "toward a kind of purity of vision." And even if the result was not exactly to Laughlin's "own special tastes," it seemed to him worthy of support. Though he couldn't possibly do a book for Creeley right now, New Directions could run his five stories plus Olson's introduction to them in their annual. Creeley was ecstatic. In reproducing Laughlin's letter to Corman, he casually offered to make sure that Cid would get the proper acknowledgment in the *New Directions' Annual*, which as Laughlin put it, got around pretty widely.

Yet the prospect of being published by New Directions did little to minimize Creeley's delight when he eventually held *Origin* #2 in his hands. It was like a small selected works of his literary endeavours so far: three short stories ("3 Fate Tales," "In the Summer," and "Mr. Blue"), four poems ("Hart Crane," "Helas," "Le Fou," and "Love"), "Notes for a New Prose," and "Letters" to editor Cid Corman. He could damn well kiss his feet, Creeley wrote to Corman. Comments to Olson were hardly less superlative. Receiving *Origin* #2 had given Creeley "a very damn fine moment" and left him "altogether bowled over." By comparison with Emerson who had kept dragging him and Olson round "all the dismal little allies [i.e., alleys], back-waters, possible," Corman, at least for the time being, was granted the status of a "fucking GENIUS for the laying on of, HANDS. He must damn well do it in a TRANCE: I can see him slumped, knocked out, the proofs in front of him, waiting for the, WORD!"

To be sure, publication also brought the inevitable disappointments and putdowns. Former Harvard associate Mitch Goodman, now married to poet Denise Levertov, for some time just wouldn't comment at all. Vincent Ferrini remarked that Creeley had a fine hand at prose, thanks to Olson. Larry Eigner, a paraplegic confined to a wheelchair, with whom Creeley had been corresponding since February 1950, attacked his prose for its cleverness and screwy grammar, wondering whether Creeley actually talked like he wrote. Also there was Williams's response as relayed to Corman and sent on to Creeley, that Bob was very unformed and on dangerous ground. It was important that Creeley not only search for but also find things, Williams argued.

Predictably, Creeley vented his spleen by cursing, as in Goodman's case, or mounting instant counter-offensives. Ferrini's problem, he explained to Olson, was that he couldn't distinguish imitation from influence. And there was absolutely nothing wrong with the latter. Olson, as Creeley assured him, had been the only *possible* influence on him. Somewhat more difficult to deal with were Eigner's snide remarks, especially since he admired the man's fine wit and shrewd head. It "shocks, damn well cuts in damn deep," to be accused of cliquishness or of pulling "some kind of protective cover" over his head "in lieu of seriousness," Creeley confessed to Olson.

It was a different story with Williams's letter which, Creeley thought, was very precise and had helped him assume responsibility for what he was writing, whatever the reservations. Thus he was taken aback to receive a letter from Olson who felt hurt by Williams's comments about himself and Creeley being unformed and searching. What also had annoyed Olson was Williams saying that one ought not to just search but also find, and that whether he or Creeley would manage that depended on their intelligence. According to Olson, the remarks merely proved that Bill had been the most valueless enthusiast of the time, that his *Paterson* failed imaginatively as well as language-wise, and that his lack of intellect was sabotaging their positions.

"Goddamn it," Creeley wrote back, "you slap this man too hard, and too easily ... jesus, we have, don't we, our *own* humilities, any of us." Although Olson instantly asked Creeley to forgive him, the matter proved deeply unsettling to him, and he even asked for some time to regain his sanity before replying. Three days later he did. He had met Williams and loved him, but the man's peculiar concentration had always been a kind of terror for him. Perhaps this was because it unmasked his very being: people like himself, that is, were "always fucking generalizers, however the appearance." In this *mea culpa* mood, even defensiveness turned self-accusation: "I don't know what the Christ you meant by 'we do have our humilities, any of us.' And how! – or do you think I buy that fucking tone of mine (that tone which buggers me as much as I damn well know it drives everyone off me – everyone, goddamn it, however they may even praise – except you, damn you."

It was the first time since starting to write to each other in April 1950 that Olson and Creeley came close to a falling out. Meanwhile, they hadn't even met. There had been attempts at such encounters, but none worked out. Twice Olson had planned to go see Creeley in New Hampshire, but each time these visits had had to be cancelled at the last minute: in September 1950 because of a rebuff Olson had suffered at the hands of his "She Bear," in January 1951 because of the death of his mother.

So all they could do was inspect each others' photographs, and guess at their respective ages (Olson giving Creeley six years too many). There was the rare phone call, the first of which Bob described in a letter to Cid Corman. Even though Olson had called to tell Bob about his mother's death, he had sounded so clear and wonderfully firm. Meanwhile, Creeley had stuttered and writhed, unable to think of anything but platitudes. To make matters worse, the crow in a cage by his phone had been making a racket throughout the entire conversation.

11

Going to Europe.

Paul Blackburn, in Creeley's opinion, was the first major poet of his generation he ever knew in person. That was in New York City in May of 1951, just prior to the Creeleys' departure for France. "We talked non-stop, literally, for two and a half days," Creeley remembered in 1981. The honour more appropriately should have gone to Denise Levertov. Three years older than Creeley, she shared many of his basic convictions and, as the future would show, was to acquire more fame and status than Blackburn. Creeley had met her as early as 1949. But she was a woman, and his relations with her both as poet and person were fraught with tensions from the start.

Born 1923 in Ilford, England, Denise was the daughter of a Russian Hasidic Jew who had converted to Christianity, become an Anglican minister, and devoted himself to the unification of Christianity and Judaism. She had written poems since childhood, corresponded with T.S. Eliot and Herbert Read, and published her first volume of poetry, *The Double Image*, as early as 1946. After marrying Creeley's Harvard friend Mitch Goodman, she moved to New York, where she and Creeley first met. In the meantime she had discovered William Carlos Williams, begun to search for ideas in things, and to write in her new American idiom. Kenneth Rexroth, who compared her to Dante's Beatrice, included some of her poems in his 1949 anthology, *New British Poetry*.

Her first impression of Robert Creeley, who had gone to see the Goodmans in their tenement apartment on 52 Barrow Street in New York's East Village, was anything but favourable. Though embarked on a Bohemian existence herself, she was put off by his unconventional behaviour and appearance, featuring work clothes and a blue woolen watchcap. He seemed to be talking to himself rather than to them. Here he was, amongst educated and highly articulate people, rambling on in his mixture of razzle-dazzle hipster jargon, and tight-lipped, country-folk lingo which even Mitch didn't find easy to follow. It was difficult not to feel insulted by him. What a strange creature, Denise remarked to her husband.

As usual, Creeley was unaware of the impression he had made on them. Reporting to Cid Corman, he praised Denise as an exceptionally fine young woman who wrote well. She and Mitch made a rare couple. And now they had a wonderful little son. He shed tears thinking of them.

In turn, the Goodmans were to revise their image of Creeley when, after corresponding with him, they finally went to visit him at Rock Pool Farm in August 1950. Unlike the unkempt, inarticulate hooligan they had met in New York, they found a man who obviously relished his paterfamilias role. He liked playing with his young son, David, doing the odd bit of gardening, or letting fly his roller pigeons, everywhere followed by dog Lina. Otherwise, he was a busy man of letters, reading, writing, and carrying on an enormous correspondence with present and future celebrities like Ezra Pound, William Carlos Williams, Kenneth Rexroth, Charles Olson, and Cid Corman. In fact, most of the time they saw little of him except his back bent over his desk with the typewriter by the window looking towards the river. To his left was the constantly going radio with a few marijuana plants on top; around him a bizarre assemblage of *objets trouvés*. There were two cut-outs featuring Cocteau, and three postcards shoved into the sides of the thermostat: one of a Mexican market, another of Foch and Joffre on horseback during the World War I victory parade in Paris, the third displaying Absalom from the Bible reproduced from a late medieval print. On the other side of the room was a wood relief carving of a dancing girl made for a Sparks Circus Wagon aroud 1900.

The Creeleys got up at irregular hours, neither of them bothering to serve their visitors breakfast or lunch. There was a lot of tension between them, Mitch Goodman remembered in 1993 – you could feel the daggers flying. The guests, including their little boy, Nikola, were starving. But finally, praise the lord, there was dinner. Bob had gone to the corn patch and come back with several dozen ears to be boiled in a big pot and then served with butter and milk. But Creeley's guests were in for another surprise. Their host gobbled up the corn like a raccoon, never once looking up. Mitch had never seen anyone go through so much corn so fast in his life. In fact, Bob ate so much of it no one else got enough.

Creeley had his own complaints about his demanding and prissy guests from the city. He felt physically attracted to Denise but at the same time repelled by her self-confident, bourgeois manner. The laudable sentiments she tended to utter seemed designed to control her husband.

In the spring of 1950, Bob had sampled some of her recent poems for the *Lititz Review*, found them good, and decided to print at least one. But by the time of the Goodmans' visit to Rock Pool Farm, his feelings about Denise's poetry as well as her theoretical ideas had changed. Her language was lacking in bite; her ideas about poetry were drivel, much like Rilke's whom she adored.

Nonetheless, Bob stayed in contact with the Goodmans, especially after they had moved to Southern France. Largely because of problems with Rock Pool Farm, they had thought of moving there themselves. Though they had cleaned up the outside as well as put on a new roof and wood floors, much else at the farm remained in disrepair. The actual pool above in the forest was often invaded by tourists sent by the neighbouring motels and turned into a garbage dump by them. Also, they could hardly afford the place. The original plan had been to buy it, but they were simply unable to pay the remaining $5,000. Owner Bill Gordon told them to either pay up or get out. They decided to do the latter. A representative of Ann's trust company convinced them that the property wasn't worth another $5,000 and that they stood a good chance of getting back their original payment.

Also, Bob and Ann had come to associate Rock Pool Farm with death. In May 1949, Ann had lost a child there. Born two months early, it had only lived for two days. Ann, Creeley speculated, suffered from the Rhesus factor whereby her body destroyed the unborn baby's red blood cells. The same thing might recur should she get pregnant again. In early 1950 she did, by October experiencing continual dragging pain. Bob was pondering the dire prospects ahead. Would she need a Cesarean section? Would the baby be stillborn, or full of edema or "blue" blood requiring a complete blood transfusion? Luckily things worked out better than anticipated. On 16 December at 7:30 p.m., Ann gave birth to a baby boy after a short labour with minor complications. The new child struck the happy father as enormous. A brute! They called him Thomas.

By that time Bob had made up his mind about leaving Rock Pool Farm. But where would they go? In January 1951, they looked at a cheap property in nearby Raymond, New Hampshire, about sixty miles from Boston. Alternatively, Buddy Berlin, now playing the saxophone in Albuquerque jazz clubs, had told them colourful stories about that boomtown during a recent visit to Boston: Albuquerque had grown to over 100,000 inhabitants almost overnight. Everyone was drinking around the clock. Buddy himself was in touch with a local gangster with his arm in a sling, driving around in a Lincoln Continental, out on bail for two murders. Would that be their kind of place? Sounded hopeless, Creeley decided upon contemplating some more of the information Buddy had provided. The mountains near Albuquerque, it was rumoured, had been burrowed out to harbour nuclear stockpiles plus pertinent equipment. The whole place was crawling with police of every kind. Come to think of it, perhaps they'd better leave their warmongering country altogether.

For a while, he sat poring over maps of Mexico. Charles Olson was there, living in a house on a bluff overlooking the Caribbean in a small Yucatan fishing town called Lerma. But would Southern Mexico with its subtropical climate and dubious politics be the right place for a young baby? Obviously there were plenty of other opportunities. By 7 February Bob found himself in correspondence with some thirteen government agencies in four different countries. Less than a week later he had finally made up his mind to go to France. The Goodmans found them a house towards which the Creeleys sent a deposit. They booked their transatlantic passage and began work on the immigration formalities. The anticipated departure date was to be as close to 1 April as possible.

Their plans were made without due respect for the intricacies of the French bureaucracy. At the beginning of March the French Consulate informed them that even after receipt of their passport numbers and forms, it would take another five to six weeks to secure visas for a one-year stay. A masochistic ritual helped Bob to endure the resultant frustrations. He let a full book of matches burn in his left hand and felt "considerably better," even though typing with the bandaged hand was difficult, he reported in a (typed) letter to Cid Corman.

Before leaving, they had to dispose of their animals (including dog Lina), store the bulk of their belongings, and pack up the rest for the trip. The problems never stopped. On 5 May their luggage was stalled in Boston. The trucking company hired to haul it from there to docking in New York harbour refused to proceed until Bob had sent them seventy-five feet of rope wherewith to tie it. A neighbour who had promised to help move their fridge and other items decided to go fishing instead. The lawyer Bob called to discuss the Rock Pool Farm business took off early for the weekend. Thomas's vaccinations didn't take, so they had to be repeated. A lady at the French consulate told them there was little chance that the visas would be ready for their departure date, leaving them with the uncertainty of having to straighten things out once they'd got to France.

There were unexpected pleasures as well. Upon arrival in New York two days ahead of departure on 12 May, Bob met poet Paul Blackburn at his place on 30 East 22nd Street. Blackburn too came from a repressive New England background, and the stories he told about his childhood sounded familiar enough, except they seemed even worse than Bob's: especially those about his grandmother who, obviously prompted by some psychological problem, used to repeatedly whip him for the slightest provocation. This strict family background had taught Paul phenomenal discipline, which perhaps explained why, at only twenty-four he had managed to turn himself into a "far more accomplished craftsman" than Creeley. He showed Creeley "his edition of Yeats' *Collected Poems* with his extraordinary marginal notes, tracking rhythms, patterns of sounds, in short the whole tonal construct of the writing." Certainly, Paul was a hard, serious worker. A different facet to this self-confident yet sensitive man pointed to his mother, Frances Frost, a novelist and poet who had lived through the "painful vulnerabilities, the alcoholism, the obvious insecurities of bohemian existence in the Greenwich Village of her time." Once, embarking on a new sexual relationship, she had taken Paul along "to a veritable tropic isle off the coast of the Carolinas."

In France, before the family headed south to Fontrousse, they spent a few days in Paris. But after the days in New York spent in Blackburn's company, it proved a disappointment. Walking through the tract of the Louvre from which Catherine de Medici had given the signal for the slaughtering of the Huguenots, Bob was struck by the "LIMITS of renaissance intelligence" as well as the "rigidity" and "frightful containment" of the city's architecture. Such gloomy perspectives were reinforced by a cold which, however, didn't stop him from distributing ten copies of *Origin* #1, or from searching out the work of three young American painters exhibiting at the gallery of Paul Fachetti.

Of the three artists, neither Lawrence Calcagno nor Sam Francis made much of an impression on Bob, but Jackson Pollock did. Bob would recall the paintings – "small canvases giving some sense of the *mode* but without *scale* that finally seem[ed] crucial" to the father of abstract expressionism – for decades to come. The discovery brought a major confirmation to the search Olson and himself had been engaged in for some time now: "Possibly I hadn't as yet realized that a number of American painters had made the shift I was myself so anxious to accomplish, that they had, in fact, already begun to move away from the insistently *pictorial*, whether figurative or non-figurative, to a manifest directly of the *energy* inherent in the materials, literally, and their physical manipulation in the act of painting itself. *Process*, in the sense that Olson had found it in Whitehead, was clearly much on their minds."

Creeley's first impression of their new abode in Southern France was one of pure delight. Fontrousse itself – then and now little more than two rows of stuccoed, interconnected houses lining a narrow street curving up towards a roadside chapel – seemed to provide the kind of ruralism they had enjoyed in New Hampshire. At the same time everything seemed so different: the reddish earth, the checker-board pattern of vineyards and wheat fields stretching east towards the hilly horizon dominated by a mountain looking like a boat, which turned out to be Sainte-Victoire, immortalized in Cezanne's paintings. There were ancient ruins all over, the foot of Sainte-Victoire, as Creeley found out, being the place where the Romans had put an end to the invasions by the barbarians. And the fantastic sharpness of the light, especially after a thunderstorm had cleared the air, so that one could make out the wash flapping on a line some three miles away! No wonder he kept thinking the sea might be just over those hills. Even their living quarters, though much smaller than at Rock Pool Farm, seemed very beautiful. From the kitchen below, a winding stair led up to two bedrooms with weirdly angled ceilings, everything painted a flat white. And all, including the view of Sainte-Victoire, for $5 a month! The place was a real wonder. In the back, they had a little garden all to themselves.

Their rural neighbours seemed not much different from farmers anywhere – like someone loading hay next door in what struck Creeley as a kind of "dutch oven" arrangement. It was equally delightful to meet the nearby townfolks while going shopping in Aix in the company of Ann, Dave, and Tom, Bob himself carrying the basket, trailing behind and exchanging glances with "all these so damn *pure* women, looking, how they do, the eyes so very deep, so fine." Though his French was limited, he noted the peculiar way in which the locals rolled it.

However, his initial exuberance quickly faded. Like Olson in Spanish-speaking Yucatan, he felt locked up in his prison of American speech and its habits. "I speak no french more than: pardon!" he confessed. If anything, France made him feel more than ever "AMERICAN, more damn well REAL," whatever that meant. The charm of Southern France soured: it was all fantastically beautiful but static. "Jesus, how it's fenced: Europe. The damn neatness," he complained. More and more he found the domesticity of the landscape as well as their living conditions enervating. And the solitude! He realized that after the sudden outburst of compulsive talking at Harvard and on Cape Cod, he had been lapsing back into the speechlessness of his teenage years and childhood. "Have been, more or less, silent for the past 4 years," he explained to Olson. That, of course, included the years in New Hampshire. But at Rock Pool Farm he had at least enjoyed the odd chat with neighbours like Kenneth Ainsworth. Here, the only person he could really talk to on a daily basis was Ann, or perhaps his son Dave, who was picking up French more rapidly than himself.

As on similar occasions earlier and later in life, his isolation made Creeley ponder his past by way of starting yet another largely autobiographical novel. Once again the attempt was doomed. After working at it for no more than a day, he found it a miserable effort. Even so, he was determined to finish it, planning to work eight hours each day until the job was done. Yet with some sixty pages completed a week later, it began to eat him up.

Encouraged by James's *Art of Fiction*, he toiled on, finished some four chapters by 13 July, planned to complete two more before sending the typescript to a publisher, and then to wrap up the second part upon receiving the latter's verdict. Meanwhile, he sent a sample chapter 3 plus a new story, "A Sort of Song," and his "Notes on the Theatre" to Olson. (None of these was ever published as such, but they are now accessible in volume six of the Olson-Creeley correspondence.) While impatiently awaiting Olson's answer, Creeley kept on reporting to him on both Ann's praise of the novel ("that it did hang together") and his own continuing frustrations with it. Yet curiously, he paid little attention when Olson's lengthy response did arrive. Olson felt that Creeley was oscillating between either the strictly subjective or the totally objective and hence didn't achieve the intensity of, say, "Mr. Blue." Creeley didn't agree. The main thing for him was to toil on in just the same way he had laboured for five years before managing to write a short story he could be proud of: "I can date it … It was, simply enough, a journal I'd kept 5 yrs back, & then reading it, 3 yrs back … Well, I tell you: this novel, slack or no slack, will continue the damn base premise of, form is the extension of content … What the hell else cd I write."

Such defiance was dampened when Adele Dogan at Morrow's Publishers turned down what he had sent them. Creeley, Dogan wrote, could be "wonderful on mood, and on atmosphere, with the small descriptive phrase, the telling sentence." Also, he obviously had "a definite, individual style." This, however, tended to be "a little self-conscious." What she and her two editors had found discouraging was the obscurity of the writing.

Another letter from Olson identified the main trouble with the novel as its being hung between two different methodologies which, at a later point, Creeley himself was to define as the total "NARRATOR IN" *vis-à-vis* the "total OUT." This time Creeley agreed, only wondering if there might not be a "meeting, somewhere, between the two ways." For the time being, he concluded, writing stories decidedly remained his "surest occasion."

But the sense of having wasted the better part of the summer lingered on. "Frightening thing. All the past months I've felt I'd lost all of it, and setting down to something, lifted only phrases, or sounds I know by heart." Also, his isolation had intensified. The only friend he could talk to was Mitch, who with his wife, Denise, lived in nearby Puyricard. Recommending him to Olson for a possible teaching position at Black Mountain

College, Bob had described Mitch as a man in his late twenties of great tenacity, good presence, and great "clarity in the bean." Hence Mitch had a "damn good head for teaching." Especially, he was "no damn arty bastard, no bullshit from this man. NONE. None." He had a degree in economics from Harvard and, like Creeley himself, was trying to write a novel.

Yet even Mitch eventually got on Bob's nerves. It was one thing for him to take four days in order to comment on *Origin* #2; for when he finally did, singling out the "3 Fate Tales" as the best story of the lot, his remarks were appreciated all the more. But it was quite another to constantly hold Bob at arm's length, as it were, or to respond to almost everything with that studied lack of enthusiasm, a quality reinforced by the presence of his increasingly irritating wife Denise, who, however, continued to attract him sexually. On one occasion in Puyricard, they had a debate pro and con the social involvement of the poet in which Bob, using Camus's *The Plague* as an instance, lashed out against the use of social diatribes of precisely the kind that delighted "Madame." Had he come bicycling over in the sweltering heat for that? The encounter left him so frustrated and "castrate" he could have given Denise the knife right there and then, he raged to Corman.

Otherwise, his antagonism toward her vented itself in more reasonable forms of mockery and contempt. Rexroth, he scoffed to Olson, thinks she is "Dante's Beatrice returned, but I have my doubts." Rather than a true poet, Denise was a "lady" confined to her moral fervours, her self-consciously manipulative benevolence, and social airs. Such hostility came to a head whenever the Goodmans tried to rope Bob into one of their socialite activities. On one occasion, a Mozart festival at the Bishop's Palace in Aix-en-Provence, Bob demonstrated his disgust with such bourgeois reverie by walking out of an opera in the middle of the performance.

How much he depended on the Goodmans' companionship only became clear to him once they left. Very quickly the self-styled "lone wolf" turned into a timid recluse. "See no one," he confessed to Olson on 4 Octobe, "and when someone goes by, feel very shy, & sometimes duck back on the stairs, so as not to be seen."

A more recent acquaintance came to feel the full brunt of Creeley's loneliness. Ashley Bryan, a black painter in his late twenties living in Aix, had met Bob around the beginning of September. "I spent the night there with him in Aix, & was going, again, well before breakfast," he reported to Olson. Ashley was a man of real intelligence who had perceptive things to say about art and literature alike and who, once he had read Bob's stories, made comments echoing Olson's. He could read them *"any way, i.e.,* from this end to that or the other way round," Ashley explained. Creeley, according to his new friend, had broken through "one aspect of 'time'" and reached out for a "dimension of *weight* beyond 'Time'."

Unlike other painters Bob knew, Ashley expressed himself with care and precision. His voice, too, was extremely pleasant: rather deep and with that typical "underwarmth a Negro so very often has in his speech." Yet naturally, the newness of their friendship entailed certain restraints. Also, Ashley lived some ten miles away in Aix and loved to travel. So even during the first six months or so of their friendship Bob didn't see him more than some half a dozen times.

A visit from Buddy and his wife, Mary Anne, offered further distraction. Buddy seemed the same as ever, filling Bob's heart with yearnings for the world of bullfights, jazz clubs, and *demi-monde* glamour frequented by his restless, dare-devil friend. A welcome incident allowed Bob to show Buddy that he too had preserved some of the Yankee bravado that had inspired their joint escapades back at Harvard. This was on the occasion of a visit paid the Creeleys by their landlord.

Upon moving to Fontrousse, they had been warned that they'd have to vacate their place by September 1951. Now, at the end of October, the man had come to tell them that he would have to move his mother-in-law in with them unless they left voluntarily. Barely able to follow the man's French, Bob cut short the argument in typically Creeleyan fashion: he "went for his throat, & pulling him round ... shove[d] him thru the door, then booted him, to the street, etc."

Another party to join the two couples was painter René Laubiès, the first to translate into French sections of Ezra Pound's *Cantos*. Laubiès came from an obviously upper-class background, had apartments in both Nice and Paris, and entertained contacts with Gallimard and *Cahiers du Sud*. After receiving the painter's address from Pound, Bob had written to him, hoping he would not turn out to be another glumly self-righteous Poundian.

What struck Bob right away was the clear, light character of Laubiès's eyes. There was luxuriance in his demeanour, perhaps stemming from the exotic Indochina surroundings in which he had been raised. That background also seemed to have given the slightly older man his distinctly colonial manner. Laubiès's self-conscious kindness made Bob acutely aware of his Yankee gaucheness. It created "a distance more damn dulling than even the hate; it follows you like a skin, it mocks you with agreement."

Even Buddy came to rub Bob the wrong way. Flaunting his married bachelor's lifestyle à la Hemingway and running to see every bullfight in the area, Buddy seemed to resent Bob's and Ann's children. Also, with so many persons now inhabiting the three-room house, things had become awfully cramped. But worse was the loneliness that once again settled around Bob after the Berlins left. Ever since coming to France, he had hated the loss of his own language, he explained to Olson. More to the point, he felt "a very damn muddled man" with an unsatisfied "hunger for speech."

It got worse once the beginning winter turned their house into a damp stone tomb. By the end of November, Bob came close to suffering a nervous breakdown. The whole of Europe, even six years after the war, seemed like a continent of death, with World War III clearly on the horizon: "there is the war coming, so surely you can *smell* it; death everywhere I have been." By now, he rarely left his cell. And when he did, reawakened phobias from adolescence quickly made him flee back to its protective shelter. People, the few he saw, made him nervous and jumpy.

Even his creativity seemed to have dried up. The "final sweep of any surety or authority" he'd commanded in New Hampshire had gotten lost "damn bitterly." A week might go by without his ever leaving his room except to go to the outhouse. Then, in the evening of 27 November, he suddenly realized he had done nothing except stare out of the window for an entire afternoon. It made him feel "dirty, even sick," yet he was unable to pull himself out of his self-reflective inertia. "It is a hellish damn thing to get caught with," he wrote Olson two days later, "this willfulness, this deadness of the attentions." More clearly than ever before, he came to understand Coleridge's "Dejection":

> A grief without a pang, void, dark, and drear,
>   A stifled, drowsy, unimpassioned grief,
>   Which finds no natural outlet, no relief,
>   In word, or sigh, or tear –

Ann, putting up with her share of miseries – doing the laundry on a washing-stone, tending a stove for which the fuel had to be gathered every day – wasn't too reassuring: "When will you get famous, so we can get *out* of here?" she snidely asked.

Christmas in this foreign country brought them plenty of gallows humour but little cheer. For a tree, they had to make do with what Bob could steal: something that looked like spruce loaded with prickers. Shopping in Aix with his family on Christmas Eve suddenly made him realize how run-down they looked. Standing on a streetcorner holding Tom, and David beside him, he noticed two young boys run past them, then come back to push two francs into Dave's hand. He knew he looked bad, Bob joked to his mother – just not how bad.

Like most everything, looking for presents for Ann's birthday shortly before Christmas quickly exhausted Bob's patience. Ashley told Bob to just go home to Fontrousse. He would take care of things, find the potholders Ann wanted, get the cake, and then bring them out to them on the bus. Yet nothing seemed capable of pulling Bob and Ann out of their by now habitual morass of morbidity. On one occasion, they were discussing what they would do if one of them should die. If Ann were the corpse, Bob would dig a hole and push her in, he proposed. Would she be able to get a hole dug if Bob died, she wondered. Never to worry, Ashley would help her, Bob countered without thinking.

It was time for the couple to take off time from each other. The first one to get the much needed break was Ann, who went to stay with an aunt in the outskirts of Paris. Her absence brought unexpected change to Bob in allowing him little time for indulging in self-reflective miseries. At night he was kept awake by David who insisted on sharing his bed. During the day, he had to feed Thomas who at some point scrambled out of the highchair and fell. "I made, what's known as a shoestring catch," Creeley reported gleefully, – "his head a clear inch from the floor, and going down fast at that – by one leg, hauled him up, and finished whatever it was I was doing with my left hand – cooking something I think – without a damn break! Anyhow, I want a medal, etc." Domestic chaos had at least reawakened his sense of humour.

12

"For Rainer Gerhardt."

Things were improving all around. A small gas heater acquired in late December provided the upstairs study with some warmth. A sketch sent to Olson by 9 January 1952 gives a sense of this cosy scenario: Creeley sitting by the window, his face turned to the right towards Olson's "This" broadside and an unframed photograph of Olson himself.

The recent friendships with Ashley Bryan and René Laubiès were starting to bear fruit. Bryan had done a whole sheath of drawings for Creeley's story "The Party," planned as a Black Mountain Workshop pamphlet. Bob liked the drawings and decided to use three of them. Eventually, René also produced a set of art works for the stories. Though puzzled by them, Bob covered a large stretch of the wall behind him with them. His personal relations with René improved accordingly. The man, he found, was not just coldly polite but had a sense of humour that Bob could "make, & enjoy completely." Ann's absence also gave him time to reflect upon his marriage and women in general. He was "born to be lonely," he concluded, and "best so," a sense confirmed by Ann's return towards the middle of February: "I never once slept with a woman who didn't throw me back at myself," he mused.

Even the problem with their landlord which Bob rightly feared might turn out badly for him resolved itself in a totally unexpected way. At the last minute, Bob's lawyer pulled "a real goofy deal" on the opposite side: the Creeleys, he argued, had been welcomed on the premises as friends but then told to leave. The result: the Creeleys' lease was extended, and rent-free from September 1951. "Too much!" Creeley wrote to Olson. "Damn well PLEASURE to see the prick ... get it and good."

Most encouraging were Olson's extensive comments on Creeley's "For Rainer Gerhardt," later published in *Origin* #6. To Olson the poem marked Creeley's breakthrough into the ranks of major poets like Arthur

Rimbaud and D.H. Lawrence. Like Lawrence, Creeley had discovered "a form of verse ... absolutely local to his own message." Shedding his prior concern with drama, plot, and image, he had finally managed to give his verse that instantaneity of strictly personal experience, which, in a different way, also marked his stories. Like Rimbaud's *Illuminations*, Creeley's "For Rainer Gerhardt" let his innermost thoughts enact themselves "with all turns, & backups," without allowing any preconceived notions of prosody, form, or ideational conjecture to get in the way of such kinetic automatism. That's what he ought to continue to do in the future, Olson urged: "Let me make this guess, that the more you use the form of verse to lay home just such severe inside experiences as this one ... the more you will be swinging your own cat by the tale."

To be sure, only poets with Creeley's and Rimbaud's instinctual penchant for form could abandon themselves to such randomness, and still produce great poetry: "for it comes, finally, to kinetics: your sense of the physical world is so strong that I value yr judgement on verse beyond any one's. Therefore, I say, there can be no question that somewhere there is this form. And what makes the Rainer G/ stand up for me is, that I think HERE IT BEGINS." Naturally, Creeley was delighted, but also worried about how he could live up to such praise. Olson's letter had been a terrific boost, Bob wrote back. "You would have wept (I mean it) seeing me holding on" to it.

"For Rainer Gerhardt" provides a first instance of a henceforth typical kind of Creeley poem. It "defines" a subject matter using key words which, through repetition and permutation, increasingly empty themselves of referential content and meaning. The poem also was prophetic of things to come. After reaching its greatest intensity during the weeks ahead, the friendship between the two men would suddenly suffer the petulance, indifference and annihilation suggested by the poem. Its beginnings have already been touched upon: Gerhardt, at the instigation of Pound, establishing contact with Creeley by late 1950; the German impressing Bob by what he was doing and planning; his asking Creeley to become the American representative of *Fragmente*; and his offering to publish two of Creeley's short stories in its second issue. Gerhardt had expressed his great liking for Creeley's prose. The company in which Bob was to be published seemed promising indeed: Ezra Pound, William Carlos Williams, Henry Miller, Aimé Césaire, etc. At a later point, Gerhardt even offered to publish a whole volume of Creeley's stories.

One thing made Gerhardt's efforts particularly impressive to Creeley: while pursuing goals so obviously congenial to his own, Gerhardt had undertaken a Herculean labour in the service of his country. Almost single-handedly he was trying to bring Germany back into mainstream world culture, a continuum that for over a decade had been interrupted by Nazi rule. Ernst Robert Curtius, one of his age's greatest scholars, had hailed *Fragmente* #1 as "the most hopeful sign to come out of post-war Germany."

The trading of photographs and personal details, as their epistolary relationship deepened, brought intriguing surprises. The parallels between the two men's lives were close to miraculous. Both were twenty-four, married with two children, the second one in both cases having been born on 16 December 1950! Were they fated to join their lots? Already, Gerhardt had made several attempts to come visit the Creeleys. He'd even made plans to move his entire family to Southern France. But the family's most recent attempts at coming to Aix during the winter of 1951–52 were cut short by Rainer being offered work on German radio, and his wife, Renate, accepting a job as an interpreter. They had run up considerable debts in publishing *Fragmente* #1 and hoped to defray some of them before bringing out the second issue with Creeley's stories.

Creeley decided to go see Rainer instead. Now that Ann was back to take care of the children, he found more than the obvious reason for doing so. For one thing, he absolutely had to break the deadening routine he had been stuck with for so long.

In late August of 1951, Creeley had acquired a second-hand car which promised to last the journey to Freiburg, from there to Paris to renew contact with René Laubiès, and hopefully back to Fontrousse. It was a twenty-three year old coupé, with a total of four horsepower, hence very low on fuel, which was essential, gasoline being very expensive in Europe. All he needed were reliable tires, one of them having recently exploded on Cour Mirabeau in Aix. That taken care of, he and Ashley Bryan were on their way.

They reached Freiburg, a city in South West Germany on the edge of the Black Forest, in the second week of March. It would take Bob weeks to recover from the horror of what they saw: almost every other building bombed out, the ruins barely cleared away, weeds and brush everywhere. And to imagine the inferno of a single night's bombing raid which had caused such devastation. It stopped Bob dead. Never, not even back in Burma, had he felt so confused and helpless in the face of human misery.

They found Rainer, Renate, and their two sons, Titus and Ezra, inhabiting a single room, which now had to accommodate Bob and Ashley as well. In fact, Rainer and Renate insisted on sleeping on the floor so that the guests could have their bed. Obviously, they were used to worse. Only three months before in the depths of winter, they had spent almost three weeks just lying in bed with their kids, desperately short of both firewood and food. Meanwhile, Bob had been cursing the taciturn Rainer for not answering his letters more promptly. How indeed was one "to define these / conditions of / friendship," given such circumstances?

Two weeks later Bob still had to admit to his inability to confront what he saw. It helped that Ashley could buy food and wine at the local army store. Or that Rainer and Bob hit it off as well as either of them had expected – "like an electrical current," as Renate Gerhardt remembers, "plus and minus." Bob did most of the talking, usually until deep into the night, when he would suddenly drop off, to jerk erect again the next morning like a folding knife and, with a "by the way," resume his argument exactly where he'd left off. But as compulsively as he talked, as attentively did he listen. And there was enough in what Rainer told him to keep him spellbound: about his growing up in the *Hitler Jugend*, being drafted into the army at a time when he had become staunchly opposed to the Nazi regime, his defecting to Tito's army in Yugoslavia, and his struggling since the end of the war. Meanwhile Renate did everything to make their American friends feel welcome. Bob had come in a pair of old scuffed combat boots and, to his surprise, found them polished to a high shine waking up the next morning.

Yet somehow the pall of horror and misery surrounding them, as well as Bob's sense of impotent helplessness in the face of it all, would not let up. With other friends like Buddy Berlin one could discuss one's tribulations, but then rise above them in defiant humour, making sure that the real work would remain ultimately unaffected by one's worries. But with Rainer the burden, however heroically he struggled with it, never lifted. It had penetrated his very core and tainted his poetic work. His was a tragic dilemma, intrinsically admirable, yet at the same time alien, even repulsive to Creeley. Gerhardt seemed close to defeat, to which Creeley could only react with rage. To his delight, Gerhardt responded in kind, the two men suddenly starting to quarrel. Some nights, as Creeley remembered shortly after the trip, it became "almost ugly, and [they] were very close to fighting, though it would have been even a love in that:"

> friendship, the wandering & inexhaustible wish to
> be of use, somehow
> to be helpful
>
> when it isn't simple, – wish
> otherwise, convulsed, and leading
> nowhere I can go.

Their joint trip to Paris, then to Fontrousse, where Rainer stayed on for about two weeks, did little to dispel Creeley's sense of helpless emotional ambivalence towards his friend. Sure Rainer was planning to move to France. There was no way he could survive in Germany: because of the split into East and West, the country itself couldn't survive, Bob speculated. The French consulate had informed them that it would take a mere six weeks to handle the formalities before they could immigrate. Rainer and Bob discussed optimistic plans of bringing Rainer's hand press to Fontrousse and printing a series of magazines in German, English, and eventually French, as well as separate editions of literary works.

However, was Rainer the man to pull off what Olson and Creeley had planned? His last day in Fontrousse had boded ill – as if he was taking his leave forever. He had come down in the morning and looked "out through a window in the door, at the long side of Sainte-Victoire, that faced our house across the fields. He was crying without sound, one could see the tears on his face."

For days afterwards Bob would "mull over the biz with Rainer, or what that came to." Their friendship, or rather its failure, became an obsession. In one way or another, it had to be exorcised. There was no point in remaining stuck in the helpless confusion into which the affair had plunged him. He had been so very shocked, gone damn well dumb and stupid in his reaction, he confessed on 31 March. Four days later he resumed discussion of the matter to Olson. The problem with Rainer, as with Germans in general, was that he was "cursed with a *public* conscience." Rainer's hell was one of history and fragmentation. Listening to him, Bob remembered, he had frequently sensed Rainer's confusion of not knowing to which extent an experience was either truly personal or mere public posturing.

Such confusion, now that he felt "sound" again, sat ill with his recently acquired sense of a poet's responsibility or "what a man can deal with as his own, where to act on it, and how." For someone to base himself on his own disintegration was the ugliest of all human acts, and worthy of special hatred when the culprit happened to be oneself. His comments turned the more negative the more successfully he managed to purge himself of his former feelings towards Rainer. What had frightened him about Gerhardt, he wrote Olson, was to realize this "destruction, complete, of the man as particular reality."

A subsequent letter from Rainer merely confirmed his sense of the man's dilemma. Judged by "the utter flab of current European work," Gerhardt still earned points for having taken on "in one damn gulp, – Pound, Williams," and Olson. Otherwise, as where he spoke of the isolation of the American poet, there was little else than confusion. Instead of speaking on his own behalf, Rainer was making "generalization[s] from immediate hell:"

but not friends, the
acquaintances, but you,
Rainer. And likely there is
petulance in us
kept apart.

Meanwhile Bob had reason to feel confused himself. They would have
to vacate their place by the end of April, and, in spite of diverse efforts,
had not yet found a new one. Ann was pregnant again, with a baby expected as early as July. A $600 cheque they had sent to Bob's mother to-
wards the end of March had vanished, perhaps been stolen. Yet somehow,
at bottom, where it counted, Creeley felt sounder than he had in a long
time. Had observing Rainer's confusions helped him regain his own bear-
ings? Also, he was writing poems again. In fact, for about two weeks early
in April, he was throwing them off in a burst of creativity he had never
before experienced. Even the obvious strains in his domestic situation
found a voice in them. A poem like "The Crisis" was an attempt to feel
his way into irritation.

Let me say (in anger) that since the day we were married
we have never had a towel
where anyone could find it,
the fact.
            Notwithstanding that I am not
simple to live with, not
my own judgement, but no
matter.
            There are other things:

to kiss you is not
to love you.
            Or not so simply.

Laughter releases rancor, the quality of mercy is not
strained.

Perhaps one had to be married to appreciate the poem, Creeley mused.
"Something for Easter" was another of his intimately private poems written in a moment of bitterness for Ann:

I pulled the street up as you suggested
– and found what?

       1 nickel
       2 pieces gum
etc.

    But we are practical
    – but winter is long & however much one
    does save, there is never
    enough.

Almost as quickly as he wrote it, Creeley subjected "Something for Easter" to a sound and stress pattern analysis, revealing "play-backs on divers previous rhythms" in an elaborate chart. Similarly, the plays on "not" echoing through "The Crisis," he explained, gave the reader a sense of the speaker's anger. Altogether, this type of verse, with its various techniques of repetition, was based on rhythm rather than melody, analogous to the jazz of Parker, Miles, Chano, Roach, or Jackson – or to the way Sebastian Bach "managed the variation of rhythm units."

Meanwhile, the poems continued to come to him fast, on 15 April over half a dozen the same day: "The Riddle," "The Echo," "The Cantos," "The Rhyme," as well as others which remained unpublished. "Keeps going, like ice in the spring," he wrote to Olson. "Even pursued to the john, viz. the enclosed bit of toilet paper." Yet after writing "The Innocence," he knew he had passed the peak of his creative outburst. Here was a new kind of Creeley poem he would only master on very rare occasions. Its speaker seemed to name things in a spirit of first discovery as if trying to find his place among them.

    Looking to the sea, it is a line
    of unbroken mountains.

    It is the sky.
    It is the ground. There
    we live, on it.
    It is a mist
    now tangent to another
    quiet. Here the leaves
    come, there
    is the rock in evidence

    or evidence.
    What I come to do
    is partial, partially kept.

"The Innocence" was himself talking, or speaking, in his own tongue. "What lifts, for me, item like THE INNOCENCE is that it makes *no sense whatsoever* unless it be *this sense*," Creeley oracled to Olson.

In the meantime, neither the $600 affair nor the "christly house biz" showed any signs of resolution. By 12 April D.D. Paige, a writer living in Rapallo, wrote that there might be a possibility in that city. A trip there in late April allowed Creeley to locate the top floor apartment once inhabited by Ezra Pound in a building overlooking the Mediterranean. But otherwise he came to agree with Kenneth Rexroth wondering how Pound could have endured this Atlantic City of Czechoslovak yachtsmen and Swiss gamblers for twenty-five years. No way Creeley would ever live there himself.

Luckily, there was good news greeting him after an overnight drive back to Fontrousse. Ashley had found Ann a place on the outskirts of Lambesc, a small provincial town about twenty kilometres on the road towards Avignon – "has plenty of room around it, pleasant garden, etc., etc. In short, will do. Rent is fair enough, people decent & distant, – so it should be ok."

13

Lambesc, 1952.

Their new home offered some of the amenities missing in their Fontrousse cave: electricity, plenty of room, a big garden, and a quiet attic where Creeley hoped to revive the creative streak of early April: "Up under the eaves … Kids can't find me, which is half of it. Low ceiling about four feet, and a fine little window, at one end, looks out on the trees, etc. Birds & the works; most idyllic." The front of the house was walled in, so the kids couldn't get out onto the road. Creeley planned to stay there for at least a year.

This time he would make sure to get properly settled: put up his bookshelves, spread five of Laubiès's drawings on a spacious wall behind him, and order, per $10 cheque, some much-needed items from his mother back home: one or two pairs of grey size 31 work pants, the usual underpants, two or three work shirts (14 1/2–15 neck), size 11, sneakers for Dave, a jar of mayonnaise, and seed-corn and soldier beans for the garden. When the seeds didn't arrive quickly enough, Bob sent an urgent reminder, plus another $10 cheque asking his mother to mail them by air – enough for one hundred feet of beans and two hundred of corn, which were impossible to come by otherwise. Europeans didn't eat corn – only for animals, they thought. The Creeleys also hired a *femme de menage* to assist a now heavily pregnant Ann with the household. With somewhat less success they checked out the local nursery school for Dave: though beautifully equipped, it was run as a mere sinecure by the tax collector's wife with no interest in kids.

A good size reservoir at the back of the house, its two feet of mud crawling with tadpoles, might serve as a swimming pool during the upcoming summer. Creeley drained it, watching the tadpoles die in the hot sun, pondering the "idiotic" biblical injunction to "do unto others as you would have them do unto you." Once cleaned out and refilled, the restored reservoir also allowed Dave to sail a toy boat which his father had equipped with a keel and high mast – "wind catches it, sails open way out, I have the jib almost like a balloon, etc., very fine! Me & Leonardo, only I buy mine at the store."

When the missing $600 finally came from the u.s., Creeley made some long overdue purchases for himself: plenty of books from England, among them Graves's translation of Apuleius's *The Golden Ass*, as well as Ovid in an Elizabethan translation by Golding and Marlowe. He also purchased a radio which he had lacked during the year at Fontrousse. Now he could listen to a u.s. Army station, and other stations from England, France, Germany, Italy, and Spain.

This time they even had neighbours they could talk to: Marti, a Spaniard; his French wife, and their four kids, who shared the other half of the garden. Considering the exotic character of French horticulture – all kinds of little bushes, hedges, most of it weird tropical stuff – Bob willingly yielded the care of their share of the garden to Marti as well. It was a good decision. Given Marti's Mediterranean expertise, the North American seeds soon shot up into full-fledged corn and bean stalks. "I got six rows of corn – and feel like Louis Bromfield," Creeley bragged.

Marti had to travel some thirty miles a day by bicycle to work as a mason's helper. Meanwhile, he was friends with Pablo Casals, and back in Spain had grown up with Garcia Lorca. Though he refused to teach himself proper French, his strange mixture of Spanish and French, accompanied by vivid gestures, made his many anecdotes come alive all the more colourfully. As they drew closer, Marti revealed other, unexpectedly terrifying parts of his life.

As with Rainer Gerhardt, Bob found himself slumping into impotent numbness listening to such horrors: Marti's grandmother nailed by her hands to a wall, buried alive. Marti saw such atrocities as the work of a latter-day alliance between the fascists and the Catholic church. After the defeat of the Republicans, the Spanish authorities had sent him to a German concentration camp where he'd spent four whole years.

Marti knew entire poems and plays by Lorca by heart. One evening, after hearing him recite a Lorca poem first in Spanish and then in French, Bob composed an English rendering he entitled "After Lorca."

for M. Marti

The church is a business, and the rich
are the business men.
          When they pull on the bells, the
poor come piling in and when a poor man dies, he has a wooden

cross, and they rush through the ceremony.
But when a rich man dies, they
drag out the Sacrament
and a golden Cross, and go *doucement, doucement*
to the cemetery.

And the poor love it
and think it's crazy.

One day, 14 July, there was an unexpected pleasure. Walking down Cour Mirabeau in Aix, Bob was struck by a small but solidly built older man in a poorly cut French suit, sitting with his pretty young wife and kids at a table of a sidewalk café. Bob stared at the stranger, who looked straight back at him with an odd intensity. After he had passed on, Bob realized it was Picasso. His eyes were "lovely damn things" he would never forget. Even in photographs, there was that quality, but faced, they were incredible. "It was damn well worth all the christly hell of the past year, etc.," he wrote to Olson.

Southern France during the summer of 1952 was experiencing its worst heatwave in years, and Ann might give birth any day now. Bob aired his worries in writing to his mother. As a nurse, she might have some useful advice. After the year in Fontrousse, Ann was run down. She needed glasses, and they'd get her a pair as soon as someone would give her a decent prescription. More urgently, her teeth needed fixing before getting badly ruined. Most serious of all, her uterus had been damaged by numerous pregnancies and miscarriages. MacGregor, their long-time New Hampshire family doctor, had suggested that already having gone through some ten pregnancies, she should have her tubes tied.

What did Genevieve think? Was it safe? A doctor in Aix had been reluctant to discuss the issue, probably for religious reasons. Also, he had turned out to be a cheapskate, predicting the birth for August and claiming one prior visit in late July would be sufficient, obviously because such visits brought him little cash. Ann decided to try someone else. The new doctor predicted the baby would be due between the end of June and the middle of July. The Creeleys' third child was born on 27 July, a Sunday. All went very simply, and quickly. As Ann had hoped, it was a girl. Name's Charlotte, Creeley wrote Olson. Someday she'll get married, and "Creeley" won't be any further worry for her.

On the publishing front there were some pleasant surprises too. *Fragmente* #2, featuring Creeley's "The Lover" and "The Seance," delayed when the Gerhardts lost their room in Freiburg, was reported to be in press. Richard Emerson, whom Bob had come close to writing off, suddenly wanted to publish a small book of his poetry, containing over twenty poems instead of the eleven originally planned. Would Bob have enough on hand? Emerson was using a hand press and seemed eager to get cracking. Taken by surprise, Creeley was one more time struck by the meagreness of his past poetic output.

In addition to some of the poems written in early April, he decided to include everything of any use up to "The Rites." "It was a very damn lonely business," he reported to Olson: "spent one night at it, spread them out on the couch downstairs, and tried to pick them up again in some order or other. Not at all happy." *Le Fou*, brought out by Golden Goose Press, duly appeared in October 1952.

More and more journals printed his poems, stories, and critical prose. Kenneth Lash, editor of the *New Mexico Quarterly*, an acquaintance of Buddy Berlin and Race Newton in Albuquerque, accepted Bob's review of John Hawkes's *The Beetle Leg* and his story "Jardou" for publication in the summer and autumn issues. Vincent Ferrini printed "Divisions" in the first issue of his new magazine, *Four Winds*, of Summer 1952. Editors who had previously published Bob proved more loyal to their cantankerous contributor than expected. Corman published another short story, "The Party," a note on René Laubiès, and three poems, "The Innocence," "For Rainer Gerhardt," and "The Question," in *Origin* #6 and #7. Horace Schwartz, after printing a letter by Creeley attacking Schwartz in the second issue of his magazine, *Goad*, published "After Lorca" and "The Festival" in number three. The squabble had been over Pound. Creeley agreed with Schwartz in branding Pound's anti-Semitism. But to rank the author of the *Cantos* lower than Housman, as Schwartz did, was simply ridiculous. Housman? By comparison with Pound, he was "a cheap little prick."

The matter almost turned ugly when Leslie Woolf Hedley, editor of a magazine entitled *Inferno*, accused Creeley of behaving like a fascist. Creeley went for Hedley with characteristic belligerence. He asked Corman to get hold of any letter in which Hedley called him a fascist directly. If he could nail him, he would sue Hedley for libel. He had already tracked down some of this possibly incriminating material himself, and was about to write to his lawyer. But nothing came of it.

He also developed promising new literary connections. Canadian Raymond Souster had reprinted part of *Origin* #1 in his auspiciously titled *Contact: International Magazine for Poetry*. Vincent Ferrini's tie-in, Robert Cooper, living in Liverpool, England, was planning to bring out a series of literary pamphlets in the coming winter. Most importantly, there was a poem, "All Devils Fading," by another Englishman Creeley had discovered in a magazine, *The Window*. Expecting to find one more instance of the dum-de-dum school of British poetry, he was surprised. This poem was very lovely and graceful. Involving two lovers thriving upon their mutual hatred, destructiveness and contempt, its content too struck him as particular to his "own emphases." The poet had a natural head for rhythms, rare amongst the English.

Creeley had immediately written the man and by 3 May, just after moving into his Lambesc house, received an answer. Born in 1928 in London, Martin Seymour-Smith had been awarded a B.A. (with honours) at Oxford, and was now tutoring Robert Graves's oldest son in Deya, Majorca. Soon the two poets were conducting an intense correspondence. "I like him," Creeley told Olson, "he writes straight – no damn jamming, or any need to be sly." What's more, Seymour-Smith might be a substitute for Rainer Gerhardt, who was just too consumed by problems to ever realize Creeley's many plans, as well as for Cid Corman who, once more, had reached rock-bottom in Bob's esteem – this time for the unlikely reason of planning to publish a poem dedicated to Robert Creeley.

Seymour-Smith was set to launch a magazine as well as a series of pamphlets under the imprint of Roebuck Press. The first three pamphlets originally planned at thirty-two pages, later at sixteen pages apiece, were to feature Paul Blackburn's Provençal translations as well as two British poets. In 1953 he was to enlarge his original project to encompass a regular list of some sixteen books. Before long Creeley was appointed U.S. editor for these far-flung endeavours.

He instantly got to work, requesting aid from former friends and enemies alike. Perhaps Corman might help with his contacts for subscriptions. Trying to enlist Olson's assistance for the same project, Creeley unceremoniously unearthed a much maligned fellow poet. He had completely misjudged Duncan, Bob concluded after rereading him – though weak on content, he had "an incredibly firm structure." But what if the San Francisco poet, after Olson's and Creeley's endeavours to have him counted in in spite of his disreputable demeanour, ended up rejecting *them*? Already, one of Bob's letters to Duncan had remained unanswered.

There was another setback when Seymour-Smith surprised Creeley with an "idiotic" attack on Pound. Seymour-Smith also thought that pamphlets featuring American poetry would not sell more than a couple of copies in the U.K. But Bob's resultant reservations were quickly forgotten when Martin suggested he might collaborate with Robert Cooper on the pamphlets. For some time now Bob had wanted to go to Majorca to see in person what Seymour-Smith was up to. With prices steadily rising in France, they might end up moving there altogether.

Lambesc, like most places Creeley ever lived in, quickly soured on him. After less than a month the town made him feel too displaced to manage any real work. I miss any stimulus, he complained to Olson, who held out various possibilities of teaching at Black Mountain. Creeley responded in kind. By December at the latest, he'd have the loot for the passage to cross the Atlantic. Perhaps even in company. Most likely he would bring along René Laubiès as well as the Gerhardts, all of whom had academic degrees qualifying them for teaching at the college. Perhaps they could jointly launch a Black Mountain College magazine to replace *Origin*.

In the meantime he kept cursing France and life in general. Worst of all, there was hardly any new poetry or prose. "I am so goddamn disturbed somewhere, nothing at all happens, or nothing I can get hold of," he told Olson.

A visit from the Berlins brought some relief. With Ann a post-puerperal invalid, Buddy's wife, Wuzza, took over the cooking while the men conversed. But the heat wouldn't let up and, to make things even more unbearable, the local canal broke, so their water for the garden and the reservoir was cut off. The only solution would be to escape from it all. Buddy filled Bob's mind with alluring images of bullfights and matadors out-bravadoing Belmonte and Manoletti, and, naturally, Bob wanted to see it all. Buddy also taught him about flamenco. Or there was the prospect of acquiring a new wardrobe at considerably less expense than in France.

So off he went with Buddy and Wuzza less than four weeks after Charlotte's birth, not without feelings of guilt for being so callous towards Ann. They went first to Bilbao and then Madrid, the days away turning out to be some of the most enjoyable since Bob had come to Europe. He once again experienced how great conversation can be. Spain, too, proved a pure delight. It was a crazy, crazy place. The ladies had tremendous bosoms, the men wore pants, not shorts. And the *corridas*! For five days Bob sat spellbound, at one point literally breaking into tears.

Once returned home, the old gloom settled around him with a vengeance: The pleasures of fatherhood were utterly beyond him at this point, he complained. Charlotte was yelling every other minute. And when she wasn't, Dave and Tom figured it was time for their kicks.

He considered longingly a possible further visit with Buddy and Wuzza in Madrid, perhaps in time for the next big corrida featuring Posada and Ordoñez, scheduled for 25 September; maybe they might move to Spain altogether. Reassured by such hopes, he enjoyed a short-lived reprieve from nearly six months of creative sterility. There were only two poems, "The Question" and "The Kind of Act Of," but the latter represented a long-awaited breakthrough as well as the greatest so far. "The 'tongue' of that poem," Creeley remembered as late as 1967, "is still the one I am given to speak with. More I *like* this poem – in that it has continued to speak both for and to me, for all that time." As usual, minimal creativity sparked extensive theorizing and exegesis. In contrast to the typical British dum-de-dum poem, "The Kind of Act Of," he explained, showed how rhythms arose directly from the sense to hand, and how such sense should emerge from a quick, hard juxtaposition of data. Thus verse could provide multiple instances of any one emotion while at the same time reacting to multiple stimuli.

A couple of weeks later he found an opportunity to discuss such matters in detail when Martin Seymour-Smith came to visit during his honeymoon with his wife, Janet de Glanville. Seymour-Smith, self-styled "shameless young Englishman," remembers their first meeting in Marseilles where Bob had gone to welcome the visitors. Seeing Bob wipe his left socket, he asked: What's the matter with your eye? Then, upon closer inspection: How did you lose it? I'm sorry, I should have worn a patch, Bob replied defensively. Seymour-Smith's tight-lipped manner of speaking made him appear devious, almost sinister. Even more ominous, his wife simply kept glaring at Bob. It was like a meeting of undercover agents checking out on each others' code words.

But a few glasses of beer imbibed at a local café brought the necessary relaxation. As it turned out, Martin's conspiratorial, frozen mien was due not to his Machiavellian temper but to an abscessed wisdom tooth which one of Majorca's *practicantes* had broken in labouring to extract it. And how defensively solicitous Martin was in trying to placate his stone-faced spouse. There suddenly was a totally different man, tired, worn, and smiling, with his "shuffling gesture, the sidewise manner, the edged, confidential voice." After several hours of drinking beer even Janet relaxed, until Bob, suddenly mindful of Ann, suggested they should head off towards Lambesc.

Here Martin revealed more of his multi-faceted personality, behaving like the impeccable guest, keeping Ann company in the crowded kitchen back of their dining room, or the storybook Englishman, entertaining Bob with his witty aperçus and anecdotes as both men took refuge from the women and children in Bob's cramped study upstairs.

Before long, Bob decided to leave Lambesc and join Martin in Majorca. Here finally was the man who might offer him what he had vainly tried to realize through his troubled friendship with Rainer Gerhardt: fascinating conversation; a joint publishing venture; the prospect of meeting Robert Graves; and the male companionship between men rooted in their respective families.

Bob could hardly wait, and in his impatience seemed ready to eliminate whoever obstructed his chosen path. He "all but strangled a clerk in a travel office ... who had refused to have a friend's baggage taken to Marseilles after his promise to." He later fictionalized the incident in *The Island*:

Their whole afternoon was a tension of getting the bags to the office by the time the clerk had told them, but once there he tried to put them off, saying they had made a mistake. [Bob's] awkward French could not keep up to their talking, but he saw his friend begin to wilt under the man's sneering refusal. He stood waiting, helpless. Then he had his hands on the man's neck, squeezing, saying, *à Marseilles!* until a policeman pulled him off with the comment that he should contain himself.

According to eyewitness Len Corman, the man who pulled Bob off the travel agent was not a French policeman but Len himself. Len had searched out Bob via a bar whose owner, after making out Len's description of Creeley, responded with undisguised disgust. Once arrived at the house, Len was told that Bob had gone to Aix, so he decided to go there himself. A young French painter Len figured was gay offered to come along. Once in Aix, the two stopped at a sidewalk café in the city's centre to see if Bob might turn up. And sure enough, there he was, chugging along in his old, boxy Peugeot, looking neither right nor left, the beret, the cape, and the patch on the eye, all of them black like the car, except for the knuckles of his hands clutching the steering wheel, which were white. Len caught up with him at the travel bureau just in the nick of time: Bob was clutching the agent's throat. His victim, a little shopkeeper-type Frenchmen who had been forced down on his knees, was vainly tearing away at the strangler's wrists. Bob, looking like the devil incarnate, was screaming: "*Vous! Vous! Vous!*"

14

Majorca, 1952–53.

We find Palma life no hardship. The ordinary townfolks go to bed early, as we do; and never use knives, or coshes, or revolvers. A few noble families remain locked away in their decaying mansions ... No social distinction is acknowledged in Majorca between the rest of the native population: peasants, professional classes, and merchants. Everyone is a gentleman or gentlewoman; because all consider themselves bound by the same high standards of politeness and rectitude implied in the adjective "formal" – which invariably carries a good sense. Informal though I am by nature, I try to pass as a *caballero muy formal*: doing nothing in public to shock my neighbours' susceptibilities.

To the author of these lines, the Majorca before the tourist invasion had a bit of Gonzalo's utopian commonwealth in *The Tempest*. A world-famous novelist, poet, and mythographer, Robert Graves was fifty-seven by the time Robert Creeley, age twenty-six, invaded his peaceful island.

Graves, in his shrewdly observant manner, later told the young American about how he had first met Ezra Pound. It had been T.E. Lawrence who had introduced them, saying: Robert, this is Ezra, Ezra, this is Robert. You will not like one another. Which they didn't. Martin Seymour-Smith might have introduced Creeley to Graves in similar terms. Creeley, while suspicious of Graves's innocent sentimentality, made no secret of his own murderous impulses towards the older man, who reminded him of surrogate father Slater Brown. Feeling very damn young and American, he wanted to kill somebody and felt it should be Graves, he reported to Ann who had stayed behind in France with Dave, Thomas, and Charlotte. Graves was quick to sense the young poet's hostility. That's a very angry man, isn't he? he remarked to Martin. What's wrong with his marriage?

In principle Bob found Graves a decent, kind, and generous person. But his initial antagonism lingered on, causing him to find fault with the older man at every turn. While pretending to like Hart Crane, Graves didn't really understand him; while acknowledging Williams's honesty, he found his rhythms too urbane. Moreover, Graves's treatment of history and myth reminded him of the basement of the Peabody Museum, Creeley remarked to Olson.

The Canadian poet Irving Layton, who found Graves's poetry "virile, intelligent, individual," enquired whether Creeley knew him. The request unleashed all of Creeley's pent-up aggression. Indeed, he did. But Layton was much too kind – Graves was "really one hell of a bore, albeit kind enough," blown up by egomania like most great men. Granted, Graves's poetry, because of its use of assonance and half-rhyme, might be of greater interest to Layton than to himself. But apart from its occasionally felicitous rhythms, it "was very damn dull, and slight finally." Especially obnoxious was its "pretension in the address" and occasional "cute flippancy." And it was getting worse by the minute.

In revising the dedication poem to *The White Goddess*, Graves had simply killed it by turning everything that was particular in the earlier version into pompous generalizations. His most recent poems in *Poetry* and the *Hudson Review* were horrible, and so was his new collection, *Poems* (1953). Bob had seen the proofs: "not one literal *poem* in the whole damn thing." Worst was a series of love poems addressed to a young girl, Graves trying to be likewise young but sounding "so pompous you'll lose your supper."

Creeley conceded that perhaps he was banging Graves by virtue of his own ambitions, but resumed his barrage in subsequent letters to Layton. "I saw Graves a few days ago," he reported on 31 July 1953, "and he shook my hand four times, held me painfully by one shoulder for abt 3 minutes, and didn't, I think, see me. Very friendly man in any case. Just back from England, sold a book, radio talks, the works. Our time will come ..." Graves's somewhat lukewarm response after reading *Le Fou* further sharpened Bob's antagonism. Graves granted Bob honest work in evolving his own rhythms. He noted that "Still Life Or" was saying "all there was to say about mobiles." Who else but an old and foolish man would make such pronouncements?

Physically, he is a long man, not too heavy. A long heavy face, blue eyes with greyish curly hair, i.e. almost curls like D/ Thomas. His mouth is full, somewhat babyish, big though, and apt to look undetermined. His nose strong, heavy again. In profile he is apt to look somewhat cruel, or priggish. Most of the fineness, or most mobile & intelligent part, occurs around his eyes & forehead. The rest is sensual. He walks with a sort of antagonistic thrusting movement, never too easily, i.e., he always strides. He is impatient out of nervousness, and his voice has a desperate edge to it, and again nervous. He speaks in rushes. He can, at times, be utterly kind, and he is always, I think, well-intentioned. But he is a very damn blind & closed man. Hence one must not trust him.

Besides enmity towards Graves, the description reveals Bob's unprecedented self-assurance. Moving to Majorca had been the right decision. After his preliminary foray to the island in the company of the Hellmans, the Seymour-Smiths, and "horrible, horrible" Len Corman, Bob had moved his family there and found a temporary abode in a Deyá pension. Meanwhile he and Martin had gone scurrying around Majorca in Bob's old Peugeot, looking for a house, but more often than not just enjoying the scenery or stopping off to drink beer in roadside cafés.

Eventually they found a place in Bañalbufar, a small town some twenty-five kilometers north east of Palma. It counted some 1,500 inhabitants, their houses perched on the side of a mountain slope, about a quarter mile above the sea, and terraced down all the way towards the cliffs. At their bottom where the sea came in to form a cove, the locals sheltered their boats in caves among the rocks. Apart from fishing, the main trade was growing tomatoes. Tomatoes were everywhere, even in the attic of the Creeleys' three-storey set-up above a barber's shop, from where a gruff old woman came up to inspect them at regular intervals. That loft, huge, with eight windows, four each front and back, one side overlooking the Mediterranean, would serve visitors like René Laubiès as living and/or working quarters. On the floor below were the Creeleys' bedrooms, three in all, plus another room, facing an outside stucco wall, that became Bob's study. The first floor divided up into two large rooms, one a kitchen also used as a dining room, and a smaller room for the children.

Altogether, a very lovely place. And the prices! two pesetas or a nickel for a shot of cognac; twenty-five pesetas, about fifty-six cents, to have the car fixed, which took the mechanic close to a full day. In France, the same job would have cost $6 to $8, in the u.s. more like $10. Madeleina, a strong, staunch lady whom they hired to help Ann with the household, worked for two pesetas an hour. Any job involving labour, Bob reported to Cid, was dirt cheap, pathetically so.

Nonetheless, Majorcans were cheerful as well as nice and ingenuous. For the time being, even their treatment of foreign visitors as objects of an amused and unabashed curiosity was intriguing rather than annoying. For a week or so, the locals followed the Creeleys like a small parade. They stared straight into their faces, showing no concern about the Creeleys looking back at them.

As usual when moving into a new place, Creeley found everything interesting: the olive trees' twisted shapes, the pigs running off the road in front of his car, the horse in a downstairs stable which performed mysterious duties in its owner's nocturnal smuggling ventures.

Mesmerized by the Mediterranean, he soon felt tempted to try its perilous waters in a boat he acquired early in 1953. To the watching townsfolk, who gathered in unexpected numbers on the neck of a rock overlooking the beach, the excursion seemed a daring success. But Bob, who at one point got hit in the neck by the boom and nearly strangled in the lines, knew better. He felt the whole boat lift and they started moving hell-bent for leather out into the sea. It was at about this moment he woke up to the fact that the rope from the boom was looped round his neck, he reported to Olson. But none of this was the fault of the boat, which, on the contrary, had a feel of rock under him, Bob decided. He loved her utterly, but would either have to learn better Spanish, or sailing, before he could get what she had to give. He did neither, and about a week later set out on his second trip, this time with five-year-old son, Dave. It turned out worse than the first. A fine wind that took them to the open sea suddenly dropped almost completely, what was left of it turning direction and blowing against them, as Bob and Dave desperately paddled the damn tub back into the harbour.

Not even repeatedly having to row the boat back amidst the increasing hilarity of the townspeople diminished his obsessive fascination with the new sport. By May it had become an almost daily two-hour activity, usually alone and during the afternoon when Ann and the kids were sleeping. And once in a while, his boat would afford him the excitement that he craved of shooting along like a bat out of hell.

Other matters contributed to his happiness. By October 1952, Golden Goose Press had brought out *Le Fou*, his first book of poems. To its author it looked like a lovely damn thing. It had been well worth the wait. Emerson had done him proud. The Roebuck Press, Bañalbufar, Majorca, Spain (so the specially printed letterhead) was ready to bring out Paul Blackburn's *Proensa*, and, with the help of a Palma press run by a certain Mossen, was soon ready to tackle numerous further books.

Creeley also planned to turn *Origin* #8 into a Charles Olson "Selected Poems." The only obstacle might be the journal's editor, Cid Corman. Somehow or other, Cid would have to be convinced that Roebuck Press should print the issue, that Creeley and his collaborator Martin Seymour-Smith would see it through the press, and that René Laubiès could do the cover.

When Corman, utter prick that he was, showed some resistance, Creeley felt like crushing him. Unable, for reasons of distance, to perform this feat himself, he advised Olson to call him around ten in the morning when he would either still be sleeping or too groggy to respond with any intelligence or cageyness. Meanwhile he would find ways to "fuck" Cid regarding copyright matters and the physical layout of the issue. As so often before, his contempt for idiot boy Corman's horribly condescending manner, questing enthusiasms, and insidious muddling was running amok.

This time it even produced a poem which Creeley sent to Olson. Addressed to Sidney Corman, it speaks of his loathing for Cid's officious face, of his hatred for his yellow guts and tailed ass, and concludes in the hope that their future relationship, or rather the lack thereof, should be one of sheer and luxurious hate.

Such hatred which Creeley repeatedly felt for Corman never, of course, went long without giving way to its proverbial counterpart of love, or at least guilt and repentance, a volte-face which on this occasion was caused by a "miserable" coincidence. By this time, he had long expanded the audience for his Corman-bashing beyond Olson, and even to those who were close to his victim. One such was Paul Blackburn who in early 1953 received a le tter from Creeley, opened it in Corman's presence, read it out loud, and, before long, stumbled upon one of Bob's more violent diatribes against Corman's poetry.

Creeley hastened to apologize, asking Cid to send him a big batch of his poems so he could do a decent job of comment. Yet how could Cid ever forgive him? For once, Creeley had to admit to being (and always having been) damn two-faced *vis-à-vis* Corman. He doubted he could ever make up for it, except with his dead body, he wrote to Olson. Someday he'd learn, at least he hoped so. But learn he didn't. Within a few days he was sending Corman a stiff list of conditions to be sent back to him signed by return mail regarding the printing of *Origin* #8. Within less than a month he again denounced Corman's poetry as little else than a pastiche of stealing and imitation. Clearly, his apologetic moods were more short-lived than ever.

Meanwhile, he also fell out with Seymour-Smith over plans for the Roebuck Press. The immediate occasion for the split was provided by Seymour-Smith's contracting to print Derek Stanford and, worse, former Harvard acquaintance Donald Hall in the poetry series. Bob was outraged. For one, Hall's poetry was utter crap. More importantly, his recent article on "American Poets Since the War" had poured scorn on William Carlos Williams as well as on the few benighted souls who called themselves his followers: "Only a small group of poets, Charles Olson and Robert Creeley among them, continue to fight Williams' battles – battles fought and won twenty years ago," Hall had written. "It seems to me, in direct contradiction to William Carlos Williams, that the American

language is characteristically highly ornamental – and not at all hard and
bare as the imagists wanted it to be; it is often irrelevantly extravagant in
its use of rhyme; in its punning and playing with words, one is reminded
of the Elizabethan manner."

And this was the man Seymour-Smith proposed to print in their series!
Obviously, their association would do more harm than good, Creeley decided. Hence he would print the American work on his own under the
new name of Divers Press. Otherwise, all his plans, as he informed Corman, remained the same.

Suddenly, the tone of resolute, sometimes megalomaniac, self-
confidence is everywhere. Ann was attacking him because he thought he
was God, and insisted on being that sure, he wrote to Olson on
30 January 1953. The time for utter coolness was at hand, he pontificated
two months later. Somewhat superfluously, he announced that he was not
a humanist. And that Virgil was shit. He didn't think Rabelais was funny.
He couldn't make Donne. Henry James was a horrible old bore. He hated
Beethoven and had started to hate Mozart. Shakespeare? Too slow on the
page. He couldn't get into his content sufficiently to move to a proper
study. Altogether, he had decided he would no longer read what didn't
damn well involve him.

What was left? Bach, "the Bird," and Williams ought to be enough for
any poet – Charlie Parker being granted the privilege of having exerted a
greater influence on him than any other man, living or dead. Whatever
else he stumbled upon that did not match his convictions was dismissed
in similarly summary fashion. He felt sickened by the fortieth anniversary
issue of *Poetry* with its unprecedented concentration of deceit and corruption. He hated those people in *Poetry*, he wanted to kill them, tear them
up, shit on them so they'd never wipe it off. Ian Fletcher's prosodic
moanings and F.T. Prince's love poems written in Donne-like conceits reflected the deplorable state of letters on the other side of the Atlantic.

From such spiritual wastelands, there was the reassuring retreat into
what a friend, watching Creeley read Olson's letters like an early Christian receiving personal letters from Jesus, called the "Church of Projective Verse." From its superior vantage point, one could suitably limit the
field of argument and keep the assertion of one's own needs clearly to the
front. That saved time and effort wasted in trying to argue each point
with everyone. It also made it easier to decide who would be counted in
and who out. Once again, Duncan, being a prime prick, was to be
counted out. On the other hand, there was Katue Kitasono who had recently written a very great poem; oddly enough, Irving Layton, who
could make it; or, by now less so, Paul Blackburn, who didn't very often,

but maybe would soon. Yet ultimately there were only two poets who were really making it, and they are "you & me," he assured Olson.

Such self-congratulatory bliss was subject to moments of doubt. It was easier to bury an attack like Donald Hall's under one's contempt than come to terms with criticism of one's work that, however analytically astute, was not unequivocally positive. Such an ordeal was Creeley's in reading Steven Marcus's brief piece on his short stories in the December issue of *Commentary*. Creeley, it said, "has removed the 'aesthetic distance,' the effort to control experience": "for it he substitutes his own person – immediate and easy to identify. What he is saying is that experience is so difficult to grasp that the traditional attempt must be given up." Pleased at first, Creeley found that the piece began to "corrode" on him upon subsequent readings. Critical snipes like "[i]narticulateness, however striking," convinced him that Marcus simply didn't like the stories.

Even more distressing were Creeley's dealings with Grove which, as he'd thought, was a courageous press with an interesting list of reprints and new materials. Donald Allen, one of the press's editors, had searched out his stories and asked him to send in a partial manuscript of them. But after a six week waiting period came the let-down. While expressing admiration for Creeley's writing, Grove turned down the stories.

Even their new abode, so very, very lovely at first, started to wear on Bob. Come late autumn, the chill and damp from the stone walls crept into one's bones. The *braseros* were apt to roast one's feet rather than warm one's body. By mid-December he was imbibing cough medicine and receiving penicillin injections administered to his buttocks by Ann; the doctor was treating as a mere flu what Bob thought was a renewed outbreak of the malaria he had first caught in India. With most of the family sharing various colds, Bob's constant low fever plus usual sinus trouble lingered on until mid-February 1953 when he spent a week in bed. He was becoming a hell of a hypochondriac, he confessed to Olson, and wasn't being paid appropriate attention. If he were there, he'd be wheeled into the grand hall, to suffer in public. He had always dreamed of giving death-bed injunctions.

Instead there was the depressingly sombre house with its uncongenial co-inhabitants – "the darkness of the place, the bareness of the heavy walls, the criss-cross meaningless mosaic which covered the third floor, and the noise, constant, from the barber and his family. And the angry, ugly old woman who stamped through on her way to inspect the tomatoes above." Once out of bed again, there was his desk facing an absolutely rigid stucco wall. He got a glimpse of the sea by way of tiles and a horridly quaint chimney, perhaps to sober him, he speculated.

Although *Le Fou* had been a pleasant surprise in terms of the printing and general layout, it apparently had been a failure, with a total of three people bothering to send him their rather vague comments. It was small comfort to imagine Odysseus passing through this island in the midst of his toils and troubles. Whatever it had been to the Homeric hero, Bañal-bufar, to Creeley, felt like the end of the world. The place was a hellish vacuum.

The worst was still to come. Around the beginning of May, Ann and Bob had gone to Palma to have dinner at a restaurant, when Ann was overcome by sudden pain. Bob found her a few minutes later in the wash-room, crying silently, trying to answer his questions, but instead doubling up with pain. "He felt her forehead quickly, there was no fever, and then her pulse, which was quick." On the way to the doctor, Ann's pain wors-ened. Arriving at the clinic, they found the doctor was out. Another rush through the night and "the muddling cars with bright headlights," Bob trying to comfort Ann, "but the pain heard nothing." At last he saw the red cross bright above the door of the other clinic. By now he was carry-ing Ann in his arms. A doctor, small, muttering, said it was nothing seri-ous. She should take twenty drops of something in a glass of water daily. Bob "grabbed the man by the throat." Then back to the car, Ann cradled in his arms. By now she was limp. Would she die on him before they could find help? But help where? In desperation, he drove back to the first clinic. Once again he was carrying Ann, stumbling under her weight, terrified, screaming for help. Down the hall came a nurse, then other people. They took Ann away from him. Later a doctor told him "how very close it had been. A cyst had broken, as big as a fist, and flooded the intestinal cavity with pus. It was lucky it had not been worse."

Even preliminary measures to control the infection with penicillin took about a week. Thereafter, Ann was allowed to go back home to Bañalbu-far, to recover towards an operation some seven weeks later. Before the cyst could be removed it had to encapsulate, the doctor explained. "You are not the first, he said, and smiled at them. You have already three fine children. And you, he said to [Ann], have been living only with half your life. This thing (he made a fist) has been eating you up inside. You'll see. Once I get that out of you, you'll feel like dancing all the time."

Creeley's fictionalization of the incident in *The Island* changes the time frame and adds dramatic elements for which he may or may not have drawn on personal memories. While foreshortening the waiting period until the operation to a mere week, the novel provides vivid accounts of Bob giving Ann antibiotic injections, and of Ann's anguish before returning to the clinic. Unlike his contemporary reports to friends, it also describes Ann's illness as the turning point in their marriage. Ann's suffering, her bodily injuries, and mortal fear opened an unbridgable rift between them. The mirror of their relationship had broken. "Each thing he now did, right or wrong, could not be placed in that reflection any longer. She had fallen out and broken too."

Six months more and Ann would have been dead, the surgeon explained. "You are both very lucky." But Bob wasn't. According to the novel, he was flooded with physical revulsion. When he applied the needle to Ann's upper buttock, the "flesh looked blotched to him. There were small pimples, scratches." It got worse after the operation. Looking at Ann's unconscious body, he felt mere nausea and estrangement:

She was white, or more accurately, a greyish white. Her hair had streaked into lines on her forehead, apparently with sweat. Her mouth was open and she made snuffling, gutteral sounds, breathing. He took her hand but it felt heavy, indifferent. Around her middle there was a large bunch, made by the bandages. All the flesh seemed to be listless, heavy. The sound of her heavy breathing made him feel uneasy, and he stepped back.

Who are you, then.

"The Operation," a poem written at the time, speaks in even more callous terms.

By Saturday I said you would be better on Sunday.
The insistence was a part of a reconciliation.

Your eyes bulged, the grey
light hung on you, you were hideous.

My involvement is just an old
habitual relationship.

Cruel, cruel to describe
what there is no reason to describe.

The wish for the woman's death, which John (alias Bob) ends up feeling for Joan (alias Ann) in *The Island*, was a small step from such ruthless disgust. But for the time being, Bob's cruel fantasies vented themselves on an unsuspecting visitor from Britain. Robert Cooper, editor of *Artisan*, a journal Creeley hoped would play a significant role in his network of world-wide literary contacts, arrived in Majorca towards the end of May 1953. As described in Bob's letters to friends, the visit quickly turned into a visitation for all of his past sins.

Twenty-one, fattish, tall, pasty-looking, very white, and English, Cooper instantly announced he hated all things American. He insulted the Creeley family collectively, then one by one. As Bob was taking Ann to the doctor, Robert almost shoved her through the side of the car. What particularly got on Bob's nerves was Robert's constantly emitting self-satisfied little snuffling grunts of approval and disapproval of everything and everybody.

There is a major difference between Bob's epistolary accounts of Cooper's visit and its later fictionalization in *The Island*. What the letters tell with typically and-fuck-that-too sense of humour, the novel recounts in a vein of at times anguished seriousness. Creeley's "revenge" on his increasingly hated visitor provides an example. In a letter to Blackburn it takes the form of causing Cooper to move from a Bañalbufar pension to another in Palma which was not only cheaper but the dirtiest in town. Other letters suggest Creeley's hatred of the man in quips like: Let's hope I can get him out alive! or: I'd see him dead first! But they omit the murderous prank he plays on Cooper in the novel.

"Some revenge seeming reasonable," Cooper (alias Willis) is taken to a remote part of the Mediterranean and almost left to drown in the waves breaking against the rocks. "From within their own ease they watched him, and said without thinking, or speaking, let him go. Watch, but let him go. For minutes they saw the large head go under, reappear, go under, reappear. René's [i.e. Laubiès's] eyes were watching sharply, with a bright, open calm. He looked at nothing but the struggling man some twenty feet away from him, as he treaded water, rising, falling, easily with the waves. He is smiling, John thought."

One witness testifies to a possibly unauthentic event recounted in neither Creeley's letters of the time nor in *The Island*: Creeley, suddenly realizing Cooper's terror and jumping in to rescue the man whom he hated with such passion.

15

The Island.

As usual when depressed, Creeley started another novel. This time it was to deal with his present rather than past life: A husband, his wife and kids have settled on an island of vaguely asiatic character. While the parents are consumed by internecine warfare, the children are set adrift in the village. The husband wants to commit suicide but cannot, his wife helplessly standing by trying to preserve her sanity. He convinces himself that his wife is against him, which she is not, consults with another couple who give advice, but ends up disliking them. He wills his wife to die. One night, after an intense argument, his wish seems to come true. She announces that she is going down to get a drink of water. The husband reads on for about an hour, then around two in the morning he goes out to look for her in the pitch dark. His search is unsuccessful. The morning finds him standing on top of a steep rock cliff. He still cannot see her. But fishermen out in the sea have "legitimately" spotted her body, one of them looking over (towards him?). For fear of being seen and suspected of having murdered his wife, he backs off, dropping onto his knees in the bush, but all the while watches out through the low scrub pine branches. Then he walks back to the house (convinced that his wife is dead, i.e., that his wish has come true). He will be punished.

Here then, outlined to Olson on 21 July 1953, is the core of *The Island* which Creeley started writing over seven years later during September and October 1960 in Guatemala and which he finished during the 1962–63 Christmas break in Canada. Naturally, there are differences. Husband John (alias Robert Creeley) in *The Island* never seriously contemplates suicide, nor does his wife, Joan (alias Ann MacKinnon), truly die. But the portrayal of their broken marriage and, above all, of the husband who convinces himself that his lethal feelings towards his spouse have come true, are common to both.

For the moment nothing came of it, and by 23 August the original idea was replaced by another. The day before, a novelist and war reporter named Godfrey Blunden, along with his French wife and their three kids as well as Blunden's widowed sister-in-law and her son, had arrived in Bañalbufar to look for a house. They had been sent there by Robert Graves. Finally there'd be a small writers' colony. Perhaps this finally would give him his novel, he wrote to Olson, praying that Stendhal might be with him.

Noting Blunden's straightforward though perhaps weak nature, his handsome wife's gothically overbearing remoteness, the sister-in-law's eccentrically imposing manner, and her son's goat-like Oedipal attachment to her, Creeley began fantasizing about the strange liaisons among them as well as their possible reactions to his family. Here his autobiographical bias once again focused on his own family as seen through the disapproving eyes of the French wife: on his poor, abandoned children, little Charlotte covered in dirt, sitting on the ground up the street, playing with an eighteen-year-old boy suspected of being a homosexual, etc. Maybe he could sell it to the movies yet!

Once again, no novel came of it, Creeley deciding instead to record his relationship with the newcomers in a short story, "A Death." In any case, the expected friendship between the two men proved an embarrassing *non sequitur*. Blunden found himself unable to read Douglas Woolf's novel *The Hypocratic Days* which Creeley planned to publish; Creeley thought Blunden's *A Room on the Route* a "goddamn horror," feeling "quite literally" embarrassed for him.

Not surprisingly, "A Death" is a bitter, Ivy Compton-Burnett-like satire. It depicts Blunden as a kind but fumblingly evasive and browbeaten husband, and his thick-legged wife as a constantly smiling virago who either ignores or provokes her husband. She is out to inflict the lethal wound on his sister (alias his real life sister-in-law), portrayed as a semierotically overprotective mother. Her six-year-old, misshapen son is "an obscenely precocious goat," who gigglingly holds onto her skirts or explodes in sudden acts of violence like pelting a stone at Blunden's daughter and inflicting a wound which the easily forgiving father hastens to bandage.

Creeley looked forward to the point when Blunden, who left Bañalbufar after about three months, would one day discover the story and find out what Creeley "was thinking." If not entirely out of the urge to "get even" with the Blundens, "A Death" was certainly written by way of "using them," Creeley admitted. What had inspired the story, he explained to Olson, was his one-eyed, dispassionate "knowledge of people,"

– hence his writing at such a level of coldness that he couldn't possibly be "misread."

At least two other stories of the early Majorca period were prompted by a similarly unsympathetic attitude. In one, significantly entitled "A Betrayal," Creeley squared off with Martin Seymour-Smith; in the other, "The Boat," he vented his hatred of women's, and his wife's, self-deceptive reliance on allegedly intuitive insights.

Mrs Peter, a mother of three children who semi-intentionally contrive to run their father over with a boat, ponders running off with another man. In spite of what has happened to her husband, William, she continues her adulterous "business in hand," having "no doubt that it was, despite the difficulties, an act that could be transacted as elaborately and as completely as the buying of potatoes." Inducing the other man to make love to her while William lies in pain, she finds she hates her lover as much as her husband: "Then she said, love me, very simply. And, as she asked it, he brushed off his pants, and came to her, and then led her back to the field, where they lay down. I want you to be for me, she said, but she hated him. As his hands touched her, she felt cold finally, and thanked him for that."

Similar elements went into the making of *The Island*. There is the often hateful portrayal of Joan, whom the protagonist John suspects of at least two potentially adulterous relationships, one with René Lely (alias René Laubiès), the other with Artie (alias Martin Seymour-Smith); there is John's hatred of Joan's "sureness," which was "particularly vicious, because it was always necessarily so *right*;" and finally there is the squaring off with Artie, that "fumbling, disjointed poor fellow" with his "thin hopes" and "bare affronteries," who, once he gets into the business of printing magazines "for a number of hopeful people," contrives the credit "by a kind of domino stagger of leaning obligations," but accomplishes little else but to create "a shoddy mess," "leaving horror on the one hand, and bills on the other."

Other characters complete the novel's *déjà vu* autobiographical scenario borrowed from the earlier stories: the good-natured, slightly pompous "writer" (alias Godfrey Blunden) who, after covering the siege of Stalingrad and living a hectic life in New York, has come to Majorca with a grant to find "a little peace and quiet" to "do" his book; his good-looking French wife who clearly "knew men and particularly her husband;" the writer's sister, "thin, wiry, a grotesquely cheerful woman," and her goblin son whom she kept "dragging back of her like an animal, a goat."

Yet in 1953–54 a larger effort like *The Island* remained beyond Creeley's scope, however hard he tried. "I can't write a novel," he complained to Irving Layton. "I'll stick to short stories for the time-being, i.e. they're short." Nonetheless, he was at it again a few days later, hoping that his past years of marital unhappiness would at last pay off and be exorcised in the process. In order to be able to remain sane and as happy as possible, he would deal with other people's unhappiness rather than with his own. Yet again, every effort of trying to talk the novel into existence or of claiming that its protagonist would become distinct from the author – to the point where Creeley imagined his hero walking into the room to see what he was writing about him – proved fruitless. Only a month later he once more announced that he had started another novel. This time he got to page four or so before the endeavour was swept aside by the hectic effort to put together the first and second issues of *Black Mountain Review* just prior to his departure for the college by mid-March 1954.

Nonetheless, the content as well as the narrative impulse evident by the later half of 1953 stayed with him until he finally wrote *The Island* between 1960 and 1963. By that time he had changed the chronological sequence of events, even altered or reinvented them in minor ways; but otherwise, most major occurrences experienced or remembered by the protagonist of *The Island* relate to what happened to Creeley during his Majorca period and in France or America before that. A contemporary photograph bears witness to one of these events. It shows Creeley high up on a roof terrace, sitting on a bench, on his right knee a child wearing a huge papier-mâché head. Bob and Ann had made the mask so Dave could wear it during a local Fiesta del Cine held in late February 1954. With Dave staggering around inside his mask, they brought down the house, Bob reported to Corman.

A less cheerful account of the same event is given in *The Island*. John feels bitter because Philip (alias Dave) has been denied first prize, which he thinks is tantamount to "the town's rejection" of the entire family. Joan makes light of the matter, to spite her husband:

So even she chose to twist it, and wanted to settle for the small portion, and would take the outrage he felt and make it another charge against him. Wrong again.

The next day they all went up to the terrace, put the head and coat on Philip, took pictures of him, and then put it all away. It was a relief to be done with it.

Like most characters in *The Island*, John is no hero. A "writer on perpetual vacation on his wife's money," he suffers under "the grossness of his own incapabilities, the treachery of his self-assurance." He "shudders with a sense of his own uselessness," again and again feels "a weary loss of all his confidence" and is plagued by guilt for having made his wife fall ill from the numerous pregnancies he caused her. He "secretes resentment like puss," vents his frustrations over his wife's growing estrangement from him onto his children, or he indulges in cruel fantasies watching the wound which surgery has left on Joan's belly: it "looked like a long puckered mouth, with jagged tight teeth made by the black thread of the stitches. He wanted to tear it off, leaving the skin again white and free. He thought that if she pushed, or strained, it would talk, obscenely, that it would spill out on them all the hate and pain he had, obscenely, forced into it." Again and again, he feels "dirty, vicious, tired." In finally convincing himself that his quarrels with Joan have driven her to kill herself, he can think of little else than his own miseries: "She was dead. He hated her. She left him with all of it, she had left him to explain his failure, her death, to their children, to the town, to her vicious guardian who would attack him, and would take the children away from him, and he couldn't now have them anyhow. She had taken everything."

Obviously, the subsequent breakdown of Creeley's marriage exacerbated his memory of this battle of hatred, making him caricature the two combatants with even greater brutality. Ann becomes "an old hag," hair growing around the nipples of each breast butting from the tight barrel of her chest, himself "the night monster, who is let out only with the dark to wander, howling, through the empty halls." How much of all this is fiction and how much fact?

Creeley has pointed out that whatever people might call his fiction was really a kind of faction or mere "prose." He disliked the sense of "something made-up," or any "intentional distortion of the 'truth'." This distrust, he explained in his "Autobiography," was largely due to his mother's insisting that he always tell the truth, while at the same time telling him two crucial lies – "the one covering my father's death and the other the necessary removal of my eye, left truth a peculiar authority."

Creeley's alleged distrust of fiction makes one wonder about how he portrayed himself and others, including Ann, in *The Island*. As we have seen, both John and Joan are frequently shown in a negative light. However, the disgust we are made to feel for Joan is often physical, while regarding John it remains mainly psychological and/or moral. Altogether, we learn little about John's physical appearance. By contrast, we are told a lot about Joan's, especially during her illness. She is disfigured by surgery, has blotchy flesh, and behaves in a sluggish, heavy manner. Meanwhile, John's negative sides tend to enhance the general image of the bungling but ultimately honest, unpretentious ingenue. "Grubby and out of place" amongst "the brisk, tanned men," owners of yachts, and "their lovely tanned ladies," he solicits our sympathy much like Holden

Caulfield in Salinger's *Catcher in the Rye*. This is also true of his self-dep-recatory sense of not being "a very real writer" like the condescending Duddon (alias Robert Graves) with his "long, childlike face [and] curl-ing, greying hair" or the busybody journalist (alias Godfrey Blunden) announcing he's "got a book to do."

Marge (alias Janet Seymour-Smith) finds John attractive and likes him. Joan loves his smile and considers her husband a brilliant conversational-ist. Artie pities him for his innocence. Even where his qualities are not unequivocally positive, we are invited to view them charitably. Like the persona Creeley projects in some of his poetry, John is shy, easily dis-turbed, upset, or embarrassed. He tends to fumble things, drinks his beer "with a persistent, awkward care, afraid he might spill everything all over the table;" he feels uneasy, even a little frightened in cities, but moves quietly and reverently in local bars; and he is so charmingly awkward to make even Joan smile. By comparison with his overbearingly self-assured wife, who is somewhat older than he, John is the eternal adolescent still waiting to grow up and become "one of, the men."

To compare John's relationship with Manus (alias Alex Trocchi), as de-picted in the novel, with its counterpart in real life shows in detail how such self-projection works. Unlike charmingly fumbling John or devi-ously inefficient Artie, Manus is a man driven by "a black, clean purpose." There is "the beak-like strength of that nose, then the eyes, blue, sharp in no simple sense, set into the projecting forehead." Manus deals with the bungling Artie in a "short, sure manner," holding him "very nearly by the scruff of the neck." John "liked the man on the instant, he wanted to be liked by him also." As Creeley remembered in 1969, he had "given a brief, personal sense of [his] relation to Trocchi in ... *The Island*, where he figures as 'Manus.'"

Creeley's 1953 assessment of Trocchi, the editor of a magazine, *Mer-lin*, and of a series of books that promised publication in the company of celebrities like Samuel Beckett and Jean Genet, was more realistic, not to say hard-nosed. Physically, Trocchi looked to him like a desiccated or decadent hawk. He was certainly a very shrewd man, perhaps too shrewd. Creeley felt that *Merlin* was shit, and he had severe objections when Collection Merlin proposed to print a book of poems by Christo-pher Logue. However, to get published in a journal that sold 1,700 an issue, or be featured in a series that was the most interesting instance of American publishing in evidence, would obviously have been a break for Creeley. And since Austryn Wainhouse, a man included in that col-lection, had told Trocchi that Creeley was the best prose writer in the u.s., that chance was real indeed. Whatever Creeley's objections, Troc-chi was a man worth courting.

It is the reverse in *The Island*: Manus courts John, who is so preoccupied with his loyalty to poor Artie that when Manus offers to publish his stories, he fails to hear him:

We want books, Manus said, we'd like to do one of yours, of the stories, if you'll agree.

What was that. He didn't quite hear it. He said, but Artie, you must take care with what he says he'll do. He means well enough, but things, for him, are an awful mess.

Manus said, I'm surprised you put up with him.

When Manus repeats his offer, John retreats behind a screen of arguments typical of his awkwardness and modesty. Manus hadn't read the stories; all he'd done was pay him "an impossibly kind complement." "Manus, confused, but persistent, asked again," only to be refused a third time. So he finally had to leave and did so "with a quiet, kind decency, John thought."

Only after talking to hard-headed Joan does John realize that Manus really wanted to publish the stories which, too late, sends him on a melodramatic and futile chase after Manus's motorbike. Back home, John is advised by Joan to send Manus a note explaining his mistake. But "he couldn't write the note. The error was too deep and he had to live as things were, he thought. He sat small in the room looking out at the darkening color of the sun going down."

Pathos played a lesser role in real life. Before meeting him in Bañalbufar, Creeley had convinced himself that Trocchi was a sharpster. Trocchi proposed to print "The Gold Diggers" in *Merlin*, suggesting it would be advance advertising for the collection of stories to be published under the same title. But Creeley mistrusted the offer: Trocchi was making false promises in order to get the story he wanted so as to fill seven miserable pages in his miserable magazine. Trying to turn the suspected ruse to his advantage, he therefore suggested that Trocchi use "The Gold Diggers," but only on condition that he also publish the volume. Otherwise, he offered "The Betrayal" (unpublished to date) as an alternative.

Trocchi's resultant silence proved unbearable. Bob stewed for a week waiting for Trocchi to write to him from Palma, then went there himself. When he found that Trocchi hadn't even bothered to leave word for him care of Seymour-Smith, he went to the printer of *Merlin* and took back his story. What other rights did an author have? To hell with it. Trocchi drove out to Bañalbufar the following day to see what was wrong, making Creeley feel like someone who had acted in "almost hysterical" fashion. He was probably very unfair to Trocchi, he admitted to Olson: he came out the next day on a motorcycle which, on such roads, was a sign of a really good intention. They talked to some extent, but Creeley was unable to overcome his own confusion, and give him the story again, or even let the collection go back to Paris for them to look at. Which admittedly was all very vague. But, anyhow, that was over now.

A letter to Cid Corman written the same day clarifies the confusion. He couldn't tolerate waiting for Trocchi to take the manuscript to Paris. He also wanted "The Gold Diggers" to remain unprinted until its eventual publication in the book. Meanwhile, his last-minute retraction of the story had indeed complicated things for Trocchi. But he assured Bob there were no hard feelings. He didn't want to mention the bloody subject again. Nor did he at all blame Bob. On the contrary, he had gotten very fond of Bob in the short time he had known him.

The relationship between John and Artie (alias Seymour-Smith) in *The Island* provides a similar instance of fictionalized self-projection. In the novel, it is dominated by money, or more specifically, by Artie sponging off John. Money is "a painful bore," the "knot between them." Borrowed "money trickled out ... vaguely" to Artie, who, rather than repay it, tries to placate John with tabulated calculations of his debts, an elaborate instance of which is given in the novel's seventh chapter. Warned by Joan that he is always "the sucker, the one left with the messy bag," John temporarily avoids Artie. However, he falls back on him out of inveterate weakness, only to be once again hit for money as well as to be reprimanded by his wife for allowing the friend "to use" him as always. In the meantime, Artie has considerably enlarged his strategies of embezzlement by printing "magazines for a number of hopeful people," using shoddy materials for the purpose, and "pocket[ing] the change."

In spite of it all, John remains essentially loyal to his friend and wants to help him. Throughout the novel, he generously volunteers his (or rather, Joan's) money whenever Artie comes sponging. Right to the last, "John said, can I help you, do you need money." His only reservation: "John could not allow that his only use to Artie was money" rather than friendship. "He had to have the friend, this friend." Driven by this need, John resigns himself philosophically to being unable either to "place" this "fumbling, disjointed poor fellow" or to sort out the "shifting vagueness of friendship" between them.

After all, he did "love" Artie, to the point of finding it "impossible ever to criticize this impeccable man, so immaculately fumbling all the terms of his life." He even takes a perverse delight in watching Artie embezzle others: "John couldn't blame him, in fact he respected the crazy invention of such will," while others in the novel, like Joan or Manus, to John's dismay, take a less forgiving view of Artie.

The actual relationship between Creeley and Seymour-Smith was far less romantic. Since their falling out over the Roebuck Press, there was little love lost between them. It wasn't that he didn't love Martin, Bob might protest to Olson, but their friendship had become hellishly tenuous. When Martin agreed to print *Origin* #11 for Cid, matters at first still looked "cool" to Bob. Martin, though fed up with Trocchi's *Merlin*, seemed deeply concerned and worried about *Origin*, and at the same time very much in control of things.

However, things changed rapidly from then on. Martin wasted more time and money drinking and fucking around than someone in his position ought to – a behaviour pattern Bob ruefully confessed to have been his own long ago after first getting married. But that was when he had been nineteen. Martin, by contrast, was twenty-five, married with a daughter, which hardly allowed for such self-indulgence. As a result, Martin muddled all possible angles of bringing out *Origin* #11 – the layout, the shipping, even the personal relationships with everyone involved. What's more, an American lady who had asked Martin to do a little book of poems for her had come rushing to Bañalbufar in desperation to ask Bob and Ann for their advice. Apparently, Martin had cashed a traveller's cheque for her, coming back 150 pesetas short and saying that he would give it to her later, but never showing up again.

The story only confirmed what Bob had long known about Martin's character with respect to money. There was the instance (later to be re-told in less incriminating fashion in *The Island*) of when, going to buy a big, expensive radio, Martin had asked Bob to lend him 250 pesetas, saying he didn't want to break his 1,000 peseta note. He promised to return the borrowed money as soon as they got to the apartment. The 250 as well as a good 1,000 pesetas more were still outstanding!

Urging Cid to arrange to pay Martin via himself, Creeley two days later provided further instances of outright deceit on Martin's part. Cid had better let Bob take over the job entirely, while of course keeping Martin in the dark about everything so as not to hurt his pride and get his back up: Martin might cause an awful damn mess otherwise. Creeley further warned Corman that Martin, little prick that he was, wanted to grab his commission before Cid would see the work. Martin was dragging his feet on the typesetting process, going at a rate of four pages a week, with about one-third of *Origin* #11 left to do. Meanwhile, Cid should listen to him whining to Bob and Ann – it was utterly nauseating. If it hadn't been for Ann who, during Bob's illness, had grabbed Martin by the scruff of his neck (in the manner *The Island* would attribute to Trocchi), things might have turned out worse.

An admission, made on 24 January 1954, that he might have been too hard on Martin was withdrawn three days later. Though Martin came through in writing an article on Roethke's poetry and a note on Dylan Thomas, interim relations of a more business-like kind had confirmed Creeley's sense that Martin was the most deceitful, malign, and tale-bearing little prick imaginable. The main reason for such name-calling this time was the horrible way Martin had printed Trocchi's *Merlin* and Ferrini's *Four Winds*, using ink with too much oil in it. Bob's account to Cid reflects both moral indignation and psychological ingenuity. Rather than from his father, a plain, sober, serious, and likeable sort of man, Martin's problems derived from his mother. Acting the fading lily but a bitch at heart, she had trained her son to pay her all the expected compliments, and in the process jammed his head with deceit, contempt for honesty, and similar attitudes. What a hell of a mess she had made of Martin's brain!

As we have seen, John's reaction to Artie's producing a barely readable "wad of oily blur" instead of print, as recounted in *The Island*, is almost admiring: "John watched the whole process with a feeling akin to satisfaction, albeit stunned. He was amazed, and to his own confusion, pleased, that Artie could get away with it."

To continue the story in real life, Creeley rapidly stepped up his charges and accusations. Convinced of his former friend's moral depravity, he easily persuaded himself that Martin had actually stolen one hundred dollars as advanced by Cid towards paying the printers of *Origin* #11. Though allowing for some doubt regarding this theft, Creeley instantly set about to devise strategies of how to recuperate the money, should Martin indeed have stolen it behind their backs. They would get their cash back somehow!

For once the roles were reversed, Cid Corman instead of Olson being the witness to Bob's Machiavellian schemes and to his glee in pursuing them, Martin instead of Corman their target. Bob assured Cid that, at a later point, he would provide him with a full account. In fact, he had already started to write about it in a novel. For the time being, Cid had better just follow Bob's advice of how to get back the stolen money, preferably by secretive means: he and Cid should keep him believing they didn't know anything about the $100.

The main lever Creeley proposed in this scheme was a book of poems, *All Devils Fading*, that Divers Press was then printing for Martin. One could delay that process until *Origin* #11 was done and paid for.

Martin had a fine new English typewriter, which would net them just about the 4,000 pesetas they lacked. If that was not enough, the poor impoverished little shit also had a nice radio. The next step, actually implemented, was to suspend all proofing on Martin's book until *Origin* #11 was done. Though still without *de facto* evidence, Bob kept taking the matter for granted, threatening personal showdowns with the culprit.

Finally, after some delays, *Origin* #11 did appear, Bob having to admit that it didn't look at all hopeless. In fact, he took responsibility for some of its less appealing features such as the paper and the cover that had been stapled rather than sewn on. The rest, however, was Martin's fault – the cuts he had made against Bob's advice while pretending otherwise, the broken letters, the delays. As a result, Martin had totally forfeited the right to any commission, particularly since he had already embezzled the $100. Though granted the job wasn't that bad, etc.

In any case, he'd shortly go into Palma himself and get the story on the $100 Cid had sent Martin. The result, reported in literally parenthentical fashion on 15 January 1954, was as follows: The bill for the printing was 8,750 pesetas, 4,000 of which had already been paid (Cid's $100, "thank God"). That left them with a balance of $118.75. No word of apology or at least clarification for having suspected Martin of theft in such vehement fashion.

On the contrary: that charge dropped, Bob instantly came up with a new one, i.e., Martin's devious proposal to ship packages of the copies via his friends at the post office without properly registering them. Once again, Bob was ready to apply his previously established arsenal of intimidation and blackmail to make the culprit pay up for any losses his devious schemes might cause them – including talking to Graves, though Bob hated to bother him.

No wonder the story of the alleged embezzlement lingered on. Corman himself repeated the allegation in the introduction to *The Gist of Origin*. Martin's handling of *Origin* #11, he writes, "aged me rapidly. After a prompt initial example of a page proof, there was no further word, despite letter after letter seeking news. The issue was overdue. I wrote Ann Creeley and then Bob, who finally told me of Martin's absconding with the funds for various reasons, but Bob feeling responsible, took it upon himself to do the issue for me at his own expense and labour." In an interview in February 1981, Corman added a colourful detail. Martin Seymour-Smith, he claimed, went down on his knees during a publisher's party in London by way apologizing for his past misdemeanors. Seymour-Smith, in an interview in March 1993, denied both allegations, adding that Creeley had probably had more of his money than he had of Creeley's. "But it doesn't matter."

Creeley's most recent portrait of Seymour-Smith is found in his 1990 collection, *Windows*, a poem entitled "For an Old Friend."

What became of your novel with the lunatic
mistaken for an undercover agent,

of your investment of the insistently vulnerable
with a tender of response,

your thoughtful wish that British letters
might do better than Peter Russell –

Last time I saw you, protesting
in London railway station

that all was changed,
you asked for a tenner

to get back to Bexhill-on-Sea.
Do you ever think of me.

16

Black Mountain Review.

While using Corman as his main confidant in discussing Seymour-Smith's alleged embezzlements, Creeley proposed to employ a different scheme behind Corman's back. This was because of his fears that *Origin* might go under or be continued by a new editor less sympathetic to the Olson-Creeley duovirate than Corman. Creeley's rescue plan, as proposed to Olson, was to circulate a rumour that Black Mountain College might start its own quarterly in the coming summer. Thus, a lot of the *Origin* poets possibly left floundering around for some alternative outlet would naturally gravitate towards the hoped-for new journal. For the time being, Creeley offered to act as a mere "drummer-boy to the wars" of the proposed venture. More realistically speaking, he could fill such a magazine, roughly the length of the *New Mexico Quarterly*, tomorrow, he assured Olson. The scheme gained additional momentum from Creeley's plans to go teach at Black Mountain College – just to get away! Majorca had long lost its charm. He felt sick of being the perpetual foreigner. As a person generally very dull to "landscapes," the gauntness of New Hampshire was really the only thing he could relate to, he mused.

Even the move from their large house to another had brought little relief. Initially the new place had promised more privacy and warmth as well as some more romantic attractions. It was located on the second floor of a beautiful mansion, La Baronia. But the water supply proved to be discontinuous and gave frequent trouble. Also, there was no hot water whatsoever. Even privacy turned out to be less than expected. The beautiful terrace above their apartment was shared with the "pension-keeper" who allowed his guests to enjoy the view of both the Mediterranean and the mountains. Worse, Creeley was experiencing another writing block, staring out the windows as earlier in Fontrousse. Going to Black Mountain College, the sooner the better, and preferably without wife and kids, promised the only way out.

But an unexpected letter from Black Mountain College threw everything into reverse. Apart from approving his appointment, it stated that the college wanted him to start a review for them. What he had proposed as a mere rumour, in case *Origin* should shut down or change editors, had become a reality. The suggested "drummer-boy" of a fake journal had been nominated chief editor of the *Black Mountain Review*. Deadly inertia exploded into hectic activity which, between the beginning of December 1953 and the middle of March 1954, propelled Creeley into accomplishing the near impossible, i.e., launching a new literary magazine while also absolving numerous other chores: to publish Charles Olson's *Mayan Letters*, Irving Layton's *In the Midst of My Fever*, his own *The Gold Diggers*, and Martin Seymour-Smith's *All Devils Fading*, as well as prepare for publication H.P. Macklin's *A Handbook of Fancy Pigeons*, Katue Kitasono's *Black Rain*, and the second issue of *Black Mountain Review*.

Bringing out the first issue proved far more difficult than the overnight job he'd expected. Mindful of Pound's advice regarding the solid core of contributors around which one could let the journal run wild to a degree, he instantly tried to set up a board of advisory editors which, under the general guardianship of Charles Olson, was to include Paul Goodman, Irving Layton, Paul Blackburn, and Kenneth Rexroth. There were to be problems even with that.

The only one ready to accept right away was Paul Blackburn. By 2 January 1954 neither Goodman nor Rexroth had responded – Rexroth, as Creeley suspected, out of rivalry with Olson. Meanwhile Creeley had received an evasive reply from Layton who, after discussing the request for reviews and articles with his friend Louis Dudek, had reached the conclusion that neither of them had the time required for such a job and that "a review of a Canadian book appearing in a mag published so many hundreds of miles away from the scene of the crime [could] do little good." At least, that's how Dudek had put it.

No doubt Layton was taken aback by Creeley's response. Their by now ten-months-old epistolary friendship had never so far reached an impasse, so the Canadian had yet had to learn what Creeleyan furies were like. Creeley had wanted Layton "in at the very first," just as he had wished to publish his poetry earlier. "I *liked* it. And thought that, by god, here is a man who can make it, and who has made it ... In any case, it is you now that I want, in, on this thing." And now this from Layton's friend Dudek, and even from Layton himself! The refusal prompted a tirade of cursing, primarily of Dudek's poetry, extreme even by Creeley's standards. It also produced Creeley's probably longest exercise in close reading, a six-page single-spaced put-down of Dudek's poem "For I.P.L." The usual apologies for having flipped followed.

In replying, Layton had assured Creeley that he was 100 per cent behind him. He also offered to provide the requested critical writings. But before the good news reached Majorca, Creeley wrote again. One more time, he apologized for having flipped, assured Layton how much they needed him, dropped a hint that none of all this, of course, would jeopardize the publication of Layton's *In the Midst of My Fever*, and casually mentioned that one or two short reviews of anything interesting to him "would be a tremendous help."

After finally reading Layton's letter, Creeley dropped his request for review material, merely appointing the Canadian poet as a contributing editor. Although Layton had called him "a bit harsh on D and, finally, unfair," Creeley was more than glad to forget the matter. In fact, he hoped to visit them both soon and, if possible, "haul Olson along" to Montreal too. Also, his review of the Contact Press books and the magazine would be printed in *BMR*. Undoubtedly, Layton and Dudek would find it "fair." Otherwise, Layton's "very damn kind & generous" letter simply added to the shame he had felt for over a week.

Finally, a note came from Rexroth saying that he'd be glad to be on Creeley's editorial board. Every time Creeley produced a new book, he read him on the radio, Rexroth added in the margin. Creeley breathed a sigh of relief. Rexroth, forty-nine year old poet, critic, translator, and inveterate maverick with his regular program on KPFA in San Francisco, certainly would be an important hook-up for the West Coast. Certainly, he would provide a useful counterbalance to Olson. Though watching each other like hawks, Olson and Rexroth tolerated each other – thank God!

Ironically, the man most helpful in the editing of *BMR* had not even been invited to be on its editorial board. Yet Cid Corman was an unlikely person to bear grudges or turn down Creeley's requests for help regarding translations from the French, reviews, and general contacts. There would be no competition with *Origin*, Creeley assured Corman – *BMR* would simply open another front, a notion Creeley kept repeating to others.

An early plan to call that second front *Noah's Ark: A Quarterly* was quickly abandoned in favour of the more academic-sounding *Black Mountain Review*. After all, it was the college that backed the venture. Volume one, number one, of Spring 1954 featured Charles Olson's "Against Wisdom and Such," Robert Hellman's story "The Quay," eight reproductions of artwork by René Laubiès plus Creeley's note on him, Martin Seymour-Smith's note on Dylan Thomas and his article "Where Is Mr. Roethke," as well as poems and reviews by, among others, Irving Layton, Paul Blackburn, Mason Jordan, Larry Eigner, Charles Olson,

William Bronk, and Thomas White. A note explained that White, an un-familiar name among the others, was working on a collection of Heine translations in Germany. By the winter of 1954 he was to transfer to Tap-pernoje, Denmark, to pursue "research on pre-Christian ritual." Initiates knew all along that the person hiding behind Thomas White was Robert Creeley himself.

Starting the review as well as attending to his multiple Divers Press chores brought Creeley close to a physical breakdown. He had been trail-ing a low temperature since after Christmas 1953, and by the beginning of February had had to spend about two weeks in bed. Otherwise, it was business as usual, carrying on his ever-more voluminous correspondence from his bed of pain, or driving himself nuts over Martin's suspected em-bezzlement and incompetence. But his caustic humour never left him for long. Staying in bed, he joked, was like being in jail: very intimate, and fair enough.

Yet somehow his health would not improve, and by the end of Febru-ary he had himself x-rayed. The diagnosis: his left lung was seriously af-fected: "just found why my face was dragging on the floor," he wrote Irving Layton, "i.e., apparently bronchitis I didn't know I had – which must have been that fever at that. Anyhow I get jabbed in the ass daily, and also a miserably humiliating Suppository, for the nights – anyhow, that I have to get thru, and somehow stagger on the fucking next boat," which he did around 12 March 1954.

Other than BMR #1, there were several trophies Creeley could take on that journey. His second booklet of poems, *The Kind of Act Of*, had been brought out by Divers Press in July 1953. By the autumn Jonathan Will-iams had published *The Immoral Proposition*, containing eight poems by Creeley and seven drawings by René Laubiès. *The Gold Diggers*, a collec-tion of eleven short stories with a cover by René Laubiès, had been printed by Mossén Alcover for his own press. Creeley's Divers books had already created enough of a stir in New York to have people malign him for publishing a small clique. Via Kenneth Rexroth, Charles Olson, and Irving Layton, his writings were becoming known at Black Mountain College, on the West Coast, and in Canada. Layton reported from Mont-real that the more he read Creeley, the more he felt that Creeley would end up by "founding a distinct school of [his] own." Already he had "quite a following" in Canada, Layton assured him. "I don't think that any contemporary American poet of your generation ... commands as much interest and attention."

Coming from someone else, Creeley might have mistrusted such com-ments as flattery. But not from Irving Layton whom Creeley admired for his self-assurance and "lack of shit": no man, he protested to Olson, ever came back at him cleaner. Layton, who risked criticizing Olson's sense of "methodology" and "open verse," or, at a later point, Creeley's own "phoney" stylistic mannerisms "of leapfrogging nouns and verbs," was hardly a flatterer. Hence his praise could be appreciated all the more – as when he called Creeley's choice of contributors to the *Rocky Mountain Review* "the pick of people writing today: all lively, all down-to-earth, all angry about something." Most perceptive were Layton's comments on Creeley's poems in which, as in the prose, he sensed "a kind of ecstasy (moral? psychological?) that disturbs because its source can only be guessed at." "I look upon your poems with the same fascination that I do a surgeon's knife: all the more so since the drops of blood I see on the blade are most frequently your own," he wrote.

In sum, Creeley's stay in Europe had turned out to be a success after all. He had left America as a virtual nonentity, with less than a dozen poems to his credit, most of them printed in *Wake*, a student journal. A poetry radio program broadcast by a local St Johnsbury station had folded after a few weeks. His *Lititz Review*, after months of editorial labours, had run aground over problems with Jacob Leed's hand press. Its remnants were picked up by the more successful Cid Corman. A projected volume of Creeley's poems sank in the same debacle. Another, to be brought out by Richard Emerson's *Golden Goose Press*, seemed to have been delayed indefinitely.

But Creeley had toiled on, gradually reaping hard-earned rewards. Since arriving in Europe, he had been printed in the *New Mexico Quarterly*, the *Kenyon Review*, and *New Directions*. He had been featured in *Origin* #2 and been published in numerous other journals as wide-ranging as Japan's *Vou*, Canada's *Contact*, and Germany's *Fragmente*. Three small collections of his poems and a sizeable one of his stories had appeared. But most crucial for his growing influence as the coordinator of an international network of postmodern literary movements, he had become head of a successful avant-garde press, as well as the editor of a literary magazine. However, who could be sure how people in the u.s., and especially Olson, would receive him? What would Black Mountain be like, which on an earlier visit he had detested so much? Could he possibly succeed as a teacher?

Many people back home were eager to meet him. One was a twenty-two year old Black Mountain student, Michael Rumaker. He had learned about Creeley through Olson, who showed him Bob's poems and short stories, as they arrived with the almost daily mail from Majorca. Holed up in his Studies Building room – one wall repainted in bright yellow, a second in flat black, a third in straight white, to make him feel he was living inside a Josef Albers painting – Rumaker had read and reread Creeley's poems and stories in *Origin* #2. Creeley, unlike any other writer he knew, "came at you out of nowhere, with no antecedents (as I thought then), with his perplexing sensibilities and acute but difficult perceptions ... this sparse, subtle and indirect writing, particularly the stories, was like signals from another planet. There were no familiar ear-sounds or sight boundaries of conventional and expected plot and character, no social conscience with a social message ... no comfortable signposts pointing in any directions previously known to me."

Whatever the man was talking about, it seemed strangely negative to Rumaker, forcing him, as it were, to turn himself inside out: "I had to learn to pay attention, to empty my head of all preconceived receptions of what writing ought to be, of my own expectations. Creeley's compositions imposed the necessity of an almost total reordering of aural receptivity."

Yet with what almost coercive power Creeley's stories seemed to accomplish this transmogrification of one's mindscape! Especially whenever "a bit of environmental detail, rarely, or a glancing thought, often, slipped into his narrative." Such mirage-like oases in the arid desert of Creeley's writings activated the reader's own resources by energizing them in almost magical fashion – "like detonators that spark and explode your own involvement. Mindscape and mind-action being the main agilities, the untouched and uncharged territories inside your own skull became populous with possibilities of discovery."

How would a man whose writing could cause such turmoil in your brain affect you in person?

17

Black Mountain, 1954.

Life on the boat, after the hectic weeks and months behind him, provided Creeley with a much-needed rest. Heading down the Guadalquivir River towards the Atlantic from Sevilla's inland port on 12 March, they were expected to reach New York harbour eleven days later. But tempestuous weather slowed the crossing, and a dock strike in New York would force them to proceed on up the Hudson to Albany instead, on the evening of 27 March.

Leaving Spain, he was still experiencing the odd kickback from the flu or whatever he had suffered from but was starting to feel better by the hour. And thank God, no sign of any seasickness in spite of the stormy, wet weather during the first few days. Apart from doing a bit of copy-editing, or writing letters, mostly to Ann – the typewriter about to be tossed off the table at any moment – Creeley, for once, took it easy. Holed up in his cabin, he read detective stories, stared out of the window at the big smokestack, and the sea beyond it, enjoying the boat's voluptuously soothing roll. He talked to the other passengers, then returned to his cabin to write about them to Ann: like the man with his ageless complexion, hair slammed down pompadour-style, neck almost twice the circumference of his head, wanting to tell dirty jokes, and making predictions about the weather which his wife wrote down to prove him wrong the following day; or the relaxed colonel-type aging joker and his wife who insisted on telling Bob that she was younger than her husband. All of them – like the couple bragging about their family's past grandeur in Italy, the young man from Syria on a UN scholarship to an American college, as well as Oriental-looking Mr Rubin from New York – seemed plagued by boredom, and took possession of the newcomer as someone odd enough to be interesting. One would buttonhole Bob to have a drink in his cabin, another, a car salesman, try to talk him into buying a Plymouth with only 30,000 miles on it, a third make him play checkers. In sum, it was a fine rest, the days lazy and simple, giving him a chance to set himself for the business ahead.

Due to the delay, his prearranged schedule for, say, attending Paul Blackburn's and Freddie's wedding, had been thrown into disarray. The truck he had ordered fixed in his absence still needed new front-wheel kingpins, a muffler, and an exhaust pipe. Just before his arrival in Littleton a storm had dumped a foot and a half of snow. He had to shovel in the bitter cold to get at the storage space and retrieve some of the things Ann and the kids might need later – crib, toys, bicycle, cart, phonograph, records, odds and ends. Also, their two cats, Elizabeth and Hercule, had become too much of a bother to Ira Grant, so Bob decided to take them with him to Black Mountain College.

Dog Lina, thank God, was doing fine. So were their birds, also in Ira's custody. There were pleasant reunions with Ira himself and Alice Ainsworth, as well as his lawyer Edes. During supper at Edes's, Bob made it clear that all he was willing to do regarding the yet unresolved Rock Pool Farm business was to pretend to sue owner Bill Gordon. While willing to gamble, neither he nor Ann had funds for any court business.

His trip down to New York City was beset by mishaps. In White River Junction, some fifty miles from Littleton, he backed into a taxi at one o'clock in the morning and had to pay the owner twenty dollars to settle. The truck's generator and fan-belt gave out, costing another fifteen dollars, courtesy of a mechanic found through the father of Blackburn's new wife, Freddie. She and Paul had just been married the same Saturday Bob's boat had docked at Albany. With her slick New York manner Freddie put Bob off a bit, but he liked Paul more than ever. Also, he had a chance to see Mitch, man to man, Denise being away in Brooklyn, thank God. He had a fine talk with William Carlos Williams over the telephone, and made some new acquaintances like sculptor Mike Lekakis, who had been working with Williams "on measure."

But it was all a rush, driving through the night to New York City, then, again at night, on to Washington where he spent a mere two days visiting with his mother and sister. Then, after another all-day and all-night drive, he and the two cats arrived at Black Mountain College in the morning of 5 April, early enough to find the Olsons still in bed. As Creeley remembered it later, he knocked on Olson's door, and "was confronted – their first meeting – by a mountain of a man wrapped in a towel but otherwise naked."

Olson had let it be known that he would like some time alone with Creeley when he arrived. So Black Mountain was abuzz with expectation. Here is how Michael Rumaker remembers it: guided by curiosity rather than necessity, he had sneaked past Olson's house on the road winding towards the farm after borrowing some sugar from the Husses next door. And sure enough, there were the two writers, "Charles and a younger man in a dark blue beret, an eyepatch over one eye and what looked like rough, loose-fitting workclothes, sitting side by side on the park bench in Charles's front yard ... They didn't see me approach at first and I watched Charles talking earnest and close in Robert's ear, his huge body swung half round in relaxed and easy confidentiality. Robert, sitting stiff, listening with bowed head, stared down at the ground."

Rumaker was waved over to meet Creeley:

the first glimpse of him was of some awkward, sturdy peasant, like a Basque, his face pale and tense, his movements jerky, agitated ... My immediate sympathy with Creeley was enlarged by seeing in that one dark eye staring out at me – the one beneath the patch began watering rapidly and he dabbed at it in quick self-conscious swipes with a wrinkled dirty handkerchief – an attractive vulnerability, a desperate desire to be liked. In his eye was a mute appeal of the painfully shy (magnified by his low, barely audible words) to overlook his clumsiness and shortcomings, to look beyond them.

A student who scrutinized the newcomer with different eyes was Cynthia Homire. In her early twenties and separated from her husband, she had spent the last three years with painter Dan Rice and had been persuaded by Olson to stay on at Black Mountain to study writing. She had glossy long hair, wore faded Levis, and walked barefoot early spring to late summer – a youthful Mother Courage, the part she played in Huss's production of Brecht's play. Dan had corresponded with Creeley while he and Cynthia had lived in Yucatan. At the time, Cynthia had read some of Creeley's writings and seen a photograph of him, and found both intriguing. She was one of the small group of students who would be waiting for Creeley to teach his first class in the large conference room on the second floor of the Studies Building on the evening of 6 April. Others included Tom Field, a painter and writer, Karen Karnes, the resident potter, Laurie Forest, a millionaire's daughter with short cropped carrot hair, Don Cooper, a music student studying with composer Stefan Wolpe, Jorge Fick, painter, and Jonathan Williams, publisher and poet.

According to a later account, Creeley's first class proved a near disaster: the students bunched up at one end of the large table filling most of the room, he, at the other end, "forlorn, alone, staring sideways at the wall, mopping at his eye with a handkerchief" and talking "in a nonstop monotone so low and gravelly, that no one could understand what he was saying. After ten minutes or so, Karen Karnes asked him if he could speak up; he lifted his voice for a few minutes, but it soon sank back into a monotone."

But memory tends to overdramatize. Creeley's first class, as he remembered it a few days afterwards, wasn't quite as bad as all that. In the thirty hours or so after his arrival, he had gotten to know most of his students and found them to be an ingenuous and malleable lot who promised to be putty in his hands. He had little concern about his personal and vocal presence. The problem lay elsewhere. What was he going to teach his students? Of course, he could talk to them about Pound, Williams, Hart Crane, and D.H. Lawrence. But teach them writing? What was that? he groaned in a letter to Ann. Yet even here, things turned out all right. When he wondered if anyone had brought some writing, Michael Rumaker volunteered to read excerpts from his journal. Creeley liked two of them, one about a middle-aged drunk getting out of a taxi in Greenwich Village, a blonde on each arm, hollering *"Toujours l'amour,"* the other about a lonely woman staring out of the upper windows of a downtown office building late at night. Any remaining tensions were resolved after class when Jonathan, Dan, and Cynthia took their new teacher out for a drink. The only one equal to what followed was Dan. Although the others dropped out, he kept listening and responding to Creeley until six o'clock the following morning.

Teaching, after the years of self-imposed silence in New Hampshire, France, and Majorca, allowed Creeley to unblock his long pent-up loquacity. At first afraid that his barely audible voice might actually fall silent, his students soon found that they simply couldn't stop him from talking, either in or out of class. As one of them joked on 29 April: How about shutting the lights off, so you can keep talking – and we can go to bed.

By 13 April Creeley found that although *he* was talking, his students were not responding in kind. So he "flipped," first in class, then again afterwards, telling them that something had to be done about it. They agreed to blame the problem on the oversized classroom with its long table and blackboard. Creeley suddenly remembered the room was conspicuously close to where he and Ann had spent a miserable few days in 1944. So off they went to a smaller room where he resumed his pedagogical endeavours by discussing the meaning of the word "flip." The effort proved liberating all around. One student suggested recapitulation, another ecstasy. They were off again.

A rare dark spot in the early days at Black Mountain was the decline of Hercule the cat. The shock of the move, Bob noted, had been too much for him. Had Bob taken action at the right time, he might have saved him. Instead, Hercule died, leaving just Elizabeth to share his spacious apartment towards the end of the top floor of the Studies Building. In a letter to Ann, Creeley draws a melancholic picture of himself at the typewriter, the lone survivor sitting on his lap and pawing the keyboard.

Back in Majorca, Ann received a somewhat less bucolic account of life at Black Mountain from Jonathan Williams. In mid-spring, the campus was wild-looking indeed. The days were great, though they tended to miss a lot of them because Bob, himself, Dan, and his girl, Cynthia, often sat up "beering" until dawn. Luckily, Bob's classes, by now five evenings a week Monday through Friday, were at night after dinner.

Before long Creeley developed his own teaching style, which for casualness, intimacy, and brevity contrasted with Olson's who would often go on for hours or oblige students to bring some of their writing as a condition of being admitted. Creeley's classes, Michael Rumaker remembers,

never met for more than two hours ... we read and discussed at length William Carlos Williams' earlier poems as points of departure towards our own possibilities in American speech, as well as the poetry of Hart Crane and the jazz of Charlie Parker and Bud Powell. Now and again a student would read a poem or piece of prose they'd written ... and we'd spend a little time talking about it, Creeley careful not to impose any absolutes or dogmas, respectful to leave space for openings. But mostly it was Creeley talking, and Creeley talking, on his best days, was plenty good enough.

By the end of his course on 9 June, Creeley felt he had achieved more than he'd ever hoped for. People believed in him, he wrote Ann. Some even looked up to him, making him almost cry with relief that he had come through at all.

Meanwhile he had taken several trips to New York City to meet old and new acquaintances. On one of them he for the first time went to see William Carlos Williams in person. Creeley knew he would not encounter the poet in one of the happier phases of his life. Williams had had to undergo an examination as a "red," which he had never been. The "stink" made at the Library of Congress had done him out of a job and thrown him for a financial loss. He was still recovering from a major stroke he had suffered in August 1952. Psychoanalysts had helped him overcome the mental derangements that had been an unadulterated hell, but his right hand as well as his eyesight remained considerably impaired.

Creeley visited Williams on 20 May 1954. Cynthia Homire, who accompanied him, remembered Williams as a little shaky on one side but charming and animated. During dinner there was a moment of embarrassed hilarity when Williams referred to Olson's "The Kingfishers" as that poem about woodpeckers. "The Kingfishers" was one of the few of Olson's works which, he felt, was exempt from the intellectual and consciously literary qualities vitiating most others. Williams at one point took Creeley upstairs to show him his old office desk and typewriter from the time he had been in practice, as well as the prescription pads he used to write on. They stayed with him most of the afternoon as well as part of the evening.

Creeley, after his more or less isolated existence of the past several years, increasingly turned his life into a non-stop carnival of old and new relationships with their concomitant enthusiasms, disaffections, intrigues, and enmities. Denise and Mitch, whose friendship he had tried to reclaim during an earlier visit to New York around April, were just about as he had known them in France, but their son Nik he diagnosed as an obnoxious and demanding problem kid. Or there was Seymour Lawrence, former editor of the Harvard *Wake* and a visitor to Bañalbufar, who had become a little heavier in the jowls and was stuttering more than before.

Another old friend, Race Newton, had suffered a breakdown in the Army, causing him partial amnesia, and had been given a pension. His face was heavier, his voice deeper. Yet he seemed to have more of a centre to himself, although things remained difficult enough for him. Another person to have emerged into a kind of troubled maturity was Eleanor, a former girlfriend of Buddy and briefly of Creeley himself. She was a lovely woman, yet a very sad one too. Working a nine-to-six job during the day and another at night while also trying to do some acting, she was involved with a man presently believed to be in Cuba.

More refreshing than these somewhat saddened relics from Creeley's past were several newcomers to his constantly regrouping friendships and literary allegiances. One such was Larry Bronfman who, for the time being, struck him as a quiet and decent man. Larry was helping with the New York distribution of Divers Press publications. Or there was a very odd but lovely girlfriend of Race, living across the courtyard from his place on Spring Street in the Village, Julie Eastman. Otherwise known as the witch from El Paso, Julie owned a copy of Graves's *The White Goddess*, was interested in magic, and wondered if Bob was an alchemist. Intrigued by her make-believe storytelling, eccentricities, and voluptuous curves, Bob eagerly followed her on her esoteric missions around Manhattan to meet both new friends and enemies. One of them, John Altoon, would briefly play a fateful role in Bob's life as his wife Ann's lover.

"The Musicians," a story written at the time, involves Creeley himself, his friend, pianist John (alias Race Newton), and "her" (alias Julie Eastman), "a small crouched figure, on the roof next to their own." The story compellingly captures the mysterious ambience surrounding the two men caught in the gravitational pull of the elusive yet omnipresent witch from El Paso.

She was saying, he's there, although the hall was empty. If there was someone there, then he was not there now. He stopped to say, you see, and continued, no

one. There's no one here at all. But she closed the door, hard, and left him standing, facing to the stairs.

So at this moment he saw the other man, like, as he thought, that now of
course there he would be, to be alone with him. It was where he hadn't looked,
above him, the stairs going up obliquely, to the roof.

Back at Black Mountain College, there were Cynthia and Dan, living in
the rear first floor apartment in Black Dwarf behind the Studies Building
on the road towards Olson's and Huss's. Being attracted to both Cynthia
and Dan, Bob found himself eating or, as he admitted to Ann, scrounging
there on a semi-regular basis. As much as he loved and respected Olson, he
gradually found the younger Dan to be more congenial company.

A veteran of Black Mountain College who, off and on, stayed there for
some seven or eight years, Dan was a person of many talents: a gifted
painter who would contribute several of his agitated but tightly controlled inks to Creeley's *All That Is Lovely in Men*; a trumpeter who had
played in Stan Kenton's and Woody Herman's bands; a gourmet cook;
the college's "most expert shoplifter;" as well as, according to Black
Mountain historian Martin Duberman, a Don Juan. Certainly Dan was
handsome. Seen by the caressing eyes of a gay fellow student, he

had a smooth boyish face, epicanthic folds of dawn-blue eyes, a tight face that
rarely smiled and when it did, a small smile, very tight. Small, baby-like teeth,
perpetually stained with nicotine; short in stature but muscular in arms and chest
and legs – Dan, stripped to the waist in Levis on a hot summer afternoon, carrying on his back several of his large abstract canvases, almost as tall as himself, on
his way to his studio in The Eye; blond close-cropped hair, blonder in summer,
tanned like a brief god in summer sun, boy-angel sailor (he had actually served in
the u.s. Navy in World War II), Billy Budd incarnate, in a way as innocent, only
with brains and artistry, seeing his beauty as an affliction because of the many
certain men, inside and outside Black Mountain, who turned on to him; Dan
puzzled and disturbed. Was he one of *them*?

Photographs show Dan's handsomeness, a James Dean-like vulnerability, shyly insistent rebelliousness as well as self-destructive bravado.
Without lifting a finger he had the power to affect the lives of those
around him, Rumaker remembers, "like a beautiful and helpless vulnerable male babe, strong in its ability to capture and maintain the attention
and ministrations of others, the permission to do so as the allowance of a
great favour like Rimbaud's 'fabulous invalid'."

Highly strung himself, Dan was taken aback by Creeley's being even
more tense and aggressive. "Look," Dan once told him after someone

they'd just barely met had left the room, "the intensity with which you're forcing this person to react or to admit you is really getting a little scary." For the time being, those most affected by that intensity were Dan and Cynthia.

Both had had their difficulties lately. Cynthia found Creeley's writings fascinating and the man even more so. How he came on to her with his low-toned but implacable persistence! Where others saw shyness and vulnerability, she sensed tough-mindedness. Where some felt Creeley was talking too much, she realized that in telling story after story or sometimes the same story over and over again, he was working things out in his own mind. But most intriguing to her was how he wrote his poems.

A possibly apocryphal story tells how Jonathan Williams, at a later point, complained that Creeley had not yet written enough poems towards the projected *All That Is Lovely in Men* to be published as *Jargon* #10. So Creeley sat down at his typewriter, started banging out poems, and throwing them over his shoulder on the floor one after the other. Thinking they couldn't be any good, Jonathan wasn't even going to read them. But all of them, including "I Know a Man," as Cynthia would remember in 1982, were terrific and would appear in print just as he had typed them.

He also looked the part: Spanish corduroy suits, long hair and beard, his one eye sizing you up when you were least aware of it – altogether the *poète maudit*, especially compared with handsome Dan with his dapper jeans and closely cropped hair. Cynthia cut Bob's hair in late April. The Samson-and-Delilah ritual aroused his suspicion while eliciting the approval of composer Stefan Wolpe, then resident at Black Mountain College. Much better, Wolpe remarked. Now you don't look like a poet.

Cynthia and Bob's sexual relationship began soon thereafter. The initial encounter happened the night before his 1 May Black Mountain College reading, for which Dan had made the announcements. As Creeley remembered a little later, Dan and Jonathan had gone for a drink while he and Cynthia went swimming in the river, then had a party on the sundeck behind his place in the Studies Building. The rest was a foregone conclusion: their driving to Ashville, a flat tire on the way back, the resultant exertion trying to get the truck back uphill to Black Mountain College, the rest of the night spent in bed. At the reading Bob felt exhausted but otherwise very "cool." Whatever may have been wrong with it was blamed on the glum audience. He hated it more than any group he had ever witnessed, he reported to Ann. An unsuspecting target for his hostility was Dan. Friend or not friend, he had to cut him, Bob felt.

Cynthia left Black Mountain to stay at her mother's in Croton-on-Hudson. Creeley, confused, decided he needed to get away from Black

Mountain. Yet as usual, his tribulations prompted instant, hard-headed decision making. Under the pretense of having to sort out Divers Press distribution problems in New York, he obtained a "leave of absence" from his teaching obligations. How to get up to New York? It took little to convince Dan, who was drawn in the same direction, to make the journey in Dan's MG. Once arrived in New York City, the two parted company. Bob stayed in Manhattan, Dan went up to Croton to see if he could reconcile himself with Cynthia. When that failed, it was Bob's turn. More successful, he first spent a weekend with Cynthia in Croton, then another full week in New York City.

Those few days proved to be the high point of their short-lived amours. It was a magical time (as evoked in "The Musicians") spent in the company of old and new friends like Race, Eleanor, Mitch, Dennie, Julie, Larry Bronfman, Joel Oppenheimer, or William Carlos Williams. It was a week of continuous visiting, bar hopping, talking. Even a potentially nasty incident resolved itself as if by magic. Dan had decided to hang around New York, where Cynthia and Bob ran into him at the Cedar Street Bar, then the preferred hang-out for avant-garde poets and artists. The two rivals, facing each other in Cynthia's presence, decided to go outside and have a fight. Instead they just talked, then returned to the bar together. Strangely enough, Bob continued to like Dan a lot. The worst was that it was Dan who had to be the one he was knifing, he pondered. At the same time, it was the best it could be, in making it so "clean."

The leave of absence over, Bob and Dan returned to Black Mountain. The two men, with Cynthia remaining at her mother's, became closer friends than before. They were like "twins, inseparable," Rumaker remembers, "non-identical though, since Creeley was dark-haired and dark-eyed, the taller of the two, with the look of a Spaniard," Dan, blue-eyed and blond, looking Nordic. Bob felt Dan was the only one at the college who trusted him, the only one in a room full of people he could speak to without saying a word, the only one who really knew him and cared for him.

It was time for theorizing his relationships, both marital and adulterous. Cynthia, rather than Ann, was very much it to Bob. However, she would have to come to him out of her own free will more than she had done so far. But Cynthia didn't. By 28 May she still hadn't written him, which, for the time being, he was ready to take with a sense of humour breathing a lovelorn sigh. Three days later, his yearning for her already made him feel goddamn lonely. His exuberance upon returning to Black Mountain – wild flamenco blaring from his speaker in room 101 at "Goof's Hollow" – had evaporated.

Once she did write, it hardly reassured him. It wasn't that she didn't love him. She did so a million times and terribly, terribly much sometimes. But she was also terribly afraid of him. She admitted to being a sentimental person who liked everything. In turn, she was always glad when people liked her, which they certainly didn't always. How different Bob was! While also liking to be liked, he'd always try to get there first and hate people if they didn't like him, she observed astutely. Smash, crash.

      I
club
people in

my mind, I
push them this
way, that

way, from
the little
way

I see them
up
the length,

for fear
of being hurt
they fall.

Cynthia feared that hate and aggressiveness. Bob would make a scene just to get attention, a hideous scene, and she wouldn't know what to do except crack a joke, or wait it out, because he never did jump out of the window finally. She couldn't take it, she wrote to him at a later point. What she wanted was to live quietly some place, cook things and eat them, sleep, and love, and never, never hate.

At Croton-on-Hudson Bob had tried his habitual technique of deflecting his hostility towards Cynthia on someone else, in this case her allegedly miserable, drunken mother, yet without the accustomed success. Proposing to rescue his beloved from this maternal ogre, he met with stiff resistance, then suddenly – horror of horrors – realized it was the mother in Cynthia who was talking back to him. Paranoia and pent-up violence between the three was captured in "The Suitor," another short story written out of his goddamn compulsion to confess while simultaneously taking a writer's revenge on the objects of his contempt. Its style, he admitted to Olson, was as close to "vicious" as he would like to get.

A first person narrator in an earlier version, protagonist George is a jobless, drunken good-for-nothing whom mother and daughter employ for menial tasks around the house. He "overhears" a conversation about what the coal dumped by a bulkhead is for: "The voices said, first we will take knives and cut little bits out of his knees, eyes, and toes, and then we will cover him all over with flour, and lard, and push him into this nice big oven, for which we have ordered one ton of coal."

Such fairy-tale nightmares mingle with household horrors of a more tangible kind. The mother accuses George of having sloshed in his bath to explain the water dripping from a crack in the ceiling; George muses impotently on his loathing for the mother ("Ratface, he thought, ratface, ratface, ratface. I hate you, ratface"), shows the daughter letters he has received from potential future employers in the attempt to get her "away from all this" ("Many men have started with less"). Or he daydreams about shooting them all: "A gun anyhow was what he wanted. A cool deliberate aim, to lift it, to hold it, pressed close against his shoulder. Here they come, he said. Pam, pam! You're stoned, George, said mother. Ok, he said, I give up."

Again there is the usual difference between fiction and reality. Like John in *The Island*, George in "The Suitor" more often than not is the defenceless, fumbling victim of his oppressive entourage. In real life, Creeley was mostly on the offensive. Reminiscing upon the goddamn power that bitch (i.e., Cynthia's mother) could manage for herself, and on how Cynthia was having no criticism, like they say, of dear old Mom when he had been paying his respects, Creeley, a few months later, narrated the following sequence of events: One very wild night, being a little weary and also drunk, he had tried to "explain" how this mother was not the greatest, all very, very carefully and kindly – death! Then he'd gone to sleep and next morning thought Cynthia was rather sour. Finally, about noon, she said he'd told her such horrible things about her mother, etc. And to this day he could not remember one goddamn word nor even the Christly sense that he had damn well come on with any viciousness.

Less easy to forget was his tendency to pick fights when drunk. A published interview attributes that propensity to a wish to relieve his "frustration of social ineptness" which made him drink in the first place, as well as to a "feeling of absolute incompetence and inability" which made him pick the fights. With obvious fondness, Creeley dwells on the weapon he used to brandish on such occasions: "a big wooden handled clasp knife, that in moments of frustration and rage – I mean I never stuck anybody with it, but it was, like I'd get that knife, you know, and I don't think I tried to scare people with it, but it was like, when all else failed, that knife was … not simply in the sense I was going to kill somebody, like a gun [sic], but I loved that knife … I've still got one like it."

People who actually had to face this indecisive person fumblingly handling his beloved knife without the least intention to scare, let alone kill, remember a somewhat more forceful man. One such was terrified Cynthia, who kept wishing her lover wouldn't chase people with knives and throw bar stools. At the same time she found that Bob was never quite real until he engaged in such activities.

In 1982 she recalled an incident that happened near Bellow's Falls, New Hampshire, where the two had spent about a week in another house owned by Cynthia's mother. Bob was racing a car through the countryside while she was entertaining old friends. One of them, when she finally went to sleep, had lain down beside her and, being drunk, fallen asleep as well. When Bob got back, he threatened to kill him, then sat in the kitchen brandishing his knife at everybody. Strangely enough, the fellow died shortly after, as if Bob had put the hex on him. Bob later sent the knife to Cynthia herself.

In Cynthia's memory, it was incidents like these that destroyed their relationship. Her worst fear, that the magic that had brought them together would turn nightmare, was fast becoming tangible reality. She couldn't fight with him, she wrote to Bob. She was no good at smashing things. If he wanted to smash, he would have to smash someone else. Goodbye. Goodbye. Creeley, out of an urge somewhat untypical for him, asked her to return all his letters to her so he could destroy them. His final reaction, once it was over, was one of incomprehension, bitterness, and resentment.

18

The Tarnished Lover.

Jocularly outspoken on most things, Creeley as a rule carefully screened out his marital problems in writing to friends. Even in corresponding with "Dear Lover" Paul Blackburn, an anecdote like the following is a rare exception. Typically, it was meant to show up visitor Jonathan Williams's timorousness rather than the Who's-Afraid-of-Virginia-Woolf domestic scenario that was the Creeleys' before his departure for the u.s. About to leave for Palma one early morning, hung over from the previous night's drinking, Bob tried to gulp down some coffee, found it too hot, and, with the bus horn sounding outside the house, "flipped" and threw first the coffee and thereafter the empty cup across the room, eliciting an appropriately irate response from Ann. And all throughout, Jonathan Williams was sort of mumbling heartfelt assent, trying to act as cool as any man could under the circumstances. Probably he thought he might be next, Creeley speculated.

Up to 11 May 1954, his letters to Ann observe a similar guardedness. He might apologize for his clumsiness in giving her needles, protesting that he was not a sadist; or mention her goddamn theories of a necessary separation only to dismiss them with a parenthetical (ha!), protesting that he'd never felt this thing between them so clear. Otherwise, what wife ever received greater assurances of being loved and desired?

The second day out at sea he already missed her so goddamn much she wouldn't believe it. After another three he felt sufficiently lonely to remember the night when he "couldn't." Now the very fact that he was unable to hear or touch her filled him with longing. Ann had given so much to him, he wrote on 21 March, he'd like to be able to give her something in return. Maybe they could live on a goat farm in the u.s., a favourite notion of hers. The night of 25–26 March he allegedly spent awake from midnight or so till 6 a.m. thinking of her. He'd even lean over to kiss her, only to wake up to the fact that she wasn't there. Instead, he implored her to kiss the drawing of the lips where he had kissed the letter, assuring her that he loved her very, very, very much.

Ann's letters, which he picked up in New York, only intensified his devotions. She was wonderful. He'd give anything to touch her. Life at Black Mountain College, for all its gregariousness, only made him feel lonelier at heart. Cynthia, one of his pupils, had remarked on how he'd already shown her the pictures of his wife and kids five times. He loved Ann so much he suspected he was hysterical.

If only she were there, she'd find out what man he was. His goddamn pathetic prick was getting hard thinking of it. HA! Anyhow, it had all been his fault for not recognizing all those seven damn years what he'd had in her. She was beautiful, had been so, and would always be. He'd known her always, right from the moment of holding her in his arms at that ridiculous party when they'd met for the first time. Even though she was far away, he could feel her mouth, eyes, the breasts he would like to bite while kissing her all over her wild, wild body. She was the only woman he'd ever seen so much in her body, and not just as a dull, dull animal. He loved her.

She had no reason to worry about other women. He was a very severe, cold man, he joked. What's more, he couldn't even see other women, busy as he was pondering more than ever before, and so gratefully, all her past constancy and devotion in having taken him through all the bumps, and, more generally speaking, all her wild, wild fucking wonder. Of course, there were a few women at Black Mountain College, or even in his class, like Cynthia, who often cooked for him, or even cut his hair. Or that pathetic student of his he contemptuously referred to as "the girl."

What a cliché she was! Daughter of filthy rich parents, her sister married to a faggot, herself hating men or being scared to death by them. Already "the girl" had tried to commit suicide once, by gassing herself. Now she wanted Bob to study Freud, she being a horror of psychiatry herself. Somehow he had been handed the job of giving her driving lessons. But just talking to her, bluntly as he did, he might fuck her up worse than she was already. After one such conversation she had had to give her Boston analyst a rush call to ask him for help. The only things attractive about her was the seventeen-foot sailboat she had up in Vermont. He had talked to her about bringing it down on a trailer and putting it out at Cape Hatteras. But as a woman? At best she'd make some young business executive a "nice" wife. As far as Bob was concerned, he'd rather jerk off than get into that. So never to worry about her. In any case, all that counted was him and Ann. Just that, forever.

But suddenly on 11 May the tone changed drastically. Bob, as he explained, had become very confused and still didn't know what had happened, except that he had gone through a shift since coming back to America. In any case, he didn't think he would see Ann now even if he could, ugly as that might sound.

The follow-up letter the next day opened the floodgates to a veritable torrent of disgust for their marriage and everything associated with it. Even New Hampshire in retrospect struck him as a hard, flat, ugly, barren place he loathed. Never, anyway, would he want to live on a farm again, or be forced into any life he had no use for, or do what he had done all throughout their seven-year-long marriage. So no more letter-writing, wheedling, or scheming to justify himself. The more he could shed what reminded him of those cold, unhappy years of their being together, the better. He had recently lost his beret, and what a pleasure it had been to be rid of it. Thereafter, all week long, he had been losing things, and found it very exciting. A letter to Olson put it more bluntly. It felt as if all the shit of years was pouring out of him.

Already it struck Bob as next to unfathomable how either of them, compelled, miserable people that they'd been all too often, had been able to endure it. And yet how carefully he used to insist that the past years really hadn't been so miserable. In fact, they'd been godawful! So that was that. Ann was treated to some more analytical reflections on his avowed disgust with what their living together had turned into. Certainly it had become unendurable to him, even rendered him impotent. The main cause had been her making him feel guilty for all he'd done to her, his past cruelty, like the business of her cysts.

She would be wrong to imagine that with all his sudden loathing for their relationship he was feeling disturbed or unhappy. He'd never felt better. All too long he'd supposed himself to be this repulsive thing, had thought that his appetites were ugly and unreasonable, had been making boxes for himself, had been jealous and possessive. That was all over now. For the first time he knew what actual peace was, in himself. Everyone was telling him how well he looked and how happy. And he was. He couldn't hide it, even if he wanted to, which he did not. He felt his own balls, and was not afraid of them. He felt how a man could be, without guilt. Ann was advised to do likewise. She would have to find herself for herself, just as he had.

After reading Bob's letter, some fifteen hundred words long, Ann was still left wondering what had happened. Was it a slow process of megalomaniac self-aggrandizement that caused Bob to look back on his former life with such contempt? There had been a streak of that running through his letters since his departure. On the boat, to his surprise, he'd disliked none of the people on board, perhaps due to shedding the old rabbit-wolf complex he had suffered from earlier. The car salesman told him that people thought he looked very distinguished – like Errol Flynn. Alice Ainsworth thought he had the most wonderful voice, as she had reported back to Ann in Majorca. Arriving in Manhattan, he had met with further events to boost his self-confidence. Making the rounds of old and new friends, he found that he was the Messiah there. Finally, there had been the 1 May reading at Black Mountain College. The day after had been a turning point in his life. Now, in the letter of 12 May, he remembered how it had made him feel almost exultant: it had felt so incredibly good to be what he was, and to say it like that.

Not a word about anything that might have caused his sudden disenchantment with their marriage: like his also being in love, "like they say," as the same letter finally announces in its seventh paragraph. Anyway, she was Cynthia. As Ann knew, Cynthia was living with Dan, and Bob and Jonathan had been eating over there a good deal.

The whole thing was really silly because Dan was a very decent man whom Bob liked very, very much. Except that under the circumstances it was of course impossible for Bob to like Dan just as it must be impossible for Ann to like Cynthia. On balance, the wildest part of it had been Dan and himself driving up to New York together. Meanwhile, Dan and Cynthia were both staying in Croton-on-Hudson, some thirty miles north of Manhattan.

Another, even longer letter written on 13 May gave detailed accounts of Bob's visits with Race Newton, Buddy's former girlfriend Eleanor, Mitch, Denise, their problem kid, Nik, Seymour Lawrence, and new friend Larry Bronfman. It also articulated his prior sentiments about the miseries of their relationship, the guilt he had felt in it, and the very deep pleasure of simply being allowed to be himself. Other than that, there was a fleeting mention of Cynthia to the effect that none of that was final or even very hopeful.

Ann had to wait for over a week for Bob's next, brief letter. It announced that he would be leaving New York and go back to Black Mountain the coming Sunday. He told her about his visit with William Carlos Williams, gave her instructions towards the printing of BMR #2 (which she was handling in his absence), and hinted that he had changed his mind about her coming to the States. Earlier, he'd still spoken of her joining him in June, and that the sooner they could see each other, the better. Now she was advised to think twice about coming back – particularly if there wasn't enough money.

Ann's letters in response before and after 12 May are marked by a rupture in sentiment almost as radical as in his. There is nothing in those sent before that date to suggest the dismal view of their marriage she remembered afterwards. On the contrary, Bob was the bravest and most intelligent man she had ever met. He was marvellous and she loved him like anything. She was happy when he sounded self-confident, sad when he was depressed. She fretted over his health and tried to cheer him up with whimsical anecdotes about the kids and things in general. Above all else, she loved him so much. She fondly remembered even their former quarrels. She and Dave obediently kissed the drawing of his lips he had sent her. In return she sent him her own hopeful kisses.

She again and again told him that she wished him back, wanted and missed him, swore to her faithfulness, and implored him to not get entangled with anyone else. If he so much as looked at another woman, she would claw him to death. Even after his enigmatic letter of 11 May she still loved him, adding that her life hung completely on his, however nasty she might have been to him in the past. She loved him very much, and didn't really know what to say except that she did.

Only after finding out about Cynthia did she suddenly remember the horror of the last three years of their marriage. Otherwise, her replies to Bob's letter, which reached him upon his return to Black Mountain around 25 May, mainly showed her open-mindedness and understanding. Taken aback, Creeley praised her kindness, calling her a terrific and very damn fine woman.

Though hoping they could start again, Ann offered him a divorce and complete freedom under the sole condition that he help her get settled into a new house in the u.s. Of course, she would finish his remaining publishing business first. She even took some of the blame for what had happened. After all, it had been she herself who had made Bob go, so as to allow him to find himself; if it weren't for Cynthia, his having found himself so completely would make her happier than she had ever been before. She had sent him away, even anticipated that he might fall in love with someone else. She was not at all angry about Cynthia. It was his only life. He had to decide what to do with it.

Delighted by her response, Creeley suggested that perhaps he might even get back with her. He once again asked her to come as soon as possible. Cynthia exerted no pressure to the contrary.

What was happening regarding Cynthia? Four more letters of 26, 28, 30, and 31 May brought Ann little further enlightenment. All she found out was that Dan, after staying with Cynthia in Croton, had returned to Black Mountain where he and Bob had become friends again. Hearing that Dan was staying with Cynthia in Croton had revived Ann's hopes of her reconciliation with Bob. Would he be living with Cynthia when she and the kids got there, she asked. Wondering whether Cynthia and Dan were still living together, she admitted to how disgustingly jealous she had become. She didn't dare go to bed because she would lie there thinking about him and how close she had come to losing him.

Whether or not he was living with Cynthia was hardly the point, Bob replied testily. Did Ann realize that two young ladies had seriously wished to come down to Black Mountain to live with him? To put it mildly, that wasn't his problem any longer. So why put up with a marriage that had turned into a mutual process of self-castration. Perhaps mindful of Ann telling him how scared to death she was of his letters, he apologized for being so ugly about it. He would never want to hurt her. Goddamn it, he did love her in his way. He did try. And he would try again if he thought it would help, but he didn't think it would.

A second letter written the same day announced that he was tired of love; in yet another, the day after, he apologized for his past spitting and finally volunteered a brief account of his relationship with Cynthia. Once again, he held out the possibility that he might come back to Ann after all. If Cynthia "was it," then he would say so. If Ann, he'd be sorry he'd had to do it that way. Though there could be no guarantee of anything, Ann was asked to bear with him in the meantime.

She was a very beautiful woman, he added, always had been and would be. But beautiful women were a goddamn dime a dozen, literally. What really mattered was who could bear him and continue breathing. And she couldn't, or at least she hadn't been able to these past years. There had been too much death in it. To convince herself, she should reread his goddamn poems. He had done so himself and been dumbfounded. He'd never realized what the hell he was actually saying in them. And he had thought everyone lived that way.

While tantalizing her with his cryptic comments, he increasingly used her as a mother confessor regarding the troublesome aspects of his affair with Cynthia. When he'd go back to New York, it would hardly be to run off with Cynthia. She had her own problems, and would do what she could as she could, and so on. Perhaps he might even come back to Ann. He loved Cynthia, but he also loved Ann, and that was true. Yet for the time being, he just damn well didn't know, and honestly for once. Essentially, he just felt tired like someone who had had his bellyful of the goddamn process of love. Perhaps Ann had had a bellyful of his vacilating, he conceded.

The next two weeks would break it one way or the other, he announced on 6 June. For another four days Ann was left guessing at what that might mean. Then, on 10 June he told her he was about to leave for New York for a week or two. Twelve days went by before she received his next letter. It curtly announced that he would see about getting a boat back to Majorca as soon as possible, if that was agreeable to Ann. Otherwise, he had spent a week near Bellow's Falls in New Hampshire. But that was a long story. He would tell her when he'd see her, like they say. A postscript conceded that things regarding Cynthia were not at all clear. Or rather quite impossible. In any case, as he had already explained (he guessed) to both Cynthia and Ann, he could love fifty women. So to hell with it. Ann shouldn't worry about it, because, one, it was his affair.

A mere two days later Ann was told that he would sail on 16 July. She was rechristened "Darling" instead of the formal "Dear" of recent weeks. The fare was $214.96, roughly the monthly allowance on which she, Bob, and the kids continued to survive. To make his volte-face complete, her tarnished lover even seemed ready to once again shoulder the guilt for all the miseries of their marriage. He was beginning to feel huge remorse that Ann and the kids couldn't come to the u.s., but really that was no good at the moment. Otherwise, he felt like an ass, though still manly. Also, he had certainly done it the hard way, and never could see it any other way.

Ann, in spite of these dubious announcements, was so happy Bob was coming back she didn't know where she was at, she admitted. Terrified, too. She hadn't been able to stop jumping up and down, and when she tried to walk normally, her legs buckled, she confessed. This time she would go all the way. She was full of praise for recent poems he had sent her. She just couldn't get over them. "I Know a Man" and "La Noche," in her opinion, were the best he had ever written. She promised that he would find her very unserious and unspiritual. Even the possibility of his having caught syphilis didn't phase her. On the contrary, the very thought of sitting on his lap, vd and all, made her so happy, she didn't know what to do. Would she have to give him shots?

More of a worry were her looks whenever she stared into the miserable mirror. She was frantically redesigning her wardrobe to make herself look attractive, and she worried about what to wear for his arrival in Barcelona. She promised to mend her ways, vowed to never again scold him, felt a little foolish after receiving his angry letter about the magazine, or awfully sorry about being so stupid about it. Also, she was ashamed to have betrayed him by telling the Blackburns about Cynthia, thereby causing Freddie to propose that Ann go to New York, abandon her kids, and lead a life of sin, starting with Larry Bronfman. More generally speaking, she admitted to being a fool, and always getting taken in by everybody.

Bob, in return, was prepared to focus his anger and contempt on everyone else but her. Hearing how Paul Carroll, then visiting in Majorca, got drunk, took off his shoes and announced he was Christ, made him curse the lush who was a goddamn conceited prick into the bargain. First time Paul would get stoned in his presence, out he'd go. What Ann told him

about their Bañalbufar neighbours made him fear he would have to confront a lawn party upon his return. But the main new bugbear turned out
to be Freddie, who had threatened to attack Bob for what he had done,
and talked Ann into buying slacks. Jesus Christ! If there was anything he
hated more than ladies with pants, it was men with dresses. So would Ann
please throw out the slacks! Soon he'd be there to rescue her from her female tormentor. If it was fighting Freddie wanted, he was in exact mood
to hit back.

Meanwhile the u.s.a. was a hell of a country. Even the houses looked
like paper. Horrible! His sister Helen, whom he had visited toward the
beginning of July, seemed to him thoroughly fucked up. Certainly, both
she and their mother didn't sound too happy these days. Newly recruited
best friend Larry Bronfman had turned out to be goddamn pompous.
Cynthia was not spared. Dan, she, her miserable mother, plus the latter's
suspected paramour Victor Kalos (poor man to eat so much shit for so
goddamn little!) were planning to go to Mexico together. How pathetically devoted Cynthia was to her mother. Reflex conditioned like a dog.
So fuck it. It was a dull, dull thing at this point.

Clearly, things between Bob and Cynthia hadn't worked out. On 22
June the two had finally decided to call it quits. To make sure he wouldn't
come back to haunt her, Cynthia had brought his suitcase and typewriter
to Grand Central Station. Within hours of kissing her goodbye, Bob had
written to Ann that he would see about getting a boat back to Spain if
that was agreeable to her.

19

Majorca, 1954–55.

News of what had happened just prior to his return to Majorca sped ahead as Bob crossed the Atlantic. What he had done merely confirmed Paul Blackburn's sense that he basically cared very little for people. Only a few months ago, Bob had spent a whole week in New York studiously avoiding friends like Cid, Ted, Mike, and Larry. Now, a few hours before his departure, he had given a kick in the teeth to the one man who, together with Blackburn himself, had selflessly sold his Divers Press books as well as offered to take care of distribution in the future. The reason: Larry Bronfman had dared inform Bob that the new person he had thought would do the job might not have sufficient storage space. Was this reason enough to snarl at Larry that he should have told him about this problem earlier? Or to say, that the whole trip with Larry to Black Mountain and back to New York had been one horror of smothered feelings, Bob being forced to feel grateful. Blackburn couldn't understand any of it. And it griped him, he wrote Cid Corman.

God only knew what would happen once Creeley came back, which was to be any minute. Ann had left to meet the boat in Barcelona several days before, so young David had been expecting them back for the last two days. And what a time they'd had with Ann! A goddamn eternal tea party, her playing the gracious hostess, shoving damn donuts down people's throats. To tell the truth, Paul had never met anyone more selfish. Amazing how Bob had put up with it for all those years, or simply not seen through it! What Ann had done to Freddie was worse. But the specifics of that were so long and involved that, rather than being reported in a letter, they should be talked about over drinks in Paris. Depending on how matters unfolded, they might leave in a couple of weeks. Already Ann had spoiled two months of their stay in Majorca.

In the middle of typing this tirade, Blackburn heard a knock on the door and in came Creeley and his son David. Paul quickly let the unfinished letter to Cid disappear in a folder. Conversation over cognac revealed little that was new. Bob acknowledged the kindnesses and favours Larry had done him, but said he felt irritated being asked to accept them under Larry's conditions. He had been annoyed by Larry reading aloud one of his poems without any attention to lines. Larry was a man of quickly fading enthusiasms whose only worry was to get laid.

None of all this, Paul countered, was grounds for what Bob had done. Larry was one of the fairest, sweetest-natured men he had ever known. Bob disagreed. After about two hours, the two men parted, neither yielding an inch.

The first meeting of the two families was even more glacial. Continuing the same letter to Cid Corman dated 29 July 1954, Paul described it as round one of an ongoing boxing match he rightly expected to unfold over the next week. Ann and Freddie were barely speaking, Ann was nervously chewing her nails. Freddie, the bitch, got in a few cracks, Ann, in retaliation, only one that Paul noticed. To be continued.

Two letters from Larry Bronfman, responding to what Blackburn and others had said about Bronfman and Creeley, arrived to aggravate matters. The rumour mill was grinding away. Bronfman felt Creeley was overrated. He was annoyed about Bob's claim that he worried about nothing else than getting laid – and that from the man who, married with three kids, had first fucked Cynthia, abandoned his job at Black Mountain for her, and while chasing Cynthia, fucked Julie as well.

Creeley felt there was plenty for him to be angry about on his side. After seeing him in New York, Paul had written to Ann that he would fail at Black Mountain because he spoke with his hand over his mouth. Upon arrival in Majorca, where Ann had had a freshly whitewashed house ready for the Blackburns, Paul had displayed a childish standoffishness and offered next to no help with Divers Press. Was it his Fullbright grant that made him act like a goddamn professor? All the posturing, the carefully modulated tone! Speaking to Paul had become a completely tight-lipped, suspicious, self-protective, and unpleasant business.

But the main culprit for their estrangement was Paul's Freddie. Bob hated "couples" in principle, and these two were veritable professionals at it. Paul primarily devoted himself to his wife's obtrusive conversation instead of concentrating on his writing. After destroying his integrity, that bitch with her goddamn ugly sureness and overbearing nothing-is-worth-shit manner was about to cost Paul his poetry as well. Deterioration was evident in the self-satisfied tone of his recent translations or in the influence he had exerted over Paul Carroll in doing an equally miserable Catullus translation. No wonder Paul looked like a tomato about to explode whenever Creeley approached him.

Tempers flared on both sides, with Creeley eagerly fanning the flames. As always, it made him feel better to hear the bullets whistling around his noggin rather than to sit like a bowl of Wheaties, ready to be eaten. Cursing Larry Bronfman as a pompously charitable and self-righteous little prick, or Carroll's Catullus translations as awkward, stuttering, and pompous, he by no means limited himself to addressees like Joel Oppenheimer, who, though probably taken aback by Creeley's vehemence, could be expected to sympathize with his general sentiments. As in discussing Dudek's "For I.P.L." in writing to Layton, Creeley knew that, if sent to Cid Corman, his put-down of Carroll's translations would reach the translator's ears. For better measure, he included parodies of the items in the same letter.

> My old lady is a goof at heart,
> she tells me she loves me, we'll never part –
>
> but what a goofed up chick will tell to a man
> is best written in wind & water & sand.
> ...
> Love & money & a barrel of mud,
> my old man gives out for a stud,
>
> comes home late from his life of sin,
> now what do you think I should tell to him?

Unpredictable as ever, Corman offered to publish the pieces in *Origin*, an idea Bob promptly decided to enlarge upon in his *Black Mountain Review*. A letter to Joel gleefully announced that the next issue would contain a series of parodies, some funny, others as vicious as things could get.

For all the unpleasantness of his break with Paul Blackburn and his followers, Bob was determined to enjoy himself while getting ready for the final showdown. By 10 September, he had gone as far as to convince himself that Freddie should go die, and that Paul, who had not said a word about BMR #3, should be helped towards the same destiny. His silence made Bob feel like choking him, he confessed to Oppenheimer.

Hours later the battle was on. Paul and Freddie were about to leave for France, so Bob and Ann brought some issues of *Origin* #11 over for them to take to Paris. What followed was a jabbing sort of conversation of about an hour, with Freddie constantly needling Ann. When Ann said something about the low rent their servant Madeleina paid for her house, Freddie called Madeleina a thief. At this point, Bob, admittedly acting on a secret wish he had harboured for weeks, let Freddie have his drink in her face. Then all hell broke loose.

Immediately afterwards, still shaking with rage, Bob fired off several detailed accounts of the horrible goddamn scene. He jokingly took the blame for the fight, even confessed to feeling a little silly about it. He also expressed regret at wringing the neck of a man who, only half his size, had tried to rise to his spouse's defence. But rather than by such sentiments, his abandoning Paul's neck was prompted by the urge "to land one in the sneering face of this bitch [Paul had] for a wife." That feat filled him with a pleasure he would "damn well savor till the grave." Language was such filth in some people's mouths as in Freddie's, you had to use your hands to stop it, he repeated to several addressees.

Characteristically, his most unrepenting accounts were sent to those likely to relay the information to the Blackburns. What he had wanted most was to get his hands on Paul's wife, he wrote Cid. And indeed, he'd had the deep pleasure of landing one swat on Freddie's sneering face. As if to make absolutely sure Paul and Freddie would find out about his total lack of regret about what he had done, he added several afterthoughts. Never, he announced, had he wanted to kill anyone so much as he did Freddie. He would gladly kill that bitch anytime and anywhere, forever. He would fight every goddamn sign of that woman for as long as he lived. Nor would Paul be exempt from his wrath. For Freddie was so much in his body, it had turned to filth in him too. What a pleasure it had been to give Freddie what he had wanted to for two months, he told Alex Trocchi. Which was hardly civilized, of course. But civilized he had never pretended to be. Okay, he was not "mad," etc., as Trocchi knew. So he'd better shut up – and to hell with it.

But shut up he didn't, following up on letters written the same day with increasingly formulaic accounts to Irving Layton as well as to an even more bewildered Larry Bronfman the day after. He wanted a goddamn chant to commemorate all this, he wrote to Olson.

With the story spreading like wildfire, the cohorts of the opposing camps took sides in increasingly partisan fashion. Paul Carroll hastened to congratulate Paul Blackburn on the "rumpus." Did Freddie really biff Ann? he wondered admiringly. Good girl! He had never been interested in Creeley's poetry and doubted if he would like the man. Creeley's poems told him little else than that he was sorry for himself.

Naturally, the fight aroused some concerns as well. Paul was worried that Creeley might not come through on his promise to publish his second book (which duly appeared in March 1955 under the title *The Dissolving Fabric*). Cid Corman felt Creeley must have been completely off his rocker, and came to suspect that he was trying to create a break between them, a rift encouraged by an increasingly ambitious Olson who was beginning to openly and callously use people. Corman also feared that *Black Mountain Review* instead of representing a second front *vis-à-vis Origin*, was becoming a major opposition.

Creeley himself was worried about the loss of yet another contributing editor. About a month before the fight with Paul, Rexroth had requested that his name be removed from the BMR masthead and that the review print a statement to the effect that he had nothing to do with Martin Seymour-Smith's criticism of Roethke and Dylan Thomas in the first issue. He certainly did not believe in such spiteful truculence masquerading as criticism. Further, Roethke was, as the reviewer knew, a sick man. Did Creeley remember what Yvor Winters's review of *The Bridge* had done to Hart Crane? Otherwise, Rexroth found the magazine lively and interesting, though much too inbred – like everything Creeley, Olson, Jonathan Williams et al. did. Though Creeley disagreed with Rexroth's views on Thomas and Roethke, he was sorry to see him go. Rexroth "could get angry with good purpose, god knows," he told Layton.

Creeley's worries about the journal had long turned to outright paranoia. People were after his neck, or worse, not writing to him any more. He had sent out some forty-odd letters and not received a single answer. Even Olson hadn't written, let alone reported on how people responded to BMR #1. What was bugging people? Probably himself, Creeley concluded.

Waiting for letters that wouldn't arrive, he received an unexpected one from Renate Gerhardt. Contacts with Rainer, after so many of his projected visits to Lambesc and Majorca had come to nothing, had turned more and more elusive over recent months. A friend had seen Renate hitchhiking in a heavy rain to a nearby city where she had hoped to sell some of Rainer's scripts. She had said that Rainer went for long periods of time all but unable to speak, or that he'd sit by himself in the park, with Renate next to him, trying whenever he could to continue the multiple tasks he had undertaken. Now Renate wrote what seemed impossible to believe: Rainer was dead. Tired of fighting for things others took for granted, he had suffered a physical breakdown, then committed suicide.

Inevitably, Renate's letter brought back all Bob's memories of his troubled friendship with Rainer. How much affection and, at the same time, how much strife there had been between them! Rainer had been one of the few men he could love. In so many ways – age, family circumstance, towering ambition, self-destructive energy – Rainer had been like a disturbing double. Now that he was dead, Bob himself, selfishly, felt that much more afraid. He was in a blind, irrational fury, wishing somebody else than Rainer had died, or vowing vengeance on those who destroyed him. Some day, he wrote to Olson, he would get his hands on the throats of men who did this to those he loved and kill them.

Bob invited Renate to come stay with them and sent her $25 for immediate relief. Meanwhile, an attempt to write a poem in memoriam of Rainer came out so bitter and ugly, he tore it up. Clearly, Bob had reached one of his periodic low points. He hated going to Palma, found it near unendurable to walk down the street, hardly ever left his room. He kept wondering why he couldn't make it with those he loved.

Even the move to a very cheap, comfortable, and pleasant new house, overlooking the Mediterranean, only twenty minutes by trolley to Palma, brought him little relief from his loneliness. With Paul Blackburn and Robert Hellman gone, the only person left he could call a friend of sorts was decent and thoughtful Alastair Reid, a Scottish poet, essayist, and translator of Bob's age. As for Graves, whom he had finally come to like a lot, Bob never quite knew what to say to him. Meanwhile, Kenneth Rexroth, so Jonathan Williams reported from San Francisco, was calling Bob an "assassin" and spreading rumours that he was writing all the reviews for BMR himself.

Rexroth had a point, Creeley joked to Robert Duncan: he might end up writing not just the reviews but the poems for BMR as well. Already, he found himself writing an unnecessarily long review of Williams's *Selected Essays* just to fill five pages in the magazine. Things felt little better once contributions did arrive. His judgment had become so jaded that the sight of almost any poem was enough to make him wince. Was he getting old before his time? To solve part of these problems, he proposed that BMR be switched from quarterly to bi-annual publication, which Olson, after some resistance, agreed to.

Creeley's gradual estrangement from Williams and Pound further exacerbated his sense of isolation. Pound's Sophocles translation seemed to him very brittle, superficial in texture, in sum a complete disappointment. So was whatever he had seen of Pound's *Book of Odes*: he disliked their scramble of vocabularies as evident in a line like "Throw out the punks who falsify your news."

Williams's recent work as well showed flaws to bewilder the former disciple. Graves had pointed out certain linguistic incongruities in Williams's Theocritus translation. Also, Creeley had become wary of Williams's sense of measure. In Creeley's view, measure amounted to patterns that minor poets derived from their betters by way of perpetuating their own failure. For this he had found support in Elizabethan Sam Putnam's essay "On Proportion" (pointed out by Alastair Reid) as well as in certain lines by Thomas Campion that made Pound's sound like a church organ. In a more recent experiment (pointed out by Graves), people had tested the actual reading of poems with a seismograph, and to their horror, been unable to discover any demonstrable patterns whatsoever. Words were lumped together, lines ran into each other, the whole thing simply bobbled up and down. But Creeley loved it! No doubt, Graves was right in arguing that men's rhythms were essentially God given. Rhythms were as personal as skin, to be used as everyone could or would. By contrast, "measure" amounted to little else than a pedant's way of stealing what he couldn't manage.

Williams's *Selected Essays* turned out to be a disappointment for other reasons as well. The volume left out much that Creeley valued, like "With Rude Fingers Forced," Williams's attack on Eliot, while it included several pieces in which Williams, to Creeley's surprise, was found hobnobbing with men like Dylan Thomas, W.H. Auden, or Karl Shapiro.

A letter airing these complaints to Williams met with an unexpected reply. Williams deeply regretted having permitted the editor to make the actual selections. He was particularly ashamed for not insisting on the inclusion of "With Rude Fingers Forced," yielding to the argument that to attack Eliot would be in poor taste. It was a weakness of his to hide behind that sort of excuse and then regret it later.

As a result, half of what he had planned had been cut. Also, he had always had a tendency to consider much of what he thought and said as unimportant in the end. But that extent of modesty was stupid. As for the inclusion of "Karl Shapiro Is Right," he pleaded extenuating circumstances. At the time of writing the piece, Shapiro had struck him as a young poet worthy of support, only to disappoint him later. Otherwise, he'd be grateful if Creeley's review would dwell on what he found good in the book but mercilessly attack its author's faults. He was ashamed to reveal the person that he was, he wrote to Creeley.

Creeley's follow-up letter, broaching his disagreement with Williams's sense of measure, met with a different response altogether. Campion's verse, which Williams knew well, merely clinched his argument that without measure the line becomes chaotic. The relative or variable foot gave the key and measure with which the Greeks began it, the dance, one foot placed before the other.

In his reply, Creeley quoted from a long statement by Olson who had entered the fray in characteristically overbearing fashion, deciding that it was best to throw words like metre, measure, foot, and rhythm out of the window because they described a usage, not a fact of language. While endorsing Olson's view, Creeley added that, rather than measure, they needed some more general sense of the elements of poetic form. Otherwise, poets might end up meeting the fate of the man singing down on Houston Street who was kicked to death by some kids for not being able to answer their question as to why he was singing. But Williams had grown tired of the discussion, advising that they forget the whole thing. Probably they were in essential agreement and were merely employing different terminologies.

Meanwhile, Creeley hardly spared efforts trying to repair old friendships and create new ones. With Julie Eastman failing to help with distribution, Denise Levertov was called upon to take on part of the task. In return Creeley made a tentative offer to publish a book of her poems (a proposal that never materialized.) Dutifully, Denise went around New York placing BMR with diverse bookstores and newsstands. Territories outside Manhattan, Montreal, and San Francisco were largely desert anyway.

There was an opportunity for displaying generosity and forgiveness when Larry Bronfman wrote to Creeley about having become the innocent victim of a gossip campaign. Allegedly, Larry had offered a brutish criticism of a Levertov poem somewhere up in Maine where Larry had never been in his life. Bob duly wrote to Denise suggesting that both of them intercede on Larry's behalf. Turning to more serious and painful affairs, he also assured Dennie that he neither wished Paul Blackburn ill nor sought to boycott his work; he wondered, somewhat gratuitously, whether Paul still wanted Divers Press to bring out his volume of poems. Denise, with her well-known moral commitments and growing reputation as a poet, was a force to be reckoned with in the future, especially regarding such matters as all this nightmare business of friendship between men.

Bob was trying his best. Martin Seymour-Smith, considered a colossal shit a little over a year before, was suddenly remembered as someone whom Bob liked very much and who, as he assured Trocchi, had been a very good friend in an utterly perverse way. He told Cid Corman, another of his one-time confidants in unmasking Seymour-Smith's suspected perfidies, that he had never been able to stop either liking or respecting Martin.

Life on the domestic front was giving Bob further reasons for trying to rebuild his network of friendships. Coming back to Majorca had been a mistake, he decided. Past bitter arguments with Ann clicked in like clockwork, with Bob accusing her of letting the place go, and she retorting that writing was hardly enough of a contribution to the household. As early as 13 August 1953, he inquired to Olson about possibilities of returning to Black Mountain, insisting that if he were to be rehired, he would not "fuck off" on other things this time.

20

The Misogynists.

Around 5 November 1954 fate sent Creeley an unexpected visitor. Reading one of the man's books back in 1950, he had reacted with unmitigated disgust and horror. *The Flea of Sodom* struck him as stinking, vile, dead, and hopeless. One morning, the author of this bilious vilification suddenly turned up on the Creeleys' doorstep, early enough to find Bob and Ann still in bed. Tall, casually yet elegantly dressed, with an aquiline, obviously Jewish profile, a Chaplinesque (or Hitlerite) moustache, his sharply lined mouth and nostrils suggested contemptuous severity, the right, fiercely penetrating eye sizing up Bob, the other obviously blind. Or was he wearing one of those glass replacements Creeley had used years ago? Alex Trocchi had given him Creeley's address.

Edward Dahlberg was fifty-four when he introduced himself to twenty-eight year old Robert Creeley. "He stalks words, women, wisdom," Olson had said about Dahlberg. "This man can only, in withering tenacity, stalk after life and because he never reaches it stalk finally his own life." Dahlberg had been Olson's closest friend and mentor back in the 1930s and '40s, but unbridgeable differences of opinion as well as temperament caused them to quarrel, even to accuse each other of plagiarism.

Pound and Williams, Olson's one-time heroes, were "miscreants" to Dahlberg. Pound was an "artistic mountebank who puts Topeka and Telemachus together to make a canto," Williams a "baby doctor with the obituary satchel of pills." In a published review Dahlberg had called Williams "an enormous deceiver, not because he tells almost everything, but because he reveals almost nothing of fundamental importance to the spirit. Williams writes that he always has been a liar. But a man of sixty-eight is too old to lie … He has lost his true memory and has become a weathervane admirer … He has become mellow, which is another word for moldering."

To Creeley such comments were simply outrageous. And yet there was much about Dahlberg he liked: such as his calling T.S. Eliot "the beadle of aesthetics," Richard Aldington's and Witter Bynner's memoirs of D.H. Lawrence "two bickering gadfly books … written out of envy"; or himself that "sick nervous jew" or "base and whoring issue of Noah, Seth and Japheth." Also, he soon paid Bob the obvious compliment of calling him a "lonely young man with no symptoms of worldliness" – such as he had obviously been himself.

What a desolate, versatile, and uncompromising life Dahlberg had put behind him by the time he had reached Bob's age. He was the bastard son born to a mother of dubious repute and multiple professions such as barber, masseuse, and quack physician "who treated any and all ailments," particularly those afflicting prostitutes, with a "violet ray lamp." At one point in his childhood, he had refused to eat in protest against having to share his mother's affection with so many men. He brawled with the Italian neighbourhood boys who beat him black and blue; he was locked away in various orphanages meant to discipline his prematurely delinquent and rebellious behaviour; he spent his teenage *Wanderjahre* crisscrossing North America, jumping freight trains at forty miles an hour, getting lost in the Mojave desert. Six feet tall, yet withered to a mere hundred-and-ten pounds, he joined the u.s. Armed Forces during the final weeks of World War II, so as to be able to pay back debts; and finally he lost his left eye either by gouging it out with his rifle butt during practice or in a brawl with a comrade – something prevented this otherwise so confessional autobiographer from ever revealing the truth, even to one-eyed Creeley. In 1926 there was his precipitous marriage to Ruth Gross, his securing an out-of-state divorce two months later so as to be able to run off with Fanya Fass, and his getting into a furious argument with Fanya's mother which cost her two teeth and him a civil service job. After a widely publicized trial during which Fanya proved her unwavering loyalty to her lover, Dahlberg was given a ninety-day suspended sentence and ordered to make bond for $500 and keep the peace for six months.

Fame came to Dahlberg at the age of thirty with the publication of his novel *Bottom Dogs*, for which a reluctant D.H. Lawrence wrote an introduction that would haunt Dahlberg for the rest of his life. "It is a genuine book, as far as it goes, even if it is an objectionable one," Lawrence commented. "It is, in psychic disintegration, a good many stages ahead of *Point Counter Point...* It is, let us hope, a *ne plus ultra*. The next step is legal insanity, or just crime … The style seems to me excellent, fitting the matter. It is sheer bottom-dog style, the bottom-dog mind expressing itself direct, almost as if it barked … I don't want to read any more books like this. But I am glad to have read this one, just to know what is the last word in repulsive consciousness, in a state of repulsion." Advised to drop the preface from the novel's American edition, Dahlberg characteristically decided to include it in every one that would appear.

Just as he inflicted himself on others, he willingly suffered for his convictions. Still a communist in 1933, he went to check out the newly installed Nazi regime in Berlin, where his semi-rabbinical appearance – receding curly hair, dark-rimmed spectacles, nose over-hanging the small moustache – provoked the predictable storm-trooper violence. A bruised and frightened Dahlberg fled back to the u.s. to give testimony in the *Times*. He warned about what was happening and what lay ahead: the suppression of the German trade unions, the harassment of Jewish businessmen, and a censorship of the press so rigorous that the American newspaper reader, however ill-informed, knew more about conditions in Germany than most Germans.

Creeley's identification with the older man grew with every conversation. He too wanted to become "that very particular kind of American writer" who, like Dahlberg, devoid of any social privilege, had to make up a language particular to himself. Initially Dahlberg didn't realize Creeley was a follower of Olson. When he found out, he quickly decided to turn the young poet into a disciple of his own. What had Bob read? Pound and Williams, of course. How about the Bible, the Pre-Socratics, the Hindu, Chinese, and Japanese classics? Whatever his talent, a poet without learning would never become an author worth anyone's time. He lent Bob books and drew up lists for further reading which Bob, to his horror, lost the following day, a fact he never dared admit to. Yet he remembered the pre-Socratic philosophers, which he began studying immediately. He was all too glad to pick up on whatever Dahlberg had to offer. It got him out of the rut of the weeks since the fight with Blackburn; but also out of his goddamn ignorance about anything back of Chaucer.

Inevitably, Dahlberg met Graves. The first encounter seemed like a meeting of two Mack trucks. Creeley was amazed to observe how two men so obviously opposed to each other could so quickly hack out the brush, as it were, to see what each was up to. In *Do These Bones Live* Dahlberg had argued that Judas became a kind of "saint" for shouldering the guilt of carrying out Christ's behest to betray him, which Graves, in similar terms, had upheld in his most recent book, *The Nazarean Gospel Restored*. In an unusually generous mood, Dahlberg conceded that Graves had made a scholarly leap forward, even advising Creeley to read Graves's book. Obviously moved by the fact that this notoriously cantankerous man paid him such tribute, Graves gave Dahlberg a copy of the study with his marginal corrections. Otherwise neither of the two veterans had yielded an inch.

Thereafter Dahlberg became a frequent visitor to Graves and his wife, who were temporarily staying in downtown Palma on Calle Guillermo Massot. But the truce between the two was of short duration. Creeley soon had the pleasure of watching his new mentor act out some of the aggression he had so often felt towards Graves himself. Perhaps this will interest you, Graves told Dahlberg one morning, handing him a copy of *Punch* in which he had published an article. In response, Dahlberg slapped the journal on the table, saying: It's bad enough to publish in such a magazine, but to expect another man to read it is absolutely insufferable. Then he stomped out of Graves's house.

Put on his guard, Graves took the next opportunity to feign surprise at Dahlberg's lack of Greek. Never short of a retort, Dahlberg charged Graves with hiring others to do most of the scholarly work for his books. *The White Goddess* was a "farrago of blowsy polysyllables which neither quenches the soul nor delights a learned palate." Altogether, Graves was an "author for hire" writing "venal prose to finance his poetic interests." Clearly Dahlberg was capable of stirring up more trouble in less time than anyone Creeley had ever known, including himself. "I can't say I'm a peaceful man, etc., but he *never* gets tired," he wrote to Layton. "He fought with everyone, yesterday refused Graves' hand."

That happened at Bar Formentor, Palma's meeting place for artists and writers in the old part of town, where Creeley and Dahlberg had gone to talk.

It was one of those days when everyone Dahlberg chose to castigate suddenly appeared out of the blue. The second such person happened to be Graves who, after shaking hands all around, finally turned to Dahlberg to do the same. But Dahlberg refused him, making a little speech about how he had once been refused by Graves. The latter flipped and said, keep him, and took off. Dahlberg, undaunted, more than ever seemed to be in his element and for the rest of the time entertained Creeley with his diatribes against everyone imaginable.

Another person whom Dahlberg, to Bob's delight, sought out for his diatribes was Ann. Their meeting had meant hate at first sight for both. Most irritating to Ann was Dahlberg's pontifical manner, especially when, obviously to provoke her, he expatiated on his biblically embroidered hatred of women.

What nerve she had to dare contradict him when, rash and dogmatic, he threw out an offhand criticism of Bob's writing. Young woman, he told her, I've been reading and writing for a long time, and I don't have to read all the work to have a sense of what a writer is. The second night, as Dahlberg ranted about pederasts, Ann remonstrated again. He told the "young lady" that she simply knew nothing. Ann left the room, then came storming back in a towering rage to tell Dahlberg he was a homosexual. Rising to the occasion, he shouted back: Young woman, when your bones are moldering dust, mine will be carried through the streets by the cheering multitudes! Next he turned on Bob: What a disgrace! Didn't he know how to control his wife?

Never again, Ann decided, would that misogynist be allowed back into their house. So for several weeks the two men met in cafés or at Dahlberg's rented quarters. On the one hand, there was the fascination with a man in whom Bob saw himself as if in a distorting mirror, on the other, the wish just to get away from home. Bob's relationship with Ann – the infernal trull, as Dahlberg called her – was definitely nearing its end.

Another visitor to the island gave the *coup de grace* to whatever fondness and respect Bob still entertained for Ann. Robert Duncan, with his life companion, Jess Collins, arrived in Palma towards the end of March 1955. For a long time Creeley had entertained sharply divided feelings about the homosexual poet from San Francisco. While admiring his craft, he felt repulsed by his Byzantine pomposity, an ambivalence reinforced by Duncan's recent complaints about the articles on Patchen, Thomas, and Roethke in *BMR* #1. To diffuse the tensions of their first encounter, Creeley decided to entertain the newcomers with a story about some "cross-eyed son of a bitch," then suddenly realized, to his horror, Duncan was suffering from that condition. There was a moment of glacial silence, glumly reticent Jess worriedly watching his friend, who, however, did everything to put the blunderer at ease.

From then on Creeley's admiration for Duncan grew with every encounter. Rather unexpectedly, Duncan proved to be completely the friend he had never had in Majorca. In conversation he was like a stone on which to sharpen one's brain. Creeley felt more awake than he had in months. Reading *The Venice Poem*, he convinced himself of Duncan's greatness as a poet. Mainly, he admired Duncan's very careful clarity. Next to Olson, he'd never known anyone sharper. Definitely, Duncan would be counted in from now on as a member of the innermost group of those who "made it." These, after some reshuffling, included Creeley himself, Olson, Duncan, Layton, Blackburn, and, *mirabile dictu*, Denise Levertov, with Olson and Duncan holding pre-eminence as the most able. In more practical terms, Robert Duncan, along with Robert Hellman, would replace Kenneth Rexroth and Paul Blackburn as *BMR's* contributing editors.

Creeley's admiration for Duncan was mutual. Robert and Jess liked Bob very much indeed. Duncan was glad to have been quite sure of Bob's stories before meeting him instead of being won over to them by their author. At least temporarily, dear, dear Bob was granted the role of an attendant upon Duncan's soul journey on its way to the end. In another flight of mythologizing, Creeley was equated with Christ as he offered himself in the host. For so, Duncan argued, Bob offered himself to those of his short story readers who were properly engaged in their task.

Duncan felt less enthusiastic about Bob's wife. Ann, to him, was an embittered, stupid, obstinate, and pathetically vulnerable woman with a highly negative influence on her poet-husband. Bob's writing, he found to his horror, was submitted to her judgment. So were friends like Blackburn, Corman, Dahlberg, and, of course, himself. If it hadn't been for Ann, Bob probably would never have quarrelled with Paul. He advised Bob to write to Paul so as to get him back into the magazine, which Bob did. The result: Ann was outraged. As if Bob had promised to cut all contact with Paul forever.

Two further men, Black Mountain student Victor Kalos and painter John Altoon, played central roles in the break-up of Creeley's marriage. Altoon, whom Bob had briefly met in New York, arrived on the island at about the same time as Duncan. He found a house with a garage on the hill slope back of Creeley's Casa Martina. Here Bob would observe him battling with the wind that occasionally knocked over his easel, sending the canvas crashing into the gravel; or watch him paint with a peculiar kind of substance chosen, it seemed, out of an inveterate habit of making things difficult for himself. "It was an incredible sight, these piles of dry pigment, then the sizable can of linseed oil, then John, his eyes on the canvas, reaching out with his free hand to get hold of the oil which he'd pour, still without really looking, on one or more of the piles. Then, with his brush he'd sop some of it up, and off he'd go – remarkably, altogether articulate."

John was an energetic man in every sense. Passing through Copenhagen, he had found it to be the new Sodom. The more Bob got to know John, the more he liked him. With Robert and Jess beginning to seem a little over-intellectual and stand-offish, Altoon gradually replaced Duncan as the person Bob felt truly akin to. As soon as *BMR* #5 was in print, the two would go to Paris, they decided.

By mid-May, they were on their way. Bob found John was the ideal travelling companion: a complex person and storyteller full of wit and humour, even when talking about the grimmer aspects of his life. And unquestionably John's life had been grim and traumatic, his mother dying of cancer while he was growing up, himself turning semi-delinquent, "always in some trouble or other, cutting school, hanging out, testing the edges." Meanwhile, Altoon had begun copying the covers of magazines, the older members of the family admiringly looking over his shoulder. John clearly had talent. Perhaps he would become a successful commercial artist one day. But then there was the other John, of a smouldering, volcanic energy, self-destructive, hanging out with an L.A. gang searching for James Dean-like, gratuitous challenges, so dear to Bob's own sensibility: "like riding motorcycles no hands at speeds exceeding 100 m.p.h., or driving souped-up cars at like speeds, blindfolded." No wonder, Bob was "a very attentive listener," prepared to allow for the necessary suspension of disbelief.

In Paris, Bob found further distractions from memories of home. He had a chance to observe the *Paris Review* editors, for the most part shyly aggressive young men of good breeding with their wives and children, making a kind of post–F. Scott Fitzgerald scene. More to his liking was the *Merlin* gang, including Alex Trocchi, American translator Austryn Wainhouse, Patrick Bowles, who translated the first of Beckett's French novels into English, and Richard Seaver, later an editor for Grove Press. Trocchi and his friends virtually checked the passenger lists of arriving boats to see what available American women might be conned into putting money into *Merlin*; or they held meetings to decide who amongst them might be most attractive to this or the other of the newly arrived ladies.

Equally congenial was Christopher Logue, who to Bob looked so English he seemed like the Mad Hatter in *Alice and Wonderland*. His first words, yelled at Bob in a noisy Paris café, were: Tell me about Olson. Later, Logue showed Bob his Pound books, finally giving him a carbon he had made of the master's Cavalcanti translations as a farewell present.

On the train back to Majorca, he had a disturbing dream about things happening in his absence. And sure enough, Ann met him in Barcelona, to Bob's surprise, in the company of Victor Kalos, newly arrived from New York. As agreed beforehand, Ann and Bob went on towards Cordoba, Victor trailing behind. They got as far as Madrid where Creeley found out that Victor and Ann had had an affair.

Apart from feeling tired, sick, beat, fucked up, and intent on his own humiliation, Bob predictably reacted with plain anger. The whole thing was so ugly, so deeply cheap, cheap, cheap, he hated the damn stain of it and felt tempted to smash his goddamn typewriter. Moral indignation provided a less self-destructive relief. It made him aware of certain roots he had largely treated with either contempt or at least neglect so far. He'd never had a clearer sense of what was in him as he did then, he explained to Olson, i.e., New England, all of it, which by God was sheer physical *joy*. That was on 5 July, just under a week before his departure for North America.

Pragmatic, especially in adversity, Creeley had made sure to be welcomed back at Black Mountain before revealing to Olson what had happened. Olson was sworn into secrecy about the "bitter" details;

Creeley has kept similar secrecy regarding a poem he wrote about his marriage breakdown and sent to Olson on 5 July 1955 with two others. Entitled "A Commentary," it is a numerological conundrum playing on one, two, and three while also, so Creeley thought, telling what happened between his wife, himself, and one more.

In spite of Creeley's efforts to keep things under wraps, news of Ann's affair quickly became a hotly debated gossip item in Palma's artistic community. Via visitors from abroad, it also spread to foreign lands. Ann, Duncan explained to Levertov, had slept with Victor mainly to punish Bob. Worse, she had demoralized herself in the process. Since Bob's departure, the household had turned into a nighmare, with Ann neglecting, misusing, even abusing her kids. One visit there when she was away from home confirmed Duncan's hostile feelings towards her. Her abandoned children seemed busy re-enacting the past violence and melodrama of the Creeley household. Playfulness suddenly turned into blows and tears. Lying on the floor, David got kicked in the head by Tom, Duncan trying to ward off further acts of savagery. Little Charlotte looked like an abandoned child, her hair uncombed, the face besmudged, a sty growing on one eye.

For all his faults, Creeley, once free of Ann, might yet advance to self-knowledge and, however belatedly, to the holy precincts of parenthood and of marriage, Duncan pontificated. Meanwhile, Ann's chances of reaching comparable heights of self-realization and domestic bliss looked as dim to him as Madame Bovary's. In sleeping with Victor, she had wanted freedom, not in order to find herself but so as to lead a life in which Bob could no longer play a part.

Playing the councillor close to dear, dear Robert's heart, Duncan sent him running accounts of Ann's parental misdemeanours and adulterous tomfooleries. She acted like an older sister rather than real mother to her children, slapping them around, demanding their loyalty, accusing David of being a thief for taking some of her money in order to buy a friend a pair of shoes. To her new lover John Altoon, she played the anti-muse, turning him against his art, once again using a rival to revenge herself on Bob. Admittedly, Duncan had never loved Ann the way he did Bob. But such lack of affection had turned into sheer loathing, hatred, and outrage after what he had witnessed recently: the falseness and meanness of things between her, John, and the children, the derelict shambles of the rooms they lived in. Duncan got so worked up he had a showdown with Ann over her accusing Dave of being a thief.

Duncan probably exaggerated. At the beginning of October Ann and the children came to see Robert and Jess in Bañalbufar, and, to the two men's surprise, the children looked fine. Charlotte was lovely and radiant as ever. Tom, while Duncan was writing to Creeley, sat at a small table cutting out paper designs with great seriousness and attention. Even David, at age seven the worst affected by the adult crises, had shed the brooding insecurity of two months earlier and once again went about his concerns of boyhood. The only person left out of the picture was the mother. The self-appointed reporter on the ongoing tribulations of the fatherless Creeley household wasted no effort on trying to guess at the extent to which Ann might be to thank for the unexpectedly wholesome state of her allegedly maltreated children.

Robert Creeley's parents; photograph from
original portrait: Ekbert Faas.

Bob Creeley as violinist.
Courtesy of Ann MacKinnon.

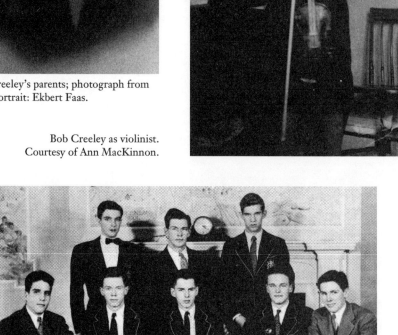

Robert "Whitney" Creeley (middle front row) as chief member of the board
responsible for the publication of *The Dial*, *The Yearbook*, and *The Bull*. Holderness
School Yearbook, 1943. (See page 25.)
Courtesy of Holderness School, near Plymouth, New Hampshire.

From left to right: Bob's sister Helen, his mother, Bob, a friend, and Aunt Bernice.
Courtesy of Ann MacKinnon.

In the American Field Service, 1945.
Courtesy of Ann MacKinnon.

Robert Creeley, ca. 1946-47.
Courtesy of Ann MacKinnon.

From left to right: Race Newton, Mary Ann Bottomly
("Wuzza"), and Buddy Berlin.
Courtesy of Ann MacKinnon.

Denise Levertov and her husband, Mitch Goodman.
Courtesy of Ann MacKinnon.

From left to right: David, Ann, Ashley Bryan, and Thomas in Aix-en-Provence, ca. 1951.
Courtesy of Ann MacKinnon.

Cid Corman, 1981.
Photograph: Ekbert Faas.

René Laubies.
Courtesy of Ann MacKinnon.

Rainer and Renate Gerhardt.
Courtesy of Ann MacKinnon.

Martin Seymour-Smith.
Courtesy of Ann MacKinnon.

Robert Graves with Martin Seymour-Smith at a Palma bullfight in 1952.
Courtesy of Martin Seymour-Smith, *Robert Graves: His Life and Work*.

Bob and David sailing. (See page 126.)
Courtesy of Ann MacKinnon.

Bob and Thomas transporting their sailing boat on the roof of their 1928 Peugeot.
Courtesy of Ann MacKinnon.

Ann Creeley, ca. 1951.
Courtesy of Ann MacKinnon.

21

Black Mountain, 1955.

To the locals, Black Mountain College was fast becoming a ghost town. Its few surviving occupants, people whispered, were headed by a giant stalking the roads at night. A local redneck eager to verify the rumours brought back stories that only worsened the college's reputation. Rector-designate Charles Olson, taunted beyond endurance, lost his temper, socked the fellow, and apparently broke his jaw.

The campus's growing desolation attracted eccentrics, freaks, and psychotics, offering them a refuge and emotional correlative. "Quail and wild mountain aster [Olson's biographer writes] were repossessing the college grounds. Mountain lions were said to lurk the winter hills, foxes ran the main road and rattlesnakes nested in the bushes along its margins; copperheads and kudzu vines were infiltrating the foundations of the cottages." Even the children had started to emulate their atavistic surroundings. One winter day Olson's daughter, Katie, and Huss's son, David, were found naked in the snow on top of a coal heap. One armed with a pitchfork, the other with a rake, they were trading curses "that might have come out of an uncensored gangster movie." On another occasion, a guest found Katie holding a dead mouse. The "fucking owl did it," Olson's daughter explained.

There was plenty of natural beauty, but the college's remaining inhabitants couldn't have cared less. According to newcomer Don Mixon, they might as well have lived in downtown Manhattan. A few took a downright hostile attitude towards their surroundings. One painter covered up the windows of his studio because he found the view distracting. Two others spent an entire night whitewashing tree leaves.

Others took things out on themselves. Michael Rumaker slashed his wrists. Robert Hellman, after breaking up with his wife, overdosed on sleeping pills. Olson, after temporarily separating from Connie and fathering a son with his new lover, Betty Kaiser, went into isolation at Jalo house above Meadows Inn. He refused to meet with his students directly, communicating with only a few of them via the school mailboxes. "A Bibliography on America for Ed Dorn," which reached the addressee one morning at breakfast, was one of the results.

Returning to Black Mountain in July of 1955, Creeley found its general atmosphere of desperation surprisingly congenial, almost useful. Much here was clearly in tune with his own frustrations and confusions. Olson seemed stuck in an inchoate state of bewilderment about being involved with two women. Asked for his advice, Creeley passed. He hardly knew how to help himself. Methods he unsuccessfully tried along these lines included talking off pressures, parading his miseries, and bewildering others. He'd tell whoever could be buttonholed to listen about the most intimate details of his breakup with Ann. "He would look at you, his eye glaring and watering, a bit mad, but coaxing the sympathy out of you, as he shook his head in disgust, his brow wrinkling in bewilderment. 'Can you imagine a woman saying *that* to her husband?'"

Also there was dope and booze, Creeley doggedly walking the three odd miles down to Ma Peak's Tavern to get drunk, often becoming oblivious of everything including his teaching. Luckily, rescue was at hand. Taciturn Grey Stone, a lanky painting student from Tennessee, would pack Creeley into his pickup truck and then hand-deliver him to his classroom, saying: Now, teach!

Creeley took his miseries out on others. "He was a real genius at taking the skin off somebody, word by word." A female witness testifies to the red-hot fury he could provoke by his needling. Taunted by him, she smilingly moved her lighted cigarette directly towards his one good eye. The incident was a rare exception: Creeley drew back. Most people, like Michael Rumaker, were unable to stand up to him. One day in class, Creeley just sat in his chair under the windows of the Reading Room, "stiffly, acidly drunk," then rose to his feet and walked up to his students, one by one, providing each with a "quietly vicious and menacing appraisal" of their "shortcomings as human beings and hopeless lack of abilities as writers." To Rumaker, Creeley sneered: What's the matter, Rumaker, taking too many baths?

A similar needling session outside class provoked an accident that marks the nadir of Black Mountain College's bleakest period since its opening in 1933.

As one of the four men directly involved in the event, Creeley, a few days later, described himself as a passenger in a car being driven into a house at forty miles an hour. The result: a twisted shoulder, a bang on the nose, and an unforgettable "view" of a house rushing out to meet them. Somewhat like a Triumph of the Home, at that. The car was a complete wreck, the house without a dent. Among the human casualties, Jorge Fick, though he had occupied the death seat, was hurt least of all. Tom Field, who'd been driving, dislocated a hip. Dan Rice, who, together with Creeley, had occupied the back seat, had fractured a vertebra.

Michael Rumaker was sitting on the wooden front steps near the exterior fieldstone chimney of Meadows Inn as the fully loaded Buick sedan came racing towards him through the dark. He heard voices from inside the car, one hollering: Whatta ya doing man? Hey, Tom; another, Tom's own, screaming: If this is what you want, you're getting it. Jumping inside the house, Michael heard the "sickening punch of metal tangling against stone" in a "crunching impact that shook the entire house from the cellar up." He gradually recognized the victims amidst "the steam and smoke swirling up in the fractured beams of the headlights:" Jorge, his pallid face even whiter than usual, stumbling about, clasping and unclasping his hands to his head; Creeley, inside the car "fumbling awkwardly around Dan, who seemed unconscious, his head twitching from side to side, his face ashen and deathlike;" Tom, "slumped forward, his glazed eyes staring out the windshield, his face red and glistening, muttering to himself: I told them to stop – I told them I'd do it – I told them – ."

Told them to stop what? Once again, there are different versions. According to one, the decisive remark to make Tom race the Buick and its four passengers towards the fieldstone chimney and possible death was Dan's saying something to the effect that Tom had cheated death again. In fact, Tom's hitting the gas pedal in response had been so sudden that Dan who, along with Hellman, was being dropped off at Black Wharf, was scooped back into the back seat.

But a single such remark could hardly have caused the murderous and suicidal fury it unleashed. What did was a merciless barrage of taunts to which Tom had been subjected by the others after leaving the tavern. In this Creeley had played the ringleader, "going on and on in his soft, implacable way about how Tom had to give up the absurd pretense that he was incompetent."

Some time after, the state troopers arrived, wearing Smokey the Bear hats, grey-blue uniforms with shiny buttons, leather belts weighed down with gun holsters and bullets. They took photographs of the Buick "slammed up against the chimney like a crushed accordion." To the Black Mountaineers looking on, it was an unusual sight. During the McCarthy era, they had gotten used to the occasional button-down, insurance salesman-type FBI agent, not the police.

They had agreed upon what to say. Tom, though in severe pain, played his role like a hero. So far, he had held the lowest rung in the college's merciless macho pecking order. But suddenly he had proven himself. He had risked death and lived to laugh about it, had shown that he was one of the men. He told the state troopers that the gas pedal had gotten stuck as he had driven it from Black Wharf towards Meadows Inn – an implausible story, since the incline between the two buildings would have allowed him to simply roll the car with next to no acceleration at all.

The injured were taken to the Veterans' Hospital in Swannanoa. "Tom it turned out had a broken leg and Creeley came out of it with a severely wrenched shoulder, but didn't require hospitalization. Dan, the unluckiest, had his back badly dislocated and would be in the hospital for a longer period of time, and in a back brace even longer after that."

If Creeley's behaviour leading up to the accident struck people as demonic, what followed it gave them reason to doubt his sanity. Come to visit Dan in hospital, Rumaker suddenly found his hand seized by Creeley, who was already there. He was forced to sit next to him on the edge of the bed. His one eye riveted on the captive, Creeley began to talk in his "harsh quick voice," not about the accident but about himself and his wife, in a "nonstoppable rush of words," his hands squeezing Rumaker's "tighter and tighter." Tears began to trickle down his cheeks, Creeley letting them run instead of mopping them up with his handkerchief, his words still pouring out of him in a "low rasping torrent" sounding as if he was choking with rage, fear, and hurt. He finally asked Rumaker for forgiveness. You're a lovely man, Mike, Tom is a lovely man – they were all lovely men.

Confused, dismayed, even insane as Creeley struck others, he was hardly suicidal like Hellman or Rumaker. The previous month had seen a pathetic number and variety of such attempts "to make it," Bob laconically reported to Duncan: using sleeping pills, slashing wrists, and crashing the car. The mere thought of committing suicide and then failing brought on his absolute horror of the ridiculous, he added. His own dilemma invariably took on a different cast. For plagued as he was by intense confusions day by day, he had learnt how to live in and with them.

Others like Tom Field – usually such a mild man – were increasingly drawn into the maelstrom of recklessness that had become Creeley's natural habitat. Another victim was newcomer Ed Dorn, a man eaten up with guilt and pride, as Creeley remarked in another letter to Duncan. Though married to a seemingly lovely and decent woman, the poor devil had no money to support her, the two kids she had brought from a former marriage, or the third they had had themselves. Now Bob was appointed his examiner. Among the poems he had submitted, one was dedicated "To Robert Creeley, a plea to his put out eye." It seemed he had a disturbing effect on Dorn, Creeley remarked.

It would soon become worse. Within days of the car accident, Creeley was sleeping with Ed's wife. It all happened thanks to his pushing and behaving in an admittedly very ugly way, Creeley conceded. He was never a hero. Meanwhile, he had obviously managed to improve upon the skills acquired in taking Cynthia away from Dan. He was getting on better with both Ed and Helene than previously, he found once the affair was over. Ed had a wild head, and she was okay too. Wow.

Trips to New York brought further distractions of a similar kind. One night spent in the company of Peter Stander, Bob ended up in bed with a girl in a posh apartment on West End Avenue, people walking in and out of the room as though the lovers weren't there. Or there were the nights spent at the Cedar Bar. Here Bob listened to Franz Kline tell stories, admiring how the painter could "locate the most articulate senses of human reality in seemingly casual conversation." When friend Earl Kerkham was there to keep Kline company, the two would weave their "endless variations ... on the 'It only hurts when I smile' saga" which struck Creeley as *the* "instance of initial story telling."

A more sobering, benignly paternal influence came from Willem de Kooning. A man of just fifty who had acquired fame and prosperity, de Kooning had retained his Bohemian insouciance, carrying a wad of bills in his pocket thick enough to "choke a horse," Bob observed admiringly. De Kooning might sneak Bob and his friends into an opening at Janis's, but he would not let them "off the hook of [their] pretensions, bullshit, faking, laziness, you name it." He'd "demolish the whole Black Mountain *mystique*" with an offhand comment. The only trouble with Black Mountain is that if you go there, they want to give it to you, he commented.

Creeley's most intimate contact with the painter occurred one evening when de Kooning was feeling depressed. Mutual friends suggested that Bob have a drink with him and keep him company. The two ended up in de Kooning's "meticulously shipshape apartment" on 10th Street "entirely occupied by his stuff for painting except for the cot and small place to cook." Staring at the paintings on the walls and another still fresh on the easel, Creeley "felt like being where we were all first made, so to speak." Then he figured de Kooning must have fallen asleep, "because he was now fully out on the bed, but one extraordinarily valuable leg had not made it, and was off the near side, looking very uncomfortable. So with intensively deliberate care, I got a hold on it, and tried to lift it so as to place it alongside the other, on the bed. Then, for whatever reason, I looked up at his face – to find that he'd been watching me all the time, with a lovely, wry smile."

Creeley's relations with another famous painter had an altogether less paternalistic opening. This happened at the Cedar Bar after Bob had left his friends' corner booth to knock back a quick one at the counter. Suddenly a very solid man came in, dominating the place with his intensity. For a person as territorially minded as Creeley, even the way the intruder placed his glass on the bar became a provocation. Before either man knew what was happening, both "were swinging at each other." Characteristically, their fury didn't abate until both found a joint new target in one of the owners, vaulting over the bar to separate the combatants. "Do you guys know each other?" the man asked, and since they didn't, introduced them. Robert Creeley – Jackson Pollock. "We were instantly very friendly," Creeley remembered in 1967. "I was showing pictures of my children and he was saying 'I'm their godfather.'"

For all his tough-mindedness, Creeley felt more and more confused. After another drunken night he had crashed at Julie's, sitting on the edge of her bed, holding her but refused the full physical contact he craved. Instead, he had to content himself with whatever non-sexual magic the witch from El Paso might weave. Once on their way to see Cocteau's *Blood of a Poet*, both passed a lady wheeling along a large baby carriage with inside it a fat little boy holding two cards. As Bob turned around to look, he recognized one card: the four of hearts. A little later he found to his amazement the sinister role the same card played in the film. A woman asks a man if he has the four of hearts, for otherwise he is doomed. He hands the card to her, then shoots himself.

The strange coincidences that happened in Julie's company never stopped. Nor did Bob's eagerness to provoke his evil fate. He felt compelled to cut cards, first in the company of Dan and a friend, then, another three times upon his return to Black Mountain. The result: the four of hearts on all four occasions. They want you to land on all fours, Olson commented.

Creeley made light of the matter, but to Robert Duncan he confessed to a sense of dread that had long weighed on him. Again and again, he felt signs coming to him with the same terrifying insistence with which, on the train from Paris, he had foreseen that Ann, in his absence, had had an affair. And how strange Ann's lover Victor had seemed when Bob saw him again in New York, ugly and heavy like synthetic wood. Vacuum Victor. Bob was making life very hard for him, Victor had told Bob. He was making him lose his friends. As if Bob had wronged him, not the other way around. Gradually the very sky above Bob began to look treacherous.

Another seemingly fated encounter, so hopeful at first, ended in similarly disconcerting fashion. Bob and a friend named Joy Aiken, both on their way back to Black Mountain, were thirty or forty miles out into the New Jersey Turnpike when one of the car's connecting rods broke. Bob left Joy to take care of the car, phoned some Manhattan friends from a neighbouring garage, then hitched a ride straight back to 8th Avenue and 18th Street. From there he walked the remaining three blocks to the Goodmans', where he'd been staying in Mitch's workroom, then went strolling around Manhattan. Since he had already said goodbye to everyone, it would have been too embarrassing to visit people.

Fate decided otherwise. Once returned to Mitch's apartment, he found Joel Oppenheimer had called. Joy was at Joel's place, desperately trying to find Bob. He had forgotten to return the car keys to her. So Bob rushed over to Joel's apartment on 236 West 10th Street. Shortly after, in walked Cynthia. Creeley had been apprehensive about such a reunion. Would they have anything left to say to each other?

But seeing Cynthia so happy and seemingly oblivious of all the past bitterness between them changed all that. Trading joint happy memories, Bob realized he still loved her. Somehow she made him come alive again, even feel he could walk through walls. The next morning she had to go back to where she was staying. So Bob, with much regret, kissed her goodbye, for some time watching the back of the bus taking her across Manhattan. For better or worse, he was used to seeing things go away, he mused to a mutual friend, Fielding Dawson, in an unusually sentimental tone.

Perhaps Cynthia might come to live with him at Black Mountain, Bob thought. Yet to her, things looked altogether different. Talking to her former poet-lover through an entire night had been one thing; the prospect of once again sharing her life with this bar-stool-throwing and knife-brandishing person was quite another. Creeley sent her letters with poems and collages, but Cynthia chose to ignore them. When she finally did reply, the letter was so ugly that Bob was left wondering if it came from a different woman. She told him about being a terrible drunk. She was too horribly involved with people in New York to dare go back there, she confessed. Instead, she was planning to go to California to marry the proprietor of a fashionable liquor store, she joked.

Meanwhile, she said almost nothing about her relationship with Bob. Sure, she loved him, though less so his letters, especially one received in late November, the saddest one he had ever written her, full of this death business. At the same time she continued to be afraid of him. Hence she would write drunken, slobbish letters to him at night, then flush them down the toilet the next morning. She was even afraid to say that she loved him. But what she feared most were his fits of violence.

While her former demon lover kept planning their future together, she put more and more distance between them: St Louis, New Orleans, finally Vera Cruz, in Mexico. Sure, in this day and age such distances meant little. A plane was very fast. Should they make a plan, she wondered teasingly. Bob used to be so good at planning things! In early January she wrote him from Vera Cruz. Bob phoned the airlines to book a ticket but found he was short seventy dollars. Afterwards he quickly settled back into his by now habitual routine of getting drunk and bugging people. The following day, he, as ever, taught his class, this time about commas, as it turned out.

A tentative affair with a twenty-two year old student from Canada provided comic relief but little else. Even before it started, Bob caricatured the girl in several letters to friends. She was a painter, pardon the expression. Bob didn't dare look. She seemed about eight feet tall, like an overgrown, good-natured Dane threatening to push him over at any moment. A true daughter of the Empire. Wait another ten years and she would be everyone's matron. Trying to sleep with her had been something like a mismanaged construction project. Lots of laughter, but no sex. Bob simply couldn't. Hence the two ill-matched would-be lovers decided to continue their amours in a strictly platonic fashion, Bob's blond admirer lying in bed, he sitting on the edge of it, reading "The Gold Diggers" and "The Boat" to her and feeling pompously good. Less reassuring was the girl's telling him that no woman could ever live with him, or even be in his life. Who the hell was he, Creeley wondered.

He had more to wonder about than that; the hideous matrimonial war during the past summer had finally hit home. Why did things with Julie not work out? He most likely bugged her finally. He got so goddamn fumbling and wanting, or pushy, without ever knowing how to say things. At the same time, he was perhaps the most niggardly man possible as a lover, he confessed to Duncan. Even after things had gotten entirely hopeless, he could not let go. More generally, he felt confused, tired, disorganized, bored, or amazed at how quickly things disintegrated into little bits. Perhaps he was a mere creature in a story that was gradually falling apart.

How desperately he wanted to take hold again, and yet how rootless he felt: drinking too much, falling on his face like a Bowery bum, cutting himself above the eyebrow and hurting the shoulder he had previously injured in the car crash. He had come to loathe it all. The staggering about with arrows protruding, the moaning, the confessing himself with its insistence on "I" that came from these present confusions. Or the ugliness of taking the rage he felt over Cynthia out on poor Tom Field. Why else would he have hit Tom? Simply because Tom had asked Bob to turn down his phonograph? How he wished he could have gotten his goddamn hands on faraway Cynthia instead! But in lieu of that there would just be another drunken, ugly letter teasing him about joining her in Mexico, even offering to help him with the fare. God how she provoked him, Bob groaned.

Yet there was much that would have caused him real joy under different circumstances: like the appearance of *All That Is Lovely in Men* or Jonathan Williams's photograph of Dan Rice just peeping out of a large barrel and of Creeley sitting on an uprooted toilet bowl. Yet nothing now brought him satisfaction. His poems merely revealed to him what he seemed almost completely unaware of otherwise; the photograph – showing his index finger pushing up wrinkles above the cheekbone, the sidewise face looking strangely introverted – struck him as equally disconcerting. Never had he seen himself look more oddly serious.

Most of all, he was starting to feel alienated from himself. Staring at his face in a bathroom mirror one night in a bar, he saw someone so monstrous he feared the image might haunt him to his dying day: his one eye surrounded by concentric circles of fine deep wrinkles. Suddenly the eye started moving to the centre of his right cheek, the wrinkles spreading all over his face. Had he been smoking dope or drinking too much? He couldn't remember having done either. Suddenly, the face smiled, the wrinkles deepening into a grimace that kept him petrified by its nightmarish stare. He tried in vain to break the spell. Thank God he was alone. That obviously was his real face, gathered together from its several masks. Finally he tore himself free and rejoined his friends.

Clearly it was also time to tear himself free from whatever had been building up over recent months. Rather than stare at monster images of himself, he should look out the window of a bus heading west. Yet before he could do that, a number of mundane problems had to be taken care of.

22

Albuquerque, 1956.

One thing he'd have to resolve was the business with Rock Pool Farm. The Creeleys had paid $5,000 towards buying the place, but even before moving to France nearly five years before, they had abandoned that plan. Now they wanted their money back.

At first, owner Bill Gordon seemed ready to settle out of court – but hardly for lack of nerve. An eccentric, speculator, self-made man, and author in his own right, he was more than ready to go to trial. If nothing else, it would afford him an experience he'd never had. Such playfulness turned belligerence after Gordon consulted with John Cheney, an industrial designer who had at one time wanted to turn Rock Pool Farm into an art centre. That plan had folded when Cheney visited the place shortly after the Creeleys' departure. What he found had been anything but encouraging: doors taken off the hinges, window panes broken, the few remaining pieces of furniture severely damaged, walls and ceilings in disrepair, the plumbing plugged or otherwise nonfunctional.

What in God's name had the Creeleys been doing here? The place reeked with animal odour; doors and frames had been gnawed at. An upstairs closet, to all evidence, had housed an unspecified beast, a bedroom been used to keep fowl in, and most other rooms, though primarily inhabited by humans, looked as if they'd been frequented by animals as well.

Encouraged by Cheney's written testimony, Gordon now argued that the damage the Creeleys and their animal park had done to Rock Pool Farm was in excess of the $5,000 they had laid out towards buying it. The hearing would be in late January 1956. Bob and Ann were advised to prepare statements as to the condition of Rock Pool Farm when they had moved in and when they had left it.

For Creeley such worries were dwarfed by others regarding Ann. When, how, and under what circumstances would she divorce him? With

Ann not writing, his impatience grew by bounds. He hated that deep ugliness of silence which hurt like nothing else, always, he complained to
Olson.

Suddenly, there she was in person, newly arrived in New York by boat
from France. Creeley fictionalized their reunion in his short story "The
Book":

"Don't," she was saying, and she was crying. "I don't want to go through it all
again. I can't tell you more. I don't know more. There isn't any more to tell."
Explain. I was raped on the boat, not raped but like that. I lost a thousand dollars in a purse, on the train. I bought a lot of Italian blouses. I do what I want
to, now.

Wearing new clothes, she seemed like someone he had never met before.
They had become very separate from each other, Bob realized.

Luck, which had so often favoured him, did not abandon him now. The
Rock Pool Farm affair was settled out of court. What's more, Ann let Bob
have the refund, even though the original $5,000 dollars they had paid
Gordon had all come out of her pocket. Next, she single-handedly obtained an out-of-state divorce by going to Alabama, paying for it as well.
She even offered Bob an interim loan in case the refund was not forthcoming quickly enough.

Otherwise, she was glad things were going so well for Bob. She reported to him on seeing off Olson and Betty Kaiser in New York (their
car had to be pushed, but they looked happy!). She confessed to not having hit it off with Victor Kalos when they had met again. She mentioned
writing a story not worth copying. Give my love to Buddy and Mary Ann,
she concluded. Though not to Cynthia – for form's sake. She hoped Bob
would have a very good trip out West.

Creeley's response was less generous. Apart from the fictionalized portrait he drew of Ann (alias Joan) in *The Island*, there is a more direct one
in his 1974 "On the Road: Notes on Artists & Poets, 1950–1965." The
piece describes one of their final encounters. He and Ann were walking
along 8th Street in New York not far from the Cedar Bar when they
bumped into Philip Guston. Creeley had recently met the painter
through Franz Kline and found him "a deeply generous and articulate
man." What followed, according to "On the Road," seems odd to say the
least.

For years Ann had supported Creeley financially. She had seen him
through his various crises as a writer, every inch the admiring and supportive wife. She had shared his diverse enthusiasms for other poets and
artists. However, more recently, Creeley claimed, she had become suspi-

cious of what she felt were the "true incompetences of [his] various heroes." William Carlos Williams wrote the way he did, for instance, because he couldn't rhyme. Franz Kline painted the way he did because he couldn't draw. Now here was another of these charlatans "she could physically confront, and she didn't waste any time about it."

What happened? Guston took Bob and Ann to a newly opened restaurant which to the men's delight offered free *hors d'oeuvres*. There's no mention of Ann's reaction. But once they were seated, "she let him have it." How, painting the way he did, did Guston know when a painting was finished? she asked him. Guston gave a clear and open answer to this, one might say, equally clear and reasonable question: "Given the field of the painting, so to speak, given what might energize it as mass, line, color, etc. – when he came to that point where any further act would be experienced as a diminishment of that tension (when there was nothing more to *do*, in short), that was when he felt the painting was finished."

Guston's explanation, if one can trust Creeley's memory, seems as plausible as any put forward by painters and poets of their generation. Ann "let the matter rest." But deep down, so Creeley convinced himself, she knew otherwise. Far from accepting Guston's explanation, she "felt almost complacently dissatisfied." Creeley even claims to remember (at an almost twenty year distance) what she actually thought on the occasion: "He doesn't know what he is doing – he's just fooling around!" Ann, "like so many others then and now, did feel that there must be an intention factually outside the work itself, something to be symbolized there, some content elsewise in mind there expressed, as they say. But that a *process* – again to emphasize it – might be felt and acted upon as crucial in itself she had not considered. So a statement such as Olson's 'We do what we know before we know what we do' would be only a meaningless conundrum at best. I guess she thought we were all dumb."

But at least there was little to fear from Ann regarding support payments for herself and the children. Bob had neither a job nor money, but under the law this did not exempt him from these obligations. Given the conditions of his Alabama divorce, he might at any point be ordered to pay out sums he didn't have and hence get caught under the uniform support law. To lawyer Edes, who had represented Ann and Bob during the Rock Pool Farm affair, that danger was real enough to make him want to scare his client by explaining what could happen. But Bob wasn't worried, and he was right.

So he was free at last, and on 13 February 1956 boarded the bus to Albuquerque, New Mexico.

For some time he had had a standing invitation from Buddy and Wuzza to stay at their home for as long as he wished. Buddy, now manager of an

Imported Motors, Inc. dealership on 610 Central SE, even offered to send Bob a hundred dollars should he need it to make the trip. The town itself, seat of all atomic and radioactive culture, Buddy had warned, was hardly an ideal habitat. But with Race Newton now living in Albuquerque as well, it might turn out like old times. Buddy said Race had become an incurable drunk whose endless wining was starting to melt his brain. But from recent contacts in New York, Bob knew that even countless booze-ups hadn't robbed Race of his inimitable deadpan humour.

As Bob stared out of the Trailway bus and watched the unfolding of the North American continent, other pleasant prospects lingered on his mind. Perhaps the Guggenheim Foundation would award him the grant he had applied for. Referee William Carlos Williams had put him first on his list of four, all of them close friends. Another referee, Robert Duncan, had spoken of his genius. What was most important to him, Duncan wrote to the Foundation, was that in Creeley's work, shaping and disturbing, was a genius of his time. Writing that vitally influenced the speech of others was rare indeed, and Creeley's work was of this order.

But the thought of the months to come, now that he was deprived of Ann's financial support, admittedly filled Bob with complete terror. Or there were his memories, both sentimental and resentful, of his final encounters with Ann: just a few days before, eating spaghetti with Dan at Tony's restaurant in New York City, Bob had unexpectedly broken down in tears, Ann accusing him of feigning them to elicit her sympathy. Within a few days of arriving in Albuquerque, he fictionalized the scene for Olson, casting himself in the role of the former unsuccessful husband who, even on this occasion, ends up paying the bill with his ex-wife's money.

The newness of Albuquerque initially dispelled such gloomy memories. Come to meet him at the bus depot was Race Newton who took him directly to Buddy's Imported Motors. From there they drove "out, in an old, white, boatlike Jaguar with open top, across the river to the west mesa, and off on a side road, then a dirt one, into a box canyon," where they stopped, the "immense blue sky overhead and no end to all that arching space."

For a New Englander like Creeley, Albuquerque, with its racial mix of Indians, Mexicans, and whites, proved an intriguingly bizarre place. Dope, mescal, beer, and shrimp, consumed in the company of Buddy, Wuzza, and Race, helped enhance these new impressions. Race, in spite of the bad things Buddy had written about him, struck Bob as completely the old friend. He had stopped drinking, and looked in much better shape than when Bob had last seen him two years earlier in New York. He was playing piano at a local night club run by Petrino, reportedly the last survivor of a local gang. Soon Race and Bob would take a trip down to Mexico, they decided.

But nothing worked out, mainly because the New Hampshire lawyer wouldn't send the money promised Bob by Ann. So the old gloom settled back all too quickly. After the hectic social rounds of his last few weeks in New York, he felt lonely. Going about their various chores, Buddy, Wuzza, and Race had little time for him. In the morning, he would wake up just as Wuzza was leaving for work, talk to her for a while, then sit in the empty house, play records, and drink coffee. A brief visit from Race was enough to whet his appetite for talk, but little more. Soon his friend would be off on another errand, advising Bob to just keep talking – he'd be back in an hour. Or Buddy might drop by, quickly turn on with Bob, but then be off again to his dealership.

Loneliness of this kind was something new to Bob, and within less than two weeks he had reached rock bottom. At one point, three entire days passed without his being aware of it, sitting under an electric bulb, all the shades drawn, the bright February sun glaring outside.

He couldn't even write. The lone exception was "The Letter," a poem then entitled "For Ann":

> I did not expect you
> to stay married to
> one man all your life,
> no matter you were his wife.
>
> I thought the pain was endless –
> but the form existent,
> as it is form,
> and as such I loved it.
>
> I loved you as well
> even as you might tell,
> giving evidence
> as to how much was penitence.

He was trying to play with rhyme and to devise variations on relatively worn forms such as the quatrain, Creeley had written Corman a little earlier. Such technical devices were supposed to provide an ironical perspective on the contents he could presently manage. Yet this program remained largely wishful thinking. "For Ann" reflects Creeley's preoccupation with rhyme and form but lacks the ironical distance he strove for. With its tone of wistful regret and longing, the poem differs markedly from the "Ballad of the Despairing Husband," in which Creeley, earlier at Black Mountain, had turned with superb self-derision upon his own self-righteous sentimentality.

> Oh wife, oh wife – I tell you true,
> I never loved no one but you.
> It never will, it cannot be
> another woman is for me.
>
> That may be right, she will say then,
> but as for me, there's other men.
> And I will tell you I propose
> to catch them firmly by the nose.
>
> And I will wear what dresses I choose!
> And I will dance, and what's to lose!
> I'm free of you, you little prick,
> and I'm the one can make it stick.

Spanish-born Ramón José Sender, whom Bob met around 8 March, provided temporary distraction from his loneliness and bitter memories. An internationally famous novelist in his mid-fifties, Sender reminded Creeley of Picasso, whom he had once seen in an Aix café: the short body, the magical eyes, and the macho Spanish bearing. Sender spoke in a sputtering, half-swallowed English mixed with Spanish. But talk he did, nonstop, especially about himself and his opinions: his days as foreign literary editor of a journal publishing Ortega y Gasset and Lorca, his fighting (as a Loyalist) in the Spanish Civil War, his dancing with a female lunatic who mistook him for her doctor. Or he would go on about the beauty of mad people, the magic of Spain, the makings of great writers (i.e., those most aware of their own weaknesses), as well as his preferences (e.g., Thomas Wolfe) and dislikes (e.g., Hemingway) for fellow novelists.

Particularly appealing were Sender's opinions on women. What he had to say about men designing the "form" in which women serve them no doubt reminded Bob of his poem "For Ann." In a fight between a man and a woman, it was always the man who must win, Sender felt. For the woman to win would only make her unhappy. The woman must serve the man. That was her form, much as it was his to make form. Or did Bob, writing to Fielding Dawson, report Sender's sentiments in the words he had used in the earlier poem?

Before long Bob also met Judson Crews, who for years had bombarded him with contributions, first to the abortive *Lititz*, and later to the *Black*

Mountain Review. There was something about Crews's loner wisdom, wry laconic perceptions, and good-humoured persistence that had caused Bob to maintain contact. Crews worked as a pressman for a local newspaper at one dollar an hour in Ranchos de Taos, New Mexico.

The trip there with Race in one of Buddy's cars – through the desert up into the mountains, along the bed of the Rio Grande passing several Indian pueblos – was an experience in itself. Taos too, in spite of the growing tourist industry, was lovely: the mountains surrounding it to the back, the air fine and brisk, the light of an eerie brightness and clarity.

Crews, with his wife and two daughters, lived in a big rambling adobe house. A Texan in his mid-thirties with a very western face, he spoke a little like a preacher. At the same time, he had a self-deprecatory sense of humour which Creeley characterizes in a preface to Crews's *Nolo Contendere* (1978). With his peculiar persistence, Crews kept publishing little magazines – *Suck Egg Mule, Poetry Taos, The Naked Ear* – as well as his own books, usually putting "a photo reproduction of a naked lady in each one, as much as to say, if you can't 'understand' these poems, you might test your powers on this person; i.e., I'm sure that God loves us all."

The liking Creeley felt for Crews was mutual. For a man that Crews came to consider the major male poet of his generation, Creeley behaved with impeccable modesty. They couldn't have wished for a better guest; especially the way Creeley related to their two daughters, attentively watching one of them draw pictures with crayons on a pad of yellow paper, making wheezing noises and laughing to herself. So perfect were Bob's house-guest manners, he would later be allowed to share the children's room for several weeks.

At least things were moving again. Bob climbed a mountain near Albuquerque from which he could see the desert for miles and miles around with the Rio Grande a "very small line though it all." He flew to Los Angeles to pick up two Porsches. L.A., where they arrived at 3:30 a.m. before being whisked off to a place on Temple Hill Drive back of Hollywood, certainly was a place all its own. Even without the pot they continued to smoke throughout the visit, it all would have seemed strange enough: the house way up above Hollywood looking down upon hazy, smog-covered fields, the intense heat, the old man, all wrapped up, answering the phone at the bottom of the house, and, whenever the call was for Creeley's hosts, pulling on a rope to ring a cow-bell contraption below their window; or the about twenty-year-old Kansas hustler walking in the following morning off an abalone boat and claiming to have met Bob in New York City in December. The rest, especially the drive back through the Mojave Desert under the moon, was lost in an hallucinatory mirage. It also helped remind Bob of what he'd been missing over the past few weeks. Almost back in Albuquerque, following Buddy, he over-took an orange-cream car resembling a beachwagon with half a dozen people inside. And there was Cynthia sitting in the back seat, staring at him.

Not that Bob hadn't looked for a replacement for her. But somehow everything had turned sour on him. On the immediate hunting grounds was his host's wife, Wuzza, a nice, bright, and sharp woman. Buddy being so entirely preoccupied with his dealership, she and Bob had ample op-portunity for tête-à-têtes. One night, while staying up to watch some films, Wuzza confessed to Bob that she really should have married him instead of Buddy, although she conceded Buddy was "much nicer." The problem was, Creeley reported to Olson, he didn't love Wuzza – although he liked her very much. Also, of course, there was the problem of his being so close to Buddy and living in his friend's house without a cent. So to hell with it. He didn't really love anyone, at the moment, he protested.

Then another woman, wife of a smallish, slightly pedantic, and timo-rous English professor, mother of four and about to give birth to a fifth, quickly changed all that. Almost instantly, Bob decided he loved her very much. The lady's wonderfully sharp blue eyes reminded him of Cynthia's – very Irish in their fierceness. Also there was her humour, the way she laughed, and her beautifully clear head. Paradoxically, she felt that Bob thought like her husband who, seemingly intent upon assuming the role of the obliging cuckold, drove him home one night insisting that he call them so they could meet again. It would be horrible if she knew what he was thinking, Creeley wrote to Fielding Dawson. But everything re-mained mere fantasy.

Shortly before his departure for San Francisco, a very nice woman bar-tender offered to accompany him on his trip. In San Francisco she would make more money, the lady explained. Her proposal plunged Bob into a dilemma similar to the one he had experienced with Wuzza. For the time being, at least, the woman belonged to a friend. It was an ugly tempta-tion. But the whole thing would have been hopeless anyway. So to hell with it.

His mind the usual "quagmire of unresolved / confessions," Creeley reported each and every one of these entanglements to his friends. To Fielding Dawson he wrote that if he saw a woman, he couldn't do much but want her; to Charles Olson, that seeing someone like the friend's wife it got impossible, immediately, and pathetic. The person most perplexed by such confessions must have been Duncan. Creeley admitted his hopes were directed backwards, even to Ann, certainly to Cynthia, or recently to a girl (wife) he had met briefly but had quickly diagnosed as a sort of impossibility. More to the point, he admitted that he was following any pleasant-looking woman he saw.

To make matters worse, Cynthia continued to bombard him with bizarrely dispassionate news releases and provocative conundrums out of limbo. She hated everyone who wrote like Bob, and everyone did, therefore she hated everyone. Also, she had fallen in love with someone else. As for Bob, he couldn't let go, Cynthia continuing to haunt him in his hallucinations as much as in reality. On his return from Los Angeles he heard via Fielding Dawson that Cynthia was in St Louis en route to New York City, and instantly decided to go to St Louis. His remaining cash was just enough for the round-trip bus fare. Again Cynthia eluded his grasp. A phone call from Fielding informed him that she had already left for New York. Cynthia had decided to try her luck there, make lots of money, and become a successful woman.

A letter, probably Creeley's last in that tumultuous affair, records his response to that final rejection. What was this business re "success" all about, he wondered. He couldn't see why women had to do these things at all. The mere thought of Cynthia becoming a successful woman was "terrifying" to him, he told her.

One thing was certain: he had to move on. He planned to go to San Francisco, he announced to Denise Levertov, recent confidant of his more bourgeois-minded effusions. Ed Dorn (with whose wife, unbeknownst to Denise, he had had a brief affair) offered to give him shelter. There he could perhaps hope to get some work, and so begin to provide for himself. He couldn't write, it seemed, until he had done that.

23

San Francisco, 1956.

For a writer there was no place quite like the San Francisco of 1956, Creeley recalls. But who could have anticipated that "all those to be blessed, truly" managed to be present in the city that year? The San Francisco Poetry Renaissance, launched by the now legendary Six Gallery Reading on 13 October the previous year, was still a pristine event. Its mass-media trivialization, the rivalries and schisms that would soon divide it, were only about to begin.

Already the movement was starting to celebrate its own achievements. Within weeks of Creeley's arrival in the Bay area, the Six Gallery protagonists staged a repeat of their earlier reading in a Berkeley theatre housed in the converted office of a trucking company filled with old movie-house seats. Artist Robert LaVigne, like Jack Kerouac just back in town, had made a seven-foot-high Lautrec-like poster and plastered the hall with pen drawings of Allen Ginsberg and Peter Orlovsky making love. On the stage was a row of throne-like wooden chairs, one for each poet. "It was the same lineup as the Six Gallery reading, a repeat by popular demand for Berkeley."

There were minor variants, like Kenneth Rexroth, master of ceremonies, wearing a white turtleneck instead of the bow tie and cutaway pinstripe suit he had worn at the Six Gallery. But then and now, Allen Ginsberg reading "Howl" played the star role, a "thin, rumpled figure in a raveling dark sweater" under a "bright white stage light." The audience passionately reacted to every line, the performance ending with a tumultuous finale after someone threw on all the lights, making his body vibrate in a chaos of flashing colours. Jack Kerouac, who would fictionalize the original reading in *The Dharma Bums*, again collected donations for wine and passed bottles up and down the rows.

To an extent, Creeley knew what to expect before he arrived in the Bay area. Robert Duncan had told him about the pre-Beat Renaissance centred around Ruth Witt-Diamant's Poetry Center, and Kenneth Rexroth's literary soirées at his home on 250 Scott Street. Some years back Creeley had also been in touch with and published in Horace Schwartz's *Goad*. Most importantly, he had long been corresponding with Rexroth, San Francisco's *eminence grise*. An enthusiastic promoter of the up and coming, Rexroth in 1951 had hailed Denise Levertov as Dante's Beatrice reincarnate. More recently, he had assured Creeley that Duncan, then newly arrived in Majorca, was a major personality as well as a very good poet, and he had recommended *Howl* by Ginsberg, as well as two other new poets, Gary Snyder and Philip Whalen.

Reports about Rexroth and the San Francisco scene had also been pouring in from a long-time Rexroth devotee who more recently had come to suffer the strains of his over-zealous devotions. Jonathan Williams, a poet, publisher, and literary envoy networking new poetic movements around the continent, frequently passed through San Francisco and at such times sent Creeley witty cameo portraits of the older and younger players in town. "Horace the Schwartz" was the polite and not immediately offensive middle European you might expect; California's "vestigial camerado Kenneth the Waxroth" insisted on being truculently and perversely wrong.

News of a possible tie-in of the *Black Mountain Review* and *Jargon* poets with the growing media attention lavished on their San Francisco peers set Williams hot on the trail. He had received an urgent phone call from *Time & Life:* Rosalind Constable, after learning about *Howl*, was eager to read Layton, Olson, Zukofsy, and Creeley himself. Also, one of the journal's photographers had covered a soirée at Rexroth's.

Creeley of course knew Duncan's poetry well and more recently had come across Jack Kerouac's "Jazz of the Beat Generation" and "The Mexican Girl" (an excerpt from *On the Road*) in the *Paris Review*. Of the other young poets' work, most of which remained in manuscript, he had seen next to nothing. However, that would change quickly. After two months in San Francisco he had not only read but collected a great deal of material from both younger and older poets local to the city, some of which he hoped to publish in BMR #7.

Creeley's arrival in San Francisco one mid-afternoon started the hectic rounds of social activity that would not cease for weeks:

Ed and Helene gave me a whirlwind tour of the city, in their tiny Morris Minor, and we drank a lot in celebration. Ed told me that Rexroth had generously invited us to dinner but that he had to go to work at the Greyhound Bus Terminal at six. I in the meantime was getting drunker and drunker, and recall vomiting heavily in the street before going up to Rexroth's apartment. People had already eaten, but tactfully made no point of my late arrival. Later that same night, returning to the Dorns' apartment, I was charmed by the arrival of Allen Ginsberg at midnight (he got off work at the Greyhound Terminal at that hour), and we talked much of the night about writing and "Projective Verse" and his own interest in Kerouac and Burroughs.

Rexroth moved him very much, he wrote to Zukofsksy a few weeks later. As a man of letters, he seemed so wilfully gregarious, yet at the same time so patently lonely and disengaged. The remainder of the story would wreck Rexroth's marriage as well as sow dissent among the San Francisco poetic community.

Shortly after his arrival, Creeley was taken over to the McClure household – an early commune which Michael McClure, his wife, Joanna, and their baby daughter, Jane, shared with Ronnie Bladen as well as Jim Harmon and his wife Beverly. McClure and Harmon were editing *Ark II – Moby I*, like its predecessor, *Ark*, a journal dedicated to philosophical anarchism and new literary expression. Creeley remembers McClure as a "physically articulate young man, level voice, eyes remarkably clear and crystalline, viz. as with diamonds a cool *light*. Already *going about his business* with undistracted singularity. At one point asks me, generously, if I'd like to go with him to Vic Tanney's where he worked as an instructor to *work out* – which scared me, first, that I'd have to *expose* my distraught carcass to possibly pitiless glares and, second, that I might get hurt!" Similar fondness which he expressed for others like Madeline Gleason or Jimmy Broughton was clearly mutual. Back in Majorca, Duncan was delighted to hear (via Ida Hodes) that Jimmy and Madeline as well as Marthe all had taken Bob to heart, a joyous fact Duncan at once relayed back to him.

Through Allen Ginsberg, Creeley met the person who was to become his closest friend during his brief but eventful stay in the Bay area. Ginsberg, after he finished work at the Greyhound baggage room around midnight, introduced the two men at The Place, a North Beach bar. Arriving there early, Creeley noticed a handsome young man seated against the back wall, part of a group but at the same time strangely detached from it. The man's head struck him as "remarkably manifest," his extraordinary physical presence fascinating like Picasso's. Suddenly there was Ginsberg's voice saying: "Haven't you met Jack yet? He's sittin' right over there!" Unfortunately, they had little conversation during their first encounter. Kerouac, as Creeley recalled later, was "pretty comatose from drinking" that night, "and when we all got back to the apartment he was sharing with Al Sublette to eat – the large steak, I remember, kept getting dropped on the floor in the process of being cooked – Jack passed out on a bed, and when I was delegated to wake him up, he regarded me with those extraordinary eyes and I felt like a didactic idiot."

Reading "The Mexican Girl," Creeley had been impressed by the curious skipping and merging of images, the real continuousness of changing impressions, as well as by Kerouac's ability to invest lowly persons with dignity and worth without moralizing about or sentimentalizing them. Obviously, none of that was fake. Asking Creeley about his family background, listening, while speaking little himself, but looking straight at him with sharp blue eyes, Kerouac obviously practised the same empathetic powers in real life. At the same time there was something brooding, uncanny about him. Why had he killed his wife, Creeley wondered, confusing Kerouac with Burroughs. Ginsberg had talked so much about the genius of both men that the two had fused in his mind.

Ginsberg attributed the instant bond between Kerouac and Creeley to their being two "New England, milltown writers." Probably he was right, but there was more to the close affinity between the two men. Kerouac's poetry, Creeley found, was like a shorthand of perceptions and memories using some of the same kind of word-play and rhythmic invention to be found in his prose. Both revealed his aversion to the "story" of usual thought. More so even than himself, Kerouac had the ability to translate present sensation into immediately actual language.

As Creeley observed over the following days and weeks, much of that could be attributed to Kerouac's constant close attention to what was going on around him. Appearances to the contrary – his football player physique, his excessive drinking, his reluctance to talk about literature – he was more seriously committed to his writing than those who talked nonstop about theirs. He was known to withdraw for writing marathons, typing his novels on continuous rolls of teletype paper or locking himself into a hotel room to compose a series of seventy-nine poems called *San Francisco Blues*. Evidently he was "writing" in his head. Putting the words on paper to him was no more than a mechanical extension of this ongoing mental process. Creeley remembered one such occasion. Ed Dorn's children were having a conversation while a hummingbird hovered in an empty window frame, and there was Jack whisking out his notebook and starting to write, capturing what was happening with "no impedances." Rewriting or revision, other than by slight deletions and additions, could only spoil the result, he felt.

At the same time, Kerouac showed little interest in surrealist poet Éluard or the French Symbolists recommended to him by the American surrealist Philip Lamantia. Mallarmé seemed obsessed with his epistemological despair and idiosyncratic modes of intellectual perception rather than concerned with real experiences. Instead of having words suggest things, he used them to point to abstract ideas beyond them. His own literary models, Kerouac explained to Creeley, were men like Balzac and Hugo who, in "the great French narrative tradition," used common language spoken by ordinary people in common situations. Like Creeley himself, he believed in William Carlos Williams's "no ideas but in things."

There were other young writers with whom Creeley shared similar concerns and felt linked by comparable, even deeper affinities. One was Kerouac's friend Gary Snyder, the protagonist of *The Dharma Bums*, a poet even then already set in his spirituality and writing. Creeley met him shortly before Snyder's departure for an extended stay in a Japanese Zen monastery. The world Snyder lived in and wrote about, so others could inhabit it as well, was "a successful relation of hope" both beautiful and painstaking. Perhaps Snyder's fascination with the *Dhammapada* and other Buddhist texts stemmed from an obsession, like Creeley's, with the self as "a self-isolated event, yet one which must find relationships." Certainly, Snyder's poetry showed a strong awareness of what emerged when that contact was severed: the interior hell which, in the twentieth-century imagination, had replaced obsolete fantasies about a hell where sinners go.

With Philip Whalen, the same preoccupation with self or intelligence as a point of entry to the real took on a cast even more congenial than Snyder's. Whalen's poetry, like Creeley's own, made clear that the self "being so used ... is almost necessarily suspect, and so must be itself examined." It used a language reflecting "the shaken egos" of our time: "Poetry, beginning with the protest of the thirties (a self-centered evaluation), moving through the chaos of the forties, loss of meaning and the huge arrival of apparently non-human activity ... comes through the fifties finding a language in a common hysteria, a nervously singular presence of mind, in which feelings are dominant as they are felt, are registered as static blurring the voice of ordinary explanation, which says that everything is all right (when it is patently not at all right)." In that sense, Creeley found Whalen the closest to his own nature among all the poets he had met in San Francisco – with a single exception: Kerouac, who, so Creeley confessed to Duncan, was at times like coming home.

Within days Kerouac joined the newest inner circle of Creeley's closest friends including Olson, Duncan, Franz Kline, and Dan Rice. He liked Jack very very much, Creeley wrote to Charles Olson. In turn Kerouac would remind Creeley that he loved him, or reminisce on the pretty weird times during the month they knew each other in the town of Mill Valley in the Bay area – the shack, the stews, the walks to the wine store in the "dog-biting night" or the way Creeley drummed on all the furniture with that great futuristic jazz beat!

What epitomized their relationship to Kerouac was a phrase Creeley uttered one morning after waking up in Kerouac's sleeping bag. Hearing Kerouac yelling, Be enlightened! Creeley answered: That's like asking water to be wet – a phrase Kerouac never forgot. The only reason why neither this event nor Creeley himself became part of *The Dharma Bums*, Kerouac assured him, was because to include him in that story would have meant writing another novel.

Kerouac had reasons to say so. There was another side to Creeley which Kerouac would remember as distinctly as his being "pure" and "enlightened." Like his voice getting hoarse and ugly when he was drunk, so that he scared princesses away; or his tendency to get into fights, his one eye beginning to glitter, his wanting "the world to narrow to a match flare," his being "too much too minded too destructively zapped head-tripping."

For godsakes don't get into any more fights! Be a happy drunk like me! Kerouac advised Creeley a little later. Write big poems about what you want to love in this eternal nothingness. Then and earlier, Creeley heeded neither. To fight, create turmoil, and sow divisiveness gave him access to insights others sought in peace and quiet. Not for him the pseudo-Buddhist serenity of the pre-hippie dharma bums of his generation! Though interested in the intellectual aspects of Zen, he felt it was just one more puritanism. Having grown up in New England, new rules were the last thing he needed. Zen involved the ability to yield ego and will to an authority, a new kind of submission almost unthinkable to an American. After spending half your life getting out of yourself, you were supposed to give yourself back to your father? Just being in situations involved with Zen conduct frankly made Creeley feel a little fakey.

And there was plenty of that to be found, especially around Locke McCorkle, a twenty-two year-old carpenter living in a house on the slopes of Mount Tamalpais outside Mill Valley. An ex-college student working part time as a manual labourer, Locke spent most of his time with his family studying the Buddhist sutras. His house had little furniture but lots of Japanese straw mats and books and an expensive hi-fi. Locke's wife baked her own bread and cooked large pots of vegetable soup. With two kids, they lived what Kerouac's *Dharma Bums* called "the joyous life in America without much money." Via Kerouac's novel they would provide a model for hippie life all over America during the 1960s.

This was also thanks to co-labourer Gary Snyder, who occupied his own shack a little further up Mount Tamalpais, the floor covered with straw mats, burlap-lined walls with prints of Chinese paintings as well as area maps of Marin County and northwest Washington, the whole place full of bouquets of mountain flowers. Frequently the cabin would also house friends like Philip Lamantia, Jack Kerouac, and, more recently, Robert Creeley.

Creeley eventually rented his own place in San Francisco at 1108 Montgomery for $27.50 a month and tried to earn odd bits of money. He applied to be a blood donor but was refused. He had also tried working for Viking Food but found it so ugly and useless that he quit. He ended up taking various typing jobs which Marthe Rexroth found for him through her employment with San Francisco State College. He also made ditto copies of Allen Ginsberg's still unpublished "Howl" for use in a poetry workshop. Some of them Ginsberg sent to T.S. Eliot, Ezra Pound, Mark Van Doren, Lionel Trilling, Richard Eberhart, William Faulkner, and other celebrities, with letters asking for comment.

Most of Creeley's spare time was spent in North Beach bars and, increasingly, with Kerouac in Mill Valley. It was a constant swirl of events:

Great parties at Locke McCorkle's house out in Mill Valley – Allen and Peter charmingly dancing naked among a dense pack of clothed bodies, flowers at the prom! Jack and I sitting on the sidelines, shy, banging on upended pots and pans, "keeping the beat." Gary Snyder's wise old-young eyes, his centeredness and shyness also. Phil Whalen's, "Well, Creeley, I *hope* you know what you're doing ..." Visits to Mike McClure's with Ed – Ronnie Bladen upstairs in their undesignated commune. Mike practicing the trumpet (in the cellar?) – anyhow, blasts of sound, and talk of Pollock, *energy*. Lawrence Ferlinghetti, standing outside his great and initial City Lights Bookstore, asking me what living was like in Mallorca – cheap? He'd had the care to review *The Gold Diggers* for the *San Francisco Chronicle*, and that was surely a first. Walking around the city with Allen and Phil, Allen reading us *Howl*, which he had in a big black binder notebook, each time we'd stop at a curb or in a cafe (Mike's – great Italian food) or just on a bench in the park.

Snyder's departure for Japan, scheduled for early May, was approaching fast, with his friends eager to give him the proper send-off. It took the form of a three-day party, the last major event before the San Francisco group, once united by pre-hippie euphoria, would disintegrate into rivalling factions. Rexroth expounded on poetry, Snyder, Ginsberg, and Orlovsky walked around naked. John Montgomery, sporting a new suit, was seen reading *Mad* magazine. People danced, others took turns pounding bongo rhythms on overturned cans. A bonfire was lit in the yard, music blared into the night. One by one the celebrants disappeared into their sleeping bags only to continue the party the next morning. On the third day, Snyder and Kerouac went on a final hike together. They discussed Buddhist philosophy, Snyder predicting the "great world revolution" that would "take place when East meets West finally, and it'll be guys like us that can start the thing. Think of the millions of guys with rucksacks on their backs tramping around the back country and hitchhiking and bringing the word down to everybody."

Gary was going East to prepare himself for the dawning revolution. For a while now he had been pondering his role in the Beat movement. Beat, whatever else, meant an "utter beatness to work up from," meant reducing one's life to barest essentials, meant being beaten by the Zen master's stick. But, above all, it meant the discipline too many of his friends lacked. Kerouac was exhorted to stop drinking or it would ruin him.

On 5 May the moment arrived to say farewell. It was the last time, there at the harbour, that Kerouac and Snyder ever saw each other. With the boat already swinging away from the dock, Snyder's girlfriend Neuri climbed back on board to give him a last good-bye kiss. Snyder tossed her ashore into McCorkle's arms. Kerouac gave the little scene saintly dimensions in *The Dharma Bums*: Gary had renounced carnal desire in favour of spiritual discipline.

Romantic sentiments had been running high – too much so for at least two men. One was Rexroth. Christ, Snyder, he'd warned his disciple, you know what they do in those Zen monasteries. You'll come back with your asshole stretched the size of a wagon tire.

The other was Creeley. To dispel Kerouac's melancholy about Snyder's departure, they went to The Cellar to hear a favourite jazz pianist, and before long started hammering away on the table top, their "fourth-dimensional counterpoint" drowning out the music. For Creeley it was time for a fight. When they were asked to leave, Kerouac had trouble getting his friend – the eye aglitter, the voice hoarse and ugly – out the door. The bouncer landed his fist in Creeley's face, driving a tooth right through his lip.

But more was required to lay to rest Creeley's evil demons. His lip still suppurating from one fight, he had to get into another, this time with former student Ed Dorn. He wanted to introduce Kerouac to him, he told Dorn. But Dorn would have none of it. All they had come for, he said, was to hustle free food and start something with his wife, Helene. He tried to throw them out, but Creeley resisted, making Dorn attack him with his fists. The rest followed well-rehearsed lines. Helene, angry with Dorn, ran out, Creeley in tow so as to "pacify" her. Dorn and Kerouac ended up talking through the night and into the late morning hours, by which time they had become intimate friends.

Next there was a tiff with a policeman. Creeley called him a fascist for asking his friend Ron Loewinsohn for i.d. As a result, he ended up in jail, where he spent the next few days, at last finding his peace in utter exhaustion. For days he had been punishing himself. It was nothing but penance, and ridiculous, he confessed to Duncan.

Kerouac decided it was time to get Creeley out of North Beach to Mill Valley where he would nurse him back into normalcy with peppermint tea and honey. Another charge Kerouac had to take care of was Bob Donlin who, after collapsing from a binge, had had a vision of being led into paradise by three Bodhisattvas – Neal Cassady, Ginsberg, and Kerouac himself. However, the demonic gales sweeping across the Bardo plains of earthly existence showed no signs of abating. They next hit in the form of a surprise visit from Bob Kaufmann, a black Jewish Haitian poet steeped in Catholicism and voodoo. Kaufmann came accompanied by his girlfriend, as well as by the Beat movement's godfather, Neal Cassady. Kaufmann had brought some peyote which they took in milkshakes while listening to a record featuring Mescalero Indians performing a peyote ritual. Cassady enacted for the assembled company what he would do if he won a million dollars at the race track, mimicked the routines of various workers on the Bombay Express, and impersonated a "lovely, hokey evangelist preacher" who could "take you right out of your head and bring you back again." While reassuring like Kerouac, he had a hard edge, like Creeley. Also, there was the man's superior macho prowess, intimating to everyone not to tangle with him, or "take the consequences."

Creeley rallied to give his first and only reading to the San Francisco community. Kerouac, playing his by now familiar role as his older brother, came along but wouldn't stay. He placed Creeley in his seat with a jug of wine and reassured him, pointing out all their friends in the audience. Then he excused himself, saying, "Your poems are really sad – I don't like to listen to you be in so much pain. I'll be down at the bar."

On balance, the reading went all right – as did almost everything else that Creeley had done in San Francisco. He had come to know some fascinating poets, made several good friends, even met men like Ginsberg and Kerouac who shared his aspirations as well as his restlessness. San Francisco was the most interesting city he had ever known. The architecture was enough to keep you occupied for months, he wrote to Denise Levertov. Neither jobs nor housing were anything like the problem in New York City, because San Francisco was still a small town. Twenty minutes from the city you found yourself in the countryside, deer at a stone's throw distance.

Yet in the final analysis San Francisco didn't agree with Bob. He was too much a country boy, he somewhat disingenuously alleged to Denise. The actual reasons for his disaffection with the city lay elsewhere. One was a temperament totally out of tune with San Francisco's easy-going atmosphere, or "looseness," as he put it. What relaxed most other people exasperated him. Witness to this bizarre response was his memory of cars stopping to let him cross the street in the middle of the rush hour. On the surface, such behaviour could seem immense courtesy, he explained, but in himself, it bred a feeling of almost hellish uncertainty.

However, the major cause for his coming to resent and flee San Francisco after roughly two months in the city was a personal one.

24

The Creeley Formula.

A liaison with a friend's girlfriend or wife – like Bob Leed's Alison, Buddy Berlin's Eleanor, Dan Rice's Cynthia, or Ed Dorn's Helene – was nothing new for Creeley. Yet none of these previous entanglements had entailed major consequences beyond the private sphere.

Creeley's affair with Marthe Rexroth was different. At fifty-one, Kenneth Rexroth had achieved nation-wide, even international fame. Locally he had done most of the spade work leading to the Poetry Renaissance of the mid-1950s. Writing to Pauline Kael as early as 1946, Robert Duncan described him as paterfamilias of his circle of artists, poets, and anarchists: "We learned only this last week that he reads the Encyclopedia Britannica from cover to cover yearly. Only something like that would make credible the fund of knowledge he has on almost every subject. And that is coupled with a high style in the Johnsonian tradition, a never ceasing to delight and astonish gift of the burlesque, a caustic and affectionate wit. He is, finally, so much the devotee of his devotees."

Little had changed since; Rexroth, a decade later, still acted as self-appointed apologist for the younger generation. Over the years his devotees had increased in number, and so had their devotion to him. Robert Duncan, Denise Levertov, Jonathan Williams, Gary Snyder, Philip Whalen, even Jack Kerouac and Allen Ginsberg, as well as many lesser-known writers paid grateful tribute to the man to whom they owed so much.

Naturally, there were tensions, such as those caused by a general anxiety of influence. Also, there was the occasional squabble – as on the occasion when Rexroth dismissively informed would-be Buddhist Kerouac that "everybody" in San Francisco was a Buddhist, and Kerouac pulled Rexroth's moustache in return. Or there was the time when Kerouac, Whalen, Snyder, and Ginsberg, shortly after the Six Gallery reading, arrived late and drunk for a dinner to which Rexroth had invited them, Kerouac, to make light of the situation, asked for a drink,

Rexroth exploded, Ginsberg called himself a better poet than Rexroth, Kerouac called Rexroth a "boche" and "dirty German," and Rexroth finally threw them out. But just as often Rexroth would have dinner guests wait for a meal that wouldn't be forthcoming, while he and his wife withdrew to the bedroom to make up after a fight started earlier in the day. Where he and his devotees quarrelled one day, they patched it up the next: the Six Gallery poets, after their fight at the Rexroths', happily reunited with him to stage the repeat reading in Berkeley.

All that changed after Creeley met Marthe and Kenneth Rexroth during the fatal dinner party shortly after arriving in town. Rexroth, for all his eagerness to get to know this young poet, had reasons to feel apprehensive. After resigning as one of *BMR*'s contributing editors over Martin Seymour-Smith's attack on Dylan Thomas and Theodore Roethke, he had officially reconciled himself to Creeley. But deep down he never forgot his feelings at the time, or the insults he had heaped on Creeley in writing to Denise Levertov. While appreciating Creeley's affinities with Mallarmé, he found him personally disagreeable and just plain mean. Strictly a literary thing – as ugly and abusive as a Stalinist, he had called Creeley, his review a mere insult sheet, his followers fascists. And now this compound of truculence, envy, and ignorance was having an affair with his wife. What's more, he was becoming friends with most of the major young poets of his innermost circle.

Events that would turn this closely knit network of friendship into a spider web of hostility, vindictiveness, and intrigue precipitated themselves with astounding rapidity.

When Marthe came home at night, Kenneth would be waiting for her outside their apartment screaming obscene imprecations. He threatened violence to Creeley and her, called her unbalanced, or proposed to kill himself. Rumours about Creeley's previous sexual exploits and present feats of drunkenness, being beat up by bouncers or getting thrown into jail, added more fuel to the conflagration. Creeley, in Rexroth's manic fantasies, was a debauched Svengali trying to spirit his wife off to his mud hut in Albuquerque. Following Creeley's evil demon, "gangs of people" were fucking Marthe. Someone "with a strong (fake) muffled Negro accent" periodically called to tell him that Creeley and Marthe were at The Cellar on Green Street.

Ginsberg, telephoning to discuss a new poem, was called one of many sons of bitches abusing Marthe and Rexroth. He felt as if he'd walked into a candy store and got beaten up by a bunch of juvenile delinquents, he screamed, then slammed down the receiver. When Ginsberg called back, Rexroth explained he'd heard Ginsberg and his friends were having "orgies with Marthe" in their cottage – "you, Creeley and Kerouac."

Kerouac, whom Rexroth came to blame for much of his misery, and, in revenge, to haunt with his critical pen for years to come, had little to do with it all. As Creeley's friend, he just happened to be around when Bob and Marthe were together, for instance, in Snyder's cabin.

Others played more active roles. Kenneth's former wife, Marie, a nurse by profession and temperament, took care of him medically while also befriending Marthe and her children, Mary and Katharine. After Creeley returned to New Mexico around the beginning of June 1956, Marie accompanied Marthe on a short trip away from home while Kenneth and the kids stayed with his old friends Frank and Shirley Triest in Sebastopol. Later Marie took care of Kenneth's deteriorating physical and mental condition, found doctors to treat his ailments, offered to donate $500 towards setting him up in the bookstore business, and asked James Laughlin, Lawrence Clark Powell, and Ferlinghetti for additional donations. She finally pleaded with Marthe to return to Kenneth, if only for the sake of the children and, for that purpose, sent her money for the plane tickets.

Frank and Shirley Triest played more dubious parts. After first giving shelter to Kenneth and the kids, upon his return to Scott Street they next extended the same hospitality to Marthe and the children. Creeley briefly returned to San Francisco to help Marthe move, then returned to New Mexico expecting her, Mary, and Katharine would soon join him there. His sending a $600 check (he had finally received his Rock Pool Farm refund) precipitated that decision. Marthe decided to drive from Sebastopol to the San Francisco airport and fly to New Mexico without saying goodbye to Rexroth. But none of the four cars on the Triests' property would start. Frank Triest, whose loyalties were with Rexroth rather than Marthe, had disconnected the batteries. When Marthe became frantic, he confessed what he had done, reconnected the cables, and drove her to San Francisco. The flight would leave at midnight, so she phoned her boss at San Francisco State College to allow her and the children to spend the evening at his home. Meanwhile Frank rushed over to 250 Scott Street to tell Rexroth what had happened.

Before Marthe and the kids arrived in Taos, Creeley had located a small place for $10 a month at a safe distance from Taos proper: a charming old house with low doorways surrounded by beautiful landscape. It was empty, but neighbours offered minimal furniture. He had also applied for a caretaker's position at the nearby D.H. Lawrence ranch, now owned by the University of New Mexico, as well as for a Wurlitzer grant that would help him with housing expenses. With $400 left in hand, he felt sure that he, Marthe, and the kids could easily bridge the two months or so before he would secure a regular job. The four spent the first few days at Judson

Crews's, Creeley nailing together a few more pieces of furniture. Then they moved into what Rexroth had feared would be a mud hut and Judson Crews described as a very small adobe cabin. A very solid beginning, Creeley augured contentedly.

But neither Rexroth nor his various helpmates let them rest. "I *must* have all the money I can raise right away," Rexroth wrote to his New Directions publisher James Laughlin, "for Christ's sake hurry – a really awful disaster is impending. Everyone in SF is prostrate after 8 weeks of lies, tricks, evasions – especially Frank, Marie, & the Wheelwrights whose trust she betrayed to kidnap the children. She is a woman possessed." Should he take legal action to get custody of the children?

Laughlin, after consulting with his lawyer, advised against it. The interstate legal procedures would be too time-consuming and expensive. What he proposed was both more practical and less costly. Rexroth would drive Marie's car as far as Santa Fe, and, once there, rent another so that the California licence plates wouldn't betray his approach. Then he would kidnap the girls. As a first line of defence, should he end up in jail, Laughlin sent him a letter of introduction to the publisher of Santa Fe's *New Mexican*, Bob McKinney, a wealthy man with clout in local politics. Once back in California, there was little chance that the courts would award Marthe custody of Mary and Katharine. The couple had not been legally married at the time the children were born, which was frowned upon under the law.

But Rexroth couldn't face it. Instead, he turned to friends for help and advice. Michael and Joanna McClure tried to calm his paranoia about the spell Creeley had cast on Marthe; psychiatrist Jane Wheelwright, who had first helped Marthe make up her mind as to whether or not she should leave Rexroth, now helped him come to terms with the result.

His misery showed no signs of abating. He appointed Frank Triest the executor of a testament he said he had made out. His friends started to fear for his life. Marthe realized that it would be partly her responsibility if he killed himself. Marie called long-distance begging Marthe to come back and sent her money. Creeley and Marthe decided that her returning to Rexroth, at least for the time being, would be the only wise course of action. Creeley accompanied her and the children to San Francisco, then once again returned to Taos, hoping they would come back to him.

A frustrating waiting period of several weeks followed. In between writing letters and making phone calls, he tried to keep as busy as possible. With poet Max Finstein, a friend from way back in Boston, he moved into the Little Rose Cupboard Cottage, a two-room wood plank cabin with a porch overgrown with rose vines in nearby Ranchites. In lieu of paying rent, he took care of a couple of horses and thirteen Black Angus cows which repeatedly broke out of their pasture. There were several job prospects that never materialized: driving Chevies up from Santa Fe, or teaching at a nearby uranium mine. He also began his editorial labours for BMR #7, hoping it would turn out to be the most relevant issue he had yet managed. Meanwhile, he met Ed Corbett, a friend of Jess and Robert, who would do the issue's cover. Creeley liked Corbett very much, he dutifully reported to Duncan. A Texas Irishman, roughly in his mid-thirties, Corbett struck him as solidly American.

To escape his various frustrations, Bob also re-enacted masochistic activities developed earlier in San Francisco: he and Corbett got drunk at a Taos fiesta, were asked to leave, but quarrelled with the bouncer, who knocked Creeley out after being stared at by his blind eye. To complete the cathartic process, the two friends got into the car, were picked up by police, and thrown into jail until Judson Crews's wife, Mildred, went to bail them out by paying the fine.

In mid-August, after Creeley had once again rushed to Marthe's assistance, there was another showdown with Rexroth. Life with him had become so unbearable to Marthe that she kept her bags packed to be able to leave him at any point. She did so briefly while Creeley was in town, but this time without the children. Rexroth had learned his lesson: if Marthe left him again, Mary and Katharine would stay behind. So Creeley went back to Taos still hoping that Marthe, either with or without the children, would join him. But in fact it was time to say good-bye, which they did shortly thereafter. Their turbulent romance had ended as abruptly as it had started.

What survived it, at least for a while, were their letters, which point to a somewhat elusive but nonetheless essential aspect of their relationship. Especially illuminating here are Marthe's letters to Bob. They suggest that what cast the decisive spell on her were Bob's voice and way with language rather than the Svengali powers attributed to him by Rexroth. Used to being shouted at by Rexroth, she learned to love Bob's intimate and reassuring way of talking, she writes to him. She muses upon the wonders of hearing his voice, even the surprise of being able to do so. We soon find her like Cynthia, though more pervasively, parroting some of Creeley's verbal idiosyncrasies.

She liked the bus ride up to Seattle, or rather thought it was good physically to get through space really mile by mile. Kenneth's former wife, Marie, she reports, though usually in a state of well-intentioned hysteria on behalf of everyone, did love Mary and Katharine, selfishly. What Bob was telling her about life in Taos all sounded very possible. Also, he'd made *her* possible. Altogether, Bob was very great himself, and it was very great to hear him over the phone. She loved him not just very much, but very very much.

Her linguistic impersonation of Creeley reaches a point where her letters to him recall his to Ann shortly before their breakup. Certainly, there are the same high-flown protestations of love and affection. She missed and loved her Bob darling all the time, with all her heart, always did, and always would. Typically, such protesting became the more fervid the more Marthe, after having left Bob in Taos so as to rejoin her husband, began to extricate herself from the commitments to her lover: she loved Bob so much, she assured him. To touch him made her come alive. She loved him completely and transformingly, himself with all appurtenances – to prove which point, she even sent him a doll for his daughter, Charlotte.

Alongside the hyperbole is the rhetorical progression, equally Creeleyan, from seeming carefreeness through syntactical equivocation towards a point-blank assertion of the brutal facts. Initially, she hadn't been worried; it all had sounded very possible; it could be gotten through, mainly because she had to. But then she got worried after all. And with worry came the see-saw motion of denying what she'd affirmed, of affirming what she'd denied, or of hedging in what she was saying with conditions, qualifications, and inversions. Had she attempted a parody of Creeley's manner, she couldn't have done better.

For too long, she explains to him, she'd been doing things out of defiance. But marry him out of the same impulse she could not; anyway, not here or like this. He couldn't nor wouldn't want to imagine the desperate spitefulness of her shouting at Kenneth: I am going to marry Bob! He wouldn't want it, because if she wanted to, then for Bob and her, but not for "them," whoever "they" were. She wanted very much the place Bob made for her in his world, but not as a reflex action of her refusing another. No matter how muddled and incompetent this was, she had to do the refusing her own way.

For once in Creeley's life, the disciple got the better of the master, Marthe increasingly using his own verbal tricks. In the process he was paradoxically cast as someone who brought, or had brought, only clear open acts, positive ones. Meanwhile, Marthe donned Creeley's favourite mask of the charmingly incompetent fumbler who constantly weighs the pros and cons of his options without ever being able to make up his mind about them. After repeatedly assuring herself that she could get through it because she had to, she finally decided she didn't know how to get through – any of it. Being in San Francisco was impossible for her for a hundred reasons; coming to Taos seemed also an impossible desertion – or rather, claim.

Though she continued to insist that she was nowhere she could tell, her decision had already been made. She couldn't leave the children to go herself. Claiming not to know why any of this was written, she states the reason for it in the very next sentence. It was meant only to say good-bye. She'd call him Friday night to tell him so in person without all this paralysis of writing.

Creeley was stunned to find how completely his irresolute sounding beloved severed all ties after that phone call. For a long time he didn't hear from her at all. And when she finally did write, she said little. She wrote the letter in a restaurant, in between quitting one job and looking for another. How could her life continue like this? As it turned out, the story was far from over.

25

The Midsummer Night's Mare.

For several months Creeley was in danger of losing more than just Marthe. He and Rexroth shared numerous friends, some of whom threatened to remain loyal to the injured party and to turn against Creeley. One was Robert Duncan, for some time now part of the innermost circle of Creeley's literary associates but also an old admirer of Rexroth.

Naturally, Creeley hastened to inform Duncan of his affair with Marthe. Taking him into his confidence, he confessed to the deep and "patiently actual" feeling between them, embroidering upon it in detail. At first, it had almost frightened him to feel that way because all last year had been so much confusion. Yet since deciding to neither worry nor plan too much, each day was turning into a new delight of some kind – as when Marthe and he had had lunch in the park with the huge merry-go-round, and in walked a duck, to look at them. As for Rexroth, Duncan could be at peace. After all, Bob was no Victor Kalos (who had slept with Ann). He liked Rexroth, in fact much more than he'd been prepared to.

Duncan's initial response was ambivalent, to say the least. Acknowledging Creeley's damned business of the other man's woman, he was uneasy about his allegedly deep and patiently actual feeling towards Marthe, but about little else. The phrase smacked too much of victory, he felt. Thank God, Marthe had enough intelligence to decide for herself whom she should go for. Whatever the outcome of that choice, it would be a difficult one. If Creeley needed Marthe – and a woman like her could do much for him – Rexroth needed her too. Be that as it may, Creeley, as far as Duncan was concerned, had papal infallibility.

But all that changed due to a number of events. Shortly after Creeley's letter speaking of the patiently actual feeling between himself and Marthe, Duncan received another one from Michael McClure reporting on the affair, telling him that Rexroth was upset as hell and adding that, in a funny way, he had regained a lot of dignity in all of it. As a result, Duncan hastened to assure Rexroth of his allegiance. What Rexroth was embroiled in was a midsummer night's mare as bitter as any Shakespeare had ever put on stage.

Next, Duncan received a long-distance call from Rexroth who told him that Bob and Marthe were planning to go to Mexico. He pleaded with Robert to either speak or write to Marthe. Duncan consulted with his companion Jess Collins upon the proper course of action. The two agreed on Creeley's hypocrisy and expressed their outrage at the sordidness of whatever life he would offer Marthe.

Then Duncan wrote three letters: one to Marthe, who for the time being had fled to Seattle, a second to Creeley (enclosing a copy of his missive to Marthe), and a third (containing the same enclosure) to Rexroth, whom he assured of his unwavering support.

Marthe was warned: over the last two years, Creeley had had a long series of affairs, all of them with the wife or mistress of some man whom, like Kenneth, he claimed to like and respect; in each case, whether it was in New York, Albuquerque, or Black Mountain, he had been forced to flee the site of his adulterous amours. To prove his point Duncan gave copious citations from Creeley's own letters to him. What kind of hypocrite, Duncan wondered, talks about patiently actual feeling in the face of the actual facts? His taking Marthe to Mexico would simply duplicate the Majorca scenario: Bob's smoking marijuana, his phobia about not speaking Spanish, his mistrust of the partner who did, his relying on her financial support, his acting the older brother rather than the father to the children, and his finally abandoning them, as he had abandoned David, Thomas, and Charlotte.

Why, if Creeley loved Marthe, would he want to take her to such an obvious hell?

If she brought along the children, she would take them into all the mess of the Creeley household. That is, unless she could single-handedly cook, teach, earn the money, and keep some kind of happy order; not to mention the cruelty of taking them away from Kenneth, who meant so much to them. If she didn't bring along the children, what a cruel thing to leave them in the name of love for Bob.

Next, Duncan wrote to Creeley. Before cursing him to his face, Duncan volunteered a peccavi. After all, he himself had put the bee into the bonnet of Creeley's evil demon by suggesting how much a woman like Marthe could do for him. All the more so, he now wanted to dissociate himself from Creeley's hypocrisy and emotional brutality. Creeley had been successful in a number of recent sexual exploits. What he hadn't managed so far was actually loving. Money was part of the problem. Only once he made a life for himself to be able to offer some kind of happiness rather than ask for it; only once he found himself in love with a woman who didn't provide the added excitement of being the wife or lover of a friend, could he be sure to enter a free relationship rather than follow the Creeley formula as so far.

Finally, Duncan wrote to Rexroth. Jess was adamant that Creeley never be admitted to their house again, and rightly so. Meanwhile, Rexroth had his creative strength to see him through the worst. And his companions would stand by him.

The opposite proved to be the case, with Duncan as one of the first to start reversing himself. After another long-distance phone call, this time from Creeley, pleading his case in his intimate voice, Creeley's friendship became a primary concern to Duncan, while his commitment to Rexroth turned ambivalent. Duncan vowed to stand by Rexroth as best he could during the coming year; on the other hand, he was glad that his absence from San Francisco exempted him from having to choose sides. Siding with Rexroth would do the gravest injustice to the manly qualities one respected in him.

This matter taken care of, Duncan gladly turned to literary concerns such as Ginsberg's *Howl* and its cosmic megalomania, journalistic derivation out of Whitman, and facile dramatization of the miserable. Otherwise, he thought the poem was terrific, expressing surprise at the fact that these *lumpenproles* can howl.

Creeley, who hastened to agree, won Duncan back one by one.

Over the years he had learned his lesson, realizing that Duncan, whatever moral stance he might take, would first consult with his fellow arbiter of moral decorum, Denise Levertov. Hence both were plied with Creeley's accounts of his amours with Marthe. To Duncan, Creeley talked about Rexroth's poor state of health and his own impotence *vis-à-vis* a bitterly messy situation; or, once the affair was over, about how very desperately he had wanted to take care of Marthe. To Denise and Mitch, he expatiated on the more spiritual aspects of the affair. Marthe was a very good woman; she hadn't so much saved his life as given it a place to be. She had made him do and see things never done or seen before – like merry-go-rounds and parks (already dwelt upon to Duncan), or hands, eyes, children, growing up, love, and what was due.

His moral guardians lent an open ear to the pleas of their erring but repentant charge. Duncan's mood was slowly swinging. He was partisan of Bob, he wrote Levertov, because he thought of him as tougher and independent; but he was an antagonist of Bob because of his keeping double accounts and embezzling with the funds of the actual. However, Rexroth, in being unprepared for the loss of Marthe, was essentially guilty of the same untruthfulness.

Levertov, in turn, was apologetic for feeling sorry for Rexroth and willingly adopted Creeley's justification of Marthe in proposing to leave her husband. While commiserating with Rexroth for losing his children, she was glad Creeley was not responsible for Marthe's deserting her husband, i.e., Creeley had said Marthe was leaving anyway.

Eventually, Duncan reversed his attitude towards Creeley completely, in spite of Jess, who continued to insist that he remain *persona non grata* in their household – just as he had recently thrown out Allen Ginsberg and Peter Orlovsky. Poor dear Bob! His poems showed real longing for Marthe. Meanwhile, Rexroth's Marthe poems mixed true feeling with sentimentality, showing that he lacked moral knowledge of himself. Obviously, he could only acknowledge his, not Marthe's, moral knowledge. Nor did he ever allow that Bob and Marthe might be in love. In retrospect, Duncan felt horribly betrayed for having flown to the protection of Rexroth's household.

But little of this was communicated directly to Creeley, who consequently kept worrying that Duncan might ultimately turn against him. Creeley wrote him several letters, even admitted to the duplicity, viciousness, and insolent forgetfulness he might project. But Duncan remained non-committal – or worse, not answering Creeley's letters at all.

So Creeley turned to Levertov. He fully understood that Duncan, like others, had been affected by his affair with Rexroth's wife. But so had *he* been, to put it mildly. And he very much wished he could stay clear with Duncan.

Although Duncan finally did write, he didn't fully assuage Creeley's fears. So Creeley once again turned to Levertov. During a Christmas visit with the Goodmans in Mexico, he got a chance to air his remaining worries to Denise. He knew what was at stake, and, contrary to his usual habits when with the Goodmans, behaved with impeccable charm. Both Denise and Mitch were sufficiently impressed to congratulate Bob and themselves on the specialness of their friendship. Cid once had said that Bob was part of his own kin, and that's exactly how Mitch and she felt, Denise wrote to him. Or more simply put, they both loved him. Unlike the usual friendships of habit, theirs not only endured but renewed and refreshed itself in an exciting and lovely way.

The day after Bob's departure, Denise received a letter from Duncan expressing his feeling of betraying Bob by having flown to the protection of Rexroth's household. Reluctant to send on the actual letter, Denise decided to let Bob know the gist of it. Although Jess remained antagonistic to Bob, Denise summarized, Duncan himself had only felt his love for Bob and his poetry deepen.

A few months later, Duncan decided to break relations with Rexroth altogether. His attitude towards Marthe had extinguished immediate human respect, in Duncan's opinion. Worse, Rexroth had deteriorated as a poet, as well as started to attack Marianne Moore and Charles Olson, both of whom Duncan admired. Such critical misdemeanours left in shreds his last reserves of fondness for Rexroth. The fronts were drawn. Denise Levertov and Robert Creeley were declared foremost among Duncan's immediate peers, Charles Olson, Marianne Moore, William Carlos Williams, and Ezra Pound his literary elders. Kenneth Rexroth was not even mentioned.

There was more of the same in the years to come. The politics preceding the publication of *The New American Poetry* of 1960 provide an instance. In a 1981 interview editor Don Allen conceded that Rexroth might easily have headed this influential anthology. But due to the pressures brought to bear on him from various quarters, that place of honour was given to Olson instead. As in the 1967 anthology *The New Writing in the u.s.a.*, edited by Don Allen and Robert Creeley, or the 1972 *Poetics of the New American Poetry*, edited by Don Allen and Warren Tallman, Rexroth was excluded, a *persona non grata*.

What helped Duncan, Levertov, Creeley, and others close ranks against Rexroth was his continuing obsession with his wife's one-time lover. While praising Creeley as a poet in print, he did everything to bad-mouth the man in private. He spread rumours that Bob had once promised Denise to leave his wife and kids if she would come live with him. He continued to believe that Creeley, like a snake hypnotizing a bird, wielded evil powers over Marthe.

A "Special Extra" Denise sent Creeley around April 1958 warned him what the jealous husband might be up to. Rexroth, while on tour in New York, had found out that Creeley had been in San Francisco and renewed contact with Marthe. He was threatening to go to Albuquerque and shoot him – in New Mexico it was all right for a husband to kill his wife's lover. Denise felt she had to warn Bob.

And the filthy stories Rexroth had been pouring out about him! Dope and orgies! Granted some wild things must have happened to Creeley since leaving Majorca. But the sheer filth Rexroth had spewed forth just the day before – it couldn't possibly be true. Denise had cried, first in anger, later in pity and horror, then finally felt mere contempt. Rexroth, taking advantage of her innocence, probably took pleasure in shocking her with his graphic stories of debauches. Until Allen Ginsberg let her read his diary, she hadn't even known what homosexuals did, for instance. In any case, even if Creeley had as many sides to his person as a diamond, she wouldn't take Rexroth's word for anything ever again. He was obviously a madman.

Creeley hastened to assure her that she was right. An orgy would scare him to death, not to mention debauches. Sure, he had smoked marijuana, but he was hardly a dope fiend. Nor anyone's lover. As for his threats, Rexroth was much too cowardly to carry them through. On one occasion he had told Creeley over the phone that he was going to shoot him. So Creeley had said he'd come over in an hour, whereupon Rexroth had mumbled that he didn't want any more trouble. As for his ranting to Denise and Mitch, he remembered Rexroth haranguing the Dorns in similar fashion for six whole hours. People were finally beginning to realize what he had known about Rexroth all along, Creeley continued: the viciousness, threats, anonymous phone calls, compulsive need to titillate, outrage, and shock his emotional system after the actual story was already dead.

The letter had the effect of a well-timed *coup de grace*. Denise apologized to Creeley for bringing the whole thing to his attention at all. Obviously, it was all old hat to him. In the meantime she had reread some of Creeley's old letters. And by Jesus, they made Rexroth look more filthyminded and/or insane than ever. How could one feel sorry for him any longer! Insanity so dehumanized people one couldn't relate to the respective person even with pity.

Duncan had long reached the same conclusion. The man was deranged. He couldn't think of ever having known a more furious man. Creeley had expressed a similar notion even earlier. His image of Rexroth, he wrote Duncan on 27 July 1957, was of an insane loneliness that scared him and struck him as malignant.

Marthe's attitude towards her estranged husband had long been similar. She describes him in letters to Creeley as sick, frightened, despairing – a latter-day Lear frantic with terror over the possible loss of his children, aimlessly walking around the house, absent-mindedly picking up and putting down books. But all she felt was fear, resentment, and loathing. Kenneth would tell her about his absolute agony of being separated from Mary and Katharine; or he'd write to her begging for the peace they had enjoyed in their former love:

> Speak to me. Talk
> To me. Break the black silence.
> Speak of the tree full of leaves,
> Of a flying bird, the new
> Moon in the sunset, a poem,
> A book, a person – all the
> Casual healing speech
> Of your resonant, quiet voice.
> The word freedom. The word peace.

But to Marthe it was all a cheap and ultimately dishonest trick.

Her attitude towards Rexroth hardened into contempt. She wrote to him that his suspecting her of having renewed contact with Creeley had merely made her waste an hour of psychiatric therapy. First she had had to explain to the analyst her fears of telling Rexroth that Creeley was in San Francisco, then about her fears of not telling him. For if Rexroth found out from someone else, he might come to suspect that she and Creeley were meeting secretly. What was the use of it all? Neither she nor Bob had any desire to stir up old flames.

Marthe's new analyst, Steven Schoen, "helped her understand" (to quote Rexroth's biographer Linda Hamalian) "that as long as she remained married to [Kenneth], she might be miserable." In the process of therapy, Marthe and Steven, himself a married man with three children, "fell in love." Encouraged by this joyous course of events, Marthe left Rexroth in late January 1961. Half a year later, she sued him for divorce "on the grounds of extreme cruelty." Rexroth refused to contest her plea. In the divorce agreement their joint savings of $6,000 went to Marthe, while he was allowed to keep his ten-thousand volume library as a "security blanket." In addition, he was ordered to make alimony and child support payments to the then considerable sum of $275 a month. Marthe and Steven Schoen married a few years later.

In September 1962, Rexroth had the gratification of seeing his daughter Mary appear unannounced on his doorstep at Scott Street, suitcase in hand. She was going to stay, she insisted. Living with Marthe, Katharine, Steven Schoen, and *his* three children had made her miserable. Marthe, writes Linda Hamalian, "had not wanted [Mary] to leave, but she felt enormous pressure – from Kenneth, from Mary, and from her new therapist – to honor Mary's preference for living with her father."

26

The Schoolteacher.

Separation from Marthe left Creeley feeling lonely, even in slight shock, he confessed to Mitch.

To have found a job that would have supported him, Marthe, and her children only made things worse. It had been a precipitous affair: Mercedes Garoffolo, in the company of Sender and his wife, coming up to Ranchites and telling him about an opening at a small boys school in Albuquerque, Creeley making a phone call, and, two days later, finding himself, beard and all, teaching English and French, grades seven to nine.

Just as quickly he had to rent a new place. He found a decently furnished three-room adobe house with two fireplaces and whitewashed walls at 601 Montano, N.W., right on the edge of the desert, about ten miles from the town centre and two from the so-called Albuquerque Academy for Boys. A water pump had to be fixed before he could move in. He also needed a car and by the end of November bought himself a '49 Mercury.

At least he had money now, $300 a month, $250 after taxes. Teaching wasn't so bad either. He found the boys generous in spirit, and they liked their warm, open-minded, and strikingly unorthodox new teacher. Irritated by the constant giggling, Creeley one day surprised the pupils by an unexpected measure of calling them to order. He briefly stared at them, turned to the board, and wrote on it, in letters as large as he could, the word *SHIT*. Some of the boys blushed, all of them fell silent. *SHIT*! That was the word. Were there any others they would like to consider? The boys were too abashed. So Creeley continued with "some vague lecture on 'power' words, and how of course we all make use of them, and are also, equally, attracted to them."

However, there was a major problem if Creeley wanted to continue in his new job. He didn't have a B.A., so he had to be paid as a janitor. Perhaps he should go back to Harvard during the summer of 1957 and complete his degree. The headmaster volunteered to loan him the money, and a colleague offered a ride east in early June.

In the meantime, he tried a different scheme. He wrote to Olson, wondering if Black Mountain College would award him any kind of degree, even as just a stop-gap. Olson managed the impossible in little over a month, sending the headmaster of the Albuquerque Academy for Boys a transcript of the record of Robert Creeley. Creeley, the document alleged, had been provisionally graduated from Black Mountain College on appointment to the faculty, March, 1954. The candidate's graduation had been satisfactorily completed in December 1955 on the basis of three writing tutorials (graduation project, English major, and finish of graduation respectively), in all of which he received A's. Certified by Charles Olson, Rector, Black Mountain College, for the Registrar, 10 November 1956. An accompanying letter also informed the headmaster about Creeley's ongoing editorship of the *Black Mountain Review* as well as about his past teaching load as a faculty member, to wit: fifteen hours a week during the spring quarter, 1954, eighteen hours during the summer quarter, 1955, fifteen in the fall of 1955, and again eighteen hours during the winter of 1955–56.

The headmaster remained unconvinced. To Creeley's chagrin he continued to insist that he return to Harvard. By 8 December, Creeley had finally made up his mind to do so. He would go back East to get his "union card."

Yet how, if ever, would he be able to resume his actual work as a poet? Teaching, he found, left him little time to write, or rather to get out of the writing block he had been experiencing for some time. He had typed dittos of Ginsberg's *Howl* and collected other people's material for BMR #7 but done little of his own work. When he was still back in San Francisco and a certain Henry Evans had offered to print eight of his poems for Porpoise Bookshop, Creeley realized he didn't even have that small number of new, yet unpublished poems. Pressure produced the needed results, and after a weekend of talking and drinking, he'd started writing poems and "feeling" them as he hadn't in months. He wrote eight in one wild day, he bragged to Olson. Among the samples sent for Olson's inspection, "Just Friends," "The Picnic," and "Please" made it into print, while several others ("Never Seek to Tell Thy Love," "I Don't Think So," and the superb "How about That") remained unpublished. None of them were included in the pamphlet *If You* ultimately brought out by Henry Evans. The alleged "break-thru" proved a dead end.

Once he'd arrived in New Mexico, there had been little more than further plans and expectations. After talking to novelists Kerouac and Sender, he had hoped to write a long piece of prose projecting an image of his own kind, but nothing came of it. Or he thought he felt the sort of vaporousness that heralded the writing of poetry. But once again, his hopes proved null and void. What poems he managed to write after a long day of teaching he mostly threw out again after a week or so – mere finger exercises to keep himself ready for the next burst of creativity.

Restless as ever, he used weekends for travel: to the Mexican border town of Juarez, which made him see America as more tangible and appreciated; or to the D.H. Lawrence ranch near Taos, where he visited Frieda's grave, caught a glimpse of Lawrence's typewriter by pulling himself up by a window with bars, and admired the ocean-like view spreading out towards the desert far below.

Finally, there came the long-anticipated Christmas trip south to visit Denise and Mitch in Mexico. In the last few months of 1956 he had put behind himself a sort of poor man's odyssey, covering some nine thousand miles, not counting side trips such as to L.A. with Buddy. But he had never taken a journey like this: by bus straight from Juarez to Durango and from there west across the Sierra Madre Occidental, the road skirting fathomless drop-offs on numerous curves. "Mabel: A Story" gives a colourful, Ginsberg-inspired account of the remainder of the trip before he joined Denise and Mitch and their son, Nik, in Barra de Navidad on the Pacific.

Move by means of third class buses from El Paso to Durango, then turn right over mountains, ghost forgotten lumber camps at twenty thousand feet turn blue in the dust as driver, Indian, shifts into neutral for the descent into Mazatlan. Stone out, stagger into cheap hotel with no doors for night's sleep, onto bus again in some time of day or night, at stop get off and go in for drink and in patio have vision of the redeemer at sight of older man's great dignity at back table under tree with traditional white clothes on, in the moonlight. Approach respectfully for wisdom. Find he has passed out.

In Guadalajara, Christmas eve, high-ceilinged one room, hotel, fly circling old light bulb hanging from traditional center on frayed cord. Read Beckett's *Malone Dies* and get its message entirely. Feel confused about purposes and other aspects of being. Very physically close to people, as on bus, but seemingly no viable response. Continuing on bus, this time with roped-up madman, very vocal, and some chickens and small pigs, to coast, land mellows out as bus gets closer, banana trees, mud, lots of stuff growing with big splayed dark green leaves. Air wettish and hot. Blue ocean, lagoon, palm huts ...

Creeley reached Barra de Navidad, a stretch of low-thatched houses on a strip of land between the sea in front and a lagoon in the back, at around nine p.m. in the pitch dark. He found a room in one of the so-called hotels for people from Guadalajara. It was like a huge crypt with no windows, a

dirt floor, a table, a candle, and an army cot. All night he could hear the
breakers hitting the beach about fifty feet from where he was sleeping.

He next went in search of Mitch and Denise, found the South Sea-type
long wooden building à la Somerset Maugham, in which they had rented the
upper floor. He went up the dark stairs, then down a corridor towards a glow
of light behind a door, and knocked. There was Mitch reading to his son
Nik, and, stepping in from the next room, wonderful Denise in a wrapper.

The next two days they spent on the beach talking, from time to time
going back to the house to cool off and then out again to the small bay,
full of papayas, coconuts, and lots of pigs. Watching Dennie stirred up
old emotions in Creeley, but temporarily all of a favourable or erotic
kind. One early afternoon on the beach, wearing a summer dress instead
of a bathing suit, she nonetheless decided to suddenly run in to have a
swim with the men. And there she was, dripping, laughing, her hair wet,
as she came stumbling out, the dress clinging to her body.

But for once Creeley decided to focus his libidinal energies on other,
unmarried women; the beautiful natives walking along the beach, or at
night during dinner in the big room for the "visitors," a girl with long
hair, thick and heavy down her back, who seemingly in spite of herself
turned to look at him with huge black eyes, wide open with curiosity. After the bitter turmoil with Marthe or the solitary constraints he'd been
living under since, it was a tremendous relief. He felt exuberant and reck-
less as he hadn't in months.

Let's go for a swim, he announced to his hosts.

You don't go for a swim here after twilight. There are sharks out there,
they warned him.

Don't worry about sharks, he insisted, and swam out into the darkening
ocean. Denise and Mitch watched from the beach, worrying he might go
out too far.

At last he was back, so the three of them went up onto their little balcony overlooking the Pacific. And there they were, good-size sharks cutting slowly back and forth through the waters. Denise recorded the
experience in a poem, "The Sharks":

Well then, the last day the sharks appeared.
Dark fins appear, innocent
as if in fair warning. The sea becomes
sinister, are they everywhere?
I tell you, they break six feet of water.
...
It was sundown when they came, the time
when a sheen of copper stills the sea,

not dark enough for moonlight, clear enough
to see them easily. Dark
the sharp lift of the fins.

Talking to Mitch and Denise reawakened Creeley's sense of who he was, or at least ought to be – a writer. It was high time. What had he accomplished of late except teach teenagers English and French (a language he didn't even know) or get entangled in an impossible affair? And here was Denise, showing him her new poems, in her broad handwriting, in an oblong copy book, a picture of a tiger on its cover – thick, beautiful poems of a density rooted in the growing sureness of her experience of things.

Perhaps he would quit his job at the Academy for Boys and do what they did! Live on less money, but write. One could carve out a decent living with little effort teaching English to Mexicans either in Oaxaca or San Cristobal de las Casas, Mitch told him. Bob's present teaching job would be appropriate for supporting a family. Without one, it made little sense. Once back in Albuquerque, he would tell the headmaster that he'd quit at the end of the school year in 1956–57 and go to live in Mexico by June.

Yet the urge to get married again remained as strong as ever. Before saying good-bye to the Goodmans after a little over two days, he left behind a surprise. He had been occupying Mitch's work room, using the typewriter, seemingly writing letters. After his departure Mitch found three of them, crumpled up, not in the waste basket but beside it on the floor. Naturally, he couldn't resist, and read them. They were addressed to three women – Cynthia, Julie, and Marthe – each one proposing marriage in unequivocal terms.

The long bus ride back gave Creeley time to reflect upon his past and future life. He thought of his children, now safely installed with their mother at Rosebud Farm on Pine Hill Road, New Fairfield, Connecticut. Like himself when a child, they were probably sleigh riding and skating while he was rambling through tropical rain forests on ramshackle Mexican buses. He thought of Ann, the first woman he had ever made love to. He remembered the years they had lived off her trust fund – like heavenly bird droppings – himself embarrassed for not supporting her or the children but covetous of the time it gave him to write. He recalled Williams's "I *am* a poet. I / am. I am." That's what he would have to get back to himself. He also recalled the grimmer moments of his married life, like the time Ann miscarried and he delivered "what there was, of the baby"; or the prematurely born baby who died, so he and the undertaker stuck it into a plain white pine box and went to bury it in a hole in a local cemetery by the road between Rock Pool Farm and Littleton.

Back in Albuquerque he found a letter from Ann. Over the past few months they had been corresponding regularly, and had spoken at least once over the telephone. Ann, writing to Bob, seemed much the same person as ever: humorous, chatty, and self-deprecating. She'd tell him about the children, the presents they would like, and their joy in receiving them. She expressed surprise at hearing his voice over the phone – he sounded more sure of himself; she was planning his visit with David, Tom, and Charlotte and offered to let him stay for a couple of days at Rosebud Farm while she'd go away; she even fretted over his health. Slater had dropped by, looking years younger; her former guardian, Connie, had spent a pleasant three days with her; and they'd soon be expecting Bob's mother whom Dave was anxious to see. Terribly, John Altoon, Bob's close friend and briefly Ann's lover, had tried to commit suicide by throwing himself in front of a train. For three weeks he had been confined in a Barcelona insane asylum. Afterwards he'd had to be watched continually, because he kept trying to do it again. He was so thin and weak, Ann reported, he couldn't even walk straight.

She was sorry about not sending the children, she had written on 26 July 1956. She was mostly worried about school and about unsettling them. She meant no harm really. The kids weren't forgetting him at all.

Bob had every reason to believe her. Speaking to her over the phone in early August, he had sensed no bitterness whatsoever. Only occasionally, when she mentioned, say, her pal the psychiatrist down the road, his feelings towards her curdled. Ann's most recent letter contained suggestions of that kind. She was learning to trade on the stock market on a pittance and to read the *Wall Street Journal*, a neighbour giving her lessons. Was the *Wall Street Journal* suitable reading for a woman as lovely as Ann often was? Bob wondered. All in all, he found the image of what was left of his former family hard to manage. In any case, his hopes lay in the future. On New Year's Day he made a vow: He'd like to find a new wife this coming year and at last write a novel.

Considering the paucity of new poetry and prose he had produced for over a year, his writing career was not going badly. Frederick Eckman had recently hailed him as "the best poet under forty now writing" in the October 1956 issue of the prestigious *Poetry* magazine. "He is also the most *conserving* poet I know," Eckman wrote. "He wastes nothing – in fact, at times, rather too little. Creeley's poems are characterized by constriction, the partially revealed vision, economy of utterance – to a degree that would be very nearly a fault, were it not for his exquisite sense of the collapsed rhythm, the precisely right degree of flatness, the stabbing flicker of wit: almost a negation of poetry in the act of poetry. Creeley is a desperate man, artistically speaking, a purist's purist who utters not one grunt more than he actually knows."

If You, the pamphlet of eight of Creeley's poems published by Henry Evans, had just come out in San Francisco. Another small volume of his poetry and prose, entitled *The Dress*, was supposed to appear soon (but never did). Part of of the *Black Mountain Review #7* was already at the printers.

Now, upon returning from Mexico, he found a letter from Gael Turnbull in England offering to bring out a good-sized volume of his "selected poems" for Migrant Books. He was ecstatic, again and again thanking Turnbull, congratulating him on his sense of selection and assuring him he was not the least concerned about format – as long as it was plain and legible and decent. For the time being, his not having copies of all his previous publications was his only worry. But he would immediately write to Duncan, who either owned them or could easily borrow them all from others.

The magnitude of what was at stake caught up with him four days later when he sent Turnbull a rejoinder to his original thank-you letter of 31 December 1956. To have the volume printed in Italy, as Turnbull had suggested, was not up to what a "selected poems" called for. Granted, it was presumptuous for him to say so but it was a book he had waited for and wanted done properly. It had to be formal and complete in every possible way.

He had also changed his mind about format. He didn't know what kind of money Turnbull had to work with, but what he would suggest was something along the lines of the BMR page dimension, paper weight, and cover (not the fold over). With the review costing $4.50 at 226 pages and 600 copies, the *Selected Poems* should run about $125 to $150, that is, if Turnbull would use his Majorca printer, Mossen Alcover, which Creeley thought would be his best bet. He would immediately write to Mossen himself to get a price.

While waiting for Turnbull's response, he wasted no time in preparing the typescript for the projected volume. By the end of the month it was ready, thirty-nine poems plus a short preface. For a title he had settled on *The Whip & Other Poems (1950–1955)*. He liked Turnbull's idea of putting a photograph on the cover but suggested it be used both front *and* back. Incidentally, Frederick Eckman had called him "the best poet under forty now writing" in *Poetry*, which seemed good for publicity as well as vanity, he added casually.

Buoyed by success, he was definitely going to leave for Mexico by June. Why waste more time teaching and taking degrees when his career was so clearly headed for success without these bourgeois props?

But something unexpected that happened early in 1957 reversed these plans.

Cynthia Homire.
Courtesy of Jonathan Williams.

Robert Creeley and Dan Rice, Black Mountain, 1955. (See page 196.)
Courtesy of Jonathan Williams. Martin Duberman, *Black Mountain*, 1972.

Charles Olson, Betty Kaiser, and their son, Charles Peter, in the summer of 1956.
Courtesy of Gerald van de Wiele. Martin Duberman, *Black Mountain*, 1972.

Edward Dahlberg with his wife, R'lene, 1956.
Courtesy of R'lene Dahlberg. Charles DeFanti, *The Wages of Expectation*.

Robert Creeley and Paul Blackburn.
Courtesy of Joan Blackburn.

Robert Creeley and Robert Duncan, ca. 1955.
Courtesy of Ann MacKinnon.

Victor Kalos with Thomas and Charlotte Creeley, ca. 1955.
Courtesy of Ann MacKinnon.

Jack Kerouac, Tangier, 1957.
Courtesy of Ann Charters, *Kerouac. A Biography*. 1974.

Allen Ginsberg.
Courtesy of Gerard Malanga.

Kenneth Rexroth, Marthe, and their daughter Katharine, 1958.
Courtesy of Harry Redl, Linda Hamalian, *A Life of Kenneth Rexroth*, 1991.

Bobbie Louise Hawkins.
Courtesy of Bobbie Louise Hawkins.

Bob and Bobbie.
Courtesy of Bobbie Louise Hawkins.

Bob and Bobbie.
Courtesy of Bobbie Louise Hawkins.

Robert Creeley, his third wife, Penelope Highton, and their son, William Gabriel, 1981. Photograph: Ekbert Faas.

From left to right: John Wieners, Robert Duncan, Robin Blaser, Allen Ginsberg, Robert Creeley, 11 August 1968 Courtesy of *Brick* (Winter 1993).

27

Bobbie.

Getting to know Bob Creeley had been a strange affair, almost as if the encounter had been fated. Before meeting him, she had met three of his close friends, all of them through different channels.

First, Race Newton: coming back from Japan, Bobbie had needed work to support herself and her two daughters, Kirsten and Leslie. Perhaps she would sing in a nightclub. She was sexy looking and, at twenty-five, still young enough for that. But she would first have to work up a proper repertoire with a pianist. When she phoned the Musician's Union, they suggested Race. For three months, the two of them spent a couple of afternoons together every week, he playing the piano and she singing – and paying him.

Second, Buddy Berlin: that happened a few months later while she was working as an account executive for television, with Buddy's Imported Motors as one of her clients. Later she ordered a car through his dealership, and met Buddy himself.

Third, Max Finstein: that again happened several months later. She was now working as a radio disc jockey, doing the so-called psycho shift, twelve to six a.m. Lots of crazies phoned in, sometimes even some nice guys. One of these, a city planner, was allowed to come over to the station to chat with her while the record was playing, in between doing ads and the news on the hour. Next the city planner brought his friend Ned, who ran the grain store up in Taos.

You look like you ought to live in Taos, Ned told her.

I couldn't afford it, she said.

But life's very cheap there, Ned insisted.

That's right, said the city planner. Ned's just given a house away to a couple of guys. Mind you, it isn't much of a house, water from a hand pump, but it's got electricity.

One of those two guys, Max Finstein, called her up a week later. Ned had suggested she might be able to help him. Max wanted to divorce his ex-wife in New York, and was looking for a job to pay for it. Next, Max dropped by the radio station to see Bobbie and pick up some addresses for potential jobs.

On the day she went to pick up her car, all three of them were there: Race Newton, Buddy Berlin, and Max Finstein, as well as a fourth guy Race introduced to her as Bob Creeley.

Bob struck her as completely wonderful and extraordinary. There was something about his intelligence and how he articulated it she had never met before. A lovely flash sense of words, a weird twist of phrase that made her laugh. When would she meet him again? Somehow she knew they had some unfinished business to take care of. Creeley delighted her from the "first sight of him. Diffident and quiet he [threw] a look as bright as color through crystal." Even four years after they met, "his conversation could still catch [her] imagination and sling it distances." Any other man was "negligible" in her eyes.

One day Bob and Max returned to the radio station for a chat with her after the bars had closed. Max went to get coffee, and Bob asked if she had a couch he could sleep on. She said yes, so he stayed there, and then went home with her.

How different he was from Olaf, Bobbie's first husband. Almost the polar opposite. Bob was moody, intense, but never boring; Olaf was controlled, manipulative, and infinitely tedious.

Olaf had been thirty-one when they had married, Bobbie only nineteen. A Danish architect who had come to Albuquerque to give a talk, he had only just taken Bobbie to lunch a couple of times when he started proposing to her. Could she ever really love him, she wondered. Though he was good looking, and obviously well situated, her mother, Norah, was against the marriage. She had run off with Bobbie's dad just shortly before turning sixteen. He vanished when Bobbie was eleven.

But Olaf insisted. One didn't have to be in love to get married: perhaps she would fall in love later. It was true that Bobbie and he hardly knew each other, so he understood why Norah opposed his marriage proposal. Why not have a trial marriage for a year, and then decide after.

How sophisticated and worldly he looked, Bobbie thought, watching Olaf talk to Norah, who was only some five years older than him. Sleeping with him a couple of times hadn't been all that exciting, but at least he would take her out of Albuquerque. Bobbie was an art student with ambitions but little money. She couldn't even afford her own painting equipment or lunches, let alone tuition fees. Marriage to Olaf would be like a business deal, a ticket to the world. Shortly thereafter they were married by a black preacher in Norah's living-room.

Some of Bobbie's wishes did get fulfilled. For a year she studied painting at the Slade in London. Then the couple spent two years in British Honduras, which Bobbie would remember as some of the happiest of her life.

She became pregnant and had a daughter, Kirsten. Olaf was a good husband, consistently considerate and reasonable. He also had decided opinions about the role of a wife – as well as about the roles of mistresses and prostitutes. And of these latter, Bobbie discoverd, Olaf had an endless number. From that moment she felt she could never love him, and asked for a divorce.

But she was pregnant again with Leslie, and Olaf advised patience. She would have their second child, and then they'd see. In the meantime they had gone to Tokyo. Olaf was often away in South Korea building low-cost housing for North Korean refugees. Once when he returned, she announced she wanted to go back to the United States. But that was impossible, he explained. They were both on a diplomatic visa from the United Nations, which would only pay for her return if he agreed to it. And he didn't. Instead, he advised patience. They would take a trip around the world, go back to Denmark, and then discuss the divorce. The same old story. Wait and see, with nothing ever happening except the way Olaf decided.

Bobbie had had enough of playing the role of the wonderful, teachable wife. She dreaded the prospect of going around the world with Olaf, or worse, of ending up in Denmark where Olaf's dad was the all-powerful chief of the country's police, a personal friend of the country's king. Instead of obtaining the wished-for divorce, she would just get trapped, with everything stacked against her: an unknown language, unfamiliar customs and laws, and an infinitely manipulative husband.

She had to act resolutely. After Olaf had flown back to Korea, she sold the car, went through some unorthodox currency transactions, and flew back to the States. That brought the much-coveted freedom from Olaf but also enormous new responsibilities. Olaf had diplomatic immunity and couldn't be forced to send money to help support Kirsten and Leslie. She had to look for a job to support herself and her kids, which was how she met pianist Race Newton.

From Creeley's perspective, getting to know Bobbie and marrying her were almost one and the same.

Once
you were

alone and I

met you. It was late

at night.
I never

left after that.

Their meeting at the radio station happened sometime around 20 January. His friend Max Finstein, Creeley reported to Ginsberg, knew a girl working there as a disc jockey. Tired and drunk, he mainly wanted a quiet place to relax, then found himself sitting across the booth in which Bobbie was spinning discs. He stayed until she was finished, accompanied her home where she fed him, then went off to teach, the kids asking him if he'd been drinking. Wow. A few days later, he made up his mind. He thought he ought to marry her, just like that, he wrote to Denise. The letter also gives us a glimpse of their early relationship: Bob working at the Academy for Boys, Bobbie, while taking care of her daughters, continuing her psycho shift on the radio. They seemed most together over tables and dishes. While he was writing to Denise, Bobbie was asleep.

They took out a marriage licence, but as the time approached, decided otherwise. Both had a broken marriage behind them, and ultimately didn't believe enough in the official wedding ceremony to want to go through it again.

His new family made Creeley feel more settled and self-assured than he had felt in years. Bobbie was very able and pleasant. A determined and substantial Texan Irish lady who cleared away many of his old cobwebs, he reported to friends. Her six-room house at 1826 Griegos easily accomodated all four of them. Bobbie also had her own car, a VW.

But "getting married" had its drawbacks too. For one, it threw most of the plans he had made upon returning from Mexico into reverse. Rather than go south after June, he had to hold on to his teaching job. As of the beginning of 1957, that meant teaching seven classes a day to groups of ten to fifteen boys between twelve and fourteen years old. His subjects included French, English, and (because of the headmaster's stomach trouble) American history and geography. The kids were nice. Most of them being from single-parent homes, the job had socially interesting aspects as well. However, a day at school left Creeley so wrung out at night that there was little leisure for seeing his family, let alone for writing.

Creeley had more worries than that. Even the grim enough prospect of continuing to teach school was not guaranteed unless he got a proper B.A. The New Mexico Board of Education wouldn't recognize the degree that Black Mountain College rector Charles Olson had awarded him. Creeley was advised to take teaching practice after hours, or go back to Harvard after all. There were problems even with that. Harvard held general examinations once a year only, so he would not be able to take his degree before 1958. Perhaps he, Bobbie, and the kids should spend the summer in Mexico after all.

But increasing family pressure wouldn't allow for it. At the end of March, Bobbie quit her job as a disc jockey after her manager paid her only $25 instead of the promised $35 a week. For the time being, she was working angles for a possible TV show. She was also pregnant, the baby expected by November.

Perhaps Bob should try to get into the University of New Mexico graduate program, instead of returning to Harvard. Once again Olson was called upon for help, provided the required documentation, but failed to impress those it was sent to. The dean of Graduate Studies criticized Bob Creeley's deficient knowledge of Shakespeare and of the history of the English language. A State Board registration officer told him that his Harvard years left him twenty-six hours short in "education" and dismissed his plea that having taught seven classes a day for a year now ought to count for at least half of that.

They were already packed and a day short of leaving for Oaxaca when the headmaster came over to tell Creeley that the board would likely cancel his job at the academy for the coming fall unless he went to the local graduate school for the summer. So the trip to Mexico was definitely off. Without pay after the official school year, he also had to take on a job working nights as a janitor. Finally he was notified that he had been admitted into the graduate program of the University of New Mexico.

Ten years older than most of his fellow students, Creeley at first felt somewhat out of place. But at least this university was less of a factory than Harvard. Also, his courses proved more interesting than expected. He took three of them: one on early American colonization; a second on the history of the English language, full of interesting concrete information; a third, his favourite, on Twain and Whitman, taught by John Gerber, a visiting professor from Iowa State. In asking the students to do a thematic outline of "Song of Myself," Gerber managed to drive home a point Creeley would remember for years to come: "The room in which we met had large blackboards on all four walls and on the day they were due, we were told to copy our various outlines on to the blackboards. So we all got up and did so. When we finally got back to our seats, we noticed one very striking fact. No two of the outlines were the same – which was Professor Gerber's very instructive point. Whitman did not write with a systematized logic of 'subject' nor did he 'organize' his materials with a logically set schedule for their occurrence in the poem."

The main annoyance was that studying, like teaching school, left little time for writing – especially since Creeley, to get by financially, also had to do some private tutoring.

Things got worse with the beginning of the school year. Shortly before, the Latin teacher had died of a heart attack, and Creeley was asked to take her place. That meant fewer hours and students but more preparation. The little Latin he had learned at Holderness, before ultimately failing the subject at Harvard, was all but forgotten. Also, how could he possibly convince his students, however good humoured and trusting, of the relevance to their lives of being able to rattle off Latin conjugations, or of reading Caesar? Not to speak of the indignity he felt for being cast in the role of a jack of all trades in the scholastic system. His patience snapped when the headmaster asked him how he would take to teaching German next year. The proposal tempted him to curse like Götz von Berlichingen. It made him feel like something out of the last century, Creeley commented to Duncan.

At night it was back to the university, a slum in most respects, as Creeley concluded after studying there during the summer. However, his course on the American Civil War turned out to be interesting and informative. The instructor knew how to make things come alive by such unconventional means as setting off charges of black gunpowder in the classroom. Nonetheless, Creeley could hardly stay awake as he sat there, night after night, sometimes so tired he hardly knew where he was, the professor's voice fading out into the slides he used. A worse experience was the Shakespeare course which merely revived his disgust, first developed at Harvard, for the university as a concentrated scene of self-betterment. How ridiculous to have to sit out an arbitrary hour each night to listen to bullshit.

Above all, he had no time, with more and more new chores piling up on him every week. Kirsten was hit by a truck (though not seriously hurt) near their place downtown, so they looked for a new house further out. They found one in Alameda north of Albuquerque by mid-September. It cost as much as their present one but offered more space and solidity. The walls were very thick, the windows inset, the whole house had a usefully asymmetrical feel to it. By the end of October when they moved in, Creeley was suffering from one of his periodic colds aggravated by an almost permanent state of exhaustion. The garden offered pleasures he hadn't enjoyed since leaving Rock Pool Farm: a small-sized animal park consisting of four ducks, numerous rabbits, and a turkey left them by the previous tenants. Creeley's plan to add some goats had to wait until Bobbie, by now nine months pregnant, was properly back on her feet. She was a little bugged with being so full with him, Creeley remarked to

Olson. Women's affairs, as they say. The expected boy turned out to be a girl. Sarah was born 17 November 1957, a Sunday, as Creeley, "grandiosely enough" sat reading Freeman's book on General Lee about soldiers defending their positions with rocks picked from the enbankment behind them.

Time flew, week by week, and month after month: teaching during the day, classes at night, in his spare time cramming either for his next Latin lesson or towards his "union card" at the "local factory." If he got lucky, there was the odd moment for playing with the kids, especially with Sarah, or for dashing off a letter to a friend, mostly complaining about a more and more unbearable situation. Like years before at Harvard, his general exhaustion was threatening his academic performance. By 23 November 1957, his grades had dropped from A's for three English courses taken during the previous summer to B's in both the Shakespeare seminar and the American Civil War course. Was it worth it?

Once in a while, Bob, seated at his desk, looked out, say, at two old men with black hats and their dog stumbling along the dirt road past his house, or at the ever-changing spectacle of the desert fading under the sun or taking on a compacted density from the clouds piled above. Then on he went studying, however pointless and demeaning it seemed at times. Older by ten years, he would not repeat his failure at Harvard but instead try, New England-style, to be a man. With most of the family pulling through a drawn-out period of sickness, Bobbie with a serious ear infection from the flu, he ploughed on. By February 1958, he had pulled his grade average back up to an A, a level he maintained from then on. The samples he submitted as qualification for departmental approval of his candidacy for a Master's degree in Creative Writing were unaminously endorsed by the three readers. Creeley had already achieved considerable reputation from his published poems, and the work submitted was excellent and publishable, commented one. Very interesting, exciting, and amusing, added a second. His final comprehensive examination earned him a B+, his examiners decreeing that, except for a B- in the eighteenth century period, his answers had been of an A or high B quality throughout.

In the meantime he had signed up for another year at the Academy for Boys at an increased annual salary of $4,800. So for ten months more he would be back there teaching Latin, doing his bit as the exhausted, "absent-minded" Latin professor who would forget what it was he wanted to tell them by the time he'd gotten them quiet.

More than ever, Creeley had reason for such perseverance. Bobbie became pregnant again. Their new daughter, Katherine, would be born on 6 February 1959.

28

In Limbo.

Adding to his frustrations, Creeley was once again turned down for the Guggenheim. Paul Blackburn had had a Fullbright, Irving Layton a Canadian Foundation fellowship, Jonathan Williams a Guggenheim. Why everyone else but him?

Just as he had started teaching school, news arrived of the San Francisco Beat poets' meteoric rise to fame. The *New York Times Book Review* had given them nation-wide accreditation. Ginsberg's *Howl*, in Richard Eberhart's estimation, was the "most remarkable poem of the young group." Others like Lawrence Ferlinghetti, Gary Snyder, Michael McClure, and Philip Whalen, as Whalen put it, were given smaller tin wreaths as well.

Reports of other people's successes, parties, and travels reached Creeley thick and fast. New York City, Joel Oppenheimer wrote on 5 January 1958, was popping, new poets, mostly five years younger than Oppenheimer himself, reading all over the place. A single letter from Kerouac or Ginsberg often told of more excitement than Creeley experienced in a whole year. Like Ginsberg spending a night with Oppenheimer and family in the Bronx, then going to see Fielding Dawson; or, on the level of business, approaching Louise Bogan of the *New Yorker*, William Phillips at *Partisan Review*, Don Allen at Grove's *Evergreen Review*, Sherry Abels at *Mademoiselle*, and Arabelle Porter at *New World Writing* – all that in between visiting art shows of Pollock and Balthus or having lunch with Salvador Dali: Kerouac, Orlovsky, and himself had sung "Why Do Fools Fall in Love" for Dali, while the latter talked "about ze higher espiritual rocknroll of ze San Juan de la Cruz." Dali was surprisingly intelligent, Ginsberg remarked. In two weeks, they would all be off, probably on a Yugoslavian freighter bound for Casablanca and Tangiers where Burroughs was getting so inspired he kicked out his Arab boys and took a revolver to his typewriter. Was Bob all right? He didn't answer letters and would soon explode like a great black mushroom over Albuquerque, Philip Whalen had remarked to Ginsberg.

Jack Kerouac was worried too. Bob had written him such a listless letter. Was he bugged about Jack's fame and success? They would last for about two years after which he'd be like Melville, Kerouac oracled, and return to his pots, beans, and shacks. Yet in the meantime Jack seemed to be having a ball, being dined and wined by his London literary agent, picking up an advance for the English publication of *On The Road*, and travelling in Europe and Morocco.

Like Kerouac, most of Creeley's friends, while enjoying their Bohemian lifestyle, found major or at least up-and-coming publishers as well. Levertov's *Here and Now* (1956), Ginsberg's *Howl* (1956), and Corso's *Gasoline* (1958) were done by City Lights, Ferlinghetti's *A Coney Island of the Mind* (1958) by New Directions, Kerouac's *On the Road* (1957) and *The Dharma Bums* (1958) by Viking, his *The Subterraneans* (1958) by Grove.

Creeley's response to it all was ambivalent. Seeing a picture of Kerouac and Ginsberg in *Mademoiselle*, or hearing Ginsberg on NBC inclined him to share Denise's sense of how the whole San Francisco fanfare was starting to make her a little sick. She thought Ginsberg behaved too much like a promotion salesman, a sentiment Creeley had come to agree with. Ginsberg had written him about his approaching Grove Press and New Directions; apparently he had even seen James Laughlin, Creeley confided to Duncan. Ginsberg was so ambitious to make him wonder. To Olson, Creeley voiced a sudden dislike for the historical and social manner even of Kerouac. The San Francisco school's all too quickly and loosely historical mode had turned BMR #7 into a hodgepodge with the inevitable leakage.

Creeley's letters to Ginsberg, that swinging cat with the helping hands, struck a markedly different note. Again and again, he thanked "Dad" Ginsberg for reading his writings in various places as well as for recommending them to his multiple literary contacts. What else was Creeley doing in his isolation than gyrate out of oblique undersided centre of what he was learning from Kerouac and Ginsberg! In the meantime, he also cashed in on Ginsberg's fame for BMR #7. Without prior notice, he appointed Ginsberg contributing editor by simply letting him know he had done so. That was presumptuous, he admitted. But there simply hadn't been time to ask. He was just about to mail copies of the finished issue to Ginsberg in Europe.

Meanwhile, Creeley himself was meeting with little else than setbacks. *The Dress*, a small volume of prose and poetry, though already proof-read, never made it into print. Sending a manuscript of poems to Lawrence Ferlinghetti for publication by City Lights proved a dead end. BMR #7 which, Kerouac thought, ought to make history, ultimately struck its editor as too much blood and thunder, thanks to the San Francisco school contributions. Plans for a follow-up which Creeley discussed with Olson, Ginsberg, and others folded just after Jonathan Williams had procured some of the necessary funds and the program director for a group of Christian and Congregational Churches, whom Creeley had contacted via Ginsberg, had offered help as well. Creeley simply didn't have the time to continue his editorial labours.

Most of Ginsberg's many plugs either didn't work out or backfired. Louise Bogan returned Creeley's poems with a curt note saying she was the *New Yorker's* poetry reviewer, not an editor. *Harper's* turned down another manuscript. Critic M.L. Rosenthal, after rejecting a batch of Creeley's poems plus a story, asked him to write a general piece on the present literary scene in America. To make matters worse, Rosenthal published an article in *The Nation* praising Blackburn, Levertov, Duncan, and Olson but speaking in rather more ambiguous terms of Creeley's "prickly little patterns." He had been described to Creeley as a shy and humane person, and now this! Obviously the man had something against him, Creeley concluded.

Most frustrating to him were his relations with Guggenheim grant winner Jonathan Williams. Who else ever made it so much with so little? Having published two small pamphlets of Creeley's poetry, *The Immoral Proposition* in 1953 and *All That Is Lovely in Men* in 1955, Williams had begun acting like his publisher, sporting him like a necktie or Sunday school pin. By late 1958 James Laughlin more or less offered to publish a book of Creeley's poetry. However, he made the offer subject to Jonathan Williams's approval, not wishing to take an author away from Williams as had happened to him in the early days of his New Directions venture. But Williams, instead of encouraging Laughlin to publish the Creeley volume, promised a Creeley book for the fall. He turned it all dirty, knowing full well what a book done by Laughlin would mean to Creeley, no matter how much it made him seem covetous, Creeley complained to Olson. He'd soon have to start looking for a new publisher, he decided.

He was feeling more isolated than ever. He hardly had time for his family. His correspondence with friends had become sporadic. What could he tell them in return for their stories of travel, adventure, and literary success? Like never before, his letters turned formulaic to the point of interchangeably repeating the same small number of trivial events to friend after friend. Again and again, he apologized for not writing, claimed lack of time, and complained about his loneliness.

Both at school and university he found himself clogged with pedantry and dull conversation. The whole scene was as flat as a pancake. Buddy

Berlin had just left his wife, Wuzza, and Race Newton had found himself one by the name of Lucia. The result was identical, Creeley groaned. Marriage stopped conversation. Other attempts at social contact had him frantically walking back and forth between the tequilla bottle (kitchen) and friends (living room) till it all got pretty damn relative. So he would leave to drive up and down the goddamn streets till all the bars were closed or indulge in his by now happy addiction of talking to himself, finding that his interior monologue had started to flip around in useful ways.

Visits from friends were few and far between. Olson, his wife, Betty, and their baby son had spent two days with the Creeleys in March 1957. Olson had been reading his poetry and lecturing on "The Special View of History" in San Francisco, where Duncan was assistant director of the State College Poetry Center. By the time the Olsons reached Alameda, Charles sporting a beard and a wide-brimmed green felt hat, he and Betty were exhausted and quarrelling. Travelling with a one year old had taken its toll on Betty; Charles's nerves were strung out from the strain of reading in front of his contentious San Francisco peers as well as from too much drinking.

The party arrived at 10:30 at night, Bob just over being sick but already back at work, Bobbie anxious to make her new husband's revered friend feel welcome. Bob noticed that they were all tired, Betty looking nervous and worried. Nonetheless, the two men settled down to talk. Bob showed Charles the little he had written, stressing how anxious he was to throw off prior senses of form and content. They talked until about 5 a.m. A few days later Bob already couldn't remember what they had told each other. They had been too exhausted. Whatever else it accomplished, the visit made Olson use the rest of his cash for a first class Pullman sleeper berth out of Santa Fe. Once back at Black Mountain, he would have to attend to the legal business of the college's dissolution.

Most of Creeley's own attempts at travelling were fraught with problems like everything else. The long awaited trip to Mexico in the summer of 1957 had been cut short by his having to attend graduate school. All he could manage instead was a brief trip East to finally visit his children. It was their first reunion in two years. Shortly before, Ann had written to congratulate him and Bobbie on their marriage and the expected new baby. He shouldn't think she didn't want him to see the children, she once again assured him.

Creeley set out by car around 10 August 1957. Once arrived in New York, he was taken aback by Ann's tight-lipped tone of voice over the phone. Perhaps it would be most convenient, she suggested, if he saw Dave, Tom, and Charlotte for an afternoon in New York City. But to have driven all that distance from Albuquerque for no more than that? Reluctantly Ann granted that he come for two days to Connecticut instead. More would be inconvenient for her. She had just bought a farm in Great Barrington, and she and the children were in the process of moving there.

Ann seemed exhausted and hostile when they met. By contrast, he looked in great shape, she told him. Unlike the letters they had continued to exchange, their conversation was defensive and monosyllabic. Eager to avoid the predictable scene, neither volunteered or prodded for unnecessary information. The emotional involvement between them was clearly dead, which unexpectedly came as a relief to Creeley. He'd rather not find out what she felt. God knows it was none of his business to find her looking like she was in pieces. Or it certainly was, but what to do about it?

Anyway, the children were much grown and seemed decently settled. The exception was Charlotte, who displayed some disconcerting behavioral patterns. She was both very controlled and frightening in her intensity, Creeley found. Tom was, as ever, heartbreaking, while Dave, to all evidence, had taken over the fathering where Creeley had left off years earlier. On balance, he was glad to have re-established a clear line to the children. Little did he realize that he would not see them again for over a decade.

Back in New York City where he was staying at Dan Rice's it was the usual rounds of seeing as many friends and acquaintances as possible: Fee Dawson careening around in familiar fashion, seeming older and impressing Creeley with a longer piece of his writing; John and Elaine Chamberlain with their very wild and "thoughtful" baby; Joel Oppenheimer seeming bugged and getting curiously harsh; Ann's ex-lover Victor Kalos as ever angling but pleasant, working at a bookstore; and last but not least, Cynthia. She and Creeley met for an afternoon and evening getting happily drunk and sentimental, he saying that she looked very, very lovely and clearer than he had ever known her, she assuring him that he was famous and the best. Given their limited time together, her former lover successfully controlled the violent outbursts she used to be so afraid of.

That happened later when Creeley got into trouble with the police and had his car impounded. Bobbie, by now familiar with some of her husband's idiosyncrasies, took action. She contacted Buddy Berlin for the necessary cash to bail Bob out, asked the local police to teletype the New York Commission regarding the car ownership, and sent two wires to her husband care of the Cedar Bar. Contact Police Department, one said. Buddy sending money this address. If sober come home. Bobbie. The second telegram, including a money order, asked him to wire her if the car remained impounded. Otherwise hurry home. Love. Love. Bobbie.

He did hurry, driving the over two thousand miles from New York non-stop, reaching Albuquerque on 27 August. In his absence a local paper had written up his trip as a celebrity's journey in pursuit of further fame and fortune. Robert White Creeley, called by critics the foremost poet under forty in the United States, was "in New York consulting with publishers regarding his newest book, *The Dress*, and the 1957 fall edition of *The Black Mountain Review*, of which he is the editor." The article, about seven hundred words, with a large photograph of the poet, discussed his diverse publications, touched on the major stages of his life such as Holderness, Harvard, Burma, and Europe, and gave a brief account of his "varied career in writing." It alluded to his Divers Press publishing venture in Majorca as well as his time spent at Black Mountain, "the outstanding experimental school in the country," which awarded him "his degree in English." Currently Mr Creeley was studying toward a Master of Arts degree at the University of New Mexico. If nothing else the article was a clear local triumph good enough to impress his mother-in-law, Norah Hall, Creeley joked to Olson.

His next major trip some seven months later was due to chance. Part of the Academy for Boys needed sudden repairs and there were rumours everyone would be given a week off. Creeley made arrangements for a short visit with Duncan in San Francisco. It would be Bobbie, Sarah, and himself, Kirsten and Leslie staying behind with grandmother Norah. They would bring some bedding for Sarah. Bobbie and he required nothing but floor space. They were off on 28 March.

It was the first reunion between Duncan and Creeley since the summer of 1955 in Majorca. Because of Bob's affair with Marthe Rexroth, their friendship had passed through some dire straits. But by the time Creeley arrived in San Francisco, even Jess's decree that Bob would never again be allowed to step across their threshold had been lifted.

The visit was brief but intense, the dialogue between the two compulsive talkers being interspersed by Duncan's reading of his *Medea* or their listening to a Levertov tape, previously broadcast on KPFA. It took his head off, Creeley wrote to Denise; he had tears in his eyes, looking out of the window and hearing her move through it. Duncan also arranged a Creeley reading at Joe Dunn's, which turned into an unexpected success. The place was packed right back to the bathroom with people listening spellbound as Creeley read his poetry and prose flat out, feeling in control and amazed at the real delivery tactics he had developed.

Then he, Bobbie, and Sarah were off again, heading towards Los Angeles for another two days with John Altoon who since last seeing

Creeley in Majorca had had an affair with Ann, thrown himself in front of a train, and spent three weeks in a Barcelona insane asylum. As with Duncan, Creeley was glad to find that it had not shattered their basic friendship.

Finally, during the summer of 1958, he took the often-postponed trip to Mexico. Having traded Bobbie's car for a VW van complete with home-away-from-home facilities, they decided to bring the whole family including Sarah and Kirsten and Leslie. The results were predictable: what had been planned as a relaxing holiday turned into another ordeal. Sitting on Mexican buses jammed in between exotic locals and dreamily peering at the landscape in December 1956 had been a real relief. Being cooped up in a VW van with three children, skirting potholes and dodging foolhardy Mexican drivers, was an entirely different story.

The first major stop was Los Molinos, Oaxaca. Against his usual habits, Creeley even played tourist, going to see Mitla, the thirteenth-century religious centre of the Zapotecs, famous for holding their own against the warlike Aztecs of central Mexico. He was intrigued by the unusual design of the temple. Unlike the pyramidal structure of most Mesoamerican architecture, it consisted of low, horizontal masses enclosing several plazas, more than twenty different patterns of a simple motif – the stepped spiral representing Quetzalcoatl, the plumed serpent – covering the walls. The rigidity of the design terrified him, but the structure as a whole was altogether to his taste, sitting so squarely on a low hill in a valley. The natives with their quietly menacing yet at the same time strangely unfocused temperament had a similar effect on him. He felt both scared by and drawn towards them.

Back in Los Molinos, he was annoyed by the American tourists crowding in on the plaza. So after a week there, they continued towards Tuxtla Gutiérrez and then wound their way up into the mountains surrounding San Cristobal de las Casas, a fabulous place, in Creeley's opinion. Franz Blum, an ingenious old Dane, told him about studying the effect of the trans-American highway on the native tribes, eight of which, each with their separate language, lived in the immediate neighbourhood. One Indian who was studying with Blum came in as they were talking and with an intriguing smile took the hand which Creeley in embarrassed surprise had stretched out to him.

Later memories gave the encounter near mythical dimensions. Never before had he met anybody like the Lacandone Indian, Creeley recalled in 1978. The man was "so completely where he *was*" and so "absolutely alive in the moment of each instant" to become a model of unmediated consciousness. Creeley's "Autobiography" of 1989 recalls the encounter in even more fervent tones: "momently an inexplicably contained person came into the room. But I mean by 'contained' that he was *all* there, all of him was present, as an intensive animal might be, a tiger, but not the least threatening. All the seeming capacity of his senses was alert to the fact of his existence, not to its projection or recall. I can't now make clear how impressive and how tender that human capacity was. So far beyond thought, or belief, or any eventual abstraction at all, requiring no exercise or intent, no commitment or reason. Paradise must be a faint echo indeed."

Creeley's retroactive transformation of the Lacandone Indian into a supernatural embodiment of alertness and self-containment owes a debt to a long tradition of American thought reaching via Olson back to Emerson and Thoreau. "I have never yet met a man who was quite awake," remarked Thoreau. "How could I have looked him in the face?" It was the same question a flustered Creeley came to ask himself facing the Lacandone Indian in San Cristobal de las Casas.

A young English professor by the name of Harold Holden provided a less elevating experience. He insisted on inviting Creeley to his thirteen-room, twenty dollar a month mansion, advising him that with a bit of searching he could do just as well himself, and offering him drinks. As a special token of their day-old friendship, Holden gave him two presents: one a carefully mimeographed sheet of nineteen examples of enjambement, the other a specially autographed offset of a poem published by *Sewanee Review*.

Bobbie's short story "Enroute" fictionalizes the encounter, casting herself as Maggie, Harold Holden as Henry (or Hank), his sycophantic disciple as Chuck, and Creeley as Patrick, a "shapechanger extraordinaire" bluntly contemptuous of his host's poetic efforts:

"Okay, Hank," Patrick rose with the finality of a brown bear rearing onto its hind legs, "it's time for the cantina."

Before they left, Henry added a thirty-one-page poem – "romantic theme, ballad form, personal innovative method" – to the stack of items given over for Patrick's consideration. Patrick being caught here until Tuesday meant there would be time to discuss all of what was close to Henry's heart. Patrick turned the pages in quietly increasing despair.

"Lots of enjambment in there, Hank," he said.

Henry smiled, then frowned.

Next follows a scene in the cantina to which a reluctant Henry and Chuck are dragged by Patrick, who manages to strike up a friendship with a Mexican drunk and troublemaker contemptuously welcoming the "gringos."

They made a charming picture, Patrick and the Mexican. The Mexican's arm was laid over Patrick's shoulder and left there while the Mexican talked, his face screwed into a villainous expression, his mouth spitting. Their faces were a scant inch apart. At intervals the Mexican would wave his free arm at the other three and glare and Patrick would also look at them, his face angelic and delighted. A friend at last. Whenever the Mexican stopped talking as if he had asked a question, Patrick would say "y pues" and bob his head sympathetically, and after a moment of puzzlement the drunk would continue.

Back at his house Holden finally rose to Creeley's continuous insults and threw him out. With the tropical rains and abrasive high elevation temperature changes providing additional irritants, Creeley decided he had had enough of San Cristobal de las Casas and left the following day.

Towards the end of July the Creeley caravan reached Vera Cruz, west of Mexico City on the Bahia de Campeche, where they decided to spend the remaining weeks of their holiday. They found a decent apartment for the same monthly rent Holden paid in San Cristobal; what's more, Vera Cruz, rather than a rainy hole in the mountains, was a far-flung city along a beach offering metropolitan pleasures such as good beer and shrimp. Otherwise, it proved as frustrating as the entire trip.

It was great fun for the kids but less so for the adults, Creeley trying to concentrate on reading Rousseau's *Confessions*, which he admired, and Lowry's *Under the Volcano*, which he found pretentious and childish, half a dozen radios blaring around him at all times. How much he had intended to write during this long awaited vacation! And yet next to nothing had gotten done. Around 25 August they headed back towards Albuquerque where he was facing another year of teaching school and the now-familiar drudgery towards obtaining his academic "union card." The main thing was to not give up. For all his frustrations and setbacks during 1957–59, he had managed to maintain a narrow continuum of writing and publishing that would bear fruit later.

Most importantly, he had cultivated contacts with Henry Rago, editor of *Poetry* (Chicago), which in its October 1956 issue had proclaimed him "the best poet under forty now writing." Initially, Rago had requested more poems than Creeley could provide. After he had sent one early in 1956, Rago asked for half a dozen. Creeley responded with another single one, apologizing for not being able to come up with more. By June 1956, he was still unable to send the requested six. In September 1957 he inquired if he could contribute reviews, Rago in reply suggesting he do one on a bilingual anthology, *Ten Centuries of Spanish Poetry*. Gently, Rago reminded Creeley of deadlines, prodded him for new poems, with judicious good sense chose one or the other for publication, and, through

his consistently polite and supportive behaviour, earned himself his pro-
tegé's respect at a time when Creeley felt some real despair about his abilities as a writer and poet. No other editor, he assured Rago, offered him
the same good humour and good will. *Poetry*, publishing more and more
of his poems and reviews, became his lifeline during an otherwise barren,
frustrating period.

At the same time he experienced strange interior rumblings or even the
odd outburst of creativity, writing like one possessed, as during the 1958
Christmas break. Perhaps the present dry spell would soon be over. Even
recent literary developments, which had so far favoured friends like Ginsberg and Kerouac rather than himself, sooner or later might swoop him
up in their momentum. The whole scene was beginning to swing their
way, he had assured Olson as early as 11 April 1958 – and that was by
almost nobody else showing up.

Meanwhile, the urge to live down south, free of the drudgery of studying and teaching, had never left him. As early as the summer of 1957, he
had noticed an ad regarding a position of tutor on a plantation in Guatemala, and had applied. What seemed a long shot then turned more concrete by June of the following year when he was offered an annual salary
of $1,800 plus free lodging in a place some two hours from Guatemala
City in a surrounding of dead volcanoes and beautiful lakes. In return he
asked for $3,000, suggesting that they increase the class size, a demand
met a year later. Intent upon little else than being able to write again, he
accepted without a thought. With the University of New Mexico finally
awarding him his M.A. – his "union card" – he could always come back to
seek an academic teaching post later.

29

Guatemala, 1959–60.

My country, let us walk together, you and I.

I will descend into the abysses where you send me.
I will drink your bitter chalices.
I will be blind so you may have eyes.
I will be voiceless so you may sing.
I have to die so you may live,
so your face emerges flaming on the horizon
of each flower born from my bones.

It has to be this way, unquestionably.
......
Ay country,
The colonels who piss on your walls
we must pull them up by the roots,
hang them from a tree of sharp dew,
violent with anger of the people.
For this I ask you that we walk together. Always
with the peasants
and the union workers,
with he who has a heart to love you.

My country, let us walk together, you and I.

Guatemalan poet Otto René Castillo, the author of the lines translated
above, was born in 1936, ten years Creeley's junior. Raised during the
revolutionary period 1944–54 and drawn by the vision of a new Guatemala, he became a youth activist in the Guatemalan Workers' Party in
high school, but with the overthrow of reformist president Jacobo Arbenz, sought exile in El Salvador where he became a member of the local
communist party. Moving in and out of Guatemala, he finally returned to
his native country in 1966 and joined the rebel armed forces fighting in

the mountains. In March 1967 he was captured by the army, tortured for four days, and burned alive.

The 1954 overthrow of Jacobo Arbenz, which turned Guatemala into the leading u.s. laboratory for counter-insurgency in Latin America, had been masterminded by the u.s. Central Intelligence Agency. "Voice of Liberation" programs, allegedly broadcast by rebel transmitters from inside the country accusing Arbenz of incompetence, de facto came from powerful CIA stations. "Rebel" pilots, some of them provided by the CIA's secret Civil Air Transport, flew bombing missions against Guatemala. Defying the risk of blowing the CIA's cover, President Eisenhower personally authorized additional air strikes. Arbenz's attempt to arm the peasants and workers was foiled by army chief Carlos Enrique Diaz. Abandoned by the military which he thought would remain loyal to him, Arbenz resigned on 27 June. With the support of u.s. ambassador John E. Peurifoy, Castillo Armas became Guatemala's new president. It was the first time in history, American Vice-President Richard Nixon proclaimed, "that a communist government has been replaced by a free government. All the world is watching to see who will do a better job."

One person watching closely from a prison cell on the Isle of Pines in Cuba was that country's future revolutionary president. Fidel Castro read an early magazine report of the Guatemalan overthrow. What he observed over the next few months became possibly the most important lesson in his political career.

Within weeks, all major unions and political organizations of the Guatemalan revolution were declared illegal. By conservative estimates "9,000 were imprisoned and many tortured under the government's virtually unlimited powers of arrest." The prime targets were "United Fruit Company union organizers and Indian village leaders. As many as 8,000 peasants were murdered in the first two months of the Castillo Armas regime."

There were further measures to make Guatemala a "showcase for democracy." The press was censored, literacy programs were suspended, hundreds of rural teachers fired, "subversive books" such as Dostoyevsky's novels and Victor Hugo's Les Miserables outlawed and burned in street bonfires. The new government returned 99.6 per cent of the land expropriated by the revolutionary government to its former owners, including the United Fruit Company. New concessions and privileges were granted to foreign investors. In a "diplomatic crusade that had the persecutorial overtones of a Torquemada," Secretary of State John Foster Dulles took an active part in the operations. Not content with overthrowing the Guatemalan revolution, he felt that all leftist elements had to be torn up by the roots. The u.s. embassy provided lists of "communists" to be eliminated, instructed the government forces to treat them harshly, even reprimanding a man as repressive as Castillo Armas for respecting the right of asylum.

Long before Creeley and his family arrived in Guatemala in 1959, the job of repression had all but attained its goal of exterminating the revolutionary elements in the population – though not quite.

Castillo Armas was murdered by one of his personal guardsmen in 1957. The five-year presidency of his successor, Miguel Ydígoras Fuentes, prepared the ground for further trouble by turning into "a farce of incompetence, corruption and patronage." At $150,000 a year, Ydígoras paid himself the highest salary of any head of state in the western hemisphere. His daughter was appointed ambassador to France, his cousin minister of education. On 13 November 1960 an officers' revolt broke out in Guatemala City, spreading from there to other parts of the country. It was quickly defeated, but two of the leaders, Captain Marco Antonio Yon Sosa and Lieutenant Luis Turcios Lima, escaped to head the Guatemalan revolutionary movement of the 1960s.

Creeley heard of the ferment that would explode into full scale rebellion on 13 November: over sixty bombings in Guatemala City, declaration of martial law, tanks patrolling the main avenues; people caught in suspicious places having their heads shaved for easy identification; finally an insane asylum set on fire, some said by the government, people screaming all night, many burned to death, others dragged about the city to other quarters, the resultant six days of mourning allowing the government the period of peace in which to quell what remained of the rebellion.

The Creeleys reached Guatemala by circuitous routes. Their rental lease in Alamada having lapsed on 20 June 1959, they spent a few weeks at Judson Crews's home in Ranchos de Taos before taking a side trip to San Francisco for Creeley's reading at the State College Poetry Centre on 16 July.

Program director Robert Duncan did his friend proud. A leaflet entitled "Robert Creeley. Reading and Commenting on His Poems" featured a list of Creeley's publications, autobiographical notes from the poet, as well as an extensive introduction by Duncan outlining the development of their literary friendship and highlighting Creeley's special talents. None of his peers rivaled him in the movement of the line, Duncan declared.

As usual, the admiration was reciprocal. Duncan, Creeley found, resembled a powerful patriarch ruling supreme over a spirited bustle of poetic activity. The excitement over the Beats, in Duncan's *mise en scène*, had at last been placed in proper relation to Black Mountain, with Charles Olson providing the centre. At the same time Duncan kept both schools uncontaminated by academia. Outstanding amongst Duncan's friends was Jack Spicer, walking bearlike, shaking his head in objective disapproval.

Allen Ginsberg and Peter Orlovsky came along for the ride back to Albuquerque. They went via Big Sur and the Pacific coast, stopped over to peer into the Grand Canyon, and, above all, Creeley and Ginsberg talked. Like never before, the two literary strategists found the time to hash over rumours from the *demi-monde* as well as the actual politics of the literary scene. Ginsberg, Creeley found, made more sense of it all than anyone else. The two poets saw eye to eye on most issues such as distribution, general events, who did work that counted. Jonathan Williams, they agreed, was doing the general cause a disservice by bringing out books that were too expensive and few in numbers.

From Albuquerque, where they picked up the children at Norah's, the Creeleys headed through Mexico down to San Cristobal de las Casas and on to Comitan near the Guatemalan border. The road had been washed away by the tropical rains the night before they arrived, and they had to backtrack nearly 250 miles from the mountains down to Arriaga near the Pacific coast, from where they completed the journey towards Patulul, south of Lake Atitlan, partly by train, partly by a maze of dirt roads ravaged by torrential rainfalls.

Their destination, Los Tarrales, the coffee plantation belonging to the Burge family on the jungle-covered slopes of volcano Atitlan, was buzzing with horror stories when they got there. Mrs Burge was recovering from a bout of typhoid. The finca's administrator had been attacked by a boa constrictor while out in the jungle. Eight frogs in the swimming pool of Tito Bressani, Creeley's co-employer, had been exterminated on site by the irate *finquero* one early morning. The newcomers weren't spared this onslaught of wildlife. Sleeping on low-lying mattresses in the east wing of the Burges' mansion, Bobbie noticed a big spider and managed to kill it before it bit them.

Los Tarrales looked to Creeley like a Burroughs scenario mixing Connecticut landscaping with a backdrop of dripping jungles and giant ex-volcanoes. Equally surreal was the swimming pool surrounded by flower bushes, bamboo trees, and grassy slopes. It was the centre of an early champagne and vodka party uniting the Burges' casual crowd of farmers, oil company pilots, divorcees, and politicians from the city. They launched an aluminum boat with a huge outboard motor, making it spin round and round, spilling lots of gas.

The Creeleys' place was much more modest but no less exotic, teeming with ever-changing varieties of plants, insects, creepy-crawlies, and larger animals. A huge leaf clung to the bathroom door; a young ocelot whose hair refused to grow in properly – it lacked its mother to lick it (thank God!) – gambolled about the living room; a huge orange and green parrot sat like nemesis above the kitchen door. Various stray dogs and cats walked in and out, occasionally depositing litters.

The house with its front porch faced out over a rolling valley lined by several distant volcanoes. In front was the main road connecting Patulul with Panajachel on Lake Atitlan some ten miles to the north, with trucks, cars, and people endlessly passing the house. To the back was a small garden which they learned to cultivate via a self-built irrigation system, Creeley delightedly watching the water crawl down various mud channels, or once when things started to grow, the caterpillars eating so fast that everything they walked on vanished.

The Creeleys were shocked by the prices of things: $2.10 for a box of crackers or a three pound can of Crisco; $6 for thirty-six bottles of beer which, however, was sharp and dry. Liquor was altogether beyond their budget. When Kirsten was suffering from intestinal sickness, the doctor's visit cost $25.

Sizing up the newly arrived tutor, *finca* boss Tito Bressani reviewed some recent cultural history. First we had a homo, he said, then a lesbian, and now we've got a beatnik. Joe Burge was similarly outspoken. The reason why he paid Creeley less than the man running the *finca* store was because the latter was more important, he said. But otherwise they were friendly enough – that is, to the Creeleys. Tito Bressani, son of a hard-headed North Italian feudal patriarch holding his clan in an iron grip, affected a Roman-style pre-eminence. Joe Burge flaunted his own more twentieth-century style ex-Kentucky grandeur. Joe had someone bulldoze a parking space for the Creeleys' car, gave back part of the doctor's fee for Kirsten, handed Creeley a $50 bill on a drunken night, or took him along for the odd trip up into the jungle covering the steep slopes of Mount Atitlan – like a Japanese movie, bamboo trees coming in and out of the fog rolling past, deep valleys clear for a moment, then back in the rain.

But otherwise, the life of the *finqueros* struck Creeley as a jazzed-up, obscene, and ultimately evil modern feudalism: racing along one-track dirt roads with their Mercedes Benzes; wailing drunkenly overhead in their airplanes; bullshitting each other or even President Ydígoras whenever they could get hold of him. They fixated on a mythical balance of $1 million dollars in their bankbooks, extorted from Indians they were afraid of and who feared them. Ultimately sick, bored and profoundly unhappy people, Creeley concluded. Neither of his two bosses, he wrote his mother, were out to harm him, yet otherwise, there wasn't an inch of common ground between him and his employers. Joint social occasions required a major effort "not to rock the boat." But he and Bobbie went anyway, whenever asked, just to have a bit of variety and distraction.

One of his employers claimed to be a member of some political "Union of Christian Agriculturalists," which seemed the ultimate irony. What would Jesus say, Creeley wondered. Joe Burge, he estimated, grossed between $200,000 and $300,000 a year. Meanwhile, the monthly salary he paid his Indian labourers housed on the *finca* and picking coffee beans ranged from a monthly $15 to $20 maximum. He could see them walking the road in front of his house all day long: poor, downtrodden creatures, their eyes dead, or furtive, aware that a white man like him would barely consider them human.

"*El país de eternal primavera*," the postage stamps called it: the land of eternal spring, as indeed it was if one looked past the miseries of its worn-out natives. What had seemed like a luscious paradise soon came to look like a green hell, cultural swamp, and burial ground. The ancient Mayans, Creeley speculated, no doubt were the last of the original inhabitants of Guatemala to ever witness what kind of paradise this land potentially was.

He also felt unexpectedly trapped. The roads were so bad that he would have ruined their VW van driving around the country. Guatemala City, where he had to go to sort out various bureaucratic tangles and stock up on shopping goods, was disappointing as well: no life, just business, ugly modernistic Mayan cartoons disfiguring public buildings, the rest like Mexico City suburbs. It's where you went to see the president or get laid, he reported to Denise Levertov. Nice whorehouses in nice neighbourhoods.

He also felt the separation from David, Tom, and Charlotte, whom he hadn't seen for over two years. Probably his coming to Guatemala had been a bad mistake, he concluded by late October 1959. His employers were breathing down his neck. Trying to maintain a semblance of day-to-day order was like holding on to a strap on the Boston subway, he mused incongruously. Most unsettling to him was the scarcity of letters from friends. Did his mail get censored or stolen? Or had his friends finally found out what a petty shit he really was?

Yet in spite of it all, they managed to settle in. Life went on, Creeley concluded stoically, and got more agreeable. Economically speaking, they had little to complain about. The house was their best ever. Caught in the exotic wonders surrounding them, the kids had a ball. A maid, Juana, helped Bobbie with the household. The Calvert courses he used in his teaching were well outlined and easy to follow. His pupils, though a little uppity, were as much fun as children everywhere.

Katherine Burge, who was Leslie's age, called her new teacher Mith-ter Creepy Crawly. Martha, the oldest, was the primmest and most standoffish. She was shy but interested. Both sisters, like their brother, Andrew Joseph, spoke a polyglot sort of garble, were well fed, and basically good natured. Mark Bressani was a hefty blond boy sweating over his English. The only real problem was his seven-year-old brother who reminded Creeley of nightmares of vacant eyes and sprawling limbs he had had as a kid, or of seeing an actual idiot child who used to block the sidewalk when Genevieve went to bank her earnings on Saturdays. Idiots, let's face it, were idiots, Creeley explained to Ed Dorn. Though this one was still young and less gross, he already exhibited the typical sprawl of attentions and movements that finally blocked all one's responses except care. Classes included Bobbie's daughters, with Leslie simply devouring everything that was handed to her.

Most importantly, the teaching job left him ample time to write, and he did more of that than he had in years. The poems were speaking in a new tone. His earlier ones had fed off the emotional tensions with Ann and hence were like springboards for comment. No matter how vicious the occasion, all of them were "social personal crucifixions" in one sense or another. In Bobbie's presence, by contrast, he was learning to relax, to quietly observe the world, and to focus on the poem's structural and formal character rather than have its words describe a subjectively felt reality.

Examples of that sort of poetry he thought poorly of included the depressive realism of Robert Lowell's *Life Studies* (1957) and the new school of confessional poetry spawned by it. To have heard via Allen Ginsberg that Lowell called him "painfully restricted" exacerbated Creeley's response to this new plague. From the point of view of the contented paterfamilias, confessional poetry amounted to a reinvestment of the old ego centre, familiar from the worst of the Romantics but now compounded by the wreckages of modern family life. Confessional poets, blasted in their everyday experience, tried to secure themselves in the poem.

His response to deep-image guru Robert Bly, who had published an eleven page essay, "The Work of Robert Creeley," under the pseudonym Crunk in the second 1959 issue of his journal *The Fifties*, was more ambivalent. Bly's praise of Creeley and his work came close to Frederick Eckman's calling him "the best poet under forty now writing." Creeley himself, while being "difficult and stubborn," had "considerable integrity." His *Black Moutain Review* was "honest and intelligent" and "in some ways the most interesting magazine in America." In using really up-to-date language as in "I Know a Man," Creeley was ahead of almost every other American poet. Altogether, his poems had "distinct originality." Reading them, one was led towards new thoughts; the reverberations they sparked in one's brain placed them far above "the barren work of such earlier men as Larsson or Lowenfels."

Whatever Bly found to criticize was America's fault rather than Creeley's. In this Bly anticipated Rexroth, who a few years later would blame American poetry past the mid-century for not being able to "produce a more major poet to overtake and surpass Robert Creeley." To Bly, American poetry, and with it Creeley's own, was found wanting in its isolationist disregard of the four major modernist traditions: "the simple description of life in modern cities" as in Baudelaire, Rilke, Eliot, or Benn; the "daring in self-revelation" as in Gautier, Corbière, or La Forgue; "the going deeply into oneself, and returning like an explorer" such as in Trakl and Rilke; and, above all, "the heavy use of images" as in Baudelaire, Rimbaud, Mallarmé, Eluard, Char, or Lorca. Hence, Creeley's poetry, though the perhaps most avant-garde in the America of 1959 was "really not *avant-garde* at all," Bly wrote. "The poems seem quite isolated from the great richness and daring of Spanish poetry, or French poetry ... Mr. Creeley has great sensitivity to the American language, and great honesty, but it seems at the service of a too narrow and barren tradition. These poems, and those of the entire Black Mountain and San Francisco groups, are based almost entirely, it seems to me, on the American tradition. The American tradition is not rich enough, it is short, Puritanical, and has only one or two first-rate poets in it and the faults of the lesser poets are always the same – a kind of barrenness and abstraction."

Nonetheless, Creeley was flattered and grateful. Denise Levertov, who had become a personal friend of Bly, felt positively about the piece. Not so Duncan, who thought "The Work of Robert Creeley" was one "crappo" job of insincerity. He even suspected that Crunk might be a pseudonym for Corman.

But the three instantly set about to work out a compromise acceptable to each. Creeley insisted that Bly, like Corman, was motivated by real respect and love for the work as well as by a will to be serious, both extremely rare with others. Where Duncan had used a baseball bat, a quiet scalpel was called for to dissect Bly's academic tone, blundering generalities, and half-baked theorizing. Levertov agreed, while at the same time paying due respect to Duncan's criticism. She continued to like Bly as an endearing person, but he had made a complete ass of himself by acting in tactless and opinionated fashion in rejecting some of Duncan's poems which, God knew, went further towards substantiating some of his claims than most others he had printed. Nonetheless, Bly ought to be given another chance. What he needed was *educating*, precisely by someone like Creeley or Duncan. Otherwise she wished she would have had the good sense to stay out of these embroilments.

Nonetheless, Duncan's negative view of Bly by and by began to prevail with both Creeley and Levertov. When Bly committed the unpardonable sin of not answering letters, Creeley concluded Duncan was right after all. Bly was a mere floater in the academic scene like Emerson, only more glib and never quite there somehow. Certainly, the man was neither a real revolutionary nor a poet of major inventiveness.

On the general front, Creeley's increasingly negative views of other poets' talents were reinforced by the ever more numerous compliments paid to his own. As he had predicted over a year previously, the literary scene had started to swing his way. Rosset of the *Evergreen Review*, to whom he had sent a piece, wrote back saying he was impressed and wanted to see more. James Laughlin suddenly started sending him nice letters. Jack Kerouac wrote that everyone had the highest regard for Caro Roberto, the secret magician. Even M.L. Rosenthal who, Creeley thought, would be putting flowers on his grave by now, accepted "Kore" for *The Nation*.

A Form of Women, his most substantial collection so far, reached him in early November. Having read the proofs in a rush upon arriving in Guatemala, he had overlooked an error in the last verse of "Sing Song." But otherwise, he was scared by his own accomplishment. If nothing else, the volume marked a completion of sorts, he mused to Zukofsky.

The biggest triumph came in the form of a telegram that reached Creeley in early February. For some time Creeley had been hunting for his next job, had applied for the D.H. Lawrence fellowship, tried to arrange various readings, even taken steps towards doing a PhD at the University of New Mexico. Now a telegram sent him by Scribner's put a temporary stop to his financial worries. At the suggestion of his former Black Mountain pupil, Michael Rumaker, the prestigious New York publisher was offering to reprint his short stories, as well as to send their author a $500 advance. For once, though only for a day or two, Kirsten and Leslie were very respectful of their writer papa, Creeley noted.

More than ever before he could feel confident about his future literary career. Besides seeing his stories reprinted by a major publishing house, he had over forty new poems on hand, more than he had written in the preceding three years. What's more, he was awarded the D.H. Lawrence fellowship, carrying a stipend of $329.92 and a free stay at the ranch during the coming summer. Finally, there was a tempting offer from the Academy for Boys. The former headmaster had been picked up drunk in a public bar soliciting and been replaced by a colleague close to Creeley. The good Lord was really making it this year, Creeley commented to Ed Dorn.

But more important than salary and security, he had found out, was time to write. Also, the exotic country was beginning to grow on him – like the view across the hills, folded in against each other towards the volcanoes, the bright light deepening the shadows where it couldn't reach. The night before they had had a fiesta, marimba music blaring all night, their maid Juana dancing till three a.m. Relations with Joe Burge, too, had become more amicable. So Creeley accepted his offer to teach there for another year. The University of New Mexico was informed that his plans towards a PHD and, he hoped, a teaching assistantship in the English department, would have to be put on hold until 1962.

There were minor and major complications before the Creeleys set out on their journey north to Taos around 30 April 1960. Towards the end of February Bobbie had gone to visit an old friend in British Honduras, bringing back intriguing tales of old battered Englishmen walking battered bull terriers along the breakwater. They thought they might all go there for an extended visit, but a hoped-for house deal failed to materialize. Meanwhile a number of calamities struck. A $200 tape recorder, then Creeley's jacket with his passport, were stolen from their VW van. There were problems with securing a residence permit for the coming year. To their surprise, they also needed visas to leave the country. Although Creeley applied right away, no visas were forthcoming for several weeks. Repeated assurances that they would arrive *mañana* reduced him to a jelly-like pulp of resentment. But finally there they were, and within hours the Creeleys were on their way.

30

Guatemala, 1960–61.

After writing plenty of poetry during the preceeding months, Creeley hoped to concentrate on prose during his teaching-free summer. Ensconced behind the "Do Not Disturb the Writer" sign at the D.H. Lawrence cabin near Taos, he would finally start the novel he had been planning to write for a decade. But as often before, Creeley's, plans were thwarted by actual events, the expected working holiday dissolving into endless rounds of conversation and drinking.

A nomadic waiting period before he was allowed to occupy the Lawrence ranch by late June helped launch him on that wasteful track. He visited the Dorns, admiringly read Ed's recent writings, or in Ed's company went to Las Vegas where he discussed his poems to a class of summer students. Used to teaching children, he froze facing an amiable but disinterested audience of adults focused on picking up credits rather than on the subject matter at hand. Would he ever be able to teach at university level?

Dorn's fascination with early American history proved eye-opening to Creeley as well. He read John W. Powell's account of travelling through the Grand Canyon or during his own trips looked out for whatever bits of local history he met with. On the way to visit William Eastlake in the company of Ed Abbey, author of *The Brave Cowboy*, he explored the Rio Grande gorge and the surrounding desert. He talked to friends of men like Hank Williams and Ernest Tubbs, or in a bar just outside Cuba, New Mexico, met the son of a man whose father had been one of Sheriff Pat Garrett's deputies in the massacre that Billy the Kid was caught in – an old guy with faded blue eyes, wearing an old fashioned hat with the high round crown. As a child the man had accompanied his father on cattle drives to Kansas, swapping horses with Billy. Other originals who attracted Bob's attention included a sawmill owner writing science fiction as well as a placidly drunken Mexican who, when confronted by the bar owner's giant pistol, just stared at his opponent remarking that it was easy enough to hold one of those things but much harder to fire it off. He would be a historian, Creeley mused to Charles Olson.

A reunion with Sender brought Creeley up against some of the limitations of contemporary American writers. How narrow they seemed when compared with this old-style man of letters! How hedged in by their momentary obsessions and arbitrary sense of self! Sender, by contrast, a man in his late fifties, was finalizing volume twelve of his miscellaneous writings and continuing to pronounce himself on everything from love, music, and painting to aesthetics. Obsolete as it might be, his ongoing attempt to define himself in relation to history, the tradition, and mankind at large aroused Creeley's admiration and envy. He found equally admirable the man's single-minded, compact energy, working long hours in total isolation while keeping faith with a wide network of friends and, for all his machismo, being a real lover of women from whom he drew much of his creative energy!

Once the Creeleys had settled in at the Lawrence ranch, there was an unceasing stream of visitors. Their living quarters, already cramped for a family of six, became overcrowded. Before long Creeley simply gave up on his plans to withdraw and write.

An unexpected and, as it turned out, unwelcome visitor was Max Finstein with, in his trail, Joel Oppenheimer's wife, Rena, and her two children. Max, from Creeley's new perspective as the self-righteous breadwinner, was proposing a vicious set-up. When Max's first wife had asked for support for their child, he had complained to Bob about unfairness. Yet now he wanted Joel to send regular support for the children living with Rena and him, pleading that they were Joel's children, not his. Max Finstein, the great poet who wouldn't deign to work for a living like Joel or Bob himself! And yet how much he had begrudged Bob his annual $3,000 when Bob had started teaching at the Albuquerque Academy for Boys. The memory revived another from the time Max had taken Bob to meet Bobbie at the Albuquerque radio station. Just prior to that, Bobbie had written a letter on Max's behalf and found him a job. Max had never showed up to take it.

More positive, though ultimately ambivalent, was Creeley's response to visitor Gael Turnbull, whom he had been in touch with for several years but never met. At first, he liked Turnbull very much. Particularly dear to him was the image of the man sitting on the porch of the Lawrence cabin making a pastel sketch of the mountains across the mesa, seemingly unperturbed by the Creeley kids whooping around him. But something about Turnbull made Creeley feel jumpy. Was it the endless resentments he suspected must be churning away under the veneer of Turnbull's civilized equanimity? He and Turnbull certainly were miles apart on literary issues. To Turnbull, a poem was a complete unit and finished work of art. To Creeley, it was a pragmatic instance of use, the new American poetry going hand in hand with the new departures in the language, a conviction corroborated by Harvard linguist Whatmough's sense that the radical differences dividing the American from the English language also affected their respective literatures. How ironic that Turnbull, while seemingly treating Creeley as a kind of fractious colonial, admired his poetry to the point of publishing a whole volume of it!

After a pretty "floppy" summer, Creeley was glad to head back to Guatemala. There were a few disasters on the way: running out of fuel about forty miles from the nearest gas station; losing all but the third gear about a hundred miles from Los Tarrales when a pin in the connecting rod to the transmission dropped out; finding that three bridges on the northern route were unusable, and having to pack family and VW van onto the train at Tonala in the sweltering heat. But then they were back at last, finding everything as they had left it, and, thanks to Bobbie's expert housekeeping, settled in in no time at all. It would be a good year, Creeley augured – erroneously.

One of the few boons it brought, paradoxically, came from his hurting his knee on the bedstead. The bruise turned into a horrible infection that had him bedridden for several days. After two unsuccessful shots of penicillin, the knee was bandaged with fresh compresses every hour, a little field hospital working with clockwork precision around him. Meanwhile he had started the novel he'd failed to begin during the summer. His sick leave from teaching allowed him to finish five whole chapters. Wyndham Lewis and Joyce Cary were his declared masters in the endeavour.

A first look at what he had written struck him as heartbreakingly funny. The opening scene had Artie, alias Martin Seymour-Smith, arriving drunk at the Creeleys' place in Bañalbufar at five a.m. by taxi from Palma to explain in elaborate detail what had happened to him and asking Creeley to pay for the cab. Seymour-Smith, Creeley projected, would serve both as pivot to the entire novel and as comic cicerone to the protagonist. He hoped he wasn't misusing Seymour-Smith, he mused to Gael Turnbull. Did Turnbull know where Seymour-Smith could be reached these days?

Rereading the same opening scene a few days later brought Creeley's efforts to a temporary halt. What had struck him as hilarious at first suddenly seemed contrived, cooked up, and cute. But with a board on one knee, the other throbbing with pain, he carried on undeterred, managing another two single-spaced pages the same day. If nothing else, prose might free him from the constrictions he had come to feel in writing poems. It would allow him to talk about things rather than be seized by them as in an apoplectic fit. So on he went, hoping to develop a feeling for a longer form and for a variety of tones ranging from a relaxed goofing via a flat-out style towards a sharp, quick pace, trying to nail things through back-ups in the phrasing. Then, suddenly and unexpectedly, there were certain brief, almost surreal-istic bits of recorded feeling popping up with seeming disregard for ar-rangements of any kind. He was delighted, wilfully starting to indulge his penchant for melodrama, pointed out by Zukofsky.

After beginning the writing process on 7 September, Creeley com-pleted chapter four by 23 September, and chapter five by the beginning of October. At this point he came up against a new problem. All his previ-ous creativity had happened in isolated bursts. Even a short story had al-ways been a half-desperate clutch at something. But in doing a novel, he suddenly had to give coherence or at least sequentiality to whatever might follow. As urgently as it presented itself, the problem would remain unresolved for months.

After finally starting to teach around 21 September, Creeley received re-assuring news. *Poetry* had awarded him its prestigious Levinson Prize of $100 for his ten poems published in its May 1960 issue. By contrast, Scrib-ner's reprint of his stories in *Short Story* 3 turned out to be an irritating dis-appointment. While allowing eighty, one hundred, and yet another hundred pages to the three other authors, Scribner's had squeezed his con-tributions into the volume's final thirty-five pages, making them appear like a mere supplement. Yet how hopefully it had started – the telegram, the $500 advance, and finally the tentative offer that they do a *Collected Poems*.

Since then nothing much had happened, Scribner's prevaricating in re-sponse to his letters. With predictable perversity, he almost hoped they would reject the typescript he had sent them. Getting published in the "wild" company of the New Directions authors, though it meant fewer financial returns, seemed more attractive after all. But finally Scribner's delivered its positive verdict. Ecstatic, Creeley couldn't sleep the entire night, sitting up, staring out at the sky – it felt so very singular. Getting his poems published by a big house like Scribner's meant an acceptance he had never thought possible. For a while his exuberance knew no bounds. He had come through, he announced.

The second year in Guatemala was fast turning into his *annus mirabilis*. By the beginning of January, he received Scribner's enthusiastic report on the five chapters of *The Island* he had sent them. As long as he could bring himself to finish it, the novel's publication was a *fait accompli*. Obviously eager for his writings, Scribner's less than a month later sent him a contract plus advance for the poems as well as a $500 advance plus option for the novel. There would be two further payments upon his sending in the first half and finally the completed typescript of *The Island*.

For a mainstream publisher like Scribner's to solicit prose and poetry that ten years before they wouldn't have considered literature pointed to a general restructuring of the cultural climate in America, perhaps worldwide. Creeley's prediction of 11 April 1958 had come true. The literary scene was certainly swinging his and his friends' way. Richard Eberhart wrote from the Library of Congress that they would like to have a tape of Creeley reading his poetry. Responding to Alan Brownjohn's "Notes on Larkin and Creeley" in *Migrant* #6 (May 1960), the London *Times Literary Supplement* oracled that composition by breath unit might well be the route to be taken by young British writers. Creeley's "I Know a Man" was singled out as a possible model. Donald Hall, who had spoken dismissively of Creeley and Olson in the *World Review* of December 1952, sent Creeley a personal apology.

In terms of his career, everything was going Creeley's way as never before. He felt accepted and respectable at last. He talked to friends about how happy and contented he was. The year, after starting so auspiciously with the writing of five chapters of *The Island*, promised to be as productive as 1959–60. Life upon their return to Guatemala felt more settled. They had brought along various things difficult to obtain locally, knew how to do things, and enjoyed better lighting from a new AC generator.

But suddenly everything turned sour. Work on the novel came to an abrupt halt. Trying to write poetry instead, Creeley was forced back into mere finger exercises. The job he had found so easy the first year turned into a grinding ordeal. From January onwards he started ticking off his remaining days like a prisoner in his cell, again and again announcing in letters to friends the foreshortening time span until his return to the United States. To know that wasting time was an essentially self-destructive business did not stop him from literally killing what was left of that miserable year bit by bit.

> It is simple
> to confess. Then done,
> to walk away, walk away,
> to come again.
>
> But that form, I must answer,
> is dead in me, completely,
> and I will not allow it
> to reappear –
>
> Saith perversity, the willful,
> the magnanimous cruelty,

which is in me
like a hill.

One of his perversities, Creeley explained to Duncan, was to qualify pleasures to the point where they almost became displeasures. His spleen vented itself on whatever least deserved it – the intentional bleakness of people, the constant vacuity of things, a landscape that seemed like a constantly smiling idiot, the crazy idyllicism of Guatemala's almost nightmarish weather, or the ubiquitous green of its finally stultifying flora.

His negative mood exacerbated his impatience with other poets, and especially with the deep imagists. While officially exchanging letters of laboured politeness with them, he privately felt disgusted with their theorizing. What they claimed was missing in, say, William Carlos Williams's poetry, amounted to little more than a vocabulary borrowed from Celan, Lorca, and others. Robert Kelly's proposal of striking a balance between deep image and Olson's breath rhythm physiology of sound was a red herring for several reasons. To start with, it was based on a widespread misconception: What Olson meant as a tentative suggestion had turned into a formal ultimatum in Kelly's and other people's minds. How could a mere psychology or, worse, symbology of reference grounded in something as nebulous as vision ever be matched with Olson's genuinely physiological suggestions? No wonder the deep image school had all the characteristics of a clique while those who, like Duncan, Levertov, or Creeley himself, shared the same breath rhythm theory in practice, wrote poetry as different from each other as could be imagined. What Bly, Kelly, Rothenberg, et al. were heading for was a progressive generalization of the poem's terms. They were stepping back before the major revolution that Olson, Creeley, and their associates had brought about ten years earlier.

Certainly there was nothing of a like revolution happening now. Those who laid claim to such had better sharpen up and listen. Even some of Creeley's former associates showed symptoms of slacking off. Fielding Dawson's prose (unlike his letters) had acquired a self-conscious tone. Oppenheimer's poetry had slowed down. Like several others, both Oppenheimer and Dawson were beginning to sound as if they were preparing for the grave. Sadly, literary history, with Creeley and a select band of peers including Olson and Duncan firmly at the helm, was entering a new era full of back-scratching fellow travellers, pseudo-revolutionaries, and epigones. Nine-tenths of the poets echoing Creeley's own manner, for instance, evidently hadn't read a single one of his poems with any intelligence. By parroting his phrase patterns and lines, they cheapened everything he had achieved.

Needed for proper new guidance was a journal that would play the uni-fying and disciplinary role that BMR and, to a lesser degree, *Origin* had played in the past. What they had built up over the years might otherwise disintegrate more quickly than it had arisen. Literary history now, just as when these magazines had given a sense of continuity to Bob's own devel-opment, was a cumulative and communal activity.

Creeley hastened to explain this much to Cid Corman, who was out to resume editing *Origin*. But mulish as ever, Corman refused to toe Cree-ley's line: instead of printing Olson, Creeley, and their disciples, he would concentrate on younger writers. So it was time for some more Corman-bashing amongst Creeley's friends. His smirk made you think you were talking to two other people, Dawson quipped. What kind of a goddamn fucker was this anyway, wondered Dorn. Creeley recalled how, in order to keep his temper during Corman's first visit at Rock Pool Farm, he re-peatedly had to leave the room.

Caught in his Thersites-like tailspin, Creeley could think of little else beyond the still unresolved problem of where – Texas, Puerto Rico, or Albuquerque – he might find a university teaching job and the chicaneries he was experiencing at the hands of Guatemala City bureaucrats. Yet for once he really had little to worry about. A lawyer easily managed to re-solve his car and exit visa problems; given the total of $1,000 in advances from Scribner's and an additional amount Bobbie had managed to save from his salary, they were financially secure for some time to come. A last minute offer from the University of New Mexico would allow him to supplement these resources by part-time teaching; until mid-July they'd be able to live in the house of William Eastlake's brother-in-law who'd be away in Africa.

Nonetheless, Creeley continued to feel like a shaking mass of inertia and worries. His perverse dislike for everyone and everything blinded him to the real worries of those around him. Since the 13 November 1960 officers' revolt in Guatemala City, the people had been subjected to renewed atrocities, murders, and disappearances at the hands of their government. Matters such as these held less interest for Creeley than ever. While teaching his pupils the American Civil War and eagerly not-ing Jackson as his favourite war hero, he dispassionately acknowledged the recent political businesses, the general unrest, the jet planes buzzing overhead – like old times in Albuquerque. Politics here was much as else-where, if not more so, he observed vaguely. Like the social horrors, they were too sick to watch.

He disdainfully commented on certain Guatemalan poets he didn't bother to read, because most of their work was concerned with history rather than anything as yet happening. Philip Whalen, who had tried to get him interested in Gary Snyder's view that poets ought to commit themselves politically, met with a rebuff. The content of a man, Creeley argued, could not be abstracted into segments of commitments. More to the point, he felt a sick vagueness in trying to approach his responsibility in political activity. Recent Guatemalan politics, he admitted to Olson, simply brought out his complete non-sense, or rather, "out-of-it pattern," of such things.

But his friends wouldn't let him rest. Allen Ginsberg too wanted to know what ken of politics Creeley had developed in Guatemala. Having spent time with communists in Chile and realizing they were the only ones to really want to help the poor, Ginsberg wanted to know more about Guatemalan politics. According to his informants, American suppression of the left-wing Guatemalan government back in 1954 had left the country a sort of u.s. Hungary, a feat the Americans were now trying to repeat in Castro's Cuba. Gary Snyder's reports from Japan confirmed Ginsberg's sense of America's pernicious role world-wide. What did Creeley think?

Creeley, in his reply, reported on the recent bombings in Guatemala City, the declaration of martial law, how captured suspects had been shaved and painted to be easily identifiable, how an insane asylum had been set ablaze with many patients burnt to death to deflect attention from the general unrest, etc. In short, Ginsberg was right: Guatemala was what Yucatan had been when Olson had lived there: loaded like a gun rammed for firing. Otherwise he didn't have much insight into local political "bizness," he admitted. All he knew was that he wanted out of there. Come the end of April, the Creeleys started their impatiently awaited journey home to the United States.

31

New Mexico, 1961-62.

A quick reading trip back East was to provide the long-missed opportunity to talk to friends, renew old contacts, and establish new ones. But everywhere Creeley met with setbacks and disappointments. In Dartmouth he walked out of a reading after getting into an argument with a certain Hirschman who, he thought, behaved in an ambitious and ugly fashion. It was great fun, he reported to Dorn. He could still see Hirschman's face suggesting: But you can't give up the $100!

A two-day visit with Olson in Gloucester was depressing in a different way. In letters to friends Creeley calls it "the greatest" or draws an idyllic picture of Olson sitting at the kitchen table listening to a Dorn tape, taking notes on the "proverbial" envelope, and snorting. But tensions between Olson and Betty as well as the dire poverty they lived in were all too evident. When Creeley volunteered a $10 bill, Olson mumbled: Hell, I want ten thousand. A later suggestion Creeley made also fell flat. Creeley had recently sold some two hundred pages of his papers featuring old poems, stories, and a short journal to the Lilly Library at Indiana University in Bloomington for the considerable sum of $750 and suggested Olson do the same. But nothing worked out for Olson.

The greatest disappointment was New York City where Creeley gave another reading. The exceptions were reunions with Louis Zukofsky, Paul Blackburn, and deep imagist Robert Kelly, who Creeley found was surprisingly intelligent. But too much else proved mere ambition and socialite routine. Dan Rice had come drunk to the reading, his girl-friend acting like a lead shield. Meeting LeRoi Jones was all very vague somehow; Creeley decided he could no longer trust him. An irritated Denise Levertov asked why *Origin* hadn't been credited in Scribner's *Stories 3*, suggesting he was unfaithful to old friends. She seemed *obsessed* with personalities including her own. Out of the blue she started telling him about what an impressive person Muriel Rukeyser was, while never bothering to talk about her poetry.

In the two years since he had left, people had lost direction and begun to lean on their oars. But perhaps there was still hope. Once returned to New Mexico, he would see what he could do to remedy this sorry state of affairs. Never mind that Corman, in reviving *Origin*, was unwilling to provide the much-needed countering force to all such greasy slides. If need be, Creeley would have to tackle the task himself. The time had come for a final sprint.

Meanwhile, he was mainly running low on energy. The endless travelling, the deadlines, the overnight talking sessions with friends had taken their toll. Yet being so obviously in demand was an irresistible pleasure, leading him to follow through on various assignments to the point of virtual exhaustion: readings, an official interview by David Ossman with Bobbie and Paul Blackburn present in the studio, a consultation with Library of Congress poetry consultant Richard Eberhart. People who might have sneered at his theorizing a few years earlier were consulting him like an oracle. Would Williams and his followers (like Robert Creeley himself) prove to be the significant tradition? Eberhart asked him. It wasn't that simple, Creeley replied with appropriate modesty. However, Roethke and consorts certainly would be given a great deal less prominence in such a future context than, say, half a decade before.

Once back in the South-West and safely installed in the house of Bill Eastlake's brother-in-law George Gaylord Simpson in Cuba, New Mexico, Bob was ready to collapse. As it turned out, it was more than mere exhaustion. A severe chest cold from a virus caught in New York, he speculated. Although the suspected bug proved curiously unresponsive to the usual antibiotic treatment, he announced his readiness to resume work a few days later.

But an elderly woman doctor with a good straight manner to whom he paid a precautionary visit warned him he might be suffering from tuberculosis or worse. After reacting "positive" to a tuberculin test, he anxiously awaited the x-ray results to tell him what havoc past and present illnesses has wreaked on his lungs. Was he suffering from cancer? The specialists' terminological huggermugger hardly assuaged his worries. Markings on the plate in the left lung area, it was explained to him, might merely represent a subsiding pneumonitis. Nonetheless the possibility of an endobronchial obstructing lesion had to be considered.

At least all of it would be free of charge. Given his status as an unemployed, married father of four, he could claim welfare medical treatment for himself and his family. Also he was genuinely recovering. After weeks of testing that lasted until early September, the doctors concluded that what had caused his illness were remnants of former diseases he had essentially lived with since childhood and would continue to do for the rest of his life: old scars from both severe pneumonia he had had as a kid, and attacks of pleurisy he had suffered in Majorca and earlier that year in Guatemala. He was off the hook after all, he announced to Denise on 14 September.

By then the Creeleys had moved into their new home on 1835 Dartmouth NE, Albuquerque, a ramshackle, old two-storey house of unusual size by New Mexico standards. It had a basement as well as a large upstairs which would serve as a workspace where Bob could write and Bobbie could paint. Opposite was a quaint old windmill especially attractive to Leslie and Kirsten, who also liked to play in the nearby Embudo Arroyo sandbank on a mesa facing the mountains.

On the road to full recovery, Creeley had geared back into action with indomitable energy. He tried to resume work on the novel which had come to a total halt a year earlier. He made preparations for a monthly newsletter, edited by himself with Olson, Duncan, and Blackburn as contributing editors, that might allow all of them to move through the present mess and keep sane. Talking to Jascha Kessler at the KHFM radio station, he explored the possibility of a poetry program, "The Single Voice," with possible tie-ins into Los Angeles.

Also, he had managed to get himself appointed visiting lecturer at the University of New Mexico. There would be lots of preparation, like reading Freud, Whitehead, Darwin, Marx, Toynbee, and Eliot as well as Greek tragedy, modern fiction, medieval to modern drama plus *A History of Western Art*. But on the plus side, his teaching of two freshman and one honours course would be compressed into two afternoons a week. Meanwhile, Bobbie was frantically busy framing pictures towards her show beginning in early October.

After the past deadly summer, the coming year would be a good one, Creeley predicted. But an unexpected disaster put a sudden end to his hopes. It struck on 1 October, a Sunday.

Someone came running to the house where Bob and Bobbie were working. Leslie had vanished under a collapsing sandbank. Where? When? Only moments ago, in the Embudo Arroyo, two hundred yards north of their house. Kirsten, Leslie, and John Rathburn, a neighbour's son living at 1837 Dartmouth, had been digging small holes into the sandbank when it started to shift. John shouted a warning. He and Kirsten jumped back, but eight-year-old Leslie was trapped under the sand. They had tried to find her but couldn't, then ran home.

Grabbing a shovel, Bob and Bobbie rushed to the site of the accident, finding Kirsten trying to dig out her sister. The Embudo Arroyo bank was about twelve feet high, with a slight overhang at the top. A thirty foot

section of it had collapsed on top of Leslie. As they dug, police and fire-
men arrived. Exhausted, Bob stood back, petrified with horror, watching
Leslie's body emerge out of the sand, first her shoes, then her legs, face
downward. People looked on from the bluff of the arroyo, observing the
diggers, the Creeleys, as well as a TV cameraman filming Leslie as she was
rolled over. A physician tried to revive her using an inhalator and artificial
respiration. But it was too late. After lying some twenty minutes under a
heavy layer of sand, Leslie had died from suffocation before she was unearthed. He watched with such intensity that even as he "did things,"
he was all that perverse act of recognition, so hungry for the exactness of
the "sight," Creeley later wrote Olson.

Creeley's immediate response to Leslie's death was rage: how could
someone so full of possibilities and with such a wild honest mind be cut
down so blindly? His fury vented itself on a too-eager onlooker. Creeley
threatened him with the shovel, saying he would smash him if he didn't
get back. His rage was unabated over nine months later and prompted
another scene that holds pride of place in Creeley's twenty-two
page "Autobiography" of 1989. He had come out of the nearby super-
market and was about to drive away when someone knocked on the car
roof, trying to get his attention: "I opened the window and looked out to
see a man beside the car staring down at me with an angry face. He said,
do you remember what you said to me a year ago, when you were trying
to find your daughter? I couldn't at first quite believe he was saying this. I
was the man you threatened, he continued, and I would like an apology. I
don't now remember just what I answered, but something to the effect
that if he didn't go away immediately, I'd give him far worse. He left, disgruntled."

Bob and Bobbie tried to control their grief by keeping busy. She went
ahead with her show, he with his various chores. Although the doctor had
advised him to go easy on reading tours, he was hectically planning a new
one which, by the following month, would take him to Toronto, New
England, New York, and Texas. He pushed ahead full steam with preparations for a monthly newsletter and "The Single Voice," his radio program on KHFM. Equipped with the station's recorder and tapes, he would
engage individual poets in informal conversation and have them read
whatever seemed pertinent. Local poet veterans Winfield T. Scott and
Witter Bynner were the first targets.

He was particularly taken with octogenarian Bynner, a "crazy" old
man, almost blind, suffering from shingles but still retaining an impressive coherence and urbanity of manner. Talking to him opened up unexpected perspectives. Eighty-three year old British laureate John

Mansfield had just written Bynner complimenting him on his *New Poems* (1960). Marianne Moore, to Bynner, was an "editress" who, as he had found to his surprise more recently, was also writing poems. And the stories Bynner told about Pound, Lawrence, Isadora Duncan, and others! Perhaps he would do an oral memoir, Creeley considered, Bynner's secretary transcribing their dialogue from the tapes. Other poets to be presented on KHFM would include Ed Dorn, Max Finstein, Paul Blackburn and Louis Zukofsky.

"The Single Voice" was launched on Sunday, 8 October 1961, just a week after Leslie's death. Creeley thought it went well enough. Several days later, he was off on his reading tour in the East.

His Torontonian hosts struck Creeley as nice and straight. But New York was a different story. Of all people, M.L. Rosenthal had been chosen to introduce Blackburn and Creeley at the prestigious YMCA Poetry Center. Creeley had not forgotten Rosenthal's snide remarks in *The Nation* of 1 November 1958, or that in republishing the piece he had cut out references to Creeley altogether. Rosenthal's introduction, culminating in a "loaded" thanks, was obviously an attempt to make up for the earlier attack.

Then there was the usual rush of seeing too many people too quickly: LeRoi Jones, Basil Bunting, Blackburn, and Zukofsky, with whom he made a tape for "The Single Voice." John Chamberlain, having gone through a psychiatric therapy, had become happily domestic. He was drinking less and driving more slowly, Creeley noted approvingly. Other former friends fared less well in his esteem: Dan Rice with his new girlfriend remained unreachable, former flame Cynthia struck him as rather sad.

Relations with an even older friend reached a crisis that had been building up for some time. By late 1959, Creeley had begun to notice that Denise Levertov was not responding to his letters, in the same way Duncan had ignored him in 1956 because of the affair with Marthe. As he had asked Levertov to mediate then, he suggested the same to Duncan now. She finally did write, unleashing a harangue of long pent-up grievances. At some point Mitch had wanted him to read his novel in manuscript, but Bob had had no time to do it. Her suggestion that a good letter from him might help Mitch out of a depression had been answered by silence. Meanwhile, Bob had lavished indiscriminate praise on others, as on Allen Ginsberg who had gifts but whose work, including *Kaddish*, was for the most part sloppy and exhibitionist, not what Denise considered poetry, but rabble rousing; or on LeRoi Jones who was a very pleasant and disarming young man, but whose journal *Yugen* was a shameful mess and certainly not deserving of the admiration Bob professed for it.

A letter from Bob to Jones handed around at a party of Don Allen's in September 1959 had been the proverbial straw to break the camel's back for her. Here were phrases expressing warmth and friendship for a person Bob hardly knew in just the same words he used in writing to old friends like Mitch and herself; or protestations of extravagant gratitude just because LeRoi approved of his writings. There was too much bending over backwards, too much humility. His relations with Ted Enslin fitted the same pattern of approval-seeking from all. A few years before, Bob had spoken with contempt both of Ted's work and of his making such a song and dance about living in the country and chopping wood. Now Bob was corresponding with him in the same meretricious tone he used with everybody.

Meanwhile old loyal friends like Race Newton (who together with Lucia and her kids had ended up joining the Goodmans in New York) were complaining that Bob no longer behaved like a real friend towards them. Instead, Bob and Buddy had tried to put Race down in Lucia's eyes. Bob was wrong to protest his innocence regarding such matters. Even his close friend Ed Dorn (whom Mitch had seen in October) no longer quite trusted him, although he might not admit it to Bob himself.

Creeley defended himself as best he could. Ginsberg's *Kaddish* was often exceptional writing; *Yugen* was a good magazine, useful, variable, open to material he was anxious to read himself. When people told him they admired what he wrote, that's the way he reacted, sounding fawning perhaps or covetous of such approval. As for his letters, they often were clichés from start to finish, as everyone knew. Denise herself had seen him write them in the same old phrases year in year out. Hadn't she herself noticed and missed it when he had once cut out his idiosyncratic wows and etcs? What letters to Ted Enslin was she talking about? The thank-you note he had sent Ted a month and a half earlier for a book Ted had sent him two years before? And after all, people did change, himself as well as others. As for not behaving like a good friend towards Race and his wife, the allegation was absurd – Race and Lucia who, while in Albuquerque, had been able to depend on the Creeleys for whatever they could offer them!

Regarding Mitch, he entered a partial plea of guilty. Asked to read Mitch's novel, he had been wary and dodged the issue. So he was sorry to have hurt Mitch.

Little of it was to any avail. Denise, as Creeley kept complaining over the following months, no longer trusted him. Their break-up of 1959 was turning viciously solid. He lapsed back into some of the resentment he had felt for her all along. Dennie was too didactically poetic and self-concerned. She was stumbling around like a drunken idiot, dispensing or withholding her favours right and left. He no longer trusted her. Her asking him to have Scribner's send her the proofs of *For Love* so that she could have it reviewed before her term as poetry editor of *The Nation* expired was typical. What did "the mother of them all" really have in mind, he wondered. He couldn't help suspecting she wanted "to take care" of *For Love* before leaving.

Meanwhile, he came under attack from other quarters. Lucia wrote him about how cruel he was, how everyone thought so, and how he didn't realize what he was doing to people. Creeley hated it all – the unfounded accusations, the backbiting, the gossip, the hysteria. As for his cruelty, how much time did he have to be cruel, taking care of four children? Wow. As for putting down Race Newton, all he might have done was joke about Race turning incommunicado since getting married, or fast becoming a real businessman – the poor old dog. Race-bashing was Buddy's sport, not his. Of course, Race had been asking for it, having Buddy act as best man at his and Lucia's wedding, and then trotting off to play the piano in some bar right after the ceremony. Buddy naturally engaged in his favourite pastime in Bob and Lucia's presence.

As Mitch Goodman remembers, this went on until Race finally packed his family into the car and drove to New York where they were put up by the Goodmans, Denise taking a fancy to both Lucia and her two sons. But their persecutors wouldn't let them rest. When Creeley read in New York in September 1961, Buddy somehow happened to be in the city as well.

What happened that day seemed more than coincidence to Mitch. When he walked up to say hello to his old friend after the reading, Creeley simply glared at him saying: I don't need you. Just like that. Out of nowhere. Back home, Mitch checked on Lucia in their apartment on the floor below theirs. He knew Race would still be at work. He called Lucia's name, but no answer. He entered: the apartment was in chaos. There was a note saying: Buddy came and got me, and we're gone. Lucia had bundled up her kids and left.

Race was devastated. Denise and Mitch tried to help him as best they could. But he finally couldn't stand it any longer and just had to leave the country. He went to live in Tangiers.

Lucia's own fictionalized account in "So Long," the title piece of her *Stories 1987–1992*, bears out Mitch Goodman's memories on several points. For instance, Race goes off to work after the wedding, leaving Lucia alone with best man Buddy Berlin; at a later point, Race abruptly decides to go to New York to escape what was plaguing him in Albuquerque. Then, Buddy calls:

Hello, he said. I'm right around the corner in a phone booth.

He came with roses, a bottle of brandy and four tickets to Acapulco. I woke up the boys and we left ... I felt not the slightest regret at the time. This was just one of the many things I did wrong in my life, leaving like that.

Naturally, there were details unknown to Mitch. Rather than the result of diabolical seduction, Lucia's and Buddy's running away together was the dramatic climax of a love story that had started even before Lucia actually met Buddy. "I had listened to him play saxophone ... watched him race Porsches at Fort Sumpter. Everybody knew who he was. He was handsome, rich, exotic." According to "So Long," her marrying Race had been a panic reaction after her first husband had abandoned her and their two children:

I married [Race] then, a thoughtful man with a dry sense of humour. He was a good person. He wanted to help me bring up my two baby sons.

[Buddy] was our best man. After the wedding, in the backyard, [Race] went off to work, where he played piano at Al Monte's bar. My best friend Shirley, the other witness, left almost without speaking. She was very upset about me marrying [Race], thinking I had done it out of desperation.

"Shirley" had been right. A year later Lucia and Buddy had an affair. "It was intense and passionate, a big mess. [Race] wouldn't talk about it. I left him to live by myself with the children. [Race] showed up and told me to get into the car. We were going to New York." Months later, Buddy appeared to take her away from Race and grinding poverty. They flew to Mexico with the children. According to "So Long," she was happy, and so was Buddy.

A letter to the same effect from Buddy, sent from Mexico, reached Creeley on his return from his reading tour. Buddy sounded happier than he had in fifteen years. What's more, his ex-wife, Wuzza, seemed to have finally come to terms with things. As for Race, Creeley tried to sympathize as best he could, but he just couldn't get that excited over the affair. In a perverse way, his detachment seemed to have had a useful effect on those involved.

Soon the scenario shifted again. Wuzza, far from having come to terms with things, relapsed into her former desperation. Creeley's patience with her was starting to wear thin. She wouldn't move, act, or do much of anything. Just like a lump, dull and drunk. By contrast, Lucia and Buddy, back from Acapulco, looked extremely happy. Irritated by maudlin Wuzza, Bob found a new heroine in Lucia who only a while before had irritated him by accusing him of cruelty. It was impossible not to like her.

Of all the people involved, Creeley decided, she had somehow risked the most and most deserved what she'd hoped for.

An allegedly vicious postcard from "fucking nosey" Mitch Goodman, reported on by Ed Dorn, confirmed Creeley in his general attitude towards everyone involved in the affair. Goodman might be a good man in other areas, Dorn commented, but the Buddy-Lucia-Race story was really none of his or Denise's business. Meanwhile, Goodman obviously knew nothing about the cruelty Race had displayed towards Lucia's kids on several occasions. How Lucia had put up with it for so long was beyond Dorn. Anyway, it was a relief to find she had finally cut out of it.

32

Canada, 1962–63.

Success and money enabled Creeley to acquire two telephones which – unhappily for the biographer – consigned to oblivion much of what previously had been committed to letters.

One unexpected phone call had long-ranging results. It reached Creeley on 28 November 1961. Just hours before, he had received some good news: John Calder in England was offering to publish his stories in book form. When the phone rang, Creeley and Bobbie were celebrating, and stoned. A certain Warren Tallman from Vancouver, associated with an Arts Festival in that city, was asking Creeley to read for the then unusually high sum of $200, over expenses. Creeley mumbled something like: Just expenses would be fine. At that point, Bobbie's voice cut in from the second phone upstairs. After all, Bob had to eat. Tallman reassured them: if everything worked out, it would be something over literal expenses.

Hung over but sober, Creeley put two and two together the following day. Warren Tallman, a University of British Columbia English professor, was married to Ellen, a close friend of Marthe, who had found refuge with the Tallmans in May 1956 during her affair with Creeley.

Then, in December 1959, Robert Duncan had accepted Tallman's invitation to read to a group of some thirty to forty people in the professor's basement. Duncan's self-effacing manner, when compared to the poets or lecturers officially invited by the English department, struck an instantly sympathetic chord with Tallman's students. He realized most of them didn't know who he was, Duncan had said by way of introducing himself. By the time he had finished reading, his listeners, among them George Bowering, Fred Wah, and Frank Davey, wanted more. There was another reading in February 1961, then a series of lectures on 23, 24, and 25 July again delivered at Tallman's Vancouver home.

Under Duncan's influence, the loose association of young Vancouver poets had pulled together into a closely knit group. Duncan told them about Corman's *Origin*, Creeley's *Black Mountain Review*, and Diane di Prima's *Floating Bear*. Publishing their own newsletter might gain them the freedom from establishment standards and limitations these journals had secured for himself and his friends, Duncan suggested. The Canadians decided to do so the Saturday after his last lecture. The newsletter was christened *Tish*.

The San Francisco poet also provided the group with its major theoretical premises. A walking and talking university of verse lore, Duncan "filled the air with his most influential predecessors (Ezra Pound, William Carlos Williams, H.D.) and his closest contemporaries (Charles Olson, Robert Creeley, Larry Eigner, Denise Levertov) ... Tone leading, rhyme, sound resemblances and disresemblances, the musical phrase, composition by field and correspondences, as well as linguistic, musical, dramatic and choreographic analogues to writing – all these began to buzz about like bees. From which hive TISH was immediately born and for the next twenty months issues kept up a steady hum."

Above all, Duncan created a myth. Lionel Kearns, after listening and talking to Olson in Toronto, came back to Vancouver resembling Gulliver after Brobdingnag, Warren Tallman observed. *Origin* editor Cid Corman's reading in Seattle had the *Tish* poets drive down in squadron. By the time Creeley read his poems at the University of British Columbia Arts Festival, there was an audience of over 450, the room itself packed, people lining up in the halls.

Used either to cut-throat bohemian careerists à la Manhattan or to stodgy academics sluggishly disapproving of things on principle as in Amarillo, Texas, or Portland, Oregon, or Seattle, Washington, where he had read on the way, Creeley found Vancouver alive with an enthusiasm that reminded him of his, Olson's, and Corman's a dozen years earlier. He was enthralled by the Tallmans as well as by Canadians in general. The dignity Canadians allowed people was better than the slip and slide back home in Albuquerque; the provincial but open and decent atmosphere of Vancouver was preferable to the alleged sophistication of the New Mexico boomtown. Canada was the new frontier. Perhaps he would go live and teach there.

Warren Tallman, though seemingly shy and humble, proved a surprisingly astute *habitué* of university politics who would find Bob a job. The *Tish* cohorts waiting like sky rockets for Creeley's return provided an ideal platform for such lobbying. What's more, diverse faculty members, among them chairman Roy Daniells, and another poet, Earl Birney, were eager to welcome the rising star on America's poetic firmament among their ranks. Creeley's work, his performance at the UBC arts festival, and what referees like Donald Hall and Charles Olson had to say about him were genuinely impressive.

What ensued was the typically North American bidding war, one university suddenly outdoing the other in competing for an object to which they had earlier paid little attention. The University of British Columbia's offer was topped by the University of New Mexico's, spurring on the Canadians to come up with an even stronger counter-offer. Creeley found himself in demand as never before. Other than the seemingly lighter teaching load and marginally better pay, several further points swayed him in favour of UBC: teaching from September to April, a month off at Christmas, and last but not least, socialized medicine.

Loneliness back in Albuquerque was another motive driving him north. With Ed Dorn gone to teach in Pocatello, Idaho, he had only occasional visitors to talk to. Fee Dawson and his young wife, Barbara, came to visit several times during February and March; Lawrence Ferlinghetti passed through town and impressed Creeley with his unexpectedly shy, ingratiating demeanour; or new friend, filmmaker Stan Brakhage, along with his wife, Jane, and their three daughters, came to see the Creeleys in May.

Via Duncan, Brakhage had long heard about Creeley, read his works, and admired both. Now, during a conference on world affairs at the University of Colorado in Boulder, he saw a chance to actually meet him. Creeley was scheduled to share a panel with no less a man than Buckminster Fuller. Not invited themselves, Stan and family decided to crash a party. Bobbie remembers their sudden, incongruous appearance amid the crowd of cocktail-swilling, formally dressed conference attendants: Jane, a kind of tall, nut-brown maiden, her hair in long heavy braids, big Stan in Billy-the-Kid fringed leather jacket, one daughter perched on his right hip, another on Jane's left, a third between them holding both parents' hands.

Never before in their lives, Stan decided with characteristically overbearing enthusiasm, had Jane or he made friends so quickly, so deeply as with the Creeleys. The feeling was mutual, though less flamboyant on Creeley's side. He instantly liked Stan, finding he was a very decent person. The filmmaker also gave him a pretext for escaping the socialite rigmarole of the conference. Both families withdrew to the Brakhages' cabin in a mountain canyon high above Boulder, where they talked and screened several of Brakhage's films. As it turned out, the two men shared crucial artistic concerns. Just as Creeley insisted on the linguistic seriality of poetry as, essentially, a sequence of words in time, Brakhage considered movies as, above all, sequences of rapidly changing, single images.

They also shared distinct domestic problems. The Brakhages were delighted to find their counterparts openly discussing what other couples kept to themselves: like having fights in front of the children, or domestic violence more befitting a horror movie scenario than the suburban life of a university lecturer. Creeley's heavy drinking and concomitant rabidness played a role in most of these anecdotes: one, possibly apocryphal, had Creeley crouching on top of their car hammering at the roof with a beer bottle, and Bobbie starting to drive, then slamming on the brakes, making Creeley topple forward over the hood and hit the ground in front of the wheels. All this with the kids cowering in the back seat of the car. Would mom next run over dad?

Before setting out for the new frontier, the Creeleys took a hurried trip East. It turned out to be as depressing as the last in the previous summer. This time Creeley saw his mother but not his kids. In Gloucester he found Olson contending with worse poverty than ever. The household's broken refrigerator stood "marooned beside the plaster Virgin in the tall grass of the backyard. Betty fished off the pier to supplement the family's thin food rations. From the same spot, under cover of darkness, Charles himself threw out the household trash to avoid the collection charge." Olson's hopes of securing a university appointment at Dartmouth had collapsed: all the college had been looking for was a one-year replacement for a professor on leave.

Visiting New York was more *déjà vu*. Aside from pleasant visits with old friends like Zukofsky, Blackburn, Rumaker, and Chamberlain, the rest seemed driven and bleak. Fielding Dawson, whose visit had lightened up Creeley's life back in Albuquerque, had become part of the city's deadening routines – the constant rush, the going about one's business, the bleakness. As so often before in Creeley's life, it was time to take stock of his absolutes in friendship like Dorn and Olson. He really couldn't make the crowd at all these days, he complained.

A visit to Scribner's threatened to turn into the ultimate let-down. For about a month he had been waiting for the verdict on the new chapters he had completed recently. At the publisher's he was told to come back a few days later: Charles Scribner was out of town. Worse, he hadn't yet gotten around to reading the manuscript. Creeley went into a tailspin which reached its climax the night before their scheduled return to Scribner's.

They were driving along, Bobbie at the wheel, John Chamberlain next to her, Creeley occupying the back seat. Bobbie wouldn't let him drive in the drunken state he was in. So he started in on her in familiarly unnerving fashion. When needling failed to produce the desired effect, he suddenly leaned forward and spat into her hair. Steering with her left and looking straight ahead, she hauled out with her right, let fly at him hard, and hit his one good eye. The result was stunning. Looking at normal people you'd switch back and forth between their two eyes. But with Bob you'd focus on only one, and that had turned huge and black, she remembers.

However, the spell was broken. The next day at Scribner's Creeley got his contract and another advance. Afterwards they were invited to spend the weekend at Don Hutter's. Nobody, not even the editor's kids, asked the obvious question about Creeley's eye. Everyone politely enquired with Bobbie how her husband was feeling; or with Bob as to what plans he had for the remainder of the novel. It turned out he had none. But that was no great matter. He was having a great time regardless.

The rest of the summer was a drag of endless driving – some 2,000 miles from New York City back to Albuquerque, then another 1,500 odd miles, kids, household junk, and all packed into the Volkswagen sedan which they had got in trade for the van. But once arrived in Vancouver in the middle of a lovely, moist, and blooming summer, the Creeleys were delighted. Canadians were so agreeably quiet, polite, and careful of other people's dignity. The Creeleys' rambling, six bedroom house on 2527 West 35th, just two blocks from the Tallmans, offered ample space for the family. His study allowed Creeley a glimpse of the mountains as well as of a little edge of both the sea and the harbour.

Plenty of good news helped brighten his outlook on the coming academic year. *For Love*, his major book of poems to date, had appeared in April 1962, and the reactions from friends and reviewers, most of them positive, were pouring in. One of the first to write was Duncan who would review the collection for the *New Mexico Quarterly*. Every reading, Duncan raved, deepened his wonder and sense of how much he had always taken for granted. Charles Olson, in a somewhat nebulous review for the *Village Voice* (of 13 September 1962), called *For Love* a "delightful volume" covering an "uncanny range … of subjects and areas." By contrast, Denise Levertov read the collection's poems as the continuous sound of a bird repeating five or six notes. However, this was a strength rather than a mere weakness. What cumulatively and read in bits had seemed like wryness, self-pity, and willful exclusion of things, had suddenly struck her as agony – not what Creeley would say but what he must say.

Rexroth's review for the *New York Times Book Review* of 4 November was similarly double-edged. He ranked Creeley as "second only to Denise Levertov among the younger poets now writing in America." Certainly, his poems stood out from the merely "competent" verse by well established minor poets like Christopher Middleton, Byron Vazakas, or Edwin Honig, who all three appealed to "bookish minds of a moderate learning and limited experience." His was "poignantly, sometimes excruciatingly personal," its polished *objets d'art* surface à la Mallarmé hiding "little traps to wring the nerves and conscience of the reader." It was not Creeley's fault that American poetry past the mid-century could not produce a more "major" poet to overtake and surpass him. That criticism "should be levelled at America, or poetry, or the mid-century." Creeley was "not to blame for his eminence."

Finally, there were the run of the mill reviews in journals from the *New York Review of Books* to the *Nashville Banner*. They called Creeley's poems "nervous shudders," their effect pure, elegant, and indelible, the poet's seriousness "dark, hypnotic, laconic, sometimes painful," his sensibility "subtle, almost feminine." One reviewer felt Creeley ought to be the leading contender for next year's National Book Award for poetry; a second, though unsure whether Creeley was "the best poet under 40 now writing," found he was certainly one of the most interesting; a third decided he had written some of the most moving and important poetry of his generation; a fourth that he was "one of the most originally perceptive and disturbing" among young American poets.

Naturally, there were negative voices too. Critics noted the occasional incoherence or mistakes of grammar and punctuation, the failure to put question marks where appropriate, a complacency in the use of certain effects, or an exaggerated reticence and over-reliance on private reference. Yet even at their most negative, reviewers had to concede to Creeley's growing reputation or, as David Bromige put it, to his being "one of the most exorbitantly overrated poets practising today."

Internationally, his reputation was growing as well. Feltrinelli's *Il Verri* published Glauco Cambon's short piece on Creeley plus four of his poems. Germany's *Carl Hanser Verlag* seemed ready to bring out a collection of his stories, then the poems, as well as the novel as soon as it was ready. Klaus Reichert, who was to render them into German, had already translated four of the seven poems included in Hanser's *Junge Amerikanische Lyrik*, edited by Gregory Corso and Walter Höllerer. He had also presented Creeley in a forty-minute radio program.

Creeley had every reason to count his blessings. But with the term barely started, his perspective on things suddenly darkened. A continuous stream of visitors to his office, however friendly, left him little time for preparation or his own work. His class load, though only nine hours, was spread over the entire week. Most irritatingly, he had clashed with the department over how to teach his section of English 202, Introduction to Writing. The existing course outline would have him start from formal categories of structure which, in his projectionist view of the writing process, ought to derive from, not be imposed upon, the basic sense of what words can or cannot do.

Rather than make the students compose a poem, a story, or a one-act play, he would ask them to commit themselves to a certain project. Instead of having them write in a preconceived form, genre, or structure, he would allow them to express themselves in whatever form the material under hand chose for itself. Above all, students ought to learn to address specific problems such as connectives in relation to general structure, tone of vocabulary, or the objective/subjective treatment of content.

When Creeley's pleas fell on deaf eyes, he reacted in habitually paranoid fashion. Canadians, who only weeks ago had seemed so gentle and respectful of others' dignity, were incredibly dull, almost without exception. Moreover, they were distinctly hostile towards Americans like himself: the Canadian manner tended to cheapen what took on its own condition, like Creeley their teaching job. The Canadian dilemma was a faked Englishness and all-consuming vagueness. Canadians had an inferiority complex from being squeezed in between the authorities of British and American attitudes.

His colleagues, except for Tallman, were hopeless. Certainly the administrators were. Even the students, though open and ingenuous, were beginning to get on his nerves. What they lacked in background, say, about Kafka and Joyce, they tried to make good for by asking a lot of questions. One student, after Creeley had spent considerable time explaining what the Black Mountain poets were all about, dropped by his office to tell him he didn't like them.

Another, George Bowering, aroused Creeley's special antipathy. Already Bowering had talked Creeley into writing an introduction to a small collection of his poems. Most disconcertingly, Bowering's manner – the incongruous combination of towering ambition and self-stated shyness – reminded Creeley of his own. The man seemed like a veritable *doppelgänger* embodying his worst image of himself: a sort of malevolent Uriah Heep obscenely rubbing his hands, an image marking an "awful, self-consciously recognized limit" to his sincerity. Bowering irritated him in a way he was ashamed to admit to. Why, Creeley wondered, didn't he just tell the man straight out that he detested him?

That imagined confrontation took a predictably more violent turn when it happened. Watching Bowering dance with his "vacant" wife at a drunken party, Creeley, before he could think, found himself pushing his loathed double off the dance floor. A greatly embarrassed Creeley hastened to apologize by phone. An easily forgiving Bowering dropped off another batch of his poems in Creeley's office, requesting help with them. The encounter did little to cure Creeley's phobia about the "possibly frightening identification of [himself] with Uriah Heep." He feared hypocrisy, he told Cynthia Edelberg in 1975. "I hate its locations in terms of my own sense of myself."

Canada's established poets, as he got to know some of them, for the most part aggravated his contempt for the country in general. Louis Dudek aroused his fury by his mere physical presence, the way Dudek's poems had enraged him years earlier. Just watching Dudek made him shake with anger so that people remarked on how nervous he had seemed reading his own verse. He saw Dudek's poetry, like Al Purdy's, as a social mechanism to make other people swallow whatever attitudes, political, social, or worst, provincially Canadian, their authors had formed themselves.

Purdy himself struck Creeley as a nervous animal caught in a small trap, which incidentally explained whatever lyrical powers he possessed. Phyllis Webb was a more accomplished poet than either Purdy or Dudek because of her better ear, the best, in fact, of any Canadian poet except Layton. And at least she was intelligent. An older Creeley would remember other, more appealing aspects to his tangential contacts with Webb – how on their way to the classes they both hated, she would save him from despair by her ironic and pointed wit. But to the thirty-six year old Creeley, Webb was stuck in a complication of devices and intents. She probably was a bitch to boot, he reported to Gael Turnbull.

In the fall of 1962 he finally met Irving Layton, having first started to correspond with him some ten years earlier. "He came in quickly one night in the fall, sponsored by Canada Council, at war with the chairman of the english department etc, and came to our house with his 'agent' – a sort of bland man etc – and Phyllis Webb came over, and we sat drinking, sizing one another up. It was impossible not to like him, and I was really much biassed in his favor anyhow. I love that intensity, and the size, i.e., the whole man so compact and vigorous." At the reading Creeley got to know Layton's "'great man' manner, with the quick general statements, always a little vague, and now unhappily habitual." But his faults, Creeley felt, undoubtedly were as much Canada's as his own. On the whole Layton was a godsend in that environment.

To compound Creeley's general disgruntlement were his problems as a writer. Since Leslie's death he had felt locked in a vice creatively. He had written next to no poems in almost a year. Then finally there it was, a poem entitled "Death," about precisely the incident that condemned him to silence. Worried it might consist of banal platitudes, he submitted the forty-four lines to Duncan who, after discussing them with Jess, wrote an elaborate critique. He suggested various changes, even rewrote the fifth stanza. Primarily, he found fault with the ending: after talking about Leslie's personal death, Creeley wound up pontificating in speciously edifying manner about a triumph over death that seemed tagged on rather than emotionally derived from the rest. Did he realize that triumph (as Jess had pointed out) was a military term implying some form of conquest?

Creeley agreed: the poem's resolution was fake in terms of the poem's base feeling. He attempted a new ending. After all, "Death" was the only poem of any interest he had written in a year. He let it sit for over four months, then looked at it again. It didn't live up to the emotions involved, in Leslie's death, so he threw it out. Was he finished as a poet at only thirty-six? In a paranoid fit he had gone through his unpublished poems in early March and thrown out most of them. The exercise had left him with a mere half dozen poems from the past two years. Increasingly he found that much of what he wrote duplicated his own clichés. He hated to go on imitating himself, and at the same time couldn't see avenues for change of any kind.

Finishing the final chapters of his novel during the 1962 Christmas break was more productive but hardly less traumatic. Writing the earlier parts had been like dredging up his life's paranoid sludge, causing him nightmares when he normally didn't dream much at all. Completing the novel was worse. The last four sections were the most painful – the protagonist John, wishing his wife dead, then imagining her to have thrown herself down a mountain cliff, even thinking he can see her dead body, clearly was the most excruciating personal episode in an admittedly autobiographical novel. In fact, it was his own experience, Creeley insisted to his editor, Donald Hutter. He remembered seeing just that "body," an error rendered possible by the vagueness of the time and place. In other words, he saw what he wanted to see.

His sympathetic identification with his alter ego's wishful thinking was more apparent in the original ending than in the printed version. In the former, John actually spots what he takes to be Joan's (alias Ann's) dead body in a cradle of rock below. Hence, Hutter was led to believe that Joan had really committed suicide.

Hutter's misreading, or rather his so obviously identifying with John's homicidal thoughts, had personal reasons, Creeley speculated. Mrs Hutter (whom Bob, sporting his big black shiner, had gotten to know that previous summer) was a wife who, though less didactic than Ann, was like her in every other respect. No wonder poor Hutter was perturbed and misled by the novel's ending. His incredulity at Joan's still being alive, and his saying so in his letters were an exact replica of John's incredulity and of Creeley's in real life.

Creeley ultimately felt purged. Now that it was finished, *The Island* appeared to him as a snake's skin of old habits he had gotten rid of. Never before had he experienced such emptiness. To relive, in writing the novel, marital problems he had happily gotten out of, also had brought some real joy. Seeing his previous self turned "fiction" in John was a special relief. So, at Hutter's anxious suggestion, he was not averse to doing a little more fictionalizing, even if that meant going against the autobiographical facts. In the rewritten, published version, John is never in a position to physically look down and confirm what he suspects to be there, i.e., Joan's dead body. His wishfully searching eyes are blocked "by an unexpected ledge."

From here on, things proceeded with unusual rapidity. Once the new conclusion was approved by Hutter, the novel instantly went to press. The proofs reached Bob just as he was packing up to leave the Canada he had come to detest so intensely. The decision to do so had been made long ago. Lending a sympathetic ear to his complaints about UBC and the Canadian dilemma, the University of New Mexico, as early as December 1962, had made him an irresistable offer: a three class load, a starting salary of $7,000 a year, plus a $500 moving allowance. Once again, as in Guatemala, he was counting his days like a prisoner serving a sentence. Come the end of term, the Creeleys travelled back to New Mexico.

By 8 May 1963, they were safely installed in a house complete with swimming pool in Placitas, some twenty miles north of Albuquerque.

33

Vancouver Poetry Conference, 1963.

Since he'd arrived in India in mid-February 1962, Ginsberg had succumbed to various illnesses: chronic bronchitis, kidney infection, influenza, dysentry, and pinworms. Though none of them proved fatal, they deepened his lifelong obsession with death. Irresistibly, he had been drawn towards India's burning ghats. There he walked around the fires, corpse fumes whirling round his head, and stared at the phantasmagoric spectacle of brain pudding blackening in the fire, gleaming teeth and dark eye sockets scorched clean by the flames, fat dripping from bloated feet and toes, funeral attendants with long bamboo poles pushing the corpses back into the pyres.

Then he ran out of money and was unable to leave India. By late September there was a letter from Creeley suggesting a possible way out. Would he be willing to teach a three-week poetry workshop at a UBC poetry conference during the coming summer? The offer of $900 for the job, plus up to $500 for travelling, was more than generous. It sent Ginsberg scurrying around Calcutta travel agencies trying to figure out a proper itinerary. For 6093 rupees (changed at the black market rate of 6.50 to the dollar), he could buy a round-trip ticket with stopovers in Saigon, Bangkok, Japan, Vancouver, Europe (to see William Burroughs and Gregory Corso), and Moscow (to visit Yevtushenko). That is, if UBC would advance him the money.

The university did, and by 26 May he was on his way. In Saigon he met Buddhist priests protesting Diem's persecution of Vietnamese Buddhists, talked to everyone from newsmen to army officials, and celebrated his thirty-seventh birthday. In Cambodia he visited Angkor Wat, in Kyoto, Gary Snyder and his wife, Joanne. On the train to Tokyo he had an ecstatic experience that was to mark a turning point in his life. He would have to renounce his previous metaphysical quests, even his Blake visions, and instead live in his body. He would have to accept its mortality which India's burning ghats had revealed in all its horrific detail. Trying to come to terms with his body, Ginsberg urged others to follow suit – "I am that I am I am the / man & the Adam of hair in / my loins."

Ginsberg, writes Barry Miles, "arrived at the University of British Columbia, jubilant in the knowledge of his new realization and clearly in a delicate emotional state, crying all the time and fondling people, demanding to be loved for what he was and loving everyone in return." Adds Michael Schuhmacher, "With his long Naomi hair, Abraham beard and cracked eyeglasses, he was a different-looking Ginsberg, as well." Yet to other conference members like Duncan, Levertov, and Olson, the old showman prophet had simply changed costume.

Also, they had more urgent problems to deal with. The falling out between Levertov and Creeley was as solid as ever. Olson, afflicted by poverty and recent illness, felt increasingly estranged from his former friends. His relations to the Beats were worse. How could he forget Gregory Corso calling him a "hip square" and "mental gangster," or his being needled during a Harvard appearance of Corso, Ginsberg, and Orlovsky. At the time, Olson had put an end to the debate by wordlessly ramming his skull into Corso's, leaving Corso with a big lump that lasted for days. The Beats were "hexing" him, Olson felt. Ginsberg, in spite of his fame, was a crowd-pleasing rabble-rouser rather than a real poet. But then who was *he*? Perhaps he was not "a *poet* at all" but merely "some creature of Duncan's and Creeley's long years of admiration," he told Betty.

Ginsberg was in no mood to be overwhelmed by others' defeatist or antagonistic attitudes. Sensing Olson's hostility, he asked him difficult questions about God, even disrupted his sacred morning slumbers to pump him about his dream life. "Get that guy outta here," Olson was heard screaming at one point, "he's trying to steal my dreams!" So Ginsberg came up with a new scheme. When Olson declared that he was one with his skin, Ginsberg hastened to interpret the words in the sense that Olson, too, had returned to his body.

Others reacted less philosophically to Olson's conundrum. Hosts Warren and Ellen Tallman silently repaired to separate couches while their six-foot, eight-inch guest usurped the master bedroom. The UBC personnel waited on Olson hand and foot as he held court on a scenic balcony overlooking the majestic mountain peaks of the North Coast range. He was "ordering everything," Warren Tallman remembers. "He wanted a stack of sandwiches. He wanted to know, 'Do you have milkshakes in this club? What kind of cigars do you have now?' He didn't want a *glass* of Scotch; he said, 'Why not bring the bottle!' And the staff did as he said.

The academic faculty were sitting inside with no one to wait on them because all five waiters and waitresses were out on the balcony with Charles."

Officially a day-time credit course in poetry writing ($66), an evening non-credit course in contemporary poetry (11 sessions: $12) plus four Friday evening poetry readings by Duncan, Ginsberg, Levertov, and Olson open to the general public (series fee $5), the conference increasingly degenerated into a "lovely union of souls" with freewheeling personal intermingling between students and faculty. Royal Canadian Mounties coming to investigate a noise complaint walked in on a poetry "'bacchanal' ruled over by the benign satyr Maximus, who disported on a bed with four or five comely female conferees, 'giggling and mildly feeling each other.'" Ginsberg informed his father that he had rediscovered the female sex. He seemed to be back on girls again, he wrote. Maybe he would bring home some baby Ginsbergs after all.

Ginsberg's euphoria, despite others' resistance, proved infectious. Olson's final four-hour reading marathon on 16 August, the last day of the conference, was a resounding triumph. It was the best reading he had ever done, he told Betty. Once it was over, Tallman found him hiding from his followers, tears streaming down his face.

Emotions ran highest during the closing celebrations. At a huge party Ginsberg once again held centre stage. He chanted "Hare Krishna," "weeping and ecstatic, kissing everyone and feeling everybody's stomach." The Vancouver Poetry Festival had turned into a *"Liebesfest,"* conference organizer Robert Creeley observed afterwards. Everyone had arrived paranoid and left euphoric. More personally speaking, the conference, thanks mainly to Ginsberg, had marked a turning point in Creeley's life.

The record of an exchange between the two poets shows Ginsberg steering Creeley in the new direction. Why not talk about his physical habits of writing, he suggested. Creeley explained: on a typewriter, always, typing with two fingers, but as fast as he could talk, on eight-by-eleven inch sheets, "the yellow copy paper that's not spongy, but has a softness to it, so that when you type, the letter goes in, embeds a little." Somewhat incongruously, he next expounded on a multiplicity of issues such as contemporary American reality being dominated by the Negro, or the "deep change in consciousness" transforming the world in general. All the terms of consciousness that he had grown up with, he explained, were "disappearing momently, daily." These ongoing changes were far more significant than those caused by World War II, because they were transforming *all* terms of our thousands-of-years old human relationships. Even a course like the present one (Creeley's somewhat anticlimactic example) would not have been possible ten years earlier.

Ginsberg, the obvious addressee of these sentiments, ignored them. What would Creeley do, he asked, if, say, sitting on a train, he suddenly had "a great seizure of realization" like Ginsberg's travelling from Kyoto to Tokyo? Arrange his paper and typewriter first?

Of course, he was right. But given Creeley's social shyness, his "being so worried about keeping himself together in public," nothing less than the protective cocoon of specific domestic circumstances, preferably in complete isolation as in New Hampshire, Fontrousse, Lambesc, Bañalbufar, Los Tarrales, or recently, Placitas, could allow him to venture forth like a snail from his shell. Only then could he "open up this equally small thing ... feel it with the intensity of all the perception that ... the ego bit can recognize, and then destroy the ego by its own existence. It's shy in other words."

Or rather, it's "situated where there is no threat," Ginsberg countered.

No question, Ginsberg was right again. Far from trying to make excuses, Creeley realized he was deeply dissatisfied with the writing habits he had created for himself; they had given him a million excuses for doing nothing nine times out of ten. They had forced him into a situation in which only certain kinds of feeling would come through – "no wonder the poems are short! I'm amazed that there are any at all!"

Slowly, over the months and years, he would find out what Ginsberg had taught him. He began writing in different states of consciousness, tried pen and pencil, used notebooks, first very small, then larger ones. Most importantly, perhaps, he attempted to avoid making instant decisions as to the poetic quality of what he was writing.

It took time. The advice he had received from Ginsberg, Olson, Duncan, and Levertov, even his feeling of once again occupying his place in their company, as well as his general new sense of happiness and exuberance, did not enable him to extricate himself from feeling locked in, which still made him tear up most everything he wrote. Right after completing a poem, he would see the facile ease with which he had written it and realize that he had simply written another "Creeley" poem. He kept telling himself that the novel had absorbed what otherwise would have found its way into poems. So why not try another novel? For a while he had been making plans towards one. Entitled *The Market Place*, it would be about the time spent in Guatemala – the complexity of disjunct senses of living, the randomness, the people in affluent, "free" worlds and their diametrical opposites. Predictably he would eschew any sociological perspective, he assured his friends. He would even try to avoid the moral tightrope he'd been walking in *The Island*. There he'd tried to, as best he could, render justice to everyone involved – Ann, Martin Seymour-Smith, Alex Trocchi, himself. In the new one, he would move beyond all such moral, or worse, sociological concerns, and simply record the surreal chaos of people crowded into the same jungle.

In spite of such announcements, the actual writing was postponed from week to week. He felt too unsettled in Placitas. Or he wondered what role he would play as narrator. Even an advance from Scribner's did little to help him get started. Besides these literary problems, there were more mundane ones; a house purchase he had planned upon his return from Vancouver fell through when the vendor upped the price. Their dog, Brody, was hit by a car and broke his left hind leg. In spite of it all, Creeley felt great. As never before, his letters show how relaxed, happy, even complacent, and solid he felt. Everything was swinging. It was good to be alive. He thought this generation was theirs, he confided to Olson.

To add to his cheerfulness, there were the reviews of *The Island* as well as of the stories ("Mr. Blue," "The Grace," "In the Summer," "A Death," "The Dress," and "The Book") LeRoi Jones had included in *The Moderns: An Anthology of New Writing*. The *New York Herald Tribune Book Week*'s comments on the anthology highlight Creeley's growing acceptance by an establishment that continued to pour scorn on his immediate associates. While Kerouac, Burroughs, and Eastlake are dismissed as successful, notorious, and hopeful, Creeley is called "excellent." After damning Michael Rumaker, the reviewer extolls "the sweet, jazzy toughness" of Robert Creeley: "He has a male malleability that pleases itself, calm and loose, and his tone is in the mainstream of American literature."

Several of the reviews of *The Island* were superlative. "Few writers," Terry Southern wrote in the *New York Times Book Review* (22 November 1963), "have shown so consistent a dedication to their work, their 'care of phrase' and creative integrity, as has Robert Creeley over the years ... So it is with considerable expectation (or anxiety) that one turns to his first novel; and it is a pleasure to find that he has succeeded miraculously, where most poets fail even to begin." Others called *The Island* "excellent" (*Poetry*, April, 1964), "sustained, coherent, and generally good" (*New York Review of Books*, 14 November 1963), or they spoke of a "notable first novel" whose "author writes like a man crossing a minefield – every word a grim step, an act of difficult trust – but genuineness is the effect" (*Harper's Magazine*, December 1963).

Creeley's friends too were exceeding each other in superlatives. Duncan felt transported into the critical hallelujah stage. *The Island*, to him, came as a fulfilment of something he had wanted to happen in the novel generally. Some of its passages, like the one about Martin dancing, were so unbearably good he felt like dancing around the room and hugging Bob. His prose in *The Island* had put writers back where their poems would have to measure up to his novel.

The hyperbole never stopped. Witter Bynner praised Creeley's uncanny skill as a storyteller. To Charles Tomlinson, *The Island* matched Creeley's short stories in terms of providing the most distinctive prose of its decade. Nothing of this astonishing tautness, accuracy, and tact in handling had come into view for years. Alex Trocchi, business-minded as ever, phrased his comments about Creeley's immense influence on modern Western culture as a possible plug that might help sales of future publications.

Others like Denise Levertov were more guarded. *The Island* was painful to read but never boring or blurry like some of Creeley's earlier prose in which, out of sheer terror of saying anything obvious, he had sometimes not said enough. The novel was clear to the point of fright – full of those hard edges suddenly seen by someone shortsighted upon first putting on glasses. Yet excellent as it was, the book could have been more so if Creeley, instead of sticking so close to the facts, had invented and transformed them. Its shocking realism inclined Levertov to read *The Island* in straightforward autobiographical terms. John's lack of self-confidence and trust in his own value as a human being was Bob's. The ghastly bind and terrible drive that thrust Joan into all those abortions was Ann's. After all, Denise and Mitch had long known some of the novel's major characters in real life. Even where this was not so, Denise was prepared to take such factual authenticity on trust. Seymour-Smith's most recent book of poems, she gleefully reported to Creeley, had a hilarious picture of the author on the jacket flap. My God, it was Artie ready to cadge ten pounds. Would Bob like to see it, or would it give him the creeps?

Creeley's frankly autobiographical method had a different effect on Gael Turnbull. Granted, the picture Creeley had drawn of Bob Cooper, alias Robert Willis, in *The Island*, was devastatingly true. But who else but Cooper had had the guts to walk the back streets of Liverpool with Gael? Cooper had a courage probably not apparent to Creeley at the time. And who else but Seymour-Smith had sent Turnbull the longest and most cheering letter he ever received while lying with polio in hospital? In that sense, *The Island* struck him as neither a novel nor a piece of writing, but as an experience. However, perhaps that's what a novel or any piece of writing ought to be, Turnbull added diplomatically.

Creeley gobbled it up like the rest, proclaiming himself very moved by Turnbull's reading of the novel. He'd wanted it to be the fact of the experience, autobiographical or otherwise, which in very large parts it was. Luckily he had been able to resume contact with Seymour-Smith before the book was out, and sent him a copy fearing he might be offended, fears that happily had proven unfounded.

Buoyed by all the praise, Creeley was quick to dismiss those who disapproved in major ways. To tell him, like Cid Corman, that there was something missing in *The Island*, or that he had sold out as a poet, was like waving a red flag, Creeley confessed to Levertov. As always, Corman proved to be the person who could frustrate him more completely than anyone else he had ever met. Fielding Dawson was a close second. His intriguing argument that the poems, the short stories, and the novel each projected a separate Creeley persona or attitude – a reactive self, a keenly angered perception, a vividly revengeful self – met with even more summary dismissal. Creeley acknowledged Dawson's sense of his multiple personality but said he couldn't follow him on *The Island*. After all, "me" was "me," "I" was "I," and "mine" "mine." As for the rest, it got pretty historical. He dodged Dawson's suggestion that *The Island* (like much autobiographical fiction) was the author's way of getting back at people he had come to dislike. Instead, Dawson was treated to variously reiterated but partly inaccurate accounts of the novel's genesis. *The Island*, he was informed, was completed in three different sittings, each involving roughly five days of writing straight, with at times a year or so between.

Throughout the autumn things continued to go well, Creeley feeling relaxed, for once enjoying his teaching, and telling friends about his clear, lovely wife as well as his equally pleasant daughters. To make his happiness complete, there was the long awaited breakthrough into once again writing poetry. It followed a by now well-established pattern: restlessness, the first stirrings, then the sudden outburst, reaching its peak around 14 December 1963, when he completed a whole clutch of poems in a single afternoon. Never before had he written poems of either the breadth or disturbingly private outspokenness of "The Dream," "Anger," or "The Woman." At the same time they clearly differed from what he had denounced as the depressive realism of Robert Lowell's *Life Studies*. His new poems were confessional, not in the sense of revealing intimate details from his private life to the reader, but of unveiling so far unfathomed secrets to their author.

Paradoxically, this period of unprecedented happiness allowed Creeley to articulate matters such as a tendency towards domestic violence in "One Way," or his proneness towards all-consuming rages in "Anger." The latter, in which the speaker fantasizes about cutting off his wife's head or twisting each of her fingers until it breaks, reflects something far more sinister than the "frustrated, impotent" emotion Creeley admits to in his "Autobiography." The anger in the poem is bottomless, blind, wilfully locked in itself and perversely searching for the horrible place of its self-fulfilment.

It is black.
It is an open
hole of horror, of

nothing as if not
enough there is
nothing. A pit –

which he recognizes,
familiar, sees
the use in, a hole

for anger and
fills it
with himself

Like "For Rainer Gerhardt," "Anger" and kindred poems written around the same time seem to anticipate what lay ahead rather than reflect the author's moods at the time they were written.

34

Anger.

Creeley's success continued throughout 1964-66. A Guggenheim during 1964–65 was followed by a Rockefeller grant, freeing him from teaching for the spring term of 1966. By January 1966, he received an offer for an annual $17,500 visiting professorship from SUNY Buffalo. On the publishing front, Rago took numerous of his new poems for *Poetry*, and Germany's *Insel Verlag*, after publishing *Mister Blue: Sechzehn Geschichten*, offered to do *The Island* as well.

His reading at the Guggenheim had people lining up along Fifth Avenue. At a Buffalo symposium he debated poetry with W.D. Snodgrass and Robert Graves in front of over two thousand people. Gregory Corso, watching from the sidelines, gave him a wide grin whenever he scored. And he did. A surprised Graves told Bobbie that Creeley seemed much less confused than he remembered him. At least to Creeley, his side won in this and in other panel discussions with Julian Symons and Jack Lambert, literary editor of the *Sunday Times*. He and his friends were becoming a cultural empire, Creeley announced to publisher John Calder. If not occupying its throne, Creeley would at least play *eminence grise* behind it. At a Michigan State University conference on approaches to twentieth-century literature, Creeley and his work hogged the discussion. His fame was rapidly spreading throughout North America as well as major European countries like Britain, France, Germany, and Italy. Still under forty years of age, he was moving into literary history, a role he would embroider on over future decades.

It was time to fraternize and make concessions. Donald Hall, the former "idiot" of Cambridge days, whom Creeley went to see in Ann Arbor, turned out to be a pleasant man surprisingly devoid of the stuffy arguments and dreary ambitions typical of such men's academic entourage. Creeley had learnt his lesson in resigning as co-editor of *New American*

Story after the anthology's main editor, Don Allen, squabbled with Field-ing Dawson. Finding that Dawson no longer behaved like a true friend, Creeley realized the futility of his gesture and resumed his editorial la-bours. Henceforth he would accept the politics of the occasion and work within it as effectively as possible. Duncan, with his reservations regard-ing anthologies as well as with a non-poet editor like Don Allen, was ad-vised to do likewise. For all their shortcomings, anthologies provided a range of writing, theoretical statement, and biographical reference that would all be hopelessly dispersed otherwise, Creeley explained. In that sense, Allen's *New American Poetry* of 1960 had been more useful than any comparable anthology in the past twenty odd years. Though a non-poet, Allen had strong sympathies for Olson, Duncan, and himself, which should be made use of. The whole publishing business was and always had been an active battleground. The main point was to win.

Naturally, concessions made in the battle for fame and fortune had their limits. Aware of how the assassination of John F. Kennedy had been turned into a media event, Creeley refused Basic Books' request for con-tributions to a volume of poetic tributes to the murdered president. It was a different story when the u.s. State Department invited him on a six-week trip to Pakistan. Never one to be overly concerned with his socio-political role and adamantly opposed to seeing literature contaminated by such issues, Creeley needed some nudging from his moral guardian Dun-can to make him find the politically correct path. But so he did, rescind-ing his acceptance of the State Department's invitation. One reason, as communicated in an official letter, was the growing dilemma in Vietnam, a second, his not wishing to be seen as supporting a president whom he deeply questioned; a third, most plausible under the circumstances, was the peer pressure from politically minded fellow poets.

Other than that, there was little to impede Creeley's increasingly fran-tic pursuit of fame, acceptance, and money – not even his admitting that he was becoming bitterly greedy. Major occasions brought on the bellig-erence of a contender facing a title fight, minor ones his contempt for, say, a cattle-auction book fair like Frankfurt's or the show-business atmo-sphere of the increasingly numerous poetry circuits. His trip to Europe at Calder's invitation, for instance, had him scared to death, in a damn flut-ter at nearly everything: like the young English men with their fishy wise-ness, or possibly having to meet Monsieur Gallimard in person.

Also there was a new tone of self-righteous indignation for being treated with less respect than he deserved. As early as 25 July 1964 he ha-rangued Calder over delays with the British publication of *The Island* and the planning of his trip to England. He wanted to know truthfully what was happening. There were contradictions in Calder's letters. Why couldn't Calder oblige him with clear terms of responsibility and clear answers to what Creeley felt were his clear questions? In expectation of the money due to him, he had bought a house in Placitas and started building an additional room, which, because of the delays with the novel, remained in a half-finished state, lacking an adequate roof and plaster. Creeley was very concerned to know when *The Island* would be out, so he could damn well finish the room. Otherwise it would be a shambles once the rain hit it and throw him for a loss of some $900.

More generally speaking, Creeley really was not pleased at all with how Calder had left him with such a vagueness of blurred misinformation. All he wanted was clarity, and he couldn't understand why it seemed so persistently lacking. A subsequent letter written some two weeks before his expected departure kept up the barrage. Too many questions regarding the proofs of *The Gold Diggers*, the travelling schedule, and his income from readings while in England remained unresolved. He wanted to have these things a little clearer before leaving, though he left the matter to Calder. But would Calder please not neglect to answer his questions in his next letter, at his earliest possible convenience.

Predictably, Creeley's fears proved mostly unfounded. Calder's arrangements got him around with a very helpful exactness, Creeley had to admit. Everywhere he went he found evidence that his side was winning, even in Central Europe. Though Germany, as usual, turned into a spooky drag, the *Insel* people were charming and kind, and had a usefully and pleasantly old-fashioned seriousness about books. Translator Klaus Reichert struck him as especially enthusiastic and intelligent.

Most delightful were London and England. The anticipated smart alecks for the most part turned out to be open-minded fellow poets and critics interested in the new American poetry and Creeley's proposals. If anything, the general welcome from the younger generation or from an old-time loner like Basil Bunting deepened Creeley's contempt for establishment figures like Cleanth Brooks, then cultural attaché at the American Embassy in London. To Creeley, the famous critic seemed like a small-town, midwestern merchant. Brooks went on and on about having been unable to help W.C. Williams with the mess surrounding his appointment as poetry consultant at the Library of Congress; he expressed surprise at how so many of Creeley's generation found Pound of such interest. Creeley felt very smug and vindicated by it all, he reported to Levertov.

Whether exciting like the trip to England or tedious like touring the Michigan Poetry circuit thereafter, the search for recognition exacted a price. It never let up: the continual rush at airports, bus depots, and train stations, the interminable driving to meet deadline after deadline, often

several the same day; the endless social rounds with old and new acquaintances, the luncheons, dinners, and receptions, the long nights, and finally the drinking. In Michigan, bourbon in water glasses knocked
straight back kept Creeley seated after the reading, for fear he could not
stand up. Then, back home, there was the onslaught of exhaustion before
lapsing into a restless sluggishness making him hanker for more of the
same. Sluggishness, boredom, frustration, and restlessness are the most
frequent terms he used to describe his state of mind during 1964–66.

There was an added factor to make him feel frustrated upon his return
home from England in the fall of 1964. Like much else in his life now, it
had unfolded in a *déjà vu* fashion. As with Ann between 1947 and 1954,
he had been sharing life almost uninterruptedly with Bobbie during 1957
and 1964. Hence, his trip to Europe in 1964, like the one to Black Mountain College in 1954, meant his first escape from roughly seven years of
continuous conjugal domesticity. More so even than in 1954 in New York
City, he was welcomed like the "messiah" in Britain. In addition to the
fame he enjoyed within his group, he had won national recognition as a
poet and novelist. As he did with Cynthia then, Creeley started a relationship with a woman considerably younger than his wife, in this case
with an up-and-coming novelist, Ann Quin. Like Creeley himself, she
was published by both Scribner's and Calder.

Friends in England responded differently to the affair. Alex Trocchi
didn't care, while Martin Seymour-Smith disapproved. Creeley defended
himself, in much the same way he had regarding Cynthia or later Marthe.
He was Irish, old, and man enough to stay with what he felt in all its complexity for both Bobbie *and* Ann, he told Seymour-Smith. Quin, a very
pleasant woman and very good novelist, he mused to Denise, had saved
his life more than once while over in England. What he brought on himself, as ever, was a uselessly complicated scene, he admitted to Olson.
Travelling did just that to him, opening him up, perhaps not altogether
happily. But to hell with it.

If travelling to England had opened Creeley up, the return home shut
him down. He loved Bobbie very much, but the world was at moments so
very large, or else small, he wrote to Ginsberg. After the great, wild time
he had had there, he very much missed England. He felt restless, frustrated, even a little bitter. Bobbie was told about all the lovely English
women wearing black leather coats and immediately wrote to Marion Boyars at Calder's about where and at what price she might get one, then
decided it was too expensive.

During Bob's absence, Bobbie had done a great amount of work on
their new house. She had almost finished an outside structure as well as
remodelled the kitchen, involving the removal of several walls. Yet all of

that only deepened the adulterous husband's feelings of guilt. He could only look at it blankly, he complained to Olson, his whole sense of things being totally numb. Suddenly the emptiness was of no use at all, and he was left bored and damn well stiff.

Perhaps he would go back to England in a year or two. Or there was the possibility of bringing Ann Quin to New Mexico via the D.H. Lawrence Fellowship awarded by the University of New Mexico; Creeley himself started negotiating on her behalf in early January. Volunteering his services as one of her referees, he approached Charles Tomlinson, like himself a previous D.H. Lawrence fellow. Ann Quin was duly awarded the fellowship, then, looking rather battered after a stay in New York City, turned up in Placitas around 20 May. She stayed for about a week.

A woman obsessed with triangular relationships, she arrived carrying the manuscript of her new novel, *Three*, about a young woman, S, coming to stay with a married couple, Ruth and Leonard. Outwardly, husband and wife present an image of conjugal stability while really feeling frustrated and bored. S's feelings towards them are ambivalent. On the one hand, she eagerly seeks recognition and acceptance, on the other she wishes to expose the couple's complacency, and in the process is driven to commit suicide. Ironically, her death achieves what S couldn't manage alive: Ruth and Leonard become obsessed with her, blame each other for her suicide, and in increasingly violent fashion, question each other and their marriage. An intrigued Creeley read seventy odd pages of the manuscript and duly reported to Calder that he was very, very impressed.

It was not the only time Ann Quin would foreshadow her destiny in her writing. The hero of her last novel, *Triptychs* (1972), suffers an attack of aphasia, as she herself did shortly after completing it. Haunted by periodic attacks of psychosis, she had another major breakdown and spent a month in a London hospital, unable to speak. In August 1973 she died, probably by committing suicide.

Ann's relations with Bob and Bobbie unfolded in less novelistic fashion than those between S, Leonard, and Ruth. However, they seem to have initiated the break-up of a marriage that deteriorated rapidly from then on. For Bob there were some happy, even idyllic moments with Ann, like driving her up to the D.H. Lawrence ranch on 27 May, trees blooming, birds warbling, the mesa stretching out immensely against the backdrop of the mountains. But otherwise her visit to New Mexico brought him little of the fulfilment he had experienced with her back in England. A local friend, poet Larry Goodell, witnessed the Creeley household while Ann Quin was there. Bobbie and Ann were stolidly adversarial, while Bob and Ann had an argument, she complaining that the hum of the refrigerator got on her nerves, Bob, in habitually quixotic fashion rising to its defence, saying something like: That's a refrigerator. I like that hum.

The Berkeley Poetry Conference proved similarly disheartening for Ann. Goodell, her chauffeur to the Bay Area, remembers her as an obsessively conscientious, talented writer as well as beautiful woman. Barely managing a perilous psychological balance, she yet seemed in permanent search of the unexpected and unknown. Travelling was an adventurous quest, a courting of imminent disaster. The tensions of her unfulfilled affair with a man she seemed to worship, compounded by North America's crass materialism, ideological jargon mongering and strait-jacket pop psychology, which she would satirize in *Triptychs*, brought her close to a breakdown. By the time they arrived in San Francisco, she had to see a doctor.

Meanwhile, Creeley was caught up in the hectic two weeks of the conference. A hoped-for repeat of the Vancouver precedent, it unfolded in reverse order. At Vancouver the major poets – Olson, Duncan, Levertov, Ginsberg, and Creeley – had met in a mood of mutual diffidence but ended on a note of reestablished trust and triumphant accomplishment. At Berkeley things started off hopefully, quickly turned into an over-organized grind, and ended in a stunning anticlimax.

On the positive side, there was Robert Duncan receiving a ten-minute standing ovation from a crowd of over a thousand people, causing Creeley to describe the conference as exemplifying the recent "peak years" in poetry. Organized on the basis of Don Allen's 1960 *The New American Poetry*, the gathering also gave him a chance to meet or hear in person some of the poets assembled under his, Olson's, and Duncan's leadership in that anthology. Ted Berrigan's poetry, for instance, while deriving from that of Frank O'Hara, John Ashbery, and Jackson Mac Low, displayed linguistic characteristics much like his own. In it "words [were] returned to an almost primal circumstance, by a technique that makes use of feedback, that is, a repetitive relocation of phrasing, where words are curiously returned to an almost objective state of presence so that *they* speak rather than someone speaking with them."

Also there were the reunions with old friends: conversations with Duncan and Olson, two pleasant afternoons with Don Allen and Gary Snyder – but all of it in too much of a rush, Creeley trying to attend as many events as possible, lest his absence as one of the movement's elder statesmen should be taken as a put-down. It should have been a lovely congruence in every sense, he remarked, but the university had them all so categorized and "dealt with," conference participants scurrying down corridors, exchanging nods and quick words but finding little time for real conversation.

The biggest disappointment, particularly to his followers, was Charles Olson. By arrangement of conference co-host Robert Duncan, he had been tacitly granted quasi-papal status as in Vancouver. Preceded by Dorn on Tuesday night, Ginsberg on Wednesday, and second-in-command Robert Creeley on Thursday, Olson was to deliver his "anchor-man" reading on the final Friday night. It turned into a debacle.

After attending first the Spoleto Festival of Two Worlds, then the PEN International Congress in Bled, Yugoslavia, Olson had arrived exhausted to the point where, as he put it, he had no more to feed on than himself. To Creeley he gave the impression of a man intent on "working his way through the whole history of drugs in America in about two weeks." While consuming heavy doses of stimulants and/or tranquillizers, he drank brandy and Cutty Sark on top. The "anchor-man" reading in Wheeler Hall unfolded accordingly. After reciting two poems, Olson launched into a drunkenly rambling monologue on poetry and politics, as well as his running for President of Poetry, semi-seriously proposing appointments to his cabinet like Ginsberg as "Secretary of State for Love." He overruled heckler Lew Welch who had asked for more poems, protesting that he was "addressing the convention floor" instead. "The only convention I care of in the whole earth," he announced, "is occurring tonight."

Duncan had already walked out. As more and more people followed suit, Olson's tone became threatening. "If you don't know, brother, that poetics is politics, [that] poets are political leaders today, and the only ones, you shouldn't have come," he jeered at one defector. Another, conference co-organizer Professor Thomas Parkinson, wittily remarked that "Duncan left at the Moscow trials, I left at the Finnish War." Even loyal faithfuls like Creeley felt increasingly upset. "Is *this* the Charles Olson we all know and love?" he asked Ed Dorn. The show, which Olson proposed should have gone on all night, came to a sudden end when two university policemen entered Wheeler Hall, tapped Olson on the shoulder, and politely asked him to stop. Even a young, beautiful woman whom the fifty-four year old Olson had singled out as his after-conference bride, had fled in dismay.

In the final analysis the Berkeley Poetry Conference left Creeley sick to death of poetry as a subject and apprehensive about how the university was appropriating what had been created in protest against it. To vent his immediate frustrations, he gratuitously screamed obscenities at a clean-cut young Berkeley policeman, later counting his blessings for not being thrown in jail. There was little time for more. He suddenly remembered that he had committed himself to a speaking engagement back home and drove the 1,500 odd miles back to Albuquerque non-stop. They got there by 30 July. Bobbie had accompanied Bob during the entire trip.

Shortly thereafter Ann Quin was off to the Bahamas. She was beginning to enjoy America, Creeley remarked to Calder. Otherwise, his letters hardly mentioned her. Their affair had definitely come to an end, though not so the frustrations it left in its wake.

35

The Unsuccessful Husband.

Towards the end of October 1965, Fielding Dawson received a letter from his old friend Robert Creeley. Bob had no interest, it told him, in maintaining a friendship in which there was so much questioning and confusion.

In all fairness, Creeley had multiple reasons to feel annoyed with his friend. Dawson and his wife, Barbara, during another visit to the South-West, had more or less snubbed him. Prior to that, there had been Dawson's squabble with Don Allen, causing Creeley to first resign, then resume his co-editorship of *New American Story*. Dawson had attacked *The Island*, first in letters to Creeley, then in a short work of fiction, *Thread*. He had even had the nerve to ask Creeley to write a "note" for the book, which Creeley had done, praising Dawson's general "abilities as a writer" and more specifically, his sense that stories, "unless they *take a turn on their own* ... come to nothing." For "if one write[s] only what one intends," Creeley explicated, "then intentions are really all one ever comes to."

Had Creeley read *Thread* before writing his "Note," he might not have said so. Subtitled "The Witches," Dawson's story features an "old friend" who, unable to learn from experience, has produced an "acidly angry narrative" about two married couples, written out of "the frenzied rage of himself blinded by his memory of jealousy and desire and fear and failure." Creeley's portrait as a person having multiple faces and personae (including the "frenzied hag in him") is highly unflattering: "His hair seems longer, he rather stoops, his skin stretches tightly over the bones on his face, neck, his blouse bags forward and I see his scrawny chest and shoulders, his lips are drawn back and his teeth are bared and smeared with blood and lipstick, he will kill his experience and his life, and as his killing goes on he will naturally reach out to kill me."

A similarly surrealistic scene has Mr Hyde reappear as Dr Jekyll, or the frenzied and murderous hag don various disguises as the wise councillor ("You can't change anything by intention"), the concerned friend ("I care for you"), and the reassuring, more successful writer ("You'll make it"). The only one unaware of what's happening is the Creeley figure himself. The narrator, as he watches him frantically exchanging one mask for another, continues to see the frenzied, bloodthirsty hag looming behind the other personae, or the grimace of hostility beyond the seemingly benign faces:

He stepped into the one to his left and nodded drunkenly, she rubbed her hand across her mouth and drew blood, and the face of flesh which identified the man I once knew as my friend, one out of several faces of his own that did care for me, looked a little hauntedly at me as if he was seeing us together in a photograph, laughing and loving each other a long time ago, and was now condescending to me, "You'll make it," he said, yet that strange tall child clinging grimly to him for him as if he was his own son and father of same, hated and feared and loved and needed, and his face became a complicated and brilliant hostility, but looking at himself he thought he was one man.

Reading *Thread* must have brought back Creeley's memories of writing an introduction to a volume of poetry by George Bowering and of the impotent rage he had felt towards this Uriah Heep-like *doppelgänger* before pushing him off the dance floor. Now, he had written in support of a book that caricatured him as a Dr Jekyl and Mr Hyde monster. The damage was done. Though limited to six hundred copies, *Thread* had long found a wide and influential readership. The list of over forty donors who had made publication possible included friends and/or future celebrities like Tom Clark, Donald Davie, Anselm Hollo, Eric Mottram, and Jeremy Prynne.

Once apprised of the facts, Creeley decided it was time to act, and decisively. Given this and the numerous other affronts he had suffered at Fee Dawson's hands, he had no interest in continuing their friendship, he wrote. Dawson's response was emotional and irrational in the extreme. He had crucified Creeley, he confessed. He felt ill with guilt for not letting him know. For fifteen years they hadn't communicated with each other except when drunk. Once in the company of Bob and Dan, he as the youngest, had suddenly realized what was going on. Creeley was not talking to him at all. His face, like that of a Shakespearean witch, had suddenly become alchemical and hateful, causing Fee complete uncertainty as to where he stood within Bob (except outside him). It made him feel like the victim of Bob's perception. Hence his sudden anger, his resentment and jealousy over Bob's success, Bob's getting everywhere where Fielding's stories and emotional frenzies were getting him nowhere.

Meanwhile, Bob had failed to tell the truth about Victor Kalos in *The Island*. In sum, that's how he felt, although anything he was saying about his emotional reactions to Bob was an understatement.

In the mood Creeley was in, such pleas merely sharpened his fury. Dawson's contentions were unacceptable in every sense. How could he tell the truth about Victor Kalos in a novel in which Victor didn't even appear? Dawson was distorting the facts in alleging that they had never talked to each other except when drunk. To tell the truth, they had had as many conversations sober. He liked drinking as much as Dawson, but he had learnt that one couldn't drink and at the same time manage, say, a university job. He could understand Dawson's sense of envy and jealousy, but hardly liked to be their cause. At the same time he couldn't tolerate Dawson's making use of him as "a character" or accept his distortions in an exchange of letters like the present one. So better stop it all.

Feeling increasingly distressed, Dawson promised to comply, while continuing his emotional pleas on behalf of their friendship. He wasn't rational towards Creeley, he admitted. They were involved in a valuable conflict that might engender great questions along with great answers. He'd prefer that Creeley, rather then punish him with silence, would shout at him in anger.

His wish remained unfulfilled. The man who all his life had stood in utter dread of no longer being spoken to by relatives and friends imposed a ban of silence on Dawson.

The rage

is what I
want, what
I cannot give

to myself, of
myself, in
the world.

Creeley's rages were by no means spent. Their next target was the English department at the University of New Mexico where he was teaching between time off through grants and ever more numerous reading engagements. Students and colleagues increasingly got on his nerves despite the admitted lack of real pressure. He kept complaining regardless. There he was, a Guggenheim plus Rockefeller grantee, and all the university did was penalize him by not counting the free time these grants gave him towards tenure. Inflated class sizes were another problem. In his view it made creative writing courses next to impossible. How could one teach poetry to housewives who had simply grown tired of television? The creative writing set-up needed complete restructuring. Given his superior qualifications, he naturally expected to be appointed director of the new program. Who else but he had been invited to attend a presidential council on the teaching of writing in February 1966 at the Sarah Lawrence College in Bronxville? His lack of ambition along the lines of PMLA publications and, frankly, inter-departmental politics, should not blind colleagues to the quality of his own accomplishments – of which he included a list. He'd like an explicit answer in writing.

The teaching made him feel paranoid, bugged, and frustrated. He "flipped" in class and verbally assaulted a student in front of eighty-two others for daring to call T.S. Eliot the accurate measure and W.C. Williams stupid.

Tensions at home were increasing too. Like his first wife once she found out about Cynthia, Bobbie, after finding out about Ann Quin, was distancing herself from him. His response was jealousy, then rage. "A Day Book" recalls his "fantasies ... of Bobbie being fucked by others" with admirable candour. In one instance he is back from a reading tour, self-righteously pondering how much he continues to accomplish for his family. He arrives with "the usual nervous hysteria and demand, to be, hopefully, comforted by [Bobbie], his laundry seen to," before rushing off again, "to make more money in a manner he found egocentrically pleasing and hateful, by public lecture."

> It is like a monster come to dinner,
> and the dinner table is set,
> the fire in the fireplace,
> good luck to good humor –
>
> The monster you love is home again,
> and he tells you stories of the world,
> big cities, small men
> and women.
>
> Make room for the furry wooden eyed
> monster. He is my friend
> whom you burn.
> Amen.

Next time Bobbie would come along for at least part of her famous husband's engagements. It was carefully planned in advance. They would meet on 23 April at the airport in Chicago, where Creeley, on invitation from Robert Bly, had been participating in a reading. Then they would fly on to London where they were scheduled to arrive the following morning.

But jealousy determined otherwise. Bobbie had hardly gotten off the plane when Creeley asked her "if she had fallen in love with anyone in his absence." He was "dumbstruck" at what he found out (just as he had in mid-1955 when during his absence in Paris Ann had had an affair with Victor Kalos). Perhaps most disconcerting to him was how the disciple had adopted the master's argument that loving a second partner did not stop one from continuing to love the first. Even before they managed to settle down at the table, Bobbie "in her usual truth" told him that she had fallen in love with somebody else but "that she continued to love him also." "A myriad of possible details, pruriently, demanding, flooded his head."

Drunkenly he insisted on details. In the ensuing argument they missed their plane and went to spend the rest of the evening at a friend's. But nothing now would still Creeley's fury. "They fought there too, himself falling and cutting one wrist on a glass that had been broken in their struggling together. The friend got them to a hospital where his wrist was sewn up by a contemptuous young doctor, without anaesthetic, possibly to make him feel the ugliness he was exuding."

Open battle turned into long, drawn-out confrontation. There were "insistent flarings of temper and irritation" in London. "Friends put up with them, with him in particular, and at one point late at night in an alley retrieved the garbage he drunkenly poured out of the cans standing along the edge of the street." A few days later a chastened Creeley delivered a "brief and confused lecture" at the Sorbonne, then proceeded on to Lake Como. However, the sedate, elitarian atmosphere of Villa Bellagio where they arrived chauffeur-driven from the Milan airport to spend a month on a Rockefeller grant only revived hostilities: "Both realized that it was markedly difficult to be long alone with each other in that his obsessively recurrent questions brought them again and again to bitterly useless argument." One incident recaptured in "A Day Book" reads like a potential re-enactment of the final chapter of *The Island*:

One night, after a particularly nattering attack on her, his wife left their room, still in nightgown and robe, and went off through the interminable corridors and passageways to escape him. He thought to go after her, but at the door, looking out at the silence of the dark halls, he could not. Later she reappeared, smiling, to tell him that one of the eldest servants, an old man who worked as night watchman, had seen her and deferentially offered to follow with his lamp so that she might find her way. How simple the intrusion of factual needs upon affairs of conjecture and assumption.

Creeley decided to break off their stay at the villa to go back to London. At the height of his fame, he was within days of his fortieth birthday.

Marriage with Bobbie ended less abruptly than that with Ann. It was not until May 1976 that they decided to separate. On a trip to the Far East, Creeley, while in New Zealand, had met Penelope Highton, who would become his third wife. They were married in 1977. Their first child, William Gabriel was born on 5 February 1981.

In the meantime, Creeley and Paul Blackburn, the latter now divorced from Freddie, had agreed to blame the fight of September 1954 that had caused such a bitter rift between them on their respective ex-wives. That wild evening in Bañalbufar had really been "women's work," Creeley decided; Ann had been paranoid. Blackburn agreed, shifting the blame to *his* ex. Freddie couldn't help chipping, did it to everyone; she'd been a tough chick, still was. His final emotion towards her had been frankly murderous.

Though he never reconciled with Ann, Bob managed to re-establish contact with their children David, Tom, and Charlotte. Less fortunate than they, two of Bobbie's daughters, Kirsten, from the first marriage with Olaf, and Kate, from that with Creeley, both struggled with emotional illness. Sarah, Creeley's other daughter with Bobbie, was made of sterner stuff. Whenever her parents started quarrelling, she used to crank up the stereo.

Finally, death struck those close to Creeley in unexpected ways. Olson died on 10 January 1970, Ann Quin in August 1973, his mother, Genevieve, on 7 October 1972. Creeley's "For My Mother" is one of the most moving poems he ever wrote.

> "Death's
> let you out –"
> comes true,
> this, that,
>
> endlessly circular
> life, and we
> came back
>
> to see you one
> last
> time, this
>
> time? Your head
> shuddered,
> it seemed, your

eyes wanted,
I thought,
to see

who it was.
I am here,
and will follow.

Creeley's fame and success, though reaching their peak around the late 1960s, have continued with him ever since. So also has his deeply divided attitude towards it. Though it has not brought him peace, it has proven useful for pulling rank. Typical is an instance that occurred in 1968. His car with its New York State licence plate was pulled over, first by the New Mexico State troopers, then twice again by the Albuquerque police. To Creeley the matter seemed sufficiently grave to make him air his indignation in an Albuquerque paper. "What must I do," he protested, "short of altering my personal appearance, to be allowed free access to Albuquerque streets. I am not a criminal, I am forty-two years old, the father of three daughters, – one of whom is an entering freshman at UNM, the author of many books, published in many countries, the recipient of a Guggenheim Fellowship, a Rockefeller Foundation grantee, and a tenured full professor at the State University of New York. I am also listed in the *Who's Who in America*! Where did I go wrong?"

Over the past decades Creeley has charted up ever more distinctions, honours, and publications. Made tenured full professor at SUNY Buffalo in 1967, he became Gray Professor of Poetry and Letters in 1978, and Samuel P. Capen Professor of Poetry and Humanities in 1989. He was granted another Guggenheim in 1971, the Shelley Memorial Award in 1981, a National Endowment for the Arts grant in 1982, a DAAD fellowship of the German Academic Exchange Program in 1983, the Leone d'Oro Premio Speciale in 1984, and the Frost Medal in 1987. That same year he was inducted in the American Academy and in 1989 appointed State Poet of New York by Governor Mario Cuomo.

Starting in 1980, Black Sparrow published his so-far ten volume *Complete Correspondence* with Olson, McGill-Queen's University Press his letters with Irving Layton, the University of California Press his *Collected Poems: 1945–1975* and *Collected Essays*, and Boyars his *Collected Prose*. There has been a carefully researched bibliography of his work by Mary Novik as well as several critical monographs by Cynthia Edelberg, Arthur L. Ford, Tom Clark, and others.

Creeley has never taken his success for granted. Even in his sixties and seventies, he continued to give talks and readings all over North America and the rest of the world, to the tune of dozens of such engagements a year, often more than one a week. Some time ago, a friend, critic, and admirer, facing Creeley just off a plane and about to address a room full of people, asked him what it was that made him push himself so hard. "I'm a Puritan," the poet answered.

Afterword.

Creeley's essay, "Robin Blaser's Holy Forest," comes with a photograph featuring himself and four other poets at a reading on 11 August 1968. There is John Wieners, smilingly disengaged from the rest; Robert Duncan, taut and withdrawn but seemingly ready to jump at anyone who might cross him; Allen Ginsberg in a meditational pose; between Duncan and Ginsberg, Robin Blaser, wearing a hat, limbs twisted, as if overawed by his famous elders; all of them ignoring each other except one: Robert Creeley who, seated to the far right, stares at the other four. The face is familiar from other photographs of the late 1960s onwards: severe and observant, like a latter-day Grand Inquisitor, a Spanish grandee. The whimsical tension revealed in earlier shots has yielded to an expression of mastery. As so often before in his life, he seems to be assessing his flock of faithful running mates and followers.

The essay itself reveals a similarly custodial attitude. Blaser, like numerous poets and artists Creeley has written about since the 1960s, is not so much scrutinized critically as assigned his place in a new literary hierarchy. The praise of others follows by now well-established formulaic patterns largely reflecting the critic's idealized self-image. Blaser is quiet and "certainly ... modest"; his "consummate poetry," rather than defining "'progress,' or a skilfully accomplished enclosure," deals with "a life that is inexorably human, the adamant given of our common fact." Other poets and artists are "deeply generous" and "articulate," "singular in all respects," "very warm" and "intensely reassuring," or at least possessed with a "lovely wit" or "lovely, wry smile."

In one way or another all these congenial fellow poet-artists share the same "deep gentleness," "shy, intensive warmth," "determined dignity." Or they display an intensely quiet, "dear, particular care," especially "with words." Like Blaser, they are concerned with the "singular, the communal," as well as "rooted in the fact of the human." Almost without exception, they are dear, lovely men and women eager "to know how and why and what it is, to be *human*."

They also share a quasi-manifest destiny. Speaking of Blaser, Creeley knew him first as a survivor of a "legendary Berkeley"; then as a member of the pre-Beat "San Francisco school;" and finally "as one of an almost mythic band, a triad composed of himself and his fellow poets, Robert Duncan and Jack Spicer."

Such local myths feed into the larger one of an all-American if not world-wide poetic revolution, pioneered by *Origin* and BMR, and then, once the battle was won, consolidated by Donald Allen's "momentous anthology, *The New American Poetry*" of 1960. This Creeley points out, turned out to be his and Blaser's "first meeting place," with a poem like Blaser's "Herons" making "actual where [they] were and had to be."

Other fellow authors Creeley has written about have the added good fortune of being members of the great revolution's pioneering army. One such was Michael Rumaker. Though one of the "least recognized," like Blaser, he eventually found his place "compact with a company which is finally ageless." The main cause for such benediction, bestowed in Creeley's "Afterword" to *Gringos and Other Stories*, is Rumaker's contributions to Creeley's *Black Mountain Review* where they are flanked by those of Rumaker's betters like Jung, Zukofsky, Olson, Duncan, Layton, or Creeley himself. To quote Blake, "the authors" – or rather those of Creeley's election – "are in eternity." It's one of Creeley's favourite citations.

Considering earlier times when he and Olson would repeatedly hail each other as the only ones that mattered, Creeley's critical appreciation of others' work has seemingly become more catholic. But definite restrictions remain. Thus he keeps nominating an ever-increasing number of "geniuses" ranging from immediate running mates like Olson and Duncan to more remote or unexpected figures like Marsden Hartley, Larry Bell, R.B. Kitaj, Edward Dahlberg, Larry Eigner, Ted Berrigan (for his *pathos*), or John Altoon (for his drawing "extraordinarily, always, no matter the occasion"). Meanwhile, the label is noticeably absent from his writings about some of his closest associates, who have to content themselves with being called "deeply gifted" or provided with an intensity of "careful thought and weighed insight" instead.

Similarly, a former *persona non grata* like Kenneth Koch might suddenly receive Creeley's blessing for virtually "*all* he's written" because "it's kept the faith immensely, and the *human* world its own significant fact, in mind, in heart, in common;" another, Robert Lowell, once denounced for his depressive realism, at least gets laudable mention for isolated aspects of his poetic oeuvre. What earns Lowell such unexpected attention, however, is not so much his intrinsic poetic achievement as the fact that, say, his "droll and often violent ironies" contrast with the "playful, persuasive ear" of William Corbett who, through his diverse though remote affiliations with the proper company, has earned himself a place, if not amongst, at least close to the eternals. Creeley explains: "If one thinks of specific friends of his life, Clark Coolidge, for example, or Bernadette Mayer, or Michael Palmer, Lewis Warsh, Lee Harwood, et al., then one may recognize a continuity from elders such as Ashbery or Schuyler to the younger Charles Bernstein and Michael Davidson."

More than all else, our example shows how the older Creeley extols a virtually endless number of followers and partisans while ignoring or perhaps remaining ignorant of several major non-partisan figures of his age. His belated discovery of Patrick Kavanagh (pointed out to him by Olson) at the London International Poetry Festival of July 1967, while seemingly testifying to a widening of his appreciative scope, provides another instance of the continuing partisanship of a poet-critic who, with the death of peers like Olson, Lowell, Duncan, Burroughs, Levertov, and Ginsberg, has increasingly become the principal literary chronicler of his age. A mere glance at the index of his *Critical Essays* with its near one thousand entries confirms this impression. No mention of Ted Hughes, Sylvia Plath, Seamus Heaney, to evoke only three of our age's more prominent poets in English; none of celebrities like Octavio Paz or P.P. Pasolini writing in Spanish or Italian.

Creeley's endeavours during the last three or so decades of promoting his and his confrères' accomplishments go hand in hand with his turning into an ever more autobiographical poet and writer. His earliest publications rarely ventured into confessional self-revelation. It took him years, he said, to find out that most of his early poems dealt with subliminal aspects of his married life. Analogous claims one feels tempted to make regarding the short stories may apply to one like "Mr. Blue," but less so to others like "The Unsuccessful Husband," "In the Summer," "The Boat," "The Musicians," or "The Book." Instead, these mark the transition to the consistently *roman à clef* autobiographical writing of *The Island*.

From here it is only another step to the overtly autobiographical mode of some of his more recent work, his "Notes on the Autobiographical Mode" of 1973 and his "Autobiography" of 1989. There are the poems dealing with remembered events (e.g., "I" or "Something," both 1963) or with clearly identifiable, not to say descriptively rendered, occurrences in the poet's ongoing life (e.g., "The Messengers" of 1963), then the journal-like jottings of *In London* (1970), republished in 1972 back to back with an actual "day book" in prose. What remained unclear in the volume of that title was clarified when "A Day Book" reappeared as the first part of *Mabel: A Story & Other Prose*, with each entry being given a separate date. "A Day Book," so the introduction explains, "is precisely what it says it is, thirty single-spaced pages of writing in thirty similarly spaced days of living."

The poet, his first wife, Ann, and diverse friends who in *The Island* appear under pseudonyms such as John, Joan, Artie, or Manus, now make their personal entry as I, Bobbie, Allen, Ed, or John [Altoon]. Nameless locations become real ones like Teel's Brook on which Creeley as a child used to skate from West to South Acton, or Nokomis, Florida, where Aunt Bernice lies dying in a "crunky, derelict" trailer park. Only when dealing with potentially contentious matters, cursing his ex-wife ("all that cagey, double edge of statement is so insistently distasteful, all that dull 'I know better' that comes in her voice") or describing a threesome, does the authorial "I" refrain from naming people. Or it seems to escape into the anonymity of the third person singular, viz. "His cock was already hard, excited by even what he was saying, that he wanted to fuck her with the other."

In spite of appearances, as suggested by his publishing record, Creeley's autobiographical impulse goes back to his beginnings as a writer. As early as 1943 his prep school journal, *The Dial*, of which he happened to be editor-in-chief, states that Creeley "hands in the best material when writing upon personal experiences." Starting in 1946 he makes repeated, involuntarily confessional attempts to start a novel which, as he kept protesting, would get more objective in the process. Around the same time he begins studding his ever more numerous letters to friends with autobiographical vignettes, a habit that would continue until the gradual petering out of his correspondences with the consolidation of his fame in the late 1960s. Or, as a rare exception, a relatively graphic reminiscence might, oasis-like in a desert of linguistic abstraction, make its incongruous appearance in Creeley's early poetry:

Ducks in the pond,
icecream & beer,
all remind me
of West Acton, Mass –

where I lived when young
in a large old house
with 14 rooms
and woods out back.

By contrast, the first major opportunity to go public with his life presented itself much later. That was in an interview of May 1961, conducted by David Ossman in a studio in New York City. It was a pivotal moment in Creeley's career. Scribner's had reprinted his short stories, committed itself to publishing *For Love: Poems 1950–1960*, his first major collection, and had bought the option on his yet unfinished novel, *The Island*. The stunning success of these two volumes was as yet a matter of the future.

Meanwhile, he had long convinced himself of his crucial role in the movement that was evidently winning the day. Always a person with a strong sense of his mission, he had augured to Layton as early as 31 July 1953 that their time would come. Less than five years later he had noted to Olson that the whole scene was swinging their way. Those who'd sneered at him a few years earlier, he remarked around the time of the Ossman interview, were consulting him like an oracle now.

So did Ossman. What was Black Mountain like? Had Creeley's extensive correspondence with other poets exerted an influence on them? Creeley later claimed that he was so tired on the occasion he hardly cared what he said. Yet, rereading the piece, it is hard to believe that this was his first major interview. Rather than Ossman, it is Creeley who is in control. He gives an erudite display of his wide international reading of modern poetry; he relates Burroughs's concern with control to Skinnerian behaviourism and Whatmough's statistical analysis of languages; he lavishes praise on Paul Blackburn who happens to be present in the studio. He carefully leads the interviewer on to ask him questions about his involvement with starting *Origin*, his running Divers Press, editing *Black Mountain Review*, views on deep image, and (via repeated hints) his New England family background.

At the same time, he sets up the major bases of an autobiographical legend he would expand on over the coming decades: his growing up in the "huge global nightmare" of the 1940s, his poetic derivation from elders like Pound and Williams, one considered a fascist traitor, the other a "paranoid mumbler," and his apprenticeship under Charles Olson who (using a phrase he formulated in an essay the previous year) he calls a "practical college of information and stimulus." And yet how far he and his band of fellow travellers like Blackburn, Levertov, and Ginsberg had come from such humble origins. Unlike Kenneth Rexroth, who had spoken of a minor renaissance in the *New York Times*, Creeley prefers to think of it as a full-fledged revolution.

At the same time, he sounds like he's talking about things that are already past and gone. Personally speaking, the "somewhat broken emotions" that had prompted the "seemingly broken line" of his early poetry have smoothed out. As he's beginning to relax, feel more settled and at ease in the world, he tells Ossman, his verse has become "more lyrical, less afraid of concluding." Similarly, Don Allen's anthology marking 1945 to 1960 as the borderlines of "The New American Poetry" strikes him as a kind of "tombstone."

Creeley's interviews and critical writings after 1961 project an increasing sense of such finality, and finally nostalgia. A still euphoric Creeley interviewed in 1965 talks about "the peak years" that have left him like someone who has everything he wants. He triumphantly looks back on the "last ten or fifteen years in American poetry" as "perhaps the most rich of any." A decade later, the same glorious years have definitely become a thing of the past. "Possibly the complex of circumstances which made the years 1950 to 1965 so decisive in the arts," he mused in 1974, "will not easily recur."

Similar sentiments recur throughout Creeley's critical writings and interviews. Reminiscing, as early as 1960, on how one night in Littleton, New Hampshire, he heard Corman's radio program "This Is Poetry," then went down to Boston to read on it while exhibiting chickens at the Boston Poultry Show, he adds: "Literary history is like that, and this event would be altogether unnotable, were it not that a magazine which I then tried to start ... but could not get printed, was absorbed in the first two issues of Cid's *Origin* – and that among the contacts so contributed were Charles Olson, Paul Blackburn, and Denise Levertov."

Talking about the same early network to Ossman the following year, Creeley adds: "and that began it, I think." Eight years later, writing the introduction to the 1969 reprint of the *Black Mountain Review*, his sense of historical achievement has become even more decisive. For who other than himself first published the Black Mountain and Beat poets between the same covers in the seventh and final issue of that review? That, he notes, meant "unequivocally a shift and opening of the previous center, and finally [was] as good a place as any to end. Other magazines had appeared as well, with much the same concerns, among them *Big Table* and the *Evergreen Review*. Whatever battle had been the case did seem effectually won." Recalling BMR #7 in 1990, and particularly Rumaker's review of *Howl* along with W.C. Williams's introduction to Ginsberg's yet unpublished *Empty Mirror*, he adds an elegiac note: "Those were the days."

Those indeed, at least, from Creeley's perspective, were his days. Screening his published and unpublished correspondences, interviews, critical, and other writings for references to his private life subsequent to, say, 1970 is like looking for proverbial needles in a haystack. Earlier autobiographical events are told and retold with sometimes obsessive frequency: his family back to great-grandparents of Irish, Scottish, and French origins, the eye injury, Four Winds Farm, Holderness, Harvard, Burma, Rock Pool Farm, the chicken raising, the puritanically deprived habits of New England speech, right up to 1956 San Francisco,

Guatemala, the Vancouver and Berkeley poetry conferences, or the time at Lake Como. Then about his life from the 1970s onwards almost nothing – as if his existence had come to an end in the middle of a long lifetime. Occasional exceptions only prove the rule, like the poets being up early in the morning while everyone else is still asleep at Ginsberg's farm, the odd anecdote told by a friend he writes about, or the mention of a major change – "I mean, *all* of it" – without further specifics, leaving the reader to wonder about what momentous change might be involved: except that Creeley was about to marry again.

> There's no surprise now,
> not the unexpected
> as it had been. He's agreed
> to being more settled.

Creeley's moral stance has undergone a similar change. The youthful author of poems like "The Operation," "The Warning," "The Hill," or "Anger" had reason to find that a poet was not "necessarily a nice person," and he had the courage to say so in print. He repeatedly protested against poetry's sociopolitical or otherwise didactive involvement and attacked our traditional Judeo-Christian humanist agenda. His more recent writings belie that earlier bias. They suddenly rediscover old values like "love's surety," the "forthright, good / natured faith of man," or loyalty, generosity, and "wise, good-natured clarity" as the essence of what's human. Watching a movie by Robert Bresson, he is moved to find "that / life was after all / like that. You are / in love." Such sentiments go hand in hand with the occasional grandstanding *vis-à-vis* the "foetid stink of human excess," "the cheapshit world of / fake commerce, *buy and sell*," or the "truly *evil*" way public language is used as a mere "instrument of coercion, persuasion, and deceit." Half listening to the House Judiciary Committee while writing an essay on the nature of poetry, he feels "angered, contemptuous, impatient, and possibly even cynical concerning the situation of our lives in this 'national' place." In the same breath he proposes a solution: *"Trust to good verses, then ... Trust to the clarity instant in being human, that knows and wants no other place."*

A cynic might wonder about Creeley's motivation for uttering such sentiments. Is the poet trying to relieve his conscience? Yet if that is so, what possible benefits can the reader draw from moralistic question and answer games like the following?

> Why not be more
> human, as they say,

more thoughtful,
why not try to care.

The bleak alternative's
a stubborn existence –
back turned to all,
pathetic resistance.

Here, as where the poet discovers "the straight line right / to God" who "must be some- / where, maybe taking / a walk on the comforting / earth," the reader appreciative of Creeley's earlier verse is desperately waiting for the twist that will throw everything into comic relief and reversal. But in vain. "There's no surprise now, / not the unexpected / as it had been." What's more, the older Creeley seems eager to impart his new moral stance to others: "Had I lived some years ago," he explained as early as 1965, "I think I would have been a moralist, i.e., one who lays down, so to speak, rules of behavior."

No wonder he has turned against his former self. Rereading "The Whip," written in the mid-1950s, he remembers the "bleak confusion from which it moves emotionally." Speaking of his early poetry he similarly recalls its "twisted, compressed" mode that tended to "singularize" and "isolate" him. Such isolation, he theorized later, made him search out "a way of doing things which found company with others" like W.C. Williams, Pound, H.D., Stein, Zukofsky, Olson, Duncan, Levertov, Ginsberg, Dorn, Bunting, Wieners, McClure, Whalen, Snyder, Berrigan, "and so on." The idiosyncratically "authoritative poetry of [his] youth," from this gregarious perspective, seems to him to project a "crotchety purview." Accordingly, this once most singular poet of his generation discovers a near paranoid fear of getting "stuck in the solitary thing," protesting that the last thing he wants is to be different.

You
have always wanted
to be friends, to be
one of many.

Creeley's poetry, in the same revisionist purview, underwent a major change from anguished, singular, and crotchety to relaxed, general, and ordinary, a change grounded in a parallel transformation of the poet's sensibility. "The intensive, singularly made poems of my youth faded as, hopefully, the anguish that was used in the writing of so many of them also did … So writing, in this sense, began to lose its specific edges, its singleness of occurrence, and I worked to be open to the casual, the commonplace, that which collected itself. The world transformed to bits of paper, torn words, 'it/it.'"

It's been a slow but inexorable process: Creeley's early creativity, which, when charged with the full vehemence of his annihilating and self-destructive fury, breaking through the commonplace to a stripped-down freshness of vision, probably unparalleled in contemporary American poetry; then, in the early 1960s, his beginning to repeat his own minimalist formulas, a danger he became aware of as early as 1963; finally, echoing the age's moralistic platitudes and/or assuming postures of self-congratulatory lassitude and moral superiority. The poet has relaxed his asphyxiating grip on himself and the world – an urge which, beginning in the 1960s, he turned into a new poetic credo.

Certainly we have come a long way from the younger Creeley we have tried to resurrect in the preceding pages – the poet who, like his alter ego in *The Island*, wanted "a clarity, something stripped of the deadening pull of relations, all the facts and figures of people and their times and places." Sharing the artist Arakawa's "delight in *zero set*, the real nitty gritty for any head-trip," he wanted "the world to narrow to a match flare," being admittedly "too destructively zapped head-tripping." The world to him broke "open in a beautiful way when there can't any longer be assumptions about it" because the poet has either destroyed or rejected them. "I [had] some insistent pattern in my own nature," Creeley stated in 1974, "that [made] me extremely restless and, not so much bored, but just that the moment something [became] familiar to me, known to me and relaxing to me, I simply tend[ed] to reject it, I don't know why."

To this younger Creeley, writing a story was always a half-desperate insistence on or clutch at something he had to hit hard and fast or else it might escape him. It was a stripping, an attempt to annihilate the facts. The writing of a poem resembled an apoplectic fit, seizing the poet. What he did to the world he did to himself. After deranging all his senses à la Rimbaud, he worked "toward a final obliteration of himself." He felt the poem with the intensity of all the perception "that the ego bit can recognize, and then destroy[ed] the ego by its own insistence." "I have long experience of my own restlessness and impatience," he recalled in 1976, "and have managed quiet and a feeling of centeredness only when the *here and now* literally discovered it for me. Elsewise I have battered myself and the surroundings with seemingly useless energy, pleased only that something at least was 'happening.'" As Rimbaud put it, "The soul must be made monstrous. He exhausts all poisons in himself and keeps only their quintessences."

324 · ROBERT CREELEY

Perhaps poems and stories like Creeley's greatest (e.g., "I Know a Man," "The Moon," "The Suitor") can only be written by someone whose iconoclastic fury is unbroken by the natural debilities of middle and old age. Short of that, his more recent poems increasingly read like those of an aging Rimbaud who, instead of ceasing to write, is pondering in verse the degeneration of his youthful powers or even deploring their once demonic drive. There is something narcissistically obsessive about the poet portraying himself and the world in the "fat doldrums / of innocent aging," pondering his loss of hearing, staring "at the backs / of [his] hands" and their "slightly mottled / swollen flesh," imploring his "sad, sagging flesh / and bones gone brittle" as well as his "mind's collapsing / habits" to stay awhile, so he can continue to talk to himself "in a fond, judgmental murmur."

Creeley's recent touting of the commonplace as the closest, yet admittedly trite analogue to the stripped down, de-anthropomorphised objectivity of his earlier work points to a more general lapse into the sentimentally self-reflective and banal. Being "devoid of originality or novelty; trite, trivial, hackneyed," to this older Creeley, has become a badge worn with pride or at least ostentatiousness. "Possibly it's attractive, you know, being sixty-four, that being trite," he pondered in 1991 – "I mean, if one lives to be old, then presumably one *will* be trite, trivial, and hackneyed. And what's the problem in that, my friends?"

Life and Death (1998), Creeley's latest collection of poems to date, is nothing if not that. Inside his head, he tells us programmatically, is

> a common room,
> a common place, a common tune,
> a common wealth, a common doom.

The volume's *dramatis personae* as well as their joys and woes stand for "Humanness, like / you, man. Us" – his sister's metal knee replacement, a daughter's pregnancy, the wife's "social / suitors," old and new friends and acquaintances, people met by chance, and, of course, the poet himself following through on the humdrum routine of "*Things to do today*," like going shopping, visiting the beach, ogling women "with huge tits, or come-hither looks," and enjoying his domestic bliss – "your bottom tucked tight against my belly or mine lodged snug in your lap."

> There is nothing to wait for
> that isn't here, and it will happen.

Considering Creeley's post-midlife mode of writing prose and verse, other of the book's idiosyncratic aspects strike one as similarly habitual, not to say "hackneyed." There's the embroidering on diverse episodes from childhood and early adulthood, some of it familiar, like his grandparents' deaths or his first time making love to a woman, some of it new, like a near-death experience in a Calcutta hotel in 1944 after a "lunch of prawns." There is the repeated reference to how and "where it had all begun;" the invoking of famous elders, peers, and fellow travellers from Louis Zukofsky to Timothy Leary; or the looking back with dismay, even disgust, at the younger man's implacable single-mindedness, cruel perversity and "crotchety purview" on life.

> I didn't know then,
> had only an avarice
> to tear open
> love and eat its person,
> feeling confusion,
> driven, wanting
> inclusion, hunger
> to feel, smell, taste
> her flesh.

By contrast, the older Creeley feels "included" by company, surrounded by things "provided," or connected to his fellow human beings by holding hands, all the while protesting, "I want no sentimentality / I want no more than home."

Clearly the young poet's bravado, provocativeness, and fatalism have gone defunct; the periodic punctuating of his discourse with a defiant "Ha!" or a dismissive "And fuck that too!" have gone silent. Instead there is the increasing obsession with a decrepitude strangely at odds with the robust looking Creeley on the book's dust-jacket photograph. Even the poet himself seems occasionally taken aback by his "curiously / solid body" and general health:

> You're not sick, there are
> certainly those older.

All the more surprising is the portrait of old-age morbidity he repeatedly draws of himself: "neural circuits" fading, the mind "slipping cogs," his heart causing "awkward, gasping convulsions," the "battered" and "shedding body" growing thinner, arms "collapsing," the "moldering hands" "looking like stubble, rubble," his "skin soft as a much worn leather glove."

Naturally, Creeley's penchant for the commonplace has found its subject matter *par excellence* in what, when compared with the gratuitous wonder of birth and life, appears as the definitive banality of decay, and, finally, death. Death, rather than life, dominates the 1998 volume. Historical personalities like Ponce de Leon devoured by alligators, or the German "conceptual" artist inadvertently committing suicide, an anonymous man dying on television with his wife "sitting by" and commenting, the poet's grandparents, Aunt Bernice, Mitch Goodman, and, last but not least, his dog Maggie – the list of the commemorated dead is sheer unending. Death, on the one hand, is the "indifferent, inexorable, *bitter* / affliction" striking us down and, on the other, the great reconciler. Along with such firmly established notions Creeley invokes several well-worn literary topoi familiar from a *memento mori* literature popular during times long gone such as Shakespeare's. Like a figure in a Renaissance emblem, the poet holds colloquy with a skull which beckons him to " 'Come closer. Now there is nothing left / either inside or out to gainsay death.' " Elsewhere, he asks "Where have all the flowers gone?" or gives an answer that is as rhetorical as the question:

I see the white, white petals of this rose unfold.
I know such beauty in the world grows cold.

Missing from this roll-call of *loci communes* is the Dylan Thomas-like raging against the dying of the light one might have expected from the younger Creeley. The older one's attitude towards death is an entirely more compliant, even collaborative one of being able to anticipate the "coming night / like an old friend who sets all to rights" and of trying to learn "to let go of, give entirely away." It is an attitude of mystical self-exhortation and hope:

Lighten the load. Close the eyes.
Let the mood loosen, the body die,
the bird fly off to the opening sky.

Excerpts from Ann MacKinnon's Memoirs and from Her 1944 Diary

Ann MacKinnon's Memoirs.

My life has been a series of extravagances, some good, some bad, which are not duplicated in the lives of any people I know. The big question is why? I have always had a yearning for peace, security and solitude. They seem to slide away as soon as I start to achieve them ...

Perhaps I seek adventure in protest against my strict Yankee upbringing. Perhaps because underneath the Yankee I am a Pole, and I have heard it said that Poles have a talent for catastrophe ...

I was one of a number of children belonging to the Toronto Children's Aid Society. We were warehoused either in a series of private homes or sometimes in their institution. I remember being in one of many white cribs side by side, tended by smiling young ladies whose names I never learned and whose faces were never familiar. My mother had left me there at eleven months of age. Thus I had no one to tell me who I was. I remember on one occasion being led by the hand along a crowded city sidewalk and there coming face to face with a strange woman. My conductress said, "Here she is." And I went off down the street holding a new hand. No hellos or good-byes were said to me, no explanation given; I was a kind of package.

On another occasion I found myself naked in a large room with twenty or so other naked children. I had a small piece of adhesive tape glued to one shoulder. Another child advised me seriously not to lose my tape, because if I did they wouldn't know who I was. I watched that tape with some anxiety. I was, however, sure that my name was Ruth. It said so on another piece of tape stuck just above a hook in the bathroom. There hung my very own blue toothbrush.

I also knew that I was Two. (Whatever that meant.) There was a day when I was led from a dark room into a light one where I found a cake and candles sparkling on it, surrounded by a number of strange shouting children in paper hats. This was a little daunting, and when I asked for an explanation I was told that I was no longer Two but was now Three. I wailed that I was not Three but Two and would not be comforted until they agreed with me.

I think that I enjoyed the institution more than I did the private homes. There were other children to follow about or play with. Only those raised en masse or in a very large family know the joy of being bathed in a tub full of slippery friends like a row of orphan monkeys. Also the institution did not go in heavily for discipline. In one private home I was in the habit of greeting myself every morning in a mirror which hung at the foot of the stairs. I would smile and wave. One morning I greeted an ugly thing, the rough board back of the mirror. Of course I did not know what had happened to my little friend and I cried in fear. They told me it served me right for my vanity and that I was not to look at my face again …

The next thing I knew I was riding in a train heading south. I asked to take my toothbrush with me, but I was told I would get a new one. I also had to leave my name behind. It was a curious sensation, watching the landscape change and change outside the train windows while reciting over and over:

"Ann MacKinnon, Hallowell House,
Wellesley."

My new mother impressed on me the fear that we might get accidentally separated, and I would not have been surprised if I had changed hands again on some busy street.

My new mother was a calm gentle person of somewhat untidy appearance. She wore a pince-nez dangling from a cord around her neck and resting on her generous bosom. She usually had a Phi-beta-kappa key attached to her somewhere and her shoes were very unusual. I knew her feet better than her face because I was so small. She was a professor of philosophy at Wellesley College …

My mother unexpectedly took sick. She asked me for a drink of water one morning. She wanted me to run the water to make it very cold, but I was impatient to get back to her bedside and it was still lukewarm. When I returned from school she was gone and I never saw her again. They had taken her to the college infirmary to die. Connie and I drove there and I was ordered to remain in the car while she went inside. I slipped out and ran behind the building looking for a window to climb in or at least see into. But they were all high over my head. I thought that perhaps if I had run the water a little colder it might have helped her fever and she could have lived. I knew that people went to heaven when they died; I could see her setting out in her green knitted dress and her pince-nez and Phi-beta-kappa key. I figured that she had been in such a hurry she had not had time to say good-bye to me.

Uncle Will arrived at our house. Connie was waiting for him at the door. He was crying and said something incomprehensible to me. "She doesn't understand," said Connie and they agreed that the best thing would be to send me out to play. But of course I knew about it, Peggy Proctor had whispered out her window to me that my mother had "failed" three times during the night.

I wandered along the street and tried to think of some way to play. A little girl I hardly knew popped out of her front door and cried jeeringly, "Your mother's dead!"

"No, she isn't," I insisted ...

I knew that my mother had made the journey to heaven but until that moment I had not realized that I was all alone in the world. I ran for home as fast as I could. But I was blind with tears and fell, but tried to keep going on my hands and knees with my mouth full of gravel ...

Nobody mentioned my mother. I think they thought I wouldn't notice she was gone. I found Connie had moved into her room; she had also taken away my pretty dresses and put some ugly black ones in their place. The only people who said anything at all to me about her death were the children. They looked frightened and talked about heaven.

After a while I took the train back to Canada, but with Connie this time. I was willing to go along with the pretense that nothing had happened. My cousins told me in whispers that my mother's coffin had been laid in the dining room and that the room had been completely full of flowers. I surmised from this that I had not been wanted, else they would have let me come to the funeral to say good-bye. This was the last time I saw my cousins until we were nearly grown. For something terrible had happened. My grandfather had shared out the money he had got from the sale of his factory among his children. But they had all spent most of it except for my mother, and she had left it all to me. Connie and Uncle Will were my joint guardians, and Connie was to move permanently in with me ...

Connie's tastes in religion led her from Low Episcopalian to medium high and then to Stratospheric Anglicism. We set out for the Mission Farm in Sherburne, Vermont, to stay for a few days. It was a pretty little stone church with an attached farm which had been endowed as a mission to the heathen Vermonters. Truman Heminway was the rector and he lived there with his wife, Gertrude, an Englishwoman, and their four children. Lynette and Olivia Heminway were a year older and a year younger than me, and we made an instant happy sandwich ...

The Heminway children, however, like most clergymen's children, had received an overdose of religion mixed with lessons in propriety. I think Trumie, Honor and Lynette were already in full rebellion, though all but Trumie put on a pious manner to avoid confrontation. He laughed scornfully, having gone to Lennox School, an Episcopalian institution, and had been fed religion for breakfast, lunch, and supper. We told wicked irreligious jokes among ourselves and sang naughty songs ...

Connie decided to go to a dude ranch in Wyoming, and I was to spend the summer at Camp Marlin in Plymouth, New Hampshire. She had a very exciting time, went on long trail rides and even had some sort of romance with a ranch-hand named Bill. I knew because I could not resist peeking at the letter that came later from the ranch. It was loving but illiterate. I knew at once that it had just been a summer's fun because I was sure she would never ally herself in such a non-prestigious way. I think he gave her a little Indian doll, for she kept it all her life and never let me play with it ...

My camp was another matter. We had to get up at dawn and run naked into a cold lake. We slept in shelters in the woods with just roofs overhead and screens for walls. We played nasty things like baseball and jumping out of canoes. Worst of all, Connie had assigned me to the diet table and I lost weight. And worse than that, there were no books. And even worse, I excited the sadistic interest of a girl named Joy Gerhart who falsely informed the authorities that she had caught me defecating on the lid of the toilet. Of course they came and asked me ever so gently not to do it again. For the rest of the summer she leered nastily at me and I lived in terror of further accusations, and went about with my head hanging for the shame of it all ...

I do not know exactly why Connie took me away from my beloved farm, but I expect she thought I was not shaping up the way she wanted me to. I was a little bookworm who wrote poetry and plays, loved solitude and talked to herself. She scolded me for having that terrible fault, a strong imagination. She gave me a book by Dorothy Canfield called *Understood Betsy* about a nervous imaginative wreck who was sent to a farm in Vermont and who became absolutely normal after a course of hard work. That may have explained why she sent me to Vermont in the first place. But all that hard work and country living had not improved me at all. Perhaps she thought that summer camp with its absence of books would turn me into a dynamo who was lean and mean and dove off boards into the water with shouts of joy and called back and forth to her friends ...

Alas, to every little girl comes the day when she starts to become a woman. I developed a slight shape and Connie bought me a bra. That was fine for a few days but then it became a bore so I took it off. I was horrified to learn that I would have to wear it permanently. I got taller too ...

At least I still had the Heminways. I found Lynette very grown up that summer. Her golden hair was curled in a pageboy and she had developed a superior tone from her first year at Northfield. But she got over it in a few days. It was an especially interesting summer, we attended square dances, and Trumie, their brother, gave a barn dance for his contemporaries in their early twenties ...

I was allowed to go on the next trip to the Berkshires and found it very exciting ... I wrote Connie every detail of the trip including descriptions of the pictures on the walls of my room where we stayed the night, and what we ate ... But there was one thing I did not write to Connie about. Trumie was with us for most of the summer and of course joined us in our nightly games of hide and seek. One night I dove into a hiding place under some stairs in the barn and found Trumie already in possession. I was going to look elsewhere for a good spot but he kindly pulled me the rest of the way in and let me share. It was a very good spot and we were not discovered. It was a cramped space and one thing led to another; I found him murmuring endearments and stroking and kissing me. I was surprised, but it was very pleasant, for I was not used to being made such a fuss over. There were no particular improprieties to alarm me and we met there night after night, leaving separately of course at the ally-ally-in-free. Sometimes he made little nests for us in the hay during the day and would show them to me at night; we were never discovered.

One night he came into my room and slid into bed with me and started stroking me. He said, "I love you," and I started to cry and said, "I'm so glad. You're the only person in the whole world who loves me." Then he said, "You poor little kid," and patted me and got quickly out of bed. After that he just gave me affectionate hugs and let me go around with him while he did his chores. He thought I was funny and laughed a lot. When I saw him put his arm around a big girl who came to visit I was so horribly jealous that I just curled up inside, and he saw that and laughed at that too. He called me Dolly Dimple and teased me until I smiled and showed my one dimple in the middle of my cheek. Then he would crow with delight while I stamped my foot and ordered him to stop.

I was not careful to hide my feelings for him and I think his parents or Connie suspected something, for that was my last summer; I was not to go back to stay there any more. Only once I drove up with Connie in the winter and stayed two days. It was a big piece of my life that just

disappeared, like my school. I do not know why I did not register a protest; perhaps I did and I was just ignored…

The Wellesley Junior High School was no replacement for what I had
lost. I never felt in the least that I belonged and usually stood out of everyone's way and replied only if I were spoken to. I think I had grown
suddenly in the summer for it turned out that I did not have a dress to
wear the first day of school. I had to wear an old faded dress of Connie's,
a former high style dress from the twenties with abnormally huge buttons, and it did not meet properly in the front. I was deeply ashamed and
felt that everyone had noticed. That feeling stayed with me during my
years at the Wellesley public schools. My clothes were hopeless, I was too
fat and an outsider to boot …

Connie insisted that I wear a girdle to school and it was very uncomfortable when I rode my bicycle the three miles to school, for I had found
that it was quicker to pedal than to walk and take the bus. But I felt suffo-
cated and chafed, which was just one more reason for resenting Connie
and her control over me. She used to look at me in a puzzled doubtful
way but never asked me what was wrong; a great silence had descended
between us years earlier.

Of course she consulted her friends, for by now she was a bona fide social worker in charge of adoptions at the Boston Children's Aid, in control of the lives of any number of children and their adoptive parents, and
she was surrounded by psychologically inclined associates. I am sure that
their professional opinion was that I needed treatment, for Freud and
psychoanalysis were all the rage. One problem was that it was an expensive process. But Connie was an experienced haggler and she found the
perfect solution; she had discovered a school run by an authentic female
Austrian psychiatrist, a former pupil of Freud's who could be counted on
to deal with any behaviour I might come up with for no more cost than a
normal boarding school fee.

This was the Windsor Mountain School, a Swiss school which had fled
Europe in war time complete with teachers and students, though of
course some had been lost on the way. It was now located in Manchester,
Vermont. In Switzerland it had been an academically successful school
under the leadership of Max Bondy. But in America they read the omens
correctly and emphasized Mrs Bondy's connection to Freud. Another
connection they advertised was the approval of Dorothy Thompson and
of Dorothy Canfield Fisher, a mismatched team if you ever saw one.
However, Connie wanted to test the waters first and sent me to spend the
summer at their camp to reconnoitre.

The two Doctors Bondy came to look me over. Mrs Bondy had snapping
eyes and a determined smile, but aside from formalities she only wanted to

know if I had had my appendix out yet, and seemed disappointed at the answer. Bondy was a tall man, mostly bald, with a sensitive, spiritual face. He sat on the edge of a straight chair in embarrassed silence like a farmer who had strayed into a lingerie shop. It turned out that neither one of them could speak English well enough to understand more than the simplest statements. I had never met school officials with so little aplomb, and my heart went out to them at once. Dr Bondy looked as though he thought Connie might actually go for him and nip him, for he jumped when she spoke to him. I was delighted to be turned over to them ...

My Latin classmate, Hugo Moser, was very sorry for my stupidity and helped me with my homework. He was absolutely brilliant. Not only could he speak several languages but his English was faultless except for the pronunciation. His father was an art dealer in New York. He set out on the uphill task of trying to lift me to his own educational level. He started by giving me a copy of *Madame Bovary* to read. I did not like the heroine or the unfortunate doctor either. So he switched to Dostoyevsky. That was more the ticket, and I devoured five of his books without waste of time. There was also a set of Thackeray left behind by the former owner, and I plunged into that ...

Since it was a German school we had breakfast, second breakfast, lunch, tea, dinner and a before-bed snack. With so much food we were all in a state of energized excitement.

We put on a lot of plays. I wrote a melodrama, creating it to fit my actors. Harry Singer, a horribly repressed English boy who always wore a suit and tie, was the hero and he formally removed his gloves before bopping the villain on the snout. And then he put them back on again and smoothed them. It really was the fulfilment of poor Harry's dream to be an immaculate hero, for he was an unappetizing sort of idiot who had a bad habit of rocking on his heels and sniggering hopefully. The villain was played by the best-looking boy, Don Mayer, who stroked his moustache and leered. I, of course, was the heroine: I had been elected to the weekend entertainment committee and made the most of it. I was very much attracted to handsome Don, but Anne Arrin of the flashing eyes was now my bosom friend and she had confided to everyone who would listen that she was madly in love with Don. So I turned my face away from him when we met, in the spirit of comradely sacrifice ...

Hugo had invited me to New York to visit his family during the spring vacation, offering tickets to the opera and an introduction to Bruno Walter and I was wild to go, but Connie put her foot down. The best I could do was spend a morning with him visiting museums and art galleries. By this time we were inseparable. Whenever I sat down anywhere he would appear beside me, usually followed by most of his friends; he seemed to be a sort of mentor to the other boys, no doubt directing their reading along with mine. He was very serious, not much on laughter and gaiety, which was to be expected as his family was Jewish and had probably narrowly escaped with their lives. He told me that one of his fears was that America would lose the war and he would be shipped to Madagascar to live in the jungle. I said hopefully that the jungle might be very nice, but he said it wouldn't. He had been accepted at Harvard and he advised me to select Radcliffe so that we could be together. I had already filled out forms for Smith on Connie's orders but the word Radcliffe sounded much more romantic, like a gothic novel; who would willingly attend a school named plain Smith? By this time he had total moral and intellectual ascendency over me, and I followed his slightest suggestion without quibbling. As soon as it was dark we would rush outside and hug and kiss, but that was as far as it went, which showed remarkable self-control on his part, because being blissfully unaware of what I was doing, I flirted, and teased him outrageously. Mrs Bondy referred to him as "your suitor" and beamed upon the match. I think she thought it a nice blending of IQ's ...

Hugo came to see me every Sunday. He was enrolled at Harvard in the summer school, wasting no time in frivolity. But he made the long trip to Wellesley each week and stayed all day. Connie looked at him not exactly askance but in a sort of disbelief. She spoke to him in a subdued tone almost as though she were in awe of him. He was gracious to her, almost condescending ...

Peggy Proctor had been accused of being "boy crazy" by the wise old heads of the neighborhood, so I figured that she would be the best person with whom to discuss my problem, because of her wide experience. I told her that I suffered from strange and terrible feelings when I was with Hugo. Did that mean that we were not "compatible" and that we should break it off? (I had been reading women's magazines also in my search for knowledge.) "Of course," she advised, "if you are not comfortable together, you should break off." I begged for advice on what to say to him for I knew that I would never be able to best him in an argument. "Tell him quickly," she said, "as soon as he comes to the door. Say you can't see him any more." Peggy was a year older than me and her bad reputation was probably unearned and her knowledge, like mine, was from the same magazines.

I did exactly as she suggested. Hugo came bounding joyfully up the path to the front door and I latched the screen door between us to make sure that he would not bound right in, seize me, turn me to jelly, and ruin my intention. He was dumbfounded, pleaded with me to talk about it, but I was adamant and he walked sadly away with his shoulders hunched. I certainly owed him an explanation, but as I did not know myself what the matter was, how could I explain it to him? I was afraid of him and afraid of myself.

He wrote me a letter offering undying love and advising me not to kiss any more boys. As a pre-med student he must have had some inkling of the truth. My ignorance was total, as I had refused to take biology in school because it was rumored that we would have to cut up frogs. I was certainly not adverse to having a big boy admire me, and it gave me a lovely feeling to have my canoe paddling done by someone else and having someone under my thumb who was highly respected, even by Connie. I didn't mind being offered books to read, and being lectured and taken on trips to museums, but I was not going to tolerate any strange emotions or feelings of going mad. Connie looked at me strangely when I told her the news, but said nothing …

It was odd that the one boy I was interested in paid no attention at all. Now that Anne Arrin was no longer there, I thought that I could have a chance at Don Mayer, whom I had secretly admired from the start. I placed myself in his way often but without result. Mrs Bondy asked me who it was that I loved, since I didn't want Hugo and didn't like the other boys. I confessed to loving Don. She was aghast. Don was her favorite of all the students. After seeing what I had done to Hugo, she trembled for Don. She told me that he had a hard row to hoe ahead of him and he was very young and she didn't want anything to happen to him, so as a personal favor would I please keep my hands off. I think she considered me a kind of femme fatale. When I had told her about my summer experience with Hugo, she had said, "Poor Hugo" and had not said, "Poor Ann." I felt that I was dangerous and might pass on a disease, so I began to leave the room when I saw Don approaching so as not to infect him. And when circumstances forced us together, I tried not to look at him. It made me feel a little better when she promised that I could renew the onslaught when he reached twenty (he was seventeen), but though I resolved to wait patiently and only love him from a distance, the thought that my love was evil cut into my self-confidence …

Graduation should have been a sad occasion for I was saying good-bye to my friends and to the Bondys, but Mrs Bondy was not ready to let me go yet. She invited me to return in the summer as a camp counselor … Ulla and Don Mayer were also counselors. Ulla and I exchanged rooms for a few nights and I found myself next to Don's room with only a makeshift partition between. We talked most of the night about books and things we thought. I was very happy and allowed myself the joy of being close to him, believing that if he could not see me I could not be a danger to him. During the day I was careful to keep my distance, but at night I let myself go as we lay side by side with the wall between us. Soon he went away and came back in his army uniform to say good-bye. I sat across a table from him where I could memorize his face but did not dare speak to him.

That summer I learned to smoke ... Looking back from the vantage point of today, I might just as well have gone to sleep in a pipe dream for the next seventeen years, for I lost my ability to concentrate, my curiosity and my speed both of movement and thought. I became slow, timid, and lazy and my ability to notice things and keep track of them left me and did not return until I stopped smoking at age thirty-five. I do not mean to say that I was paralyzed by the smoke; to the casual eye I must have seemed only lazy and a little depressed. I got along, made friends, and had some surprising experiences. But I could not make decisions, for my judgment was impaired, and I totally lost my interest in learning which till then had been a major occupation ...

I was so proud to be going to Radcliffe. I knew that Harvard was considered to be the pinnacle to which aspiring students must struggle, therefore Radcliffe would be also. I pictured Radcliffe as being made up of the best parts of all my other schools. It would be gracious, leisurely, rich and refined like Tenacre. Like the Mission Farm it would be full of sweet gentility and beautiful to look at besides. As at the Windsor Mountain School, I would mingle with the sophisticated International Set, music would waft through the corridors, string quartets at supper, motets in the gymnasium. At last I would learn to play the piano, study ballet. Instead it was a continuation of Wellesley High School, with increased discipline. If anything, it was barer and more unattractive. I had never seen the place before enrolling.

Connie had bought me a very cheap black crêpe gown which I was ashamed of, so I mostly went to afternoon dances in a green dress I had made which I thought had come out fairly well. I had a silver necklace of silver balls which was interesting enough to make up for the rest. I think it had belonged to my mother for Connie let me have it ...

I had quietly pledged myself to Don Mayer, though he did not know it, and I was waiting until he got back from the war, all grown up. I knew that he intended to go to Harvard and that he would show up one day if I were patient. Meanwhile I intended to be popular and have dates and amuse myself ...

In addition to cultivating our minds, Radcliffe paid some attention to our bodies. The first thing I failed was a stress test, so I was relegated to folk-dancing and bowling. Next there was a posture test, or so it was called. We were ordered to strip and then walk one at a time into a little room walled in mirrors. There I was politely introduced by a formally clad lady to two men, Doctors "X" and "Y." One was a smooth looking older man and the other was a very young and good looking man. We all said "How do you do," and I would not be surprised if we had shaken hands, though I was too dizzy by that time to notice much. I was ordered to stand up straight while they stared. What with the mirrors, there was nowhere to look but down. I tried to have good posture but still remained hunched over in cringing despair. They tut-tutted and awarded me a C- ...

I went merrily off to audit a course on Dostoyevsky for I had read several of his books by then and wanted some opinions on them. I was the only girl in the class and was sent to the back of the room. It was a nice first lecture but the professor announced at the end of the hour that the next lecture was to be on the subject of sex and he glared at me in a most unpleasant manner so that I was afraid to return ...

I ran into a girl in the choral society who seemed to be a monotone. Her name was Alison Lurie, and like me she had set out to do the impossible. I think she had had a stroke for there was something a little wrong with her face and she spoke oddly. She liked to walk along beside me in my coat ...

Christmas was approaching so I went to a carol sing at Harvard. It was not much of a sing, I think it was just an excuse for a "mixer." A boy standing next to me shared my book; he had a dismal thin hesitant voice. I edged away from him but he followed and extracted the information that I was going to a house dance the next evening. I had a nice partner for that dance, for we had both been to dancing school and we ostentatiously performed "dips." But at the dance I found Bob Creeley again, buoyed up by drink and determined to cut out my partner and keep me for himself. While we danced I observed that he had very strange eyes, but as usual I kept mine lowered and did not learn at once that one of his was made of glass.

This was the beginning of a determined pursuit. He was to be found nearly every day at the Henry House door demanding that I drop everything and come out with him. First I was flattered by his attentions but I explained to him that I was not available as I had given my heart to Don Mayer and was just waiting for him to return. But that did not deter Bob; he told me that I was his exclusively and when I protested, accused me of pride, appealed to my pity, and even threatened to kill himself ...

When I tried to withdraw, he accused me of hating him because of his ugly eye, and out of mercy I lied and said that he was very attractive, and having lied to him and having established a tangled web I had to keep on lying to lie to myself also. Alison Lurie, who was already producing short bursts of her distinguished satirical prose, described his repulsive drunken behaviour as he "spat inexpertly into the gutter." His best feature was his very distinguished nose, and his playful, disrespectful gift of the gab, and his total disregard for the usual conventions. Thus I could be both amused and a naughty child when I was with him ...

Excerpts from
Ann MacKinnon's Diary,
1 January – 24 June 1944.

1 January: Every year at about this time I make a resolution to keep a diary; faithfully and permanently. But always before, I was hampered by the diary itself, a small leather object with a very weak lock. There was never enough space to write anything interesting and there were always days on which nothing had happened but for which a page had to be written. It said so irrevocably in the book. This is a lovely big book with so much space that I may feel tempted to tuck in a few pictures and odds and ends just to fill it …

6 January: … I got four telephone calls this evening and only two from the same person. Two from Bob with whom I'm going out on Thursday and Saturday, one with Manny Holman who is taking me out tomorrow, and one person whose name doesn't click and who wanted a date for Saturday. I had a charming talk with him about Bobbie and I think they must be in some way related but I'm darned if I have any idea who he is.

… Bob called up and said he couldn't come over tonight because he had a cold and would probably drown in one of the twenty foot ponds that separate Adams house from Henry House.

7 January: … A telephone call from Bob found me in the bathtub washing my hair. Cecily tried to make tactful excuses without telling the truth and it sounded as though I were trying to get rid of him, goodness knows I was not, but I think he was a little hurt …

8 January: … Feeling by this time very young and plain I put on my lovely new cotton stockings with designs all over them. They look ridiculous but they still intrigue me very much. Then in my best coat and flat shoes I went off with Bob to have tea with the German teacher from Holderness school. The German teacher, whose name is Werner, and his wife are altogether delightful. They come from Vienna and have such strong accents that they remind me forcibly of some of my schoolmates. It was wonderful to know that they know of my school and that they are friends of Thomas Wiener, Mrs Bondy's nephew.

Bob was almost broke so we went back to Adams House where he borrowed some money and where I met Steve Becker, one of his roommates, who is very nice. Bob gave me an old licence of his sister's which says that I'm twenty-one and which will let me into any bar. Now I'm Helen Caroline Creeley and I was born in 1922 …

Bob told me that he was in love with a girl named Penny Kingsley who doesn't like him at all. So I told him about Don …

11 January: … Last night Bob came to see me entirely without warning. He had called me up to tell Bobbie about it, but not me. I was just on the point of getting into the bathtub when he arrived …

19 January: … Bob told me quite simply and unhappily that he didn't love Penny Kingsley but that he loved me. He said that there was no hope because I loved Don and that he had made up the story about Penny to find out if I loved someone else. He said that he was weak and needed somebody to cling to and that he wanted me. He knew he couldn't have me and so he said that his life was pointless.

And what did *I* do? I got drunk on *one* rum coke! I drank it very fast because I was so upset and lost control of myself for about 20 minutes. He spoke of serious things but I sat there and smiled happily into space, not hearing him. My brain felt as if it were full of soap suds and my knees wobbled alarmingly until a walk in the cold air brought me back to my senses. I admit that I was terribly frightened, that I was afraid of doing some foolish thing that I would regret ever after. The only foolish thing that I *did* was to smile when I should have frowned.

I didn't know what to do at first. He said that he ought never to see me again and that it was the only way to forget me, but he won't go away. I stumbled helplessly into the house and cried myself to sleep, for a thing like this gives me a constricted and horrible feeling. I blame myself terribly as I should have seen it coming and somehow prevented it. It was the same with Sandy and Donald Finlayson who both loved me. It is a feeling that won't go away, a feeling of blame and guilt and despair that is like a heavy rock on my chest, that no amount of crying can remove. The only help is in forgetfulness and it is hard to forget such a thing. Why am I so vain that I must make myself attractive to people? and why can't I be cruel and without conscience like Bobbie, who can be unkind and who could have solved everything by saying to Bob, "Go away, I don't love you, and by being near me you make me unhappy"? I certainly can't say that, and yet he *must* go, because much of our wonderful friendship has been lost through this.

20 January: ... Bob came in the evening and I was much relieved by his actions. He acts as though nothing had happened last night. Indeed, it seems almost like a dream except that I know how he now feels and can understand him when he acts strangely toward me. I have entire sympathy for him. It was hard at first to talk.

22 January: Today was a long and wonderful day spent with Bob. We ate a supper that we made ourselves, in his room as I was terribly tired of eating in dull restaurants. First of all we went shopping for food at various little stores. Penny Kingsley gave us 5 meat coupons so we ate in style. We did very well as we found three black markets in a row. I almost burst with rage when Al's Place, the lovely delicatessen, wanted to sell us some cheese without ration points. We had a huge ham and I had a thorough lesson in cooking it from Bob who is a better cook than I am. I told him of my love for Chillion my darling kitten, so he and Steve Becker his room-mate promised to get me another one and to keep it there with them. Neither Harvard nor Radcliffe students are allowed to keep pets but it will be easier to hide it in Adams House than in Henry House because the maid in the former can be fixed.

We went to see Chekov's *The Cherry Orchard* and I can say without reservation that it is the greatest play I have ever seen ...

Bob invited me to go to Manchester to ski with him in Spring vacation. I jokingly said that Don might be there at the same time. It was then I discovered that Bob can be very jealous when I speak of Don. He was furious and quite frightened me.

As usual I had forgotten my house key and this time I had to wait alone until Lena came home because Bob had stamped away in a great rage.

24 January: ... This evening Bob came over in a vile mood. He was still angry from Saturday night because he was fearfully jealous of Don whom I had described in glowing colours to him. He threatened to go away and never see me again if I didn't use one of my last three one-o'clock permissions. I did and we stamped crossly away. He asked me if I would marry him and I said no. He was terribly unhappy but tried to be gay and change the subject. I finally told him that I loved him and it took a lot of convincing. Then he kissed me on the observatory steps. The same ones where Manny had so uselessly attempted the same thing the night I met Bob. I was wonderfully happy but somehow it was as if I were completely detached and observing the whole thing as a spectator. I arrived late at about 2 ...

25 January: ... The funniest and most awful things happen to me! This evening I got a visit from three solemn and slightly embarrassed girls. They were Penny Kingsley, Barbara Abrams and Betsy Mulany. From their position as ex-girlfriends of Bob's they had come, as they frankly admitted after nudging each other and passing the buck, to look Bob's "latest" over. They released him and said that their affairs with him had been purely platonic. Then they said that he needed the other kind and that I was just the right girl for it. They sat in a serious row and looked at me like an inquisition as I blithefully said that our love was platonic. Ha! Ha! Then they offered me a chocolate peppermint and a lemon as a peace offering and quietly filed out. To an outsider the affair would seem highly ridiculous and even to me, a definite insider, it seemed so. I told Bob about it in the evening and he was highly amused too ...

30 January: ... Besides being tangled in my working life, I find that my love life is in rather a complicated state. I'm quite at a loss, knowing that one can be a hypocrite just so long and no longer. After that it must be stopped. I cannot let Bob kiss me anymore because I really don't love him. I know that he is infatuated with me, it may even be love, but I cannot let it continue in this one-sided manner. When he said to me that he loved me and so to speak dumped his life in my lap I had to reply that I loved him too. There was an awful look in his eye before I said this to him and although I knew quite well that he would not, if spurned, fling himself off one of those charming bridges that span the Chas, I realized that he would be quite capable of flunking his English A and quitting the college. Last Monday I had not prepared myself for an occurrence of the kind, and not having thought it out at all objectively I didn't know what I wanted. But now I have. I love Bob dearly and hope that he will be happy. I will try to help him in this but I know that I love Don Meyer with a much greater love, I want to marry him and that is the real test of a love. The poor blind fool (Don) doesn't have an idea that I am in love with him. I remember that he kissed my hand twice and I will never forget it but that is rather a thin thing to pin a memory on ...

Bob came over in the evening and we chatted and bickered pleasantly about this and that. He is protesting against my command that he grow out his crew cut.

2 February: ... I have also the realization that I am hopelessly inconsistent to haunt me. Today I am in love again with Bob. In the clear light of day I don't love him at all, but when he begins to kiss me, I am lost. It's a horrid unsettled sort of feeling to have.

3 February: ... Bob and I bickered pleasantly about our hair. He wants a crew cut and likes my hair over one eye. I like his hair long and mine neat. So far I'm winning and he had consented to grow his out. This is a great concession for him to make for I realize that it must be disagreeable to have one's friends call one a bear ...

5 February: I began to be really tired when I crossed the Chas, but before then I was having a beautiful time without any thought as to my personal safety. One very well dressed man thought I was a prostitute and was much abashed when he discovered that I wasn't. A number of sailors tried to pick me up which goes to prove that a sailor loves any girl because I certainly looked horrible. My face was coated with dirt, my hair was stringy, and I had a general down-trodden look.

The nicest part of the whole journey was the half hour or so I spent walking along the river. There was nobody there to molest me and the night was beautiful and very warm for February. I sang gaily to the frozen Charles and felt that I was dancing lightly in the air ...

6 February: Today Bob and I went to Wellesley for the day. Somehow nothing happens as planned with him, and we missed our train and when we did catch it we rode too many stations. We took the bus back again and bought a prodigious amount of food in the square from Mr Frangoulis who was very grumpy.

Mrs Arnold gave us more food and we spent a lovely afternoon and evening eating and trying to play boogie-woogie on our creaky old Steinway with the silly carving ...

Bob was rather grumpy because both the dean and his mother are putting pressure on him to take the next term off. He won't do it and is in a fearful mixup.

We both ran out of money as usual so he sent me home on the subway and walked back from Park Street alone. It isn't a very long walk and since I did it yesterday with little trouble, he ought to be able to do it today ...

7 February: ... After supper I played innumerable games of solitaire at Whitman. When I came back I found Bob waiting patiently for me. He is almost a permanent fixture in the house. We went for a carefully timed walk and talked about congenial nothings ...

> Do others know the things
>   that you have taught me?
> Do others know the joys
>   that you have brought me?
>
> They can't know! Yet,
>   If they should,
> I'd care not,
>   Even if I could.
>         ~~~
> I walked alone. And then
> I saw a figure come
> From out the shadows shaped
> Grotesquely by some fearful one.
> It slowly passed me, and

The shadows shrank in odd
Respect. They felt, though I
Did not, the hand of God.

~~~

The window's open – jump! No pain
Will mock you.
They will not call you fool again.
Nor will they longer
Stare with snobbish eyes to see one
Wonder why
They hate, when hate alone has done.
What only Death should do.

~~~

[Marginal note:] Juvenilia by Robert Creeley in his very own hand!

9 February: ... Bob dropped in although I had told him repeatedly to stay home and study. He had written some poems so I had him write them for me in this book. I wouldn't tell him what was in this book although he was dying of curiosity. It is just as well that I didn't as he said he hoped it wasn't a diary because he hated people who kept them. This doesn't seem like a real diary to me, but more like a record, or sheaf of notes that will tell me enough of my thoughts to keep me from losing them as soon as they are thought. I guess I can't ever show this book to him, he would be angry.

... Bob hasn't cut his hair yet and I think I may even win in the battle between his friends and myself, the length of his hair being the "objective." He threatens to cut it from day to day, but he hasn't done it since I met him. If he does finally get his way and cut it, I'm sure that his face and head will look just like an egg.

10 February: ... No Bob today, I really find myself missing him when he doesn't come to see me at least once a day. The rest of the house has quite accepted him as a permanent fixture. Mary Ford said, "Bob? Oh yes, the boy downstairs" (It was about midnight and we were in my room.) I jumped!

Lydia and I discussed our marriages, we decided on our wedding gowns and weddings. Currently I want a brocaded taffeta with a mile long train and a lace veil just as long with the same motif. Then the conversation switched to living with your husband, especially sleeping with him. I changed my mind about getting married. I think I will be an old maid, thank you just the same.

11 February: ... Bob called me up in default of not appearing in person. I had the longest talk with him I've had with any human on the phone. I'm so completely used to him that I had not a trace of my usual receiver fright.

13 February: … Without informing me in advance, Bob appeared as usual. The snow was beautiful and we walked around admiring it. We even found a garage with a Latin inscription on it.

Bob asked me to marry him and I said that I would but only after he is through his education, and I am too. It was a very funny scene: he said "Would you ever marry me?" I said "Oh sure, someday when you grow up, many years from now." He got angry and said, "Dammit, I'm proposing to you – will you marry me?" That squelched me finally and I said yes. Whereupon he kissed me beautifully for about an hour and a half and indulged in what a vile cheap magazine called "Woman's Life" would call very heavy petting: It upset me rather, as there was no defence against it, he was so gentle and loving that I didn't have the heart to slap his face, but I have heard wicked tales about young girls who have allowed such bad things of their boy friends.

I think he is very much in love with me, at least he says so at every possible moment, and for me, I'm quite sure that I'm in love with him. Don seems to have dissolved from my mind, at least for the present. Perhaps it will start over again when I see him, if I ever do.

15 February: … I do not understand how I can be so unfaithful to Bob that I am always seeking to meet new people. I was entranced by a beautiful young British sailor in the subway. He had an ethereal beauty that made me want to follow him when he got off just that I might look at him longer. He resembled Gordon Rollins but his face was still more sensitive and lovely than his. I would have tried to pick him up if I had the courage, but I didn't dare, besides the idea repulsed me, I only wanted to look at him not to talk to him or kiss him …

16 February: I had a beautiful date with Bob and wore my new aqua and navy blue dress that Connie gave me for my birthday. First we had a heavenly steak at Jim's Place. I don't believe that anywhere I have had such a delicious steak before, home not excepted. I must have consumed at least 12 cubic inches of tenderloin steak, which is a record of me even with venison.

Afterwards we went to the Tic-Toc club where Louis Armstrong was playing with his band. I had never been to a nightclub before and this was really exciting: Louis Armstrong is a handsome Negro with beautiful white teeth and his whole troupe is Negro. They played all sorts of music and had assorted singers … It was rather difficult to get in the Tic-Toc because we were both under age with no false identification. We finally got in by lying and forging other people's names to papers.

Since this was my last permission, Mrs Henry gave me a two o'clock permission, but as usual abusing my privileges I didn't come into the house till twenty minutes of four. When we got back to Cambridge it was already late but we nevertheless went up the observatory hill where Bob kissed me rather thoroughly for a long time in the manner of last Sunday only worse. However, as one might say – I perserved my virtue although with difficulty.

18 February: … Bob came over in the evening and said that he had been drunk since he left me two nights ago. He promised to go home and go to bed early tonight but I doubt if he will. He actually kissed me in Mrs Henry's living room and I was fearful that someone might come in and be shocked.

22 February: … Today was Washington's birthday. Nevertheless I went to Dorchester House, but found that everybody had gone to the zoo, leaving me behind with nothing to do. In quite a dudgeon I stamped home (I really rode on the subway) and found Bob waiting to cheer me up. He always comes over in the afternoon because he cannot remember that I work every day. Instead of going away again he stays and talks to Bobbie, with whom he has built a good friendship. They make plans for our wedding and Bobbie has said that she will take care of all the arrangements, as though one could make arrangements now for an event to take place in seven years! I feel that it will take place a lot sooner if I can do anything about it. I cannot enjoy waiting until I am twenty-five to get married.

22 February: … Bob and I discussed our forthcoming trip to Vermont and he confessed that he was frightened at the prospect of meeting some sixty new people who would judge his suitability for me. I do hope that my school likes him, although they probably won't like him so much as I do for they don't love him and accordingly will be able to see the faults to which I am blind. I love him very very much and wish that I could write poetry so that I could write a sonnet to him. I have the kind of love for him that would become a sonnet well, and it is sad that my hand is so unskilled that I cannot write more than awkward sentences about him.

25 February: … I met Bob for lunch, but the poor boy was so broke that I had to buy his for him. He told me a wild tale of being drunk last night, but that he was going to stop for a while because he expected his stomach to melt if he drank anymore beer for a week …

I came back to Henry House, packed my bags preparatory to leaving for vacation which begins today and lasts until the sixth. Then Bobbie, Bob, and I started for the station, Bob weighed down with [Bobbie's] huge bags that almost broke his back. But he got his revenge by staggering about in the South Station looking as though he were drunk and embarrassing us thereby …

27 February: Bob called me up for about a half hour to make last-minute arrangements about the trip and to chat about silly subjects. He and I and Herbert Cole, whose phone he always uses since the telephone company removed his because he didn't pay his bill, had a delightful three-way conversation that was unequalled elsewhere for silliness ...

28 February: ... All through the trip Bob kept saying that he feared my school wouldn't like him but it seemed to like him and I'm quite sure he liked it ...

1 March: This morning I was filled with energy and went down to the Old English Inn to get Bob up. He showed me his glass eye which was fascinating, and I wasn't a bit shocked by the empty space where his real eye used to be ...

2 March: ... Bob felt a creative urge coming on so he wrote a story about a Negro with a razor, which he subsequently tore up, while I sang Jubal's Lyre, Agnus Dei and my whole opera with Paula. It was wonderful to sing these songs again but they were mostly too high for me as my voice seems to have changed from a high soprano to a moderate alto ...

3 March: ... Feeling the need of a stimulant, Bob, Paula, Edith and I went to the Quality to get something to drink. I had two rum cokes and was really drunk. I felt awful and staggered visibly when I walked down the restaurant stairs.

Bob made an experiment with me. He tried to seduce me and stopped just before the end to see what would happen. I was scared at first as he had a good technique.

... Today was my last day at school and I was a fool and missed most of it by staying in bed until two in the afternoon. The lazy Bob demanded as usual that I wake him up in the morning and light him a cigarette.

I told Mrs Bondy that I intended to marry Bob and she wasn't shocked at all. She spoke to me for a while although she was very busy ...

4 March: Having had no sleep at all last night Bob and I were a trifle confused when we alighted in the North Station, and tired too. He came with me to the South Station to wait for my train with me, and while we were waiting we discussed our marriage. He said that he would marry me when he was 24 if he is drafted and assigned to limited service in this country because of his eye. If he is deferred because of his eye he will join the American Field Service (ambulance) and go overseas. In that case he will marry me right away. I am torn between the desire to have him safe in this country but unwedded to me, or married to me and in another country. The second idea is purely selfish, but there is nothing I can do about it for it is the army that has to decide ...

6 March: My greatest adventure of the day was my meeting with Bob's mother ... He had told his mother that we were to be married and she appraised me carefully, I am sure. But her glances were not half so upsetting as those of the chance pedestrians who passed us on the street while we were kissing ...

7 March: I met a friend of Bob's on the street. His name is Horace Washington and he is rather disparagingly called Horrid Horey Hocks by Gordon Rollins (Rolls) and Bob's other friend. Horey Hocks is very much perverted and it is known that he offers fifty dollars to any boy who will stay with him in his suite at the Ritz Carleton Hotel. It is slightly rumored that Duncan Eaves took his offer, but I don't believe it. I was greatly surprised when he invited me to a party in two days, and being at a loss for words I accepted the invitation …

I found out my marks. They are really quite shocking. Art D+, French D+, Psychology D, and English C. I don't believe that ever before in my life have I done so badly.

8 March: … I went to Horace Washington's party with Bob. It was in a dark depressing house and there were all sorts of homosexuals there and not one other girl. I was fearfully embarrassed and kept my eyes on the floor all the time as I didn't dare speak to them for fear they should be repulsed by me, for I cannot help smiling at the people I talk to. To sustain myself I drank two glasses of sparkling burgundy which was very nice and delightfully fizzy.

We left shortly as Horace and his "boy-friends" tripped gaily off to the ballet. Then we went up to the observatory hill and did the usual thing. We were constantly interrupted by little professors who tripped over us on the steps and by a huge group of girls who thought we were very amusing. We were both very much in the public eye, and I hope nobody recognized us.

… When Bob had left I told Mrs Henry that we were going to be married. It took great courage and I was highly annoyed when I found that Bobbie had already told her. At least she gives her approval.

9 March: … I had supper in Bob's room with Barbara Abrams and his assorted room-mates who all seem to be coming down with the grippe. I like his friends amazingly well. It is as though I had chosen them myself.

We made a flying visit to see his mother who leaves for N.E. Harbor in a few days. She is a charming person and interesting, but I'm afraid that I'm a wee bit jealous of her, as she must be of me …

13 March: Duke Ellington who is a Negro band leader gave a lecture at Harvard supposedly on Negro music. In reality it was nothing but a publicity stunt and a farce too. He told nothing about the style and played four very dull pieces on the piano. We and most of the college were annoyed because about a thousand of us came expecting something good and ended up as camera fodder. They even made some boys go up on the stage and pose with him for the photographers.

I was unbelievably tired today. I had no strength or sense of humor left. When Bob left I began to snap at everyone and actually swore for the first time in a year, and it was at Janie and Bobbie who wanted the bathtub before me. Then I wept because I couldn't find my eraser. The thing that made me most unhappy was that I couldn't blame anyone else for anything, only myself when I was calm enough to use a little logic.

14 March: I missed a class today which was a terrible thing to do. I felt so tired this morning that I quite literally couldn't get out of bed. I am a fool because I do not allow myself enough sleep to be healthy and in a good mood. Tonight I stayed out until one. Bob took me to a party at the house of a friend of his, Ferdinand J. Ach, who is tremendously ugly but very nice. He suggested a lovely course for me to audit, Contemporary Physics and Its Philosophical Meaning. I also got Dave Harris to promise to sing duets with me.

My back feels very funny and there is a queer lump there which leads me to believe that I have broken my coxix. It doesn't hurt much and it provides a lovely conversation piece. I feel just like Winnetou who used to cry "My Coxix" every time she sat down.

16 March: I felt myself very much depressed today when I discovered that I was at the bottom of my chemistry class. Even with the aid of two very patient and intelligent men I failed to understand the simplest relationships. Never before have I been the stupidest of a group of people, for not infrequently I was the brightest. It is a definite jolt to my self-esteem. Bob too, failed me. I had thought that he was only able to do English well and to write, but now it appears that he has a mathematical brain too. He helped me with my math, which was also the first time I had solicited help from a fellow student to the extent of letting him do my assignment. And he did it with such speed and sureness that I had never expected to find in people other than Felix or a few assorted math majors ...

18 March: We had a splendid and exciting party at Lay's again today. The most I contributed to it was an exhibition of drunkenness that is unequalled in my own life. I drank four huge rye and gingers which I love dearly and at the end was as unlike my conservative and inhibited self as possible. The drinks didn't make me noisy and obnoxious, they just made me very sleepy and quite helpless, so much so that I was unable to prevent Bob from kissing me in public. I was angry at him as he was quite sober at the time and should have known better. I am very glad that I was with him rather than with some untrustworthy man who might have done me permanent harm in my helpless condition ...

20 March: I felt awful when I got up, and quite feverish so I went right back to bed where I remained all day. In the evening I staggered downstairs to see Bob who brought me some food, very welcome indeed as the sick person in this place is liable to starve ...

24 March: I went to the hospital, Baker Memorial, in an ambulance, and although it hurt me I had a wonderful time. I must be a supreme egotist since the attention I received offset my discomfort which was so much greater. I found that in all this time my pain was greatest when I was alone ... They put leggings and diapers and a hospital johnnie on me (it seems to be the standard operation garb) and wheeled me, bed and all, up to the operating room but not until a very young intern, Dr. Clement, had given me a very thorough examination which embarrassed me a bit.

I had a lovely time talking to the anaesthetist who had to put me to sleep to shut me up. They gave me Nitrous Oxide and ether which was most unpleasant and made me feel exactly as though I were bursting ...

29 March: Bobbie and Bob both came to see me. Bob brought me a huge white and pink teddy bear. Bobbie upset the whole floor. She rushed around visiting strangers and upsetting my favorite nurse, Miss Lindsay, by rushing about in the hall in my bedroom slippers with her skirt lifted high and filled with orange peels. She thought that Bobbie was me, and that I was fully dressed and running away. She ran into the T.B. section which is called "precaution" and is absolutely forbidden.

Connie brought me the elephant from her office, whose name is Christopher, and now my section of the room looks like a menagerie, especially since Eddie made me some ethel and methel alcohol with the atom set which looks very much like toy animals.

1 April: I made my grand exit from the hospital in a wheelchair carrying little animals and fully dressed except for my feet because they had forgotten to pack my shoes when I came. It was a beautiful day ...

5 April: I went to the movies with Bob and I found that I could sit for a long time in the theatre without too much discomfort. Afterwards we went down to view the river which looks beautifully spring-like and romantic.

I have been welcomed back by a very great number of people, some of whom I don't remember ever having seen before. But the nicest welcome of all was that of Bob's friends who were charming. Dave Harris, the boy with the beautiful voice, said that I was the nicest girl in Radcliffe. Coming from him it was a valued compliment ...

7 April: Just for fun I went to the Catholic church for two hours with Bobbie and Janie. We were a funny trio. I had a very dirty outfit and was very informal, Janie was dressed neatly and ordinarily and Bobbie had on pumps and a hat with a veil and an orchid. I met Herbie Cole in the street.

I bought a lot of hot-cross buns because it is Good Friday – but they weren't hot and the crosses were very ragged.

I stayed out with Bob until two in the morning and we did nothing but neck – quite frankly and in a dark suspicious tool shed too. It was very funny for there occurred what we fondly called "Our little fiasco." I laughed about it all night. "Poor timing."

8 April: Today the April showers began in earnest and although there are few flowers blooming and the grass is still yellow it is unmistakably springtime. All day I missed appointments, possibly because the air was so languid and so inviting that I dawdled on my way. I missed a doctor's appointment in Boston and I took so much time standing in the public gardens in the rain singing to myself that I missed an English conference and the changing of my dressing.

I ate lunch with Bob and spent most of the afternoon playing cards and reading poetry in his room.

10 April: I finally got Bob to take me to the Old Howard. It is a burlesque of the lowest kind and there were six strip teases, mostly by fat slobs. The chorus girls were horrid and altogether it was rather sordid and dull. There was one talented stripper however, called "Peaches." And of course there were filthy jokes and juggling acts.

Outdoors there was a man preaching about Christ. He was very fiery and waved his arms around and screamed. Some nasty people in the crowd heckled him and he almost went mad. Scollary Square is a good place for a preacher and he lectured to the wandering females, but unfortunately he picked on me, the most innocent of the bunch. I felt very sorry for him. Scollary Square is certainly very interesting.

11 April: This morning I slept until a disgustingly late hour, a luxury I can't allow myself if I expect to get off probation and back into the graces of Mrs Henry and the whole college. Bob took me to lunch, on my money incidentally, as he seems to have taken over my money in a calm and self-possessed manner, a thing that surprises me very much and a habit of which I shall soon have to break him …

13 April: I decided to devote the entire day to studying, not only to accomplish anything that would help me in the eyes of my masters or to assure myself of passing my examinations, but also as an exercise in willpower to see if I was suffering so badly from inertia that I could do no work. I wasn't so was able to devote about four hours to the study of Harmony with Marty Diller at Agassiz. Marty didn't work nearly so hard as I did for he left me chewing distractedly on my pen and my fingernails while he flirted with most of Radcliffe College's musically minded maidens. He is quite a gay old thing and insisted on holding my hand while he taught me.

I was going to study math too, but Bob was very sick with the grippe or something and couldn't help me.

14 April: Bob has gone to the infirmary and I have been going crazy trying to get in touch with one of his roommates. I spent so much time looking for him that the visiting hours were up before I could reach him. I hope he won't be mad at me for not coming to see him. I haven't seen him for two whole days and am almost going crazy. I wonder how I shall manage to survive this summer when we will be in different states …

15 April: After a cursory examination of my incision the authorities decided that I need have my dressing changed only once a semi day (!?)

We have been having intermittent April showers and I was caught in a terrible one today. I went to see Bob in Stillman Infirmary and visited him for most of the day except for widely separated excursions into the rain to get food for myself and writing materials for him, for unlike me, while in bed, he does his assignments. I'm not sure what is wrong with him, he is feverish (102 – terrible) and feels just horrid although he manages to consume quantities of candy …

16 April: After eating we went to visit Bob in Stillman Infirmary. Bobbie wanted very much to flirt with all the Harvard boys there but some new and surprising modesty kept her from doing so. She had to leave after a short time for a date and I walked home in the rain beside the river singing quite foolishly to myself. After supper I went back to see Bob. I've been there so often that his roommates are beginning to stare at me …

17 April: … We stayed for the most part in Bob's room and he insisted upon bouncing up and down on his bed which must have sounded funny to the assembled listeners outside the door. The day was altogether enjoyable and I stayed a half-hour later than I was supposed to by the Adams House rules.

Mrs Henry is getting tired of seeing Bob and says so in no uncertain terms. She and Charlene are determined to reform me and make me study.

19 April: … Bob took me to see "Snow White," a revival, so now I have seen it four times. I loved it as much as ever and wept in all the right places even though the people were quite unreal.

We walked all over the bad part of Cambridge looking for a cemetery with a view of lights. It was there that Bob kissed Barbara Abrams so I made him find the very stone and kiss me on it. He said he preferred me …

20 April: Today was such a beautiful day, so windy and springlike that Bob and I fled from our studying and went to Belmont Hill which is a beautiful hilly place with farms and wonderful woods. We saw some little boys in a pasture, who thought that as lovers we were fair game for them. But they didn't realize that we were not too old to be able to remember our own childhood actions. They crept up on us but we escaped and crept up on them. This continued until all our knees were scraped and sore and our clothes tangled. The little boys finally escaped which didn't surprise us as it is easier to win in "Cowboys and Indians" provided you know the territory. A cross man saw us and chased us away. He said, "Boy take that girl home at once!" and Bob meekly replied "yes, sir," and we left. I guess he didn't approve of people like us in the woods. "In the spring a young man's fancy … thoughts of Lust (Love)" and all that.

21 April: … Bob was ill from too much drinking last night and wasn't supposed to eat anything but just the same he ate steak at Jim's Place with me. We went to the game room over in Cabot and tried to play ping-pong but he was too sick and there weren't any balls. We spent a very lonely and unhappy evening together sitting on the hard chairs. He gets terrible fits of depression sometimes. He quite frightens me then ...

22 April: Bob's mother had come to see him so I didn't expect to see him at all, but she was gone in the evening and so we went over to Adams House. Bob as usual was feeling sick. He has very poor digestion which I optimistically hope to cure when we are married. We were in his room most of the time and I was slightly rumpled when Don Mishara came in to borrow the ink. I was fearfully embarrassed and even more so when Herbie Cole almost came in when we were in a still more awkward position. But fortunately Bob warned him to stay out ...

23 April: We planned to study all day but played ping-pong in Cabot instead. I beat him in the first game which amazed me and pleased me no end. But alas he won the rest.

We sat in Henry House and studied the rest of the day. He finished his 4,500 word short story and I criticized it ...

Heroic Couplet

One time I died, and then I rose again
I looked about me, at the earth, its men
All selfish, rushing madly, helpless round
And back and forth in frenzy near the ground,
As though they sought in ceaseless searching, rest,

From human struggles. I, new from the blest
Stood near to them and looked upon the sight
And sighed to think how far from the delight
Of deathly peace they were, but could not say
The truth to them; and mourning went away.

Me

Bob wanted me to write a heroic couplet for him to pass in for English when I was in the hospital. I was nasty enough and lazy enough not to do it. And now, I, out of my meanness make one for my own amusement – but at least it is not a very good one. (Bah!)

24 April: My past had caught up with me at last. The dean called Connie up and told her that I was nearly flunking out. Connie came post haste and administered me a lecture in front of Bob. She tried to lecture him too but it didn't take. She said that I didn't have to come back to Radcliffe next term if I didn't want to. Always when I have been lectured I sit like a scolded sulky child. Today was a good example of it. Bob was furious at me because I acted like such a baby. But he comforted me very nicely too. Dr Hardy has lost faith in me too; she thinks I should go to a psychiatrist because she can't understand why I won't work. I have a good understanding of why I won't work. I am spoiled. After my years in Manchester I refuse to work unless I am happy doing it. I can't be happy here. It was a horrid miserable day and Mrs Henry intimidated me so much that I studied all day.

26 April: … Bob tried to teach me how to play football and while trying to block one of my tackles, or rather while blocking one of them, he hit me fiercely on the head. I was knocked quite silly for a minute and had a terrible headache. It must have been a concussion …

27 April: … After I had to be thrown out of Adams House because it was late Bob and I went walking on the river bank. I had no idea that the Charles River could be so secluded and wood-like. We strolled in Mount Auburn Graveyard and quite desecrated the spot. We couldn't find any nice comfortable stones to sit on.

28 April: Tonight was the Dunster House costume ball and thinking to save my permission until tomorrow night I decided not to go to it. The effort was wasted as I used up my permission anyway. Harry Phillips had a party in his room and I ate supper in Dunster House. I drank some gin and grapefruit juice which I like quite well, two glasses of it. Then Bob mixed me a drink which I didn't observe carefully. It had Brandy and gin and grenadine in it and under its influence I almost passed out. I remember doing a weird dance with Harry. Bob had to walk me up and down the river from 9:30 to 12:00 to make me sober. I protested against walking as I was fearfully dizzy but he dragged me. I am grateful for it now. If I had sat down I would have been sick or gone to sleep. It was out of the question for me to go back to Henry House at 10 so Bob called up to sign me out (I couldn't talk) and left me sitting on the drugstore stool with my head spinning …

29 April: Today was so far the most beautiful day of the year. The sun was shining and I want to roll in the grass. Instead Bob and I made a beautiful house of twigs, complete with a well and a wood pile for Mrs Henry's niece Sally Rider …

… Bob drank a lot of Brandy, and under its influence he told me that we should not get married because he was not good enough for me. I cried a little and tried not to show it for I know I could get anything I wanted through tears, and was ashamed to do it that way. But he found out and sure enough he promised to stop drinking and loafing. He said he was just jealous of all the attention I paid to Peter Longyear who is fascinated by me and flirts just the same way Sandy did. I love to have someone jealous but it is so ridiculous that I cannot but laugh at Peter.

I really must stop starving myself. I'm getting ill. I almost fainted today and when I did find some food I couldn't eat it. All I have in me is two glasses of milk, some potato chips, three spoons of chicken, four of soup, two of fruit and two of potato and cranberry sauce and a cookie. I had a violent day too …

30 April: … I spent a tiring day at Adams House and almost fainted during supper. A messy thing to do. Bob was very worried and we decided to be more careful of my waning (!) health. I decided that perhaps my inertia came from my thyroid deficiency rather than from inclination toward laziness. I decided to take my pills for a change after renewing my supply for I have neglected them of late …

1 May: … Bob and I managed to get a ping-pong ball and we played in Cabot. I won all the games and Bob was furious …

2 May: … I went out to see Connie afterwards, much to her surprise, and talked so long to her that I left Bob waiting for me more than an hour in Henry House. Mrs Henry told me that she was very tired of seeing him sitting quietly doing his homework and that he wasn't normally loud; in short that he was insipid. I think that is the one thing with which you cannot confuse Bob.

We spent a merry afternoon in Adams House and as usual emerged late, sneaking around corners and trying to avoid Chester (Chit), the janitor …

3 May: … Connie took me to lunch at the Women's City Club … My hair was dirty and so was my face. I wore no cosmetics. Some of the more sedate members of the club must have looked at me askance. I even flicked a cigarette butt away into the garden, a most unladylike thing to do. Connie asked me if there was a "necking problem" with Bob. I changed the subject hastily. I most carefully refrained from telling her of my love for Bob and that I intend to marry him. But now I'm sure that someone told her, probably Mrs Henry who is no respecter of the secrets of "Children." I had supper in Adams House but felt quite sick. I'm afraid that I lead too strenuous a life. But not in the way that Mrs Henry thinks. She thinks that Bob tires me out by talking to me and yet she calls him "insipid." If she only knew! …

… When I came in I was bursting for love of Bob and felt like writing poetry. But my pen was inkless …

4 May: … I audited a course of Bob's on the short story. It was delightful and I decided to take it next term if they let me stay.

We went to Herbie's room and I drank some rye with water as a chaser, two jiggers only, as it was far too hot to drink.

We ate at Jim's Place and went for a walk where we encountered several little boys playing "commandoes." We wanted to play too but they didn't seem inclined to let us.

We studiously avoided Henry House for Bob is determined not to go back there again since its mistress called him insipid. He is deeply insulted ...

5 May: ... Bob thought that I had gone home so didn't see me. It's horrible to be separated from him for even a day. I love him very much and I can feel it all through me but cannot speak about it without seeming stupid. I couldn't convince Dr Lindemann [a psychiatrist] of it because my tongue became very tied. To my amazement he asked me if I were sexually attracted to him. I said "yes" very confusedly. Someday I suppose that I will have to tell him about us.

He has already done a great deal for me (my Doctor). I feel now as though I had been asleep for a long time and were just waking up and seeing something beautiful ...

7 May: ... When I came back to Cambridge, Mrs Henry gave me supper, delicious. Bob had a horrid cold and a temperature. He was gruff when I tried to pity him, saying that his grandfather said boys weren't made to be pampered. This is because I told him of Connie's statement that he wasn't very masculine ...

8 May: The day was mostly notable for its games of ping-pong. Bob and I played in Cabot, he with a fury that made him want to win after the last beating I gave him. He was like a little child. When he lost he sulked and when he won he was so happy that he danced and sang. He won two games out of three and was as happy in winning them as he had been unhappy in losing the others. What a baby I am marrying! ...

11 May: The day was spent in Taunton where Bob's sister Helen is staying with Sandy as her husband Arthur is in the Army. She stays with Aunt Bernice (the mother's sister) and Uncle Wade Raymond who is a rather dull superintendent of schools there and a confirmed amateur photographer with no hope of cure. Also his views on the treatment of children are queer as he drove Sandy almost crazy when he sang to him. I sat patiently looking at the photograph albums with which the house is filled. I also didn't smoke or wear lipstick so he was much impressed by me.

Of course we were low on money and had to borrow some from Helen in order to get home.

Sandy is an angel and I love him. He seemed to like me better than he did Bob. Bob intends to go into the Army or Field Service after the 21st.

12 May: Bob and I went to Boston to the Negro section to hear Pete Brown who is a Saxophone player. He was at the Café Savoy which looks amazingly respectable but Bob said he was nearly killed there one night. The negroes take offense very easily and when offended, they are dangerous. He told me not to laugh at anything, which was hard to prevent when the trumpet player made noises like a dove. Pete Brown is one of the hugest men I have ever seen. His saxophone which was pretty large and which would have bowed me down, was like a toy in his hands. He must have weighted nearly 400 lbs and he was of an amazingly square build ...

13 May: I was waked in the morning by the arrival of Bob. We played ping-ping and he enraged me by trying to throw away a game even though I was still two games ahead of him. I was so angry at him that I almost cried. I did hit him with my fist and every moveable small object in sight. So we were in a vicious mood for most of the day. We very rarely fight but have continuous misunderstandings, especially as we are both dreadfully stubborn.

Steve's mother and Sister Myra came to visit him so we sat in A26 and talked to them. I ate lunch at Adams House and supper with Joe Greenwood because Bob had no money. It is Joe's 17th birthday which makes him eligible for dating, flirting with etc. At least Bob seems to think so. He was fearfully jealous of him and so was even crosser. He also hates Howie Dillon who is getting unfortunately attached to me. He actually gives me things which is a thing he would never do for another girl as he is very stingy ...

14 May: The day began under the most unfavourable conditions. I missed an appointment with Bob and made him miss lunch. Then while he studied I looked very mistreated and turned both the gallant H. Dillon and J.A. Greenwood against him. They both called him a cad and I didn't stand up for him because he had hurt my arm. But all was solved in the evening when I promised to try not to turn his friends against him or to befriend his enemies, a thing which I seem to be doing of late. It seems that we still love each other just as much as ever ...

15 May: It was a perfectly beautiful day and consequently torture to go to my classes. I spent most of the afternoon with Bob. We walked all over the place and stayed out until 1:00 a.m. in order to make a trip to the graveyard which is down Mass. Ave. by the railroad tracks. We desecrated it shamelessly. Graveyards seem to have a strange fascination for us ...

17 May: Bob had a new eye made today, it's lots brighter and more cheerful and by contrast makes his real eye seem dull. He had two made but the first one turned out to be cross-eyed.

We went to the movies and saw Rudolph Valentino and Thelma Banky in the silent film "The Eagle" and Charles Boyer and Hedy Lamarr in "Algie." It was fun to compare the two men. Each was the greatest lover of his age. I am inclined to favor Valentino, he was better looking and kisses just like Bob. Even though the acting was rather bad. The make up was weird. The subtitles in "The Eagle" were very funny to the modern sophisticated audience.

We ate at Al's Place and Bob told me that he hated to hear me talk because I kept wandering off on tangents. He didn't kiss me all day.

20 May: It was a beautiful day as we collected Jay and a box of chocolates that Bob's mother had sent him for his birthday, and some beer and went to the river bank to sit. Bob and Jay took turns rowing in a funny little boat and we all took turns breaking beer bottles that were floating about in the river. We presented a sort of idyllic scene that Renoir might have painted as we played on the bank. We also watched a soccer game. Dave hates Connie and wants to adopt me when he is 21, which I think is very nice of him.

Bob and I played ping-pong and never before have I seen such an exhibition of ill temper as he displayed when he lost. He broke one paddle by banging it on the table.

He hates Connie and is beginning to prejudice me too although heaven knows that I could never do otherwise than love her.

21 May: It was Bob's birthday and we went to Wellesley. We were wonderfully happy. I made him a cake and we drank Connie's wine closet almost empty in the shape of three different cocktails. Weird things made of Vermouth, gin, baccardi, lemon juice and soda water. We both got pretty well stewed and we staggered so much that we left the house in a mess and decided to clean it up sometime during the next week.

We stayed in the house in the dark until 9:30 when Mrs Arnold called up anxiously to know what had happened to us. When I went over there she read me a short lecture on necking too much with men, especially if "you are fond of them, because what is lovely now might lead to something cheap."

We were late to reach Boston and since I was a few minutes late last night, Mrs Henry says that I cannot go out at all next week.

22 May: I slept through my first two classes but didn't much care as I intend to leave college anyway. I also signed up for a futureless and pointless English major as I particularly hate the subject.

Bob and I played ping-pong again and now all is well. He is improving so much that he is well caught up and is even one game ahead of me. I'm happy now because he is so happy ...

23 May: Bob and I were very happy today. We made beautiful plans for our marriage. He actually wept from excess emotion. He bought a book for us to own in common, an anthology of Modern Poetry. There are beautiful poems there. It is the first thing we owned in common. We bought some records of Lead Belly who is a Negro ballad singer and very exciting.

Then we had a fight. I have never seen happiness dissolve so suddenly into tears before, not real obvious tears but felt and wished for tears that didn't come. I am deadly afraid that I have lost Bob. He said that his love for me before was idealistic, but now it had come into a practical sense and isn't beautiful to him anymore. I love him very very deeply and am horribly afraid. I never thought that a love could dissolve in such a short time but it seems to have melted into a dirty puddle as far as he is concerned.

26 May: I've given up the hope of passing my final exams; I am afraid that my experience in college has been a complete flop; an expensive one too. My interest has been entirely transferred to Bob. It would sound fairly bad to an outside ear to hear that my work was suffering because of a love affair. But it is more than a mere love affair; it is a care in itself.

... I am wonderfully optimistic and idealistic. It is wonderful to be so, but there are so few people like that around me that I fear it will be naturally my turn soon to be disillusioned. I hope that this will not be so. It would be beautiful to spend my life in love with life. But if I did, I should never want to die, and other people die around me and don't complain. I feel that there is something very bitter in store for me. Other people have said so. But it may not come. Would it be nice to be a happy earnest child, as I am now when I have to die? I think not. Perhaps it is a way of nature to let people be happy when they are young. I am happy now and I have Bob to fasten my hope to. Perhaps I shall have to lose him. That may be my hurt. Now we are very happy ...

27 May: Mrs Henry is furious at Bob. She said that I would have to leave her house if he came to see me any more or even called me up. We were both very angry and spent much of the afternoon plotting revenge with various members of Adams House. Jay Ach suggested that Bob call her up every night in the middle of the night and just hang up without saying a word when she answered. Bob dispatched four taxis to the house to bother her but she had gone to a baseball game and Charlene had to deal with the indignant cabbies. Don Mishara suggested that Bob pretend that his mother had died and gain sympathy from Mrs Henry. Joe said that we should build him up as an important person and say that the student government wanted to hold a meeting and needed to get in touch with all of its members (Bob). Whis's suggestion was the best. She said that he should ask for motherly advice and invent some simple problems for her to solve. He agreed to do that on Monday. But none of the plans worked very well because he finally went to Mrs Henry and asked her very plainly what was wrong. She said that we were wasting our time and that we couldn't see each other more than twice a week, at which time he would be admitted to the house. She gave no other reasons. She told him what a sweet boy he was and blamed it all on me, but a few weeks before she told me what a sweet girl I was and blamed everything on him ...

28 May: Bob and I have been forced to resort to secret meetings and the like. I have trained my friends in the house to answer when questioned by Mrs Henry as to my whereabouts to say that I am off in some corner studying very hard when in reality I am in Adams House playing with equal fervor. I ate dinner there but missed supper because we were busy doing something else. Bob had finished writing his play and has got Joe to type it. He wrote a long dedication poem in our book of poetry. He said that this was the "first" that we owned in common ...

Bobbie, Ruth and I have formed a "Bob club." We certainly lack originality in our love affairs. The people involved are Bob, Bob, Bob, Bobbie, Ruth and Ann (the Ann used to be Ruth until she was four). They even kiss the same (this fact learned through discussing not experimentation).

30 May: I was awakened by the irate Mrs Henry at some ungodly hour of the morning. She said that Bob was on the phone. He called and insisted that I meet him in the park for breakfast because he had stayed up all night talking with Stewart Kirby. We ate breakfast in Stew's room after watching an earnest and shaggy little procession place wreaths up the huge monument in the Cambridge common that commemorates Lincoln, Washington, and assorted dead.

I played chess with Stew and found out that he was a budding psychologist. Also that he knew how to hypnotize people. Remembering that Mrs Bondy had said that I would be a hard person to hypnotize, I offered myself as a subject. I got a little drunk to help it along, on five ryes and ginger ales. This was after Connie had made a special trip here to tell me not to drink with Bob because sex and liquor do not mix. She was very right but I played innocent and probably fooled her.

I got very drunk after a while and got sick – perhaps it was brought on just as much by the burning hot weather as by the rye. I lay on Stew's bed where he had carried me and got sick into his waste-basket while Don Mishara alternately held and stroked my head and/or gave me hot water to drink. I guess I passed out. I woke up a few hours later to find myself clutching Bob who was still asleep. We were all tangled up together and I found that my bra was undone. Most definitely sex and liquor do not mix.

Stew came home and wanted his bed so we draped ourselves over some cushions on the living-room floor and set an alarm to wake us at midnight. I didn't go to sleep but it was lovely to be still with him asleep beside me. Unfortunately my nose itched and my arms were occupied.

2 June: ... As I was sober and presentable I was sent for a lot of food for supper, and we ate it in Jay's room having dispensed with Ann and her date. Bobbie Freiburg proved to be rather odd. She claimed that she had the habit of smoking marijuana but Bob and Dave fortunately proved her to be showing off. Then she suggested that we all go swimming in the Charles River without any clothes on. Of course when we got there she wouldn't go in but stayed embarrassed on the bank while Bob quite im-modestly paraded about completely nude. I didn't go in either but it was because I am like a cat and hate the water. It's funny that I didn't feel a bit embarrassed.

When everyone had been thoroughly seeped in the waters of the Chas they were much more sober than before which was very good because they had been acting disgracefully a few minutes before. I, as a detached observer, could see that clearly. Bob had insisted upon kissing me publicly in the rumble-seat while Dave was driving dangerously. The ride was so bumpy that we cut our lips. Dave was the only one who didn't sober up very much so Bob drove the car while he sat in the rumble-seat with me. It turns out that he must have been cherishing a passion for me. He wanted to hold my hand and he asked Bob if he could kiss me (quite pla-tonically, of course). Bob got very angry as might have been expected. He drove the car as fast as it would go from pure rage.

We drove to Concord where Bob used to live. He was terribly unhappy at the sight of the place so he jumped out of the car and went for a walk in the woods alone. He came back after a while, quite unhappy, and we drove on. He was still a little drunk and he was homesick and fearfully jealous too so he decided to kill himself. He is very much over-emotional and I under-stand how he feels. He opened the car door and jumped out but fortunately Jay was driving slowly and he was not much hurt. The car ran over his leg though. There was no damage except cuts and bruises. After he had the physical hurt he was quite normal again. But he bothers me by saying that he knew what it is like to face death now, so he won't be afraid next time.

3 June: Bob's leg was rather stiff today but otherwise he is quite normal. But still he gets furious when I mention Dave's name. I never saw anyone who could get more jealous than Bob …

4 June: I went to the park to meet Bob as usual at 11:30. He didn't appear so I waited until I went almost crazy and then went to wake him up. It is funny that I am so used to the state of his absent eye that I didn't even no-tice that it wasn't there …

I don't like Stew very much. I don't know why, but he is very dirty minded and a lover of cheap thrills. In spite of that he is very nice to talk to although I don't like him when he is absent. Maybe I am conditioned against liking him because I was so sick in his waste-basket.

He tried to hypnotize me but failed again. Rather than disappoint him I pretended to be so doing everything he told me to even to the extent of the post hypnotic suggestion of wanting a glass of water. Bob was very upset at seeing me apparently going to sleep under the persuasion of an-other man, so he drank a quart and a half of beer from anxiety. He said that he had a horrible feeling that he was losing me …

7 June: I got a letter from Connie saying that she had finally decided to let me quit college because I would flunk my math exam and that would spoil my record. Dr Hardy and Dr Lindemann both gave me medical excuses which was nice of them and undeserved by me. Now I get no credit for this incompleted term but at least I won't have to take final exams. I've decided to devote my time to making Bob work and pass his exam now. I've been reading cases for his paper on alcoholics …

8 June: … Bob became nasty tempered as he sobered. He was jealous because Dave had taken me to dinner because he wouldn't leave his room.

For a while Jay and I were alone in 5 DeWolfe Street house and he decided to be funny so he climbed out on the garage roof and threw pebbles at passing cars. An old lady came along and scolded him. He did his best to look insane and he must have succeeded because she called the police. While she was calling he came into the house and changed his suit, took off his glasses, and put on a false mustache. Then he called Dave to bring the car so we could make a quick getaway.

The police came so he washed off the mustache and jumped out a back window and got away. But I walked out the front door and played innocent and annoyed the poor foolish police. Dave came alone and we played that Frank Forsythe (imaginary fellow) was the imbecile. "He's just like an animal, sometimes he runs around on all fours."

Bob had been building up an enormous amount of jealously and we parted in a rage. But as soon as I had left for the station he came after me, very repentant.

I think he could do well with a psychiatrist but he is afraid of them …

11 June: I saw Bob again and it was beautiful. I hadn't seen him since Thursday except for the telephone calls which he had made to me everyday. Sometimes Connie would be standing in back of me while I spoke so I couldn't speak freely which he didn't understand.

He gave me a ring, for our engagement. It wasn't a real ring for it was made from ebony and aluminum and was taken from the finger of a dead German in 1918. Bob got it from Harry Phillips. It has an iron cross like this: ✠ on it, which is very symbolic.

Connie won't let me go to Cambridge any more to see Bob because she says she won't have me chasing boys at Harvard. She has altogether the wrong viewpoint. She can't realize that one can have close friends and not lovers …

12 June: I didn't have mumps at all, just a very sore throat and a temperature all from nervous fatigue. Even my weight is going down. I weigh just 127 lbs, and I'm wonderfully happy about that even if I am sick. Dr Barton came and gave me all sorts of medicine, but I neglected to take it.

The only bright spot of the day is the telephoning of Bob. He hates Connie though and calls me spineless because I won't fight against her. But the only way I could fight against her would be to hurt her, and I don't want to do that because I love her. I only wished that she could see that she was hurting me.

13 June: ... I talked with Bob for two hours on the phone today. It was lovely but also it was torture not to be able to be near him. He invited me to come up to North East Harbour on the 23rd and I accepted at once, not thinking that there would be complications. But when I asked Connie, she said "definitely not" in an angry voice. It shocked me. She gave no reasonable reason for the refusal except that I was away so often that it was about time that I stayed home ...

17 June: Bob called me up several times in the morning and we had a fearful row. I hung up in tears so he came out to straighten it out. It was fixed in ten minutes, and I fed him lunch and we went canoeing on the lake. We started out with me doing the work in the bow, while he sat and laughed in the stern. We ended up with him working and doing all the paddling and my lying comfortably on a lot of cushions holding a water lily in one hand dangling the other in the water.

He stayed for supper and went to sleep with his head on my lap. He gets too little sleep and too little food so when he is with me I work hard to make him catch up on both ...

18 June: Bob and I wanted to have our engagement announced before we were separated. But Connie didn't want to do it formally unless Mrs Creeley approved so nothing is to be done pending her arrival on Friday when I shall be gone. It is a great pity.

Connie doesn't want me to get married because she says I'm childish and besides that neurotic. I don't see how that can be true. I don't feel like either of them. If anyone is that way, it's Bob ...

19 June: This was my last day at home and I sang passionate farewells and shed tears into my packing. Bobbie came from Cambridge and stayed through supper, then she went home and Bob came. It was a very sad leave-taking. It rained and we had to sit at home under Connie's thumb. I gave him my baby ring for a farewell present and he keeps it on his watch chain. He, poor and broke, can scarcely afford a ring for me so I start out with his picture of Sandy, his nephew ...

20 June: I left. Connie took me to Waltham to catch a train so I didn't see Bob any more. When we went past Acton I looked and looked but I couldn't see Bob's house. All this made me unhappy so I sat dismally through the trip and read Russian stories about people killing themselves. It may have been the effect of the stories or my #own wretchedness, but I suddenly felt that there wasn't any beauty in life and I wanted to kill myself. I hope I am not losing my *joie de vivre*.

The Bondys were all at school, all branches of the family including the babies Jeanette and Tommy. So are Didi and Dick. I roomed with Didi.

I smoked innumerable cigarettes and soaked in the calm of Manchester. I didn't realize before now how nervous and unhappy I was.

21 June: P.S. Bob's first letter came. It was beautiful. I was so happy that I smirked conspicuously at the table where I was reading it, so that everybody stared ...

24 June: This diary is going to end soon. When I started it, I was lonely. I had no one to write to except myself. It was fun to look back and say hello to myself. Then I had nobody else who loved me enough to listen to my rantings. Now the necessity is over, I have Bob, and he is enough. I don't need to dwell on memories for I have the present and Bob. I may lose him and only then would I return to this book for he is in it, and by reading I can relive the past, the few short months contained herein. But he mustn't die. I'm too selfish for that. I want to build my life around him and not myself. This book is only a symbol.

I can't write anymore for my heart is not in it. It used to be, but is no longer.

ANN MACKINNON'S MEMOIRS (CONTINUED):

... Before long the inevitable [had] happened, I was no longer a virgin. I was horribly ashamed; like the girls in the Victorian novels I had read, I was now ruined. The only cure for ruination was marriage to the offender. Obviously no other marriage was available to me now, for what decent man would want a ruined girl? I was also sure that my shame was written in large letters on my forehead for all to see. My posture became more slumping than ever. I knew I was the only girl in the college to do such a bad thing. Bob had proposed marriage to me but the date was so far off that it did not seem real ...

I introduced Bob to Connie. She wore her disapproving look but had no comment to make. I got permission to take him to the Windsor Mt. School to meet the Bondys. We spent three days there. The Bondys had nothing to say either. I thought he would like my friends but he did not want to mingle. He did not want to eat in the dining room so we were cast on the mercies of Susie the cook and ate in the kitchen. Paula offered to play the piano accompaniment so that I could sing all my best songs for him, but he walked out in the middle and said he couldn't stand all that screeching. In addition to our tastes being completely different (he liked only jazz, modern art, and modern writers) he disapproved generally of everything in my past, telling me that it was unworthy, dishonest, unnatural, vulgar, and so forth. I believe he wanted total ownership and control of me with no strings attached, and he came very close to getting it ...

Connie was very angry at me, her lips were never unpursed. She said that she had received a letter from the college saying that I could return some day when I was thoroughly well. She did not show me the letter. "Mentally well, also," she said. Though I might in time become physically well enough to satisfy her, I could never be really mentally well enough. So I knew that the "some day" would never come and that my days at Radcliffe were over. From what I know now of College correspondence, that letter had been addressed to me. Twenty-five years later I got to read my college transcript and found that I was still on temporary medical leave. "Why didn't you go back?" asked the Dean of Berkshire Community College. "You could have gone back at any time …"

… For the next month I spent most of my time with Bob and his friends, for as he worked at night his afternoons were free. He never needed more than six hours sleep at night. He had joined that strange group of former Harvard students who did not go home when they left the college but rather joined a kind of underground of often aging men who associated with and passed themselves off as students but who had no real occupation. As an Alma Mater Harvard was unparalleled. She must have paralysed her sons so they could not leave her …

We decided to announce our engagement at the same time and concocted a sort of notice which we sent to the newspapers. When I opened the *Globe* I was horrified to find screaming headlines at the top of the social page: "Ann MacKinnon of Wellesley to wed."

The rest of the information was the lead story. His friends had determined to give him a grand send-off. We had not made any plans to actually marry, Bob being not of age and requiring his mother's permission to marry and neither of us having any money to live on, for Connie controlled my money and would do so until I was twenty-one. I was always a little worried about getting pregnant for it seemed that marriage in that predicament would be impossible. When I missed a period Bob would get some Ergot pills from his friends and I would take them and feel sick. My periods had always been irregular, only once every few months, probably due to cysts, so I do not think the Ergot did anything to me except upset my stomach. This was hard on my nerves as I was totally ignorant of reproductive biology and did not know how to protect myself.

I set off to North Carolina by train …

[Black Mountain College] stood in the middle of a landscape of the most abject poverty. Little ramshackle huts stood on stilts in the red ground, with a cow here and there. There were no lawns, everywhere was mud. The college had been a Baptist campground next to a small artificial lake. There was a large chicken house type building designed by some Bauhaus simplist, and it was surrounded by six or seven small buildings, a pair of barracks, and a meeting hall. There was also a gazebo and a tiny stone chapel grown over in the woods. Besides Bauhaus, the architecture was woodsy, with logs, stone fireplaces, rough wooden walls, and splintered floors. Small as it was, it was far too large for the twenty-five or so students, mostly girls. Each of us had a study in the chicken house which was honeycombed with little rooms all decorated with bare plywood. I slept in a room with two other girls in one of the barracks. One of them was Beate Gropius, her father was the architect, but I do not think he was responsible for the chicken house ... Bob came to say good-bye before going off to the Field Service. He was thrilled to be able to sleep in the same room with Alfred Kazin. As he hoped to become a writer, he valued contacts with literary personalities and studied them in order to imitate their life styles, which he considered the first step in joining their ranks ...

... As the cold weather approached I lost my appetite and began to feel ill in the mornings. Some serious thought revealed to me that I was probably pregnant this time. I wrote the bad news to Bob and asked him what I should do. He sent some Ergot which I took to no avail. I wrote back to tell him that it was useless, and what should I do now? He did not answer my question but instead told me of his approaching departure and about the parties he had attended and the interesting people he had met. I realized that I was now completely alone. I felt that I was standing on the edge of a cliff and was about to perish. I reasoned that if I really loved him I would release him to a happy life while I perished alone. So I wrote to him to break off our relationship, saying that I had lost interest in him or perhaps that I had met another man, I don't remember which.

My big fear was of Connie. I felt that she would take my baby away and put it up for adoption, that she would bully or trick me into signing it away, perhaps by withholding food from me or perhaps waiting until I was in labor to force me to sign it away. I would not be able to resist her will, for I never had. From my own experience adoption could be the act of handing your child over to misery ...

I joined a car full of girls, probably led by the Quakers, who were in the habit of going weekly to a nearby Army hospital for shell-shocked or otherwise mentally deranged soldiers to cheer them up. Perhaps the thing behind these visits was that the sight of pretty girls would make the patients want to get better in a hurry and back out into the world. I figured I might as well go once, it would make a change. We wandered about in a huge crafts room where disconsolate men made baskets, or model airplanes or painted by numbers. We walked about and praised their productions to our mutual embarrassment. Then we attended a picnic in a gravel bed and ate hot dogs while a desperate young woman from Activities ran up and down the rows of men sitting in the gravel trying to stir up enthusiasm and happiness. We girls felt that it was our duty to flirt, which we did half-heartedly, and got practically no response. You could see that the men were sick to death of being encouraged by Activities and the car full of young ladies.

One young man really enjoyed flirting and immediately asked me for a date. It seemed that those soldiers who were in good enough condition to receive visitors were also allowed out on passes. His name was Eddie B. D. and he came from Oklahoma. He was handsome and cheerful, aged twenty-two and not very tall so that he was not intimidating. He told me he was not really insane but that he had been badly wounded in Italy and while still convalescent, one of his officers had spoken rudely to him and he had lost his temper and tried to kill him. The Army had had the choice of shooting him or of sending him to a hospital as a mental case. They had chosen the latter in light of his citations and decorations. He was considered pretty well cured and was due to be sent home soon. He showed me his scar and his ribbons.

He had hired a car and a driver for our date, and while we went to restaurants and while I showed him around the college the driver sat patiently outside for hours with nothing to eat. I took Eddie out onto the porch to admire the view, and after looking around to see if anyone was watching he tried to rape me while I slapped and kicked him, a silent and angry battle. This was followed by a profuse apology and a promise not to do it again, he had not known that I was a "nice" girl. He was so abject that I did not send him home at once, and promised to drive around with him the next day, now that he had learned to behave.

Aside from the fact that we were attracted to each other, we had neither tastes nor opinions in common. Also I could not understand his speech very well, he stretched my name out to three syllables, "Ay-ee-an" ...

When he finally did manoeuvre me into a room with a bed in it, I said to myself, "What the heck, I'm already ruined, pregnant and unattached. Why not enjoy myself?" Afterwards, to my surprise he proposed marriage to me at once. A light bulb suddenly went off in my head: a way out, a home for my baby! I knew it was a dirty trick to play on anyone, especially someone who trusted me, also that I probably would not be able to fool him into thinking he was the baby's father and that he would be very angry, but that it was a question of choosing between my baby's and my life, and his happiness and my conscience. But even if he became angry enough to kill me, I would be no worse off than I was now. Even if he divorced me in disgrace, I was sure that the law would not require me to return once more to Connie.

I accepted his offer at once, though I could see that he was already sorry he had made it. But a few kisses cheered him up and we started making plans. He told me about his family and his prospects and I told him about myself. "You poor little girl," he said. He could not marry without permission from the Army but would set about getting it the next day.

Early the following morning an Army car arrived for me and I was ordered to get in; I felt that I was under arrest. At the hospital I was marched from office to office, from psychologist to psychiatrist while efforts were made to convince me that I should not marry him. Once I saw Eddie in the corridor, for he too was being led from office to office. They tried everything: I was accused of being publicity mad, stupid, sex-crazed and so forth. The psychiatrist tried to frighten me: Eddie was a dangerous maniac. "In what way?" I asked. "His medical history is secret. We cannot discuss it with people who are not members of his family." They finally suggested that I settle for an engagement and a large diamond which could be bought cheaply at the PX. Then I was driven home.

Two mornings later the car was there waiting for me again. This time I was taken to the Red Cross. They had gotten hold of Connie and she had moved into furious action. By chance she had a new secretary who was a cousin of President Roosevelt. This young lady, fresh out of college and no doubt as overwhelmed by her as I was, had busily pulled strings and I learned that Eddie was to be transferred to a camp in Florida that very day, which was well beyond my reach. I was allowed to ride with him to the railroad station in the back of a truck with a group of other soldiers also being transferred. We promised to write and as soon as he was released from the army he would either come to get me or I could go to meet him at his father's house.

So there I was, alone and hopeless again ...

Connie's inexperience prevented her from discovering symptoms of pregnancy, but the sight of me wiggling in my chair were excellent symptoms of something else, and she told me that I would probably have to go somewhere for "help."

This bit of news galvanized me. If she succeeded in packing me off to some sort of mental hospital and of having me declared incompetent, which she could easily do with all the "evidence" she had collected over the years, she would not only get her hands on my baby, she would get them on me too, a sort of perpetual guardian, managing my life, my money and my house for the entire future instead of only for the next two years before I would reach my majority. I must flee to some place from which she could not drag me back. The only person I could think of was Mrs Bondy. She did not consider me insane, at worst I was a pest, and her word as an M.D. and a psychiatrist would be good against Connie's.

I was kindly welcomed at the school, which had moved from Manchester to Lennox, Massachusetts, that fall. There were no students there as it was still vacation. Mrs Bondy was clattering around as usual as fast as she could move and put me into Didi's room and left me to my own devices. The next day I became ill and aborted spontaneously. Everyone was too busy to notice my absence and when I reappeared red-eyed and subdued I suppose they assumed that my state was the natural consequence of a college failure and a broken heart ...

One day Charlotte Symonds stopped me with a grave face. Don Mayer had been reported missing in action. I could not believe it, it must have been a mistake. He had not been reported dead, just missing. He must have just been mislaid, or gotten lost. Surely he would be found and rejoiced over. Mrs Bondy tried to reason with me but I paid no attention. Even when Don's mother appeared, to wander shakily about the building and to meet his late friends with whom he had been so happy, and to establish a memorial fund for him, I would not believe it and ran from her when she tried to approach me. When a formal vote was called for to accept the memorial I rose to my feet and told them indignantly that they had better wait until he was dead before they went around setting up memorials. No one brought the subject up to me after that for I was clearly a nut case ...

I had two offers: I could go to Detroit and teach in the Roepers' school and go to the university or I could live free of rent in Mrs Campbell's house in Chapel Hill and attend the university there. I packed up my belongings and went home to discuss it with Connie.

Connie refused to allow me to go anywhere. I had demonstrated my unfitness for college. I would now stay home and attend secretarial school in Boston where she could keep an eye on me ...

I found a letter from Eddie in our mailbox. He complained that I had not answered his last five letters and unless I replied to this one he would write no more. He said he was ready to marry me as soon as I arrived on his doorstep. I thought he was lying about writing to me for I had received no letters all summer. I guessed that he had chosen this method of breaking off with me, so I did not write back to him. It was only by chance that I had been standing at the door when the mailman arrived for it was always Connie who took in the letters. It never occurred to me that she might have been taking mine. That was the end of my contact with Eddie ...

My typing was getting better. I was allowed to hire myself out to various authors who came to the school for cheap help. One had settled herself into an office next door for the sake of convenience. She was Olive Higgins Prouty, a very popular writer who specialized in novels of high life, written in a very low style. She dictated several pages to me which I took in shorthand, only wincing a little bit when she used incorrect grammar. When I typed the pages up I corrected the errors like "lay" for "lie" and misuse of the subjunctive. She was in a towering rage when she saw what I had done; I thought she might hit me. She stamped around and fired me on the spot. I told her aggrievedly that she should have been grateful ...

It was a joyous reunion at school also; students came from all directions. Mrs Bondy lent me her one evening gown as my costume. During the play Herbie had to kiss me and my legs turned at once to jelly and he had to hold me up. I was so embarrassed and apologetic. Someone complimented me on my skilful acting! How I hated myself for my "round heels." I avoided Herbie in a kind of terror that he had seen my weakness. We all crammed together into a car and I found myself next to Hugo. It was the most wonderful feeling, like coming home; I nearly cried. But he withdrew himself from me as far as he could and I felt myself despised, it hurt in my chest and I knew I was despicable. No matter how I combed my hair, that scarlet "A" was on my forehead for all to see. I could never marry.

I went home to a black future. The feeling of hopelessness would not lift, I had the feeling that I had never before experienced such depression ...

My twentieth birthday came. Instead of a letter from Eddie I got a postcard from Bob, calling me rude names and saying that he would always hate me. I got hold of the card and destroyed it before Connie saw it. I suppose that it was Bob's way of letting me know that he had returned safely from the war. Bobbie Maybank telephoned and told me that she had no date for New Year's Eve, and wouldn't I come to Radcliffe and spend it with her. There I found Jane Montgomery also. I was happy to see them, happy to be at Radcliffe. Bobbie took me to the Oxford Inn to celebrate, but no sooner had we settled down than Bob appeared, looking dashing in his English army uniform and with a black patch on his eye. It had all been a plot. Bobbie went to join her date who had been lying in wait and Bob rushed over and hugged me with great self-confidence. After that I did not feel that Bobbie was my friend any more, for she had fallen prey to Bob's fine talk.

He was much improved in appearance, for his self-confidence had increased while mine had shrunk. I felt a little dismay at the thought of renewing the relationship but I was quickly overwhelmed and later when I had collected my wits a little I decided that anything was welcome that got me out of the drab life awaiting me, epitomized at present by daily trips to Boston in a slow, evil-smelling train, with typing drudgery at the end of them. At least I would have an ally in my struggle against Connie's attempts to train me into the kind of rut she thought I deserved ...

Bob had been accepted back into Harvard and his mother had moved down from Maine and taken an apartment on Sparks Street so that he could live at home. She was a school nurse in Melrose, and Helen, Bob's sister, who was in the middle of getting a divorce, worked at various sales jobs in Cambridge and Boston. Her little son, Sandy, was dropped off in day-care. Bob's mother had a terrible time with her fledglings. Helen was tearful and prone to fall in love, despite her mother's ineffectual scoldings. Bob constantly demanded money, which he characterized as "loans," for he could not go without drinking. Both women were very friendly to me, Helen out of good-heartedness, while her mother regarded me as being "good" for her son. He was such a terrible strain on her finances and probably Helen's too, that neither one could help hoping that I would take over the burden of his education and maintenance. When Bob's uncle Hap and his wife came to meet me, Helen reported that they had nothing to say about me as a person but that his aunt had said, "I'm so glad Bob is marrying money" ...

Helen was delightful company but she was a master of broken promises, which she scattered around her like fairy dust, graciously accepting gratitude in advance of performance. She was the only person who really understood Bob. Whereas I humbly accepted everything he said as coming from his heart, she used to snap at him and say, "Don't rationalize!" I would tremble at her temerity. She would also stand up for me when he was especially unreasonable and demanding.

Bob's mother was also a little afraid of him. When he drunkenly smashed up her car and she could not afford a new one, she meekly took another job in Boston which she could reach by subway and found other day-care for Sandy. Bob was always soft voiced and polite except when he was drinking. Then he would start fights with anyone. He got many bruises and bloody noses. If there was no one else to irritate him he would start on me, no matter how I would back down to avoid confrontation. And occasionally I would find my own nose bloodied. One evening he worked himself up into such a rage that he knocked me down in the street right in front of a policeman. The policeman held him while he wept in baffled rage and self-pity. The policeman asked me if I knew him. The temptation to say no was almost over-powering; I would then have the pleasure of watching him walk off in handcuffs. But the repercussions later would have been too terrible. I did not have the courage. Bob began to wail that I had been unfaithful to him during the war and the policeman took his side and joined him in scolding me. Bob led me off triumphantly with a handkerchief to my nose. When he was sober Bob entreated forgiveness and promised good behavior in the future. I believed him, but not really enough so that I could relax when he drank. As for myself, I drank nothing at all now. It both saved money and kept me alert for emergencies ...

Bob was pleased that I had quit my job for it meant that we would have more time together. Another eight months had to go by before I was of age and could marry him. I did not see much of Connie anymore for I would spend several days a week in Cambridge sleeping over at his mother's. I tried off and on to find work, but after Bob had failed to stop at a stop sign while in a temper, and crashed into another car, I found myself with a sprained finger and unable to type. To my surprise the insurance company gave me seventy-five dollars without my even asking for it, which replaced my previous earnings. Helen, and Bob's mother came to meet Connie, and although Connie liked Helen, she looked down on his mother, whom she did not like at all.

We often had his mother's apartment to ourselves in the daytime and made the most of it. Bob's friends came to visit us there, we even had a party there. Alison Lurie and Anne Hirschon were there frequently. Even though we were engaged, Bob was still playing the field though I did not suspect it. One day Alison admired my necklace of silver balls. Later Bob took it gently from my neck as we were preparing to go to bed together. But afterwards I could not find it though I searched the room thoroughly, and even the neighboring rooms. Weeks later I saw it around Alison's neck. But such was my trust in Bob that I congratulated her on being able to find a necklace just like mine. I lamented that mine was lost and told her how much it had meant to me because it was my mother's. I think she must have been a rather heartless person not to have forced Bob to return it to me on the sly ...

Bob was still wearing a "uniform" but it was no longer from the British army. It became a permanent dress with him for many years. Grey pants, blue chambray shirt, a black beret, and a black patch on one eye. I made him some rakish pirate patches which suited him well. He also grew a rather scanty beard. What with scrapes on his face, unwashed hair and a drunken lurch, he looked pretty terrible, but he felt that he looked artistic and it was important to him not to look ordinary. One day in the subway a woman gave me fifty cents and whispered, "Give your brother a treat." We bought a sandwich and shared it ...

We planned to marry two days after my birthday. I told Connie we were only going before a Justice of the Peace. She pleaded with me to put it off. She said that people would think that I was running away from her as soon as I could and that this would damage her reputation. And because there was no real wedding it would look as though she didn't care. She began to cry, which I had never seen her do before, as she pleaded for her reputation. When I was firm she asked to come to our wedding to avoid gossip. Bob had insisted that she not be invited, not even told about it, but I was so moved by her tears that I agreed to let her come.

She spread the word at once. Some of the neighbors rushed over with hastily bought wedding presents and Connie bought me a nightgown and peignoir set. The next day she drove me into Cambridge for my wedding. I wore a black suit and not flowers (Bob's choice) and we woke Bob up from a terrible hangover, for he had been celebrating furiously with his friends the night before. He begged to be let off as he felt so terrible, but his best man, Buddy Berlin, and I dragged him out of bed. It was a dismal wedding, having nothing in common with the sweet laciness of the Bride magazine I had been reading. Connie glared, indignant at being characterized as bridesmaid, Bob's mother wept sentimentally, Bob was ill, Buddy thought it was funny, and I stood at attention and listened carefully. We had lunch afterwards in a bar as guests of Buddy Berlin. Then we set off to New York for our honeymoon. It was my first frightening trip in an airplane; the tickets were the gift of a friend of Bob's from the Field Service, who was now a travel agent. The plane trip made at least as much impression on me as had the wedding. At last I was entering the real world of adventure ...

The next thing we did was to go to New Hampshire with a great deal of expensive new equipment, to ski. It was exciting to move into a ski lodge and to fly up the side of the mountain on a lift that dangled you into the air. At the top Bob said goodbye and zipped off into the woods. I set off slowly on a treacherous combination of unpacked snow and patches of ice ... I would have to snow-plow down the entire huge mountain. I started slowly out. A few other skiers passed me at speed and Bob went by several times and waved happily.

When it was beginning to get dark the ski patrol came to rescue me. They worked in teams. One person would stand with me at the top of a slope and show me the safest route to descend, while the other braced himself at the bottom to catch me. There another team would come by and take over. Bob came by again and stopped to gaze. I believe he came in for some criticism. Though we had planned to stay for a few days, we went back to Cambridge the next morning.

I think Bob had miscalculated; he may have believed me to be richer than I was and had expected to move into a much higher sphere than he was accustomed to. The $500 that Connie had handed me was nearly gone (in those days it was an enormous amount), and he spent the rest of it on several large reproductions of Picasso paintings, precisely the ones on display in the better heeled dormitories and apartments he had penetrated ...

We moved into the Hotel Brunswick in Boston, a Harvard dormitory for married students, for the college was flooded with returning veterans and there was no place in Cambridge to keep them ...

We went to pay Connie a visit, and while there had a row of horrific proportions. I did not know that Connie had it in her to hurl insults. They flew back and forth over my head while I cringed and wept and pleaded. Finally Bob had her cornered. "You'll have to choose between him or me!" she shrieked. I went home with him desolate, for all my bridges were burned and I was already pregnant. Thus I lost the only person who could have advised or defended me ...

Bob sent me to see Connie at her office and ordered me to give her the choice of either paying rent or vacating, for my $150 a month income would not cover his tuition as well as our living expenses. If she would not pay we would need to sell the house. She stonily refused and I offered her, in a last attempt at reconciliation and against Bob's orders, a year in which to find another place. She refused this also and the next day she moved ... I sold the house and divided the furniture with Connie, giving her everything she wanted, avoiding the slightest disagreement ...

We now had money to burn. I was afraid to spend any of it, but Bob was not. His tastes were expensive. He had a suit made for him by a tailor in Harvard Square, and we bought an over-priced car. On the advice of Mr Freeman, we invested the remainder in Government bonds, which Bob carried around in his pocket to show to people. One tipsy evening the bundle fell out of his pocket; easy come easy go. A week later two toughs visited us at the hotel. They had found the bonds and being unable to cash them demanded a reward. We were quite afraid of them and I wrote them a check for $40 to make them go away ...

We drove to Provincetown to visit a new acquaintance, William Slater Brown. He was to become my friend too and one of the few influences for good in our lives for the next few years. Slater was one who clung to the fringes of literary fame. He had appeared as a character named "B" in e e cummings' book *The Enormous Room*. From then on he tottered often drunkenly around the literary world dining out on his experience. I think his only real output was a children's book named *Ethan Allen and the Green Mountain Boys* which I pat lovingly today when I pass it in our town library ...

Bob rented us a good-sized house in North Truro, the town next to Provincetown, for the summer. It was very expensive but we would need all those rooms for his many friends who had been invited to visit us. He would spend the week at Harvard finishing up his last semester and come to the Cape on weekends and perhaps one day midweek on the Provincetown steamer ... Bob would arrive with his friends and they would drink and play jazz on the huge record player put together for him by Marvin Minsky, the electronic whiz-kid brother of Charlotte Minsky, the silent, haughty, well-dressed girlfriend of Race Newton. She looked at me when she came to visit as though I were something dirty. Anne Hirschon was much more friendly and mixed me five old fashioneds in a row which I took as an anaesthetic in preparation for Bob's piercing my ears, until one of the soberer visitors stopped me. One ear was pierced properly but the other one was off at an angle which spoiled the effect somewhat. On one of the better days everyone had gone out early and I woke, not to the sound of jazz but of Beethoven. Buddy and Race were there alone and they had decided to wake me pleasantly. I cried a little with relief as the sound floated up the stairs and I had a soft spot in my heart for the two of them from then on for they were the only ones in our circle who saw me as the tired person who had been cooking and cleaning up for them ...

Among the curious people Slater introduced us to was a woman named Polly Boyden and her daughter Tut, and Tut's husband, John Jordan. They were a nest of Communists. Polly had been a Stalinist and had brought up her children in the faith, sending them off to training schools and camps. She had a little sign in her yard calling it the Garden of Culture and Rest. But then she had made a long-dreamed-of trip to Russia and had been shocked by what she had found, producing during her mental struggles a book called *The Pink Egg*, and had emerged a Trotskyite. Meanwhile Tut had married John Jordan, a trained *agent provocateur* for the Stalinists. They all lived crossly together in the Garden of Culture and Rest. Through their doors passed a steady stream of Russians; some were ruined nobles, some not. All had accents. John was a hard worker, it fell on him to organize the Progressive Party on Cape Cod. What a motley crew he assembled in his "Henry Wallace for President" campaign. He successfully mingled the artist colony with the Portuguese fishermen, none of whom had any suspicions of his foreign connections. At one meeting a lady said that she had heard a rumor that the Progressive Party was full of Communists. John put his hand on his heart and with his eyes rolled up to avoid laughing, asked rhetorically if anyone saw any Communists there. They all looked around fearfully but only saw their neighbors. It was still so soon after the war that it was illegal to be a Communist. I do not know why he was so open with Bob and me, perhaps he hoped to recruit us. I was given the task of flirting with a selectman who was eyeing me, but I refused. But we did get on an odd sort of mailing list; for years we received invitations to attend training camps for "concerned radicals" ...

Bob had been skipping classes, and the moment came when he knew he would not pass his summer courses, and therefore not graduate that year. He said he did not wish to graduate, that if he did he would have to get a job. But that if he did not graduate he would be permanently unemployable and therefore would never have to go to work. He could then become a dedicated writer without danger of a steady job. Whereas if he had a degree and were employable the temptation to work would be too strong for him to resist if we were ever in need. Thus he would save himself from temptation forever. I had to have it explained several times and even then I feebly disagreed. But his dedication to his art was too strong so I accompanied him to Cambridge where he formally withdrew from the university.

John Jordan was not only astute at handling a political crowd but could also handle naive young people. He convinced us that he would invest $5,000 for us in local real estate, as we had decided to live on the cape. We meekly passed the money to him without security except for a confusedly worded note. Two years later he returned $500 to us but that was the last we heard from him. He spent the money on a truck for peddling fish and opened a small restaurant in the garage underneath his apartment.

We rented a house for the winter from a summer resident. Like many foolish newly weds we had bought a large dog as soon as we had a place to keep it. Our North Truro landlady had been outraged by our unhousebroken Great Dane puppy who chewed on the wallpaper when she had nothing better to do. This justifiably peevish lady who had spent the summer in the next door garage where she could see and hear our streams of noisy guests, had daily cleaned up the puppy's mess from her driveway with a dust pan. In our newly rented house which was at the end of a dirt road near the sea, we felt much more at ease and could have all the pets we wanted. The mice were plentiful, and I used to sit on the kitchen floor and invite the baby mice out of their holes to climb on me and eat titbits while their more sophisticated mothers screamed and chattered at them from the doorway. I have always loved baby mice since for their beautiful translucent pink ears and their trust.

Bob stopped drinking in honor of my baby's impending birth, and being fired up by the crusading spirit shown by newly reformed drunks, invited Slater Brown to stay with us while he dried out also. He had already left Esther, probably to her relief, and was wandering about living from friend to friend. He was a good house guest, but when I discovered he had drunk a pint bottle of vanilla, I became really worried about him.

One evening he disappeared, and feeling that he might be at Polly's house I drove over to investigate. The door was unlocked and the lights were on, but no one was home. So I strolled in to look for him. When I reached the kitchen the back door was open. It was black outside and I thought Slater might be lying in the woods freezing to death, so I walked out into the dark looking for him. Instead of his huddled body I found a path under my feet. Nothing could be seen in the dark but I walked easily and quickly down the path following the direction of my feet. After some twists and turns I stopped, put out my hand and found a door knob. I twisted it, opened the door and crossed a room and put out my hand again and found it resting on Slater's face.

"I've come to take you home," I said matter of factly, and without a word he got up and followed me. Later he said that he had been terribly frightened by my powers of divination and he treated me with extraordinary respect from that day on …

Despite our efforts to keep Slater with us and off the bottle, he slipped away from us again and a few weeks later he wrote to us from Boston that he was being held prisoner there by an insane artist who was painting his portrait and who would not let him go until the picture was finished. He had also just finished a session in a hospital for alcoholics and he was now under the iron thumb of Alcoholics Anonymous as well as under that of the artist, and was a reformed man. We drove to Boston to see if he was all right and not raving. First we found the Alcoholics Anonymous headquarters on Beacon Hill where they were very cooperative and directed us to a nearby doorway. Upstairs we found a very reduced Slater huddled in an armchair facing a life-sized portrait of himself. It was an excellent likeness though he looked even more furtive in the picture and downright frightened. The owner of the apartment bounced out of an inner room, a large extroverted man with black bushy hair and beard, dressed in what we learned was his only costume, grubby red swimming trunks. But who could resist his friendliness and enthusiasm? We returned again and again to visit this wonderful artist and raconteur, and listen to his stories, some of which were almost unbelievable. Meanwhile, Slater, no longer the center of his attention, quietly slipped away.

Bob was bored and had started drinking and complaining again. One evening he became very drunk at [Jordans] and suddenly decided that his life depended on his driving to New York City that night in order to see his friends and enjoy some excitement. Of course I did not want him to go in that condition so I whispered to John that the car frequently would not start when the points were damp and would he please sneak out and pour a glass of water over them. Instead he let some air out of one of the tires and the car started all right and Bob and Lina, the dog, tore off into the night. The Jordans drove me home with the baby and the next day about noon a taxi pulled up with Bob and Lina in it. About fifty miles down the road the tire had blown and the car had been nearly destroyed. I never told him what John had done and sometimes I wonder if he had been well aware of the damage that must ensue and had been happy to think that the man who knew so many secrets as an *agent provocateur* might be taken out of the way.

As spring approached our lease ran out and it was time to get our own home before all our money had dwindled away. Bob's sister's latest boyfriend was Bill Gordon, who owned a quaint little house near Littleton, New Hampshire, that he was anxious to sell. He wanted $10,000 for it which was more than we had left, so we gave him $5,000, planning to borrow the rest from the Littleton bank on a mortgage, and receiving the usual scrambled receipt from Bill for the money ...

We spent the first few months living in the barn, for the house was not fit to live in. We spent all our remaining money on a new roof, new sills, and a heating system, and the bank refused to handle the mortgage as they said the house was not worth $5,000. Bill said he would take the mortgage himself but never got around to it. I do not think he meant to cheat us for he was nearly as foolish as we were. I was twenty-two years old by now.

The house was a gray clapboarded house, devoid of paint. There was a small barn and some sheds, one of which contained the remains of a blacksmith's shop. All the door latches were either very old, or new and of unusual iron work. Some earlier owners had built a large sunken garden, now almost ruined, behind the house and had added a tiny summer house from which they dispensed refreshments to tourists and people who came to swim in the beautiful rock pool in the nearby river. These had been artistic people who, like so many others of their kind, had come to start a little Utopia in the north woods and had been driven out by poor planning and hunger.

I set to work with my paint brush and had the upstairs bedrooms in good order. But carpentry was beyond me, and I had not done a very good job in the joints of the sheetrock which the hired carpenter had left for us to finish. Bob was very interested in the lawn, which he mowed with great devotion with a hand mower, about an acre of it. He also built pens for a horde of poultry. In his childhood he had belonged to a fancy pigeon and poultry club. Now that he had ample housing for them, he bought a quantity of chicks and pigeons in fancy breeds by mail order. They were his major interest while we lived there. He built exercise pens and flyways everywhere and tended the birds lovingly. He bought a goat who had kids and he milked her and cut her hay with a scythe. We acquired a cat and her kittens. Bob gave up drinking during this period

and became very healthy with all the outdoor work which included sawing and chopping wood to feed the fireplace when we were too low on
money to afford to buy oil …

He found an elderly chicken breeder in Hanover, New Hampshire,
whom we would visit in our ancient International pickup truck (we had
exchanged the repaired car for it), and we would usually return home
with boxes of new chickens in the back. I too was fascinated by their
shapes and colours and we both memorized the standard of perfection for
all breeds. Many of these birds were delicate and had to be brought into
the kitchen on very cold nights to protect their combs from freezing, for
we had selected an especially cold spot in the state where the temperature
regularly reached forty below. But Bob never shirked the job of carrying
them indoors in cardboard boxes.

The chicken breeder's name was Ira Grant. He was tiny and wizened
and lived with his tiny wife in the midst of countless little sheds. All his
poultry loved him and would rush up to be admired and petted. He had a
wonderful infectious little chuckle, and he charmed me as well as the
birds. He attended many poultry shows and was constantly training his
pets to strike show poses. One day we came upon him training a baby
chick so young that it had only a half dozen feathers, but the feathers
were marked in the way he wanted them. The chick grew up to be a monster of over-confidence and vanity as well as best of show at a major event.
It crowed on command. He constantly talked to the birds. One day we
found him shutting up his ducks for the evening. "Go to bed!" he
shouted and flapped his wings. With gabbles and complaints they rushed
across the yard into their house and he slammed the door on them. He
was very angry; they had been naughty all day. The geese would beg to be
picked up and carried and he had an elderly sow whom he could not bring
himself to butcher.

Ira made his living as a house painter, taking it seriously enough to
paint the four sides of a house in slightly different hues so that they
would all appear the same under their different conditions of light. He
painted pictures with his leftover paints. He made a dream landscape of
his childhood home and Dartmouth College bought it to hang in their
library for the huge sum of $400. He set to work immediately on four
copies of it to give to his children so that they could each own a painting worth $400. He made delicate landscapes and did alarming things to
them. Through a field of flowers ran a rusty railroad track; on a lovely
mountain view he pasted two gentlemen and a tent which he had cut
from a magazine so that they too could enjoy the view. One interior was
decorated by a dog of unpleasant aspect with lolling mouth and crossed
eyes. The title was written in large letters across the bottom "Our Dog

J ..." I told him that the dog looked awful, sick in fact. "I know, he died the next day," he said.

Ira also had other mysterious powers. He could dowse for water; a talent for which I suspiciously tested him when he visited our house. He found our water pipe immediately though there was no sign of it above ground. He made our new baby Tom wiggle and giggle by just looking at him, long before he was old enough to respond to his own mother. Once we bought a trio of Silkies through the mail, a feeble breed with fluff instead of feathers and dark blue skin. The male died almost at once though we kept him in the house, and later that day Ira Grant arrived in his strange old car and handed me a box with another Silkie rooster in it. He had felt that I had needed one and by chance a stranger had stopped at his house that day and given him three chickens, this one among them ...

I had two more babies while we lived in New Hampshire. The first one was born prematurely and died within a few days. I think this accident was due to my having driven the truck over a plowed field while Bob threw manure off the back of it for the vegetable garden. I had told him that I thought it would be dangerous but he insisted. I thought he was responsible for the death of my baby and I held that resentment permanently in my heart, though of course I said nothing about it. Like most bereaved mothers I cried almost continually for weeks. It seemed that I would grieve permanently and have nothing else on my mind, and that rather frightened me. But I came out of it suddenly one day when I helped our neighbors, the Ainsworths, catch their pig. I could not help but laugh ... They were a wood-cutting family. Their old Uncle Cad told me that the men in the family had always been choppers and mowers. There were three brothers, Kenneth, Howard, and Oola. Kenneth's wife, Alice, was my special friend and I used to walk over there with David and sometimes the two young geese to seek her company almost daily. In return her two children visited us almost daily. I never confided my troubles to her but she could see them and was sympathetic. They lived very poorly and took great care with their possessions, especially tools. They carved their own axes and saws, the latter having to be carved all in one day to avoid "checking" and then varnished and painted with a thin green stripe, a tradition in the family. Their deceased father's saw hung in an honorable position over the stove, and there it would remain forever. The saw blades were filed out of a smooth piece of steel. They gave us endless lectures on the correct management of the saw and the scythe ... They were part Indian.

... Bob stayed mostly at home while I did the shopping once a week either in Littleton, over the hills to the south, or Lisbon, over the hills to the north. I would take David with me and sometimes stop at a farm where I had met the people at least once before and stay to chat and make friends.

They were always glad to see me and sometimes gave us cookies and milk. It was the same with the storekeepers; they were always friendly and ready to talk. Thus I found I had friends spotted up and down the valley. My doctor and dentist lived in Lisbon and were very good to me, the doctor giving me reduced rates and the dentist also; which was just as well as I had to have all my back teeth pulled, a penalty for motherhood and malnutrition …

Buddy Berlin had been arrested when a large supply of marijuana was found in his closet, but his father, a very successful doctor, got him out of it by sending his foolish son to work on a farm for the summer. This was supposed to reform him. He spent the summer with us but no work was done. He was good company of course, and my life with Bob was unusually peaceful as he was more interested in Buddy than me. Buddy brought a supply of marijuana with him and Bob started several pots with the seeds. They spent the summer smoking it, swimming in the pool, and discussing the politics of literary publishing.

Another year Bob Leed came. He was a Mennonite from Lititz, Pennsylvania. His parents, who owned a butcher shop, unwisely sent him to Harvard. There he fell in love with a Jewish girl named Edith and brought her to visit us. He had to keep her hidden from his family. She was very sad for she had a wasting disease from which her sister had already died. He spent the whole summer with us. At one point we found ourselves totally out of money, and Bob Leed suggested that he and Bob find work. Bob Leed found work cutting wood by the cord but Bob indignantly refused to soil his hands with labor. Until that moment I had believed that in an emergency he would set to and give what help he could. "I never thought you would actually refuse," I said reproachfully. But that was as far as I got. He flew into such a rage that even Bob Leed was frightened and we both apologized for daring to try to steal away the freedom of a creative artist. Earlier I had investigated work for myself in Littleton, but when Bob had heard of it he made me stop, as he refused to have the care of David during my absence. He never took care of the children, considering it "woman's work" though he had no reluctance in having me do fully half of the heavy "men's" work like sawing and carrying fire wood …

Connie came once to visit and was very polite to Bob, and gave him little presents that would please him, made much of David and knitted him sweaters. Bob's mother came up for Thanksgiving and criticized us for having a chicken instead of a turkey (which we could not afford). Helen came bringing her new son, Alec. She was now married to Dick Axt but had continued her practice of falling in love with new men …

Seymour Lawrence was another friend who came. He brought his girlfriend Merloyd Luddington with him with the intention of seducing her.

Which he did, to my shame, for I had written a letter to Mrs Luddington as a chaperone for she had a proper old-fashioned family. I never liked Seymour, though he did marry Merloyd whose family had a great deal of money. She was a sweet girl but when I met them later in Spain she had become rather hard and sharp like him.

Our best visitor was Slater Brown. He stayed with us for several weeks and I felt comforted by his presence. He had no money to pay his way but he built me a kitchen out of scraps of lumber from the barn. There were shelves for dishes and cabinets under the sink. He made a milking plat-form for the goat and kept us both laughing with his stories. No one drank any alcohol. I would have been almost happy if there had not al-ways been the demon of hunger hanging over us ...

We had visits from two literary types that Bob had found. One was Cid Corman who had a literary magazine; he promised to publish Bob. The others were Denise Levertov and her husband, Mitch Goodman. They lived very uncomfortably in New York with their little boy. Denny was the first published poet Bob had found, as well as an authentic expatriate and world traveller. They were Communists of some sort and Denise was very loud and radical, though Mitch was the silent type. Bob was dazzled; I think he was in love with Denny also, for she was beautiful in a Merle Oberon sort of way. They spent some time together discussing poetic punctuation, rewriting her poems. She put the idea in Bob's head that we could live comfortably in Europe, for our money would go farther on the favorable exchange rate ...

...We gave Lina to a nice policeman and sold my piano to a neighbor for $15 as Bob did not want to transport it into storage. All our furniture went into a rented garage and we merely abandoned the house and Bill Gordon took it back. It was hardest of all to part with Lina, I can still hear her screams of terror when we left her in the strange house. The police-man was kind to her and kind to us too for he saw the marijuana growing in pots and said nothing ...

We gave the poultry back to Ira Grant and lent him our truck until our return. The Ainsworths took my precious figurine of the Japanese actor and promised not to break it. Helen took most of our phonograph records. The hardest chore was finding documents. They had been thrown away with some rotten goose eggs. I dried and packed the marijuana leaves in a small pillow and everything we would need was wedged into a number of grandmother's trunks and various small cases. The plastic baby carrier had not yet been invented and Tommy had to be held all the time. David was three and had to walk, though he cried a great deal when he was tired. And so we set off on our adventures ...

Mitch met us in Aix with a friend's car and we travelled to the Goodmans' pleasant home where I wished above all things to lie down and recover. Neither of us was in the mood to walk the two miles to our new home with me carrying the children while Bob and Mitch pushed our luggage ahead of them on a donkey cart ...

I thought that the cottage which the Goodmans had acquired for us would be a little house in the country, but to Denny, an Englishwoman, a cottage meant a low-grade house bordering on a street and jammed between others of the same sort. Our new home had neither water nor electricity, nor even an outhouse. For the latter we were supposed to crouch over a hole not yet dug, behind two upended shutters for privacy. There were three rooms and a cave, the latter a frightening hole leading into a hill behind the house, into which I never ventured more than a few steps as the dismal light of tallow candles, our only illumination, was not enough to explain the nature of the dark bulges within. My feelings toward Denny Levertov became profound. Her being a poetess was not enough to excuse her luring us to this miserable hole ...

To a stranger, Fontrousse was a village of incredible quaintness, entirely medieval, a living painting ... There were about ten houses, or hovels in some cases, stuck together helter-skelter except for four of them that stood proudly and saggingly alone, held together not by their neighbors but by iron rods stuck through from side to side and protruding through the pink stucco. Everything was pink or white or grey, for the soil was pink and the rocks were bleached white or were blackened by smoke and age. The roofs were all pale tile and there seemed to be no sign of modern technology except a chain hanging into one of the two wells. The inhabitants wore shapeless shabby clothes in black or dismal faded colors.

The wells provided drinking water; washing water came from the canal built by the Romans to fill their baths in Aix-en-Provence. It travelled sometimes beside the village and sometimes beneath it until it reached a tall aqueduct like the ones in my old Latin schoolbook. Though Mitch had mentioned the aqueduct I did not connect it with our little canal for I was too busy drawing washing water up from it through a pump operated by a little handle. I was conveniently near the village washing stone, a huge flat rock on which I scrubbed our clothes ...

The sun was unbelievably brilliant, we found it difficult to take pictures at first as the light was so strong. I used to travel in that sun a great deal. First I had to walk to a farm about a mile away to get the milk in the early morning, then bring it home and boil it. Then I had to walk the two miles daily to Puyricard where the Goodmans lived to buy our food. The store there closed at noon so I had to hurry. The road in the hot sun was endless and my burden was complicated by having to take David with me, for he was in terror of my leaving him. Since he was only three years old, the walk back home on the treeless white road was too much for him and I usually had to carry him for the last mile. Sometimes the sun seemed to boil my brains and things looked black in front of my eyes ...

Whether it was drugs or not which accounted for the very strange experiences I had while living in Fontrousse, I was regularly bombarded there with the inexplicable. Mitch thought it was the presence of witches in that and the nearby villages. My uncle Ian said in his dry way, when I told him about it later, that the area was noted for things of that sort.

The first irregularity I noticed was the presence of lightning in our bedroom upstairs. During the frequent thunderstorms the room would fill with blue light but the thunder would be inaudible. There might be a silent implosion which stunned me a little. Also there was a rock about a foot in diameter sticking out of the high ceiling. This did not worry me, for there were rocks sticking out of walls everywhere in the village. One day I went upstairs and found this rock lying neatly on my pillow.

It was a wonder that poor baby Tom survived. He drank boiled and frequently sour milk. For solid food he ate bananas and uncooked flour paste. We all ate a lot of bread, like our neighbors, for a car came through the village daily with long loaves of bread sticking out of its windows and trunk. It was the only food we found that really tasted good. The two big cows that lived in the cave under the floor at the farm supplied our village and part of Puyricard with milk. We bought a quart and a half a day (litres of course) but most of our neighbors got by with a half pint or less. The old lady who lived across the road with her 98 year old mother regularly walked to the same farm I did and bought a quarter of a pint for her mother. They both wore long black dresses and looked rather feeble to me. One morning I wrenched her little bottle out of her hand and told her that I was going to get her milk along with mine. She protested for a while but when she realized that it was actually true she was very happy. It was the least I could do for her as we got our drinking water out of her well on the say-so of our landlord who was not a kindly man and had probably not asked her permission before renting out her well. The bucket had a hole in it which made the drawing of water a bit futile, so we bought her a shiny new stainless steel pail and a new rope to go with it. She was so delighted you would have thought it was Christmas ...

Besides walking to Puyricard we sometimes went to Aix on the bus which passed through the village twice a week or so. We had found a place there where we could take a bath, probably the remnants of an old Roman bath for the building was shaped like those in my Latin book, a courtyard with a big hole in the roof and a little pool in the middle of it and dark marble rooms all around with huge marble tubs in them. A family would rent one and all bathe at once. So we took our soap and towels. The luxury of bathing when you have been dirty in a hot climate for a whole month! There were also little patisseries in Aix which served delicious pastry which to our starving palates was Manna. We also bought stationery supplies and fancy breads at the small unfamiliar stores ...

Sometimes when I was in Puyricard buying food I would stop in to see Denny for advice or just to sit under her tree and cool off. Denny was an experienced traveller and was quite efficient at finding a comfortable place to stay. She loved travelling and sometimes she would just drop everything, leave little Nicky for Mitch to take care of and start hitch-hiking. This used to frighten Mitch very much. And even when he was allowed to go with her there was trouble. While they were in Paris she slapped a policeman, and when given the alternatives of apology or jail, she chose the latter while Mitch went pleading about with Nicky in his arms. Finally she condescended to apologize. In addition to being a lady of spirit she was beautiful. Her face had a dreamlike quality and she moved gracefully, accompanied by flowing arm movements ... She made me feel gross and uncomfortable. When we walked on the road with little Nicky and David, she would utter gentle cries of rapture, "See, the flower, Nicky, see the lovely lovely flower!" I had not nearly such an appreciation of the aesthetic.

For some reason my passport picture had come out very well, especially my hair. Denny took it into her head to have her hair done the same way. Normally her black hair flowed dramatically down her back as had mine before Bob had cut it. One day in New Hampshire he had taken offence at my hair and chopped it off in spite of my begging. It looked terrible and he tried to even it up but failed, so I had to go to the hairdresser, who did the best she could, mourning my loss with me. He didn't like her neatness so he cut some more off here and there, while I cried for mercy. However, it did grow out in a shaggy way and that was the effect Denny wanted.

She took me with her to the hairdresser in Aix and I had to sit as a model while my hair was copied onto her head. As that cloud of elf locks fell away, the true Denny was revealed. She was a bull-necked brute with bad posture and the short black hairs on the back of her neck were coarse and looked dirty. She was horrified, as was the hairdresser. As for me I was smug at the sight of her carefully nurtured persona falling off her. Vengeance was mine without my having to lift a finger. Her husband looked at her with distaste.

Mitch was a large, kindly, vague man, a bit lazy. He was writing a book about his experiences in the war, how the u.s. had done everything wrong. He had received and spent an advance on the book and was already bored with it. But Denny marched him daily into his writing room. Bob dropped in once to see him in that sacrosanct room and found him asleep. It was Denny who was the fire-eater. She was a strident Marxist, a speech maker and a demonstrator …

As my legs got stronger and stronger I bicycled greater distances, sometimes going as far as Aix, about five miles away. I also travelled into the woods beyond Fontrousse and discovered some charcoal burners and an interesting ruin of three concentric circles which I imagined into a tiny castle. I also inspected the agriculture of the area and admired the irrigation system and the immaculate condition of the fields and vegetables. The huge flat fields were divided into strips all of which seemed to have different owners. I learned later that this was the medieval plan, with the castle in the middle and serf-owned strips all around. The pitchforks were certainly medieval, being merely saplings with three naturally growing branches at the top, whittled irregularly into tines. There were no modern hoes, the ground was tilled with a "piosh," a sort of coarse pick. The only things that looked at all modern were the motor vehicles and the electric wires, which were strung from cement pylons rather than telephone poles and travelled across country rather than spoiling the looks of the little back roads as they do in America …

It was Ashley who saved us. I am not sure where we had met. We were all sitting in some smoky room while Bob held forth on modern literature when Ashley slipped in. He was quite beautiful, his skin was a delicate light brown and his eyes were so sharp that I could not bear to look at them. But then he smiled as if he gave me permission to look at him, and we were friends. He was always there when we needed help … Ashley was an artist living in France in order to find himself. He had an M.A. in philosophy, but he was quite humble and spent a good deal of his time doing good deeds …

Ezra Pound … gave [Bob] the name of a fellow sufferer in Germany, Rainer Gerhardt. Bob set off to visit him in Freiburg, taking Ashley with him to do the translating, and found Rainer a young man determined to mold German literature into his own image. He felt himself to be the sole survivor of the German defeat and was publishing a series of books which none of us could read because of the language barrier. Rainer had a wife and two children, but he neglected them, and from the pictures I saw they were starving. Rainer on the other hand looked rather sleek. He returned Bob's visit, though we could not offer him much in the way of accomodations. We gave him the mattress from David's bed and David slept on the spring with all our winter clothes under him. These had formerly been the stuffing in Tommy's trunk and he looked very sad lying at the bottom of it. Rainer returned to Germany carrying a bag of oranges and a freshly plucked duck we had bought from one of our neighbors. But the duck began to smell before he reached home and he had to throw it away. Which I do not believe. I think he was a poet, and did not wish to be seen carrying a freshly plucked duck ...

Buddy Berlin, who had recently married Mary Ann Bottomly whom I had known only for her beautiful dresses and butterfly graces, informed us that they were coming to visit. Buddy, like Bob, had married a rich woman but his was much richer. They were on an extended wedding trip. I rode to Aix to greet them at the train. What a disappointment to find they were not there! I rode home to find them waiting, for they had taken a taxi, the last word in luxury. They had just come from Algiers where they had bought a great deal of the best hemp and gave some of it to us. They observed that we were fools to live so uncomfortably. Buddy was never one to mince words, this was one of the qualities I liked so much about him. Sometimes his comments were too abrasive to absorb, however. A year or so earlier Bob had seduced Buddy's girlfriend, quite openly, thus making it impossible for them to get together again. Buddy's comment was that the whole affair was disgusting and that the most disgusting part of it was that Bob had come back to me and apologized and I had accepted this and forgiven him. He was quite right; a better time for a break had never arisen. On this occasion he advised us to go to Algiers and improve our lifestyle. Bob dug his feet in, he said that he intended to spend the rest of his life in Fontrousse for he was quite satisfied with his lifestyle there ...

[But] Buddy's visit had filled Bob with a desire for better things. He was not satisfied with the bicycle and was determined to buy a car. We found a 1928 or 1923 Peugeot for $200. It resembled a model T but was much smaller, having only two seats, one slightly in back of the other. It had been kept alive all these years by the clever French mechanics for it was very simple in concept and would cheerfully accept home-made parts. On one occasion a flat tire was temporarily repaired by stuffing it with tree branches. And it was so small that I once pushed it uphill to start it. It took a full two months to get the paperwork attached to it done and though Bob got a licence to drive it, I as a Canadian found that so difficult that I gave it up and drove without a licence without anybody noticing.

I found myself pregnant again. This was an extra source of anxiety to me. On the advice of some Americans in Aix I got an appointment with an expensive and fashionable obstetrician. I was worried about Bob's and my Rh incompatability which the doctor in New Hamphshire had dealt with by weekly blood tests. I tried to alert the French doctor to the problem but either my French was too bad or he had never heard of the Rhesus factor. All he did was tell me not to alarm myself, everything would be taken care of. What and how? He refused to discuss it, so I walked out in a rage. His reply was too reminiscent of the old Fontrouse ladies saying, "Il faut avoir patience" whenever I asked their advice in dealing with the bureaucracy. This left me without a doctor, but there were still many months to go and I hoped I would stumble on one.

Ashley decided that it was my turn for a vacation and it was settled that I would visit Aunt Cecelia and also spend a few days in Paris seeing the sights ...

The minute I saw René [Laubiès] I fell madly in love with him. This was quite a new experience for me. His eyes were dark and liquid, I drowned in them. His every motion was graceful, I longed to hold his hand and dance with him. When he led me around to look at his pictures, every one of them seemed a reflection of his eyes ...

After David had beaten up the little six year old town bully Girard, they became close friends and went around with their arms draped on each others' shoulders. David became the leader of the Little Rascals and would erupt from the door after breakfast shouting, "Vien le David!" and his gang would assemble. They addressed him as "le David," and he thought that was his name, just as he thought mine was "Hey Ann."

But peace was short-lived. We had trouble with the landlord. During the last war the French had passed a law prohibiting tenants from being ejected from a rented house, and they also froze the rents at pre-war levels, thus effectively transferring the ownership of the homes to the rentees. This had happened to Aunt Cecelia's apartment in Paris; she still owned it but she could not have it unless the tenants attempted to sublet it or ceased to live in it. This was the case with our house in Fontrousse. The landlord was only a tenant who had sublet it to us for a good price while he paid peppercorn rent to the local family that owned it. He came one day to inform us that he was going to move his mother in with us for a month to maintain the fiction that his family was still living there. This was obviously impossible and Bob with his usual hot temper seized him by the neck and threw him out the door. Then we waited, trembling, to see what would happen.

Next day a mild little man dressed in a uniform with enough gold braid to be an admiral, bicycled up to our door and informed me apologetically that he was the *Garde champêtre*. I asked him what that was and he said he was in charge of brawls and almond stealing. I told him about the landlord's mother and he rode away saying it was not his jurisdiction. The next day an ancient black car came swaying up the road and a very polite gentleman emerged. He was the local Comte and also the Mayor of Puyricard. He inspected our house with great dignity and then said, "It is my opinion that this house is full." Then he got back in his car and swayed away. It turned out that the landlord had spent the most danger-ous part of the war in the village and had constantly begged his neighbors for food, but when he had extra food himself had been unwilling to share. They were tickled to learn he was having real estate troubles.

We hired a lawyer when the landlord took us to court. It was a vast marble palace in Marseilles. Lawyers dressed like the cartoons of Daumier, in black cassocks with white bibs, strolled up and down the huge staircase. Our lawyer would not let us go into the courtroom but brought us the good news as we waited in the echoing hall. The judge had given the house back to its original owner and ordered us to vacate in three months, but under no circumstances were we to pay anyone any rent. I was very happy that we would have to leave, and Ashley promised to find us a better house somewhere else.

As the paperwork on the car was not yet finished, I had still to bicycle daily to Puyricard. It was the stretch of road between Troujus and Cujus that gave me all the trouble. I would put on a burst of speed at the shrine and pedal fast until I plunged through the wall of icy air at the bridge. Then I was home safe. It was in that stretch that David had caught his foot in the bicycle spokes and was unable to walk for two weeks. It was there that I ran into a fiend in the shape of a magpie. David was luckily not with me that day. I saw the black bird flopping on the road ahead of me; I knew what that meant, for I had seen a brave quail pretend to be in-jured in front of a truck in New Hampshire. It meant that there were ba-bies nearby and the mother was trying to draw a predator away from them. I skidded to a stop, taking a little flesh from my leg as I tipped onto the stones, and looked for the babies. The mother was gone and so were they. I rode on. Suddenly she was there again just in front of my wheel and I stopped to save her and skinned myself on the palms of my hands this time.

The next time that she appeared in front of my wheel, I knew that she could not possibly be real. I was very frightened. I had the choice of either falling off my bicycle again and perhaps being seriously hurt or of treating the horrible illusion as it deserved. I put on a burst of speed and rode right through it. Instead of the magpie disappearing as it had before, it flew up into my face, which would have been impossible for a real magpie as it could not have been acrobatic enough to have circled over my wheel and arrived at my face so quickly. I stopped and stood in the road, and shortly saw two magpies fly across the road laughing disagreeably. Magpies, like crows, can laugh. It was just the sort of thing you would expect from that stretch of road. Mitch, when applied to, was convinced it was witches, for he said the magpie was the favorite vehicle for a witch to metamorphize into. I must have offended one of the good old ladies in my village.

Most of the unearthly experiences I have had were while I was pregnant. I have thought a good deal about this. Perhaps my feminine intuition was strongest then. Perhaps I was a bit toxic and subject to hallucinations. My favorite explanation was that there were two of us in one body, both endowed with a small amount of extrasensory perception, so that we made a bigger audience. But there is one thing I am certain of: as soon as I stopped riding that enchanted mile between Cujus and Troujus, my observations became much tamer.

We were living in Van Gogh country. I had always thought that his bright colors were an expression of himself. Actually they were a true depiction of the country. The sunflowers were that bright and the chairs just that lopsided. His blue cart stood for several days in a field near Cujus. One of his most famous pictures was of a group of magpies in a field, just pecking around. He was planning to shoot them, but instead he shot himself. A man who had reason to think that he was not quite sane might have lost all self-confidence if his magpies had gotten up to the same antics mine had. Perhaps one of those disagreeable witch-like women he painted did not like her portrait. I digress …

We also met quite a few international Americans, none of them memorable, except for Elga Lippman. We were in a large artistic group with everybody impressing everybody else by name dropping, knowledge of the latest styles, and general one-upmanship. Bob was quite good at this but I was terrible. Elga strolled in, beautifully dressed, and asked in her hoarse, drawling tones why no one was talking about anything interesting, like the meaning of things. That put a stop to all talk but it caught up again while I told Elga that I would be happy to talk about anything she wanted. But then I found that she was very deaf and she was so serious because every word she did manage to hear was of great importance to her. So we shouted profundities at each other. Bob told me that she was reputed to be rich, and being of an envious nature with yearnings toward egalitarianism, he took a dislike to her and was barely civil. So she became exclusively my friend, the first one outside the villagers that I had acquired …

When we left the village, David and I went to every house to say goodbye. We were plied with sweet white wine, and poor David was staggering and giggling by the end of the day …

The new house was such an improvement over the other one. There were occasional light bulbs in the ceilings. There was a real outhouse with a roof on it at the back of the garden. The well was right there in the kitchen so that you did not have to go out in the rain, and there were four rooms downstairs and one upstairs. There was even a fireplace in the living room. Though of course that was officially the dining room. None of the small French houses we entered had living rooms, only a stiff formal room with a table in the middle and matched chairs around the walls. Our garden had a high wall around it and a row of strawberries ready to be picked, as well as a water tank meant for irrigating the vegetable garden, for the French never grew grass but saved every inch of land for agriculture. I did my washing in the tank and sometimes stood in it to cool off. There were some large hydrangea bushes in front of the house, with little baby bushes growing under them. Our landlord, a chef from Marseilles, extracted a promise from us that we would guard these young bushes with our lives as there were some citizens of Lambesc who would steal them if possible. Since we now lived in a villa rather than a hovel we were treated with flattery by some of the shopkeepers. David and Tommy came in for some of this caressing praise too and I could see what the French authors meant who described the small shopkeeper as one of the world's abominations ...

The married daughter of the woman in Fountrousse who had tried so hard to dose me with her tisanes lived to one side of the great square before the church and I visited her frequently. Her name was Marti and her husband was a refugee from the Spanish Civil War who had settled in France to eke out a living as a hod carrier. They were very good-natured people, and David played joyfully with their young children. Madame Marti assured me that the doctor who lived next to them on the square was a good one, he had been very "douce" with her when she had her last child. So at least I had a doctor, even though he looked and acted exactly like Charles Bovary, which did not give me any confidence ...

[Martin and Janet Seymour-Smith] were a mismatched couple. Janet was a tall narrow haughty aristocratic young lady with ancestors from 1066. Her hair was very straight and almost white. Martin was short and silly and witty and drank too much. One of his grandfathers had been a Portugese smuggler. He was addicted to telling tall stories which were quite original ... I can still hear Jan's indignant scream, "Martin!" just as soon as he got well launched into a new story. Both of them were enormously intelligent and well educated, I took to them at once. Bob liked Martin best.

As the time approached for me to have a baby, Buddy and Mary Ann appeared again, for they quite rightly thought that Bob couldn't manage alone while I was out of commission. I was so happy to see them! My great fear was that I would die in childbirth and that the children would be left without friends ...

When Charlotte did not breathe, they worked on her efficiently, a well trained team. She was plunged into cold water, passed to the next person and stuck with a needle, then passed to the next and slapped, then returned to her cold bath. She went round and round the circle at high speed while I sat up and screamed for them to give her to me. I thought it would help to shake her and yell in her ear. Her trips around the circle were so speedy that I saw her momentarily unsupported in the air, which made her yelp ...

Buddy and Mary Ann thought that Bob needed a rest and a change of scene. First Bob wanted to go with them as soon as I got out of the hospital, but I begged them so hard to stay for an extra week or so that they did not set off until I was well enough to drive our car to the store ... When he returned a couple of weeks later, I was much stronger and very pleased to see the suede jacket Bob had brought back for me. He had bought himself two sharply tailored suits and had enjoyed seeing the sights and going to bullfights. We considered moving to Spain where our money would go much further and even run to some new clothes ...

In addition to being cold, a huge spider like a daddy-long-legs got into Charlotte's basket where it amused itself stinging her every few minutes and making her cry. I could not imagine what was wrong with her until I saw it rush out and sting her and hide immediately. It was very difficult to catch. Is it possible that it was trying to paralyse her, a task that could take weeks, in order to make an enormous meal of her? I found a scorpion in the kitchen, it was not in the least afraid of me and made dashes in my direction. I killed it by dropping a heavy frying pan on it from a safe distance. There had been nothing like that in the house in Fontrousse, only beautiful jeweled tree frogs jumping from wall to wall and singing. Perhaps they had been poisonous too, for the scorpion had been the same lovely jade green with bright eyes ...

René came for a visit. I was surprised to see that I still adored him. I was reduced to keeping my eyes on the floor most of the time so as not to show it. There was no way to express my love for him. But I could give him one thing. Since he was a Frenchman, I assumed that he liked good cooking ...

Death of one kind or another seemed all around me. Perhaps it was just post-partum depression. But I had had a good look at it while I watched the newborn Charlotte's attempts to breathe. I had been badly frightened, and now thought about it for the first time. I had also been reminded of death by seeing French funerals. Once a sparkling empty glass carriage with ostrich plumes nodding from its roof had bounced gaily through the street of Fontrousse on its way to another village. It was drawn by two high-stepping black horses with plumes waving from the tops of their heads, an altogether elegant and dainty equipage worthy of a circus parade. The fact that everything was black did not detract from its style. I had not realized that it was a hearse until I saw the driver in his frock coat and stovepipe hat. Then I thought that if you must die, it was a beautiful way to go ...

But Lambesc was also truly permeated with death. The town had been pretty much tidied up after the war, and so had all of France, and though people rarely spoke of it the memory was still there under everything. In Fontrousse there had been nothing worse than hunger and fear of airplanes, but Lambesc had been occupied by the Germans. Near our house was a shallow gravel pit and at the back of it was a little cave under a very large boulder. A message had been hastily painted on it:

"The six martyrs of Lambesc, gunned down by the Germans."

The date was given and their names were listed. No one ever mentioned them to me. Only one excited man waylaid me in the town and told me over and over again that he was a hero of the Maquis and that his suffering had been horrific and what did I think of that, eh? My vocabulary in French was inadequate. I think it would have been inadequate in English ...

We said a sad good-bye to the Martis and gave them most of our food and household goods as well as David's tricycle, which delighted their children. He felt that he was ready for a two-wheeler and we promised him one as soon as we got to Spain. We embarked at Marseilles in the *Djebil Djira* which plied between Marseilles and Algeria, stopping at the island of Majorca halfway between. It was an ancient ship, for I had encountered its name in a novel written in the early part of the century. You could ride in a deck chair in a big tilting groaning smelly lounge or lie upon the deck in the cold or sleep in one of the two cabins with berths. There was one for men and one for women. But as no one could afford a berth except us, we were allowed to occupy one of them all to ourselves. We took breakfast with the captain and the crew. It was our funny little square black car which shared the deck with the homesick Algerians. Many of our belongings were packed in it, and though the doors did not lock, nothing was stolen ...

Martin had found a room for us in a little hotel. Washing water was brought upstairs by the chambermaid in a pitcher. But I was too tired from traveling to go upstairs to look and collapsed onto a bench in the foyer. Charlotte was screaming with hunger, but I had no milk for her and on inquiry neither did the hotel, their daily supply not having yet arrived. I had used up her last dry diaper, she was soaking wet and so were my own clothes. So I rocked her and wept to keep her company and waited for sleep or perhaps death to come.

At this moment Robert Graves and his wife, Beryl, came in the door of the hotel. They had heard of our arrival from Martin and had kindly come to greet us. What a sordid sight we were. Bob did his best to cover this embarrassing moment by making charming and witty remarks, but Mr Graves ignored him and came over to inspect me and my huddle of children. I looked up to see a tall stout middle-aged man with a very plain face and beautiful eyes holding out his arms to take Charlotte away from me, even though I protested that she was too wet. He sent Beryl running home for supplies, and then walked up and down carrying Charlotte until she was almost quiet. He assured me that he was a very experienced father and there was no baby too nasty for him ...

The Graves invited us to their house one evening to meet some of their friends. They had an apartment in Palma and this was their summer house. Besides servants there was a secretary named Carl who lived in the house next door with his wife and baby. Those two were quite cool to us and acted very superior. Then there were Martin and Jan. All of them together constituted a kind of literary factory which had just finished turning out the Greek myths and a Bible concordance and was currently working on Suetonius' *Lives of the Caesars*. There was also another young couple there named Metcalf. They were sophisticated and elegant and looked down their noses at us as though we smelled. We found later that this was the nucleus of a kind of court around the Graves that hung so close to them that the Graves could not go anywhere without them following. I think they were so unfriendly to us because they feared that we might become new additions to the circle. Not only did the employment of most of them depend on the Graves, but all of their prestige also ...

In an effort to introduce an interesting topic of conversation to this uncomfortable group, Robert (he insisted that we call him Robert, I think that he was unwilling to be so much older than the rest of us) brought out an Etruscan medal, quite large, with two stick-like figures either dancing or fighting. Some admirer had just sent it to him, for he lived in a warm bath of admiration and flattery. As the medal travelled from person to person everyone sighed apppreciatively over its beauty, the ladies placing their hands over their heart while they gushed. Graves brought it over to me. He asked me what I thought of it. I tried to be polite, truthful, and concise.

"I think it may be one of the best looking dug up things I have ever seen."

He was electrified. "Did you hear what she called it?" he shouted at Beryl. I shrank back in terror. "That's exactly what it is, just that and nothing more." He turned to me. "How did you know it was dug up? Where have you seen others like it to compare it with?"

"Wasn't it dug up?" I whimpered, undone at being the center of attention in such company. I explained that I had spent hours as a child wandering the corridors of the Boston museum, and when I was lost I always seemed to end up at the Roman coins, and though I never looked at them I could not avoid seeing them. I was very apologetic for having had an opinion. But he seemed more interested in how I knew that it had been dug up. I said that I just knew. Did I have psychic powers? I remembered

Slater Brown's opinion on that subject and insisted that I had no powers at all for I did not wish to be stared at. Nonetheless they all did ...

We did not find a house to rent in Deya, but Martin found us one in the next seaside village. Unfortunately, though it was a short run by boat, the two villages were separated by high mountains and cliffs, and to arrive there by car necessitated a drive to Palma, an about-face, and a journey over the high mountains on a perilous winding road, narrow, rocky and unfenced. One would never dream of going around a corner without blowing the horn first and one had a tendency to hug the rock wall and not look down.

Our house, which we had rented sight unseen as we had the one in Fontrousse, was almost as inconvenient, though bigger. It was near the bottom of a steep street leading down to the sea and was very tall, narrow, and made of porous sandstone and therefore damp. The bottom floor was occupied by a horse on one side and by a barber shop on the other. The next two floors were ours and there was a large, light loft under the roof. There were some amenities: furniture, though the heavily carved bed looked like too many people had died in it. There was a sort of porcelain outhouse on a porch off the kitchen and electric lights until nine in the evening, when the young men who ran the village generator got tired of it and went to bed or strolled out serenading. They would blink the lights twice to warn people to run and light their candles. Another advantage was the presence of two small stores within walking distance. The chief drawback was in the water supply. The well was at the other end of the village up a steep hill and the washing stone in the deep valley below us ...

The village stretched from the mountain as far down to the sea as it could get, until stopped by precipices and tongues of black volcanic rock which reached out into the water and formed the sides of the little harbors and separated one fishing village from another. Bañalbufar, which means "Bathtub of the Winds," was lucky to have two harbors for its fishing fleet. Those who did not go fishing tended the tiny terraced gardens which climbed back up the side of the mountain till they could cling no farther. Besides vegetables for their own use, the inhabitants grew tomatoes which they transported over the mountain in two-wheeled carts drawn by mules, to sell in Palma. The different villages all had their own specialities; some made wine, some grew almonds and some olives. Deya's specialty was tourists who came to look at Robert Graves, and artistic types who settled there to be near him ...

Our village had a rigid caste system which took me a long time to figure out. A young lady came to call. Unlike the dumpily dressed village housewives she was neatly buttoned into a suit. My instinct equated her with identical young ladies in Wellesley and I was quite right, though she was taller and stronger. She was the daughter of the owner of the hotel and actually spoke some stilted English. She expressed horror that I did not have a servant, and sent me Magdalena Cunil, the wife of a fisherman in poor circumstances and her own cousin. We paid her two dollars and a half a week and did not miss it.

Magdalena had never been a servant before and I had never had one before, and because she was big and strong and older and louder than me, she decided what our roles were to be. She became an "aunt." She arrived in the morning, tut-tutted at the mess we had made, swept it into order, and about noon put the laundry under one arm and Charlotte under the other and disappeared for the rest of the day with the boys tagging behind her. She alway took an egg with her for Charlotte's lunch. Sometimes she ordered me sternly to go to bed, explaining to me that's what a señora "did." I was extremely grateful to her for her help and as a result of it was able to put my efforts into marketing, cooking, buying clothes ...

Martin had discovered an excellent way to help spend our money. He was in the process of having his mother's poems printed at a local press as a birthday surprise for her. We visited the printers with him. They set all the type by hand and the results were very fine ...

One of the first books we printed was a set of non-rhymed translations of Provençal ballads made by Paul Blackburn, one of Bob's favorite correspondents, a fellow plotter to change the face of literature. Paul had taught himself Provençal out of a dictionary. It was the sort of book Ezra Pound would have approved of and set a refined tone to our enterprise. Bob wrote to Ashley and invited him to do the cover for the book, as Ashley was already a published illustrator. Not only did he design a cover but came for a visit, bringing his cover under his arm.

Bob did not like it and did not hesitate to say so and I tried to save the situation by using part of it, but that offended Ashley also, and after a few days of stiffness he went home, not to return ...

I wanted to print a novel Martin had written. I had never seen anything like it. It was the cautionary tale of a pathological liar from a respectable English family who had an uncontrollable desire for any adventure and who tangled himself in his own web and died before a firing squad, convinced until the last minute that his native wit would rescue him. This character was a new kind of madman I had not encountered yet in any other book. But Bob refused, I do not know why; perhaps it was envy, as his own psychological explorations were not nearly so breathtaking.

All this writing inspired me to try my own hand. Bob had taught me by example that I had to write about what I felt and that I must not rhyme.

The New Basket

I dreamt of bright picnics
Basketfulls of goodies.
There it stands on the floor
Full of waste paper

It was not a good poem, but it was how I felt about my life ... I did not deserve to be slapped around that day for daring to say what I felt. I was also told never to attempt to write anything again so I confined myself to writing duty letters in a bright cheerful tone ... I was pretty wretched at this time. Bob slept until about noon but I rose with the children at daylight. Then I dragged myself tiredly through the day until the evening, when we would both light up the high-quality hashish which Buddy had sent us. The evening passed in riotous laughter or else with me listening dazedly to Bob expounding his literary theories. So it went, dismal days and noisy nights. By this time I was really thin. I remember sitting and looking out at the sea and saying softly to myself, "I am dying," which I knew was unreasonable because I was still so young.

One night while I was high one of my legs began to jerk uncontrollably. My goodness, I thought, am I suffering brain damage with this drug? A few nights later I heard Charlotte crying in the next room. I found the sound very funny and laughed and did not go to find out what was the matter. She kept on crying and after several minutes I became tired of this amusement and went to make her stop. I found her uncovered, wet and very, very cold. After I changed and warmed her I began to think, a process very unusual for me as I was in the habit of mostly just agreeing with what Bob said. Was it possible that the hashish was not only damaging to my synapses but was also able to numb or destroy my most basic maternal instinct?

Having reached this inescapable conclusion, there was nothing left to do but act upon it. The next morning I timidly attacked Bob's collection of hemp plants growing so large and healthy in their pots on the back porch. I hacked at the roots and hid the evidence of my invasion. But they refused to die; they enjoyed being pruned. So in a few days, with my heart in my mouth, I uprooted them, chopped them up and pushed them down the toilet.

Then I had to tell Bob. He took it very calmly, just informing me that since I had deprived him of his necessary nerve food he would probably be very uneasy for months and I could expect him to be of uncertain temper and anything disagreeable that happened to me during that period I would have brought on my own head. I tearfully promised that I would not complain. For my part I did not have any withdrawal symptons, but he indulged himself in fits of rage or demanded what I did not want to give, and it was more than I could do to be always agreeable and cheerful.

Now that we no longer passed our evenings in a drug-induced haze, they became horrible battles. Bob had always enjoyed a "scene" and had bolstered up his enjoyment of them by a complex argument drawn partly from psychology and partly from D.H. Lawrence. "Scenes" were supposed to be good for one. It was his part to rage and threaten, and mine to cry. But little tears would not do, I must be fully in despair. Sometimes it took hours of teasing and trickery to get me to disagree with him enough so that he could unleash his rage. Then he would sweetly forgive me my disobedience and we would go to bed. Sometimes I would manage to slip past him and out the door and would spend the rest of the night walking by the sea. Majorca was mostly rock and there was nowhere to lie down and sleep. Once I found a pile of garden waste and lay down on that and for once slept. I woke just as the sun came up with a glad shout. For a moment I had forgotten all my troubles and saw only the rising sun. That moment often sustained me in later troubles.

On another even blacker occasion Bob was so anxious to get a rise out of me that he followed me from room to room laughing and poking at my eyes with his finger. I was so frightened that I cowered in the back of a closet, but he dragged me out. I seized a big carving knife from the table and rushed at him with screams suitable for a Red Indian. Poor David was an onlooker. He was seated on that very table trying to keep out of the way. I had never attacked Bob before, just run away. On this occasion I stood quietly with my back to the wall and watched a screaming mad-woman flourishing a knife, with Bob fleeing from her. David put an end to this. "Ann," he begged, "Please don't kill Bob." He was speaking to me, the woman standing quietly by the wall. I realized that I was also the woman with the knife. I flung it away from me in horror and ran to find Bob to apologize. I found him at the top of the stairs where he had gone to hide. I knelt down to ask his forgiveness, but instead he kicked me down the stairs.

This was the last event of this sort for some time. It was the only time that I tried to kill him ...

The procession I remember best was the midsummer one which was celebrated with flowers at mid-day. This was the black Virgin's own procession. René Laubiès had reappeared and settled down in the attic to paint pictures. He and I went out alone to see the celebration, for Bob was tired of the whole village by this time and did not want to see any more of their antics. We waited near the altar in the middle of the rocky street and listened to the approaching singing. The wind suddenly rose and the flower-decked altar flew apart, the blossoms flying in every direction. The ladies who had decorated it shrieked and ran to repair the damage. We ran after the flowers too and helped hold it together until the procession rounded the corner. One of the ladies whisked us into her house and into an upstairs room where we could lean out the window and see the marchers. The statue, a bust only, was of old blackened wood and looked like no Virgin I had ever seen, very ugly. Some of the flowers were perched on the tops of tall bamboo poles and René said that they arranged flowers like that in the religious processions in Vietnam where he had grown up. I had not realized until then that he was one of the colonial French. Unlike most of the Frenchmen I had met he was totally unaffected and never sneered. No wonder we got along so well. We leaned out the window babbling happily until the lady of the house pulled me roughly back into the room and slapped me quite hard in the abdomen. I couldn't figure out what was ailing her, but later I realized that she like everyone else thought that I loved René ...

Another visitor arrived, one with whom Bob had been corresponding. He edited a small literary magazine in Liverpool and turned out to be a cheerful naive noisy and strong young man, the antithesis of Bob, who took a violent dislike to him. Even I could see that he was out of place in our would-be sophisticated and carping milieu. Sneers went right over his head. He went down to the beach with Bob and René and just before they left Bob said (in jest of course) that he was going to drown him; I laughed. When they returned from their swim the visitor was lavish in his praise and gratitude to Bob for having saved his life and swore him eternal loyalty. It seemed that he had jumped into one of those whirlpools so common near the rocks and found himself unable to escape. Bob was sitting on a rock an arm's length away and had debated within himself whether or not to let his visitor drown, and while he thought it over had urged the victim to try to swim harder. But René was watching from a distant rock and finally Bob had given his hand to the drowning man and by that easy movement had earned his gratitude. But he went back to Liverpool at once ...

Magdalena had found us a better house. It had been there all the while, ready to be rented, but the landlord had been suspicious of us, new as we were to the village. Now that our first year was up we had become acceptable as tenants. It was an apartment in a beautiful building with strong historical and romantic aspects, the Baronia, the home of the last Baron, who had been deposed and driven away in the late revolution. I never dared ask what had happened to him.

Not only was there a view of the sea from all windows and from the roof, which was an almost flat balustraded terrace reached by a spiral stair, there was a bathroom with a shower, toilet, and wash basin. The absence of hot water did not grieve me at all. The Baronia was built around a paved courtyard which one entered through a huge archway. The building was extremely old, and the oldest part was a thick-walled square tower left over from the days of the Moors. The landlord's son and his wife lived in the tower, and we had a long room that had been divided into five small ones. The windows came down to the floor which was made of hardwood, the only wood floor I had seen since coming to Europe. It may have once been a ballroom. The rest of the Baronia was now a small unsuccessful hotel for tourists who never came. The Baronia spread out on two sides of the court, the archway occupied another, and the priest lived in the house on the other. He was looked after by his sister, a silent black-garbed lady who kept pots of geraniums growing at the sides of her front steps. All the front steps in the court were large and magnificent, including ours, and our front door was studded with nails and was stong enough to keep off anything except a battering ram. It boomed hollowly when it was shut.

Of course we were delighted and rushed out to buy furniture. We went to the bed factory in Palma. At one door we discovered a pile of logs, peeled of their bark, obviously imported from a distance. At that end of the factory they sawed and carved and turned the logs. In another part they welded springs and in another they stuffed and sewed mattresses. You had to draw a picture of the bed you wanted, and in about a week it emerged looking curiously unlike what you had intended ...

Another visitor was Alex Trocchi who owned the Olympia Press in Paris. He wanted one of Bob's stories for a magazine he was starting. I did not know then that his press specialized in pornography, and was delighted to see him. He had the most extraordinary silver eyes and was very handsome. Behind him came his wife, a beautiful willowy but dispirited girl. Their two little daughters followed. His wife proved to be the Fair Elizabeth, once loved and lost by the bagpipe playing Sutherland. She did not look as though the change had made her very happy, though her clothes were expensive. Bob took an almost instant dislike to Alex as soon as he saw him and they quarrelled at once and Bob took back his story.

Bob and Charles Olson had become quite close through their letters and the publication of Charles's works. He arranged for Bob to come to Black Mountain College to teach for a semester. We both saw this as a break-out from total obscurity, and though it meant that I would be left behind, I welcomed this chance for his sake, and perhaps I looked forward to his absence subconsciously though I would not admit it to myself. I said good-bye to him in Seville, for I had to travel with him across Spain to where his ship was waiting as he still did not know enough Spanish to manoeuvre by himself. I was surprised that I did not grieve; instead I went peacefully to sleep ...

The next few months were wonderful, I had no duties except to the children and after resting up for a bit I found I could wander where I pleased, without having to be back in time to cook meals. I took many long walks, usually with David and often with Tommy who staggered cooperatively along until he dropped and had to be carried. Charlotte was usually left behind on the real hikes as she had been slow to learn to walk ...

Although I spent most of my time alone or with the children, I had a continual supply of English-speaking visitors. The first were three very young hiking Germans who had come to view Bob as a curiosity, as he was quite the rage in Germany among the younger set thanks to Rainer Gerhardt. Since there was no room for them to stay with us, Magdelena arranged for them to rent a pretty tiny house clinging to a cliff-side up a great climb of stone steps. Three or four hardy families lived up there. It cost about two dollars a month and the Germans climbed the hills and pressed flowers between heavy boards fastened with a chain. I fed them sometimes while they discussed literature with me in a heavy, learned way. They told me that Bob's poetry was "cryptic" which I think meant that it could not be understood unless you knew in advance what he meant.

The house was so pretty that I continued paying the rent and so had a house ready for Paul Blackburn and his wife, Winifred. Paul had got himself a Fullbright fellowship on the strength of the Provençal translations we had published and had come to Europe to learn Provençal but had decided to learn Majorcan as a substitute because the money would go further in Spain. I amused them as well as I could while waiting for Bob to return from Black Mountain.

Paul was a nice enough person, though without much talent. But his wife was very strange. She had been a call girl in New York and had been in a prostitution ring that had received much publicity. She was quite proud of her past and spent all her time talking about clothes. The local seamstress was put to work and my wardrobe was criticized and the seamstress set to work on some items for me too. Freddie assured me that I was good-looking enough to engage in her trade and that she would give me some addresses. I protested but she assured me that it was a delightful life and one could go to hotels and resorts with important men ...

One day I decided to swim a little in the pool, so I left my guests sitting on the flat rock and slipped into the buoyant water and paddled about while they watched me. That became boring so I started back to the rock.

To my horror I found that I could get no nearer than about three feet away from it. The water washed me inshore and out, and no matter how hard I swam I could not grasp the edge of the rock. I explained my predicament breathlessly to my friends and asked for help. They looked at me in a bored way.

"Why don't you swim harder?" said Paul. I said I couldn't and pleaded for help. No matter how I begged they both said they would not help, even when I told them that I was exhausted. I looked at their cold eyes and saw that there was no help there so I turned my face to the sea and the sharp volcanic rocks on which the sea was breaking with some violence, in the vain hope that I might wash up on one of them unbloodied and be spotted later by a fisherman and be saved. Also if I must die then I would not let these people see my tears or my frightened face. I resigned myself to die as bravely as I could. I would look at the sky as long as possible. Paul called my name.

"What will you give us if we save you?" I turned back with lists of my possessions rushing through my mind, trying to think what would satisfy them as I paddled back to as near the rock as I could get.

"Anything you want," I gasped. Paul lay on his face and reached for me while Freddie sat on his legs to keep him from slipping in. When they had dragged me up on the rock, for I was too weak to drag myself, I lay there and sobbed. I think Paul kicked me. I know he said, "I hope you remember what you promised." I gasped out that I would. From the way he was looking at me I was afraid that he might push me back into the water. Then he said: "Oh, shut up. Quit making a fuss about such a little thing."

I was always a little afraid of them after that, but since I had always given them everything they asked for, and since they never demanded anything special like my possessions or money, our relationship returned almost to normal. Though one day Paul came to me and glaring at me said he didn't like my "attitude" towards Freddie. I told him that I could not change my "attitude" at will, no more than could anyone else, but I could control my actions. What did he want me to do for Freddie that would satisfy her? He left in a huff ...

Relations became outwardly polite again on the arrival of ... Paul Carroll ... who was spending his vacation visiting his old friend Paul. They had been acolytes together in their Catholic childhood but had strayed apart in spiritual matters. Paul Carroll taught English at Notre Dame and was pleasant to talk to as he was an intellectual babbler after my own heart. One day he found me alone and drawing up very close he gazed into my eyes and asked me what I thought about Evil. I told him that I so disliked Evil that I got no pleasure out of even talking about it. He withdrew himself and no longer bothered to address a word to me. The three of them were self-sufficient which was a relief to me as I did not see them unless they needed help or wished to complain about Magdalena who was also "doing" for them as well as for me …

I received a letter from Bob informing me that he had found a new love and that he was never coming back. I felt a sickening rush of fear and anger. I saw before me a horrid vista of living in Bañalbufar forever, without books and raising three ignorant Majorcan children with whom I could not even communicate, a sort of kindly treated pariah in a rocky land. My anger, on the other hand, was not so much directed at Bob, whom I considered mentally crippled and therefore to be excused for some of his aberrations, but rather against his new love.

He told me that her name was Cynthia and that she was the much younger sister of Nancy Homire, my friend from the Windsor Mountain School. I could see her in my mind's eye, not as a *femme fatale* but as a girl of about twelve, skinny, dark-haired with just a blur of a face, for I had once glimpsed her at the distance, getting into the family car with her older sister on their way home during school vacation. Every time I thought of her as the fiend who had stolen my husband and directed my hatred toward her, so strongly that it seemed to fly across the ocean in the wind, the vision of an innocent little girl rose before my eyes and I had to quickly draw back the javelin of my hatred in order to avoid killing her.

These ambiguous feelings were very painful, especially as I had very little else to think about during the long warm days and nights. I was too frightened and confused to organize a rational new life for myself and the children, so all I had to think about was my anger. I wondered if I could engage in some sort of witchcraft and destroy her at a distance by my hatred. After a while I began to think I could; the method appeared to be fairly simple. All I had to do was roll my hatred up into some kind of hard magic ball with poison in the middle of it, like a missile, and direct it toward her with all the strength of my evil thoughts. I thought it might work. But then the image of the little girl rose up before me and I had to withdraw my sting again. I found myself in a constant quandary.

I took the bus to Palma to distract my mind by wandering about in the cloth and shoe stores. I bumped into Robert Graves on the street, and he must have seen something in my face for he took me home, and he and Beryl were very kind to me and gave me lunch. Since I knew that he was an authority on witches and witchcraft I presented my problem to him, quite heavily disguised, for I had told no one about it yet and did not intend to. I suppose that he saw through my disguise, for Robert advised me very strongly against becoming a witch for any reason whatever. He gave me some information about witches, that there were two kinds, white and black. Usually the neophyte first became a white witch, a dangerous condition, for at her first move to use her powers for her own advantage rather than using them for the benefit of others, she would turn into a black witch. The white witch might, with effort, turn back into a normal woman, but the black witch never could. Unfortunately thereafter the black witch would sink into a life of misery or alcoholism and would usually commit suicide.

This gave me considerable pause. Now I was on the horns of a three-way dilemma. Beryl wanted to talk about the time she had attempted to become a witch. She had gone out naked and oiled at night, drawn diagrams and everything, but nothing happened, and she was aggrieved. I told her that I didn't think she was the type. Robert laughed both loud and free, which gave me a barrier of noise behind which to do a little thinking.

I asked what I ought to do, since I had to do something. Robert sobered up. He said that one should select the deity of one's choice, and in the strongest language possible, state one's case to that deity, and then just wait. The appropriate solution would arrive without further trouble on one's own part.

I think if he had said that "revenge is mine, saith the Lord," and that I ought to pray, I would have gone home in a huff. As it was, I was impatient to leave and get by myself where I could try it out. I could not wait to get back to Bañalbufar but sat in the bus and selected a sort of shiny spot in the sky for a deity and poured out my heart to it with great violence. It seems to me that there was a kind of implosion in the air for my ears hummed and the aisle and the people in the bus seemed to shake. I folded my hands and waited impatiently though my reason told me that it would be a long wait. But I no longer had to choose any action and felt better. When I got home I penned a marvelously stiff letter to Bob, not berating him but forgiving him, and wishing him happiness in his new life.

It was not many weeks later that he informed me that he and Cynthia had broken up and that since the semester at Black Mountain was over, he would return to me. Would I please send him some money? And meet him, as he had quite a few boxes and bundles? The agitations of the past few weeks finally brought a physical result; I lost my sense of smell. I dropped a bottle of perfume into the sink and of course it broke, but no odor arose. I opened another one, still no smell. Had someone poured out my perfume and substituted water? Of course not. I ran weeping out into the soft moonlight night, weeping not so much for my marriage as for my poor nose. It did me good, for when I returned to the house it reeked of perfume.

I met him and brought him back with his bundles. He was quite jolly and friendly, he had met another poet on the ship, Alistair Reid, who was on his way to visit the Graves with his young wife. They were both attractive, sympathetic people, and associating with them had done Bob good. My hopes were high that he would remain cheerful and that indeed a new phase of our marriage would begin. All went well until we reached Bañalbufar. The Mayor turned out to greet him as a returning hero, everyone shook his hand. Magdelena snapped her fingers to summon a porter to carry his heaviest trunk home ...

After we had eaten and everyone had gone away and the children were tucked into bed we sat on opposite sides of the living room and faced each other. Bob had already had a few drinks, it was now time to soften me up, to make me cry, so that he could take his pleasure with me. But I had been alone for several months, I was well rested, my nerves were restored. Under his barrage of insults and accusations I failed to cry and ask forgiveness, I got angry instead and left the hate-filled room and went out into the night to seek my friend solitude. Then, of course, I cried with disappointment and the fear of being sucked down again into Bob's tormenting vortex. I walked up and down by the sea under the full moon, knowing that I could not go on without help from somewhere. But where could I ask for help?

I looked around, but there was nothing to see except the full moon shining down on the sea and the rocks. I remembered Robert Graves's advice to address the deity of my choice. The moon was reputed to be a deity and a female to boot, perhaps she would show me some pity. So I poured out my heart to her and begged for help. Within a few minutes I felt calm and strong and determined, quite to my surprise. I returned to the house to find Bob anxious to carry on with his scene. It was now as though he were an ugly little animal squirming and snarling in front of me. What he said did not touch me at all, I was in a protective globe, rather like the moon itself, and when he raged I laughed inside it. He satisfied his physical desire but left me otherwise untouched by his emotions. From then on I felt no love for him. He had physical control over me, could frighten me, and occasionally I admired some piece of his cleverness, but I never believed him or looked up to him again. My most generous feeling toward him was pity. He was now merely an ugly creature who had somehow become my responsibility, a sort of weight and blight on my life, and at the same time my master ...

We were up at [Paul and Winifred's] house one evening and they began to complain that Magdalena was robbing them. I laughed since it was so unlikely, but Bob took the equally unlikely position of defending her. Shouts arose and he threw himself on Paul, who was much smaller than he was, and soon had Paul on the floor with his hands on his throat. "Do you give up?" he was yelling. Freddie seized a heavy wine bottle by the neck, and advanced to protect her mate. I could easily have pulled Bob off Paul but found my hands occupied with preventing Freddie from braining Bob. I held her wrist and begged her to stop; I promised that as soon as she stopped struggling I would stop the fight. She relaxed and I let go of her wrist, but instead of putting the bottle down she hit me with it. She aimed for the back of my neck and I went down for the count. This was what stopped the fight. And all three commenced to blame me for the lump growing on the back of my head. I was chagrined, the peacemaker blamed by the combatants whose fun she had spoiled.

Magdalena insisted on knowing what had happened to my neck, and though I told her the truth, she had difficulty in believing it. But I saw Freddie only once more. I met her accidentally in the store, and when I saw her I gave a cry and jumped back in fear, which I am sure was an educational experience for the bystanders. Not long after that the Blackburns left. Possibly things had become a bit hot for them in the village, for I was a general favorite as well as a sort of foster daughter of Magdalena ...

We also made occasional trips to the Spanish mainland where we saw the sights and went to the bullfights. We flew over to Barcelona, a breathtaking experience, for the ancient rivets in the wings jumped excitedly up and down. We travelled to Madrid on the night train and talked all night to a very young bullfighter who was kind enough to give me a Spanish lesson. He pointed out the Latin words in my vocabulary and told me the correct ones. Everyone else had been too polite to expose me. In Madrid we visited the Prado. Velazquez's "Maids of Honor" was in a room that just fitted the picture so that you seemed to be in the same room with the girls. Then there were huge stone tables with all kinds of nonsense like fans and spurs and bottles inlaid *trompe l'oeil* into the tops of them. What a clutter, I wanted to straighten them out. And there were the Goya pictures of the vile shimmering nobles and the pretty peasants. I also remember the battle scenes with tiny figures in exquisite detail, probably all recognizable by their relatives.

There in Madrid we saw endless gypsy dancers throwing themselves about with unbelievable grace and speed with a most passionate effect. And we went to the bullfights. They too were violent and beautiful, and they were associated with the same music as the dancing. We usually bought the best seats in the front row. One day we found ourselves near the big archway through which the fighters would make their ceremonial entrance. The crowd began to murmur, it was time. All the men in the neighborhood left their seats and pressed up to the rail and looked down in order to see their heroes make their entrance. We wanted to see too and moved into the crowd. I was the only woman to do so and the men noticed me and asked if I was an aficionado, and when I said yes they made a way for me and I found myself in the best position of all, facing the archway.

The fighters came out dressed in their suits of lights, walking proudly, surrounded by the lesser fighters. My neighbors went wild. They shouted and called the leader by name. He was a tall very handsome young man with blond hair, a kind of graceful giant. "Here she is!" they shouted. They had brought him a present, me, a pretty girl, to bring him strength and luck. When he heard his name he looked up, straight into my eyes. All the hope in him passed from his beautiful blue eyes into my own, and I returned to his look the same. After a bit we came to our senses and he went on to dodge his three bulls and I looked around nervously for Bob. He was not to be found, for the crowd had carefully hidden him. If the sight of me had protected the bullfighter, the sight of a one-eyed man would have killed him. But the wall around Bob dispersed when the fight began. My hero was not hurt and I suppose he waited for me at the end of the fight but I felt that he would have enough admirers to keep him happy without me. But I have never forgotten him ...

We left the Baronia but kept the little house on the hill with its minuscule rent for occasional use in the hottest weather, for we were moving to the warmer side of the island. The children had to say goodbye to their friends. The hardest was to say goodbye to Magdalena who viewed our departure with foreboding. The "Man of the Store" carried our furniture in his truck and spoke very sternly to our new landlords, which made a great impression on them.

It was an exquisite little house. The former tenant had been an Englishwoman with a taste for antiques. She had lived there many years and had left her treasures to the landlord. There were chests and carved beds and a fireplace in an inglenook. There were stoves, a bath with hot water and a garden for the children to run around in. There was even an oven of a sort and an icebox with ice, firewood, and milk delivered to the door! Mr Short found us a maid who came all day every day except Sunday and did the cooking and marketing. I sank into a life of unimagined luxury. No longer did my children disappear for half the day, I brought them up myself, and I had nothing to do but amuse them, dress up the lot of us, run errands for Bob in the daytime, and shop and visit ...

About this time one of the strangest of our visitors appeared, Edward Dahlberg. Where poor Elizabeth Trocchi attracted disaster, this man carried it around with him, perhaps in the heavy boxes of books he thumped down on our doorstep when he arrived all unannounced. Bob had heard of him through Charles, and since he was a published author

Bob was thrilled to play host to him, though he had brought all his dirty laundry with him. Carmela was a good sport about that, but she dragged me into his room to view his flower and heart decorated shorts and his numerous perfumed mouthwashes, toothpicks, toilet water, etc. It was the first time she had seen such doo-dads. I know it wasn't nice to spy on a visitor, but it made me giggle too.

He had really come to get an invitation to Robert Graves from us. Robert had just published his tome on the Bible, and Edward, who fancied himself a profound Hebrew scholar, wished to meet him as an equal and cross swords with him. But the introduction could not be abrupt or seem contrived. He must meet him casually and drift into conversation. To this end he and Bob would have to wander daily in Palma until they bumped accidentally into Robert in some café (there were not all that many cafés in Palma). But it would take a long time. Meanwhile he had brought all the applicable books on Hebrew history with him and would profit from the waiting period by reading them over again.

In the evenings he and Bob would sit side by side on the couch while I watched them, bored and half asleep, from across the room. Bob was so hopeful of making a good impression (Edward knew a lot of people whom Bob would give anything to meet) that he poured on the flattery and told him that he was dropping pearls of wisdom while it looked to me that he was merely dropping names. Edward was busy flattering Bob in return. They could keep that up for hours. To my sleepy ears they almost seemed to be cooing to each other. Sometimes I would interject a comment but Edward would tell me to shut up, I was a typical ignorant woman, all women were ignorant, the ancient Hebrews held that women ... I withdrew and watched the scene before me and wondered what Edward was really up to (I knew what Bob was up to). Of course it was clear that Edward was a literary bum, he was supported by his wife who worked as a librarian and who stayed in America while he travelled. But why would he settle in to live at our house? I leaned back and mulled this over while watching Edward murmur sugared nothings into Bob's ear.

Suddenly I had a moment of inspiration. I was so delighted with the solution that had rushed into my mind that I bounced in my chair and announced it at once.

"I finally understand you, Edward, you are a homosexual!"

Inasmuch as I had been thoroughly trained to find nothing wrong with being a homosexual, indeed to think of it as being rather clever and elegant, I was astounded to see that he was furious. Bob was just as furious. He spoke through his teeth.

"What you are really saying is that it is I who am a homosexual!"

I denied everything. But it was too late. I did not feel at all comfortable watching these two men glaring at me, so I slipped out of the room and went outdoors to wait for the trouble to die down. But one gets tired of sitting on a stone wall for more than a couple of hours, so I stole around the house to the terrace where I could listen in through the partly open door to what they were saying, to see if it was safe to come back into the house.

Edward was giving Bob fatherly advice. He advised Bob to leave me. Bob agreed that he would really like to do so but that he was dependent on me for his bread. Edward thought that over for a little and then told Bob that he would have to learn to control me better. He advised beatings. Bob said that he had tried that but it didn't work very well, I was so stubborn. Edward said that he probably didn't do it thoroughly enough. At that Bob protested a little. After all, he said, I was his wife, and he had to treat me with some consideration.

I had been standing under the clothesline with wet sheets hanging down around me, listening to Bob reveal that he stayed with me only because of my money. My heart was nearly stopped with grief and horror. Bob's remark that as his wife I deserved a crumb of consideration seemed to be balm to my aching heart. I had expected nothing but now had gotten one little drop of affection. Such was my low condition that I was inordinately grateful for it, and in my typically sudden way burst into the room and sobbed to Bob that I was so grateful for his kind words.

Edward rose up in rage and shouted, "Now! Now's your chance! Hit her! Hit her!" Bob obligingly did so, hard enough so that I fell back through the door, and tangled in the wet sheets but struggled out of them and made my escape in the dark. Somehow he had torn the earring out of my ear, fishhook and all, and it was bleeding. I walked around a bit until I found a sheltered spot under a bush where I lay down and prepared to spend a cold night.

After a long time I heard breathing in the dark. Bob had found me. He begged my forgiveness, was very gentle and apologetic. But as soon as I had agreed to forgive him he dropped another bombshell. Edward was very important to him, was the key to his career, and therefore important to my future too, bound up as it was with Bob's. It was vitally necessary to Bob's well-being that Edward be happy and remain at our house. I would have to apologize to him.

I objected tearfully but Bob pulled me back into the house and sat me down in front of Edward who was pacing the floor expectantly. I apologized for my rudeness, which I thought would be enough. But it was not. He began a diatribe in which I remembered the sentence: "My bones will be carried on the shoulders of the cheering populace while yours rot in an unknown grave!"

At that point I realized that he was totally insane. The only thing I could do was humor him. In reply to his indignant statement that I was picking on him with accusations of homosexuality just because he had not made a pass at me, I assured him that he was right and that he was so attractive that no woman would be able to resist him, and yes, I was just jealous. He was mollified and went to bed.

The next morning I got up early to make breakfast. Edward followed me into the kitchen and started jeering at me and asking me if I was over my snit of the night before. It was hard to make breakfast with him in the tiny kitchen as he constantly tried to make me face him. I told him I would tolerate him anywhere except the kitchen and he started to rant that in the ancient Jewish home the kitchen was the centre of the household and that the visitor had the right to be there, even against the wishes of the wife. Indeed in some ancient Jewish households the wife herself was offered to the visitor. And that was how it should be.

This was too much, I was tired from lack of sleep, I saw no possible ending. I told Bob that I would return after Edward had moved out, dressed the children and walked them down the road to Myrna's house. Of course I was crying and she said that we could stay as long as we wanted. Bob came to get me late in the afternoon. He had driven Edward to Soller where he had inconsiderately left him at Elizabeth Trocchi's. She told me later that he had spent some time telling her how worthless she was, and then advanced upon her. She wept when she told me … Later Charles Olson's sister-in-law reported to me her experience with Edward. He had chased her round and round the kitchen table until she had seized a knife and defended herself with it.

I had to go to a pre-arranged lunch with Alistair Reid and his wife a few days after this episode, and as my eyes were still swollen with tears and I was still so shaken that I could hardly speak, they drew my reluctant story out of me. I suppose that they told Robert Graves about it, for when Bob and Edward in their perambulations finally ran him to ground, and Bob had introduced Edward, they were told abruptly, "He's your friend, you keep him." So in the end I was avenged by my good angel Robert.

Later I read the explanation for Edward's terrible behavior in his autobiography. He had been accused of homosexuality by his stepfather, but he claimed that he was an innocent and only wanted to be loved. So I had stabbed him in his most sensitive spot …

The other person whom we saw most often was John Altoon. He lived in the next town up the mountain in a very pretty house which he was slowly spattering with paint, for he was an artist. I think he first came to see us because he was hungry. He had not quite sorted out how to live up on a hill far away from Los Angeles and New York with their restaurants. It was hard to see what he looked like for all his head besides his nose and eyes was covered with a big curly black bush. He seemed to have no lack of girlfriends, though I could not understand what they saw in him ...

He was very often at our house. I thought of him as a hairy bear or a hairy dog, for he sometimes lay on the floor and extracted sympathy from me. I asked him why he had never married (he was thirty), and he sniffed and said no one would marry him. A curious thing happened the first day he came to dinner. As he was going home he thanked me for the meal and took my hand. My eyes were as usual fixed on the floor, and as he held my hand I felt him telling me to raise my eyes and look at him. I tried as hard as I could not to do it but felt my eyes being dragged up to his. They were overwhelming and seemed to be laughing at me. I pulled away with difficulty. He never did that again, but henceforth always played the part of the tame bear or floor mat and quietly become part of our lives.

Bob was now editing the *Black Mountain Review* which Charles Olson had persuaded the college to pay for. Bob would not let me help edit it except for the format, though he did print a number of pictures I had taken of the villagers of Fontrousse to bulk out the first issue. However, he would not let me put my own name on them but invented a man's name as the photographer ...

Robert Duncan appeared with his companion, Jess, and Bob agreed to print a book of his poems with collage illustrations by Jess. I did not like his poems and scarcely looked at them. The pictures also were disgusting and some were blasphemous, so I thought that perhaps Luis Ripol would refuse to print it, but he didn't mind. Robert was going to pay for his own book, so I did not much mind either. Though I found his writing revolting, he himself proved to be very sympathetic. I was always a little afraid of Jess, however.

Bob was delighted to be able to add someone so well known to his list of friends. The two of them settled in Bañalbufar at the Baronia, planning to remain until the book was printed. This would be a matter of months with all the hand-setting, sewing, and my innumerable trips on foot across the battlements and through the twisting alleys. They visited us frequently and I spent long happy sessions discussing books with Robert. At last I had found someone who had devoted his childhood to reading, just as I had. We were both unsuitably adopted children and had hidden ourselves away in books.

We shared some of our childhood experiences. But his were far worse than mine. His adoptive parents had discovered from the stars that they were to raise a child so wicked as to be an embodiment of evil. This was their karma or something. They had plenty of money to spend and so were able to locate a child whose stars foretold exactly that future. Perhaps they bought him from his father, for he never mentioned his real mother. He was constantly reminded of his approaching growth into evil; they probably ignored his training in any other skill. They kept a pile of money in a dish, and he could have as much as he wanted, a fact which struck me as inimical to a child's good upbringing. We differed on that point and he scolded me for keeping David so short of funds. But I was a New Englander! Then he told me that while he was in his first year or so of college, they wrote to tell him that he was now a full grown and fully wicked man and that they washed their hands of him. He had no idea what to do and slept in doorways for warmth.

It was a frightful story and I assumed that he had become a homosexual in order to live, in the same way that a frightened girl might become a prostitute. I was acutely sorry for him. But we did not talk much about that, but rather of things that had made us happy, for it turned out that we had both read and loved exactly the same books and for the same reasons. I had never met anyone like that before. We spent some time noisily reliving our favourites under the cold eyes of Bob and Jess, neither of whom could share in our memories. Robert usually had a kind of wall-eyed look, but when we talked excitedly his eyes straightened out until he remembered to put them out of focus again ...

It was beginning to be borne in on me that I was not at all happy, that I woke up in the mornings with dread. It was almost like a sickness. I suspected that it was not really sickness but had something to do with the circumstances of my life, that some part of my life that had been a little better in the past was much worse now. In the past I had seemed to have hope; now it was gone. I asked Robert if he had noticed this, and if he had, could he please guess at the reason why, because I could not find it. He squirmed at the question and Bob broke in with his own analysis: that I was only happy when I was pregnant or carrying around a newborn baby. That my operation had removed any source of happiness I could have. His shallow definition of me as a female animal annoyed me.

I had been looking hard for an answer. A ghost of one had come to me. Originally Bob had been fired up with the ambition to be a writer. And though he had not made much progress, he had made some and was even developing a kind of style. But since moving to Bonanova he had flung himself into self-advertising to the extent that he no longer bothered to try to write. I had backed his efforts whole-heartedly while he was trying, but how could I offer my whole life as a sacrifice to a publicity campaign?

I was rather ashamed of my selfishness, but the idea kept teasing me. Because I knew Robert was intelligent and I trusted him, I had asked him for an answer. But he only looked worried …

John thought it would improve Bob's state of mind to take him away for a trip, to go to Paris, to see the world a little. Perhaps John wanted to go for his own sake too. He shaved off his beard for the event. It was a shock to me to see what lay under it. My old friend the bear had turned into a handsome prince who smiled sheepishly as I stared at him with gaping mouth. Our easy friendship was ruined, I no longer dared look directly at him, back down to the floor went my eyes. They packed up and took off, promising to meet me in Barcelona at noon in precisely two weeks at the hotel we frequented there. When they were gone I had a very pleasant rest, enjoying the luxury of sleeping in bed all alone and singing without seeing Bob wince.

But knock, knock at the door. Another visitor. This time it was Victor Kalos, a man Bob had met in New York during the Cynthia episode. I knew that he had been invited for a visit and did not feel that I could send him away even though Bob was not at home. For one thing I knew he had very little money for a hotel. I would entertain him and he could travel to Barcelona with me when I went to meet Bob.

He was a charming house guest, an absolute treasure-chest of jokes and comic stories. It was such fun being amused. He said that I needed to laugh more because I walked about in a "flat-footed" way. He was a little like Martin, witty and silly. Like Martin he drank too much, but he never became violent or got sick on the floor. Like Martin he amused himself by teasing my gullibility. He told me in a self-pitying voice that he was a Russian Jew (the worst kind of Jew) and sang me some horrible songs he claimed were Jewish, and told me jokes in a Jewish accent. Once I looked at him at an odd angle and thought I recognized in him one of the Greek statues in the cast court of the Boston museum. I had drawn every inch of it (the Scraper) for weeks but I still believed Vic to be Jewish because he had said so.

The day came for us to go to Barcelona. Our landlady's old mother pleaded with me not to go with him, but I argued that travelling with him was no worse than having him as an unchaperoned house guest for a week. So off we went to take the Barcelona boat as deck passengers with our blankets and pillows. We settled down uncomfortably and Victor sailed off into descriptions and imaginary conversations with our fellow sufferers. Of course I was in stitches. We settled down to sleep, but after a while I felt cold and complained about it. He whipped out a bottle of rum with which he had provided himself, and though it was disagreeable, I drank some. After a while I realized that we were engaged in sex under our blankets. I was as enthusiastic as he was. And then we went to sleep.

I woke in a terrible state of mind, compounded of guilt, shock, fear, and any number of unpleasant sensations. I found myself unable to think, to plan, even to speak clearly. Victor told me to take his arm and walked me off the boat and up and down streets for several hours. We went to a hotel and back to bed, but that did not help at all, it wasn't even a pleasurable experience. We walked some more and then met Bob and John at the appointed time. I tottered blank-eyed through the door. Bob saw nothing wrong in my behavior. But John saw what had happened at once and took charge of Vic and took him back to Majorca and installed him and his luggage in his own house in order to separate us.

I was so haunted by what I had done that I confessed it all to Bob. He of course was very angry but did not let it interfere with his itinerary. We had to see the sights of Barcelona and then travel on to Valencia where we would take another boat for Majorca. We went to a Japanese movie called *Gates of Hell* about a virtuous Japanese lady who arranged for her own death rather than betray and dishonor her husband. I sank into a sea of remorse and tears. I realized from watching that heroic lady that I deserved death, but my quality and courage were too low to let me embrace it in a fine scene with a dagger. All I could do was cry. The curious thing was that Bob did not seem in the least angry with Victor, only with me. He told me that he would never forget or forgive me ...

A few days later I managed to slip out of the house after dark and walked up the hill to John's house. Vic came out on the terrace to talk to me. I suppose I wanted some sympathy or help. He thought I wanted to make love, like a cat on the tiles. I was angry at myself, angry at Bob, and now I was starting to become angry at Vic. I had nowhere to turn for comfort. I could not even pray to "the deity of my choice," for I had broken all the rules, and so no longer had anyone on my side, even myself ...

There was nothing to do now except pick up the pieces and try to put them back together. Bob seemed to have a clock inside him like a time bomb that made him explode into recriminations at regular intervals. He did make an effort to appear normal in the presence of the children or Carmela or any other auditor, but whenever he was alone with me I could expect some kind of righteous blame.

We went to Bañalbufar for a few days, to stay in the little house on the hill and perhaps recapture partial tranquility But being alone together for that long made things worse. One night I went out for a long walk to escape continual scoldings for having deliberately tried to ruin Bob's life, all delivered in squeals of rage, which sent chills of revulsion through my body.

Out in the soft night air I felt better and walked for two hours or so up and down my favorite hills in the near dark, for it was a moonlit night. Finally I judged it safe to go back and sleep, so climbed homeward down a precipitous trail from which I could slide onto our terrace. At one point I had to navigate a slick wash-out in the path, it overlooked a cliff that fell about a hundred feet into the stone edged gardens below. Something made me look up, and there was Bob seated just above the narrowest part of the path, which was only a few inches wide at that point. He had divined the route I would take home! He watched me silently. From where he sat he had only to push me gently and I would tumble down the cliff to sure death. I was fairly certain this was his intention.

I stopped about ten feet away from him. I chose that distance because at ten feet I would be able to spin around and run away when he lunged at me. Although his legs were longer than mine I knew the trail better and I felt fairly safe. We remained silent for a few minutes, each waiting for the other to make a move. Nothing would induce me to approach that dangerous spot. He finally said in a resigned voice, "You can come by me, I won't touch you," and moved away from the spot.

We had lived together enough years so that each of us could often tell what the other was thinking. He did it better than I could, for I know that he was usually able to anticipate what I was going to say or do. But sometimes a picture would rise in my mind and later developments would show that the same picture had already been in his mind. This bad moment on the cliffside was one of these. I was frightened and wisely on my guard. But even then I was not in constant terror for my life, for I was not yet thirty, a few months remained to me, because my death before that date would disinherit not only Bob but the children also. I trusted that his common sense fear of being destitute would protect me. However, I could not count on his coolness under sufficient provocation, and in his present state of indignant jealousy it would take little to provoke him. For the next few days of our stay I tried great politeness and circumspection.

But it was not enough. I found myself on my back in bed with his hands around my throat. Luckily he was angry enough to be inefficient, so that while I struggled I had time to let out a few screams, each one ending in choking gurgles. His hands found a better hold and instead of screaming, my tongue stuck out at enormous length. I was just starting to lose consciousness, and fear too, when I heard a loud Majorcan male voice shouting and there was an even louder banging on our door.

Bob let go of my throat at once, frozen in doubt. I also was too frightened to speak. He ordered me to tell the interloper through the door that I was all right. I did so, and Bob dressed and left the house. When he did not return in the morning I went down to the village, found Magdalena, and was informed that he had left on the early bus for Palma. I followed him the next day and found him at home with the children and Carmela. All seemed as usual. We never mentioned this little contretemps but we never returned to Bañalbufar together again ...

I knew I had to make some kind of escape plan for myself to get out of my intolerable position. But I was trapped by both fear and feelings of guilt. The first thing I did was think up a foundation of righteousness for my contemplated action. Was it right or wrong to flee from someone who hated you? It seemed to me that it was most right and most merciful to both sides. Not to do so was also plain stupid and the rightness of it transcended my previous contract to which I had heretofore been faithful.

The second thing I did was divorce Bob in my own mind, but of course that was not helpful because even though I told him about it he would not move away from his commanding position as husband one single inch. This brought me up against a stone wall. Because my position was not just uncomfortable but intolerable, I sought desperate solutions. There appeared to be only three. Flight, suicide, or murder. Clandestine flight would last only a small time, for I was on an island and a foreigner at that. I would be easy to catch dodging from place to place with my three noisy children. Then I would be returned to my husband, for in Spain the wife and all she owned were the man's property. I had heard a tale of a woman who had been murdered by her husband after she had begged help in vain from the authorities. Nor would I be able to obtain a divorce, as divorces were illegal in Spain.

I quickly dismissed murder as a possibility. If I had fainted while killing a bird, I could never kill Bob. Or if I could I would never get away with it. Suicide seemed to me to be the most desirable. I dwelt on my own death and escape, longing for them in the way that a hungry person longs for food or an exhausted person longs to lie down. I looked affectionately at cliffs, at the steep little cut behind the house where the tiny train came through carrying blocks of stone from the quarry in the mountain down to the half-built quay on the seashore. But I rejected the blessing of annihilation, for Bob would never take care of my children. I thought of myself as being so poverty-stricken that I could not even afford the luxury of death. But sometimes I would drift unthinking in front of the tram. The driver got out and shouted at me for ignoring his bell, which had sounded to my addled mind like birds singing. Once a stranger snatched me back just in time. I would walk on the edges of curbs, or on the tops of walls. Bob paid no attention, but the ubiquitous John saw me. One day I accidentally burnt him with a hot poker in the kitchen. I cried out that I was sorry and in my shame immediately pressed the burning poker into the palm of my own hand. John snatched it away from me and shouted at Bob,

"For God's sake, don't you ever look at her? Can't you see what she is doing?"

But Bob saw nothing unusual. John took to spending the nights at our house, sleeping on the couch. We had so many overnight visitors, Austryn, Robert Duncan and others, that this did not seem unusual. Austryn and John became friends. After all, mine was the only kitchen with a good stove available to these hungry men, and it was no surprise that we were so popular. Sometimes they hosted us at restaurants in return.

One day as we alighted from the tram, Austryn held Bob in conversation while John and I walked alone to the house. He stopped me just outside the door and whispered, "You must know how I feel about you. I'll do anything on earth that you want. Tell me what you want!"

Salvation had appeared before me.

"Help me get away from Bob," I whispered back.

"All right, if that's what you really want, I will."

Bob was quickly at our side and hurried us indoors. This was the first moment I had ever been alone with John, and that opportunity did not come again. However, though we had no opportunity to discuss my means of escape, John's behaviour subtly changed. He was almost within reaching distance from the time Carmela left in the evenings until she returned in the mornings. He hardly ever spoke to me, spending all his time listening to Bob and interjecting a thought from time to time. He mostly encouraged him to pursue his literary future in America, to seek friends and contacts in America with which John would help provide him. He built up Bob's self-esteem, encouraged him to write Charles and ask for another semester at Black Mountain. He painted airy pictures of a brilliant literary life in America …

The packing and leave-taking went smoothly. I was to accompany Bob to Barcelona to help with the luggage, and we would sleep in our usual hotel for one night. John was no longer at my side. The thought of being alone with Bob in an emotional situation frightened me, though I had agreed to go through with it. We had taken the children to Bañalbufar to stay with Magdalena and I went to the dock to get on the ship with him. I had continual pictures floating through my mind of our usual hotel room high on an upper floor and of him pushing me out of the little window, even though I was screaming and hanging on to the frame with all my might. This vision terrified me so that even though I had already placed one foot on the gangplank I could not go on and backed up and said I was not going. He stared into my eyes in a puzzled way as though he had no idea of what was happening, shrugged his shoulders, and left.

I think I went directly home and sat on the couch. All that day and night I listened to the sounds of his ship crossing the Mediterranean; I heard the iron doors clang and listened to the iron plates booming as the waves struck them, I could feel the damp fog and the steady wind on my face. Only these sensations relieved my terror that Bob had somehow escaped from the ship after I had left him there and was crouched outside the door waiting to burst in. I do not think I moved much from my position on the couch for the next two days, though the children reappeared in front of me. I do not know how they returned from Bañalbufar ...

John came every day. I did not want to talk about Bob and just drooped around. He tried to stiffen my spine by taking me about with him. We went to parties, bars, to see everyone he knew. He took us all to the beach to go swimming. I made not very appetizing lunches to take with us. He came so often that David took a dislike to him and threw stones at him ...

I began to think seriously of marrying John. First I had thought of him as my pet bear, then I had seen him as a kind of handsome god, quite beyond my reach, and as an object of worship from afar. Then he became my saviour. And then from seeing him follow me closely around and listen closely to everything I said, I began to think of him as belonging to me. The only way I had of showing my love was to wait on his every wish in silence. He objected to this. Once he said, "I should have taken you before Bob left." Another time he said that two people to be happy should approach life as a pair walking side by side, that he did not like the clinging vine stuff. I tried to be bolder, but felt doomed.

Pretty soon he ceased visiting me every day and appeared only once or twice a week. He introduced me to his other girlfriends. The result was that I became insanely jealous, and it was the first time in my life. Once when I saw that he was heading home with a plump talkative artist who specialized in "sophisticated primitives," I followed them and refused to leave the house and spent the night sulking on the couch while the two of them retired to the bedroom. I thought of him constantly and wasted many hours sitting by my door all dressed up waiting for him to appear, listening for the sound of the tram and rushing out, only to see an empty street ...

Other [of David's] playmates were the sons of women who gathered asparagus in the pasture and sold them to me. The family was raggedly poor and I always gave them too much for the asparagus. One day the mother brought me an expensive-looking pair of new sandals which she said David had bought for her son. She was in doubts whether he should keep them. I too was in a quandary for he had stolen the money out of my pocketbook. Even if it was for a good end I had to teach him that it was not right to steal. I kept the sandals and we tried to find the store where they had been bought in order to return them. But David was very young and Palma was a fair sized city so we could not find the store. Since they fitted him well I made him wear them. But he was a boy of capacity and determination. He had two or three pesetas of his own and he found a box and turned them into buried treasure, showing the children where he had hidden them. The next day he dug up the box in my presence and behold, the coins were gone. He was very satisfied.

Because Bob had gone away and left him, David was probably fearful that I would leave him also. I did not consider his feelings at the time because I knew very well that I would never abandon the children and I had told them that. I was so busy worrying that John would leave me that I had no inclination to think about anybody but myself. While David kept a close eye on me, I kept a close eye on John. One evening he had a party at his house to which I could not go because I had no one to watch the children. I told David that I was going away and that I would be back at ten sharp. They would be quite safe, for the house was built of stone and the fire in the stove was out. I gave him the huge alarm clock and pointed out the time I would be back.

I was having such a good time at the party that ten o'clock approached and I had not yet left for the two mile hike home. I reasoned that the children would be asleep and would not notice. There was a little knock on the door and when we opened it there was David, holding a very tired and sleepy Tommy by one hand and with the other he accusingly held out the big clock, which showed exactly ten o'clock …

Robert Duncan had arranged to have his mail delivered to our house and he picked it up once or twice a week. He would come without Jess and would usually sink into our one armchair and chat for a half hour. Then he would leap to his feet, say Jess was expecting him and plunge out the door. He would demand an explanation of what I had been doing since he had seen me last and would favor me with opinions on my behavior. He amused himself by pretending to be my mentor; he found fault with my conduct over the sandals. I think it was John who told me to take them back to the store. I tried to agree with both of them, being in a craven, weak-minded state. He complained about life in Bañalbufar and I comforted and advised him in return …

One day when Robert had come to fetch his mail and was settled down to read it and to talk, I boasted about a new step I had just learned in dancing school. I jumped up to show it to him. Spanish dancing is often sexually suggestive; the choreographers thought up some extraordinary moves through the centuries. But it is all in the eye of the beholder; the dancer has her own mind completely full of numbers (3; 3; 7; 4; 3; etc.) The rhythm changes constantly and there are the feet, the hands, the arms, the skirt, the neck to worry about, while keeping a smile frozen in place to denote lighthearted pleasure. It is easy to lose your balance or trip or bump into the furniture. I turned carefully round and round in front of him and on each turn his face changed. First he looked hypnotized, then stunned, then predatory. I thought it was terribly funny, a self-proclaimed homosexual who didn't know his own mind. I laughed like anything and spun a little closer, laughing right into his face. He was puzzled at first and then dismayed as he realized what was happening to him. He leapt up and rushed from the house like Christian fleeing the tempter. Of course I chased him and apologized, but he was having none of that and so it was the last time I saw him. I was very sorry that I had teased him and driven him away for I had valued his kindly meant advice ... .

I passed my thirtieth birthday. It was time for me to get my inheritance. I wrote to Mr. Chute at the Old Colony Trust Co. and told him so. About that time a gypsy woman came to the door to tell my fortune. I have never been able to resist gypsies and invited her in. She wanted me to make a cross on her hand with silver, so I did so with two spoons, and then took them back which displeased her. But after I gave her a few copper coins she seemed convinced that I was shortly to come into a large fortune. I thought it was clever of her for I had not mentioned my inheritance to anyone at all. She thought that I might be going to win the lottery and urged me to buy a ticket. I just chuckled to myself in my secret knowledge. She became urgent. If I won the lottery as the result of her advice, would I share the takings with her? I promised faithfully. Then she went away. Later I found a lottery ticket tucked into the door frame. But I never did check to see if it was a winning number. I could not believe that I would hit the jackpot twice.

But it was going to be work to get hold of my inheritance. Mr Chute hemmed and hawed and tried to get me to leave the trust company in control. Finally he said that I would have to appear in person, but sweetened the blow by saying that he would send me money whenever I asked for it. Which was just as well, for I had big bills to pay. When I dropped in at Mossen Alcover I was informed that Robert Duncan's book was finished and that he and Jess had picked up the entire edition and gone back to America with it. They had not left even one copy for me. And the bill had not been paid. Luis Ripol, under his exquisite reticence, looked extremely worried, so I paid him because I liked him. I was furious with Robert for having stuck me with the bill, and remained furious with him for years, until I realized that he had probably given the money to Bob who had kept it for himself. The same thing had happened when Elga Lippman who had returned to New York and had written her PhD thesis there wanted the Divers Press to publish it at her expense. Bob had pocketed the money she had sent for it and it was up to me to refund the amount to her. Which I did, thus gaining her trust and friendship, for the poor soul was continually being bilked by members of the artistic world. Never mind that she was quite well off: it was not fair.

All my friends were in agreement that I should go to New York, straighten out my monetary affairs, including a settlement for the New Hampshire house, and perhaps get a divorce from Bob once I was on American soil instead of Spanish. For I hated the fear that filled me at the thought of his returning to us ...

I had a unique looking black and white coat and several skirts and blouses. Even an odd sort of suit. And of course my magnificent pin-striped suit copied from Elizabeth Trocchi's. I felt that I was a perfect fashion plate. I held my head up and sneered like a model. My posture had been much improved by the dancing lessons and I think I looked very well.

I took the children to Bañalbufar where Magdalena promised to guard them with her life. I left them many presents (Christmas was just over) so that they should not miss me too much, and indeed they did not look distressed. David could read and write moderately well so we would be able to remain in contact and I could leave them with a clear conscience. John had written to invite me to stay for a few days over New Year's in his tower, and he and Keith planned to meet me at the airport. I was thrilled; perhaps he had decided he was in love with me after all, and this would be the beginning of a new and wonderful life ...

John's tower appeared to be a recently excavated ruin that had been swept at least once. There was no furniture, only canvas and quilts on the floor covering a great deal of cement dust which was somewhat softer than the bare floor would have been. There were three storeys, the upper two reached by climbing up a home-made ladder and squirming through a hole in the middle of the ceiling. John's easel was set up on the second floor and he slept on the top one. There was nothing on the bottom floor except an unused stove. He took his meals at the local café, which had a washroom with a cold water tap.

These primitive surroundings did not offend me. What more romantic spot could you find for lovers, for lovers we became. I was excessively tense for fear I would not measure up, and I could not say that either one of us was completely easy. But I had gotten my own way and that pleased me enormously; I floated on a kind of blissful cloud and ignored the scowl on the face of the woman who ran the café ...

Back at the tower, after sleeping for a full day, we went to the café to see what they were doing for New Year's. A dance was in progress, a few locals hopping around, doing a sort of polka. A young Guardia Civil came up and asked me to dance. I knew that no local girl would dance with him and that I was his only chance for a partner. So we stepped out under John's disapproving eye. But it was a Bolero, which I had not yet learned, a dance of about ten different figures. I tried to escape but my partner assured me he would teach me. And so he did, with a good deal of crashing around. But finally I had the joy of going through the figures once without a flaw ...

The ship proved to be the *Franconia*, handed over by the German government as a war reparation, newly painted and, I think, renamed by the English. I had sailed in it as a child and had been very seasick. Perhaps there was something special about the ship for I began to feel sick at the very sound of the engines ...

I explored as much of the ship as I could reach, usually in the company of my girlfriends. As we sat on the deck we became engaged in chatting with a man I thought was a friend of theirs though I found out later that he had simply slipped into our conversation. He was a reporter with a powerful talent for appearing suddenly, looking like he had always been there. He was a Canadian named Ron K., separated from his wife and on his way to the States to get funding to allow him to explore certain mysterious congregations of Russian scientists which had sprung up unannounced in various centers of learning. He had followed these scientists around for years and knew their habits and itineraries. When they met secretly he knew that there was something up ... We had some pleasant times conversing and exploring the ship, playing ping pong. He told lovely stories of his life as a reporter. I was not very alert due to all the Dramanine, and when he tried to teach me to play bridge I ruined a couple of hours for the people at our table by my denseness.

He was particularly good at getting new ping-pong balls out of the stewards, after I had paddled them overboard, and adept at sneaking into parts of the ship closed to passengers, which I found great fun. One evening he rushed me up a staircase which usually had a sailor at guard before it. We emerged on top deck and crept around so that the pilot house could not see us. I was looking about me trying to find interesting shapes in the dark when he seized me, and started to rape me. I scratched and bit and kicked and did him so much damage that I could tell that he was getting really angry. Then I became afraid. He was a large strong man and I knew he would get his way in the end. After it was over and when he had begun to think again, he might expect me to have him arrested. Why should he not just give me a shove off the unrailed deck? No one would know, for no one had seen us climb the stairs.

I stopped fighting and became very cooperative ...

John had given me two instructions for my conduct in New York, which was a place he was sure would gobble me up in no time. First that I should stay at the YMCA, and second (which I am sure was a joke) that I should always tip taxi drivers ten cents. He gave me the addresses of some of his friends and told me to visit them. I followed his instructions and found the YMCA in Greenwich Village very comfortable, and its very name discouraged several men from following me home. I felt perfectly wonderful as I settled in for it was the first time in my life I had been completely alone, answerable to no one and with no one even watching me to see if I behaved. I gleefully ran over the kinds of mischief I could get into, but alas there was nothing I could think of except wasting time looking into store windows and buying a few things I didn't need, like candy bars ...

But I was not in New York to gad about and talk. Connie, on receiving a letter describing my intentions, had directed me to her uncle Lewis Arnold, a lawyer. At the time I was not looking for a divorce, only for some legal mechanism that would keep Bob away from me. I was still afraid of him; to that end I had bought a handbag with a wide metal rim around the base of it. I had a dim idea that if he attacked me I could swing it around by the handle and deliver him some kind of blow, much as I later drove off a pair of attacking dogs by swinging binoculars. However, "Uncle Louie" told me that was ridiculous, but I was still not quite convinced to get a divorce and join the ranks of those fallen women.

Bob learned somehow that I was in New York and came north with Charles Olson and Charles's girlfriend and new baby. Bob's appearance decided me suddenly, and I rushed back to Uncle Louie and begged for help. While he was making out divorce documents I agreed to meet Bob at a restaurant, where he introduced me to Dan Rice, who I think was the fatal Cynthia's former boyfriend. Bob was indignant that I planned to divorce him and screamed that he would take the children away from me and that I would never see them again. I was so afraid of him that I believed that he would succeed in this, and started to cry. Though Dan Rice told him to quit bullying me, and so took my side, I did not like Dan Rice either, for when he had quieted Bob down he asked me in a suggestive way if I would be "around" ... Bob was staying with someone named Julie who was a former girlfriend of John Altoon's, and Victor Kalos had been involved with her too, I think ... we went to lunch with Willem de Kooning, and to his exhibition. He was a nice enough man and I got some joy out of him by getting him to agree that incomprehensible poetry was valueless, while Bob sulked. There may have been some other notables. Then we went to meet Charles Olson and his mistress, Elizabeth, a rather sensitive helpless look-ing young woman, considerably prettier than Charles's real wife, Connie, who had fled with their daughter to her sister's house near Cape Cod. Eliz-abeth's baby was very young and Charles, in fatherly enthusiasm, had come to New York to seek employment.

Charles was an amiable giant, sure-footed like an athlete and very pleased with himself. It was impossible not to like him. Peter Stander, whose apartment they occupied, had vacated it at once for their benefit, though he scarcely knew them. Charles liked me, he liked everyone, I felt greatly at ease, and we cracked jokes and made fun of each other. Bob in his presence became amiable too, even to me. I was greatly relieved to have found a sort of middleman, someone who might make it possible for me to communicate fearlessly to Bob who would not attack me in Charles's presence.

Of course out of his presence it was the same old battle. Uncle Louie had ordered me to get Bob to sign an agreement for a divorce as the easi-est method of obtaining one. He refused savagely. So I took the agree-ment with me on our next visit to Charles and asked Bob, ever so sweetly, to sign it in his presence. Bob had convinced Charles that he was a gentle and lovely person, ill treated by his wicked wife. Now he was in a quan-dary; if he refused to sign he would appear to Charles to be mean-hearted and his persona would go up in smoke; and Charles was the pivot of his career. He signed while I held my breath. And I whisked the paper away so that he could not seize it later and destroy it.

It was very hard to persuade Bob to go back to Black Mountain. When I gave him money to leave, he spent it and remained. He would not go until we had eaten a farewell dinner together in an expensive restaurant. We sat opposite each other while he ate. Try as I could, I was unable to get the fork to my mouth, the sight of him choked me so. Perhaps he re-alized from watching me that it was no go, for he accepted my money this second time and we separated for good.

Uncle Louie sent me for my divorce to Birmingham, Alabama, to avoid New York residency requirements ...

My lawyer was a friend of Uncle Louie's, and he fretted that I had been gone so long for he felt responsible for me. He was as ceremoniously polite as a Spaniard and handed me a box of chocolates with my divorce papers ... I felt spruced up with my new divorce. I decided to devote a couple of weeks to visiting around and shopping before going on to the next tedious task of prying my money out of the trust company. I had thought I would have to go to New Hampshire to settle the ownership for the house there, but that was not necessary for Bob had told me that it was all settled for a very small sum and so I had told him he could keep it for his trouble. I bought presents for the children and gifts for Magdalena, Iska, and several others ...

I had also previously made contact with Victor Kalos, for I was still suffering from the illusion that sex and love were inextricably joined and that therefore I must be loyally connected to him in some way, even though I knew that it was John that I loved. I ate a few meals with him and went to his apartment where I had some of the sex and none of the love, which puzzled me. I found out that it was difficult to even like him, for he drank a lot and told lies now instead of funny stories.

I visited Charles and Elizabeth quite often. Charles was still looking for work and in between times they were always glad to see me. Peter Stander, who owned the apartment they were borrowing, was often present. He was an artist but not a good one. Nor was he good at life, for he was living on welfare and I think also received hand-outs from his mother. But he was a clever conversationalist, and when he invited me to go to a movie I was pleased.

After the movie he invited me to his mother's apartment to listen to some records. Since he had never shown any signs of being interested in me physically, I was not worried and went with him. We listened to all of the *Three Penny Opera* and by the time it was over I was very sleepy and wished that I did not have to go out into the cold night, for it was about the beginning of February by now. So I put it off and when he offered to share a joint with me I accepted just to delay the leave-taking. It was not long before I found myself on a mattress on the floor with him. This was a shock to me in more ways than one for it was far and away the best sexual experience that I had enjoyed in all my life ...

Charles had not yet found work and they decided to go back to Black Mountain. I came to help them on their way. Elizabeth wanted to give me a gift and all she could think of was a red chenille short bathrobe. It was pretty old but I thanked her profusely and put it on over my coat and insisted that I would wear it home though I made a pretty funny looking bundle.

I helped carry boxes and the baby out to the car, gave them a little money so that they would not have to sleep in the car during their long journey, and stood back a little and prepared to wave as they took off. But the car was a wobbly old thing and it would not start. Charles knew just what to do. Across the street was a tiny church made all of marble. It was just letting out and the minister was at the door shaking hands with the congregation. Charles went straight to him and asked for a push. The congregation stopped dead and stared. Of course the minister, under all those eyes, was required to be extra helpful and gracious to this group of unreliable looking bohemians, which included me in my red bundle. He brought his car up and attempted to give Charles a push, but his bumper was higher than Charles's, who evened that out by making me sit on the minister's radiator cap. That was just enough to bring it down, and after a successful push at quite a high speed amid cheers and waves from the congregation, Charles's car shot down the street and on into history.

Bibliography.

MAIN PUBLISHED MATERIALS

Books

Allen, Louis. *Burma: The Longest War, 1941–45*. London & Melbourne: J.M. Dent 1984.

Berlin, Lucia. *So Long: Stories 1987–1992*. Santa Rosa: Black Sparrow Press 1993.

Butterick, George, ed. *Charles Olson & Robert Creeley: The Complete Correspondence*, volumes 1 – 8. Richard Blevins, ed., volumes 9ff. Santa Barbara and Santa Rosa: Black Sparrow Press 1980–1997.

Callahan, Raymond. *Burma, 1942–1945*. Newark: University of Delaware Press 1979.

Cech, John. *Charles Olson and Edward Dahlberg; A Portrait of a Friendship*. Victoria: University of Victoria 1982.

Charters, Ann. *Kerouac: A Biography*. New York: Warner 1974.

Clark, Tom. *Charles Olson: The Allegory of a Poet's Life*. New York: W.W. Norton 1991.

– *Robert Creeley and the Genius of the American Commonplace*. New York: New Directions 1993.

Coleridge, S.T. *Poetical Works*, ed. E.H. Coleridge. London: Oxford University Press 1969.

Corman, Cid, ed. *The Gist of Origin, 1 951–1971: An Anthology*. New York: Grossman Publishers 1975.

Creeley, Robert. *The Collected Essays of Robert Creeley*. Berkeley: University of California Press 1989.

– *The Collected Poems of Robert Creeley, 1945–1975*. Berkeley: University of California Press 1982.

– *Contexts of Poetry: Interviews, 1961–1971*, ed. Donald Allen. Bolinas: Four Seasons Foundation 1973.

– *Echoes*. New York: New Directions 1994.

– *The Gold Diggers and Other Stories*. New York: Charles Scribner's Sons 1965.
– "Holy Forest." *Brick* (Winter 1993), 46–9.
– *The Island*. New York: Charles Scribner's 1963.
– *Life and Death*. New York: New Directions 1998.
– *Mabel: A Story & Other Prose*. London: Marion Boyars 1976.
– *Memory Gardens*. New York: New Directions 1986.
– *Mirrors*. New York: New Directions 1983.
– *Places*. Buffalo: Shuffaloff Press 1990.
– *A Quick Graph: Collected Essays & Notes*. San Francisco: Four Seasons Foundation 1970.
– *Was That a Real Poem & Other Essays*, ed. Donald Allen. Bolinas: Four Seasons Foundation 1979.
– *Windows*. New York: New Directions 1990.
Davey, Frank, ed. *Tish, No. 1–19*. Vancouver: Talonbooks 1975.
Dawson, Fielding. *Thread*. Woolwich: London: Ferry Press 1964.
DeFanti, Charles. *The Wages of Expectation: A Biography of Edward Dahlberg*. New York: New York University Press 1978.
Duberman, Martin. *Black Mountain: An Exploration in Community*. New York: E.P. Dutton 1972.
Edelberg, Cynthia Dubin. *Robert Creeley's Poetry: A Critical Introduction*. Albuquerque: University of New Mexico Press 1968.
Evans, George, ed. *Charles Olson and Cid Corman: Complete Correspondence, 1950–1964*. Orono: National Poetry Foundation, University of Maine 1987.
Faas, Ekbert. *Towards a New American Poetics: Essays & Interviews*. Santa Barbara: Black Sparrow Press 1979.
Faas, Ekbert, and Sabrina Reed, eds. *Irving Layton & Robert Creeley: The Complete Correspondence, 1953–1978*. Montreal & Kingston: McGill-Queen's University Press 1990.
Ford, Arthur. *Robert Creeley: Two Contexts*. Boston: Twayne 1978.
Fredman, Stephen. *The Grounding of American Poetry: Charles Olson and the Emersonian Tradition*. Cambridge, Mass.: Cambridge University Press 1993.
Fried, Jonathan L., M.E. Gettleman, D.T. Levenson, and N. Peckenham. *Guatemala in Rebellion: Unfinished History*. New York: Grove Press 1983.
Graves, Robert, and Paul Hogarth. *Majorca Observed*. London: Cassell 1965.
Hamalian, Linda. *A Life of Kenneth Rexroth*. New York: W. W. Norton 1991.
Handy, Jim. *Gift of the Devil: A History of Guatemala*. Toronto: Between the Lines 1984.
– *Revolution in the Countryside*. University of North Carolina Press 1994.
Harris, Mary Emma. *The Arts at Black Mountain College*. Cambridge, Mass. & London: MIT Press 1987.
Hawkins, Bobbie Louise. *Almost Everything*. Toronto: Coach House Press 1982.
– *Enroute*. Albany, Calif.: Little Dinosaur Press 1982.
– *My Own Alphabet*. Minneapolis: Coffee House Press 1989.

Immerman, Richard H. *The CIA in Guatemala: The Foreign Policy of Intervention.* Austin: Univerisity of Texas Press 1982.

Jeffreys-Jones, Rhodri. *The CIA and American Democracy.* New Haven: Yale University Press 1989.

Jonas, Susanne. *The Battle for Guatemala: Rebels, Death Squads, and U.S. Power.* Boulder: Westview Press 1991.

Levertov, Denise. *Collected Earlier Poems, 1940–1960.* New York: New Directions 1979.

Miles, Barry. *Ginsberg: A Biography.* New York: Harper Perennial 1990.

Nicosia, Gerald. *Memory Babe: A Critical Biography of Jack Kerouac.* New York: Grove Press 1983.

Olson, Charles. *Human Universe.* New York: Grove Press 1967.

Rexroth, Kenneth. *Excerpts from a Life,* ed. Ekbert Faas. Santa Barbara: Conjunctions 1981.

Rimbaud, Arthur. *Complete Works. Selected Letters,* ed. Wallace Fowlie. Chicago: University of Chicago Press 1966.

Rumaker, Michael. *Gringos and Other Stories.* Rocky Mount: Wesleyan College Press 1991.

– "Robert Creeley at Black Mountain." *Boundary* 2, 6, no.3/7, no.1 (Spring/Fall 1978).

Schumacher, Michael. *Dharma Lion: A Critical Biography of Allen Ginsberg.* New York: St Martin's Press 1992.

Seymour-Smith, Martin. *All Devils Fading.* Palma de Majorca: Divers Press 1954.

Szulc, Tad. *Fidel: A Critical Portrait.* New York: Morrow 1986.

Terrell, Carroll F., ed. *Robert Creeley: The Poet's Workshop.* Orono: National Poetry Foundation, University of Maine 1984.

Wilson, John, ed. *Robert Creeley's Life and Work: A Sense of Increment.* Ann Arbor: University of Michigan Press 1987.

School Publications

The Dial (Spring 1942)
The Dial (Summer 1943)
The Dial (Winter 1943)
Dial Year Book, 1942
Dial Year Book, 1943
Holderness School Today (September 1990)

Journals and Newspapers

Atlantic Monthly, November 1962
Evening Sun (Baltimore, Maryland) 5 February 1963
Harper's Magazine, October 1962

Jubilee, June 1962
Nashville Banner, 25 May 1962
Northwest Review, 6, no. 3 (Summer 1963)
Oakland Tribune, 1 April 1962
Saturday Review, 4 August 1962
Vancouver Sun, 5 September 1962

UNPUBLISHED MATERIALS

Documents

Acton Elementary and High School records
Holderness School records
Harvard University papers: Freshman Application for Rooms; Reader's Report
   on Applicant; Principal's Report on Applicant; Petition of 20 July 1944
University of New Mexico papers

Correspondence

Ainsworth, Alice, to Ann MacKinnon (Creeley)
Berlin, Donald ("Buddy"), to Robert Creeley
Blackburn, Paul, to Cid Corman
– to Robert Creeley
Bloodbank to Robert Creeley
Borden, A.R., to Robert Creeley
Brakhage, Stan, to Robert Creeley
Bronfman, Larry, to Paul Blackburn
Bush, Douglas, to Dean A.C. Hanford
Bynner, Witter, to Robert Creeley
Carroll, Paul, to Paul Blackburn
Corman, Cid, to Robert Creeley
Creeley, Genevieve Jules, to D. Leighton
– to Edric A. Weld
Creeley, Robert, to John Altoon
– to Basic Books
– to his Aunt Bernice
– to Paul Blackburn
– to Marion Boyars (includes notes from Bobbie)
– to Larry Bronfman
– to Witter Bynner
– to Gordon Cairnie
– to John Calder

– to Cid Corman
– to Ann MacKinnon Creeley
– to Judson Crews
– to Edward Dahlberg
– to Fielding Dawson
– to Ed Dorn (with comments from Bobbie)
– to Robert Duncan
– to Richard Emerson
– to Ian Hamilton Finlay
– to Allen Ginsberg (with comments from Bobbie)
– to Mitch Goodman
– to Harvard University
– to Cynthia Homire (later Fick)
– to Donald Hutter
– to "Jake"
– to "Jazz"
– to Carolyn Kizer
– to LeRoi Jones
– to Robert Jacob Leed
– to Denise Levertov and/or Mitchell Goodman
– to Ron Loewinsohn
– to his mother and/or sister (Genevieve Jules Creeley, Helen Creeley Axt)
– to J.F. Nims
– to Charles Olson
– to Joel Oppenheimer
– to Dorothy Pound
– to Ezra Pound
– to Henry Rago
– to Michael Rumaker
– to Schulman
– to Scott
– to R.N. Searles
– to Martin Seymour-Smith
– to Charles Tomlinson
– to Alex Trocchi
– to Gael Turnbull
– to the University of New Mexico
– to Philip Whalen
– to William Carlos Williams
– to Zempleny
– to Louis Zukofsky
Dahlberg, Edward, to Robert Creeley

Dawson, Fielding, to Robert Creeley
Duncan, Robert, to Robert Creeley
– to Denise Levertov
– to Kenneth Rexroth
– to Marthe Rexroth
Edes (lawyer) to Ann Creeley
– to Robert Creeley
Fleming, R., to A.C. Hanford
Gerhardt, Rainer Maria, to Robert Creeley
Ginsberg, Allen, to Robert Creeley
Greenman, R.B., to the American Field Service
– to the Reverend Charles R. Peck
Hanford, A.C., to Douglas Bush
– to Genevieve Creeley
– to Robert Creeley
Homire (later Fick), Cynthia, to Robert Creeley
Horton, David, to Robert Creeley
Kerouac, Jack, to Robert Creeley
Leighton, D., to Genevieve Jules Creeley
– to R. Fleming
Lester, J.A., to the dean of sophomores at Harvard University
Levertov, Denise, to Robert Creeley
MacKinnon (Creeley), Ann, to Paul Blackburn
– to Genevieve Jules Creeley
– to Robert Creeley
– to Ekbert Faas
Nims, John F., to Robert Creeley
Oppenheimer, Joel, to Robert Creeley
Paulson, R.E., to the dean of sophomores at Harvard University
Pound, Dorothy, to Robert Creeley
Rago, Henry, to Robert Creeley
Rexroth, Kenneth, to Robert Creeley
– to Denise Levertov
Rexroth, Marthe, to Robert Creeley
Tallman, Warren, to Robert Creeley
Tomlinson, Charles, to Robert Creeley
Trocchi, Alex, to Robert Creeley
Turnbull, Gael, to Robert Creeley
Weld, Edric A., to Genevieve Jules Creeley
– to W.F. Hall
Whalen, Philip, to Robert Creeley

Williams, Jonathan, to Ann Creeley
Williams, Jonathan, to Robert Creeley
Williams, William Carlos, to Robert Creeley

Interviews

Ainsworth, Alice and Kenneth, 26 July 1981
Berlin, Donald ("Buddy"), 16 August 1993
Brakhage, Stan, 18 August 1982
Burge, Mrs J., 30 August 1995
Corman, Cid, 27 July 1981
Corman, Leonard, 2 January 1993
Creeley, Robert, 29 December 1975
Creeley, Sarah, 18 July 1981
Crews, Judson, 21 August 1982
Ferrini, Vincent, 3 January 1993
Gerhardt, Renate, 6 March 1993
Goodell, Larry, 21 August 1993
Goodman, Mitchell, 19 January 1993
Hall, Norah, 3 September 1982
Hawkins, Bobbie Louise, 30 August 1982
Homire (later Fick), Cynthia, 20 August 1982
Judge, William F., 26 July 1981
Leed, Robert Jacob, 31 August 1993
Newton, Race, 12 March 1993
Power, Helen, 29 July 1981
Saunders, Paul, 10 July 1981
Seymour-Smith, Martin, 15 March 1993

Archives and Institutions

Thanks are due to the following archives and institutions for providing me with research materials: Special Collections, Ball State University, Muncie, Indiana; John Hay Library, Brown University Library, Providence, Rhode Island; Concordia University Library, Concordia University, Montreal, Quebec; Harvard University, Cambridge, Massachusetts; Harvard University Library, Harvard University, Cambridge, Massachusetts; Houghton Library, Harvard University, Cambridge, Massachusetts; Holderness School, Plymouth, New Hampshire; The Lilly Library, Indiana University, Bloomington, Indiana; Kent State University Libraries, Kent, Ohio; Newberry Library, Chicago, Illinois; Division of Archives and History, North Carolina Department of Cultural Resources, Raleigh, North

Carolina; Special Collections, Northwestern University Library, Evanston, Illinois; College Library, Reed College Library, Portland, Oregon; Simon Fraser University, Burnaby, British Columbia; Special Collections, Stanford University Libraries, Stanford, California; Poetry and Rare Book Collection, the University Libraries, SUNY at Buffalo, New York; Special Collections, Frank Melville, Jr Memorial Library, SUNY at Stony Brook, Stony Brook, Long Island, New York; Bancroft Library, University of California, Berkeley, California; Special Collections, University Library, University of California, Davis, California; Special Collections, University Research Library, University of California, Los Angeles, California; Archive for New Poetry, University Library, University of California, San Diego, California; Special Collections, University at Carbondale, Carbondale, Illinois; Joseph Regenstein Library, University of Chicago, Chicago, Illinois; University Library, University of Connecticut, Storrs, Connecticut; Special Collections, University of Delaware, Newark, Delaware; Archives and Manuscripts Department, McKeldin Library, University of Maryland, College Park, Maryland; Special Collections, University of New Hampshire, Durham, New Hampshire; Humanities Research Center, University Library, University of Texas, Austin, Texas; Thomas Fisher Rare Book Library, University of Toronto, Toronto, Ontario; Special Collections, University of Vermont, Burlington, Vermont; Special Collections, John M. Olin Library, Washington University, St Louis, Missouri; Beinecke Rare Book and Manuscript Library, Yale University Library, New Haven, Connecticut.

Notes.

CHAPTER ONE

3 future wife: cf. C.F. Terrell, ed., *Robert Creeley*, 23.
  – was thirty-nine: according to interview with Creeley's sister, Helen
    Power, 29 August 1981.
  – Arlington, Massachusetts: cf. ibid; T. Clark, *Robert Creeley*, 15.
  – "he was head": *Collected Poems*, 401.
4 the cornea: cf. Terrell, *Robert Creeley*, 23, 206. Clark, while quoting Terrell's
  account, also reprints the slightly different version of the accident from
  Creeley's 1989 "Autobiography." According to the latter, the party was driving "through Boston" where a lump of coal hit "the side window," shower-
  ing Bob's face with broken glass. Cf. Clark, *Robert Creeley*, 8, 125.
  – into corners: cf. Terrell, *Robert Creeley*, 23, 25.
  – completely blind: ibid., 209.
  – "Tom and Phil": *Memory Gardens*, 66.
  – country altogether: cf. Terrell, *Robert Creeley*, 23.
5 far away: cf. ibid., 22, 200, 203; *The Island*, 108.
  – the Blind: cf. Terrell, *Robert Creeley*, 206; Clark, *Robert Creeley*, 15.
  – the one started: cf. Terrell, *Robert Creeley*, 205.
  – and soda: cf. ibid.
  – "lost now": *Memory Gardens*, 67.
  – *Boston Herald*: cf. Terrell, *Robert Creeley*, 205; *The Island*, 67.
  – long time: cf. Terrell, *Robert Creeley*, 205.
  – "to die": *Mirrors*, 4.
  – "spring thaws": Clark, *Robert Creeley*, 125.
6 with candy: cf. *Contexts*, 137–8; Terrell, *Robert Creeley*, 22, 204.
  – "never located": *Contexts*, 158.
  – rich old man: cf. Clark, *Robert Creeley*, 7.

7 "had died": *Collected Poems*, 279.
  – soon after: cf. Terrell, *Robert Creeley*, 22.
  – died prematurely: cf. Clark, *Robert Creeley*, 7.
  – of Massachusetts: cf. Clark, *Robert Creeley*, 49.
  – and status: cf. A. Ford, *Robert Creeley*, 15; Terrell, *Robert Creeley*, 205; Clark, *Robert Creeley*, 16, 26f.; *Contexts*, 157.

8 and quickly: cf. Terrell, *Robert Creeley*, pp. 23, 206.
  – "curious way": ibid., 206.
  – "did not": Clark, *Robert Creeley*, 125.
  – "for some time": Terrell, *Robert Creeley*, 206.
  – replaced too often: interview with Bobbie Louise Hawkins, 30 August 1982.
  – tease him: cf. Terrell, *Robert Creeley*, 24.
  – pitying glances: interview with Bobbie Louise Hawkins, 30 August 1982.
  – "stay there": Terrell, *Robert Creeley*, 211.
  – shamefully unmanly: interview with Bobbie Louise Hawkins, 30 August 1982.
  – 1930 photograph: cf. Clark, *Robert Creeley*, 54.
  – "Far East": ibid., 124.
  – the women: cf. Terrell, *Robert Creeley*, 214; *The Island*, 68.

9 in the family: cf. Clark, *Robert Creeley*, 124; Terrell, *Robert Creeley*, 214.
  – black belt: cf. Terrell, *Robert Creeley*, 214; Clark, *Robert Creeley*, pp. 28–9.
  – genuine dignity: cf. Clark, *Robert Creeley*, 28–9; Terrell, *Robert Creeley*, 216–7.
  – "pup tent": Clark, *Robert Creeley*, 33; *Contexts*, 148.
  – "sly voices": *The Island*, 68.

10 "at 65": interview with Helen Power, 29 July 1981; cf. Terrell, Robert Creeley, 27.
  – Creeley's possession: cf. Clark, *Robert Creeley*, 27.
  – "wittily quotable": ibid.
  – hear of it: this and the following according to interview with Helen Power, 29 July 1981.
  – "sly voices!": *The Island*, 68.

11 years at a time: cf. Terrell, *Robert Creeley*, 212; *Contexts*, 157; Creeley to Olson, 11 June 1950, I, 97.
  – recite poems: cf. Creeley to Olson, 11 June 1950, I, 97; 26 November 1953. Terrell, *Robert Creeley*, 213.
  – all right: cf. Terrell, *Robert Creeley*, 212.
  – fundamentalist religion: cf. ibid., 211.
  – "him again": *Collected Poems*, 456.

12 figure out: interview with Helen Power, 29 July 1981.

12 *Lena Rivers*: ibid.
   – by heart: ibid.
   – knife as well: cf. *The Island*, 160–2; Terrell, *Robert Creeley*, 213.
   – his grandmother: cf. Terrell, *Robert Creeley*, 212.
   – was dead: cf. ibid.
13 "that's why": *Contexts*, 167.
   – of anger: cf. Terrell, *Robert Creeley*, 209.
   – into disrepair: cf. ibid., 204.
   – taken out: cf. ibid., 203; Clark, *Robert Creeley*, 17.
14 "another fight": *The Island*, 71.
   – was doing: cf. Terrell, *Robert Creeley*, 24, 221.
   – "had to": *The Island*, 70.

CHAPTER TWO

15 "further world": Clark, *Robert Creeley*, 127.
   – received a B: cf. Acton Elementary School record.
   – radiant smile: cf. ibid.
   – "Tarzan": Clark, *Robert Creeley*, 127.
   – the centre: cf. ibid., 201, 202; *Contexts*, 45; Clark, *Robert Creeley*, 129.
16 special journal: interview with Helen Power, 29 July 1981;
   cf. Genevieve Creeley to Weld, 15 June 1940; *Contexts*, 55.
   – semi-pornographic book: cf. *The Gold Diggers*, 79.
   – to fair: cf. Terrell, *Robert Creeley*, 207, 202.
   – A average: cf. Acton High School records.
   – "was there": Terrell, *Robert Creeley*, 221.
17 his mother: cf. ibid., 208.
   – "hard people": ibid., 208.
   – "changed remarkably": ibid.
   – and deserving: cf. Greenman to Peck, 1 September 1942.
   – high standards: cf. Greenman to the American Field Service, 23 October
   1944.
   – and advantage: cf. M. Novik, *Robert Creeley*, v; interview with Bobbie
   Louise Hawkins, 30 October 1982; interview with Helen Power, 29 July
   1981.
   – scholarship tests: cf. Clark, *Robert Creeley*, 125–6.
   – school fellows: for this and the following, see Genevieve Creeley to Weld,
   11 June 1940. Creeley's sister Helen Power recalls that she wrote the letter
   about Bob to the Reverend Edric A. Weld herself and that she assumed her
   mother's persona in the process. This is borne out by the fact that the handwriting of "Genevieve J. Creeley's" letter of 11 June 1940 differs markedly
   from that of Genevieve's other letters of the time.

18 awarded his scholarship: cf. Weld to Hall, 26 June 1940.
19 scholastic record: cf. report card of 12 October 1940.
- their owner: cf. Creeley to Searles, 18 December 1960; Creeley's 1979
commencement address.
- benign school: Terrell, *Robert Creeley*, 219.
- his charge: cf. Creeley's 1979 commencement address.
- "perfect response": *Holderness School for Boys* history,
1954, 66.
20 shy at first: cf. *Dial Year Book, 1943*.
- classical prosody: interview with William F. Judge,
26 July 1981.
- Lake Placid: cf. *Dial Year Book, 1942*.
- "common griefs": ibid.
- Holderness's history: cf. ibid.
- alias "Hook": *Dial Year Book, 1943*.
- "marriage broker": ibid.
21 "many admirers": ibid.
- "personal experiences": *The Dial* (Winter 1943), 2.
- "to night": *The Dial* (Summer 1943), 6.
22 "at peace": *The Dial* (Winter 1943), 7, 8.
- "of air": *Boundary* 2, vol. 6, no. 3/7, no. 1 (Spring/Fall 1978), 71.
- like it: cf. ibid.
23 all particulars: cf. Creeley's 1979 commencement address; Creeley
to Searles,
5 December 1960.
- "three years older": Creeley to Olson, 19 June 1952, X, 77; cf. [27 October
1950], III, 138.
- amongst peers: interview with William F. Judge, 26 July 1981.
- "strangling him": *The Dial* (Spring 1942), n.p.
- "shut up": Clark, *Robert Creeley*, 32.
24 "were doing": *Dial Year Book, 1942*.
- "at Holderness": ibid.
- in Plymouth: cf. ibid.
- "and masters": ibid.
- and town: cf. ibid.
- bow tie: cf. ibid.
25 "tone, 'Well?'": *Dial Year Book, 1943*.
- "needed voice": ibid.
- before breakfast: cf. Creeley to Searles, 5 December 1960.
- "two weeks": *The Dial* (Winter 1943), 3.
26 his leg: cf. Weld to Genevieve Creeley, 26 November 1942.

CHAPTER THREE

27 in spirits: cf. Leighton to Fleming, 7 February 1944.
   – of publications: cf. *Contexts*, 149; Creeley's application to Harvard University.
   – to writing: cf. Genevieve Creeley to Leighton, 27 June 1943.
28 excellent promise : cf. Leighton to Genevieve Creeley, 30 March 1944.
   – but Catholic: cf. Freshman Application for Rooms, 26 May 1943.
   – "time indeed": *Contexts*, 46.
   – denied earlier: cf. Genevieve Creeley to Leighton, 27 June 1943; cf. Clark, *Robert Creeley*, 125, where Creeley inflates this amount to $9,000.
   – his studies: cf. Genevieve Creeley to Leighton, 30 December 1943.
   – by mistake: cf. ibid., 8 February 1944.
29 (both four): cf. Reader's Report on Applicant, n.d.
   – he was with: cf. Principal's Report on Applicant, 15 February 1943.
   – he travelled: cf. ibid.
   – "some sort": Creeley to Olson [28 September 1950], III, 43.
30 "and dilemmas": Clark, *Robert Creeley*, 44.
   – "a lot also": ibid., 45.
   – jazz clubs: cf. ibid., 44.
   – grounds for complaint: cf. Leighton to Genevieve Creeley, 30 March 1944.
   – was called: cf. Petition, 20 July 1944.
31 and responsible: cf. Hanford to Creeley, 18 August 1944.
   – months later: cf. Hanford to Genevieve Creeley, 17 August 1944; and handwritten notes by Dean Hanford about the arrest of 24 August 1944.

CHAPTER FOUR

32 additional worry: this and some of the following according to interview with Helen Power, 29 July 1981.
   – done to her: cf. *The Island*, 34.
   – cuter kids: cf. ibid., 33.
33 a couch: cf. ibid., pp. 33, 35.
   – let him: cf. ibid., 33.
   – "trust of him": ibid., 72.
   – "a man": *Contexts*, 148.
34 "so simple": *Mabel*, 86.
   – "a habit": Terrell, *Robert Creeley*, 210.
   – "God in": *Later*, 70.
35 "rhetorical patterns": Clark, *Robert Creeley*, 26.

35 as early as 1943: cf. *Dial Year Book, 1943*.
  – "torn, eaten": *Mabel*, 84.
  – solitary vices: cf. Terrell, *Robert Creeley*, 216, 219.
  – "about to ...": *Gold Diggers*, 80.
  – their vagina: cf. Terrell, *Robert Creeley*, 219.
  – "fuck me": Ann MacKinnon's April 1997 marginal comment in this biography's typescript reads: "EF, can you really imagine me saying this?"

36 "and relaxed": *The Island*, 171–2. Ann MacKinnon's April 1997 marginal comment reads: "Nonsense! He was reading dirty books. I think Bob, intending to seduce me, tried to cover it up by accusing me of doing the same. I was too ignorant to try."
  – "love to her": ibid., 158.
  – "the hill": ibid.
  – without hesitation: cf. Greenman to the American Field Service, 23 October 1944.
  – great strain: cf. Weld to the American Field Service, 25 October 1944.

37 the board: cf. Hanford to Creeley, 21 November 1944.
  – "exact out": Creeley to Olson [28 September 1950], III, 43; cf. [25 September 1951], VII, 187.
  – "not him": *The Island*, 107.
  – rehabilitation centre: cf. ibid., 107, 34.

CHAPTER FIVE

38 major speculated: cf. Paulson to the Harvard dean of sophomores, 11 January 1946.
  – he had been!: cf. Creeley to his mother and/or sister, 5 February 1945; 20 January 1945; 7 January 1945; cf. *Contexts*, 139.
  – for her: cf. ibid. [17 March 1945].

39 going home: cf. ibid.
  – no mistake: cf. ibid.
  – "Bob Creeley": cf. ibid., 29 January 1945.
  – the war: cf. ibid., 20 January 1945.
  – being condescending: cf. Terrell, *Robert Creeley*, 220.
  – by rail: cf. Creeley to Olson [11 February 1951], IV, 140; Creeley to his sister Helen, 20 January 1945; Terrell, *Robert Creeley*, 220; Creeley to his mother and/or sister, 8 March 1945.

40 way home: cf. Creeley to his mother and/or sister, 8 March 1945; 15 May 1945. Creeley gives a different and conflicting account of the incident in Terrell, *Robert Creeley*, 220.

40 New England spring: cf. Creeley to Harvard University, 14 December 1945; Creeley to his mother and/or sister, 8 March 1945.
   – issue belts!: cf. Creeley to his mother and/or sister, 13 April 1945.
   – "tough spot": cf. Creeley to Harvard University, 14 December 1945; Paulson to the dean of sophomores, 11 January 1946.
41 "the attack": R. Callahan, *Burma, 1942–1945*, 159; cf. L. Allen, *Burma*, 420.
   – pointlessly ugly: cf. Creeley to his mother and/or sister, 13 April 1945.
   – "won't quit": *Boundary 2*, vol. 6, no. 3/7, no.1 (Spring/Fall 1978), 40.
   – on 3 May: cf. Creeley to Harvard University, 14 December 1955; Allen, *Burma*, 480.
42 his own: cf. Creeley to his mother and/or sister, 13 April 1945.
   – "breaks up!": *Mabel*, 153–154.
   – "6 octaves": Creeley to Olson [20 June 1950], I, 112–3; cf. [8 August 1950], II, 131, 130.
43 "each morning": ibid., II, 130.
   – "without stimulus": ibid. [20 June 1950], I, 113.
   – the war: cf. Creeley to his Aunt Bernice, 29 June 1945; cf. Creeley to Harvard University, 14 December 1945.
   – gun fire: cf. Creeley to Olson [18 Febuary 1951], V, 18; 27 June 1952, X, 118.
   – a remedy: cf. ibid. [20 June 1950], I, 113; *Contexts*, 150.
44 "damn good": Creeley to Olson [18 February 1951], V, 17.
   – "very delightful": *Contexts*, 150.
   – "a trace": Creeley to Olson [18 February 1951], V, 19.
45 "damn weeks": ibid. [11 February 1951], IV, 139.
   – "Just beautiful": *Contexts*, 150, 151; cf. Creeley to Corman, n.d.

CHAPTER SIX

46 at least two: cf. Bush to Hanford, 29 December 1945.
   – at Harvard: cf. Creeley to Harvard University, 14 December 1945.
   – settled down: cf. Fleming to Hanford, 3 January 1946; A.C. Hanford to D. Bush, 2 January 1946.
47 Levin's attention: cf. Lester to the dean of sophomores, 14 December 1945.
   – been refreshing: cf. Paulson to the dean of sophomores, 11 January 1946.
   – at Harvard: cf. Hanford to Fleming, 3 January 1966.
   – one more: cf. ibid.
48 never to be: cf. Borden to Creeley, 7 August 1947.
   – "be reformed": *Collected Essays*, 367.
   – *Armed Vision*: cf. ibid., 373.

48 "at Harvard": Clark, *Robert Creeley*, 131.
49 really knew: cf. *Contexts*, 102–3.
 – the semester: cf. *Collected Essays*, 524.
 – "Stevens reading": T. Clark, *Robert Creeley*, 131.
 – most suspect: cf. *Collected Essays*, 24.
 – "as possible": ibid., 4.
50 fellow homosexual: cf. ibid., 5, 23.
 – "his students": ibid., 4.
 – obsolete genteelism: cf. *Contexts*, 35–6.
 – an idiot: cf. Creeley to Olson, 23 January 1953.
 – the tracks: cf. *Contexts*, 61.
 – to emulate: cf. Clark, *Robert Creeley*, 132.
51 Political Association: cf. *Collected Essays*, 516; Creeley to Olson [4 July 1950],
 II, 47.
 – "the job": Creeley to Olson [4 July 1950], II, 47.
 – and others: cf. ibid., 24 June 1950, I, 154; interview with Race Newton,
 12 March 1993.
52 "jazz clarinetist": Clark, *Robert Creeley*, 44.
 – in the middle: cf. Creeley to Corman, n.d.; interview with Race Newton,
 12 March 1993; interview with Mitch Goodman, 19 January 1993.
 – a band: cf. ibid., 46.
 – "the most": cf. *Contexts*, 47.
 – sordid exploits: cf. Creeley to Olson, 25 September 1951, VII, 187.
 – Eliot editions: cf. *Contexts*, 51.
 – named Curley: cf. Creeley to Olson [18 October 1950], III, 105.
 – a record: cf. ibid., 31 May 1950, I, 62.
 – "total wreck": interview with Race Newton, 12 March 1993.
53 Creeley's Cambridge circle: cf. ibid; interview with Mitch Goodman,
 19 January 1993.
 – of his building: cf. B. Miles, *Ginsberg*, 56, 80, 106.
 – "own life": *Contexts*, 46; cf. interview with Race Newton, 12 March 1993.
 – Columbus Hospital: cf. Miles, *Ginsberg*, 131–2.

CHAPTER SEVEN

54 Goodman remembers: interview with Mitch Goodman, 19 January 1993.
 – becoming legendary: interview with Race Newton, 12 March 1993.
 – struck others: interview with Cid Corman, 27 July 1981.
 – their friendship: cf. Creeley to Leed, n.d.
 – responsible for him: cf. *Was That a Real Poem*, 101; Creeley to Leed, n.d.
55 marry her: cf. Creeley to Leed, n.d.
 – "as I was": C.D. Edelberg, *Robert Creeley's Poetry*, 159.

55 "her now": *Mabel*, 136.
  – "to be": Edelberg, *Robert Creeley's Poetry*, 159.
  – "his self-assurance": *The Island*, 34.
56 "even be": ibid., 107–8.
  – would happen: cf. Creeley to Leed, n.d.
  – sexual intercourse: cf. ibid.
  – the money: interview with Mitch Goodman, 19 January 1993.
  – school otherwise: interview with Cid Corman, 27 July 1981.
  – the bride: cf. Creeley to Leed, n.d.
  – laughing fit: interview with Buddy Berlin, 16 August 1993.
57 "any day": Creeley to Olson [24 June 1950], I, 155.
  – fuse blew: interview with Jacob Leed, 31 August 1993.
  – three days later: cf. Creeley to Olson [24 June 1950] I, 154.
  – to Cambridge: cf. *Contexts*, 205.
  – *"Enormous Room"*: Clark, *Robert Creeley*, 134.
  – to leave: cf. Creeley to Leed, n.d.
  – "of repair": interview with Race Newton, 12 March 1993.
58 and quick: cf. Creeley to Leed, n.d.
  – to nothing: cf. *Contexts*, 51.
  – "father surrogate": Terrell, *Robert Creeley*, 218.
  – miniscule prick: cf. Creeley to Olson [24 November 1950], IV, 48.
  – Bob concluded: cf. ibid., 11 June 1950, I, 96; [21 September 1950], III, 13.
  – "my father": ibid. [21 September 1950], III, 13.
  – "goes sour": ibid. [6 October 1950], III, 82.
  – and left: interview with Race Newton, 12 March 1993.
59 to Truro: cf. Creeley to Leed, 14 August 1947.
  – Wurlitzer juke-box: cf. Creeley to Olson, 9 October 1950, III, 88.
  – "got in": ibid., 18 October 1950, III, 105.
  – drawn to Ann: cf. ibid., 104.
  – "a baby!": Clark, *Robert Creeley*, 133–4.
  – planning more: cf. Creeley to Leed [2 January 1948].
60 "be okay": interview with Race Newton, 12 March 1993; cf. Creeley to Olson, 18 October 1950, III, 106.
  – main house: cf. Creeley to Leed, n.d.
  – "I'd say": Creeley to Olson [24 June 1950], I, 155; cf. Creeley to Corman, n.d.
61 imminent fate: cf. *Contexts*, 144; ibid., 143.
  – any professor: cf. ibid., 52, 144.
  – stagger back: cf. Creeley to Olson [19 August 1950], II, 152.
  – "even choked": ibid. [21 August 1950], II, 105.
  – "Too much": ibid. [23 October 1950], III, 124.
  – "nize cow": ibid. [31 October 1950], III, 147.

61 of pot: cf. Creeley to Leed, n.d.
   – and New York: interview with Alice and Kenneth Ainsworth, 26 July
     1981.
62 "least taxing": MacKinnon to Faas, 30 May 1984.

CHAPTER EIGHT

63 "competence in it": *Contexts*, 52; cf. *Collected Essays*, 496.
   – *Boston Globe*: cf. Creeley to Olson [18 April 1952], IX, 272–5, for several
     anecdotes regarding Creeley's work with that newspaper.
   – compulsive talker: cf. ibid., 19 May 1952, X, 77; [27 October 1950],
     III, 138.
64 around Boston: cf. ibid. [27 October 1950], III, 139; 19 May 1952, X, 77;
   Contexts, 10.
   – at the party: cf. Creeley to Leed, n.d.
   – literary language: cf. Creeley to Olson, 19 May 1952, X, 75–6.
   – about Donne: interview with Helen Power, 29 July 1981.
   – revelation to Bob: cf. *Collected Essays*, xiii; cf. *Contexts*, 123, where Creeley
     makes it his "twentieth birthday." See also *Contexts*, 50.
   – "had to": *Collected Essays*, 29.
   – *The Wedge*: cf. ibid., 498.
65 "authenticity": quoted from *Collected Essays*, 499.
   – back home: cf. Creeley to his mother and/or sister, 20 January 1945.
   – emerging poetics: cf. Creeley to Corman [1 June 1950].
   – "of these": *Collected Poems*, 3, 5; also see Creeley's comments on the poem
     in Edelberg, *Robert Creeley's Poetry*, 158–60.
66 dedicated to them: cf. Creeley to Leed [5 November 1948]; n.d.; 2 January
   1947; [4 May 1949]; [4 October 1949]; [23 November 1948].
   – Bob felt: cf. ibid. [4 May 1949]; n.d.
   – too easy: cf. ibid., n.d.
   – possible degree: cf. ibid., n.d.
   – "at first": *Contexts*, 106.
   – every page: cf. Creeley to Leed, n.d.; [30 September 1948].
67 been his eye: cf. Creeley to Leed, n.d.
   – at all: cf. ibid.
   – first novel: cf. ibid. [23 November 1948].
   – of form: cf. ibid., n.d.
   – Farm disjointed: cf. ibid. [6 July 1949].
   – some meaning?: cf. ibid. [3 June 1949].
   – with it: cf. ibid.
   – couldn't stop: cf. ibid. [20 February 1950]; *Contexts*, 105.

67 character presentation: cf. Creeley to Leed [29 September 1950], n.d.
68 they wish: cf. ibid., n.d.
  – in character: for this and the following, see ibid., n.d.
  – remained unpublished: cf. ibid., n.d.
  – in continuity: cf. ibid., 21 June 1948.
  – he wondered: cf. ibid. [17 February 1949; 1 June 1949; 25 October 1948].
69 it didn't: cf. ibid. [4 October 1949].
  – pass through: cf. ibid. [25 September 1950]; Creeley to Olson [20 September 1950], II, 155.
  – just awful: cf. Creeley to Leed, n.d.
  – pure hate: cf. Creeley to Leed, n.d.
  – conservative *Advocate*: cf. *Contexts*, 50–1.
  – Basic English: cf. Creeley to Leed, n.d.; [4 October 1949].
70 "valued advisor": C. Corman, *Gist*, xv; see also Corman-Olson, *Complete Correspondence*, 21 and passim.
  – "around America": Corman, *Gist*, xv–xvi.
  – station manager did: cf. ibid., xvi–xvii.
  – "of profanity": ibid., xvii.
  – write to Bob: cf. ibid., xviii.
  – "damnit, did": Creeley to Olson, 21 September 1950, III, 15.
71 "This Is Poetry": cf. Creeley to Corman, 14 December 1949.
  – who Corman was: cf. ibid., n.d.
  – his mouth: cf. Creeley to Leed [25 January 1950]; Creeley to Emerson, [14 February 1951].
  – payback time: cf. ibid., n.d.
72 once a week: cf. Creeley to Corman, 15 February 1950; 12 March 1950.
  – the studio: cf. Creeley to Emerson [14 February 1951].
  – told himself: cf. ibid., 5 April 1950.
  – tired of him: cf. ibid., 5 April 1950; 12 April 1950.
73 by a nonentity?: cf. Creeley to Leed [4 October 1949], n.d.; *Collected Essays*, 506.
  – real purpose: cf. Creeley to Leed, n.d.
  – the power: cf. ibid., n.d.
  – "for people": interview with Jacob Leed, 31 August 1993.
  – their work: cf. Creeley to Leed, n.d.
74 Bob's own mind: cf. Creeley to Leed [16 February 1950] n.d.; [21 February 1950]; n.d.; n.d; Creeley to Corman [6 March 1950].
  – wrote back: cf. D. Pound to Creeley, n.d.
  – a mad house?: cf. D. Pound to Creeley, 22 March 1950; n.d.
  – system, etc. etc.: c.f. Pound to Creeley, *Agenda*, IV, ii (October–November 1965), 21.

74 the *Del Mar Quarterly?*: cf. Horton to Creeley, 9 April 1950; 28 March 1950; 21 May 1950; 30 April 1950; 21 April 1950.
 – about education: cf. ibid., 30 April 1950.
75 for transportation: cf. Creeley to D. Pound, 31 May 1950; 16 May 1950.
 – of ideas: cf. ibid.
 – "anti-semite biz": Creeley to Olson [28 June 1950], II, 25.
 – such labels: Creeley to D. Pound, 28 June 1950.
 – "in literature": W.C. Williams to Creeley [13 April 1950]; 23 February 1950.
 – *Lititz Review:* cf. Creeley to Leed [22 April 1950].
 – and method: cf. Creeley to Corman [17 April 1950]; Creeley to Leed, n.d.
76 the students: cf. Creeley to Leed, n.d.; W.C. Williams to Creeley, 13 March 1950; Creeley to Olson, 29 June 1950, II, 30–1.
 – teaching job: cf. Creeley to Emerson, 10 May 1950.
 – first issue: cf. Creeley to Leed, n.d.
 – "they ate": Creeley to Olson, n.d., II, 75; 22 June 1950, I, 129; Creeley to Emerson, 24 July 1950.
 – the grindstone: cf. Creeley to Olson, 24 July 1950, II, 75.
 – "two: worlds": ibid., 23 August 1950, II, 106; 24 July 1950, II, 77; 27 July 1950, II, 79.
77 and rage: cf. Creeley to Leed, n.d.; Creeley to Olson, n.d., II, 105; 8 September 1950, II, 129.

CHAPTER NINE

78 "one's self!": Clark, *Charles Olson*, 92. For my accounts of Olson's relationship with Pound as well as with Frances Motz Boldereff I am indebted to Tom Clark's biography, see ibid., 92–3, 107–10, 118, 136–7, 145, 148, 154–7, 160–1, 164–7, 171, 178, 180, 183.
79 "single word": Charles Olson, *Human Universe*, 100.
81 ever, encountered: cf. Creeley to Emerson, 5 January 1951.
 – "liveth for": Clark, *Charles Olson*, 166, 197.
 – this situation: interview with Vincent Ferrini, 3 January 1993.
82 been told: e.g., Creeley-Olson, *Complete Correspondence*, I, ix-x; Clark, *Charles Olson*, 179–80, G.F. Butterick, "Creeley and Olson: The Beginning," *Boundary* 2, 6/7 (Spring-Fall 1978), 129–34; Jacob Leed, "Robert Creeley and *The Lititz Review*: A Recollection with Letters," *Journal of Modern Literature* 5 (April 1976), 243–59.
 – were lost: cf. Olson to Creeley, 21 April 1950, I, 19.
 – "ex-character": ibid.
 – "amused, etc.": Creeley to Olson, 24 April 1950, I, 21.

82 told Ferrini: cf. Creeley to Ferrini, 24 April 1950.
- to Frances: cf. Clark, *Charles Olson*, 177, 178, 180.

83 "of content": Creeley to Olson [5 June 1950], I, 79, 168, note 83; Clark, *Charles Olson*, 183.
- to her: cf. Clark, *Charles Olson*, 173; Creeley–Olson, *Complete Correspondence*, III, 87, 161, n. 26.
- "Chas Olson": Creeley to Olson [21-22 October 1950], III, 113, 110; cf. [9 March 1951], V, 59; Olson to Creeley [31 March 1951], V, 115; Clark, *Charles Olson*, 188.
- "with me": Olson to Creeley [9 May 1950], I, 24; 12 April 1951, V, 136; 8 November 1951, VIII, 107.
- things up: cf. Creeley's interview with L. Wagner, in the *Minnesota Review* V (October-December 1965), 320; Creeley to Pound [6 July 1950]; Creeley to Emerson, 7 June 1950.
- "the LINE": Creeley to Olson, 7 July 1950, II, 59.
- "indigenous speech": Butterick in Terrell, *Robert Creeley*, 121, 122.

84 "a thing": Creeley to Olson, 18 July 1951, VI, 152, 151; 28 April 1950, I, 21; [12 March 1951], V, 71; [23 October 1950], III, 121; 11 April 1951, V, 158.
- "them all": ibid., 19 September 1951, VII, 173; 8 June 1950, I, 86; 3 July 1950, II, 43.
- "of 'em": ibid., 3 July 1950, II, 43.
- "done, new": ibid. [16 May 1950], I, 28-9; 28 April 1950, I, 21; [11 May 1950], I, 25.
- anti-Semitic feelings: for this and the following, see Clark, *Charles Olson*, 132-3.

85 "for himself": quoted in Creeley to Olson, 11 June 1950, I, 98.
- "spreading around": Olson to Creeley, 19 June 1950, I, 110.
- "do Jewz": ibid. [23 June 1950], I, 147; Creeley to Olson, 21 June 1950, I, 119; Olson to Creeley [22 June 1950], I, 136.

86 by construction?: cf. Creeley to Olson [18 February 1951], V, 18, 17.
- "PRO/VERSE": ibid. [5 June 1951],VI, 53; 22 November 1950, IV, 37; 3 August 1951, VII, 50.
- as well: cf. Olson to Creeley, 18 September 1951, VII, 169.
- West Coast poet: cf. Creeley to Olson [23 September 1951], VII, 184.
- "like a man": Olson to Creeley, 15 November 1951, VIII, 140.
- couldn't manage: cf. ibid., 18 November 1951, VIII, 149.
- "already out": Creeley to Olson [19 November 1951], VIII, 157.
- "Hermes himself?": *Contexts*, 142.

87 "bad, miserable": Olson to Creeley [27 November 1951], VIII, 185.
- entire poem: cf. Creeley to Olson, 31 November 1951, VIII, 209.
- "a publisher!": Olson to Creeley, 15 January 1952, IX, 37.
- "most times": Creeley to Olson, 24 January 1952, IX, 58.

CHAPTER TEN

88 of person: cf. Creeley to Leed, n.d.
  – damn well obscene: cf. Creeley to Olson [21 September 1950], III, 15; 6 November 1951, VIII, 99; [31 January 1951], IV, 118; [13 November 1951], VIII, 129.
  – utter fool: cf. Creeley to Olson and/or Olson to Creeley [11 February 1951], IV, 136; [2 December 1950], IV, 65; 12 October 1951, VIII, 43; [23 October 1950], III, 121; [12 April 1951], V, 136, 139; 23 July 1951, VI, 190; [30 June 1951], VI, 99; 18 November 1951, VIII, 146; [25 October 1951], III, 130; [21 September 1950], III, 15; 18 November 1951, VIII, 146; [10 October 1951], VIII, 120; [23 January 1951], IV, 112; [31 January 1951], IV, 117; [18 October 1950], III, 102; [31 January 1951], IV, 117; [17 October 1950], III, 100.
  – "such eunuchism": Creeley to Olson [21 January 1952], IX, 50; Olson to Creeley [27 November 1951], VIII, 185.
89 "mother. Shit!": Olson to Creeley, [17 January 1952], IX, 41, 42.
  – "their balls!": ibid., IX, 43, 41.
  – "into him!": Creeley to Olson and/or Olson to Creeley [17 January 1952], IX, 44; [27 September 1951], VII, 196; [31 January 1951], IX, 117, 118; 31 March 1951, V, 115; [18 October 1950], III, 101.
  – inside out: cf. Creeley to Leed, n.d.; Creeley to Olson [11 April 1951], V, 161.
  – "Black Mountain School": *Collected Essays*, 507.
  – Bob cursed: cf. Creeley to Corman [18 October 1950].
90 literary matters: cf. ibid. [18 October 1950].
  – the editing: cf. ibid., n.d. [18 October 1950].
  – deep end: cf. ibid. [6 November 1950].
  – the program: cf. ibid. [29 October 1950].
  – altogether ball-less: cf. ibid. [3 November 1950].
  – of purpose: cf. ibid. [8 November 1950].
91 human pertinence: cf. Corman to Creeley [12 November 1950].
  – Gerhardt write him: cf. Creeley to Olson [3 November 1950], III, 153.
  – he promoted: cf. Creeley to Corman, n.d.; [21 November 1950]; [22 November 1950]; [24 November 1950].
  – on 29 December 1950: cf. ibid.
  – Columbus, Ohio: cf. Clark, *Charles Olson*, 181; Creeley to Olson [15 December 1950], IV, 89.
  – *Golden Goose*: cf. Creeley to Corman, n.d.; [15 December 1950].
  – shamefaced apology: cf. ibid. [1 February 1951].
  – his nerves: cf. ibid. [5 February 1951].

92 confessed to Olson: Creeley to Olson [11 February 1951], IX, 136;
[23 January 1951], IV, 112.
   – printing process: cf. Corman, *Gist*, xx, xxi.
   – a minimum: cf. Creeley to Corman [9 March 1951].
   – been blustering: cf. ibid. [12 March 1951].
   – "[his] dismay": Corman, *Gist*, xxi.
   – "of printing: cf. ibid.
   – thank you: cf. Creeley to Corman [20 April 1951].
93 faith in him: cf. ibid., 15 July 1951.
   – beyond recognition: cf. ibid., 14 June 1951; 17 July 1951.
   – "special tastes": quoted in Creeley to Olson, 28 June 1951, VI, 88.
   – pretty widely: cf. Creeley to Corman, 29 June 1951.
   – wrote to Corman: cf. ibid. [20 July 1951].
   – "the, WORD!": Creeley to Olson, 21 December 1951, VI, 177;
[20 July 1951], VI, 170.
   – to Olson: cf. ibid. [19 September 1951], VII, 172; [20 July 1951], VI, 172.
94 he wrote: cf. ibid., 26 July 1951, VI, 208, 209.
   – find things: cf. Creeley–Olson, *Complete Correspondence*, VII, 260, no. 64.
   – influence on him: cf. Creeley to Olson, 19 September 1951, VII, 173.
   – confessed to Olson: cf. Creeley to Corman, 7 August 1951; Creeley to
Olson, 26 July 1951, VI, 209.
   – their positions: cf. Olson to Creeley, 10 August 1951, VII, 82, 83, 87, 88.
   – before replying: cf. ibid. [21 August 1951], VII, 108; [20 August 1951],
VII, 116–117.
   – "damn you": ibid. [22 August 1951], VII, 120, 117, 119.
95 his mother: cf. Clark, *Charles Olson*, 185, 370; Creeley to Olson [18 September 1950], II, 150.
   – too many): cf. G.F. Butterick's introduction to Creeley-Olson, *Complete
Correspondence*, I, xv.
   – conversation: cf. Creeley to Corman [7 January 1951].

CHAPTER ELEVEN

96 "half days": *Collected Essays*, 181–2.
97 her husband: interview with Mitch Goodman, 19 January 1993.
   – of them: cf. Creeley to Corman [12 March 1950].
   – August 1950: cf. Creeley to Olson [27 August 1950], I, 114.
   – around 1900: cf. Creeley to Corman [15 November 1950]. Ann
MacKinnon, in her April 1997 marginal comments in this biography's
typescript, remembers the object to have been a "worm-eaten wood relief
carving of a dancing Hindu girl" belonging to her mother.

97 got enough: interview with Mitch Goodman, 19 January 1993; cf. Creeley to Leed [6 October 1950].

98 at least one: cf. Creeley to Corman, n.d.
  – she adored: cf. Creeley to Leed, 6 October 1950; Creeley to Corman, n.d.
  – original payment: cf. *Contexts*, 56, 145; Creeley to Leed [29 September 1950].
  – two days: cf. Creeley to Leed [24 May 1949].
  – red blood cells: cf. Creeley to Corman [23 October 1950]; Creeley to Olson [16 October 1950], III, 97. Creeley, in a letter to his mother of 17 May 1952, gives a conflicting account of this matter to the effect that Ann never suffered from the Rh factor. Ann MacKinnon has confirmed the latter version and attributes the premature birth to an accident.
  – blood transfusion?: cf. Creeley to Olson [20 October 1920], III, 115.
  – A brute!: cf. Creeley to Leed, 16 December 1950; cf. Creeley to Olson, 16–17 December 1950, IV, 90.

99 country altogether: cf. Creeley to Corman [4 January 1951]; Creeley to Leed, n.d.; Creeley to Olson [31 January 1951], IV, 121.
  – French bureaucracy: cf. Creeley to Leed, 16 December 1950; Creeley to Corman [10 February 1951]; [7 February 1951]; [12 February 1951]; [10 January 1951].
  – to Cid Corman: cf. Creeley to Corman [5 March 1951].
  – to France: cf. ibid. [5 May 1951].
  – 22nd Street: cf. ibid. [30 April 1951]; Creeley to Leed, 11 July 1951.

100 "the writing": *Collected Essays*, 181.
  – "the Carolinas": ibid.; cf. Creeley to Olson, 19 October 1951, VIII, 67.
  – "frightful containment": Creeley to Olson, 28 May 1951, VI, 47.
  – Paul Fachetti: cf. Creeley to Corman, 27 May 1951; *Collected Essays*, 369.
  – "their minds": *Collected Essays*, 369.

101 those hills: cf. Creeley to Blackburn, 23 May 1951; Creeley to Corman, 27 May 1951; Creeley to Leed, 11 July 1951; Creeley to Olson [27 September 1951], VII, 194.
  – to themselves: cf. Creeley to Blackburn, 23 May 1951.
  – "so fine": Creeley to Olson [20 July 1951], VI, 171; Creeley to Corman, 31 May 1951.
  – rolled it: cf. Creeley to Blackburn, 13 June 1951.
  – "well REAL": Creeley to Olson, 28 May 1951, VI, 48.
  – "damn neatness": ibid., 22 June 1951, VI, 64.
  – "4 years": ibid. [28 September 1951], VII, 202; cf. Creeley to Leed, 11 July 1951.

102 eat him up: cf. Creeley to Corman, 2 July 1951; Creeley to Olson, 7 July 1951, VI, 111.

102 correspondence): cf. Creeley–Olson, *Complete Correspondence*, 13 July 1951, VI, 117; VI, 119–34; Creeley to Corman, 17 July 1951.
  – frustrations with it: cf. Creeley to Olson, 21 July 1951, VI, 173; 26 July 1951, VI, 205f.
  – "Mr. Blue": cf. Olson to Creeley, 1 August 1951, VII, 35–46.
  – "I write": Creeley to Olson, 8 August 1951, VII, 61.
  – of the writing: cf. ibid., 23 August 1951, VII, 131.
  – methodologies which: cf. Olson to Creeley, 22 September 1951, VII, 180.
  – "total OUT": Olson, *Human Universe*, 127; cf. E. Faas, *New American Poetics*, 148.
  – "surest occasion": Creeley to Olson [26 September 1951], VII, 191, 192.
  – "by heart": ibid., 27 August 1951, VII, 129.
103 "NONE. None.": ibid., 8 July 1951, VI, 115.
  – him sexually: cf. ibid., 25 July 1951, VI, 195; [20 July 1951], VI, 172.
  – there and then: cf. Creeley to Corman, 20 June 1951.
  – "my doubts": Creeley to Olson, 8 June 1951, VI, 115.
  – social airs: cf. ibid., 20 July 1951, VI, 172.
  – the performance: cf. Creeley to Corman, 18 July 1951. Ann MacKinnon's April 1997 marginal comment in this biography's typescript here reads: "He didn't get the seat he wanted, so he walked out dragging me after him."
  – "be seen": Creeley to Olson, 4 October 1951, VIII, 17; [29 September 1951], VII, 206.
104 "beyond 'Time'": ibid. [23 October 1951], VIII, 83, 84; 4 September 1951, VII, 149, 150.
  – "his speech": ibid. [15 November 1951], VIII, 134.
  – dozen times: cf. Creeley–Olson, *Complete Correspondence*, VIII, x.
  – September 1951: cf. Creeley to Corman [25 August 1951]. According to Ann MacKinnon's April 1997 marginal comments in this biography's typescript, the original deadline for their moving out was May 1952.
  – "the street, etc.": Creeley to Olson [29 October 1951], VIII, 94; cf. Creeley to Corman [25 August 1951].
  – "with agreement": Creeley to Olson, 29 November 1951, VIII, 196; cf. *The Island*, 78.
105 "for speech": Creeley to Olson [15 November 1951], VIII, 133; 134; cf. [5 November 1951], VIII, 135; [13 November 1951], VIII, 129.
  – "have been": ibid., 19 November 1951, VIII, 156.
  – and jumpy: cf. ibid., 24 December 1951, VIII, 252.
  – "the attentions": ibid., 29 November 1951, VIII, 195, 196, 194.
  – "or tear –": S.T. Coleridge, *Poetical Works*, ed. E.H. Coleridge (London: Oxford University Press, 1969), 364.
  – "of here?": quoted in Creeley to Olson, 13 December 1951, VIII, 244; cf. ibid, x.

105 how bad: cf. Creeley to his mother, 31 December 1951; Creeley to Olson, 7 January 1952, IX, 21; 24 December 1951, VIII, 249.

106 without thinking: cf. Creeley to his mother, 31 December 1951.
  – "medal, etc.": Creeley to Olson [4 February 1952], IX, 87.

CHAPTER TWELVE

107 Olson himself: cf. Creeley to his mother, 31 December 1951; Creeley to Olson, 9 January 1952, IX, 25, and photograph following ibid., 160.
  – "at myself": Creeley to Olson [14 February 1952], IX, 99; cf. 3 January 1952, IX, 18, 281, note 2; [25 February 1952], IX, 168; 12 April 1952, IX, 240; Creeley to his mother, 8 January 1952.
  – "and good": Creeley to Olson, 20 February 1952, IX, 160.

108 "the tale": Olson to Creeley, 31 January 1952, IX, 68, 66, 67.
  – "IT BEGINS": ibid., IX, 68.
  – "holding on": Creeley to Olson [4 February 1952], IX, 88.
  – Creeley's stories: Gerhardt to Creeley, n.d.

109 "postwar Germany": cf. Collected Essays, 279.
  – December 1950!: cf. Creeley to Corman, 4 January 1951!
  – Creeley's stories: cf. Gerhardt to Creeley, n.d.
  – their way: cf. Creeley to Olson, 13 February 1952, IX, 97; [16 February 1952], IX, 127; Creeley to his mother, 25 August 1951.
  – brush everywhere: cf. Creeley to Olson, 27 March 1952, IX, 197, 196.

110 more promptly: cf. ibid., 11 September 1951, VII, 163.
  – "of / friendship": Collected Poems, 114.
  – "and minus": interview with Renate Gerhardt, 6 March 1993.
  – "the way": ibid.
  – next morning: cf. Collected Essays, 279.
  – "in that": Creeley to Olson, 27 March 1952, IX, 197.
  – "I can go": Collected Poems, 114.

111 literary works: cf. Collected Essays, 280; Creeley to Olson [24 March 1952], IX, 188; 27 March 1952, IX, 196.
  – "his face": Collected Essays, 280; cf. Creeley to Olson, 27 March 1952, IX, 197, where Creeley gives a slightly different account of the incident.
  – "public conscience": Creeley to Olson, 4 April 1952, IX, 220; 31 March 1952, IX, 217; 4 April 1952, IX, 222.
  – "particular reality": ibid., n.d., IX, 231; 31 March 1952, IX, 218; 4 April 1952, IX, 222; 17 July 1952.
  – "immediate hell": ibid., 12 April 1952, IX, 239, 238.

112 "kept apart": Collected Poems, 114.
  – been stolen: cf. Creeley to Olson [12 April 1952], IX, 243, 242, 329, n. 293; 31 March 1952, IX, 216, 217.

112 into irritation: cf. ibid., 31 April 1952, IX, 218; 12 April 1952, IX, 241.
  – "not / strained": *Collected Poems*, 113.
  – Creeley mused: cf. Creeley to Corman [13 May 1952].
113 "never / enough": *Collected Poems*, 32.
  – "rhythm units": Creeley to Olson, 13 April 1952, IX, 250, 248; cf. Creeley to Corman [13 May 1952].
  – "toilet paper": Creeley to Olson [15 April 1952], IX, 254.
  – "partially kept": *Collected Poems*, 118.
114 to Olson: Creeley to Olson, 19 May 1952, X, 73; cf. Creeley to Corman [13 May 1952].
  – that city: cf. Creeley to Olson, 31 March 1952, IX, 219; 12 April 1952, IX, 238.
  – "twenty-five years!": Creeley to Cairnie, 29 April 1952.
  – "be ok": Creeley to Olson, 27 April 1952, X, 17.

CHAPTER THIRTEEN

115 "most idyllic": Creeley to Olson, 2 May 1952, X, 24; cf. Creeley to Emerson, 13 May 1952.
  – a year: cf. Creeley to Olson, 27 April 1952, X, 20.
  – in kids: cf. Creeley to Laubiès, 25 May 1952; Creeley to his mother, 17 May 1952; 3 June 1952.
  – "unto you": Creeley to Olson [27 May 1952], X, 118; Creeley to his mother, 29 May 1952.
116 "the store": Creeley to Olson, 29 June 1952, X, 189.
  – and Spain: cf. ibid., Creeley to his mother, 29 May 1952.
  – "Louis Bromfield": Creeley to Olson, 6 July 1952, X, 210; cf. Creeley to Corman [26 May 1952]; Creeley to his mother, 17 May 1952.
  – his life: cf. Creeley to Corman [26 May 1952]; 9 September 1952; Creeley to Olson, 23 June 1952, X, 173–4; MacKinnon to Genevieve Creeley, n.d.
  – whole years: cf. Creeley to Olson, 9 July 1952, X, 215.
117 "it's crazy": *Complete Poems*, 121; cf. Creeley to Olson, 23 June 1952, X, 174; Creeley to Corman, 9 September 1952.
  – "past year, etc.": Creeley to Olson, 15 July 1952.
  – numerous pregnancies: cf. Creeley to his mother, 17 May 1952. Ann MacKinnon, in her April 1997 marginal comments in this biography's typescript, remembers six pregnancies.
  – religious reasons: cf. Creeley to his mother, 17 May 1952.
  – of July: cf. MacKinnon to Creeley's mother Genevieve, n.d.
  – for her: cf. Creeley to Olson [31 July 1952].
118 poetic output: cf. Creeley to his mother, 14 June 1952; Creeley to Corman, 29 May 1952; 3 June 1952.

118 "all happy": Creeley to Olson, 10 June 1952, X, 143.
  – number three: cf. *Goad* 1, no.2 (Winter 1951–52), 16–19, and *Goad* 1, no.3 (Summer 1952), 22.
  – "little prick": *Quick Graph*, 94; cf. Creeley–Olson, *Complete Correspondence*, IX, 330, no. 305.
  – like a fascist: cf. *Goad* 1, no.3 (Summer 1952), 7–9.
  – came of it: cf. Creeley to Corman, 16 November 1952.
  – coming winter: cf. Creeley to Olson, n.d.; [31 July 1952]; [6 August 1952].
119 the English: cf. ibid., 4 May 1952, X, 29; Creeley to Corman, 9 September 1952.
  – "be sly": Creeley to Olson, 20 June 1952, X, 165.
  – to Robert Creeley: cf., ibid., 4 July 1952, X, 205.
  – far-flung endeavours: cf. ibid., 2 July 1952, X, 200; Creeley to Corman, 20 June 1952.
  – for subscriptions: cf. ibid., 20 June 1952.
  – remained unanswered: cf. Creeley to Olson, 30 August 1952; 6 July 1952, X, 207.
  – there altogether: cf. ibid. [31 July 1952]; 20 June 1952, X, 166; Creeley to Corman, 30 August 1952.
120 replace *Origin*: cf. Creeley to Olson [27 May 1952], X, 120; 20 June 1952, X, 166.
  – in general: cf. ibid., 13 June 1952, X, 146.
  – "hold of": ibid., 17 June 1952, X, 158–9, 163.
  – in France: cf. ibid. [21 July 1952]; [6 August 1952]; 15 August 1952; [6 August 1952].
  – can be: cf. ibid., 6 September 1952.
  – into tears: cf. ibid., 30 August 1952; Creeley to Corman, 30 September 1952; Creeley to Emerson, 13 September 1952.
  – their kicks: cf. Creeley to Olson, 30 August 1952.
  – to Spain altogether: cf. ibid., 6 September 1952.
121 so far : cf. ibid., 4 November 1952.
  – "that time": *Collected Poems*, 3.
  – multiple stimuli: cf. Creeley to Corman, 9 September 1952; Creeley to Olson, 10 September 1952.
  – replied defensively: interview with Martin Seymour-Smith, 15 March 1993.
  – "confidential voice": *The Island*, 59.
122 "contain himself": ibid., 158.
  – Len himself: this and the following according to interview with Len Corman, 2 January 1993.
  – "*Vous! Vous!*": Len Corman's account here, of course, conflicts with Creeley's own in *The Island*, 158.

CHAPTER FOURTEEN

123 "neighbours' susceptibilities": Robert Graves and Paul Hogarth, *Majorca Observed*, 29.
   – one another: cf. Creeley to Layton, 17 August 1953, 39.
   – his marriage?: interview with Martin Seymour-Smith,
      15 March 1993; Creeley to his wife Ann [29 September 1952].
124 Peabody Museum: cf. Creeley to Olson, 26 March 1953; 3 December 1952;
      7 January 1953.
   – "intelligent, individual": Layton to Creeley, 17 April 1953, 9.
   – "cute flippancy": Creeley to Layton, 26 April 1953, 9, 10.
   – "your supper": ibid., 26 April 1953, 10, 11.
125 "trust him": ibid., 17 August 1953, 39, 38; 31 July 1953, 35.
   – roadside cafés: cf. Creeley to his wife, Ann [29 September 1952]; Creeley
      to Olson, 4 November 1952.
   – the children: cf. Creeley to Corman, 20 December 1952; *The Island*, 62;
      Creeley to Olson, 30 March 1953.
   – pathetically so: cf. Creeley to Olson, 4 November 1952; Creeley
      to Corman, 20 December 1952.
   – at them: cf. ibid., 20 December 1952.
126 smuggling ventures: cf. ibid.; Creeley to Olson, 4 November 1952.
   – early in 1953: cf. *The Island*, 128; cf. Creeley to Olson, 26 March 1953;
      Creeley to Corman, 30 January 1953.
   – to give: cf. Creeley to Olson, 26 March 1953.
   – the harbour: ibid., 3 April 1953.
   – out of hell: cf. ibid., 10 May 1953.
   – him proud: cf. Creeley to Corman, 16 November 1952.
   – the cover: cf. ibid., 4 December 1952; Creeley to Olson, 16 November
      1952; 4 December 1952.
127 or cageyness: cf. ibid., 5 December 1952; 4 December 1952.
   – luxurious hate: cf. ibid., 31 January 1953; 3 December 1953;
      19 January 1953.
   – Corman's poetry: cf. ibid., 20 February 1953.
   – hope so: cf. ibid.; cf. Creeley to Corman, 20 February 1953.
   – *Origin* #8: cf. Creeley to Olson, 24 February 1953.
   – and imitation: cf. ibid., 15 March 1953.
   – utter crap: ibid., 23 January 1953; cf. Creeley to Corman, 18 January 1953.
128 "Elizabethan manner": *World Review*, nos. 5 and 6 (December 1952), 31,
      32.
   – the same: cf. Creeley to Corman, 18 January 1953.
   – at hand: cf. Creeley to Olson, 2 April 1953; 30 January 1953.
   – was shit: interview with Martin Seymour-Smith, 15 March 1993.

128 proper study: cf. Creeley to Olson, 8 April 1953.
  – or dead: cf. ibid.
  – the Atlantic: cf. ibid., 2 April 1953; 12 April 1953.
  – "Projective Verse": interview with Martin Seymour-Smith, 15 March 1993.
  – with everyone: cf. Creeley to Olson, 30 March 1953.
129 "you & me": cf. ibid., 7 June 1953.
  – "given up": review of *New Directions*, no. 13, 1951; *Commentary*, 14, no. 6 (December 1952), 576–7.
  – to "corrode": cf. Creeley to Olson, 12 February 1953.
  – "however striking": *Commentary* 14, no. 6 (December 1952), 577.
  – the stories: cf. Creeley to Olson, 20 February 1953; 3 April 1953.
  – death-bed injunctions: cf. ibid., 6 February 1953; cf. ibid., 17 December 1952; 12 February 1953.
  – "tomatoes above": *The Island*, 62.
  – sober him: cf. Creeley to Olson, 30 March 1953. Ann MacKinnon, in her April 1997 marginal comments in this biography's typescript, claims that her husband "took the only warm room in the house for his study."
130 the world: cf. Creeley to Olson, 9 January 1953; Creeley to Corman, 12 February 1953.
  – "been worse": *The Island*, 93–94; cf. Creeley to Olson, 10 May 1953. Ann MacKinnon, in April 1997, claims that the cyst was her appendix.
  – "the time": *The Island*, 97.
131 "broken too": *The Island*, 100; cf. Creeley to Olson, 27 May 1953; 19 June 1953; 5 July 1953; Creeley to Corman, 15 May 1953.
  – "you, then": *The Island*, 105, 98.
  – "to describe": *Collected Poems*, 128.
132 past sins: cf. Creeley to Olson, 10 May 1953; 27 May 1953; Creeley to Corman, 15 May 1953; Creeley to Blackburn, 27 May 1953; 14 June 1953.
  – *The Island*: cf. *The Island*, chapter 9.
  – in town: cf. Creeley to Blackburn, 27 May 1953.
  – the novel: cf. ibid.
  – "John thought": *The Island*, 84.
  – such passion: interview with Martin Seymour-Smith, 15 March 1993.

CHAPTER FIFTEEN

133 be punished: cf. Creeley to Olson, 21 July 1953.
134 with him : cf. ibid., 23 August 1953.
  – movies yet: cf. ibid.
  – "quite literally": Creeley to Layton, 18 October 1953, 56.
  – "precocious goat": *Gold Diggers*, 37.

134 to bandage: cf. ibid., 36.
  – "using them": Creeley to Layton, 18 October 1953, 57, 56.
135 be "misread": cf. Creeley to Olson, 5 October 1953.
  – "for that": *Gold Diggers*, 115, 113.
  – "the other": *The Island*, 151, 28, 11, 137, 138.
  – "a goat": ibid., 51, 53, 54.
136 "they're short": Creeley to Layton, 25 October 1953, 59.
  – his own: cf. Creeley to Olson, 27 October 1953.
  – proved fruitless: cf. ibid.
  – another novel: cf. ibid., 26 November 1953.
  – A contemporary photograph: see Layton to Creeley, *Complete Correspondence*, following xxxii.
  – to Corman: Creeley to Corman, 27 February 1954.
  – "with it": *The Island*, 177, 178.
137 "taken everything": ibid., 12, 34, 15, 117, 111, 64, 188.
  – "empty halls": ibid., 73, 178.
  – "peculiar authority": Clark, *Robert Creeley*, 142.
  – blotchy flesh: cf. *The Island*, 98.
138 "to do": ibid., 126, 52, 17, 52.
  – "the men": ibid., 155, 63.
  – "him also": ibid., 139.
  – "as 'Manus' ": *Collected Essays*, 509.
  – break for Creeley: cf. Creeley to Blackburn, 4 October 1953; Creeley to Corman, 3 October 1953.
  – worth courting: cf. Creeley to Blackburn, 4 October 1953; Creeley to Corman, 3 October 1953; Creeley to Olson, 5 October 1953.
139 "with him": *The Island*, 140.
  – "John thought": ibid., 140, 141.
  – "going down": ibid., 141.
  – miserable magazine: cf. Creeley to Olson, 3 November 1953; cf. Creeley to Corman, 25 October 1953.
  – an alternative: cf. Creeley to Corman, 25 October 1953; Creeley to Trocchi, n.d.
  – "with it": Creeley to Olson, 3 November 1953.
  – "almost hysterical": Creeley to Layton, 6 November 1953, *Complete Correspondence*, 61; see also Creeley to Corman, 6 November 1953.
140 over now: cf. Creeley to Olson, 6 November 1953.
  – the book: cf. ibid.
  – known him: cf. Trocchi to Creeley, 10 November 1953.
  – "the change": *The Island*, 63, 58, 38, 159.
  – "of friendship": ibid., 160, 58, 59, 64, 28, 58.
141 "of Artie": ibid., 58, 137, 38.
  – hellishly tenuous: cf. Creeley to Olson, 6 November 1953.

141 of things: cf. Creeley to Corman, 11 November 1953.
  – such self-indulgence: cf. Creeley to Corman, 17 January 1954; Creeley to Olson, 16 December 1953.
  – showing up again: cf. Creeley to Corman, 17 January 1954.
  – still outstanding!: cf. ibid.
142 out worse: cf. ibid., 17 January 1954; 19 January 1954; [20 January 1954].
  – Martin's brain: cf. ibid., 24 January 1954; 27 January 1954.
  – "with it": *The Island*, 137, 138.
  – back somehow!: cf. Creeley to Corman [28 January 1954].
  – the $100: cf. ibid. [28 January 1954].
143 was done: cf. ibid. [28 January 1954]; 31 January 1954.
  – the culprit: cf. ibid., 9 February 1954; 3 February 1954.
  – bad, etc.: cf. ibid., 23 February 1954.
  – vehement fashion: cf. ibid., 14 February 1954; 18 February 1954.
  – bother him: cf. ibid., 18 February 1954; 4 March 1954.
  – "and labour": Corman, *Gist*, xxv.
144 "of me": *Windows*, 100.

CHAPTER SIXTEEN

145 than Corman: cf. Creeley to Olson, 12 November 1953.
  – tomorrow: cf. ibid.
  – to "landscapes": cf. ibid., 1 September 1953.
  – the mountains: cf. *The Island*, 40.
146 a reality: cf. Creeley to Olson, 2 December 1953; Creeley to Corman, 5 December 1953.
  – Kenneth Rexroth: cf. Creeley to Olson, 12 December 1953; Creeley to Corman, 17 December 1953.
  – with Olson: cf. Creeley to Layton, 12 December 1953, 71; ibid., 2 January 1954, 86.
  – "little good": Layton to Creeley, n.d., 72.
  – "this thing": ibid., 21 December 1953, 74.
147 critical writings: cf. Layton to Creeley, 1 January 1954, 83–6.
  – "tremendous help": Creeley to Layton, 2 January 1954, 87.
  – "finally, unfair": Layton to Creeley, 1 January 1954, 84.
  – "& generous": Creeley to Layton, 8 January 1954, 91, 90.
  – the margin: cf. Rexroth to Creeley [17 February 1954].
  – like hawks: cf. Creeley to Corman, 3 February 1954; Creeley to Blackburn, 27 January 1954.
  – general contacts: cf. Creeley to Corman, 5 December 1953.
  – to others: cf. ibid., 16 December 1953; Creeley to Layton, 8 January 1954, 91; Creeley to Levertov, 3 February 1954.
  – *A Quarterly*: cf. Creeley to Olson, 12 December 1953.

148 "pre-Christian ritual": BMR #4 (Winter 1954), 37. According to her April 1997 marginal comments in this biography's typescript, Ann MacKinnon contributed "a set of photos of Bañalbufar": "But I was not allowed my name on them."

– fair enough: cf. Creeley to Corman, 27 February 1954; 3 February 1954; 4 February 1954; Creeley to Levertov, 3 February 1954.

– "next boat": Creeley to Layton, 27 February 1954, 103–4; cf. Creeley to Corman, 27 February 1954.

– "and attention": Layton to Creeley, 1 January 1954, 85; ibid., n.d., 73.

149 him cleaner: cf. Creeley to Olson, 17 February 1954.

– "open verse": ibid., 31 July 1953.

– "and verbs": Layton to Creeley, 24 October 1954, 168.

– "your own": ibid., 5 December 1953, 67; ibid., 6 February 1954, 99; 17 January 1954, 92.

150 "to me": M. Rumaker, "Robert Creeley at Black Mountain," *Boundary* 2 vol. 6, no. 3, vol.7, no. 1 (Spring/Fall 1978), 137, 138.

– "aural receptivity": ibid., 138.

– "of discovery": ibid.

CHAPTER SEVENTEEN

151 first few days: cf. Creeley to his wife, Ann [17 March 1954].

– soothing roll: cf. ibid. [23 March 1954]; [22 March 1954]; [16 March 1954]; [17 March 1954]; [19 March 1954].

152 business ahead: cf. ibid. [13 March 1954]; [19 March 1954].

– Black Mountain College: cf. ibid. [29 March 1954]; 3 April 1954; Alice Ainsworth to MacKinnon [1 April 1954].

– court business: cf. Creeley to his wife, Ann [29 March 1954]; 3 April 1954.

– "on measure": cf. ibid., 3 April 1954.

– in bed: cf. ibid., 6 April 1954.

– "otherwise naked": quoted in M. Duberman, *Black Mountain*, 393.

153 "the ground": Rumaker, *Boundary* 2 (Spring/Fall 1978), 142–3.

– "beyond them": ibid., 143.

– both intriguing: interview with Cynthia Homire (later Fick), 20 August 1982; Rumaker, *Boundary* 2 (Spring/Fall 1978), 144.

– and poet: cf. Creeley to his wife, Ann, 14 April 1954; 6 April 1954, Rumaker, *Boundary* 2 (Spring/Fall 1978), 144.

– "a monotone": Duberman, *Black Mountain*, 393, 394.

154 as all that: cf. Creeley to his wife, Ann, 8 April 1954.

– letter to Ann: cf. Creeley to his wife, Ann, 8 April 1954, 6 April 1954. Creeley similarly over-dramatized the sequence of events from his arrival at Black Mountain on the morning of 5 April 1954 to his first class.

According to two interviews he gave to Ann Charters and Martin Duberman, Olson persuaded a reluctant Creeley to teach his first class "the
same evening of his arrival," a version repeated by Michael Rumaker
(cf. Duberman, *Black Mountain*, 393, and 491, n. 21; Rumaker, *Boundary 2*
(Spring/Fall 1978), 144.) By contrast, Creeley's letter to his wife, Ann, of
6 April 1954, written the day *after* his early morning
arrival at Black Mountain, states that he'd begin teaching "tonight."

154 at night: cf. Rumaker, *Boundary 2* (Spring/Fall 1978), 145.
 – to bed: cf. Creeley to his wife, Ann, 8 April 1954; 30 April 1954.
 – off again: cf. ibid., 14 April 1954.
 – the keyboard: cf. ibid., 14 April 1954; 18 April 1954.
155 until dawn: cf. J. Williams to MacKinnon [24 April 1954].
 – "good enough": Rumaker, *Boundary 2* (Spring/Fall 1978), 145.
 – through at all: cf. Creeley to his wife, Ann [10 June 1954].
 – considerably impaired: cf. W.C. Williams to Creeley, 10 August
 1953.
 – 20 May 1954: cf. Creeley to his wife, Ann, 21 May 1954.
 – most others: interview with Cynthia Homire (later Fick), 20 August
 1982.
156 the evening: cf. *Contexts*, 29.
 – than before: Creeley to his wife, Ann, 13 May 1954.
 – in Cuba: cf. ibid.
 – an alchemist: cf. ibid.
 – Ann's lover: cf. *Collected Essays*, 434-5.
157 "the roof": *Gold Diggers*, 141, 137; cf. *Collected Essays*, 434.
 – and Huss's: cf. Rumaker, *Boundary 2* (Spring/Fall 1978), 157.
 – congenial company: cf. Creeley to his wife, Ann, 26 April 1954.
 – "expert shoplifter": quoted in Duberman, *Black Mountain*, 410.
 – Don Juan: cf. ibid.
 – "of *them?*": Rumaker, *Boundary 2* (Spring/Fall 1978), 158.
 – "'fabulous invalid'": ibid., 159.
158 "little scary": *Contexts*, 146-7.
 – his poems: according to interview with Cynthia Homire (later Fick),
 20 August 1982.
 – typed them : ibid.
 – like a poet: cf. Creeley to his wife, Ann, 30 August 1954.
 – Bob felt: cf. ibid., 23 April 1954; [5 June 1954]; 2 May 1954; Creeley to
 Olson, 17 October 1954.
159 New York City: cf. Creeley to his wife, Ann, 9 June 1954; 11 May 1954;
 [5 June 1954]; Creeley to Bronfman, 3 May 1954; Creeley to Olson,
 24 October 1954.
 – bar together: cf. Creeley to his wife, Ann, 13 May 1954; interview with
 Cynthia Homire (later Fick), 20 August 1982.

159 so "clean": cf. Creeley to his wife, Ann, 12 May 1954; Creeley to "Jazz": 2 August 1954.
– "a Spaniard": Rumaker, *Boundary 2* (Spring/Fall 1978), 158.
– for him: cf. Creeley to his wife, Ann [4 June 1954]; 11 June 1954.
– had evaporated: cf. Creeley to Bronfman, n.d.; [28 May 1954]; [31 May 1954].

160 much sometimes: cf. Homire to Creeley, n.d; n.d.
– Smash, crash: cf. ibid.
– "they fall": *Collected Poems*, 324.
– never hate: cf. Homire to Creeley, n.d.; n.d.
– drunken mother: cf. Creeley to his wife, Ann, 28 June 1954.

161 to "vicious": cf. Creeley to Olson, 17 August 1954; 17 October 1954.
– earlier version: cf. ibid.
– "of coal": *The Gold Diggers*, 130.
– "give up": ibid., 132, 133, 134.
– any viciousness: cf. Creeley to Olson, 17 October 1954.

162 "like it": *Contexts*, 151, 152.
– such activities: cf. Homire to Creeley, n.d.
– Cynthia herself: according to interview with Cynthia Homire (later Fick), 20 August 1982.
– Goodbye. Goodbye: cf. Homire to Creeley, n.d.
– destroy them: cf. Homire to Creeley, n.d.
– bitterness, and resentment: cf. Creeley to Dawson [12 January 1956].

CHAPTER EIGHTEEN

(The chapter's title is taken from a letter from Creeley to his wife, Ann, of 24 June 1954.)

163 be next: cf. Creeley to Blackburn [27 February 1954].
– and desired?: cf. Creeley to his wife, Ann, 17 March 1954; 18 April 1954.

164 very much: cf. ibid., 13 March 1954; 16 March 1954; 21 March 1954, 26 March 1954.
– was hysterical: cf. ibid., 3 April 1954; 14 April 1954.
– loved her: cf. ibid., 18 April 1954.
– "the girl": cf. ibid., 6 April 1954; 26 April 1954; 30 April 1954.
– that, forever: cf. ibid., 18 April 1954; 30 April 1954; 23 April 1954; 30 April 1954.

165 might sound: cf. ibid., 11 May 1954.
– very exciting: cf. ibid., 12 May 1954.
– of him: cf. Creeley to Olson, 12 May 1954.
– her cysts: cf. Creeley to his wife, Ann, 12 May 1954.

166 Errol Flynn: cf. ibid., 16 March 1954; 17 March 1954; 23 March 1954.
– in Majorca: Alice Ainsworth to MacKinnon, 1 April 1954.

166 like that: cf. Creeley to his wife, Ann, 3 April 1954; 2 June 1954;
12 May 1954.
- good deal: cf. ibid., 12 May 1954.
- of Manhattan: cf. Creeley to his wife, Ann, 12 May 1954; 11 May 1954.
- very hopeful: cf. ibid., 13 May 1954.
- enough money: cf. ibid., 26 April 1954; 13 May 1954; 25 May 1954; 26
May 1954; 11 May 1954.

167 hopeful kisses: cf. MacKinnon to Creeley, n.d.
- she did: cf. ibid., n.d.
- and understanding: cf. ibid., n.d.
- fine woman: cf. Creeley to his wife, Ann, 25 May 1954.
- with it: cf. MacKinnon to Creeley, n.d.
- the contrary: cf. Creeley to his wife, Ann, 25 May 1954.
- friends again: cf. ibid., 31 May 1954.

168 it would: cf. Creeley to his wife, Ann, 4 June 1954; cf. MacKinnon to Creeley, n.d.
- the meantime: cf. Creeley to his wife, Ann, 5 June 1954.
- that way: cf. ibid.
- of love: cf. ibid, 28 May 1954; 6 June 1954; 4 June 1954; 11 June 1954; 25
May 1954; 10 June 1954; 22 June 1954; cf. Creeley to Olson, 23 June
1954.

169 his affair: cf. Creeley to his wife, Ann, 6 June 1954; 10 June 1954; 22 June
1954.
- other way: cf. ibid., 24 June 1954.
- him shots?: cf. MacKinnon to Creeley, n.d.
- by everybody: cf. ibid., n.d.
- was Christ: cf. ibid.
- out he'd go: cf. Creeley to his wife, Ann, 28 June 1954.

170 his return: cf. ibid., 28 June 1954.
- hit back: cf. ibid., 14 July 1954; 8 July 1954.
- this point: cf. ibid., 29 June 1954; 7 July 1954; 14 July 1954; 28 June 1954.
- Grand Central Station: cf. Creeley to Olson, 23 June 1954.
- to her: cf. Creeley to his wife, Ann, 22 June 1954.

CHAPTER NINETEEN

171 the job: cf. Blackburn to Corman, 29 July 1954.
- feel grateful: cf. Creeley to Levertov, 10 September 1954.
- Cid Corman: cf. Blackburn to Corman, 29 July 1954.
- in Majorca: cf. ibid.

172 get laid: cf. ibid.
- an inch: cf. ibid.
- be continued: cf. ibid.

172 as well: cf. Bronfman to Blackburn, 30 July 1954; 6 August 1954.
- his mouth: cf. Creeley to Olson, 4 September 1954.
- the Blackburns: cf. MacKinnon to Blackburn, n.d.
- childish standoffishness: cf. Creeley to Olson, 4 September 1954.
- Divers Press: cf. Creeley to Corman, 3 September 1954.
- unpleasant business: cf. Creeley to Levertov, 10 September 1954.
- as well: cf. Creeley to Bronfman, 13 September 1954.
- approached him: cf. Creeley to Olson, 28 August 1954; 4 September 1954.

173 little prick: cf. Creeley to Oppenheimer, 4 September 1954.
- and pompous: cf. Creeley to Corman, 26 August 1954.
- general sentiments: cf. Creeley to Layton, 23 December 1953, 75ff.
- translator's ears: cf. Creeley to Corman, 26 August 1954.
- "to him?": *Collected Poems*, 68.
- could get: cf. Creeley to Olson, 4 September 1954; Creeley to Oppenheimer, 10 September 1954.
- to Oppenheimer: cf. Creeley to Oppenheimer, 10 September 1954.
- to Paris: cf. Creeley to Olson, 12 September 1954.
- of conversation: cf. Creeley to Layton, 13 September 1954, 132.

174 broke loose: cf. Creeley to Bronfman, 13 September 1954; Creeley to Olson, 12 September 1954; Creeley to Corman, 12 September 1954.
- goddamn scene: cf. Creeley to Olson, 12 September 1954.
- "the grave": Creeley to Layton, 13 September 1954, 132.
- stop it: cf. ibid.; Creeley to Bronfman, 13 September 1954; Creeley to Corman, 12 September 1954.
- him too: cf. Creeley to Corman, 12 September 1954.
- with it: cf. Creeley to Trocchi [12 September 1954].
- all this: cf. Creeley to Olson, 12 September 1954.
- for himself: cf. Carroll to Blackburn, 21 September 1954.

175 major opposition: cf. Corman to Blackburn, 28 October 1954.
- et al did: cf. Rexroth to Creeley, 8 August 1954; 2 August 1954.
- "god knows": Creeley to Layton, 18 August 1954, 120.
- Creeley concluded: cf. Creeley to Olson, 19 August 1954.
- committed suicide: cf. ibid., 20 August 1954; *Collected Essays*, 280.

176 kill them: cf. Creeley to Olson, 20 August 1954.
- he loved: cf. ibid., 31 August 1954; 28 August 1954; 10 September 1954.
- BMR himself: cf. ibid., 10 November 1954; Creeley to Corman, 14 October 1954; 15 October 1954; 22 November 1954; 28 November 1954.
- as well: cf. Creeley to Duncan, 21 November 1954.
- the magazine: cf. Creeley to Olson, 26 January 1955.
- agreed to: cf. Creeley to Corman, 3 February 1955.
- your news: cf. Creeley to Corman, 4 April 1955.

177 couldn't manage: cf. ibid., 22 November 1954; 4 March 1955; *Collected Essays*, 39; Creeley to Olson, 4 December 1954.
  – Karl Shapiro: cf. Creeley to W.C. Williams, 25 November 1954, *Collected Essays*, 34.
  – it later: cf. W.C. Williams to Creeley, 2 December 1954.
  – wrote to Creeley: cf. ibid.
  – of measure: cf. Creeley to W.C. Williams, 25 November 1954.
  – the other: cf. W.C. Williams to Creeley, 16 December 1954.
  – of language: cf. Creeley to W.C. Williams, 26 January 1955.
178 was singing: cf. ibid.
  – terminologies: cf. W.C. Williams to Creeley, 3 February 1955.
  – wrote to Creeley: cf. Creeley to Levertov, 25 November 1954 and 4 December 1954.
  – between men: cf. ibid., 8 January 1955.
  – assured Trocchi: cf. Creeley to Trocchi, 23 October 1954.
  – respecting Martin: cf. Creeley to Corman, 22 November 1954.
  – other things: cf. Creeley to Olson, 13 August 1954.

CHAPTER TWENTY

179 unexpected visitor: cf. Creeley to Olson, 10 November 1954.
  – and hopeless: cf. Creeley to Leed, 12 September 1950.
  – in bed: cf. Creeley to Levertov, 9 November 1954.
  – Creeley's address: cf. Creeley to Olson, 10 November 1954.
  – "own life": quoted in J. Cech, *Charles Olson*, 64.
  – to Dahlberg: cf. Dahlberg to Creeley, 12 January 1955.
  – "of pills": quoted in Cech, *Charles Olson*, 87.
  – "for moldering": quoted in C. DeFanti, *Edward Dahlberg*, 184.
180 "of aesthetics": cf. Dahlberg to Creeley, 14 July 1956.
  – "of envy": quoted in DeFanti, *Edward Dahlberg*, 185.
  – "and Japheth": quoted in Cech, *Charles Olson*, 81.
  – "of worldliness": quoted in DeFanti, *Edward Dahlberg*, 189.
  – "ray lamp": for this and the following see DeFanti, *Edward Dahlberg*, 5, 29, 53.
181 "of repulsion": quoted ibid., 70.
  – would appear: cf. ibid.
  – most Germans: cf. ibid., 110.
  – "American writer": quoted ibid., 189.
  – of Chaucer: cf. Creeley to Olson, 10 November 1954.
  – was up to: cf. Creeley to Levertov, 9 November 1954.
  – *Gospel Restored*: cf. DeFanti, *Edward Dahlberg*, 190.
  – an inch: cf. Creeley to Olson, 10 November 1954.

182 Graves's house: cf. DeFanti, *Edward Dahlberg*, 190.
  – "poetic interests": ibid., 191.
  – "Graves' hand": Creeley to Layton, 27 November 1954, 182.
  – everyone imaginable: cf. Creeley to Olson, 27 November 1954. For a different remembered version of the incident see DeFanti, *Edward Dahlberg*, 191–2.

183 his wife: cf. Creeley to Olson, 27 November 1954; DeFanti, *Edward Dahlberg*, 188.
  – infernal trull: cf. Dahlberg to Creeley, n.d.
  – in *BMR* #1: cf. Creeley to Corman, 15 January 1954.
  – at ease: interview with Robert Creeley, 29 December 1975.
  – in months: cf. Creeley to Corman, 27 March 1955; Creeley to Dawson, 21 April 1955.
  – as a poet: cf. Creeley to Levertov, 20 April 1955; Creeley to Olson, 26 March 1955.
  – anyone sharper: cf. Creeley to Olson, 26 March 1955.
  – most able: cf. Creeley to Trocchi, 23 April 1955.
  – their author: cf. Duncan to Levertov, 16 April 1955.

184 their task: cf. Duncan to Creeley, 25 August 1955; 20 May 1955.
  – Paul forever: cf. Duncan to Levertov, 16 April 1955.
  – as Duncan: cf. Creeley to Corman, 27 March 1955.
  – "altogether articulate": *Collected Essays*, 435–6; Creeley to Levertov, 20 April 1955.
  – they decided: cf. Creeley to Corman, 27 March 1955; Creeley to Olson, 1 May 1955; n.d.
  – growing up: cf. *Collected Essays*, 433.

185 "attentive listener": ibid., 434.
  – arrived ladies: cf. *Collected Essays*, 508; *Contexts*, 62.
  – farewell present: cf. *Collected Essays*, 109.
  – an affair: cf. Creeley to Olson, 5 July 1955; 1 May 1955; 24 June 1955.
  – goddamn typewriter: cf. ibid., 13 June 1955; 24 June 1955; 5 July 1955.
  – physical *joy*: cf. ibid., 5 July 1955.
  – North America: cf. ibid., 24 June 1955.
  – "bitter" details: cf. ibid.

186 one more: cf. ibid., 5 July 1955.
  – one eye: cf. Duncan to Levertov, 24 August 1955.
  – Madame Bovary's: cf. ibid.
  – did Bob: cf. Duncan to Creeley, 25 August 1955.
  – a thief: cf. Duncan to Levertov, 24 August 1955; Duncan to Creeley, 5 August 1955; 30 August 1955; 25 October 1955.

187 maltreated children: cf. Duncan to Creeley, 2 October 1955.

CHAPTER TWENTY-ONE

188 his jaw: cf. Duberman, *Black Mountain*, 400.
— "the cottages": Clark, *Charles Olson*, 239.
— "did it": Duberman, *Black Mountain*, 400.
— whitewashing tree leaves: cf. ibid., 399–400.
189 the results: cf. Clark, *Charles Olson*, 249.
— "her husband": Rumaker, *Boundary* 2 (Spring/Fall 1972), 155; cf. Duberman, *Black Mountain*, 395; Clark, *Charles Olson*, 249; Creeley to Olson, 10 January 1956; Creeley to Duncan, 9 October 1955.
— Now, teach!: cf. Duberman, *Black Mountain*, 395.
— "by word": quoted ibid., 396.
— many baths: cf. Rumaker, *Boundary* 2 (Spring/Fall 1978), 156.
190 without a dent: cf. Creeley to Duncan, 6 September 1955; cf. Creeley to Dawson, 6 September 1955.
— "told them-": cf. Rumaker, *Boundary* 2 (Spring/Fall 1978), 163, 164; cf. Clark, *Charles Olson*, 249.
— back seat: cf. M.E. Harris, *Black Mountain*, 178.
— "was incompetent": Duberman, *Black Mountain*, 400.
— the police: Rumaker, *Boundary* 2 (Spring/Fall 1978), 166.
191 "after that": ibid., 167–8.
— lovely men: cf. ibid., 165.
— with them: cf. Creeley to Duncan, 6 September 1955.
— Creeley remarked: cf. Creeley to Duncan, 20 August 1955.
192 okay too. Wow: cf. Creeley to Dawson, 6 September 1955.
— weren't there: cf. ibid. [24 September 1954].
— "story telling": *Collected Essays*, 371.
— he commented: ibid., 416.
— "wry smile": ibid., 418; cf. J. Wilson, *Robert Creeley's Life*, 355–6.
193 "their godfather": *Contexts*, 151–2.
— might weave: cf. Creeley to Dawson [24 September 1955].
— shoots himself: cf. Creeley to Duncan, 24 September 1955; Creeley to Bronfman, 25 October 1955.
— Olson commented: cf. Creeley to Duncan, 2 October 1955.
— look treacherous: cf. Creeley to Duncan, 9 October 1955; cf. also Creeley to Dawson [24 September 1955]; 14 January 1955.
194 visit people: cf. Creeley to Dawson [24 September 1955].
— sentimental tone: cf. ibid., [24 September 1955], Creeley to Altoon, 16 November 1955.
— ignore them: cf. Creeley to Duncan, 2 October 1955.
— different woman: cf. Creeley to Levertov, 19 October 1955.

194 she joked: Homire to Creeley, n.d.
   – of violence: cf. ibid.
195 wondered teasingly: cf. ibid.
   – turned out: cf. Creeley to Dawson [12 January 1956].
   – Creeley wondered: cf. Creeley to Altoon, 16 November 1955; Creeley to
     Oppenheimer, 10 November 1955; Creeley to Levertov, 7 November
     1955; Creeley to Duncan, 16 November 1955.
   – falling apart: cf. Creeley to Duncan, 9 October 1955; 16 November 1955;
     Creeley to Altoon, 16 November 1955; Creeley to Dawson, 9 October
     1955; 28 November 1955.
   – present confusions: cf. Creeley to Dawson, 9 October 1955; Creeley
     to Duncan, 30 July 1955; 25 October 1955; Creeley to Olson,
     19 January 956.
   – in Mexico: cf. Homire to Creeley, n.d.
   – Bob groaned: cf. Creeley to Olson, 7 January 1956.
196 unaware of otherwise: cf. ibid., 19 January 1956.
   – oddly serious: cf. Creeley to Duncan, 20 August 1955.
   – rejoined his friends: cf. Creeley to Duncan, 9 October 1955.
   – heading west: cf. Creeley to Olson, 22 January 1956.

CHAPTER TWENTY-TWO

197 never had: cf. Creeley to Olson, 19 January 1956.
   – otherwise nonfunctional: cf. Edes to Ann Creeley, 12 December 1955.
   – as well: cf. ibid.
198 else, always: cf. Creeley to Olson, 22 January 1956.
   – "to, now": *Gold Diggers*, 154–5.
   – Bob realized: cf. Creeley to Duncan, 25 February 1956.
   – quickly enough: cf. MacKinnon to Creeley, n.d.
   – out West: cf. ibid., n.d.; n.d.
   – the least: cf. *Collected Essays*, 373.
199 "about it": ibid., 374.
   – "matter rest": cf. ibid., 374.
   – "all dumb": ibid.; see also Wilson, *Robert Creeley's Life*, 350. Ann MacKin-
     non, in her April 1997 marginal comments in this biography's typescript,
     calls the whole scene an "imaginary meeting and conversation," insisting
     that she liked William Carlos Williams "a lot."
   – could happen: cf. Edes to Creeley, 2 March 1956.
   – New Mexico: cf. Creeley to Olson, 12 February 1956.
200 his brain: cf. Berlin to Creeley, 27 November 1955; [27 October 1954];
     [7 June 1954].

200 close friends: cf. W.C. Williams to Creeley, n.d.

– this order: cf. Duncan to Creeley, n.d.

– complete terror: cf. Creeley to Olson, 23 February 1956.

– ex-wife's money: cf. ibid.

– "arching space": Clark, *Robert Creeley*, 135.

201 they decided: cf. Creeley to Oppenheimer, n.d.; Creeley to Dawson, n.d.; Creeley to Olson, 23 February 1956.

– his dealership: cf. Creeley to Dawson, 2 April 1956; 4 April 1956.

– glaring outside: cf. ibid., 29 February 1956.

– "For Ann": cf. Creeley to Olson, 9 March 1956.

– "was penitence": *Collected Poems*, 195.

– presently manage: cf. Creeley to Corman, 1 March 1956.

202 "it stick": *Collected Poems*, 173; cf. Edelberg, *Robert Creeley*, 167.

– fellow novelists: cf. Creeley to Olson, 9 March 1956; Creeley to Dawson, 16 March 1956; 14 March 1956.

– earlier poem?: cf. Creeley to Dawson, 16 March 1956.

203 New Mexico: cf. *Collected Essays*, 301.

– and clarity: cf. Creeley to Olson, 9 March 1956; Creeley to Dawson, 16 March 1956.

– "us all": *Collected Essays*, 301.

– his generation: interview with Judson Crews, 21 August 1982.

– to herself: cf. Creeley to Dawson, 19 March 1956.

– several weeks: interview with Judson Crews, 21 August 1982.

– its own: cf. Creeley to Olson, 9 March 1956; ibid., 25 March 1956; Creeley to Dawson, 25 March 1956.

– in December: cf. Creeley to Olson, 25 March 1956; Creeley to Dawson, 25 March 1956.

204 back seat: cf. Creeley to Dawson, 25 March 1956.

– sharp woman: cf. Creeley to Duncan, 27 March 1956.

– the moment: cf. Creeley to Olson, 23 February 1956.

– mere fantasy: cf. Creeley to Dawson, 13 March 1956; 16 March 1956.

– with it: cf. ibid., 4 April 1956.

– "unresolved / confessions": *Collected Poems*, 199.

205 he saw: cf. Creeley to Dawson, 25 March 1956; Creeley to Olson, 25 March 1950; Creeley to Duncan, 2 April 1956; 27 March 1956.

– someone else: cf. Homire to Creeley, n.d.; Creeley to Olson, 23 February 1956.

– successful woman: cf. Creeley to Duncan, 26 March 1956; 27 March 1956.

– "terrifying" to him: cf. Creeley to Homire, 27 March 1956.

– done that: cf. Creeley to Levertov, 4 April 1956.

CHAPTER TWENTY-THREE

206 "blessed, truly": *Collected Essays*, 513, 567.
 – "for Berkeley": Miles, *Ginsberg*, 202; cf. A. Charters, *Jack Kerouac*, 259.
 – the rows: cf. Charters, *Jack Kerouac*, 259; M. Schumacher, *Dharma Lion*, 214; Miles, *Ginsberg*, 202.
207 Philip Whalen: cf. Rexroth to Creeley, 30 June 1951; n.d.; n.d.
 – perversely wrong: cf. J. Williams to Creeley, 26 December 1954; [7 December 1954]; 1 June 1955.
 – Creeley himself: cf. ibid., n.d.
 – *bmr* #7: cf. Schumacher, *Dharma Lion*, 230; Creeley to Zukofsky, n.d.
208 "and Burroughs": *Collected Essays*, 567–8.
 – and disengaged: cf. Creeley to Zukofsky, n.d.
 – literary expression: cf. L. Hamalian, *Kenneth Rexroth*, 257.
 – "get hurt!": *Collected Essays*, 177.
 – back to him: cf. Duncan to Creeley, 10 May 1956.
 – "over there!": G. Nicosia, *Memory Babe*, 520.
209 "didactic idiot": *Collected Essays*, 568.
 – changing impressions: cf. Creeley to Olson, 17 May 1956.
 – his mind: cf. Nicosia, *Memory Babe*, 520.
 – Ginsberg attributed: cf. Creeley to Duncan, n.d.
 – "milltown writers": Hamalian, *Kenneth Rexroth*, 258.
 – usual thought: cf. *Collected Essays*, 250.
 – he felt: cf. Nicosia, *Memory Babe*, 460, 521.
210 "in things": ibid., 522.
 – and painstaking: *Collected Essays*, 172.
 – our time: cf. ibid., 173, 174.
 – all right): cf. ibid., 173–4.
 – coming home: cf. Creeley to Duncan, n.d.
 – very much: cf. Creeley to Olson, 17 May 1956.
 – jazz beat!: cf. Kerouac to Creeley, 28 November 1962.
211 another novel: cf. ibid., 15 October 1959; 15 January 1962 (postal date).
 – princesses away: cf. ibid. [13 January 1958].
 – "head-tripping": *Collected Essays*, 178.
 – eternal nothingness: cf. Kerouac to Creeley [13 January 1958].
 – little fakey: cf. E. Faas, *New American Poetics*, 194; Terrell, *Robert Creeley*, 200.
 – "much money": quoted in Charters, *Jack Kerouac*, 258.
 – mountain flowers: cf. ibid.
212 for comment: cf. Creeley to Duncan, 2 May 1956; Creeley to Olson, 17 May 1956; Blood Bank to Creeley, 19 April 1956; Miles, *Ginsberg*, 203.
 – "the park": *Collected Essays*, 568–9.

213 "to everybody": Schumacher, *Dharma Lion*, 231.
  – "up from": Nicosia, *Memory Babe*, 524.
  – spiritual discipline: cf. ibid.
  – wagon tire: cf. Kerouac to Creeley, 28 November 1962.
  – his lip: cf. Nicosia, *Memory Babe*, 524–5.
  – intimate friends: cf. ibid., 525.
214 utter exhaustion: cf. ibid.
  – to Duncan: cf. Creeley to Duncan, n.d.
  – Kerouac himself: cf. Nicosia, *Memory Babe*, 525.
  – peyote ritual: cf. ibid.
  – "the consequences": ibid.
  – "the bar": ibid., 526.
  – stone's throw distance: cf. Creeley to Levertov, 18 July 1956.
  – lay elsewhere: cf. ibid.
215 hellish uncertainty: cf. ibid.

CHAPTER TWENTY-FOUR

(The chapter's title is taken from a letter by Duncan to Creeley of 18 May 1956.)
216 "his devotees": Rexroth, *Excerpts*, 9.
  – younger generation: cf. Rexroth to Levertov, 20 November 1954.
217 "dirty German": Hamalian, *Kenneth Rexroth*, 243, 246.
  – and ignorance: cf. Rexroth to Levertov, 20 November 1954; 7 April 1955;
    20 April 1955.
  – Green Street: cf. Hamalian, *Kenneth Rexroth*, 258, 259.
  – "and Kerouac": ibid., 259.
218 Snyder's cabin: cf. ibid., 258, 269f.
  – plane tickets: cf. ibid., 259, 261, 265.
  – had happened: cf. ibid., 260, 261.
  – housing expenses: cf. Creeley to Duncan, 7 June 1956.
219 augured contentedly: Creeley to Olson, 30 June 1956; cf. Creeley to
    Duncan, 7 June 1956; interview with Judson Crews, 21 August 1982.
  – "woman possessed": quoted in Hamalian, *Kenneth Rexroth*, 262.
  – the law: cf. ibid., 262, 263.
  – the result: cf. ibid., 265, 259, 263.
  – to him: cf. ibid., 265, 265–6.
220 uranium mine: cf. Creeley to Olson, 17 August 1956; interview with Judson
    Crews, 21 August 1982.
  – solidly American: cf. Creeley to W.C. Williams, 8 August 1956; Creeley
    to Levertov, n.d.; Creeley to Duncan, 7 June 1956; 17 June 1956.
  – the fine: according to interview with Judson Crews, 21 August 1982.
  – had started: cf. Hamalian, *Kenneth Rexroth*, 266; Creeley to Olson,
    17 August 1956.

220 do so: cf. Marthe Rexroth to Creeley [14 July 1956]; n.d.
- Katharine, selfishly: cf. Marthe Rexroth to Creeley, n.d.; [13 May 1953];
  [14 July 1956].
- *her* possible: cf. ibid. [9 June 1956]; [18 July 1956].

221 the phone: cf. ibid. [17 May 1956]; n.d.
- very much: cf. ibid. [13 May 1953]; [14 July 1956]; [9 June 1956].
- always would: cf. ibid., n.d.; [14 July 1956]; [22 August 1956]; n.d.
- come alive: cf. ibid. [14 July 1956].
- all appurtenances: cf. ibid. [18 July 1956].
- had to: cf. ibid., n.d.
- own way: cf. ibid., n.d.
- positive ones: cf. ibid. [14 July 1956].
- of it: cf. ibid.
- rather, claim: cf. ibid.

222 go herself: cf. ibid.; 31 July 1956.
- of writing: cf. ibid., n.d.
- like this?: cf. Creeley to Olson, 25 October 1956; Creeley to Crews,
  12 December 1956.

CHAPTER TWENTY-FIVE

(The chapter's title is taken from a letter by Duncan to Rexroth of 14 May 1956.)

223 prepared to: cf. Creeley to Duncan, 2 May 1956.
- papal infallibility: cf. Duncan to Creeley, 10 May 1956.

224 on stage: cf. Duncan to Rexroth, 14 May 1956.
- write to Marthe: cf. Duncan to Rexroth, n.d.
- the sordidness: cf. Duncan to Rexroth, n.d.
- one to Marthe: cf. Duncan to Marthe Rexroth, n.d.
- second to Creeley: cf. Duncan to Creeley, 18 May 1956.
- unwavering support: cf. Duncan to Rexroth, n.d.

225 Creeley formula: cf. Duncan to Creeley, 18 May 1956.
- stand by him: cf. Duncan to Rexroth, n.d.
- respected in him: cf. Duncan to Creeley, 22 May 1956.
- one by one: cf. Creeley to Duncan, n.d.
- care of Marthe: cf. ibid., 7 June 1956; 8 December 1956.
- what was due: cf. Creeley to Levertov, 4 July 1956; 4 November 1956.
- same untruthfulness: cf. Duncan to Levertov, 18 July 1956.

226 leaving anyway: cf. Levertov to Creeley [3 September 1956]; [29 July 1956].
- Rexroth's household: cf. Duncan to Levertov, 15 November 1956;
  12 February 1957.
- at all: cf. Creeley to Duncan, n.d.
- with Duncan: cf. Creeley to Levertov, 14 September 1956.
- Creeley's fears: cf. Duncan to Creeley, 24 September 1956.

226 lovely way: cf. Levertov to Creeley, 15 January 1957.
   – poetry deepen: cf. ibid.
   – Rexroth altogether: cf. Duncan to Rexroth, 23 April 1957; Duncan to Levertov, 3 December 1957.
227 Duncan's opinion: cf. Duncan to Creeley, 24 July 1957.
   – as a poet: cf. Duncan to Levertov, 12 February 1957.
   – Charles Olson: cf. Duncan to Rexroth, 11 January 1958.
   – for Rexroth: cf. Duncan to Creeley, 24 July 1957.
   – not even mentioned: cf. Duncan to Creeley, 7 December 1957.
   – influential anthology: interview with Don Allen, 18 July 1981.
   – over Marthe: cf. Hamalian, *Kenneth Rexroth*, 273, 284.
   – contact with Marthe: cf. ibid., 283.
   – warn Bob: cf. Levertov to Creeley, n.d.
   – a madman: cf. ibid.
228 whole hours: cf. Creeley to Levertov, 22 April 1958.
   – already dead: cf. ibid.
   – with pity: cf. Levertov to Creeley, n.d.
   – furious man: cf. Duncan to Levertov, 10 December 1957.
   – as malignant: cf. Creeley to Duncan, 27 July 1957.
   – and loathing: cf. Marthe Rexroth to Creeley [13 June 1956]; [14 July 1956].
   – "word peace": quoted in Hamalian, *Kenneth Rexroth*, pp. 264–5.
229 dishonest trick: cf. Marthe Rexroth to Creeley [13 May 1956].
   – old flames: cf. Hamalian, *Kenneth Rexroth*, 283–4.
   – years later: cf. ibid., 305, 307, 313.
   – "her father": ibid., 312.

CHAPTER TWENTY-SIX

230 to Mitch: cf. Creeley to Mitch Goodman, 4 November 1956.
   – to nine: cf. Creeley to Olson, n.d.; Clark, *Robert Creeley*, 136.
   – '49 Mercury: cf. Creeley to Dahlberg, 19 November 1956; Creeley to Olson, 1 December 1956.
   – after taxes: cf. Creeley to W.C. Williams, 1 January 1957.
   – new teacher: cf. Creeley to Zukofsky, 24 October 1956; interview with Paul Saunders, 10 July 1981.
   – "to them": *Mabel*, 18.
231 early June: cf. Clark, *Charles Olson*, 136; Creeley to Dahlberg, 19 November 1956; Creeley to Duncan, 8 December 1956.
   – stop-gap: cf. Creeley to Olson, n.d.
   – for the Registrar: cf. Olson to headmaster, 10 November 1956.
   – "union card": cf. Creeley to Duncan, 8 December 1956.

231 wild day: cf. Creeley to Olson, 28 May 1956.
  – "break-thru": ibid.
232 of creativity: cf. Creeley to Duncan, 7 June 1956; Creeley to Zukofsky,
  8 January 1957; Creeley to Dorn, 2 December 1956.
  – and appreciated: cf. Creeley to Dahlberg, 19 November 1956.
  – far below: cf. Creeley to Dorn, 2 December 1956.
  – man's odyssey: cf. Creeley to W.C.Williams, 8 August 1956.
  – with Buddy: cf. Creeley to Olson, 17 August 1956.
  – "palm huts …": *Mabel*, 143–4. It may be noted that Creeley's original response to Beckett's *Malone Dies* was different. A letter to W.C. Williams of
  1 January 1957, to which we owe the remainder of our account of Creeley's
  1956 Christmas trip, states that he found the novel small, tired, and not
  enough.
233 "The Sharks": interview with Mitch Goodman, 19 January 1993.
234 "the fins": Levertov, *Collected Earlier Poems*, 74.
  – by June: cf. Creeley to Duncan, 31 December 1956; Creeley to Turnbull,
  31 December 1956.
  – unequivocal terms: according to interview with Mitch Goodman,
  19 January 1993.
  – love to: cf. Creeley to W.C. Williams, 1 January 1957.
  – "I am": cf. ibid. and *Collected Essays*, 495.
  – and Littleton: cf. Creeley to W.C. Williams, 1 January 1957.
235 walk straight: cf. MacKinnon to Creeley, n.d.; n.d.; 26 July 1956; n.d.;
  13 May 1956; Creeley to Duncan, n.d.
  – at all: cf. MacKinnon to Creeley, 26 July 1956.
  – bitterness whatsoever: cf. Creeley to W.C. Williams, 8 August 1956.
  – her curdled: cf. Creeley to Duncan, 15 December 1956.
  – a novel: cf. Creeley to W.C. Williams, 1 January 1957.
236 "actually knows": *Poetry* 89 (October 1956), 60.
  – the printers: cf. Creeley to Layton, 3 January 1957, 250; Creeley to
  Turnbull, 31 December 1956.
  – from others: cf. Creeley to Turnbull, 31 December 1956.
  – possible way: cf. ibid., 3 January 1957.
  – a price: cf. ibid.
  – added casually: cf. ibid., 28 January 1957.

CHAPTER TWENTY-SEVEN

237 different channels: this and the following according to interview with Bobbie Louise Hawkins, 30 August 1982, and interview with her mother, Norah
  Hall, 3 September 1982.
238 in her eyes: B.L. Hawkins, *Enroute*, 8.

240 "after that": *Collected Poems*, 359.
 – drinking. Wow: cf. Creeley to Ginsberg, 7 February 1957.
 – wrote to Denise: cf. Creeley to Levertov, 23 January 1957.
 – through it again: cf. Clark, *Robert Creeley*, 135.
 – a VW: cf. Creeley to Duncan, 1 March 1957; Creeley to Olson,
 3 February 1957; Creeley to Zukofosky, 9 May 1957.
 – than that: cf. Creeley to Olson, 3 February 1957; Creeley to W.C.
 Williams, 1 January 1957.
241 after all: cf. Creeley to Duncan, 1 March 1957; Creeley to Levertov,
 31 March 1957.
 – by November: cf. Creeley to Olson, 21 March 1957; Creeley to Levertov,
 18 April 1957.
 – of that: cf. Creeley to Olson, 1 May 1957; n.d.; Creeley to Goodman,
 16 June 1957; Creeley to Dorn, 16 June 1957.
 – New Mexico: cf. Creeley to Dorn, 16 June 1957; Creeley to Mitch
 Goodman, 16 June 1957.
 – concrete information: cf. Creeley to Levertov, 17 July 1957.
 – "the poem": *Collected Essays*, 8.
242 private tutoring: cf. Creeley to Olson, 28 June 1957.
 – last century: cf. Creeley to Duncan, 29 October 1957; cf. Creeley to
 Levertov, 15 September 1957; 28 April 1958; Creeley to Crews,
 15 February 1958.
 – to bullshit: cf. Creeley to Olson, 18 October 1957; 18 January 1958;
 Creeley to Dorn, 5 June 1958; Creeley to Corman, 12 December
 1957.
 – previous tenants: cf. Creeley to Duncan, 29 October 1957.
243 they say: cf. Creeley to Olson, 18 October 1957; 19 September 1957.
 – behind them: cf. Creeley to Duncan, 29 November 1957.
 – piled above: cf. Creeley to Olson, 18 January 1958.
 – be a man: cf. Creeley to Mitch Goodman, 4 May 1957; Creeley to
 Blackburn [24 February 1958].
 – the flu: cf. Creeley to Olson, 2 March 1958.
 – from then on: cf. Creeley's grades from the University of New Mexico.
 – a second: cf. document of 3 December 1958.
 – quality throughout: cf. document of 27 May 1959.
 – them quiet: cf. Creeley to Olson, 5 June 1958; Creeley to Dorn, 5 June
 1958.

CHAPTER TWENTY-EIGHT

244 "young group": quoted in Schumacher, *Dharma Lion*, 239.
 – as well: cf. Whalen to Creeley, 11 September 1956.
 – the place: cf. Oppenheimer to Creeley [5 January 1958].

245 to Ginsberg: cf. Ginsberg to Creeley, n.d.
  – and Morocco: cf. Kerouac to Creeley, n.d.
  – agree with: cf. Creeley to Ginsberg, 9 December 1958; Levertov to Creeley [17 October 1957]; [4 February 1957].
  – him wonder: cf. Creeley to Duncan, 15 December 1956.
  – inevitable leakage: cf. Creeley to Olson, 28 December 1957.
  – helping hands: cf. Creeley to Ginsberg, 6 November 1958.
  – of what: cf. ibid., 18 March 1958.
  – in Europe: cf. ibid., 16 February 1958.
  – dead end: cf. Creeley to Duncan, 18 May 1957; 16 March 1957.
  – Kerouac thought: cf. Kerouac to Creeley [13 January 1958].
246 and thunder: cf. Creeley to Turnbull, 28 September 1957.
  – editorial labours: cf. Creeley to Blackburn, 25 January 1959.
  – in America: cf. Creeley to Levertov, 31 March 1957; Creeley to Ginsberg, 6 November 1958.
  – "little patterns": "In Exquisite Chaos," *The Nation* 187 (1 November 1958), 327.
  – Creeley concluded: cf. Creeley to Blackburn, 9 November 1958.
  – school pin: cf. Creeley to Olson, 19 January 1959.
  – for the fall: cf. Creeley to Duncan, 2 January 1959.
  – to Olson: cf. Creeley to Olson, 19 January 1959.
  – a pancake: cf. ibid., n.d.; cf. Creeley to Duncan, 24 March 1958.
247 stopped conversation: cf. Creeley to Olson, 5 June 1958.
  – were closed: ibid., 2 March 1958.
  – useful ways: cf. ibid., 5 June 1958; Creeley to Levertov, 28 June 1958.
  – in March 1957: for this and the following, see Clark, *Charles Olson*, 263f.; Creeley to Dorn, 9 April 1957; Creeley to Duncan, 16 March 1957.
  – assured him: cf. MacKinnon to Creeley, 1 July 1957.
248 moving there: cf. Creeley to Duncan, 27 July 1957.
  – about it?: cf. Creeley to Olson, 28 August 1957; 19 September 1957; Creeley to Levertov, 15 September 1957.
  – ever, heartbreaking: cf. Creeley to Olson, 28 August 1957; Creeley to Levertov, 15 September 1957; Creeley to Bobbie, 16 August 1957.
  – a decade: cf. Creeley to Olson, 28 August 1957; cf. Creeley to Levertov, 15 September 1957.
  – afraid of: cf. Creeley to Dorn, 29 August 1957; Creeley to Olson, 28 August 1957.
249 to Olson: cf. Creeley to Olson, 28 August 1957, plus enclosed newspaper clipping.
  – on 28 March: cf. Creeley to Duncan, 24 March 1958; Creeley to Levertov, 27 March 1958.
  – he had developed: cf. Creeley to Levertov, 22 April 1958; Creeley to Blackburn, 11 April 1958; Creeley to Olson, 11 April 1958.

250 basic friendship: cf. Creeley to Olson, 11 April 1958.
 – different story: cf. Creeley to Mitch Goodman, 28 June 1958.
 – on him: cf. Creeley to Olson, 28 August 1957.
 – towards them: cf. Creeley to Duncan, 10 August 1958; Creeley to Duncan, 10 August 1958.
 – embarrassed surprise: cf. Creeley to Levertov, 13 August 1958; Creeley to Olson, 11 August 1958.
 – "absolutely alive": *Boundary 2* (Spring-Fall, 1978), 39–40.
251 "echo indeed": Clark, *Robert Creeley*, 139.
 – "the face?": quoted in S. Fredman, *The Grounding of American Poetry*, 45.
 – *Sewanee Review*: cf. Creeley to Duncan, 10 August 1958; Creeley to Levertov, 13 August 1958.
 – "shapechanger extraordinaire": Hawkins, *Enroute*, 18.
252 "would continue": B.L. Hawkins, *My Own Alphabet* (1989), 30. For an earlier version of the same story, see *Enroute* (1982).
 – de las Casas: cf. Creeley to Levertov, 13 August 1958; Creeley to Rago, 10 August 1958.
 – entire trip: cf. Creeley to Duncan, 10 August 1958.
 – "union card": cf. Creeley to Levertov, 13 August 1958.
 – contribute reviews: cf. Creeley to Rago, 6 March 1956; 7 June 1956; 15 September 1957.
 – *Spanish Poetry*: cf. Rago to Creeley, 4 February 1958.
253 frustrating period: cf. Creeley to Rago, 28 June 1958, 30 December 1958.
 – showing up: cf. Creeley to Olson, 11 April 1958; cf. Creeley to Levertov, 17 July 1957; Creeley to Duncan, 2 January 1959.
 – a thought: cf. Creeley to Duncan, 24 July 1957; Creeley to Mitch Goodman, 28 June 1958; Creeley to Levertov, 13 May 1959.

CHAPTER TWENTY-NINE

254 you and I: quoted in J.L. Fried et al., *Guatemala in Rebellion*, 187–8.
255 burned alive: cf. ibid., 186.
 – Latin America: cf. S. Jonas, *Battle for Guatemala*, 171.
 – against Guatemala: cf. R.H. Immerman, *The CIA in Guatemala*, 161ff; R. Jeffreys-Jones, *The CIA*, 90f.
 – Carlos Enrique Díaz: cf. J. Handy, *Revolution in the Countryside*, 189, 183.
 – "better job": quoted in J. Handy, *Gift of the Devil*, 185; cf. ibid., 150.
 – political career: cf. T. Szulc, *Fidel*, 239.
 – "Armas regime": Jonas, *Battle for Guatemala*, 4; cf. Handy, *Revolution*, 193, 195.
256 of asylum: cf. Jonas, *Battle for Guatemala*, 42.
 – "and patronage": Handy, *Gift of the Devil*, 152.

256 the 1960s: cf. ibid., 153; Fried et al., *Guatemala in Rebellion*, 326.
   - the rebellion: cf. Creeley to Ginsberg, 2 October 1960.
   - 16 July: cf. Creeley to Crews, n.d.
   - Duncan declared: cf. brochure for the 16 July 1959 reading.
257 objective disapproval: cf. Creeley to Olson, 12 August 1959; Creeley to Dorn, 6 September 1959.
   - in numbers: cf. Creeley to Oppenheimer, 24 August 1959; Creeley to Duncan, 30 July 1959; Creeley to Ginsberg, 7 September 1959; Creeley to Olson, 12 August 1959.
   - torrential rainfalls: cf. Creeley to Dorn, 25 August 1959.
   - bit them: cf. Creeley to Dorn, 25 August 1959; interview with Mrs. Burge, 30 August 1995.
   - lots of gas: cf. Creeley to Ginsberg, 7 September 1959; Creeley to Dorn, 25 August 1959; Creeley to Duncan, 27 September 1959.
258 depositing litters: cf. Creeley (Bobbie's P.S.) to Ginsberg, 31 October 1959; Creeley to Dorn, 25 August 1959.
   - walked on vanished. cf. Creeley to Dorn, 24 February 1960.
   - intestinal sickness: cf. Creeley to Oppenheimer, 24 August 1959; Creeley to Crews, 7 November 1959; Creeley to Dorn, 25 August 1959.
   - the rain: cf. Creeley to Ginsberg, 7 September 1959; *Mabel*, 44; Creeley to Oppenheimer, 24 August 1959; Creeley to Crews, 17 November 1959; Creeley to Olson, 12 August 1959; Creeley to Dorn, 24 August 1959.
   - feared them: cf. Creeley to Ginsberg, 7 September 1959; Creeley to Dorn, 24 December 1959; 26 October 1959.
259 and distraction: cf. Creeley to his mother, 26 October 1959.
   - them human: cf. Creeley to Ginsberg, 7 September 1959; Creeley to Crews, 7 November 1959; Creeley to his mother, 26 October 1959.
   - potentially was: cf. Creeley to Dorn, 11 December 1959; Creeley to Loewinsohn, 27 October 1959; Creeley to his mother, 26 October 1959.
   - nice neighbourhoods: cf. Creeley to Dorn, 24 December 1959; Creeley to Levertov, 15 September 1959; 18 October 1959.
   - mused incongruously: cf. Creeley to Zukofsky, 25 October 1959.
   - really was?: cf. Creeley to Duncan, 30 October 1959.
   - children everywhere: cf. Creeley to Dorn, 16 November 1959; Creeley to Jones, 8 November 1959; Creeley to Crews, 7 November 1959.
260 to Ed Dorn: cf. Creeley to Dorn, 11 December 1959.
   - to her: cf. Creeley to Dorn, 11 December 1959; Creeley to Crews, 7 November 1959.
   - felt reality: cf. Creeley to W.C. Williams, 30 January 1960; Creeley to Ginsberg, 19 September 1959.
   - the poem: cf. Creeley to Olson, 12 December 1959; Creeley to W.C. Williams, 30 January 1960.

260 "now writing": *Poetry* 89 (October 1956), 60.

 – "or Lowenfels": *The Fifties* #2 (1959), 10, 19, 21.

261 "surpass Robert Creeley": *New York Times Book Review*, 4 November 1962, 38.

 – "and abstraction": *The Fifties* #2 (1959), 21, 14, 15.

 – for Corman: cf. Creeley to Duncan, 10 June 1959; Levertov to Creeley [9 May 1959]; Duncan to Creeley, 12 May 1959.

 – these embroilments: cf. Creeley to Levertov, 27 May 1959; Levertov to Creeley [7 June 1959].

262 major inventiveness: cf. Creeley to Blackburn, 18 November 1959; Creeley to Olson, n.d.; Creeley to W.C. Williams, 16 March 1960.

 – *The Nation*: cf. Creeley to Olson, 11 April 1958; Creeley to Duncan, 22 October 1959; Creeley to Levertov, 15 September 1959; Kerouac to Creeley, 15 October 1959; Creeley to Blackburn, 20 February 1960.

 – to Zukofsky: cf. Creeley to Zukofsky, 10 November 1959.

 – Creeley noted: cf. Creeley to Dorn, 11 December 1959; Creeley to the University of New Mexico, 18 January 1960; Creeley to Olson, 7 February 1960; Creeley to Turnbull, 30 March 1960.

 – to Ed Dorn: cf. Creeley to Olson, 7 February 1960; Creeley to Turnbull, 30 March 1960; Creeley to Duncan, 23 March 1960; Creeley to Dorn, 16 March 1960.

263 until 1962: cf. Creeley to Olson, n.d.; Creeley to the University of New Mexico, 2 April 1960.

 – their way: cf. Creeley to Dorn, 24 February 1960; Creeley to Zukofsky, 15 March 1960; Creeley to Olson, 3 February 1960; Creeley to Levertov, 30 March 1960; Creeley to Rago, 29 April 1960.

CHAPTER THIRTY

264 and drinking: cf. Creeley to Zukofsky, 15 March 1960; Creeley to Duncan, 3 September 1960.

 – university level?: cf. Creeley to Levertov, 8 September 1960.

 – with Billy: cf. Creeley to Olson, 24 June 1960.

265 to Charles Olson: cf. Creeley to Duncan, 24 June 1960; Creeley to Olson, 24 June 1966.

 – creative energy!: cf. Creeley to Turnbull, 7 September 1960; Creeley to Dahlberg, 29 October 1960.

 – to take it: cf. Creeley to Dorn, 2 February 1961.

 – around him: cf. Creeley to Duncan, 3 September 1960; Creeley to Levertov, 8 September 1960.

266 volume of it!: cf. Creeley to Blackburn, 6 November 1960; Creeley to W.C. Williams, 21 September 1960.

266 augured – erroneously: cf. Creeley to Olson, 2 October 1960; Creeley to
Dorn, 2 September 1960.
– the endeavour: cf. Creeley to Dorn, 14 September 1960; Creeley to
Turnbull, 7 September 1960.
– these days?: cf. Creeley to Dawson, 7 September 1960; Creeley to
Turnbull, 7 September 1960.

267 by Zukofsky: cf. Creeley to Dorn, 14 September 1960; Creeley to Levertov,
23 September 1960; Creeley to Olson, 2 October 1960; Creeley to
Turnbull, 8 October 1960; Creeley to Zukofsky, 18 October 1960.
– for months: cf. Creeley to Turnbull, 7 September 1960; Creeley to
Levertov, 23 September 1960; Creeley to Olson, 2 October 1960; Creeley
to Turnbull, 8 October 1960. This evidence conflicts with Creeley's later
claims that the part of *The Island* written in Guatemala was done in one
week (cf. Creeley to Olson, 29 January 1961) or in sittings of roughly
5 days of writing (cf. Creeley to Dawson, 8 November 1963).
– *Collected Poems*: cf. Creeley to W.C. Williams, 21 September 1960; Nims
to Creeley, 3 October 1960; Creeley to Olson, 2 November 1960.
– he announced: cf. Creeley to Duncan, 27 November 1960; Creeley to
Dorn, 20 November 1960; Creeley to Corman, 17 December 1960;
Creeley to Blackburn, 6 November 1960.
– *The Island*: cf. Creeley to Levertov, 5 February 1961; Creeley to Dorn,
2 February 1961.

268 friends' way: cf. Creeley to Olson, 18 December 1960; ibid., 11 April 1958.
– possible model: cf. "Breathing Words into the Ear of an Unliterary Era,"
Times Literary Supplement, 9 September 1960, 15; cf. Creeley to Olson,
18 December 1960; Creeley to Dorn, 9 January 1961.
– personal apology: cf. Creeley to Dorn, 16 April 1961; 26 March 1961.
– to friends: see, for instance, Creeley to Dorn, 16 April 1961; Creeley to
Duncan, 27 November 1960; Creeley to Corman, 17 December 1960.
– ac generator: cf. Creeley to Levertov, 8 September 1960.
– United States: cf. Creeley to Olson, 29 January 1961; Creeley to Duncan,
9 January 1961; Creeley to Dorn, 16 March 1961; 23 March 1961;
16 April 1961.
– bit by bit: cf. Creeley to Duncan, 20 January 1961; Creeley to Olson,
29 January 1961; 23 February 1961.

269 "like a hill": *Collected Poems*, 202.
– to Duncan: cf. Creeley to Duncan, 9 January 1961.
– stultifying flora: cf. Creeley to Olson, 29 January 1961; 17 February 1961;
Creeley to Goodman, 5 February 1961.
– years earlier: cf. Creeley to Dorn, 29 December 1960; Creeley to Duncan,
9 January 1961; Creeley to Levertov, 16 January 1961; Creeley to
Blackburn, 11 January 1961; Creeley to Nims, 11 February 1961.

269 he had achieved: cf. Creeley to Dorn, 21 March 1961.

270 communal activity: cf. Creeley to Corman, 17 December 1960.

– the room: cf. Creeley to Olson, 18 December 1960; Creeley to Dorn, 29 December 1960; 23 March 1961; Dorn to Creeley, 19 March 1961.

– in Africa: cf. Creeley to Duncan, 9 January 1961; Creeley to Blackburn, 1 April 1961; Creeley to Zukofsky, 11 December 1960; Creeley to Dorn, 16 April 1961; 16 March 1961.

– to watch: cf. Creeley to Olson, 27 March 1961; 23 February 1961; 29 January 1961; Creeley to Dorn, 23 February 1961; Creeley to Levertov, 16 January 1961; Creeley to Goodman, 5 February 1961.

271 such things: cf. Creeley to Olson, 29 January 1961; cf. Creeley to Blackburn, 6 November 1960; Creeley to Whalen, 18 April 1961.

– Creeley think: cf. Ginsberg to Creeley, 19 July 1960.

– he admitted: cf. Creeley to Ginsberg, 2 October 1960.

– United States: cf. Creeley to Dorn, 16 April 1961.

CHAPTER THIRTY-ONE

272 the $100!: cf. Creeley to Dorn, 21 June 1961.

– for Olson: cf. ibid., Creeley to Olson, 8 December 1961; Clark, *Charles Olson*, 295.

273 her poetry: cf. Creeley to Dorn, 21 June 1961; Creeley to Olson, 20 June 1961.

– final sprint: cf. Creeley to Whalen, 24 July 1961; Creeley to Olson, 29 July 1961.

– the studio: cf. Creeley to Dorn, 21 June 1961.

– decade before: cf. Creeley to Hall, 16 June 1961.

– days later: cf. Creeley to Duncan, 5 July 1961; 20 June 1961; Creeley to Crews, 16 June 1961; Creeley to Dorn, 21 June 1961.

– be considered: cf. Creeley to Dorn, 21 June 1961; Creeley to Duncan, 5 July 1961.

274 14 September: cf. Creeley to Levertov, 14 September 1961.

– the mountains: cf. Creeley to Dawson, 17 August 1961; Creeley to Olson, 29 July 1961; Creeley to Levertov, 25 August 1961; Creeley to Whalen, 24 July 1961.

– keep sane: cf. Creeley to Olson, 29 August 1961; cf. Creeley to Dorn, 1 August 1961; Creeley to Blackburn, 14 October 1961.

– early October: cf. Creeley to Levertov, 25 August 1961; 14 September 1961.

– a Sunday: cf. Creeley to Levertov, 25 August 1961; Creeley to Dorn, 9 October 1961.

– ran home: cf. Creeley to Dorn, 9 October 1961, plus enclosed newspaper clipping, "Girl, 8, Is Killed, As Arroyo Bank Collapses Here."

275 the "sight": cf. Creeley to Olson, 6 April 1962.
  – get back: cf. Clark, *Robert Creeley*, 140. An account to W.C. Williams writ-ten on 4 June 1962, some nine months after the accident, states that Creeley apparently pushed the man.
  – "left, disgruntled": Clark, *Robert Creeley*, 140–1.
  – first targets: cf. Creeley to Scott, 1 August 1961; 8 August 1961.
276 in the East: cf. Creeley to Turnbull, 25 August 1961; Creeley to Blackburn, 14 October 1961; Creeley to Dorn, 18 October 1961.
  – earlier attack: cf. Creeley to Dorn, 10 November 1961; Creeley to Blackburn, 18 October 1961.
  – rather sad: cf. Creeley to Dorn, 10 November 1961.
  – to Duncan now: Creeley to Duncan, 3 January 1960.
  – professed for it: cf. Levertov to Creeley, 11 January 1960.
277 with everybody: cf. ibid.
  – towards them: cf. ibid.
  – Bob himself: cf. ibid., n.d.
  – offer them!: cf. Creeley to Levertov, 15 January 1960.
  – hurt Mitch: cf. ibid.
278 before leaving: cf. Creeley to Duncan, 27 November 1960; Creeley to Dorn, 23 November 1961; 29 November 1961.
  – children? Wow: cf. Creeley to Dorn, 14 February 1960; Creeley to Olson, 9 April 1960.
  – Lucia's presence: cf. Creeley to Dorn, 6 September 1959; Creeley to Oppenheimer, 24 August 1959; interview with Mitch Goodman, 19 Janu-ary 1993.
  – of nowhere: interview with Mitch Goodman, 19 January 1993.
  – and left: cf. ibid.
  – in Tangiers: cf. ibid.
279 "like that": Lucia Berlin, *So Long*, 209–10.
  – "of desperation": ibid., 207–8.
  – those involved: cf. Creeley to Dorn, 10 November 1961.
280 hoped for: cf. Creeley to Dorn, 20 November 1961.
  – out of it: cf. Dorn to Creeley, 23 November 1961.

CHAPTER THIRTY-TWO

281 literal expenses: cf. Creeley to Dorn, 29 November 1961.
  – Vancouver home: cf. Tallman to Creeley, 21 March 1963; F. Davey, *Tish*, 7.
282 christened *Tish*: cf. Davey, *Tish*, 8.
  – "steady hum": ibid., 8.
  – in the halls: cf. Tallman to Creeley, 2 March 1963; Creeley to Blackburn, 9 April 1962.

282 teach there: cf. Creeley to Oppenheimer, 11 April 1962; Creeley to Olson, 7 March 1962; Creeley to Dorn, 5 April 1962; Creeley to Duncan, 24 February 1962.

283 genuinely impressive: cf. Creeley to Dorn, 26 March 1963; Tallman to Creeley, 21 March 1962.
  – socialized medicine: cf. Creeley to Scott, 16 April 1962; Creeley to Dorn, 5 April 1962.
  – in May: cf. Creeley to Olson, 19 March 1962; Creeley to Dorn, 25 May 1962.
  – Buckminster Fuller: cf. Creeley to Oppenheimer, 11 April 1962.
  – parent's hands: interview with Bobbie Louise Hawkins, 30 August 1982.
  – Brakhage's films: cf. Brakhage to Creeley, 3 May 1962; Creeley to Olson, 1 May 1962.
  – single images: cf. *Collected Essays*, 410.

284 run over dad?: interview with Stan Brakhage, 18 August 1982.
  – "collection charge": Clark, *Charles Olson*, 298; cf. Creeley to Corman, 17 August 1962.
  – on leave: cf. Creeley to Duncan, 7 August 1962.
  – he complained: cf. Creeley to Corman, 17 August 1962; Creeley to Dorn, 6 August 1962.
  – the manuscript: this and the following according to interview with Bobbie Louise Hawkins, 30 August 1982.

285 time regardless: cf. Creeley to Finlay, 16 August 1962.
  – the harbour: cf. ibid., Creeley to Bynner, 30 July 1962; Creeley to Dorn, 6 August 1962.
  – for granted: cf. Creeley to Duncan, 20 July 1962.
  – must say: cf. Levertov to Creeley, 23 September 1962.

286 American poets: cf. *Oakland Tribune*, 1 April 1962; *Saturday Review*, 4 August 1962; *Atlantic Monthly*, November 1962; *Jubilee*, June 1962; *Vancouver Sun*, 5 September 1962.
  – private reference: cf. *Nashville Banner*, 25 May 1962; *Harper's Magazine*, October 1962; *Evening Sun* (Baltimore, Maryland), 5 February 1963; *Saturday Review*, 4 August 1962.
  – "practising today": *Northwest Review* 6, no. 3 (Summer 1963).
  – his blessings: cf. Creeley to Dorn, 7 October 1962.
  – cannot do: cf. Creeley to "Jake," 5 October 1962.

287 of content: ibid.
  – American attitudes: cf. Creeley to Dorn, n.d.; Creeley to Finlay, 14 December 1962; Creeley to Olson, 23 January 1963; Creeley to the University of New Mexico, 2 December 1962.

287 like them: cf. Creeley to Olson, 23 January 1963; Creeley to the University
of New Mexico, 2 December 1962; Creeley to Zukofsky, 27 January 1963.
– "recognized limit": Clark, *Robert Creeley*, 142; cf. Creeley to Duncan,
27 February 1963.
– "Uriah Heep": Edelberg, *Robert Creeley's Poetry*, 165; cf. Creeley to
Duncan, 27 February 1963.
288 formed themselves: cf. Creeley to Turnbull, 27 June 1963.
– to Turnbull: cf. ibid.
– "unhappily habitual": Creeley to Turnbull, 27 June 1963; cf. Creeley–
Layton, *Complete Correspondence*, xxvii.
– almost a year: cf. Creeley to Kizer, 30 July 1962.
– to Duncan: cf. Creeley to Duncan, 29 December 1962.
289 the rest: cf. Duncan to Creeley, 3 January 1963.
– threw it out: cf. Creeley to Duncan, 4 July 1963.
– any kind: cf. Creeley to Schulman, 13 March 1963; Creeley to Kizer,
1 April 1963.
– to see: cf. Creeley to Kizer, 7 October 1962; Creeley to Hutter,
23 September 1963, to the effect that he disliked the autobiographical
excuse, but that it was, in fact, his own experience. See also Creeley to
Turnbull, 20 November 1963, to the effect that he wanted *The Island*
to be the fact of the experience, autobiographical or otherwise.
Contexts, 52: "The novel I've written, *The Island*, really gives the content
of those years. It isn't the story of my life but it makes much use of that
time."
– real life: cf. Creeley to Duncan, 24 January 1963.
290 special relief: cf. Creeley to Ginsberg, 9 March 1963; Creeley to Olson, 23
January 1963; Creeley to Schulman, 13 March 1963; Creeley to
Hutter, 9 January 1962.
– "unexpected ledge": *The Island*, 188; cf. Creeley to Hutter, 20 February
1963.
– of Albuquerque: cf. Creeley to Rago, 28 May 1963; Creeley
to Dawson, 31 December 1962; Creeley to Duncan,
8 May 1963.

CHAPTER THIRTY-THREE

291 the pyres: cf. Ginsberg to Creeley, 3 November 1962; Miles, *Ginsberg*, 318;
Schumacher, *Dharma Lion*, 379.
– more than generous: cf. Creeley to Ginsberg, 17 September 1962.
– the money: cf. Ginsberg to Creeley, 24 September 1962.
– his life: cf. Miles, *Ginsberg*, 321; Schumacher, *Dharma Lion*, 391–2.

292 "in return": Miles, *Ginsberg*, 327.
  – "as well": Schumacher, *Dharma Lion*, 398.
  – "of admiration": Clark, *Charles Olson*, 304, 276.
  – "my dreams!": ibid., 302.
  – his body: cf. Schumacher, *Dharma Lion*, 398.
293 "with Charles": Clark, *Charles Olson*, 301–2.
  – (series fee $5): cf. Creeley to Ginsberg, 23 January 1963 plus enclosure.
  – "of souls": Ginsberg's phrase, quoted in Schumacher, *Dharma Lion*, 398.
  – "each other": Clark, *Charles Olson*, 303.
  – after all: cf. Schumacher, *Dharma Lion*, 398.
  – his face: cf. Clark, *Charles Olson*, 304.
  – "everybody's stomach": Miles, *Ginsberg*, 328.
  – observed afterwards: cf. Creeley to Turnbull, 29 August 1963.
  – Creeley's life: cf. Creeley to Blackburn, 30 August 1963.
  – "a little": *Collected Essays*, 529, 527.
  – years earlier: cf. ibid., 532.
294 typewriter first: cf. ibid., 532, 533.
  – "other words": ibid., 533.
  – "no threat": ibid.
  – "at all!": ibid., 534.
  – was writing: cf. ibid., 535–6.
  – into poems: cf. Creeley to Levertov, 9 October 1963; 9 October 1963; Creeley to Dorn, 14 October 1963.
295 same jungle: cf. Creeley to Levertov, 16 September 1963; Creeley to Oppenheimer, 24 September 1963; Creeley to Scott, 5 October 1963; Creeley to Rumaker, 20 October 1963.
  – get started: cf. Creeley to Dorn, 14 October 1963; Creeley to Duncan, 10 October 1963.
  – to Olson: cf. Creeley to Olson, 8 November 1963; Creeley to Duncan, 24 February 1964; 19 November 1964; Creeley to Dorn, 20 March 1964.
  – his novel: cf. Duncan to Creeley, 15 July 1963.
296 a storyteller: cf. Bynner to Creeley, 16 September 1963.
  – for years: cf. Tomlinson to Creeley [2 September 1963]; [20 October 1963].
  – Western culture: cf. Trocchi to Creeley, 9 October 1963.
296 the creeps?: cf. Levertov to Creeley, 12 September 1963; 14 November 1963.
  – added diplomatically: cf. Turnbull to Creeley, 18 November 1963.
  – proven unfounded: cf. Creeley to Turnbull, 20 November 1963.
297 ever met: cf. Creeley to Levertov, 16 November 1963.
  – revengeful self: cf. Dawson to Creeley, 3 November 1963.
  – so between: cf. Creeley to Dawson, 8 November 1963.

297 pleasant daughters: cf. Creeley to Dahlberg, 14 December 1963; Creeley to Olson, 24 November 1963.

– single afternoon: cf. Creeley to Rago, 14 December 1963.

– his "Autobiography": Clark, *Robert Creeley*, 142, 65.

298 "with himself": *Collected Poems*, 306.

CHAPTER THIRTY-FOUR

299 SUNY Buffalo: cf. Cook to Creeley, 21 January 1966.

– future decades: cf. Creeley to Levertov, 19 April 1964; Creeley to Duncan, 4 April 1965; Creeley to Calder, 12 May 1965; 18 March 1965; Creeley to Hutter, 13 March 1964.

– academic entourage: cf. Creeley to Olson, 23 January 1953; Creeley to Dorn, 27 November 1964; 20 November 1964.

300 do likewise: cf. Creeley to Duncan, 28 August 1964.

– to win: cf. ibid.

– murdered president: cf. Creeley to Basic Books, 28 August 1964.

– fellow poets: cf. Creeley to Zempleny, 8 April 1966; cf. Duncan to Creeley,

7 April 1966; Creeley to Duncan, n.d.

– in person: cf. Creeley to Levertov, 17 November 1964; Creeley to Olson, 5 September 1964; Creeley to Duncan, 21 August 1964.

301 some $900: cf. Creeley to Calder, 25 July 1964.

– persistently lacking: cf. ibid.

– possible convenience: cf. ibid., 25 August 1964.

– and intelligent: cf. ibid., 21 November 1964; Creeley to Levertov, 17 November 1964.

– to Levertov: cf. Creeley to Levertov, 17 November 1964.

302 stand up: cf. Creeley to Calder, 21 November 1964.

– told Seymour-Smith: cf. Creeley to Seymour-Smith, 18 November 1964.

– in England: cf. Creeley to Levertov, 15 May 1965.

– hell with it: cf. Creeley to Olson, 28 November 1964.

– to Ginsberg: Creeley to Ginsberg, n.d.

– too expensive: cf. Bobbie to Marion Boyars, 21 November 1964.

303 well stiff: cf. 28 November 1964; cf. Creeley to Tomlinson, 19 November 1964.

– or two: cf. Creeley to Dorn, 18 February 1965.

– approached Charles Tomlinson: cf. Creeley to Tomlinson, 8 January 1965.

– very impressed: cf. Creeley to Calder, 28 May 1965.

– on 27 May: ibid.

304 that hum: according to interview with Larry Goodell, 21 August 1993.

304 a doctor: ibid.
  – "with them": *Contexts*, 118, 89, 88.
  – real conversation: cf. Creeley to Duncan, 1 August 1965; Creeley to Calder, 10 September 1965.
305 a debacle: cf. Clark, *Charles Olson*, 323.
  – on top: cf. ibid., 321, 323.
  – "occurring tonight": ibid., 325.
  – in dismay: cf. ibid., 324, 325.
  – against it: cf. Creeley to Seymour-Smith, 30 July 1965.
  – entire trip: cf. Creeley to Duncan, 1 August 1965; Creeley to Seymour-Smith, 30 July 1965.
306 to Calder: cf. Creeley to Calder, 11 August 1965.

CHAPTER THIRTY-FIVE

307 and confusion: cf. Creeley to Dawson, 22 October 1965.
  – "came too": *Collected Essays*, 273.
  – "kill me": F. Dawson, *Thread*, 5, 6.
308 "one man": ibid., 6.
  – he wrote: cf. Creeley to Dawson, 22 October 1965.
309 an understatement: cf. Dawson to Creeley, 25 October 1965.
  – stop it all: cf. Creeley to Dawson, 30 October 1965.
  – in anger: cf. Dawson to Creeley, 16 November 1965.
  – "the world": *Collected Poems*, 309.
310 included a list: cf. Creeley to University of New Mexico, 27 December 1965; 28 December 1965; 11–12 February 1966; Creeley to Duncan, 23 January 1966.
  – Williams stupid: cf. Creeley to Tomlinson, 19 October 1965; Creeley to Levertov, 28 January 1966; Creeley to Dorn, 3 December 1965; Creeley to the University of New Mexico, 27 December 1965.
  – "fucked by others": *Mabel*, 53, 51.
  – "public lecture": ibid., 99.
  – "Amen": *Collected Poems*, 182.
311 following morning: cf. Creeley to Dorn, 2 April 1966; Creeley to Duncan, 8 April 1966.
  – "his head": *Mabel*, 99, 100.
  – "was exuding": ibid., 100.
  – Lake Como: *Mabel*, 99.
  – "and assumption": ibid., 100, 102; interview with Bobbie Louise Hawkins, 30 August 1982.
312 fortieth birthday: cf. Creeley to Marion Boyars, 19 May 1966.
  – 5 February 1981: cf. Creeley to Hawkins, 20 February 1977; Creeley to Duncan, 5 February 1981.

- frankly murderous: cf. Blackburn to Creeley, 9 December 1967; 1 February 1968; Creeley to Blackburn, 15 January 1968.
- up the stereo: cf. Creeley to Hawkins, 20 February 1977; interview with Sarah Creeley, 18 July 1981.

313 "will follow": *Collected Poems*, 597.
- "go wrong?": clipping dated 19 September 1968 from an Albuquerque newspaper.
- poet answered: cf. Clark, *Robert Creeley*, 59.

AFTERWORD

315 "Holy Forest": for this and the following quotations from and references to the essay, see *Brick* (Winter 1993), 46–9.
- "wry smile": *Collected Essays*, 373, 435, 437, 283, 418.

316 "be *human*": ibid., 288, 70, 363, 259, 405, 453.
- "in eternity": M. Rumaker, *Gringos*, 285.
- "weighed insight" instead: *Collected Essays*, 356, 430, 405, 355, 325, 323, 436, 286, 166.

317 "Michael Davidson": ibid., 343, 326, 325. Regarding Lowell's depressive realism see above page 260.
- July 1967: cf. *Collected Essays*, 349.
- "Autobiographical Mode": cf. *Collected Essays*, 554f.

318 "of living": *Mabel*, 5.
- "the other": ibid., 37, 32, 51, 22, 26.
- "personal experiences": *The Dial* (Winter 1943), 2.
- "out back": *Collected Poems*, 82.

319 would come: cf. Creeley to Layton, 31 July 1953, 35.
- their way: cf. Creeley to Olson, 11 April 1958.
- family background: for this and the following see the reprint of the Ossman interview in *Contexts*, 3–12.
- full-fledged revolution: cf. *Contexts*, 9, 10, 7, and *Collected Essays*, 107.

320 of "tombstone": ibid., 7, 9.
- "of any": ibid., 88, 87.
- "easily recur": *Collected Essays*, 375.
- "Denise Levertov": ibid., 106.

320 "I think": *Contexts*, 11.
- "effectually won": *Collected Essays*, 513.
- "the days": Rumaker, *Gringos*, 285.

321 Ginsberg's farm: cf. *Collected Essays*, 519.
- "of it": ibid., 579.

321 "more settled": *Mirrors*, 28. The proverbial exception to the rule was prompted by a visit to Berlin during 1983–84. Too much in Berlin, Creeley wrote thereafter, was "locked echo of [his] life's failed symbols and political,

social despair." Growing up in New England, he explains, he'd occasionally witnessed people going to their graves "without speaking to one another, the dumb result of an argument, whatever – just the will left, locked in abstract place." But what had been the exception in New England struck him as standard behaviour amongst Berliners and Germans at large. How "aweful to live with that sullenness, the truculence, righteousness, sophistication, appetite so prolonged." Creeley found examples everywhere. Older women of a secure social class were mercilessly pushing, shoving, "all very discreetly yet firmly, to get their way." Mentioning to his host that several trains he'd taken had been late, he was told "that German trains are *never* late," and, intimidated, dropped the subject. The only time he met with much strength of feeling was "when [he] dumbly broke a rule, tried to get on a bus with [his] small son before the drivers had finished the very particular exchange of their authority, one coming on duty, one going off." A policeman working a stop-light was timing the action precisely to his watch, ignoring the few cars or persons passing. "It seemed the whole country was didactically committed to its procedures."

Left-wing Germans, despite their "clear seriousness," fared little better in Creeley's estimation. Women were so completely absorbed by the peace movement, they had no time left for actual feminism or gay lib. The great number of protesters of both sexes, among them many that were "older people, settled and middle class," would ultimately have little effect on the general political climate or "tone" which was increasingly moving "to the right ... neo-Nazi elements that ten years ago would have been judged criminally liable are now looked to as the firm, no-nonsense guarantors of public welfare and sane thinking."

The arts? A "contemporary show at the National Museum seemed drab echo, almost a mannered 'street' harshness, cosy political gesturing. Sad." Apart from "the landmark anthology *Neue Amerikanische Lyrik*" comprising Creeley's own, the literary scene was bleak. "So, what's poetry doing in Germany. Not very much."

"*Ich bin kein Berliner*," as Creeley might have said. Cf. *Collected Essays*, 587, 580, 585, 587, 582, 587, 582, 588.

– "nice person": ibid., 477.

– "*and sell*": *Mirrors*, 12, 36–7, 83; *Memory Gardens*, 4; *Windows*, 133.

– "other place": *Collected Essays*, 578.

– his conscience: cf. Clark, *Robert Creeley*, 140.

322 "pathetic resistance": *Windows*, 130.

– "had been": ibid., 45; *Places*, n.p.; *Mirrors*, 28.

322 "of behavior": *Gold Diggers*, 7.

– "crotchety purview": *Collected Essays*, 591, 572, 571.

– be different: cf. Clark, *Robert Creeley*, 81, 112.

– "of many": *Echoes*, 18.

323 "it/it": *Collected Essays*, 575.
  – "and places": *The Island*, 133.
  – "head-tripping": *Collected Essays*, 549, 178.
  – "know why": E. Faas, *Towards a New American Poetics*, 181, 180.
  – seizing the poet: cf. Creeley to Olson, 11 June 1950, I, 94; [7 July 1950], II, 64; Creeley to Levertov, 23 September 1960.
  – "own insistence": *Collected Essays*, 330, 483, 533.
  – "was 'happening' ": ibid., 571.
  – "their quintessences": Rimbaud, *Complete Works. Selected Letters*, 307.
324 "judgmental murmur": *Echoes*, 51, 64, 50; *Windows*, 90, 75.
  – "my friends": Clark, *Robert Creeley*, 84.
  – "common doom": *Life and Death*, 80.
  – "*man. Us.*": ibid., 25.
  – "social//suitors": ibid., 9; cf. 18.
  – "*do today*": ibid., 50; cf. 57.
  – "your lap": ibid., 49, 57; cf. 64.
  – "will happen": ibid., 10.
325 a woman: cf. ibid., 10, 29, 34, 68, 69, 71.
  – "lunch of prawns": ibid., 7; cf. 32.
  – "all begun": ibid., 27; cf. 35, 41.
  – Zukofsky: cf. ibid., 5, 8, 35, 37, 50, 63.
  – "her flesh": ibid., 70; cf. 57.
  – "than home": ibid., 10, 12, 36, 56; cf. 26, 67.
  – "those older": ibid., 49, 64.
  – "leather glove": ibid., 29, 37, 47, 55, 62, 73; cf. 17, 59.
326 sheer unending: cf. ibid., 5, 13, 15, 34, 42, 51, 63–4, 68.
  – "*bitter* / affliction": ibid., 23; cf. 31.
  – great reconciler: cf. ibid., 33.
  – "gainsay death": ibid., 84.
  – "grows cold": ibid., 37, 83.
  – "opening sky": ibid., 33, 62, 84.

Index.